BREAKING DOWN THE WALLS OF HEARTACHE

Breaking Down the Walls of Heartache

How Music Came Out

Martin Aston

Constable • London

CONSTABLE

First published in Great Britain in 2016 by Constable

1 3 5 7 9 10 8 6 4 2

Copyright © Martin Aston, 2016

The moral right of the author has been asserted.

All rights reserved.
No part of this publication may be reproduced, stored in a retrieval system, or transmitted, in any form, or by any means, without the prior permission in writing of the publisher, nor be otherwise circulated in any form of binding or cover other than that in which it is published and without a similar condition including this condition being imposed on the subsequent purchaser.

A CIP catalogue record for this book
is available from the British Library.

ISBN 978-1-47212-243-8 (hardback)
ISBN: 978-1-47212-244-5 (trade paperback)

Typeset in Stempel Garamond by TW Type, Cornwall
Printed and bound in Great Britain by CPI Group (UK) Ltd,
Croydon CR0 4YY

Papers used by Constable are from well-managed forests and other responsible sources.

Constable
An imprint of
Little, Brown Book Group
Carmelite House
50 Victoria Embankment
London EC4Y 0DZ

An Hachette UK Company
www.hachette.co.uk

www.littlebrown.co.uk

*To Mat, for continuing love, encouragement, patience, dinners.
To David Bowie,* in memoriam, *my Wizard of Oz, changing my world from black and white to colour.*
To Alan Wakeman, in memoriam.

Contents

Introduction		ix
1	The Art of Secrecy, The Sound of Lavender	1
2	The Twenties – ''T'ain't Nobody's Business if I Do': Sissies, Bull-Dykers and Freakish Man Blues	16
3	The Thirties – the Age of the Pansy Craze	24
4	The Forties – War Games and Nancy Boys	46
5	The Fifties – the Tutti Frutti Revolution	62
6	The Sixties – Gay Party Pop and the Rock'n'Roll Closet	105
7	The Seventies – Let The Children Boogie	176
8	The Seventies II – Disco, Punk and Out Come the Freaks	240
9	The Eighties – All The Nice Boys Love Sea Men – Pop Comes Out	321
10	The Nineties – Rock'n'Roll – Queer to the Core	421
11	Twenty-first Century – A Rainbow Riot	482
Acknowledgements		536
Picture Credits		539
Index		542

Introduction

Childhood memory is typically selective and there are a handful of contenders for the first piece of music indelibly burnt in mine. If any nursery rhymes sank in, they were quickly subsumed by songs imbibed from BBC radio's Saturday morning request show *Children's Favourites*; was I three, maybe four years old? Clearly music mattered, judging by the numbers that stuck: Burl Ives' 'Would You Like To Swing on a Star?' (or was it the Pinky and Perky version?), Harry Belafonte and Odetta's 'There's a Hole in My Bucket', Bernard Cribbins' 'Digging a Hole', Charles Jolly's 'The Laughing Policeman', all simple novelty stories songs that a child would enjoy.

Looking back, I realise that each of these songs were jokey, more spoken than sung and even for a child, they were irritating as much as memorable. And none triggered the kind of reaction that another song 'story' of the era managed, with a completely different style of novelty hook – the uncanny tone of an early electronic instrument, a Clavioline-style keyboard known as a Musitron, to match the singer's uncanny falsetto cry: 'I wah-wah-wah-wah-wonder!'

I could have heard 'Runaway' by Del Shannon on *Children's Favourites* – it was a UK No. 1 single in February 1961. But whenever and however I discovered it, I was thrilled, haunted, confused, possessed. And that was just the music and voice. Besides, what exactly was a runaway? The single was a portal into a new world I had no understanding of but Shannon's exhilarated and urgent delivery and racy melody touched my little beating heart.

With hindsight, I know that this was Pop Music rather than the BBC

BREAKING DOWN THE WALLS OF HEARTACHE

Light Entertainment world of Cribbins and for all the frivolity of pop – there will another ten songs along in the next half hour – there were serious emotions being exposed and exorcised. I couldn't have known that 'Runaway' was a break-up song and the reason for Shannon's pain[1] but I felt at home with the drama, his voice's pleading, aching and occasionally gruff edge and I suspect now that something about its falsetto androgyny appealed too. As soon as I was collecting singles, from the age of six, I fell hook, line and sinker for female singers or men with high, keening deliveries. *Children's Favourites* was immediately passé, likewise the banal and creepy tones and make-up of television's blackface entertainers, *The Black and White Minstrel Show* – a grown-up world I wanted no part of.

So I'm six years old and sharing my tastes with teenagers and soaking up artists who are older than that. My first seven-inch single was the Supremes' 'Where Did Our Love Go', the Motown trio's first UK No. 1 in 1964 and the first record I could repeatedly play at my own leisure. I'd found Shannon an uplifting, comforting companion; he wasn't gay but it feels like 'Runaway' spoke to the gay in my DNA. Similarly, the Supremes' dreamier, but no less lustrous voices and harmonies made me giddy with happiness.

Meanwhile, my elder brother David was snapping up early Beatles and Rolling Stones singles, a world of – and for – boys. I was building my own collection: Dusty Springfield's 'I Only Want to be With You' (sadly shattered in a Frisbee-style mishap), Cilla Black's 'You're My World', The Mamas and The Papas' 'Dedicated to the One I Love' – dynamic and sweeping melodramas all. I'd lie in front of the turntable, trying to merge my little voice with theirs as if these were my songs, my time. And when I did find other male voices that I adored, it was the Beach Boys and the Monkees. Harmonies drove me crazy, in the best way.

It was at this point that I diverted my pocket money into Marvel

---

[1] Shannon was distraught enough to eventually kill himself in 1990 with a rifle.

comics and the lure and thrill of superheroes, a different portal to another world, shinier and sexier and more unknowable than pop, an on-going soap opera with added magic powers and the ability to transform.

I mostly stopped buying records until I was fourteen and experienced another moment that embodied something shiny and sexy with the power to transform – and set in outer space. It's a memory I share with many others, one that has been widely discussed since the sudden death of David Bowie in January 2016 as I was nearing completion of this book: Bowie performing 'Starman' on *Top of the Pops* in 1972.

The soft, alluring melody, the hookline of Mick Ronson's guitar (which I later discovered was inspired by a Supremes' song), the arm slouched around Ronson's shoulder as they sang the heavenly chorus, the sight of Bowie pointing and waggling his finger at the camera as he sang, 'I had to phone someone so I picked on you' . . . this was a thrill and a swoon beyond anything I'd known. I was unable to articulate what I felt about my young gay self, but staring at this face looking straight back at me it was like some lightning bolt, the key inserted and the unlocked door blown open. As my partner Mat says, it resembled that moment in the 1939 movie *The Wizard of Oz* when the action shifts from black-and-white to colour.

A line had been drawn in the sand and, after buying the single's parent album *The Rise and Fall Of Ziggy Stardust and The Spiders from Mars*, I was off, exploring a world of musical superheroes: Roxy Music, Lou Reed, the Velvet Underground, Iggy and the Stooges, through which I could vicariously live while trapped in north-west London suburbia, lacking magic powers and even the ability to come out.

With hindsight, I realise that I had no way to align Bowie to what I understood about my sexuality, which was very little. For one, Bowie had said that he was gay and yet he had a wife and a child and, in any case, he was an alien from Mars and not from suburbia. There were two other potential gay role models at that time in the 1970s, sitcom actor John Inman and game show presenter Larry Grayson. I recognise as internalised homophobia the way their exaggerated camp frightened me because it was so far from my self-image. There was nothing to identify with, no mirror of what made me tick and so I settled down in the closet and secretly sought out evidence in literature and film.

I came out after reading two books, David Leavitt's 1986 novel *The Lost Language of Cranes* (a son comes out to his closeted father: I had to be the son and not the dad) and Radclyffe Hall's 1928 novel *The Well of Loneliness*, a pioneering lesbian saga that summed up the injustice and cruelty of the era.

By the mid-1980s, pop music had begun to mirror my worldview but while I was still closeted, Frankie Goes To Hollywood's 'Relax' was too provocative and sensual. Bronski Beat's 'Smalltown Boy' spoke more to me, lonely and vulnerable. But it was important to have music validate my feelings and, as I began to make a career as a music journalist, I began to see how pop music would reach out to embody hopes and fears, love and break-ups; from party songs to rebel songs – and, equally, how the artists themselves struggled to put themselves in their songs. Once I became an openly gay man, I sought out those singers and songwriters who were expressing their gay, lesbian and bisexual selves, to hear the stories of those who provided the visibility and validation – political, social, sexual – that I had so little of in the first half of my life.

But I didn't visualise a narrative in the music until I heard journalist and author Jon Savage's CD compilation *Queer Noises 61-78: From the Closet to the Charts*, released in 2006. It began in 1960 with a clip of drag queen and pioneering activist José Sarria from the Black Cat bar in San Francisco and ended with Sylvester's disco classic 'You Make Me Feel (Mighty Real)' in 1978.

In 2012, I was asked to write the story of the evolution of gay rock'n'roll for the UK magazine *Attitude*, compiled from moments I considered most pivotal. It felt to me as if each entry could be the chapter of a book, although focusing on rock'n'roll was limiting – did that include folk and country? Disco, house and hip hop? The full story would be broader, deeper and embrace the roots of rock'n'roll and all its offshoots. It needed to ask, How did music come out the closet?

Other books have tackled the subject of gay, lesbian and bisexual singers and musicians in popular music, albeit in different forms. American writer Boze Hadleigh's *The Vinyl Closet: Gays in the Music World* (1991) aimed to do for music what the late Vito Russo did with Hollywood in his landmark book *The Celluloid Closet*, published in 1981, the first attempt to reclaim gay and lesbian history via an art form by outing the hidden gay texts of cinema.

Hadleigh was a pioneer, starting the conversation about the achievements and influence of gay, lesbian and bisexual singers and musicians and naming names. The tone was gossipy and Hadleigh, bizarrely, finished his book with chapters on ballet and film, as if he'd emptied the vinyl closet without reaching his minimum quota of words.[1]

In 1994, fellow US writer Wayne Studer's *Rock on the Wild Side: Gay Male Images in Popular Music of the Rock Era* (1994) was a brief, opinionated commentary on individual songs with an epilogue of all the songs he didn't have room for or the patience to process. All gay UK journalists, John Gill's *Queer Noises: Male and Female Homosexuality in Twentieth-Century Music* (1995), Richard Smith's *Seduced and Abandoned: Essays on Gay Men and Popular Music* (1996) and the late Kris Kirk's posthumous *A Boy Named Mary* (1999) were vivid encounters, but in essay form, some reproducing former magazine features.

There are the academic studies too, such as *Queering the Pitch: The New Gay and Lesbian Musicology* (edited by Philip Brett, Elizabeth Wood and Gary C. Thomas), *Queering the Popular Pitch* (edited by Sheila Whiteley, Jennifer Rycenga) and Jodie Taylor's *Playing It Queer: Popular Music, Identity And Queer World-making.*

But none of these books approached the subject as an unfolding narrative, as a chronological piece of social history, to explore how

---

1 The book jacket has a quote by Madonna that she claims never to have given, which questions the authenticity of Hadleigh's revelations.

popular music came out of the closet. While researching my book, I discovered a predecessor, by the German writer Ralf Jörg Raber, *Wir Sind Wie Wir Sind (We Are As We Are), A Century Of Gay Love on Vinyl and CD*, published in 2010. Raber's authoritative study was restricted to music released in the German-speaking countries (Germany, Austria, Switzerland), just as my book has a British and American bias – partly a result of my inability to understand other languages and so comprehensively research those countries' histories, but also – to my advantage – many of the key innovators and musical genres that have formed the narrative of popular music are American and British (if anyone can name the Little Richard, Elvis Presley, David Bowie, Dusty Springfield and k.d. lang of Germany or Spain, then I'll reconsider . . .).

This is not to discount – or exclude - the groundbreaking influence of Germany's cabaret scene of the early twentieth century or the French *chanson* tradition. After all, the first recorded song about homosexuality – and before then, the invention of the term, 'homosexual' – came from Germany, as did the first homosexual rights organisation. But even in the twentieth century, society believed that homosexuality was not just a choice, but a perversion, a crime against nature, to be criminalised and eradicated, until enough individuals proved that humans must obey the laws of nature rather than ignorance, fear, cruelty and denial. It's these individuals in the field of popular music that drive the narrative of this book; those singers and songwriters who led the way by example either because they were politically motivated or simply had no alternative but to be true to themselves. Defiance was the best option and between the oppressed and the oppressors, sparks flew and extraordinary work was made.

I felt it was also important to incorporate as many personal memories of those pioneers as I could, via new interviews or archives. It makes for a long read, but popular music is a Hydra and ancient too, as the story unfolds over a hundred years, from the love that once dared not speak to the love that sings on daytime radio. There are blatant declarations,

Introduction

coded messages and examples of heterosexual songwriters who chose to address same-sex issues.

Some pioneers were unknown even to me – and I've been writing about music for over thirty years – unreported in the pre-celebrity era. If men admitted they were homosexual, it was also admitting they were breaking the law while similarly honest women simply scandalised society. Then there were the pioneers who did sell millions of records and had the most widespread impact; after all, David Bowie was the first male singer to wear a dress – 'a man's dress,' he called it, but still a dress – in public and on an album cover and the first to announce, 'I'm gay,' in any publication. But Bowie was far from the first singer or songwriter to reveal themselves – two years before him, British singer Dusty Springfield had addressed the subject in a British newspaper interview in 1970.

Still, the story I want to tell does not centre on the gay icon: this is not the place to eulogise the Top Ten of the Top Gay Pop Songs website:[1] in descending order, Alicia Bridges' "I Love The Nightlife', Madonna's 'Vogue', Olivia Newton-John's 'Xanadu', Kylie Minogue's 'Better the Devil You Know' and 'Your Disco Needs You', the Weather Girls' 'It's Raining Men', Gloria Gaynor's 'I Will Survive', the Village People's 'YMCA' and, at No. 1, Abba's 'Dancing Queen'. Several of the songs are classics and cornerstones of the mainstream gay club experience and there is one lesbian artist and one (predominantly) gay male group among the performers and their place in the story is secure. But Kylie Minogue, your disco needs you but not my book . . .

Neither is this book a mirror of the Channel 4 documentary *Queer as Pop: From Gay Scene to Mainstream*, a shallow, over-familiar and stale story. The makers completely misunderstood the term 'queer', which encompasses the whole spectrum of lesbian, gay, bisexual and transgender and a new understanding of gender fluidity that's truly the new story in this second decade of the twenty-first century; in fact, *Queer As*

---

1 www.topgaysongs.com/top-songs/top-gay-songs

Pop . . . disregarded women entirely, as if the likes of Dusty Springfield and k.d. lang weren't icons worthy of story and could be erased from history.

Talking of erasure, I was also fired up by pieces in the *Guardian* in April 2016 on gay culture that sidelined or trivialised music's contributions.[1] There is a much bigger truth to be unveiled. But I want to apologise to those who feel that exploring all the hidden details, making interpretation concrete and rationalising something as irrational as sexual behaviour, comes at a cost; as Francis Bacon said, 'The job of the artist is to deepen the mystery.' Vito Russo also lamented, 'We lose that sense of belonging to a secret world to which no one else has access.'[2] But if liberation and assimilation has meant that the various strands of the LGBTQ community now share living space with our former oppressors, Russo also acknowledged what was gained: 'The reality that fourteen-year-old gay kids in Tulsa will . . . not have the idea that they're the only ones in the world who are gay.'

Equally, many of these people have been forgotten by historical accounts; the first pioneers and the last ones too. I want to bring them back. If any art form can be cited above all others in furthering the cause and rights of LGBTQ people, surely it's music. Those fourteen-year-olds in Tulsa might do well to know about them, to realise their sense of alienation does not have to be permanent; that 'It Gets Better', in the words of the campaign to reduce the numbers of LGBTQ teen suicides.

I'm equally aware of those countries such as Russia and vast swathes of Africa, where homosexuality remains illegal and shame, humiliation, harassment and arrest, imprisonment and homophobic violence still exist as, in the worst cases, does the death penalty. Yet those communities living under draconian conditions might take heart in knowing that

---

[1] 'From Proust to Ellen DeGeneres, ten gay works that changed the world' and 'From gay conspiracy to queer chic: the artists and writers who changed the world', the *Guardian*, 8 April, 2016

[2] Joanna Cotler Books (1981)

political and social climates can improve, as this book testifies. In the words of Johnny Johnson's northern soul classic from 1969, 'Breaking Down the Walls of Heartache':

> 'Got to tear down all the loneliness and tears/And build you up a house of love.'

CHAPTER 1

The Art of Secrecy, The Sound of Lavender

I would like to see every gay doctor come out, every gay lawyer, every gay architect come out, stand up and let the world know. That would do more to end prejudice overnight than anybody would imagine.
    Harvey Milk, city supervisor of San Francisco, from a tape recording he made in November 1977 to be played in the event of his assassination

When I was growing up, just to be a musician or to think of yourself as a musician automatically meant that you were a sissy.
        Charles Ives to fellow modern classicalist Lou Harrison

It's discouraging to think how many people are shocked by honesty and how few by deceit. Noel Coward, *Blithe Spirit*, 1941

Do you know what pioneers get? Arrows in their ass.
        Charles Whyte, audio engineer, to Wendy Carlos, musician

A blurred image of a vintage radiogram pulls into focus, with a single word, 'Glacier', superimposed across its centre. The dial turns across the channels as the white-noise static in the background dissolves into a series of voices, and snippets of sentences: 'Gay people cannot be married... save our children... sexual sickness... misguided liberals... death of this young man from Wyoming sparked demonstrations...'

The radiogram fades to a split screen of images from the earliest days of cinema and photography, of same-sex couples in romantic poses and news footage ranging from demonstrations to newspaper headlines regarding police raids. Over sombre, insistent piano notes, a velvet baritone begins to sing: 'You just want to live your life the best way you know how/But they keep telling you that you are not allowed.'

More words appear on screen – 'prejudice . . . federal vigilance on perverts asked' – as the singer laments, 'They say you are sick/That you should hang your head in shame/They are pointing fingers/And want you to take the blame.'

Dating from 2013, the video was created by the independent filmmaker Jonathan Caouette for 'Glacier', an album track written and performed by the American singer-songwriter John Grant, partly in response to Russia's new homophobic laws, against what its government termed, 'propaganda of non-traditional sexual relations'. But the root of the song is Grant's formative experiences, deeply closeted within a deeply religious family in Michigan, a state where it seems as if there is a church on every block.

Persistently bullied at school with no conceivable way to admit his truth or to consider he was anything but unlovable, 'I didn't want to be gay,' Grant recalls, 'because it meant I was going to go to hell and I was a pervert and sick.'

The screen splits further into a dazzling configuration of images that can be interpreted as propaganda for non-traditional sexual relations. Bugs Bunny in lipstick. Radclyffe Hall's *The Well of Loneliness*. Christine Jorgensen, the first transsexual to go public. The pioneering glittery drag troupe the Cockettes. Actor Rock Hudson, the first celebrity to die of AIDS. Harvey Milk, the first gay man to serve political office in California. 'From the Stone Age to Stonewall to full equality', placards carried by campaigners for gay marriage.

Simultaneously, other intersecting images portray a society determined to ensure tradition is upheld. The assassination of Harvey Milk. Matthew Shepherd, the young gay man from Wyoming beaten and left to die by the side of a rural road. 'God hates fags' placards carried by members of America's Westboro Baptist church. The 'Glacier' video represents a history lesson, a century of homosexual and transgender identity and struggle: hidden romance, open persecution, hopeful transformation. The song's chorus suggests that what doesn't kill you will make you stronger:

'This pain/It is a glacier moving through you/And carving out deep valleys/And creating spectacular landscapes/And nourishing the ground/With precious minerals and other stuff/So don't you become paralysed with fear/When things seem particularly rough.'

'The image and metaphor were inspired by Iceland,' Grant explains. 'A glacier moving down a valley is one of the most powerful forces on earth. It's reaching out to young gay kids and people struggling with their sexuality and how they're special for all that.'

As Grant told *HIV Plus* magazine, 'I wished I had heard somebody talking about the fact, you know, being gay didn't make me less of a human than other people. It takes a very, very long time to undo a lot of the damage.'[1]

'Glacier' was the finale of Grant's 2013 album *Pale Green Ghosts*, the second of three cathartic solo albums that have documented, with mordant humour as well as brutal honesty, the fear, shame and anger of his closeted youth and the cycles of addiction (drugs, alcohol, sex) as he struggled to balance his outward reality with the internal damage. His efforts culminated in being diagnosed HIV-positive in 2011 – which he announced from a London concert stage the following year[2] (now *that's* pioneering) before performing 'I Tried to Talk to You', in which Grant addressed his diagnosis by both scolding himself for reaching this new perceived low and yet equally responding with empathy for the choices he'd made.

---

1 http://www.hivplusmag.com/people/2013/08/12/musician-john-grant-talks-about-hiv-being-gay-and-glaciers?page=full
2 Grant's confession came when he joined US collective Hercules And Love Affair's performance at London's Meltdown Festival. 'I Tried to Talk to You' was co-written with HALA's gay founder Andy Butler and is included on the collective's 2014 album *The Feast of the Broken Heart*.

The fact that Grant has been able to candidly chart his rollercoaster of a life would have been unthinkable in those days when people never even admitted their sexuality to their friends, let alone their weaknesses and fears. For centuries, artists had to remain silent or hide in metaphor, starved of the joy – as described by singer-songwriter Steven Morrissey (like Grant, a tragi-comic bard of isolation and anxiety) – to 'Sing your life... And have the pleasure of saying what you mean.'[1]

Societies didn't always denigrate less conventional forms of sexuality: the ancient Greeks and Romans accepted same-sex relationships, with the Greek poet Alcman writing a hymn for a chorus of virgins to celebrate the marriage of two women, Agido and Hagesichora, c. 630 BC.[2] But modern historians only acknowledge the existence of same-sex desire in a musical context from the twelfth century onwards, and, even then, it's a matter for us to interpret rather than confirm. 'Notre Dame polyphony – by composers that include Léonin, Perotin and Philippe de Chancelier – may have been written in a homosexual sub-culture symbolised in the music,' according to the *Encyclopaedia Of Lesbian and Gay Histories and Cultures*[3]. In twelfth-century southern France and northern Spain, 'troubadours travelled from court to court, singing Provençal songs of courtly love that sometimes describe love between men and between women.'[4]

It's also claimed that twelfth century abbess – and liturgical music giantess – St Hildegard von Bingen, 'had a close relationship with a fellow nun, Richardis von Stade, which some scholars believe may have been romantic in nature... Some scholars also attest to a pattern of focus on the female body and female desire throughout Hildegard's music.'[5]

---

1 'Sing Your Life', Morrissey, *Kill Uncle* (1991).
2 http://www.aaronsgayinfo.com/Ffacts.html
3 Edited by George Haggerty, Bonnie Zimmermanm (Routledge Press, 2000)
4 From 'Gay Timeline' by Aaron Rush, found at http://www.aaronsgayinfo.com/Ffacts.html
5 Found at 'girl-on-girl culture' blog Autostraddle, article by musicologist graduate Rose (no surname given), http://www.autostraddle.com/ladies-of-note-a-brief-history-of-women-composers-queer-and-otherwise-141391/

The Art of Secrecy, The Sound of Lavender

Historically, the church is an institutionalised force against homosexuality while providing accommodation to hide, or bury, unwanted urges, a place where religious ecstasy can substitute for sexual fervour.[1] One of von Bingen's most celebrated compositions, *Symphonia Armonie Celestium Revelationum*, is devoted to the Virgin Mary but subsequently interpreted as same-sex desire; likewise '*Na Maria*' by Bieiris (or Bieris) de Romans, one of the thirteenth-century female troubadours collectively known as *trobairitz*, who wrote secular music, 'where the singer and object are both suggested to be women'[2] – a gender more exalted in southern Europe, and given administrative powers, than in comparable societies, when men were busy crusading (or perhaps even cruising).

More documentation has survived from later eras so there's much less guesswork to the claim that eighteenth-century *castrati* singers, castrated before puberty to give them a sublime upper-register voice, were not only considered by their patrons to be conduits to a higher spiritual plane, but also very likely their lovers too. Letters written by Russia's Pyotr Tchaikovsky openly acknowledge his tortured relationship with what he termed his 'secret desire' and academics argue for Schubert (his unfinished symphony is a favourite for queer interpretation)[3], Handel, Mussorgsky and Chausson without the same proof, while Chopin was reputedly bisexual 150 years before Bowie. It's believed Baroque composers Jean-Baptiste Lully and Johann

---

1 Musicians were safe using devotional language so that faith and desire could not be separated; it's doubtful that *trobairitz* would have been burned at the stake (a practice that used faggots, meaning a bundle of sticks). However, the use of faggot as a disparaging slur for homosexual derives from 'fagot', meaning old woman.

2 http://www.autostraddle.com/ladies-of-note-a-brief-history-of-women-composers-queer-and-otherwise-141391/

3 In Anthony Tommasini's review of Nadine Hubbs' *The Queer Composition of America's Sound: Gay Modernists, American Music and National Identity* (University of California Press, 2004), Schubert's 'relationships with the young men in his circle still elude our understanding. Schubert's devoted friends considered the pudgy, bespectacled and sickly composer a genius in their midst. But who was sleeping with whom? We're not sure.' http://www.nytimes.com/2004/10/24/arts/music/24tomm.html?oref=login&_r=0

Rosenmüller were homosexual; the latter was arrested for sodomy, then punishable by death, and fled Germany for Italy.

Musicologists even claim they can hear queer: according to Clive Paget, editor of the classical magazine *Limelight*, 'Anyone who doubts Schubert was gay need only listen to the *Trout Quintet*. It's about the gayest music ever written this side of Tchaikovsky.'[1] The Austrian composer apparently had 'soft' or 'feminine' approaches to harmonic and melodic structures, as opposed to, 'the aggressive and hyper-masculine Beethoven, who was held up as the model and measure for composers until at least WWI.'[2]

In his study of nineteenth century homosexuality, Graham Robb writes about letters revealing gay men's tastes that regularly cited the same classical composers (including Beethoven, Chopin, Wagner, Tchaikovsky and Debussy): 'the key ingredient seems to have been a melodious melancholy and something oxymoronic in the emotions: grandiose and sentimental, ostentatious and discreet.'[3] However, the sexuality of the composer, Robb added, 'was not of primary importance. Still, American professor Bruce Holsinger claims there is a 'constant link between polyphony and sodomy in the puritan tradition,'[4] and few are informed enough to argue otherwise.

The connection between music and the sensibility of its composer created a series of euphemisms: 'Is he musical?' 'Does he play in the orchestra?' 'Does he sing in the choir?' The same guessing game has been retrospectively applied to the USA's first full-time professional songwriter, Steven Foster, the man widely known as the father of American music for the likes of 'Oh! Susanna', 'Camptown Races' and 'My Old Kentucky Home'. Though nothing in his book of close to 200 songs hint at sublimated homosexuality, Foster's personal

---

1 Clive Paget, *10 Greatest Gay Composers*, Limelight magazine, 2013, at http://www.limelightmagazine.com.au/Article/334391, the-10-greatest-gay-composers-mardi-gras-special.aspx
2 http://www.glbtq.com/arts/music_classical.html
3 *Strangers: Homosexual Love in the 19th Century* (Picador, 2003)
4 *Music, Body, and Desire in Medieval Culture* (Stanford University Press, 2001)

correspondence was destroyed by his family after his death – at 37, from a fall that cut his throat, suggesting it could just as easily have been suicide. According to one academic source, 'The failure of his marriage, his alcoholism, the gentle, dreamy, feminine nature of much of his music, and some close male friendships[1], all served to fuel speculation on his sexual identity.'[2]

There is also something about his 1862 song 'Why, No One to Love?' written two years before his death, which strongly suggests some deep fracture of unhappiness: 'No one to love!/Why, no one to love?/What have you done in this beautiful world/That you're sighing of no one to love?'

Walt Whitman was greater proof of a homosexual community, arriving in New York in 1841, documenting the men he found in parks, public baths, the docks, bars and dance halls and expressing his feelings in his poems. Europe had no such singular diarist or poet, but there's enough recorded evidence of homosexual societies across the continent, though very little support in song. In the British folk tradition, the tiniest fraction addressed the fluid nature of sexuality. In the late eighteenth-century Scottish ballad 'Willie O'Winsbury', the king is so struck by the beauty of his daughter's betrothed that he confesses he'd take Willie for himself had O'Winsbury been a woman. 'The Handsome Cabin Boy' – a cross-dressing female stowaway – is bedded by both the ship's captain and the captain's wife: a homosexual fling either way you look at it.

Women were typically adjuncts to men and any who deviated could be defined as witches or prostitutes. In the only potential lesbian saga in the folk tradition this writer could find, 'Bessie Bell and Mary Gray' are shunned and build a cottage in the woods so they can live together.

---

1 One of Foster's friendships was with the poet Charles Shiras; they were co-founders of a club they called Five Nice Young Men.
2 *The Gay and Lesbian Theatrical Legacy: A Biographical Dictionary Of Major Figures In American Stage History in the Pre-Stonewall Era*, Billy J. Harbin, Kim Marra, Robert A. Schanke (University of Michigan Press, 2005)

There is doubt too regarding the Irish ballad *'An Buachaill Caol Dubh'* ('The Dark Slender Boy'), which interpreters have claimed refers to a pint of beer craved by the (male) drinker. There is no such question about the old whaling ballad 'The Strapping Lad' (in the lyric, 'Allan became Eleanor') or the 'Highland Tinker' who fucks the lady of the manor, 'but when he fucks the butler, "twas the dirtiest fuck of all'.

Accessibility to traditional oral ballads was restricted until the invention of the gramophone and wireless radio at the start of the twentieth century, while homosexuality was not even a defined concept. 'The dirtiest fuck of all' would have only contravened the sodomy laws that excluded any sense that men could love their own sex. Women escaped the statute books because it was feared sanctions would encourage such behaviour.

At least the US laws against sodomy were no longer punishable by death, starting with Pennsylvania in 1786 and spreading through most states within a generation. Potential sodomites – or anyone who simply fell in love with someone of their own gender – still lived a miserable lie but some freedom of expression came in halls of entertainment where those of artistic temperaments gathered, and gender roles were subverted.

The art of impersonation

The first documented female impersonator was Lady Elizabeth, who performed in Los Angeles in 1848, though there is no proof that the Lady incorporated music in her act.[1] Yet music was a crucial part of the mix in vaudeville, alongside plays, comedy, mime, acrobatics and dancing, with the sexualised offshoot of burlesque also featuring dancing girls and striptease.

The minstrel show was another music-based variety show, with white performers in blackface make-up, parodying Afro-American culture. Here black performers also played their part, including Gauze, a female

---

[1] *Gay LA: A History of Sexual Outlaws, Power Politics and Lipstick Lesbians*, Lillian Faderman and Stuart Timmon (Basic Books, 2006)

impersonator belonging to the Georgia Minstrels, a crew of former slaves popular in the late nineteenth century that lampooned aristocratic figures.

Impersonating the opposite gender was lauded and well-paid, in the realms of comedy and illusion. But you'd still think most heterosexual men would not choose this vocation. In 'Our Love is Here to Stay: Gays and Musicals', John B. Kenrick asserts, 'Gays of the 1800s had something resembling a safe haven in theatre. No one really cared if a supporting actor was "that way" or if an effeminate dresser twinkled with admiration as he assisted the leading man into a costume.'[1]

Out front, there was no safe haven for homosexual men, only a secret society that required total discretion. Women could behave with more impunity. America's first known male impersonator, the British-born Annie Hindle, trod the boards as Charles Ryan, the kind of well-dressed gentleman of independent means known as a 'dyker', a term that fell into use for a manly woman. Hindle shaved until she developed a moustache, to better present songs such as 'Racketty Jack' and 'Do Not Put Your Boots on a Man When He's Down'.

In 1886, dressed as Ryan, Hindle married her dresser, Anna Ryan. A newspaper got hold of the story and the rumour spread that Charles Ryan was a man who had been passing himself as a woman for 20 years, ending Hindle's career.[2]

'I Love The Ladies' and 'He's Doing His Bit For The Girls' were signature songs by Florenze Tempest, 'America's most lovable impersonator of boy parts,' according to Des Moines *Daily News*, once Hindle's career had faded. In the UK, male impersonator Vesta Tilley (born Matilda Powles), the voice of 'Squeeze Her Gently' and 'Strolling Along with Nancy, admitted she 'felt that I could express myself better if I were

---

1 www.musicals101.com/ourlove.htm
2 Newspapers also reported that the most popular male impersonator of the era, Ella Wesner, eloped to Paris in 1873 with a female lover – from Laurence Senelick's *The Changing Room: Sex, Drag and Theatre. Gender In Performance* (Routledge Press, 2000)

dressed as a boy,'[1] a process that had begun when she was six, walking on stage in a little suit made by her father. WWI gave Tilley a fresh military identity: 'Jolly Good Luck to the Girl who Loves a Soldier' earned her the title of Britain's 'best recruiting sergeant'. Tilley's rival, Winifred Emms, who called herself Hetty King, dressed as a sailor for her signature song, 'All the Nice Girls Love a Sailor'. Ostensibly about the girl-in-every-port seaman, the song was adopted by the legions of gay men who found freedom on the water, within the navy or the cruise ships, denied by law on land.

Lesbians remained prisoners of the restrictive Victorian age, with the monarch fiercely opposed to any women in paid employment, let alone feminism. There was not even a medical – or social – concept of female sexuality at the time, let alone lesbianism.

Aware of developments in Germany, a more forward-thinking woman emerged in English classical composer Maude Valérie White, who named her 1890 *lied* 'Soft Lesbian Airs' (or 'Soft Lydian Airs', presumably for official publication). White was one of only two female classical composers – both lesbians – in *A History of British Music*[2], featured alongside Ethel Smyth, described as 'the first [woman] in Britain seriously to adopt composition as a career'. Clive Paget claims her 1906 opera *The Wreckers* was 'considered by many to be the finest British opera between Purcell and Britten.'[3] In a letter to her male librettist, she confessed, 'I wonder why it is so much easier for me to love my own sex passionately than yours. I can't make it out for I am a very healthy-minded person.'

With women routinely written out of history by male writers and the classical establishment, Smyth is now virtually forgotten, lost among male peers such as Edward Elgar, Maurice Ravel and Camille Saint-Sens on RCA's 1995 compilation *Out Classics: Seductive Classics by the*

---

1 *Recollections of Vesta Tilley*, by Lady de Frece (Hutchinson, 1934)
2 Written by Percy M. Young (Ernest Benn Ltd, 1967)
3 *The 10 Greatest Gay Composers*, *Limelight* magazine, 2013

World's Greatest Gay Composers,[1] as the record label responded only to rumour rather than fact. But Smyth was a vital part of feminism's first wave, writing 'March of the Women' in 1910, the officially adopted anthem for the Women's Social and Political Union, the organisational arm of the suffragette movement that formed three years after Queen Victoria's death in 1901.

The love that dared to sing

On the music-hall stage, Fred Barnes, born in Birmingham, was intrigued enough by Vesta Tilley's male impersonations – and gifted enough with a noble baritone voice – to refuse to join his family's butchery business. He reaped the early benefits of a post-Victorian age, dressing in a monocle, white tie and tails but also the kind of rouge make-up usually applied by women, encouraging cries from the audience of 'Hello, Freda!' As a songwriter, Barnes was a rarity among music hall performers. 'The Black Sheep of the Family', arguably the first song to come out of the closet when it debuted in 1907, was his most blatant effort to feed off his risqué public persona: 'It's a queer, queer world we live in/And Dame Nature plays a funny game/Some get all the sunshine/Others get the shame.'

The song made Barnes famous and became his signature song, secretly acknowledging those who would understand that 'shame' was slang for love between homosexual men. And shame was Barnes' reward, for persistent drinking and an arrest for drunken driving through London's Hyde Park, with a topless sailor in tow. He served time in prison, his career ruined.[2]

If the UK was still extricating itself from the Victorian age of morality, mainland Europe was encroaching on liberty. German writer Karl Heinrich Ulrichs became the first man – and the only man of the entire

---

1 It featured a contemporary cover photo of a topless man, presumably because a be-wigged and jowly nineteenth century figure wasn't deemed suitable to peddle classical music to gay men as a lifestyle accessory.
2 Barnes eventually drank away what was left of his wealth before catching tuberculosis; in 1938, after being told he had three months to live, Barnes committed suicide by gassing himself.

nineteenth century – to publicly confess to being attracted to his own sex, in 1867, having published his *Research on the Riddle of Man-Manly Love*. With the word 'homosexual' yet to be invented, Ulrichs called himself an *'Urning'* – in English, 'Uranian' – a nineteenth-century term that referred to 'the third sex . . . a female psyche in a male body', while *Urningin* applied to women. Some two years later Austrian physician Karl-Maria Kertbeny wrote of 'homosexuality' and 'heterosexuality' in a pamphlet, following what he called an, 'instinctive drive to take issue with every injustice'.

The German government nevertheless criminalised homosexuality between men (alongside bestiality, prostitution and paedophilia) in 1871. Twenty-five years passed before school-teacher-turned-publisher Adolf Brand produced *Der Eigene* (*The Unique*), the first homosexual periodical. A year later, Brand joined the Scientific-Humanitarian Committee, spearheaded by physician and sexologist Magnus Hirschfeld, the first organisation to defend homosexual rights and initiate a reform of its country's penal code. While Hirschfeld failed overall in that regard, he did inspire one of the earliest songs to address homosexuality.

Recorded in 1908, *'Das Hirschfeldlied'* (*'The Song of Dr Hirschfeld'*) was the work of the popular Berlin humourist and singer Otto Reutter. The song referred to 'one of the biggest scandals of the German empire,' when the aristocrat and diplomat Philip, Prince of Eulenburg was named alongside army general Kuno Graf von Moltke and the Kaiser himself, Wilhelm II, was implicated – an even greater scandal than that surrounding English writer, aristrocrat and dandy Oscar Wilde when he was convicted of gross indecency and imprisoned in 1895. As an academic, Hirschfeld's expert appraisal was called on in court. He felt that proving Moltke was gay would help his case for legalising homosexuality and so testified that there was nothing wrong with the officer, as 'homosexuality was part of the plan of nature and creation just like normal love.'[1] Hirschfeld fell victim to the political sensitivity that ensured that

---

[1] *The Eulenburg Affair: A Cultural History of Politics in the German Empire*, Norman Domeier (Camden House, 2015)

his studies were 'laughed at and ridiculed'. Worse, 'the whole scandal was then a major setback for the homosexual movement.' Even worse, Hirschfield's religion increased anti-Semitic agitators' feelings that Jews were to be Germany's undoing.

In 1908, too, Reutter's fellow singer/humourist Hans Blädel recorded *'Neue Ofenrohrverse'* ('New Stovepipe Verses' in English, which is only the start of the song's inscrutable humour that doesn't work in translation). But the lyric suggests that a homosexual – the first time the term has been used in a song – is an alternative bedmate given the chauvinistic certainty that a wife will grow old and lose her looks.

The same year, the most popular Brazilian tango and folk singer of his day, Manuel Pedro dos Santos, known as Bahiano, added homosexuality to his innuendo- and euphemism-laden topics of sexual practices, prostitution, adultery, masturbation, and sado-masochism. 'Açouguerio' ('The Butcher'), 'Francesco' and 'O Bonequinho' ('The Doll'), the last about a baby so pretty that the midwives (and, as he grew, his parents' neighbours) likened him to a doll – all made playful references to homosexuality, though 'Os Colarinhos' ('The Collars'), a scene set in Venice, was more direct: 'I walk behind a boy/To touch me one . . . /No wonder! I'm not married/Such a desire does not ensnare me.'

Brazilian singers beside Bahanio liked to provoke and tease, while it was only the odd exception that proved the rule of a more uptight Europe. The backlash after the Eulenberg affair put an end to any reference to homosexuality, in song, until 1919, after WWI. Hirschfeld celebrated the new era, distinguished by Germany's shedding of social conformity as part of its post-war recovery, by founding the Institute of Sexology; the same year, he co-wrote and acted as himself in the film drama *Anders als die Andern* (*Different from the Others*), featuring one of the earliest homosexual characters written for cinema.

Germany's liberation came with a thriving artistic response that included the *Kabarett*, or cabaret[1] scene, centred in the new capital city of Berlin, a hotbed of political and social satire. According to academic writer Sarah Lippek, 'Weimar Berlin was alive with a uniquely intoxicating sexual atmosphere because . . . of eroding middle-class values . . . new freedoms of expression, changing forms of womanhood, and the increased visibility of "deviant" sexual personae through popular culture.'[2]

In 1920, Russian-born composer (and Berlin resident) Mischa Spoliansky and German lyricist Kurt Schneider – billed as Arno Billing and Kurt Schwabach – co-wrote *'Das Lila Lied'* ('The Lilac Song'[3]), the first musical landmark of this revolution, a civil rights anthem that the pair dedicated to Hirschfeld. The scant biographical details of pianist Spoliansky or journalist Schneider don't refer to their sexuality, but the collaboration is a milestone; articulating the right to freely love someone of your own sex had been expressed, covertly, in books but never so outwardly or in song. The first verse of Schneider's lyric embodied the same human sentiment as Ulrichs and Hirschfeld, asking why man – who is otherwise, 'wise and well' – should outlaw anyone for being 'in lust' with his own kind:

> 'We see a world of romance and of pleasure/All they can see is sheer banality/Lavender nights are our greatest treasure/Where we can be just who we want to be.'

The second verse was more direct, political and angry, a call for change. 'Why the torment to impose morals of others on us?/The crime

---

[1] Cabaret developed in France in the 1870s and differed from the music hall by being staged in a nightclub or bar rather than a theatre. The audience sat at tables and were served food as well as drink. Folies Bergère (1869), Le Chat Noir (1881) and Le Moulin Rouge (1889) were the most famous clubs and some of the earliest.

[2] *Disrupted Values, Erupting Culture: Cabaret and the Sexual Persona in Weimar Berlin* (Central European University, 2008)

[3] Lilac – or lavender – became the chosen colour of homosexuality, inspired by the blue rose, thought to combine male and female attributes.

is when love must hide,' observed Schwabach, concluding, 'We will not suffer anymore, but we will be tolerated!'

Three versions of *'Das Lila Lied'* were recorded, one released by the suitably named Homocord label. In 1921, it released *'Küss Mich Mein Lieber Kohn'* ('Kiss Me My Dear John') by the Homocord Orchester. The idea of homosexual rights had acquired a legitimacy that seemed impossible before WWI: an end to suffering, the beginning of tolerance. Free at last.

CHAPTER 2

The Twenties: "T'ain't Nobody's Business If I Do': Sissies, Bull-Dykers and Freakish Man Blues

'My man got a sissy, his name is Miss Kate'

Ma Rainey, 1926

It was known as the Great Migration, an initial trickle of Afro-Americans heading north in the 1890s that had become a flood by 1916, freed from slavery in the southern states. By 1920, a million had made the move. They came to rest in cities such as Detroit, Chicago and Buffalo, but none of the places in which they settled were as large, or as legendary, as the plot above Central Park West in New York – Harlem.

These urban centres were not places to rest when the population density was insufferable and the poverty incurable. But the chance for a social life created a new era of play built on drink, drugs, gambling, prostitution, dancing and sex, and the soundtrack was music. The twin conduits of this cultural deluge were jazz and blues, imported with slavery from Africa and the Caribbean, born of the chain gang, spirituals and gospel music. Jazz was a mostly instrumental expression of jubilance that found employment in the minstrel shows, dance halls and vaudeville. But if jazz required instrumental skills, the blues could be sung with a battered one-string guitar, for its secular messages of woe, appeals for love, connection and salvation and celebrations of lust.

The social, cultural and artistic explosion in Manhattan's black enclave was vibrant and creative enough to earn a title, the Harlem Renaissance, 'a seething cauldron of Nubian mirth and hilarity', according to *Variety* magazine – the antithesis to the repressed, class-conscious goldfish bowl of European upper and middle-class society. The scene was aided by the economic boom of the roaring twenties, a decade of unprecedented innovation from cars to planes, gramophones to radiograms and sports to Hollywood movies. But it's a delicious irony that the Harlem Renaissance was also substantially aided by Prohibition in 1920, a nationwide ban on alcohol. Speakeasies – unlicensed venues that sold illegal liquor – flourished, not just among black communities but also drawing in white crowds to the 'seething cauldron', eager for a drink and to see black performers playing jazz and blues. Almost everyone was now officially illegal, not just anyone who acted on the urge to sleep with their own sex, which won its own description – 'in the life'.

'In the life' was carnal love, expressed lewdly rather than romantically. And homosexuality remained largely a stigma among men. But women, finding a new sense of self in the post-slavery era, could seek out other women, in defiance of men trying to control them, especially on the road. But social convention dictated those in the life generally got married so the ratio of lesbian to bisexual could never be established. Either way, the most famous blues singer of the era and the woman who mentored her, were both married and flagrantly enjoying lesbian relationships.

From Columbus, Georgia, Gertrude Malissa Nix Pridgett, who called herself Ma Rainey, was labelled 'mother [or godmother] of the blues' by record label Paramount. Rainey had toured with her husband Will 'Pa' Rainey in the Rabbit Foot Minstrels and then as a duo before she went solo, making her first recordings in 1923. She befriended and mentored the younger Bessie Smith, who made her recording debut that same year. From Chattanooga, Tennessee, Smith had joined Moses Stokes's Travelling Show, fronted by Rainey, though there's no proof that they became lovers when they made their base in Harlem.

Rainey embodied a style commemorated by her 1928 cut 'Deep

Moaning Blues' but Smith became the era's most popular iconic blues singer not a 'mother' but 'empress of the blues'. 'Nothing had as profound an effect on me as hearing Bessie Smith for the first time in the fifties,' recalls Chris Albertson, author of the definitive biography *Bessie*. Citing Smith's 'masterful inflections and timing', Albertson also heard, 'What's perhaps best described as "soul", a sincerity I also hear in Edith Piaf[1] and Carlos Gardel[2]. Some of Bessie's audience likened hearing her to a religious experience.'

Speakeasies weren't the only venues of entertainment; so-called 'rent parties', where tenants hired out rooms in order to pay their bills, hosted raucous gatherings, which Smith celebrated in 'Give Me a Pigfoot and a Bottle of Beer'. 'Buffet flats' were rent parties with a host of sexual activities on offer:[3] one such venue, run by ex-chorus girl Hazel Valentine on 140th Street and known as the Daisy Chain, became so popular with entertainers that jazz band leader Count Basie would write 'Swinging at the Daisy Chain' while blues legend Fats Waller penned 'Valentine Stomp' for the proprietor.

It seems that the first blues song to address homosexuality was Alberta Hunter's 'Someone Else Will Take Your Place' from 1923, in which she sang, 'If you didn't want me, tell me to my face/'Cause five or six women going to take your place.'

Rufus and Ben Quillian's 1930 track, the upbeat swinger 'It's Dirty But Good', recognised that women were on to something, and the brothers were missing out: 'I know women that don't like men/The way they do is a crying sin . . . There ain't no difference, it's just dirty but good'.

Perhaps women found as much comfort and tenderness as sexual compatibility in a world where, as Smith sang in one of her typically

---

1 The most legendary of all French singers, the *chanson* supreme, nicknamed Little Sparrow, though there was nothing little about Piaf's voice.
2 The sexuality of Argentina's king of tango, who died in a plane crash when in his thirties, has been the subject of speculation, without any hard evidence he was homosexual.
3 Rumour has it that buffet flats even had something to offer fans of bestiality. Maybe that's what the pigfoot was for.

downbeat blues, 'A Good Man is Hard to Find'. Women were as much under the thumb of their record label bosses as they were their husbands. But it's hard to know where Smith stood. In the downbeat 'Foolish Man Blues', she complained, 'Men sure is deceitful and they's gettin' worser ev'ry day/Act like a bunch of women, they's just-a gab, gab, gabbin' away', as if their lack of masculinity was the root of the problem. Smith's lyric went on to qualify, 'There's two things got me puzzled, there's two things I can't stand/A mannish-actin' woman and a skippin', twistin' woman-actin' man'.

Perhaps 'Foolish Man Blues' was intended to put distance between Smith and 'the life' because of her angrily jealous and violent husband, Jack Gee, who suspected what she was getting up to on tour, namely a lengthy affair with chorus dancer Lillian Simpson. Ma Rainey was also toying with disapproval. She was arrested for organising a lesbian orgy at her home and yet 'Sissy Blues' (1926) raged at her man's own infidelity – 'My man got a sissy, his name is Miss Kate/He shook that thing like jelly on a plate'. While 'Prove It To Me Blues' (1927) declared Rainey's lesbianism – 'Went out last night with a crowd of my friends/They must've been women,'cause I don't like no men' – it also dared audiences to label her: 'They say I do it, ain't nobody caught me/They sure got to prove it to me.'

The one woman who didn't require her audiences to find proof or who needed a husband was singer/pianist Gladys Bentley. She personified the mannish-acting, bull-dyker (also 'bull-dagger') enshrined in Bessie Jackson's 'B. D. Woman Blues' – a woman who emulated the well-dressed man of independent means. 'Comin' a time, B. D. women, they ain't gonna need no men,' was Jackson's core message; she also sang 'Women Don't Need No Men' under her real (married) name of Lucille Bogan. Bentley was living proof. She favoured a white tuxedo and top hat, which she might have worn in 1931 when she supposedly married her girlfriend in a private ceremony in Atlantic City, Jersey (information that she brazenly, provided to a gossip columnist).

Much more than Smith, Rainey, Jackson, Hunter, Ethel Waters or Clara Smith (who also professionally mentored her lover Josephine Baker), Bentley was the renaissance's true lesbian revolutionary. If her lyrics didn't ratify her desire, Bentley's entire persona said everything – her outfits, masculine voice and crew-cut hair, her flirting with women in the audience, her avoidance of male pronouns when half-singing and half-growling obscene rewrites of contemporary classics such as 'Sweet Georgia Brown' at gay speakeasy the Clam House on 133rd Street on Harlem's main drag, Jungle Alley. Unlike the traditional male impersonator, 'Bentley didn't try to "pass" as a man, nor did she playfully try to deceive her audience into believing she was biologically male,' said writer James F. Wilson. 'Instead, she exerted a "black female masculinity" that troubled the distinctions between black and white and masculine and feminine.'[1]

If the Harlem Renaissance was distinguished by women who slept with women and sometimes sang about it, there was no male musical equivalent to its notable poet, novelist, playwright and activist Langston Hughes or his peers such as Countee Cullen and Richard Bruce Nugent. But a small number of homosexual bluesmen existed. The first suggestive lyric from a male perspective was 'Pretty Baby' by Antonio Junius 'Tony' Jackson, recorded in 1916. The sheet music featured a female cover star but Jackson's lyrics – unusually – avoided pronouns and the pay-off, 'I'd like to be your sister, brother, dad and mother too/Pretty baby, pretty baby' didn't sound like he was wooing ladies.

Hailing from New Orleans, a city that would host the most liberal attitude to gay life in the US before San Francisco took over, Jackson was blessed with an extraordinary range and piano skills. He made his name in New Orleans' unique piano-based ragtime scene, though he also had a penchant for female impersonation; one of his reputed stage

---

[1] *Bull-daggers, Pansies and Chocolate Babies: Performance, Race and Sexuality in the Harlem Renaissance* (University of Michigan Press, 2011)

tricks was to perform a high-kicking dance while playing the piano. He later settled in Harlem with his lover Carl van Vechten, a rich socialite (and, later, novelist) famed for hosting parties for his gay pals and their straight admirers.

Jackson was dead by 1921 (probably from alcohol or syphilis), aged 38. The Harlem Renaissance exploded without him and he's been virtually forgotten; even Louis Malle's acclaimed 1977 film *Pretty Baby*, which used Jackson's song, didn't bring him back. Jelly Roll Morton, the ragtime genius who claims to have invented jazz, called Jackson 'the greatest single-handed entertainer in the world. There was no tune that come up from any opera or any show of any kind or anything that was wrote on paper that Tony couldn't play . . . His voice on an opera tune was exactly as an opera singer. His range on a blues tune would be just exactly like a blues singer.'

The blues classic ''T'ain't Nobody's Business If I Do' was first popularised by Bessie Smith in 1922 but was written by her openly gay pianist Porter Grainger; with that knowledge, the track stands as America's first gay pride anthem. Grainger was circumspect about his motive: 'There ain't nothing I can do or nothing I can say/That folks don't criticise me/But I'm going to do just as I want to anyway/And don't care if they all despise me.'

Georgia's Rufus Perryman, better known as Speckled Red, wrote and recorded the barrelling 'Dirty Dozens' in 1929, rare for its admission of bisexuality from a male voice: 'Now I liked your mama, liked your sister too/I liked your daddy but your daddy won't do/I met your daddy on the corner the other day/You know about that, he was funny that way.' George Hannah – 'openly gay' according to JD Doyle's Queer Music Heritage[1], with a lovely, high vibrato that could easily pass for a woman – was also willing to sing from the first-person perspective. In 1930, he wrote an equally concrete affirmation to ''T'ain't Nobody's Business If I Do', titled 'Freakish Man Blues.'

---

1 www.queermusicheritage.com/nov2014s.html

'Had a strange feeling this morning/I swear I've had it all day/I'll wake up one of these mornings/That feeling will be here to stay'.[1]

There were enough homo-centric songs from the first Golden Age of Gay to fill the 1989 twenty-five-track CD, *Sissy Man Blues*, without including Bessie Smith or Alberta Hunter. There was Harlem Hamfat's 'Garbage Man – or 'The Call of the Freaks' – advising, 'Stick out your can/Here comes the garbage man', Bert 'Snake Root' Hattan's 'Freakish Rider Blues' and Peg Leg Howell's 'Fairy Blues'. while 'Sissy Man Blues' itself was performed by both Connie McLean's Rhythm Boys and Josh 'Pinewood Tom' White, two of three covers that followed Kokomo Arnold's 1934 original, declaring, 'Lord, I woke up this mornin' with my pork grindin' business in my hand/Lord, if you can't send me no woman, please send me some sissy man.'

Cross-dressing also found a niche in Harlem. If Tony Jackson had left his impersonating days back in New Orleans, Frankie 'Half Pint' Jaxon, five-foot two-inches of vaudevillian dynamite, sang 'I'm Gonna Dance wit de Guy wot Brung Me' from both male and female perspectives; he also fronted the Tampa Red's Hokum Jazz Band on 'My Daddy Rocks Me with One Steady Roll' in 1929. In song, Wayman 'Sloppy' Henry wrote a similarly spirited anthem for cross-dressers, 'Say I Do It': 'Pete run with Mose 'cause he powdered his nose and even wore ladies hose' hollered Henry, whose titular heroes, 'could be seen running hand in hand in all kinds of weather.'

Female impersonators began to take cues from Hollywood royalty, with names such as Sepia Gloria Swanson and Sepia Mae West. Lavish, costumed drag balls were a feature of both Harlem venues such as the Rockland Palace and in downtown Manhattan's Greenwich Village. They were populated by both black and white, crossing the boundary

---

1 In 1931, Hannah also sang about lesbians in 'Boy In The Boat' (a slang term for the clitoris): 'When you see two women walking hand in hand/Just look 'em over and try to understand/They'll go to these parties have their lights down low/Only those parties where women can go'. His final verse spoilt the gay-positive mood by claiming that these lesbian liaisons were down to, 'the dames ain't got nuthin' to do', on account of their men were away, fighting for Uncle Sam.

of racial segregation, though the whites tended to be more voyeuristic, with special seating provided to look down on the action. According to writer John B. Kenrick, the balls featured 'effeminate, "pansies" mixed with straight-acting homosexuals and the general public . . . advertised as "unconventional to be sure . . . only be discreet".'[1]

'Harlem is the one place that is gay and delightful, however dull and depressing the downtown regions may be,' novelist Max Ewing wrote to his mother. 'Nothing affects the vitality and the freshness of Harlem.'[2]

But in actuality, the renaissance party and its pan-sexual freedoms didn't last long, as the roaring twenties hit the Great Depression the economic crash of 1929 would snowball into the thirties and across the globe, driving up religious and social conservatism. The repeal of Prohibition in 1933 decreased the numbers of and the takings in speakeasies and from its mid-thirties' vantage point, 'Sissy Man Blues' was an aberration, a ghostly echo of the glory days.

The fate of Gladys Bentley epitomised the new age. According to *Black Women in America: A Historical Encyclopaedia*[3], 'Initially, Bentley was able to hold on by cultivating her homosexual following. In the early 1930s, she was the featured entertainer at Harlem's Ubangi Club, supported by a chorus of men in drag. But by 1937, the glory days of Jungle Alley were very much a thing of the past. Bentley (now aged 30) moved to Los Angeles to live with her mother in a small California bungalow.'

---

1 www.musicals101.com/ourlove.htm
2 From http://xroads.virginia.edu/~ug97/blues/watson.html
3 Edited by Darlene Clark Hine (Carlson Publishing Inc., 1993)

CHAPTER 3

The Thirties: The Age of the Pansy Craze

'There's something about bulls that I like.'
'I'd Rather Be Spanish Than Mannish', Gene 'Jean' Malin, 1932

The post-WWI social revolution wasn't isolated to a black population in North America that had belatedly discovered its sense of self. After 1918, Europe was also beginning the rebuilding process after the cataclysmic events of the conflict, with the rise of socialism, republicanism, communism and fascism transforming the political terrain.

Britain in particular had already begun to rebuild after the death of Queen Victoria in 1901: her son, King Edward VII and his successor, George V, were more acquainted with art, fashion and travel. In Russia the 1917 revolution decriminalised homosexuality as part of a wider expansion of human rights, especially for women.

Coming together in the early noughties, the London-based intellectual and art collective known as the Bloomsbury Group was an emblem of change, with openly homosexual members at its core – novelists E. M. Forster and Virginia Woolf, painter Duncan Grant, writer Lytton Strachey and economist John Maynard Keynes. Yet none of the group were musicians. Perhaps the new sounds of ragtime and jazz were too frivolous, compared to literature, but they captured the young and gave rise to the female 'flapper' in the early twenties, the name inspired by the dance style, flapping their wings as if they were birds trying to fly.

The party-hard, fashion-conscious flapper sensibility spread through Europe and in America, Petting [making out] parties became popular; sex outside marriage was more frequent. To paraphrase the saying, 'Fuck war, let's dance. And even fuck'. Life was for living and the technological and economic boom gave people the chance.

Outside Harlem, New York's homosexual sub-cultures flourished in Greenwich Village and even pockets of Times Square, where the elaborate Ziegfeld Follies productions – modelled on the Folies Bergère revue in Paris – highlighted singers such as Lilyan Tashman, the wife of silent film star Al Lee, both bisexual luminaries of the new age.

Similar enclaves took root in San Francisco, Los Angeles and Chicago, anywhere capitalism had created large, concentrated populations that offered anonymity and an alternative to rural family life. There were dangers: the first recorded police raid on an American gay bathhouse was in 1903, at New York's Ariston hotel and seven men received sentences ranging from four to 20 years. But gay life thrived.

Female impersonation thrived too, though male impersonation waned after 1920; perhaps the war had seen women take over the roles of real men, so negating the need for illusion. Hollywood's silent film industry had appreciated the former even before the war, albeit as slapstick rather than subversive characters. The great American female impersonator Julian Eltinge (born William Dalton)[1] made sure he put clear water between his elaborate fantasy and his (equally artificial) offstage act, when he was all cigar-smoking, horseback-riding, bar-fighting machismo; at the climax of his show, Eltinge would rip off his wig to reveal the illusion. But he made a fabulous Countess Sylvia, a Hungarian belle, in the 1903 production of *Baron Humbug* and in the 1912 Broadway musical *The Fascinating Widow*, he sang both male and female leads.

Greenwich Village staple Bert Savoy (born Everett McKenzie) was more daring and suggestive: 'the very first true drag queen', reckoned

---

1 Eltinge was popular enough to have a Broadway theatre named after him.

writer Mickey Weems[1]. Where Eltinge was sophisticated, Savoy was bawdy; where Eltinge took great steps to quell rumours of homosexuality, Savoy made much of his sexuality, begging to wear make-up while in prison (for the crime of fortune-telling). After Savoy met chorus boy Jay Brennan on a streetcar, the lovers created a successful double act in 1918's *Ziegfeld's Follies* and the 1920 and 1922 editions of *Greenwich Village Follies*. Brennan was the straight man to catty, gossiping Savoy. In 1923, the pair released a single, it's A- and B-sides named after Savoy's catchphrases, 'You Don't Know the Half of It' and 'You Must Come Over'. But it was a short-lived recording career: Savoy was killed by lightning that year while walking on Long Beach. But his legacy lived on in the form of Mae West, vaudeville's queen of bawdy, who learnt her exaggerated moves from Savoy, likewise her legendary catchphrase, 'Come up and see me,' most likely modelled on Savoy's 'You must come over.'

There's very little filmed evidence of Eltinge and none of Savoy, but the UK's Douglas Byng has a presence on YouTube. A school teacher and costume designer turned actor, Byng raised double entendres and sexual innuendo to a new level. He was as openly gay as Savoy but presented himself as an old lady, as unthreatening as his signature songs 'Milly the Messy Old Mermaid' and 'I'm the Mayoress of Mold-on-the-Puddle'. But there was a message to 'I'm a Mummy – an Old Egyptian Queen' and an edge to 'Doris the Goddess of Wind':

'I blow through the bedrooms and blow out the light/I blow to the left and I blow to the right/My life's just one blow through from morning to night/It's the wind, it's the wind'.

Germany had been several steps ahead of the UK with Magnus Hirschfield's work and 'Das Lied Lied' and, by the end of the twenties, there were over twenty-five publications dedicated to homosexuality, while the rest of the world had just one – Henry Gerber's *Friendship and Freedom*. A German émigré to the US, Gerber had refused to keep

---

1 Edge Media Report, www.edgemedianetwork.com/style/grooming///77172/bert_savoy:_the_first_queen_in_the_whole_wide_world

his homosexuality secret and was sectioned in a mental hospital. When WWI broke out, he chose to join the army rather than be interned as an enemy alien; stationed in Germany, Gerber discovered Hirschfeld and, back in Chicago after the war, he formed the Society for Human Rights in 1924, America's first gay rights organisation.[1]

Neither did America develop the same strong cabaret scene as Germany, with much more intimate spaces than music halls where a select, underground crowd soaked up political satire and gallows humour, especially in the capital Berlin. Germany had its first musical too, written by *'Das Lila Lied'* composer Mischa Spolianksy, with lyricist Marcellus Schiffer (the two men had lived together before Spoliansky married). *Es Liegt In Der Luft* (*It Is In The Air*) included a duet for two women, *'Wenn Die Beste Freundin'* ('When The Best Friend'), performed in the show and later recorded by French singer Margo Lion and rising Berlin actress Marlene Dietrich[2], about best friends who find a common bond – inferred to be sexual – outside of their dissatisfying marriages.

In France, where sodomy laws had been abolished as early as 1791[3], a similar sense of freedom was lived out in the larger nightclubs and smaller cabaret scenes. The glamorous figurehead was Josephine Baker, whose lesbian affairs included Ada Beatrice Queen Victoria Louise Virginia Smith (known as Bricktop because of her flaming red hair),

---

1 Gerber found it almost impossible to sign up subscribers for *Friendship and Freedom* as US law enforcement agencies were able to access postal lists. It only lasted two issues, and his Society two years before Gerber was arrested (but not charged) and all his paperwork confiscated. In later letters, Gerber complained that most homosexuals he knew were keen on finding partners for sex rather than helping to reform the laws that forced them underground.
2 Male impersonation was a dying art, though Dietrich did her bit after her international breakthrough with *The Blue Angel* (1930). In *Morocco* (1930), she dressed in a top hat and tailcoat for a nightclub scene, albeit as a radiant, blond-curled femme rather a man. She not only flirted with a woman in the audience but kissed her on the lips.
3 Ironically, the anti-clerical feeling in Catholic countries such as France had helped repeal the sodomy laws long before Protestant nations, where church life was less dominant, and statutes that were less rooted in religion weren't repealed for centuries.

another American ex-pat who'd found her niche in Paris, as a dancer, singer and subsequently the owner of the nightclub Chez Bricktop. Britain still lagged behind. Its first nominal cabaret club, London's Cave of the Golden Calf, had opened in 1912 but went bankrupt three years later.

Yet one British 78 rpm record was willing to go public. 'Masculine Women, Feminine Men', a swinging foxtrot written by the prolific partnership of lyricist Edgar Leslie and composer James Monaco, was first covered in 1926 by the Savoy Havana Band and by Merrit Brunies and His Friar's Inn Orchestra: a subsequent five covers underlined its popularity. Leslie's verses spun examples of role reversals: she's learning to shave and he's doing his hair, she's playing billiards and he's dressing the kids; she's buying suits and he's wearing perfume. 'Masculine women, feminine men/Which is the rooster, which is the hen?' the chorus asked in earnest. 'It's hard to tell 'em apart today.'

A year later Mae West put the first openly homosexual figure on the USA stage in her play *The Drag*, inspired by her anguished gay friends' desire to live without censure, though the script featured conversion therapy and murder. Also in 1927, the musical *Show Boat*, by composer Jerome Kern and lyricist Oscar Hammerstein II, was staged on Broadway. It was set on the Mississippi river with themes of love and racial prejudice and, tellingly, 'Can't Help Lovin' That Man', which gave a voice to anyone who felt oppressed because of who they fell in love with.

The Pansy comes out...

Finally, in 1929, the first clearly delineated gay man, a flamboyant costume designer, came out front, in the first homosexual role in a film with sound. *The Broadway Melody* was set backstage at a Ziegfeld-style revue; the designer was typecast as a snippy, preening queen, a female impersonator in all but clothes. There was a butch lesbian caricature too. But they were there, in full view.

In 1929 too, Helen Kane – the model for the dipsy cartoon character

Betty Boop – released 'He's So Unusual'[1]: 'When I want some kissin'/ And I gotta have some kissin'/He says, "No! Let me go"/He's so unusual!' It was a start. Popular culture now allowed men to be effeminate, though the concept of masculine homosexuals would have been too threatening. The economic downturn after the Great Depression had yet to kick in by 1930, when the Pansy Club opened in Times Square. This was the start of a brief era that a 1930 edition of *Variety* magazine called the 'pansy craze'. If 'pansy' was a derogatory term, it gave the effeminate man an air of legitimacy, if not quite respectability. 'Mistress of ceremonies' at the Pansy Club was George Francis Peduzzi, from Baltimore, Maryland. Calling himself Karyl Norman, he was the first female impersonator to write his own songs, which made use of his octave-stretching voice. No recordings exist, but the sheet music survives; song titles such as 'Nobody Lied (When They Said that I Cried Over You)' and 'I'm Through (Shedding Tears Over You)' suggest tantalising precursors of fifties and sixties pop melodrama, though the pansy sound was defined by zippy, roguish piano tones.

Norman soon had a rival: Brooklyn-born Gene 'Jean' Malin, who recorded 'I'd Rather be Spanish than Mannish' in 1932, and on a major label (Columbia) too, which certified the pansy's fashionable status. 'I'm amazed Columbia got involved, because it was a great risk to release such a record,' says Peter Mintun, a specialist in the between-the-wars great American songbook. 'It was expensive to make records, which involved different mechanical processes. In Britain, radio was limited so people would buy recordings, but in the US, radio meant that people bought far less, so you'd get five or maybe ten thousand pressings of a single, while in the UK, it might be fifty thousand.'

Malin had performed on screen with Mae West, and did a great West impression, spoken and sung, in the 1933 film *Arizona To Broadway*, but his club outfit was tuxedo rather than a dress – less female impersonation, more assimilation. Hearst Newspapers' Broadway columnist

---

1 A 45-second snippet of 'He's So Unusual' was covered by Cyndi Lauper on her 1983 album *She's So Unusual*.

Louis Sobol described Malin as 'a baby-faced lad who lisped and pressed his fingers into his thighs'[1] and his single set a new benchmark for camp and innuendo. The B-side, 'That's What's the Matter with Me' was a direct confession: 'As far as I'm concerned, this thing is breaking up my life/I don't know whether I should take a husband or a wife.'

This *thing*, the matter with the singer, is that he's a hermaphrodite. Malin's A-side was more about metaphor: 'I am a Spaniard that's different', he declares. 'When I keep my mouth shut, there's room for a doubt/ But when I start talking, the secret is out.'

The chorus incorporated a shrieked, '*SpaaanEEESH!*' ending in falsetto. What was it about the Spanish? Perhaps the rhyme with mannish was too good to pass up. But it also inferred that America didn't cultivate pansies – they're all queer over in Europe, aren't they?

Ray Bourbon, stole the exact same falsetto inflection for 'Spanish Passion', a B-side in 1935, incredibly one of 14 singles he released that year. While Malin emulated Savoy's brief moment in the sun, killed in a car crash in 1935, Bourbon would endure, 'the *sine qua non* of pre-Stonewall drag artists, and certainly the most prolific,' according to a collector of records by female impersonators,[2] with a thirty-five-year stretch of 78s, singles and albums. Bourbon's first recording, an unreleased test pressing of 'I Want To Be Good', established his trademark bitter and barbed spoken-word, decorated with piano trills, frequent mock laughter and barrage of innuendo. Real angst, as penned by Karl Norman, or rage, wouldn't have got anyone far.

Bourbon, born Hal Wadell in Texas, inherited vast wealth in 1931 but was still committed to his act, as nature clearly intended. According to a detailed account by showbiz and comedy expert Kliph Nesteroff, Bourbon, 'joined with pansy acts George "Honey Boy" Hayes, Billy "the male Jean Harlow" Beryl and several other ambitious drag queens for a touring revue titled *Boys will be Girls*. Remarkable for its time, the showcase brought homosexual themes direct to the closeted corners of

---

1 *The Longest Street; A Memoir*, Louis Sobol (Crown Publishers, 1968)
2 http://www.blakstone.com/MainSite/Homepage.html

America – from the Torch Club in Massillon, Ohio, to the Kit Kat Club in Sheboygan, Wisconsin.'[1]

There was no lesbian equivalent, apart from cellist Gwendoline Farrar and pianist Norah Blaney, partners on and off stage. The British pair presented as women, though Farrar's deeper voice took the 'male' role in their duets while Blaney was the woman, in a knowing twist on the traditional singing couple. Farrar was romantically linked with US actress Tallulah Bankhead, and socially with Radclyffe Hall, the British author of *The Well of Loneliness*, written in 1929, the first novel to make a clear-cut romantic and political stand for lesbianism.[2] Farrar and Blaney were less forthright; though Farrar recorded 'Masculine Women! Feminine Men!' with a pianist in place of Blaney, you needed inside information to get the gist of the duo's tender ballad 'Moanin' For You'.

By the mid-thirties, newspaper ads for female impersonators featured 'All-star gay boys', the word 'gay' for 'homosexual' having entered modern parlance. Yet at the same time, the word was still used for its traditional meaning, though it was never clear when the songwriter was intent on using both meanings simultaneously. As publishers of sheet music insisted no lyric could be changed, male and female singers would respectively sing male and female pronouns (on the male side, Leo Reisman's 'Can't We Be Friends?', Abe Lyman's 'If He Cared' and the Singing Boys' 'He's So Unusual'). Vess L. Ossman's 1905 recording of 'A Gay Gossoon' was unlikely to be a pioneering act of subversion and the 1934 film musical *The Gay Divorcee* didn't have a homosexual subtext. But what of rising crooner Bing Crosby's 1929 cut 'Gay Love', a pared-back waltz? Or the swing of his 'There ain't No Sweet Man Worth the Salt of My Tears', written by the first (known) gay man of jazz, pianist and cornet player Bix Beiderbecke, Crosby's former roommate?

---

1 *Murder in Mink! The Crimes of Comedian Ray Bourbon*, http:/blog.wfmu.org/freeform/2012/07/murder-in-mink-crimes-of-ray-bourbon.html

2 *The Well of Loneliness* is much more part of gay folklore than what's considered the first gay-themed novel, 1870's *Joseph and his Friend: A Story of Pennsylvania*, written by – married – USA author Bayard Taylor.

In 1929, Crosby also recorded the swelling ballad 'I Surrender Dear', confessing, 'I may seem proud and I may act gay/It's just a pose, I'm not that way'. As Beiderbecke's pal, he must have been aware of the potential interpretation. Fellow male superstars of the era pushed camp at the expense of machismo. Eddie Cantor, whose signature tune 'Ma, He's Making Eyes at Me' was accompanied by rolling his eyes upward while Cantor's main inspiration, Al Jolson, was America's most popular entertainer and arguably first to embody the proto-rock star, 'teasing, cajoling, and thrilling the audience', according to Broadway expert Larry Stempel.[1]

Mad about the boys

The UK's thirties' superstar was cut from a very different cloth to Jolson. Noël Coward was an actor and singer, but his core strength was his writing: songs, musicals, stage plays. Though Coward moved in very different worlds to the 'pansy' entertainer, as an intimate of British royalty (most notably the bisexual Prince George, Duke of Kent), there was a similar level of arch camp and innuendo to his weaponry; the Londoner would never water down his arch mannerisms and plummy accent.

Coward's 1929 breakthrough was his own play, *The Vortex*, in which he played the cocaine-addicted son of a nymphomaniac socialite: surely enough scandal for the times, though interpreters also note a hint of repressed homosexuality. But it was his mastery of musicals – *Hay Fever*, *High Society*, *Private Lives* – that defined Coward and gave him the most freedom to let the gay genie out of the bottle. Growing up in the libertarian twenties, Coward, like his friend and musical peer Ivor Novello,[2] seemed to view the gay life with amusement instead of fear. He once said he'd like to cover Beatrice Lillie's tooth-sweet take on Rose Amy Fyleman's poem,

---

[1] *Showtime: A History Of the Broadway Musical Theater*, Larry Stempel (W. W. Norton, 2010)

[2] Novello, the most successful British writer of musicals until Andrew Lloyd-Webber, was more concerned with music than lyrics, though his final musical, *Gay's the Word*, tenuously named after its lead female character Gay, was a late-flowering act of boldness.

'There are Fairies at the Bottom of our Garden', but feared he'd accidentally sing 'There are fairies in the garden of my bottom'.

Coward's first hit musical, 1929's *Bitter Sweet*, included 'Green Carnation', a reference to Oscar Wilde's choice of flower for his lapel in the belief that the colour was, 'in individuals . . . always a sign of a subtle artistic temperament'. 'Green Carnation' chimed perfectly with pansy style: 'Haughty boys, naughty boys, dear, dear, dear!/Swooning with affection . . . And as we are the reason/For the nineties being gay/We all wear a green carnation.'

'Mad About The Boy' (from 1932's *Words and Music*) was written from the viewpoint of women queuing to see a film star:[1] 'I know it's stupid to be mad about the boy/I'm so ashamed of it but must admit/The sleepless nights I've had about the boy.' While Coward willingly recorded his own version, he never performed it. When UK singer-songwriter Tom Robinson became the first male singer to cover the song – live in 1982, on record in 1984 – Coward's estate threatened to sue because of his wish that no man could interpret his supposed 'female' songs[2]. It was as if the association would retrospectively out him. Coward never publically declared his homosexuality but lived vicariously on the edge, with enough clues for the initiated. Take his 1941 song 'I've Been To A Marvellous Party': 'Everyone's here and frightfully gay/Nobody cares what people say/Although the Riviera seems really much queerer than Rome at its height/Yesterday night.' The guests include Cecil, who wears a black feather boa, the Grand Duke dancing the foxtrot with the narrator and 'Maurice made a couple of passes at Gus'. It does sound like a great night and a really *gay* night. As long as you never discussed your sexuality, and you counted royals as friends, you could get away with it.

---

[1] The object of Coward's adulation could have been Italy's new matinee idol, Rudi Valentino, whose sexuality was often questioned, his various marriages declared fronts for his gay affairs.

[2] Says Robinson, 'Perhaps whoever was dealing with this for the Coward estate had figured it was better to let my little live album on an obscure label die its natural death rather than giving me the publicity of a court case that could have been tabloid catnip.'

BREAKING DOWN THE WALLS OF HEARTACHE

At least Coward never hid behind a marriage and his homosexuality was barely a secret: he was profiled in the first 'gay lifestyle' magazine, *Bachelor*[1], published out of Philadelphia in 1937. Cole Porter, meanwhile, was not among those profiled, presumably because he was married, having combined his fortune as the grandson of one of Indiana's richest men with that of socialite Linda Lee Thomas. But Porter was Coward's only true peer; as erudite, sharp and arch a craftsman, as coded and playful in his wordplay, though he lacked the voice to front his own songs.

Porter's wife knew about his affairs with men and dalliances with rent boys, which he wrote about in 'I'm a Gigolo', for – and about – the black bisexual s(w)inger, Hutch Hutchinson, who sang it first in 1929, noting, 'I'm a famous gigolo/And of lavender, my nature's got just a dash in it.'

Porter also wrote 'I'm Unlucky in Gambling' in 1929, his first unveiled reference to homosexuality, about a woman who falls for a croupier and takes him to a film starring US screen idol John Gilbert: 'I said, 'Like John Gilbert a lot, don't you?'/He didn't answer, but when the show was through/I realised that he liked John Gilbert too.'

In 'A Picture of Me Without You', Porter suggested trying to 'Picture Central Park without a sailor', referring to New York's prime cruising zone. He pushed things still further with Broadway's first gay love song, 1934's 'You're the Top': 'If, baby, I'm the bottom, you're the top!' Few would have got the inside gag or the reference in 1941's 'Farming': 'Don't inquire of Georgie Raft/Why his cow has never calfed/Georgie's bull is beautiful, but he's gay!'

In their moneyed worlds, Coward and Porter would have enjoyed their fame, parties and affairs, though the threat of exposure and arrest still required discretion,[2] while persistent subterfuge must have been wearying. In Coward's 1934 operetta *Conversation Piece*, the female lead sang 'I'll Follow My Secret Heart'. Neither Porter nor Coward found anything close to a settled romance (Porter's only lasting relationship was his marriage).

---

1 *Bachelor* magazine only lasted a year.
2 It's often suggested that Coward was protected by his closeness to the British royals.

The Thirties: The Age of the Pansy Craze

For the less privileged gay man, the Great Depression meant increased social hardship, more religious conservatism, and the closure of venues where they could meet others. New York's Pansy Club didn't even last two years, closed down after a shooting. In 1933, Ray Bourbon was one of seven *Boys Will Be Girls* troupers to be arrested, at Tait's Café in San Franciso (the club's manager eventually took the rap), where the police would periodically make their presence felt and reinforce the need for bribes. In 1936, Bourbon was arrested at Hollywood nightclub Reuben's, accused of an 'indecent performance'.

'Par for the course,' wrote Kliph Nesteroff. 'The indecency charge stemmed not from dirty words or descriptions of sex acts, but merely Bourbon's onstage admission that he was gay.'[1]

Other gay haunts had their liquor licences revoked and other venues declined after 1933's repeal of Prohibition. It wasn't a good year for the gays elsewhere: Adolf Hitler was appointed chancellor in Germany and initiated the Nazi eradication of socialist policy and civil liberties, from political opposition to expressions of 'deviant' art and sexuality. Hungarian ex-pat Paul O'Montis, who sang 'Was Hast du für Gefühle, Moritz' ('What did You do for Feelings, Moritz') in 1927 – in a proto-Joel Grey from *Cabaret* fashion – would flee to Austria and then Czechoslovakia before being sent to his final destination, a Polish concentration camp.[2]

Hollywood began its own crackdown, having ignored its own production code of 1930, which included a ban on any sexualised behaviour. But the Roman Catholic Church's nationwide protest finally forced the studios to buckle down. The appointed overseer, Joseph Breen, 'a devout Catholic, blatant anti-Semite and homophobe,'

---

[1] *Murder in Mink! The Crimes Of Comedian Ray Bourbon*, at http://blog.wfmu.org/freeform/2012/07/murder-in-mink-crimes-of-ray-bourbon.html

[2] One small victory against the Nazis was scored by Max Hansen, a half-Jewish Danish-German comedian/actor, who satirised Adolf Hitler as a homosexual in 'War'n Sie Schon Mal In Mich Verliebt?' ('Have You Ever Been In Love With Me?'), which infuriated Hitler. Hansen eventually resettled in Denmark.

wrote John Kenrick, 'set out to reform the content of Hollywood films with unflinching zeal'.[1]

Lacking a central body, the US songwriting industry escaped imposed self-censorship. Likewise the UK, which hadn't had the equivalent pansy craze but threw out the occasional pansy fancy. It's impossible to know what sales a record such as 'Let's All Be Fairies' by London's Durium Dance Band achieved but it would have been fun to flap – or mince – to. Over a typical slice of orchestral swing, the effete male vocalist gets his lips around the words 'tinkle', 'gresh', 'daisy', 'whimsy', 'whomsey', 'flimsy' and 'flamsey', but gets specific when singing about 'two great big burly boxers', one suggesting to the other, 'There's no reason why we should fight/So let's both be fairies'.

If 'Let's All Be Fairies' was as light as its namesakes, there was another path. Judd Rees' 'The King's a Queen at Heart' (1934) was shocking – crude, audacious and controversial, with the first English lyric to feature the word 'homosexual'. It's Rees' only recording to have surfaced, alongside a single image online[2], but it confirms he existed, and mirrored the heavily made-up look of Gene Malin. It turns out that Rees' real name was Edward Jarvis, a stage and radio actor born in Hollywood, while the record label involved – Liberty Music Shop[3] – was based in New York. That might explain the irreverent approach to the British monarchy, specifically King Edward VIII, who abdicated the throne in December 1936 after just 326 days to marry American divorcee Wallis Simpson. There was a rumour that both were bisexual, despite Edward's additional womanising reputation. Online reports date 'The King's a Queen at Heart' to 1934, two years before Edward's coronation, where Rees' song begun: 'There's something queer about this peer/his actions most complex/The way he walks, the way he talks/makes me doubtful

---

1 From 'Our Love is Here to Stay I, 1900-1940: On Screen', http://www.musicals101.com/gay4.htm
2 Of a flyer for a bill headed by US vaudeville dance stars Pat Rooney and Marion Bent, http://queermusicheritage.com/jun2004jr.html
3 Liberty had previously released Ray Bourbon records, making the label the default home for risqué club acts.

about his sex ... His troupes are a-blaze with colour, as they parade in the castle courtyards/From the swish of their stride, he has named them with pride/The king's own homosexual guards.'

Rees must have been familiar with Gene Malin's record: 'To suggest that the Spanish is more apropos than the mannish/On a new conquest gives him a start/He'll be gay till the end, till he's too old to bend/For the king's just a queen at heart.'

All of America's pansy craze releases proved to be one-offs rather than products of a steady musical career, such as Louis Powell with the Jazz Wizzards' 'Sissy' ('We're all sissies and we must stick together') and 'Man About Town', written by Sherwin Bassett and sung by Jimmy Rogers, a vocalist/pianist associated with the Club New Yorker.[1] The Coward-esque A-side has a mild gay reference – 'Don't gamble with the men at all/Just learn to play strip poker' – but the B-side 'Cellini (The Menace of Venice)' is the earliest musical reference to bisexuality, as known to J. D. Doyle of Queer Music Heritage: 'And of the women he soon grew very sick/So when he met a blue-eyed page named Dennis/He fell for Dennis like a ton of bricks.'[2]

Another one-off is documented in *Chicago Whispers: A History of LGBT Chicago Before Stonewall*[3], namely male duo Frankie and Johnnie, who performed in the city's Ballyhoo club but never seem to have made it to the studio – they exist in the memory of an anonymous contributor, with a lyric that wins outright for outrageousness: 'Whoops! My dear, even the chief of police is queer/When the sailors come to town, lots of brown, lots of brown/Holy by Jesus, everybody's got pareses[4] in Fairy Town.'

---

1 Neither Bassett or Rogers have traceable origins or other recordins to their name and they're likely to be the same man.
2 Cellini teaches Dennis how to read, 'but he couldn't wait until he got to the bottom of the page.'
3 St Sukie de la Croix, University of Wisconsin Press, 2012
4 Pareses is the medical term for inflammation of the brain in the later stages of syphilis, causing progressive dementia and paralysis

BREAKING DOWN THE WALLS OF HEARTACHE

The unknown genius of pansy: Bruz Fletcher

Not all pansy performers were transient characters. Between 1933 and 1937, Dwight Fiske, from Provincetown, Massachusetts, recorded up to thirty sides on his Fiskana imprint. Fiske earned the nickname King Leer and 'sounded like the biggest flamboyant queen,' reckons Peter Mintun, but he probably survived because he sang in subtle and veiled code, adopting animals for his party records, from 'Why Should Penguins Fly' to 'Ida the Wayward Sturgeon'. But Fiske pales next to a pansy-era singer-songwriter who raised the bar – with sharper wit and chutzpah, with extra lashings of filth with pathos and tragedy: Bruz Fletcher.

Stoughton Fletcher IV – Bruz was his childhood nickname, a mispronunciation of 'brother' – was born into one of Indiana's richest families, like Cole Porter. There, their circumstances diverged, as Fletcher's family fortune was lost and in need of work, Fletcher worked as a jobbing songsmith in Hollywoodwhere he moved in with actor and Oscar nominee Casey Roberts. Newspaper columns never inferred a romantic link but their cohabitation was there in print. The show business community looked after its own – except when it came to posterity. History, for the best part of seventy years, has buried Fletcher.

Most of what is now known about Fletcher is down to Tyler Alpern, author of the 2010 book *Bruz Fletcher: Camped, Tramped and a Riotous Vamp*[1]. He heard a cover of Fletcher's waning lament 'Drunk With Love' by American *chanteuse* Frances Faye and was intrigued to dig deeper.

Alpern learned that Fletcher recorded the track in 1934, but on the west coast and had remained undiscovered when the east coast pansy craze itself was first documented in 1993 by George Chauncey in *Gay New York: Gender, Urban Culture and the Making of the Gay Male World, 1890-1940*. Fletcher's stage show had been mostly restricted to LA's Club Bali bar and he had little luck with music publishers, only managing to copyright four of his tunes.

---

1 Blurb Books, 2010

The Thirties: The Age of the Pansy Craze

At least Fletcher found a home, at Liberty Music Shop alongside fellow risqué artists, with eight singles; he also released three albums and wrote two novels. As his relationship with Roberts showed, Fletcher embraced risk, with blatant homo-centric songs that refused to settle for the coded messages of Porter and Coward. They included 'Keep an Eye on His Business' (the B-side to his first single 'Hilly Brown'), with a lyric as phallo-centric as any freakish blues. The song, Alpern says, 'offers pointers on how to hold a man – literally. Fletcher makes it clear that he is talking about more than stocks rising and every time he says "ladies", you know that, depending on the audience and the hour, he means "gentlemen".'

Fletcher was also willing to display the dysfunctional skeletons in his closet. 'Hilly Brown' described what Alpern calls an 'Adonis-like travelling salesman' who ends up castrated, while his mother is poisoned. This was how Fletcher's mother killed herself in real life, followed by his grandmother, who died sampling the same tincture. The double suicide was compounded by Fletcher's sister dying in Paris. Systematically, his privileged world had unravelled, which blackened Fletcher's gift for frothy comedy. 'His protagonists often have terrible ends in spite of the light, happy nature of the songs,' Alpern says. 'Like the "gorgeous" gay butler in "Mrs. Lichtenfall" is shot dead and the madcap society girl turned movie star Miss Day dies young.'

Fletcher vacillated between comedy and tragedy. For laughs, there was 'My Doctor', the first anthem for size queens: 'The size of his prescription quite belies human description/My doctor, his understanding really is huge.' For sadness, 'Drunk with Love' documented Fletcher's alcoholic slide after he and Roberts had split up, resulting in what Alpern calls 'Fletcher's 'least arch and most honest lyric':

'Don't need champagne to make me spin/Love him so, is it a sin?/My hands touch his, my senses fizz/He makes me drunk with love/Now every day I stop and say I'll find someone new/Someday he'll walk out my door/Well, I guess that's what doors are for/And when I slam it, He'll say/"God, damn it! He's just drunk with love."'

In between, Fletcher used comedy as a vehicle for tragedy, in songs such as 'Hello Darling', inspired by Fletcher and Roberts' pet monkeys to lampoon the idea that homosexuality was a curable affliction: 'The new psychiatrist that I am going to in the Bleecker Building/Says that I've got a primate urge/Yens to sleep with monkeys, marmosets/Anything with a big tail.'

Fletcher was also groundbreaking, creating the first transsexual character in song, 'Peter Lillie Daisy' (like 'Drunk With Love', a mid-period single released on his Bruz Fletcher Sings label) portrayed 'a misunderstood young person with the wonderful ability to instantly change its sex from male to female and back again,' Alpern explains. 'Seeking its father's approval and searching for its place in the world, it ends up finding its own self acceptance and happiness. To a population of closeted homosexuals forced to move with great agility between the worlds of straight and gay, the metaphor of changing one's gender at a whim must have been easily appreciated.'

Fletcher also championed women, if you took 'Miss Day' and 'Mrs Lichtenfall' at face value rather than metaphors for men. Alpern sees Fletcher as 'an early feminist of sorts, creating a myriad of bold, powerful, smart, independent, female characters who were often sexual outsiders. These women resonated deeply with homosexuals who related to them on many different levels.'

Stylistically, Fletcher began closer to Coward's vaudevillian camp patter but gravitated toward Porter's more timeless sound[1] and if Fletcher never matched either's acute songwriting precision, his melodies have a subtle beauty and some lyrics still dazzle, such as 'Simple Things' (1936):

---

[1] Fletcher acknowledged his contemporaries in 'Oh, For a Week in the Country': 'With bright green tile they've lined the swimming hole/And the skunks all smell of tweed/The birds all sing songs by Cole and Noel/We were there/With the Hammond organ playing the accompaniment they need.'

The Thirties: The Age of the Pansy Craze

'I want an expensive extensive excursion/To the realms of in-, per- and di-version/It's the simple things in life for me.'

For all his hopes, Fletcher's life was never simple. Behind the wit and wordplay, his private life was like that of Peter Lillie Daisy: complicated and compromised, between the need for honesty and defiance – perhaps the loss of the family fortune meant there was far less for him to now lose – and the fear of arrest or even prison and disgrace. Since the launch of the production code in Hollywood, LA's gay community had been pushed back underground. Fletcher's residency at Club Bali was cut short and the bar shut down soon after. 'Police crackdowns made it virtually impossible for him to find work', says Alpern. In 1941, Fletcher shut himself in the garage and turned on the car engine.

Fletcher's suicide symbolised the moral shift between the twenties, when he and Casey were first together, and the renewed bigotry of the thirties. His brutal denouement preceded that of Lorenz 'Larry' Hart by two years. Hart would be another victim of the vicissitudes of a turbulent time – and this was a man at the top of his game, like Coward and Porter.

Lyricist Hart and composer Richard Rogers were the most successful song-writing duo of the age; F. Scott Fitzgerald called Hart 'America's poet laureate' while Stephen Sondheim claims Hart 'freed American lyrics from the stilted middle-European operetta technique'. But Hart's private life was, in the words of his own lyric, bewitched, bothered and bewildered. While Coward and Porter mastered what John Kenrick calls 'the combination of private daring and public tact', Hart was, 'too guilt-ridden and too frightened . . . The more he tried to suppress his desires, the more they consumed him.'[1]

Unlike Coward and Porter, Hart's family were Jewish immigrants; they weren't poor but they lacked that veneer of privilege. For whatever reason, Hart lacked the confidence of his gay peers; the nearest he came to confession, playful or otherwise, was 1936's 'The Heart is Quicker

---

1 'Our Love is Here to Stay – Musical Closets: Gay Songwriters', www.musicals101.com/gay5b.htm

than the Eye': 'Mother warned me my instincts to deny/Yet I fail/The male is frail/The heart is quicker than the eye!'

But within Hart's musical closet, *New York Times* writer Stephen Holden hears 'a heart-stopping sadness that reflected his conviction that he was physically too unattractive to be lovable . . . By all accounts, Hart, who stood just under five feet tall . . . saw himself as an undesirable freak . . . he pursued a secretive and tormented erotic life of which only hints appear in his songs.'[1]

The gender-free oddball romance of 'My Funny Valentine' and 'Blue Moon' – 'Standing alone/Without a dream in my heart/Without a love on my own' – also bear strange fruit. Given Rogers and Hart's popularity, many similarly closeted gay men would have clung to his words. The language of 'Bewitched, Bothered And Bewildered'; was also odd, because only a man, rather than a woman, would have chosen the phrase, ' . . . and worship the trousers that cling to him.'

By the end of 'Bewitched, Bothered And Bewildered', the narrator is gladly free of this giddy love: 'wise at last'. Like Fletcher, Hart retreated into alcoholism and by 1943 he was free at last, dying of pneumonia after a three-day bender, the culmination of what Hart biographer Gary Marmostein calls, 'dozens of lyrics that were less about being small than about what it's like to *feel* small – to be dismissed, excluded, denied admission and left standing out in the cold.'[2]

Under Republican mayor Fiorello LaGuardia, motivated by 'a fierce hatred of commercialised vice,'[3] wrote Rachel Shteir, gay New York was also under attack. But there were pockets of resistance. By the end of the decade, former Pansy Club MC Karyl Norman had moved to California, to LA's surviving Club La Boheme and San Francisco's Finocchio's, producing drag shows – the only way left for gay men to present on stage – but he never wore drag when singing himself.

---

1 http://www.nytimes.com/1995/04/30/theater/pop-view-just-a-sap-for-sugar-love-and-sorrow.html
2 *A Ship Without A Sail* (Simon & Schuster, 2013)
3 *Striptease: The Untold History of the Girlie Show* (Oxford University Press, 2005)

The Thirties: The Age of the Pansy Craze

The drag show still had legs and two lovers in Miami, Danny Brown and Doc Benner – billed as 'boy-ological experts' – took their Club Jewel Box on the road in 1939 (having opened in 1935). Their Jewel Box Revue, according to the *Encyclopaedia of Lesbian and Gay Histories and Cultures*[1], 'featured original music, dancing and comic sketches – but no lip-sync'. The company was run as a family business: Benner sang, Brown MC-ed and his brother-in-law was musical director, while both owners' mothers travelled with the revue. Writer Wayne Anderson calls the Jewel Box 'one of the first gay-positive communities in America, if not *the* first. It was a place where "gayness" was accepted before the concept of gay-identity had even been fully conceived.'[2] The revue sought straight punters too, to swell the numbers while evading the vice squad's hunt for 'sexual deviance'.

The singularly named Spivy operated the same policy at her club, Spivy's Roof, up and running on New York's 57th Street by the early forties. She enforced an air of maximum discretion: it was the only way to stay in business. Born Bertha Levine in Brooklyn to Russian parents, Spivy was 'a short, stout woman in a black dress and black hair combed into a stiff pompadour with a white streak going from front to back,' wrote James Gavin.[3] She was the main attraction, playing piano as she sang – with a second, more accomplished pianist hidden out back.

She recorded *Seven Gay Sophisticated Songs* in 1939. 'The Tropical Fish' and 'Alley Cat' suggested animal metaphors were still in vogue, which Spivy delivered with the familiar arch, sly style of the day. One of Spivy's regulars, Ignacio Schwartz,[4] can still recite the lyrics to 'Alley Cat', whose *raison d'etre* is surgically removed: 'No longer will I take chances with the maids/Now I pass them by/And hear them cry/There goes that pansy cat.'

---

1 Edited by George Haggerty, Bonnie Zimmerman (Routledge, 2000)
2 Huffington Post, http://www.huffingtonpost.com/wayne-anderson/the-jewel-box-revue-americas-first-gay-community_b_2228790.html
3 *Intimate Nights: The Golden Age of New York Cabaret* (Watson-Guptill, 2006)
4 'The Review of Arts, Literature, Philosophy and the Humanities', www.ralphmag.org/DJ/spivy2.html

A few last pansy tunes made it through, from the most unexpected source, as if homosexuality had taken a train out of the city and into the country. In 1927, Harold Hersey's comic poem 'The Lavender Cowboy' had been set to music by Earl Hall,[1] mocking a man 'with only two hairs on his chest'. 'I Love My Fruit', by the Sweet Violet Boys – a pseudonym for Kentucky's Prairie Ramblers, the backing band of country music star Patsy Montana – was a country bluegrass number written by their pianist Bob Miller that laughed *with* the subject. The Violets' singer declares a fondness for pistachios, pecans and cashews – 'Yes, indeed, I sure love my nuts' – and, furthermore, 'I am always hungry for bananas/That it almost seems to be a sin/They're so good that when I'm all through eating/I still love to nibble on the skin.'

At a time when America was looking across the water, to the start of WWII, 'I Love My Fruit' sounded innocent and frisky, as if the 'sweet violet boys' were an accepted part of society. But by the end of the thirties, the pansy craze was dead, its cats neutered or worse. The Jewel Box Revue aside, gay men and women were isolated; without hope, only prayers. A gorgeous, simmering ballad, 'Something to Live For', epitomised the mood. Musical ingénue and closeted pianist Billy Strayhorn wrote it as a poem in 1933 when he was just 18, and then recorded in 1939 with Duke Ellington's band after he became the jazz bandleader's invaluable arranger: 'But there's something missing . . . It seems I'm never kissing the one whom I care for . . . Oh, what wouldn't I give for someone who'd take my life/And make it seem gay as they say it ought to be.'

In hindsight, 1939 proved to be a pivotal year for gay identity. The Jewel Box Revue was a microcosm of a gay community, a concept which grew, imperceptibly, as WWII broke out that year, triggering a second wartime wave of social mobility, *carpe diem* positivity and fluid sexual encounters. The same year, the MGM film musical *The Wizard Of Oz* was released, starring former child star Judy Garland as Dorothy, but just as crucial was the film's production team, christened Freed's Fairies.

---

1 Two more recordings followed, by Bob Skyles and his Skyrockets (1937) and Vernon Dalhart (1939) respectively.

The film's producer, Arthur Freed, may have been straight, but key member Roger Edens, a gay songwriter and arranger, fought to keep Harold Arlen and Yip Harburg's song 'Somewhere over the Rainbow', after MGM claimed it was slowing the film down.

According to John Kenrick, the endearing euphemism for gay men, '"friends of Dorothy" caught on as early as WWII. However, it was not until the 1950s, when television made broadcasts . . . an annual event, that the film iconography became a widespread part of the American gay mindset.'[1]

At base, on the way to battle or on leave, the film's message would have struck a chord in gay men and women. 'Find yourself a place where you won't get into any trouble,' Aunt Em tells Dorothy, who turns to her faithful canine companion Toto and replies, 'Some place where there isn't any trouble. Do you suppose there is such a place, Toto? There must be. It's not a place you can get to by a boat, or a train. It's far, far away. Behind the moon, beyond the rain . . . '

---

1 http://www.musicals101.com/index.html

CHAPTER 4

The Forties: War Games and Nature Boys

> *'Frances Faye/Gay gay, gay, gay/Is there another way?'*
> Frances Faye, cover of Cole Porter's 'Night and Day'

Twenty-one years after WWI, the Second World War became another platform for a silent revolution; 'something of a nationwide coming-out experience,' as John D'Emilio phrased it.[1] The level of prosecutions plummeted and gay men made use of the freedom. The singularly named Tallujah, who started DJing on London's underground gay scene in the sixties, recalled asking 'the old queens' what the war was like. Was it horrible? 'No, dear,' they replied, 'during the blackouts you could wear as much make up as you liked and you didn't know who you were having!'

Few armed forces personnel questioned the bravery and contribution to morale that homosexual soldiers provided, but their superiors typically felt otherwise. Not long after America entered the war in 1941 the US Navy banned sailors from frequenting a variety of clubs in San Francisco, presumably to keep their minds on war rather than the enjoyable side of remaining alive. Among them was gay bar Chez Boheme – star attraction, Ray Bourbon – and lesbian bar Cafe Internationale. Both were both closed down when state authorities revoked their liquor licenses following their inclusion in the ban.

---

1 *Intimate Matters: A History of Sexuality in America*, edited by John D'Emilio and Estelle B. Freedman (Harper and Row, 1988)

New York City gay bar Gloria's had already been a casualty in 1940 after hiring a known gay man as its manager. The bar fought the closure, citing a state law that contained no provisions against 'sexual variants being served at a bar' – so the law was changed to make it illegal for homosexuals to congregate and be served in licensed premises. It would remain on the statute books for the next twenty-seven years.

Clubs that did survive included Spivy's Roof – where a promising young pianist, Władziu Valentino Liberace, was one of Spivy's backstage pianists – and Mona's Club 440, in San Francisco, considered the first US lesbian bar when it opened as Mona's Candlight in 1939. Its ashtrays bore the words 'Where girls will be boys'.

Gladys Bentley was a regular Mona headliner, alongside drag queens such as 'Butch' Minton and Miss Jimmy Reynard. Unlike Bessie Smith, killed in the car crash of 1937 and Ma Rainey, dead from a heart attack by 1939, Bentley had survived the decade, but the police were now strict on how many items of clothing could be worn that traditionally belonged to the opposite sex. Bentley wasn't a drag king so her signature tuxedo had to be retired and her forties' tracks were neutered compared to the licentious thrill of the past; one was titled 'Find Out What He Likes'.

Press advertisements showed the Jewel Box Revue stayed in business through the war, while Irving Berlin's all-serviceman theatre revue *This Is The Army*, staged in 1942, provided another safe haven for gay performers who couldn't avoid the draft – especially those who could better express their inner truth in drag, playing the cast's female characters.

As the war finally ended in 1945, the Athletic Models Guild opened for business, a photographic studio in LA specialising in semi-nude men in athletic poses and (initially) posing pouches. The other saviour was Frances Faye. Born Frances Cohen in Brooklyn, New York, Faye earned her spurs as a teenager in New York's speakeasies before graduating to bigger venues such as the Cotton Club; she recalled only having four weeks off in 1936, the year of her debut single for Decca. In 1937, Faye made her screen debut in the musical comedy *Double or Nothing*, playing a sister act with a terrific scat-singing face-off with lead actress Martha Raye before male lead Bing Crosby cut in for a threesome.[1]

But Faye was no Hollywood-approved pin-up and had to slim down to find a label willing to run with her. Her self-titled debut album of 1946 was 'a pretty awful record,' according to number one fan Tyler Alpern. 'It has a lot of her personality in song choice but her performance is quite restrained and her unique sound and energy did not come off well because producers tried to change her. But her live radio performances from that time are great.

'I first heard Frances after taking a chance on a two-dollar album at a used record store. The cover notes were oddly vague, yet telling [Faye], "resides in a hillside home high above the famous Sunset Strip in Hollywood which is shared with her secretary and four French poodles... she admits she's an unconventional character with a wide range of interests." But I was most impressed that someone had recorded "Barney Google" and I loved "Fever", so I bought it. She had a unique, high-voltage delivery and I was blown away by the unusual and wonderful sound; the rhythm and delivery against Jack Costanzo's bongos were instantly appealing and unlike anything I had ever heard. And then there was the saucy banter. I'd *never* heard anything so frank or gay on an album. I can only imagine what that was like to hear during the closeted era in which it was made! A bit like seeing the first on-screen same-sex kiss.'

Double or Nothing had billed Faye as 'The syncopating cyclone – originator of zaz-zu-zaz'. She had the requisite pipes, all raspy and smoky and 'a voice that could flatten the redwoods', reckons singer-songwriter Alix Doblin,[2] who heard Faye in a handful of lesbian bars while at college in Philadelphia during the fifties. One of Faye's most

---

[1] Faye's second film role was forty years later, as a wisecracking madam in Louis Malle's *Pretty Baby*, which Faye recalled, 'opens with me in bed smoking an opium pipe with a wig half off my head.'

[2] *My Red Blood: A Memoir of Growing up Communist, Coming onto the Greenwich Village Folk Scene and Coming Out in the Feminist Movement* (Alyson Books, 2009).

popular covers – recorded on her debut album – was Bruz Fletcher's plaintive 'Drunk with Love', which Alpern says served both as code for Faye's gay fans and 'for her own sexual orientation'.

Faye was married twice but made the audience well aware of her bisexuality. She'd insert her girlfriend (and manager) Teri Shepherd's name into her cover of Ira and George Gershwin's 'The Man I Love', switch gender pronouns and recast Cole Porter's classic 'Night and Day' as a terrific Latino rumble with her signature line: 'Night and say/Olé! Olé/What is there to say?/Frances Faye/Gay, gay, gay, gay/Is there another way?'

Fans knew the answer. 'Frances and her Friends', recorded for *Caught in the Act*, reprised the facts of life over a terrific swing metre: 'I know a guy named Joey, Joey goes with Moey/Moey goes with Hymie and Hymie goes with Sadie/And Sadie goes with Abie and Abie goes with Davy/And Davy goes with Howard and Howard goes with Charlotte/And Charlotte goes with Shirley and Shirley goes with Pearly/And Pearly goes with Yetta...'

Too much of a risk for conservative labels, she didn't record after 'Night and Day' until 1953; Shepherd told Alpern that Faye's openness hurt her career, 'in many ways'.

But as a nightclub act, Faye was top-tier and once she'd gained control in the studio (she funded better session musicians if the label budget didn't provide), Faye's verve and versatility was finally captured on disc. The mid-fifties album *I'm Wild Again* was followed with *Relaxin' With Frances Faye*; she recorded a version of the Gershwin brothers and DuBose Heyward's famous musical *Porgy and Bess* set in the black slums of Charleston, South Carolina and followed it with *Frances Faye Sings Folk Songs*. But Alpern still thinks her live albums, volumes one and two of *Captured in the Act*, capture the essence of her greatness. Her swagger and patter was 'peppered with double entendre and saucy modification of lyrics,' according to gay historian Andrej Koymasky. 'Faye can be deemed a precursor of artists such as Bette Midler, Phyllis Diller and Eartha Kitt.'[1]

---

1 http://andrejkoymasky.com

There was an ominous, deathly silence from equivalent male singers during the war. It was as if, in wartime, gay men couldn't do anything as frivolous as recording innuendo-laden frivolity.

Even Liberty Music Shop slowed down with releasing risqué singles, though the label worked with Nan Blakstone, who had got her break in New York's speakeasies in the twenties. She found a niche after the war as the 'world's greatest interpreter of sophisticated song', with her 'sophisticated' repertoire including 'A Lady's a Lady No Matter What Cooks' and 'Little Richard's Getting Bigger'.

A growing market for mildly salacious material confirmed that audiences, in the aftermath of WWII, again reflected the loosening of moral restrictions, but it was the fact that Blakstone was straight that she could be bolder than Frances Faye. She recorded such singles as 1947's US Women's Army Corps (WAC)-referencing, 'He Should Have Been a WAC': 'Now we all know the draft caught some fellows who would have felt more at home in the WACS/the sort of a boy who would marry a girl because he could wear her size slacks.'

A younger New York singer, Ruth Wallis, who'd broken through in big-band jazz before progressing to the cabaret scene's lounge and cocktail bars, also earned her title as the 'high priestess of the double entendre' and 'queen of the party record'. She had discovered her more risqué songs – which she wrote herself – were the most popular, including 'Queer Things (Are Happening)', in which Wallis, 'always thinks of my blushing groom whenever I see the pansies bloom.' Wallis piled on the stereotypes: her husband wears pink pyjamas and uses curlers, though he's 'so big and he's so strong'. Yet by the end, however, she's philosophical about her plight: 'He can do what he wants and I'll do what I can/but the both of us have got to get a man!'[1]

At least Wallis, Blakstone and Faye treated homosexuality as a fact of life rather than a source of conflict that threatened the natural order. They were joined by a post-war milestone of social progress that came in the

---

[1] In the early fifties, the boy from Trinidad in Wallis' calypso tune 'De Gay Young Lad' would also get away from her. She also recorded 'He'd Rather be a Girl'.

shape of a few combined sheets of A4 paper – a mere pamphlet – the first gay or lesbian publication in the USA, which debuted in June 1947.

Vice Versa was 'a magazine for gay gals,' according to its editor Edith Eyde, 'mainly to keep myself company.'[1] Eyde chose the magazine's name, 'because in those days, our kind of life was considered a vice. It was the opposite of the lives that were being lived – supposedly – and understood and approved of by society. And vice versa means the opposite. I thought it was very apropos.'

Typing out two copies with five sheets of carbon paper in quiet times while working as a secretary in LA, Eyde distributed twelve copies of *Vice Versa* around the local lesbian bars. There was even a periodic music section. In October 1947, a page headlined LYRICARICATURE was written by 'our new literary contributor "laurajean"', who re-worded the lyrics of a popular song of the day, 'My Ideal', with unaffected honesty:

'Will I ever find/A girl of my kind/A girl who's a mate to me?/Maybe she's afraid to make up her mind/If only she would, tho', I know she'd find/Someone who'd adore her ever more and more/And nothing from her conceal/Wherever she may stay/My sad heart longs there to be gay/With my ideal.'

The following page was headed UNUSUAL RECORDS and reviewed what Eyde called 'pertinent' records. One was a track she'd heard on radio, about Latin American music: a memorably haunting ballad, '*Pervitida*', by Mexican singer-songwriter Agustín Lara.[2] 'The narrator's spurned love for a woman isn't given a reason, except from the way he calls her "*Pervertida*" – she is "perverted",' Eyde wrote.

Eyde's amateur venture only lasted nine months. In February 1948, her job changed, denying her the free time at her typewriter to produce her pamphlet. But in those priceless nine issues, Eyde presented a reasoned voice to counter the idea that she was a pervert suffering from curable symptoms, a view that was suddenly and very publically

---

[1] *Making History: The Struggle for Gay and Lesbian Equal Rights, 1945-1990 – An Oral History*, Eric Marcus (HarperCollins, 1992)
[2] performed by Chucho Martinez and the Columbia Broadcasting System Orchestra.

disseminated in 1948 by US biologist Dr Alfred Kinsey's pioneering report *Sexuality in the Human Male*. This fostered the frequently quoted 'one in ten' ratio of homosexuals to heterosexuals. According to Kinsey, 37 per cent of the male subjects had had at least one homosexual experience, while he estimated that as many as 200,000 homosexuals lived in the Los Angeles region.

Only a few days after the Kinsey report, Gore Vidal's novel *The City and the Pillar* became as much of a shocker in the publishing world. It was an uncompromising portrait of love and sex between men that defied the clichéd view of effeminate victims corrupted by their unnatural libido. Vidal's book itself was quickly followed by *Other Voices, Other Rooms*, Truman Capote's southern-gothic tale of similarly intense gay experience in Louisiana.

In Hollywood, commercial expectations ensured that sympathetic treatments of homosexuality were eschewed for sensationalism; Alfred Hitchcock's 1948 film *Rope*, which entwined a murder plot with a coded homosexual relationship, co-starred John Dall (gay) and Farley Granger (bisexual). The screenwriter was Arthur Laurents (gay) and music was by Francis Poulenc (gay), but the plot entwined a murder plot with barely disguised homosexual villains. Elsewhere, Broadway and the world of modern classical music supplied supportive gay enclaves and this was where, it seems, gay musicians made their home.

As writer John Clum points out, the men who brought *Kiss Me, Kate* to Broadway in 1948 included writer Cole Porter, director John C. Wilson (formerly Noël Coward's lover) and starred bisexual Harold Lang, 'who had affairs with Leonard Bernstein and Gore Vidal, among others.'[1] Cole Porter's pointedly titled military musical, *Something for the Boys*, was choreographed by the openly gay Jack Cole.

Journalist Jesse Monteagudo wrote, 'This was a time (1940) when being gay was almost de rigueur in New York musical circles, so much so that the American Composers League was known in the life

---

1 *The Queer Encyclopaedia of Music, Dance and Musical Theater*, edited by Claude J. Summers (Cleis Press, 2004).

as the "Homintern"'[1] – a play on the word 'Comintern', short for the Communist International party.

Only out to his intimate circle of similarly gay friends, Leonard Bernstein was music director of the New York City Symphony Orchestra and a burgeoning composer across symphonies, chamber music, ballet and opera as well as a raft of iconic musicals: *Candide*, *On The Town*, *On the Waterfront* and *West Side Story*. For professional respectability, Bernstein hid behind a marriage and family life, but his great friend Aaron Copland was much more daring. The composer of 1942's 'Fanfare for the Common Man' and ballet soundtracks *Billy the Kid* and *Rodeo* lived openly with his male partner. He had multiple indiscreet affairs, all while being crowned the father of modern American music, with aural vistas as magnificently vast and rugged as his country's landscapes.

Did Copland's outsider status, his conflicted emotions at odds with a mainstream that criminalised him, affect his music? Not even the composer knew, according to his biographer Erik Johns: 'Aaron felt that his sexuality was there in the music ... but also that it was incidental to his major theme.'[2]

It was much easier to isolate the gay gene in British classical composer Benjamin Britten, given his most famous operas *Peter Grimes* (1945) and *Billy Budd* (1951), in which distinct allegories of homo-erotica and homophobia – sung by Britten's lover, tenor Peter Pears – were set against a nautical backdrop. Most of Britten's work involved emotional disenfranchisement alienated by bigotry, which fuelled his creativity. Likewise Copland; as writer Kevin Bartig saw it, 'forging the nation's musical identity through his individual genius', Copland was in reality a left-leaning, communist, Jewish homosexual who worked during a time of rampant homophobia and insular anti-communism.'[3]

---

[1] 'Leonard Bernstein: A Divided Life', http://gaytoday.com/garchive/people/111698pe.htm

[2] *Aaron Copland: The Life and Work of an Uncommon Man*, Howard Pollack (University of Illinois Press, 2000)

[3] Humanities and Social Sciences Online, www.h-net.org/reviews/showrev.php?id=13266

BREAKING DOWN THE WALLS OF HEARTACHE

The outsider was clearly motivated to reject the status quo and restlessly pursue the future; you didn't have to be gay to belong to the musical avant garde (Charles Ives, Stockhausen, Schoenberg and Berio were all straight), but it was as populated as Broadway. Music's homosexual modernists trod different paths, from radical John Cage (most famously his silent composition '4.33') to Bernstein's jazz-classical fusion and Samuel Barber's orchestrations such as 'Adagio for Strings'; from Lou Harrison's eastern influences to Harry Partch's rejection of western classicism for his own forty-three-tone scale. The fearless Henry Cowell, born in 1897, invented the first electronic drum machine, the Rhythmicon, although he was driven off course by a ten-year prison sentence for 'improper relations' with several friends.[1]

Though musical composition was clearly a man's world, fellow American Pauline Oliveros was experimenting with wire recorders before her pioneering work in electronic music flourished in the fifties. Her creativity was nourished, reckons biographer Martha Mockus,[2] through her 'lesbian domestic space,' with lover Laurel Johnson, 'contrasting it with the repressive domestic space of a typical heterosexual married woman...'

If modern classical music was an open field for gay men, modern jazz was an exclusion zone, with only Duke Ellington's right-hand man Billy Strayhorn confirmed to be gay in the forties. Black, gay and out – Strayhorn was 'a triple minority', according to biographer David Hajdu.[3]

Jazz's first acknowledged gay player, Bix Beiderbecke, was long gone; another personal life ruined by alcoholism, plus a fatal dose of pneumonia, at just 28 years old in 1931. At least Strayhorn had a community that Beiderbecke lacked. Namely Ellington, who'd taken Strayhorn under his wing in 1938, housing him as part of the family as well as his band.

---

1 Cowell composed over fifty musical works while in San Quentin jail, plus a book on melody. After he'd served five years, testimonials to his good citizenship got him released. His subsequent work for the US government eventually led to a full pardon. He also got married and toned down his musical radicalism.
2 *Sounding Out: Pauline Oliveros and Lesbian Musicality* (Routledge, 2007)
3 *Lush Life: A Biography of Billy Strayhorn* (Granta, 1997)

Through Ellington's son Mercer, Strayhorn had even met a lover, fellow African-American pianist Aaron Bridgers; the couple lived together, protected by his secondary role in the band.

Strayhorn couldn't have been the only gay man in jazz, but the prejudice ran deep. In *Jazz Times*, trumpeter Dizzy Gillespie said, 'I don't even know a jazz musician who's a homosexual – not a real jazz musician.'[1]

In theory, jazz should have incubated a liberal mindset alongside the blues, as it did in subjects ranging from drugs to promiscuity. But the all-female jazz bands that thrived during WWII were also widely shunned, considered second-class musicians by the men and none achieved any level of fame or permanence – not even the acclaimed, all-black International Sweethearts of Rhythm, whose ranks included the boldly out lesbian couple Ernestine 'Tiny' Davis (trumpet/vocals) and Ruby Lucas (drums)[2]. But they could hold their own, judging by their tootling instrumental 'Diggin' Dykes'.

Bessie Smith biographer Chris Albertson, an expert in jazz as well as blues, and a gay man himself, says he knew the jazz community, 'for all its macho talk, was not immune to homosexuality. There was such a code of silence that most people not only never knew, but didn't *want* to know.'

Jazz pianist Fred Hersch, who came out in the early 1990s, told writer James Gavin, 'Playing creative jazz music with someone demands a certain intimacy. And a lot of men, historically, have displaced men's issues by joking around or physical horseplay or various other kinds of deflections . . . I always thought it was more of a fear of intimacy issue than actual homophobia.'[3]

When, after nine years with Strayhorn, Aaron Bridgers moved to

---

1 'Homophobia in Jazz', *Jazz Times*, 2001, http://jazztimes.com/articles/20073-homophobia-in-jazz
2 *Tiny and Ruby: Hell Divin' Women* is a 1989 documentary by Greta Schiller *and Andrea* Weiss. The pair also made *The International Sweethearts of Rhythm* (1986).
3 Ibid. 88

Paris in 1947 to start over, the 'someone to believe in' that the fledgling Strayhorn had once yearned for and found, was gone. In 1948, he unveiled a song that became his signature classic. It had been in the works since 1923 and was now heartfelt. Its working title was 'Life is Lonely', but he changed it to 'Lush Life'.[1] Though its chords and mood are, undeniably, lush and the title sounded positive, Strayhorn had in mind lush's other meaning – drunkenness.

Sung in Strayhorn's charming, downbeat croon, 'Lush Life' revisited the earlier pun of 'Something to Live For': 'I used to visit all the very gay places/Those come-what-may places/Where one relaxes on the axis of the wheel of life.'

He then laid into the ideal of love with understandable weariness and bitterness: 'Romance is mush, stifling those who strive/I'll live a lush life in some small dive/And there I'll be, while I rot/With the rest of those whose lives are lonely, too.'

Records we can believe in . . .

Billy Strayhorn could have taken solace from knowing 'Something to Live For' and 'Lush Life' had comforted similarly sad and isolated individuals 'in the life.' But there were more opportunities to socialise, in bars such as San Francisco's the Black Cat and New York's Howdy Club, or the smarter hotel bars like Times Square's Astor hotel, a major cruising spot during wartime and after. The Jewel Box Revue was one place that gay men could meet without overt discretion: Kliph Nesteroff thought 1940s Miami Beach 'may have been the most sexually liberal in America. The Mexicana Bar featured "transvestite bartenders and waiters" and the Club Ha Ha, where [Ray] Bourbon gigged, featured a roster of male employees who wore makeup and sang dirty songs to the customers.'

Yet the majority of gay men, and women, would not dare to go public.

---

1 'Lush Life' was covered many times, initially by impeccable voices such as Nat King Cole, Sarah Vaughan and Ella Fitzgerald, but subsequently Nancy Wilson, Rickie Lee Jones and many more.

They lived in a climate of secrecy and shame, closeted by draconian laws, grasping whatever signs they imagined spoke to them and about them. There is no one left alive to ask which popular songs of the twenties and thirties might have provided comfort and validation. In the forties, however, more households had a radio and maybe a gramophone, spreading music's gospel. For Jack Fritscher, born in 1939, music was a vehicle for unleashing his imagination, one that would lead him to a life of journalism, editing and novels.[1]

Fritscher's earliest memories are of WWII, with its rallying anthems that tapped nascent and inarticulate feelings. Looking back, he recognised, 'thrilling masculine chills' from the rousing chorus of 'Stout-Hearted Men', sung by strapping actor Nelson Eddy. The question posed by bandleader Gordon Jenkin's 'Would You Rather Be a Colonel with an Eagle on Your Shoulder or A Private with A Chicken on Your Knee?' was 'as suggestive as it was surreal,' he recalls. 'I didn't understand the military codes of rank but I knew it meant a sexy situation. I wanted what they were having.'

More crucially for Fritscher, Nat King Cole's debut solo single, 'Nature Boy', released in 1948, 'swept little emerging me over the rainbow. Eden Ahbez's lyrics gave me fully realised concepts and words that helped me name and sort pre-teen feelings about how different I secretly knew I was.'

Eden Ahbez was a quintessential maverick. He was born George Alexander Aberle in Brooklyn to a Jewish father and British mother, but adopted and raised in Kansas as George McGrew, where he found work as a pianist and dance band leader. But he dropped out and moved to California, one of the first proto-hippies, informed by oriental mysticism and Germany's social movements *Naturmensch* (natural man) and *Lebensreform* (life reform). Styling himself eden ahbez – he considered only God and Infinity deserved capitalisation – he also wrote songs, and

---

1 In 1971, Fritscher co-founded the American Popular Culture Association and in 1977 was the founding San Francisco editor of *Drummer*, an erotic leather-based men's magazine he positioned as 'The American journal of gay popular culture'.

considered the serene croon of Nat King Cole to be the right vessel for a semi-autobiographical ode to those 'nature boys', the free spirits who believed in love, who lived without comforts, without even clothes.

Ahbez managed to get the sheet music of 'Nature Boy' to Cole via the singer's valet; the singer quickly responded to its uncanny chords and equally unusual and compelling message. Tapping into a dreamy, swimming jazz style that echoed Billy Strayhorn's 'Something to Live For', the song deployed strings and flute to mirror this 'very strange enchanted boy . . . A little shy and sad of eye/But very wise was he.'

The song's last lines, 'The greatest thing you'll ever learn/Is just to love and be loved in return,' can be interpreted in various ways: as a child imparting wisdom to adults, an adult hippie reflecting on his journey or Fritscher's version, regarding the right to love freely. He wasn't alone: in 2008, Paul McCartney told *MOJO* magazine that he'd always loved 'Nature Boy', praising 'this rather strange little song when you look at the lyrics – it's rather gay! In a nice way.'

EJ Emmons of seventies' gay duo Smokey, recalled that they and ahbez both used the same studio in LA. 'His nickname for me was, "Beautiful EJ", but I don't think he was gay,' Emmons says, although Smokey's other half, John Cordon, disagrees: 'He was more asexual than sexual, but I did always think he was gay, though he never hit on us.'

Logo TV's online feature 'Ten straight songs about gay men' tellingly placed 'Nature Boy' at No. 1.[1] For its writer, known only as Snick, ahbez's sexuality wasn't important. He'd heard the song as a teenager, 'on the car radio (when you're trapped in a car with your mom and dad, you have to listen to stuff like that). At the time, I was coming to terms with my sexuality and my first thought listening to it was, "OMG, it's about a gay man." I've never backed down from that assumption and, frankly, it doesn't matter to me anymore if I'm proven wrong. "Nature Boy" will always be my personal coming-out song.'

'Nature Boy' featured in the 1948 film *The Boy with Green Hair*, about

---

[1] http://www.thebacklot.com/ten-straight-songs-about-gay-men/04/2008/

a town's reaction to a boy (played by a young Dean Stockwell) taunted for being 'different' but whose message unites the community. 'Dean was only three years older than me at the time,' Fritscher recalls. 'The film gave me almost music-video images to go along with the lyrics.'

The power of suggestion is mirrored by a real-life story recounted in Allan Bérubé's *Coming Out Under Fire: The History of Gay Men and Women in WWII*.[1] A GI in Coolidge, Arizona in a local drinking hole spots 'a most handsome colonel drinking at the bar'. The pair exchange glances and the GI orders a beer and sticks a nickel in the jukebox, and to reaffirm his interest, selects 'If Only You Loved Me a Little Bit More'[2]. The colonel checks out the song title, after which the GI ups the ante by selecting 'Why Don't You Do Me Right'[3], after which the colonel shows his interest by choosing 'Heaven for Two'.[4]

Bérubé gave no indication if there was any happy ending that night, but men – given the opportunities for companionship both during and after wartime in a way that women were not – did find their way toward one another, as Bérubé's book makes clear. But still only heterosexual women dared make jokes about homosexual men, until a spirited and clever song from 1949, *'Ils En Sont Tous'* ('They All Are'), recorded by Frenchman Robert Rocca, a former hairdresser turned comic cabaret singer. He sung of a 'small, lovely town, like we often see around us/A main street, a lovely square with a fountain in the middle . . . But when you get off the train, the train master immediately says, "Hello, my sweetheart"/In this country, they all are.'

Rocca sang, 'It all started with the butcher/One day he brought his assistant to get meat at the slaughterhouse/He called him, "My little darling."' The notary tells his clerk he has beautiful eyes; the clerk replies that the gendarme has already told him the same. The postman sings

---

1 University of North Carolina Press, revised edition, 2010
2 I'm not sure if Bérubé has the right title in 'If Only You Loved Me a Little Bit More', as I can't find a track by that name.
3 This is most likely the 1936 upbeat jazz-blues 'Why Don't You Do Right' made popular by Peggy Lee in 1942.
4 Oh dear; I can't find a song named 'Heaven for Two', either.

under the ironmonger's window and when the grocer, 'slightly drunk, was found lying next to his wife, he had to leave the country.'

Rocca's satire knowingly implicates the old priest, 'who tries to put everybody on the right path/But, like he says, "With my skirts, what chance do I have?"' The town's women, meanwhile, 'are sad, they no longer have husbands nor lovers'. But Rocca concludes, 'Gentlemen, spend your holidays here if you're feeling sure about yourselves . . . If you have nice moustaches, the hotel owner will give you a good price/ And far away from the storm, you will discover, happily/That there is a place in this world where men live in peace.'

In other words, if men could learn to love, then they wouldn't go to war.

The US contribution to the canon in 1949 was, coincidentally, set in WWII, the Broadway musical *South Pacific* by the late Larry Hart's writing partner Richard Rogers and his new foil, Oscar Hammerstein II. They again used a story of racial prejudice – and a mass population of sailors, and drag roles – to plead for tolerance and provided coded entertainment for the gays in the audience with songs such as 'I'm Gonna Wash That Man Right Outta my Hair'.

The only other US contender would have enjoyed as little exposure as *South Pacific* got a ton. 'Truck Drivin' Man' was a slice of countrified honky-tonk from Cowboy Jack Derrick: 'When my truck drivin' man comes back in town, I'll dress up in my silken gown . . . We'll drink beer from a can while I'm with that man.'

A silken gown *and* a can of beer? Well, this *was* Texas. Derrick was known for his novelty songs but it was still an unusual lyric; this was no seasoned cabaret *chanteuse* with a select audience that would get the joke. Perhaps this was Derrick's way of saying that cowboys are secretly fond of each other.

It seemed that the only way to be gay was by hiding in plain sight, and the man who would become the most successful entertainer of the fifties, former Spivy's Roof pianist Władziu Valentino Liberace, was not holding back. Known only by his surname, the musical prodigy of

Italian and Polish Catholic descent found a niche by ditching the old classical pieces and playing all manner of popular songs in the classical style, chopped up between the most popular classical pieces; a *Reader's Digest* version of the classics.

By the end of the forties, Liberace had graduated from clubs to concert halls, peddling a level of camp not witnessed outside of the female impersonators, with candelabra on his grand piano, dressed in white tie and tails for maximum visibility, incorporating showbiz gimmicks into his show and not disguising the proto-drag-queen mannerisms of his speaking voice when engaging with his audience. In 1950, 'Liber-*ah*-chee', the most flamboyantly queer performer of his day played privately at the White House for US president Harry S. Truman.

Though the US armed forces' policy of 'don't ask don't tell' would not come into effect for another four decades, Liberace was its living proof. It seemed the only way to break through was to go for broke and see who called you out for the crime. There had to be some change, given the level of homosexuality estimated by Alfred Kinsey. How much longer could all of this be denied? And who was going to publicise it?

CHAPTER 5

The Fifties: The Tutti Frutti Revolution

'It's not us . . . it's everything around us.'
Maria, *West Side Story*, 1957

'The thing I always loved about Little Richard was that strong sense of rushing forward, of not being restrained. Because he was gay, he was black, it must have been a terrible time for him in the fifties, so he found this solution, just crash through all the walls, just go through them.'
Michael Rother, NEU!, January 2016[1]

The inexorable rise of Liberace – his one-hour show, syndicated nationally, had a weekly audience of thirty-five million – was just one of a tangle of contradictions as the forties morphed into the fifties. The pianist seemed to go out of his way to be the planet's gayest entertainer while projecting an image of a lady's man that included widely publicised date nights with women, among them Judy Garland.

Liberace's fan base was predominantly female, but would have contained a proportion of gay men (a decent quota of lesbians is less assured). The more adventurous fans would have also been aware of another contradiction; that Athletic Models' Guide founder Bob Mizer served a year in prison for distributing images of male frontal nudity through the US postal service, but freely launched *Physique Pictorial* magazine in 1951. He clothed his models in the skimpiest of posing pouches – or photographed them naked from the rear – and

---

1 Told to Andrew Male of *MOJO* magazine.

published blatantly homoerotic art that confirmed the target market was not bodybuilders.

Mizer and Liberace's efforts were paralleled by those of Republican senator Joseph McCarthy, whose anti-communist purge against President Truman's Democrat party was in full swing by 1950. As the cold war with Russia deepened, McCarthy widened his brief to weed out those government employees he had reason to believe were homosexual and thus open to blackmail by Soviet agents. 'Homosexuality, McCarthy asserted, was the psychological maladjustment that led people toward communism,' wrote author David K, Johnson.[1] Homosexuality was officially classified as a mental disorder – specifically a 'sociopathic personality disturbance' – in the American Psychiatric Association's first *Diagnostic and Statistical Manual of Mental Disorders* of 1952.

McCarthyism, which came to be defined as 'the practice of making accusations of subversion or treason without proper regard for evidence'[2] was something that homosexuals had been enduring in differing forms for decades. One victim was former Harlem star Gladys Bentley. Shorn of the male attire that she'd so comfortably worn two decades earlier and needing to support her aging mother, she'd begun to wear dresses on stage. In *Ebony* magazine, under the headline *I Am Woman Again*, Bentley admitted she had been taking female hormones and managed to cure her lesbianism, 'a hell as terrible as dope addiction', she said. After decades of psychological abuse, Bentley resorted to marriage (but soon enough was divorced) and found born-again religion as a way of ensuring she'd end up in heaven.[3]

If Bentley had been neutered, another of Mona's Club 440 headliners, Beverly Shaw, still proudly wore a suit and tails. She adopted the male

---

[1] *The Lavender Scare: The Cold War Persecution of Gays and Lesbians in the Federal Government* (University Of Chicago Press, 2006)
[2] http://dictionary.reference.com/browse/mccarthyism?s=t
[3] Bentley was about to become an ordained minister in the Temple of Love in Christ, Inc. when she died in a flu epidemic in 1960, aged 52.

spelling of Beverly and appeared as Beverly Shaw, Sir, at Club Laurel – the LA nightspot she and girlfriend Betty owned. Shaw made herself eligible for the category of male impersonator and so could circumnavigate police harassment. But when Shaw released an album, she wore a skirt (though she kept the bow tie) and abandoned the 'Sir' for the cover of *Songs Tailored to Your Taste*.[1]

Mona's 440 and Club Laurel survived McCarthyism alongside other pockets of resistance; in the late forties and early fifties, there were six gay bars in San Francisco's North Beach area alone. A landmark victory was won in 1951 when one, the Black Cat, won its liquor licence back, having had it revoked under the charge of 'keeping a disorderly house'. There had been no 'proof of the commission of illegal or immoral acts on the premises', a pattern that was persistently repeated following police raids.

Musical portraits of homosexuality were, typically, demeaning. Country-and-westerner Billy Brigg, who had already shown enlightened views with 'Be a Lady When You Walk and Talk with Me', released 'The Sissy Song' in 1951, a contagious bluegrass rhythm carrying a list of undesirable unmanly habits that included wearing a moustache and bow tie, drinking iced tea or sweet milk, holding the little finger, 'up high', sleeping in pyjamas, eating salad, washing the dishes, hanging out diapers and making up beds. Should Briggs fall prey to this behaviour, he'd have to, 'go out behind the old red barn and let a grey mule kick my brains out.'

Television historian Steven Capsuto recalled how US shows projected 'lisping, mincing, loose-wristed stereotypes of gay men', such as fashion designer Bruce on *The Steve Allen Show*, 'sissified, giddy Greenwich Village poet,' Percy Dovetonsils and 'swishy, gushing Hollywood film star' Rock Mississippi on *The Ernie Kovacs Show*.[2]

---

[1] Dated to between 1954 and 1957, but also to 1962.
[2] 'Shtikking It To Homosexuality: Radio and TV Sketch Comedy Through 1964', www.stevecap.com/alternatechannels_net/us/trends/shtikking_it.htm

The Fifties: The Tutti Frutti Revolution

The appearance in 1954 of Curtis White as the first gay activist interviewed on TV[1], would be a shock to any viewer. There was no drag, no pronounced costume or camp voice, just a plain-speaking individual man who talked about the organisation that he represented.

The Mattachine Society had been founded in 1950 by Harry Hay. Born in England but raised in Chile and California, Hay discovered the existence of Henry Gerber's Society for Human Rights and, in 1948, conceived of a similar organisation. Hay's communist beliefs had already put him in jeopardy, but he pushed on for the cause of what he called, 'Society's androgynous minority' or in the name of his gay networking group, Bachelors Anonymous. He had been encouraged by Alfred Kinsey and based Mattachine on Russian communist principles of a 'community of language, territory, economic life and psychological make-up manifested in a community of culture'. Hay might have recognised the potential folly of his concept; while researching the history of folk music, he discovered that Mattachine was the name of the secret medieval French society of unmarried men who dressed as fools as a form of social protest, while disseminating information to the oppressed poor.

By 1953, Mattachine had 2000 members, but there had been a split in the ranks over how to run the organisation (Hay's communism versus a democratic process). Those departing formed ONE, Inc, admitting women to the fold and publishing a magazine called *One*, which was sold openly in LA for 25 cents, the first such of its kind since Edith Eyde's *Vice Versa*.[2]

Hay was dismayed that both his communist structure and his manifesto were rejected; he believed that homosexuals were not like heterosexuals and rather than being an inferior group, 'homosexuals formed a unique culture from which heterosexuals might learn a great

---

[1] Curtis appeared on Paul Coates' *Confidential File*, LA's top-rated local talk show, 'a series that revelled in topics usually considered too hot for television', according to Steven Capsuto.

[2] France, Switzerland and the Netherlands all had gay magazines by this point.

deal.'[1] But he was outvoted by the argument for integration, that 'homosexuals should not be discriminated against because gay people were just like straight people.'

The crying game

Excepting Liberace, singers who wanted to step outside of the limited appeal of the cabaret and nightclub scene typically hid their homosexuality and tried to act like straight people. Certainly, Johnnie Ray looked conventional, in a suit and clean-cut, with square-jaw appeal, though he showed a surprising range of emotion for a man: 'He deflated a certain kind of machismo expected of American male singers,' says Jack Fritscher – and Ray would probably be guilty of several of the traits listed in 'The Sissy Song'. But while Billy Brigg faded into obscurity, Ray topped the national charts for eleven incredible weeks in November 1951 with 'Cry'. American society, though constantly told to be suspicious of difference, was entranced by this maverick, whose party trick was to break down on stage, pulling at his hair and falling to his knees, not just crying but '*kaaaah-rrrryyyying*'. Ray recommended that you would feel better if you cried too.

From Dallas, Oregon, Ray had been set apart since the age of thirteen after an accident at Boy Scouts had left him deaf in one ear. The hearing aid was a novelty but also ironically helped him, as his difficulties in hearing the bass had led to him developing his own rhythmic style to accompany a powerful, lustrous voice.

Having impressed a song plugger at Detroit's Flame Showbar and been signed to Columbia offshoot Okeh, Ray's debut single, 'Whiskey and Gin' was an uneventful big band blues. 'Cry' unleashed the beast, a slow and pensive crooner anthem lit up by its voluminous chorus. Ray's nicknames piled up: 'Mr Emotion' 'the Nabob of Sob', 'the Prince of Wails' and 'the Atomic Ray'. *Billboard* was impressed but also unsettled by this voice, which the magazine compared to a cross

---

1 Michael Bronksi in 'The Phoenix', www.bostonphoenix.com/boston/news_features/other_stories/documents/02511115.htm

between jazz/blues singer Kay Starr and jazz stylist Little Jimmy Scott, whose genetic condition blocking puberty had produced an unusually high contralto. Ray was an anomaly, a glimpse of something uncontrolled, maybe uncontrollable. As singer-songwriter Alix Dobkin says about Liberace, 'When something is so repressed, it just comes out sideways.'

The root of Ray's palpable angst was soon revealed after news leaked that he'd been arrested just one month before 'Cry was released, for soliciting an undercover policeman in Detroit's Stone Theater, a burlesque club known locally as a homosexual rendezvous. Ray hadn't even requested a jury trial, pleading guilty and paying a $25 fine,[1] probably in the hope it would stay undiscovered. Sudden fame changed all that, with the mercenary *Confidential* – a new magazine, the first centred on scandal, gossip and exposé journalism – digging up the charge a year later.

'People who'd never whisper the word homosexuality were all a-twitter that Johnnie Ray was queer,' Jack Fritscher recalls. A gay teenager such as Fritscher, searching for validation, shared *Billboard*'s thrilled and unsettled reaction. '"Cry" was a *cri de coeur* torch-song, a kind of cautionary tale about the existential heartbreak of outlawed homosexuality,' he says. 'I watched him on our first television set and thought that I liked him, but I don't want to *be* like him. He wasn't like the stoic, manly soldiers of my childhood. He was quivering very like the *"manazon"* Judy Garland, the ventriloquist of gay code, whom I liked from her MGM musical comedies in which she pined for the boy next door. It felt like Johnnie and Judy carried the weight of the gay condition on their shoulders for the rest of us.'

Ray seemed aware of his role. 'Above all things, a man must be masculine,' he told the Milwaukee *Sentinel* in June 1952. 'But when he has the desire to express emotion, he suppresses himself because he doesn't think it's manly. Ordinarily, a man can't be as demonstrative as I am

---

[1] It was either a fine or thirty days in prison! Ray went to trial following a second arrest in 1959, also in Detroit, again for soliciting an undercover officer. The jury, composed entirely of older women, delivered a 'not guilty' verdict.

when I sing – people wouldn't understand it. But I get fan letters from men. Women in my audiences see reflected in me all the emotion and tenderness and thoughtfulness that unfortunately the American male doesn't have time for today.' Ray was one facet of what Fritscher calls an emerging 'diversity of gay faces, voices, and identities in popular culture'. Liberace was now living in Hollywood, about to establish a permanent residency in Las Vegas, wearing ermine on stage and decorating his piano in rhinestones and mirrors.

'Everyone knew Liberace was gay and yet he was so beloved because people are just *weird*,' says Alix Dobkin. 'But it was the beginning of mass consumption on TV, which accounts for his mass popularity with women. Not that that protected him from being ridiculed in some quarters.'

Playwright Tennessee Williams was also riding a wave off the back of the 1951 film of his 1947 play *A Streetcar Named Desire*, centred on ageing Southern belle Blanche Dubois, whose husband – a closeted homosexual – has killed himself. Historian and novelist Ethan Mordden ventures that public homosexuality began when the controversial and tempestuous actress (a gay icon before Judy Garland) Tallulah Bankhead played Blanche in the play's 1956 revival,[1] but it can equally be said that the first true gay idol was Marlon Brando, then young, unknown and buff, playing Blanche's brother-in-law and nemesis Stanley Kowalski on both the stage and in the 1951 film adaptation: simultaneously butch and beautiful.

Nothing matched the coverage of the first publicised gender reassignment, in 1952, when former American GI George Jorgensen took the first name of Christine. The public's taste for sensationalism allowed her to appear on talk shows and give lectures. Jorgensen even released a single, 'Crazy Little Men' in 1957, riding the craze for novelty singles and sci-fi, 'in which a heartbroken Jorgensen, dumped by her earth-man, flies off in a spaceship to be consoled by the "crazy little men" of the moon,' wrote Charles Lieurance.[2] Jorgensen's Blanche Dubois-style

---

[1] 'Our Love is Here to Stay – WWII to the 1960s', http://www.musicals101.com/gay6.htm
[2] http://thisdevilsinterval.blogspot.co.uk/2014/03/christine-jorgensen-crazy-little-men-bw.html

drawl was accompanied by a speeded-up vocal representing the crazy little moon-men. Her operation was one giant step for mankind; her sole musical recording less so.

Jorgensen had a French equivalent; Coccinelle (French for 'ladybird'), born Jacques Charles Dufresnoy, an actress and cabaret singer. She made her stage debut as a transgender showgirl in 1953 and would have a vaginoplasty in 1958. She released two singles in 1959; *'Tu T'Fous de Moi'* ('You're Kidding Me') and *'Je Cherche un Millionnaire'* ('I Want a Millionaire'). Both Coccinelle and Jorgensen, like Liberace, found support from female fans, whose sexuality wasn't under threat. Johnnie Ray was similarly cushioned by the emerging teenage market and his audience's screams drowned out his.

Ray's marriage in 1953 was standard press damage limitation and was over in a year. He charted in the UK[1] and Australia, featured in the 1954 film musical *There's No Business Like Show Business* alongside Ethel Merman and Marilyn Monroe, but his career was starting to wind down. After 'The Little White Cloud That Cried' – originally the B-side of 'Cry'-- reached no. 2, Ray only had one more US Top 3 single (also his solitary UK no. 1), 'Walking in the Rain' in 1956. For this return bout of misery ('torture in my heart'), Ray also provided a metaphor for cruising, as if he was pacing the streets, searching for contact, any momentary distraction from the pain. This interpretation was enacted on *The Frankie Laine Show*, as Ray mimed in front of a cast of men wearing raincoats and wandering back and forth, resembling furtive, lonesome fugitives. The introduction of a male/female couple, slow-dancing together, served as a reminder of what every man should aspire to and what Ray and all the gay men watching could never attain: happiness.

Ray's performance embodied his demise, his suit and crooning style

---

1 A 1955 entry in Sir Noël Coward's diary detailed one of Ray's UK appearances: 'Squealing teenagers and mass hysteria, quite nauseating, but [Ray] gave a remarkable performance both on stage and later at the embassy, where he fondled [actress] Terry Moore for the cameras. Poor boy.'

dating him; he was no longer a rebel but part of the mainstream that rebels were trying to dismantle. In 1954, Brando had starred in *The Wild Ones*, the first 'society outlaw' film, banned in the UK for 14 years, followed a year later by the equally iconic *Rebel Without a Cause*, starring new pin-up James Dean. In music, a new, equally handsome face, but with a voice to match, made his first significant recording in 1954, when Elvis Presley released his version of Arthur Crudup's 1946 jump blues 'That's All Right'.

Outside nightclubs and bars, classical concert halls and jazz venues, the spirit of the Harlem blues continued to simmer. Under the title 'race music', blues, jazz and gospel earned its own chart between 1945 and 1949 before *Billboard* rebranded it as the rhythm-and-blues chart. Its identity was quickly subsumed by the broader consensus of rock'n'roll.

Rock'n'roll as a term was derived from the motion of a boat on water, but when Trixie Smith had sung 'My Daddy Rocks Me (With One Steady Roll)' in 1922, listeners knew what she meant. When US DJ Alan Freed first used the term rock'n'roll in the 1950s, he meant the alchemic reaction of racial integration; from the African-American side, blues and the speedier model known as jump blues, plus boogie-woogie, jazz and gospel. From the Caucasian side, hillbilly and bluegrass, Western swing and country and the speedier, bluegrass-influenced rockabilly. The continuing rise of radio dispersed the new sound to further reaches. And the individual credited with the first rock'n'roll record was a bisexual black woman.

Born in Arkansas in 1915, Rosetta Nubin was gospel-trained, but she fought the confines of the church and began playing secular spaces under the name Sister Rosetta Tharpe (an adaptation of her first husband's surname, Thorpe), accompanying herself on guitar – practically unheard of for a woman. She had released some of the earliest gospel recordings on a major label (Decca) in 1938 and 1945's 'Strange Things Happening Every Day' was considered the first gospel hit on *Billboard*'s fledgling race records chart, reaching no. 2. But Tharpe's brand was more rhythmic than gospel; she swung rather than swayed, making music for dancing rather than testifying. Soon enough, someone had awarded her the title of godmother of rock'n'roll.

Playing choppy rhythm or playing silkier notes, with a sweet, buzzing edge to her vocal, Tharpe could sound tough or vulnerable; she could front a big band (Lucky Millender's jazz orchestra) or just strip things back to guitar; she'd play intimate venues, or a bigger stage such as Harlem's Cotton Club and even Manhattan's Carnegie Hall. She also slept with men and women. One acquaintance told Tharpe's biographer Gayle Wald of walking in on the singer and two other women after her third wedding in 1951. Was her trio of husbands a case of a good man being hard to find or a lesbian who kept searching for a male alibi?

The gospel truth about 'Tutti Frutti'

Gospel music kept its gay and lesbian roots a tight secret until recently: 'The family secret has become public knowledge,' gospel expert Anthony Heilbut wrote, 'and the black church, once the very model of civil rights, has acquired a new image, as the citadel of intolerance.'[1] Heilbut first wrote about gospel music in his 1971 book *The Gospel Sound: Good News and Bad Times*[2], unearthing homosexual singers but respecting their privacy. Come 2012, its key figures having died, Heilbut felt free to discuss names, and conclude, 'gospel music was the blues of gay men and lesbians'.

By then, Tharpe and gospel legend Clara Ward had already been outed; Ward too was also keen to cross over into secular society[3] and to enjoy lesbian affairs while remaining married. But major male performers such as James Cleveland, who assisted 'queen of gospel', Albertina Walker, before fronting his own ensemble, was news to many. So was

---

1 *The Fan who Knew Too Much: Aretha Franklin, The Rise of the Soap Opera, Children of the Gospel Church, And Other Meditations* (Knopf, 2012)
2 Simon & Schuster, 1971
3 In 1963, Clara Ward became only the second singer to perform gospel on Broadway, in the Langston Hughes play *Tambourines to Glory*.

Alex Bradford, who assisted arguably the most famous gospel singer of all, Mahalia Jackson, before he formed the Bradford Singers and the Bradford Specials and incorporated choreography and costumes into their acts. Bradford Specials counter-tenor Charles Campbell was also gay. 'I heard it forever,' Heilbut notes. '"He's a great singer, but he's a sissy." Or, "He did a terrible thing, but at least he's not a sissy."'

As a former Bradford Singer and a gay man, Archbishop Carl Bean's autobiography, *I Was Born This Way: A Gay Preacher's Journey Through Gospel Music, Disco Stardom and a Ministry in Christ*[1] covers a lot of the same turf and then some. Bean volunteers the additional name of Andraé Crouch, the 'modern father of gospel', born in the forties like Bean. 'Ninety per cent of gospel was gay and lesbian, it was no secret,' he says. 'If you were gay or lesbian and you could sing, you knew it was the path you could take out of poverty. If you were black, you weren't going to be welcome on Broadway or in ballet. America was still very segregated, and the black community owned gospel by itself.'

Another traditional escape route from poverty was drag. Billy Wright wasn't even out of his teens when he joined Atlanta's enticingly titled Snake Anthony's Hot Harlem Revue, one of the so-called travelling tent shows of the rural south, where blues singers topped the bill while drag queens propped up the bill. Both set of acts would entertain in city nightclubs too, such as New Orleans' Dew Drop Inn, hosted by Irving Ale (or, to use her drag alias, Patsy Vadalia), whose duties included singing. Vadalia was good, but Wright was much better; compare the former's signature cover of Big Bill Broonzy's jump blues 'Put Your Hand Over Your Heart' (1953)[2] next to the latter's 1950 version and it's clear why the former's recording career stalled while Wright earned the sobriquet, 'prince of the blues'.

Larry Darnell was also among the singers out of drag at the Dew

---

[1] Simon & Schuster, 2010
[2] 'Put Your Hand Over Your Heart' was the B-side of Vadalia's only single 'Baby Rock Me', released under the safer name of Pat Valdelar, given the clear male identity of the singer.

Drop, a child gospel star who'd left home at fifteen to dance with the burlesque road show the Brownskin Models before returning to music. His second single, 'For You My Love' hit the top of the R&B charts in 1949 but it was more of a big band arrangement than gritty R&B and other tracks revealed more of a croon.

Wright had more rock'n'roll sass and lung power and, after being discovered by Columbia offshoot Okeh, he debuted the same year with 'Blues for my Baby', a gorgeously smoky and dolorous blues with a spiralling saxophone to parallel Wright's pining, 'Baby, I'm so unhappy/Tell me how you can feel so gay?' The single climbed to no. 3 on *Billboard*'s R&B chart, followed by another thirteen singles in four years, several making the R&B Top Ten.

For many years, Wright's drag origins didn't form a part of his narrative; performers weren't interviewed and there were no detailed reviews or discussions of artists' work. When his boogie-woogie-slanted A-side cover 'Don't You Want a Man like Me?'[1] threw in, 'I want all you girls to listen to what I got to say/I got a new way of lovin' and I'll fill you both night and day', only those in the know would have known Wright was singing to a man. Or that Wright's 1955 cover of 'Don't You Want a Man Like Me' was a brassy blues favourite among southern drag queens.

The track was covered that year by one of Wright's younger friends and drag peers at Snake Anthony's. Born an hour outside Atlanta in the town of Macon into a fastidiously religious household, Richard Penniman was singled out at school because he was born with one leg shorter than the other; the other kids 'didn't realise I was crippled,' he recalled. 'They thought I was trying to twist and walk feminine. The kids would call me faggot, sissy, freak, punk. They called me everything.' One of his childhood nicknames was Little Richard.

Penniman made up lost ground by excelling at singing and playing alto saxophone. He sung gospel with roof-raising exhilaration, and worked part-time at Macon City auditorium (selling drinks during shows while keenly

---

[1] Likely written by BB King though unreleased by the blues guitar legend until 1960.

watching the performers, including his favourite, Sister Rosetta Tharpe. She clocked the fourteen-year-old Penniman singing her gospel songs as he unpacked her gear and invited him to join her onstage that night.

Caught using his mother's make-up and wardrobe, Penniman was fifteen when he was kicked out of home by his father, a church deacon who also owned the Tip It Inn nightclub. This mixed parental message – part-sanctity and part-salacious – fed into Penniman's world as he swung between the two in a lifetime of enjoying and then renouncing his homosexuality, as God and Satan wrestled for control. But Satan played a strong hand.

A three-day prison sentence for lewd conduct – Penniman was a keen voyeur[1] – got him temporarily banned from performing in Macon, so he started doing drag across the south in various minstrel shows, under the name Princess Lavonne, such as *Sugarfoot Sam From Alabam*. Music promoter Alan Walden recalls seeing Lavonne in downtown Macon, 'in flaming glory, dressed in a tight, red suit with red shoes and a matching red parasol'.

Lavonne channelled some of Penniman's favourite gospel voices; Clara Ward, devout traditionalist (and former Famous Ward singer), Marion Williams and Dinah Washington, the decade's popular black female singer whose turbulent life – she eventually accumulated seven husbands – earned her a gay following second only to Judy Garland. Penniman admitted he got his trademark '*Whoooo!*' from Tharpe, but Billy Wright's forceful presence was as important. 'I copied [Wright], you know, for my dressin' and my hairdo and my makeup,' Penniman later said. 'I would call him a butch boy, you know, but I duplicated him really.' He also labelled Wright, 'the most fantastic performer I've ever seen.' Penniman was also smitten with Alex Bradford, another champion of the '*Whoooo!*' vamp but perhaps Little Richard's biggest influence was Esquerita. Or was it the other way around?

From South Carolina, born Eskew Reeder, Jr or Steven Quincy

---

[1] Penniman and a female friend would habitually drive around, picking up men for her to have sex with while he watched.

Reeder, Jr, the singularly named Esquerita was a madcap personality. Both he and Penniman took Wright's pompadour hairdo to extremes, almost defying gravity. It was the spirit in the air. Billy Miller, who befriended Esquerita in the eighties, says the singer claimed 'every part of [Penniman's] act, from pompadour to countertenor syllables, manic piano triplets and Pancake 31 make-up, was all conventional in the gay clubs of the south-eastern cities between 1947 and 1953.'[1]

Differences between Wright, Esquerita and Penniman could have included luck, timing or commitment. Wright might have been too early to benefit from the rock'n'roll revolution, while Esquerita seemed to be too unhinged:[2] he released his first record in 1958, by which time Penniman had been recording for six years as Little Richard. If Sister Rosetta Tharpe had carried rock'n'roll's pregnancy, Richard was to deliver the baby, whack it on the arse and send it out to wreak fun and havoc. And that baby was named 'Tutti Frutti'.

In 2007, *MOJO* magazine ran down the *One Hundred Records That Changed the World:*[3] no. 1 was 'Tutti Frutti'. It's gratifying to know that 'the biggest big bang in popular music' (adding, 'without this, no . . . nothing!') was a flamboyantly gay, cross-dressing black imp. He took the title from a song by Brazilian superstar Carmen Miranda, she of the tropical-fruit headdress who sang 'The Lady in the Tutti Frutti Hat' in the 1943 musical *The Gang's All Here*. Equally gratifying is the knowledge that this year zero classic was an enthusiastic ode to the joys of anal sex, while the US remained predominantly redneck and homophobic: 'A-wop-bom-a-loo-mop-a-lomp-bam-boom!/Tutti Frutti, good booty/ If it don't fit, don't force it/You can grease it, make it easy.'

Like Presley, Richard had his fair share of false starts. His debut single, for major label RCA, 'Taxi Blues', lacked the anarchic spirit that

---

1 *Deliberate Speed: The Origins of a Cultural Style in the American 1950s*, W. T. Lhamon (Smithsonian Institution, 1990)
2 Billy Miller: 'Esquerita was so fuckin' intense. There was nobody in the world like him, nobody.'
3 June, 2007 issue, http://www.mojo4music.com/2152/mojo-163-june-2007/

underscored his future legend and none of his first six singles truly fired. In frustration, during one session he suddenly unleashed 'Tutti Frutti', attacking his keyboard in a way that nobody present had witnessed ('I almost tore that piano out of the wall,' he recalled). Cosimo Matassa, who engineered the session, told *MOJO*: 'I describe his efforts as being the Queen of the May syndrome. He's gay, he wants to be the best, he has to be the best . . . And his performances tell that. The way he sang on stage was the way he sang in the studio. He'd bleed for you.'

Robert Blackwell, who produced the session, recognised that the music was fantastic, but that he needed to sanitise Richard's filthy lyric. Local songwriter Dorothy LaBostrie's revision, 'Tutti Frutti, aw rooty', was much more in keeping with the pop charts, which 'Tutti Frutti' entered in 1955 (after reaching no. 2 in the R&B chart), rising to no. 17. But part of Richard's original intention remained intact. It wasn't Carmen Miranda's doing, but 'fruit' had become slang for homosexual after the use of 'fruitcake' to describe male homosexuals treated for their apparent disorder.[1] According to American black history expert WT Lhamon, characters in 'Tutti Frutti' – Sue ('she knows just what to do') and Daisy ('she almost drives me crazy') – were euphemisms for transvestites.

The UK was slower to get rock'n'roll. 'Tutti Frutti' finally broke the UK Top 3 in 1957 and only then as the flipside to 'Long Tall Sally', a similarly charged and transgressive banger that referenced a drag queen: 'Well, I saw Uncle John with bald-headed Sally/He saw Aunt Mary coming and he ducked back in the alley.' The baldness referred to a drag queen without her wig while Aunt Mary was gay slang for a possessive queen.[2]

Both the UK and the USA embraced 'Long Tall Sally' and subsequent Richard singles 'Lucille' and 'Good Golly Miss Molly', which again

---

1 'Fruit' was adopted from Polari – an argot used by actors, circus performers, sailors and thieves – to mean 'queen'. It was taking the word back as 'queer' did in the eighties.
2 Ibid. 126

referenced drag queens who were quite likely prostitutes as well. For all his swagger and vocal charge, not even Presley had hit such gleeful heights; but then he wasn't inspired to exorcise the insults he'd taken at home and school. He wasn't treated as an outcast for the colour of his skin, let alone his sexuality.

But it got all too much for Richard, whose appetite for thrills[1] created a raging cocaine addiction: 'All I wanted to do was stay high all day and night and have sex. I loved sex, I wanted to do it all day and all night,' he said in 1987. 'And at other times, I didn't know what I was doing.'

The same year, Richard was also interviewed by a high-profile fan, gay underground film-maker John Waters, in which Richard described himself as 'the founder of gay. I'm the one who started to be so bold, tellin' the world.'[2]

In 1995, he told *Penthouse*, 'I've been gay all my life and I know God is a god of love, not of hate.' Yet in late 1957, Richard was in the middle of a sex-and-drugs-crazed, racially sensitive, fame-triggered identity crisis, and he scarpered back to the security of the church. Since Richard had once ventured that homosexuality was contagious and that he'd picked it up off the grocer boy, presumably he thought he could be cured with a spoonful of Christianity.[3]

Prisoners forty-seven and three in 'Jailhouse Rock' shock . . .

At least Richard had had his fiery moment in the sun, unlike Esquerita.[4] To truly bed down in the mainstream, it helped to be white. With lightning speed, Pat Boone, a Christian cut from a very different cloth, released covers of 'Tutti Frutti' and 'Long Tall Sally'. This whitewashing

---

1 One Little Richard legend concerns an alleged three-way with Buddy Holly and Richard's girlfriend, Angel, although she denies it.
2 http://www.theguardian.com/music/2010/nov/28/john-waters-met-little-richard
3 Little Richard's next move would be a handful of comparatively tepid gospel recordings. He wouldn't return to secular rock'n'roll until 1962.
4 Esquerita would have to wait a long time to be resurrected as a cult legend – 1987. Even then, tales of throttling producers and drug binges were legion. Poverty and AIDS were Esquerita's final undoing and he died that same year.

had also seen Fats Domino and Nat King Cole records similarly overtaken by white singers. Even Elvis Presley was guilty. His first year of major success, 1956, included chart-topper 'Hound Dog', previously taken into the R&B charts by Willie Mae 'Big Mama' Thornton in 1952. If nothing else, Presley sounded authentic and looked the part, shaking as if possessed by spirits, while Boone drained all the potency out of his covers. Presley was honest enough to admit that he'd learnt from Thornton – but accolades don't pay the bills and history has sidelined the likes of Thornton and Sister Rosetta Tharpe.

Ten years younger than Tharpe, Thornton had something of the Gladys Bentleys about her – powerhouse voice and personality and a fondness for menswear (though she preferred work shirts and slacks to a top hat and tails). Thornton 'tapped into a liberated black femininity through which she freed herself from many of the expectations of musical, lyrical, physical, and sartorial practice for black women,' wrote feminist scholar Maureen Mahon. 'These transgressions, central to her artistic voice, were at the heart of her musical identity, her appeal and her influence.'[1]

Thornton sung at Snake Anthony's and went on to sign to Peacock Records before Little Richard. 'Hound Dog' was her second single, written by emerging songwriters Jerry Leiber and Mike Stoller, a raucous twelve-bar blues that sold two million copies and topped *Billboard*'s R&B charts for seven weeks. But unlike Presley, Thornton would never have even one national hit.

In her essay *Queer Voices and Musical Genres*, Judith 'Jack' Halberstam wrote that Presley took 'the shout from Thornton, the defiance, the confident rejection of the "high-class poseur". He takes her confidence, her rhythm, her phrasing, even and her gender mobility.' Halberstam also claimed that Thorton 'exemplified how people deal with masculinity in female performers: The term "Big Mama" was used to domesticate Thornton and turn her masculinity into something female again.'[2]

---

[1] *Women And Music: A Journal of Gender and Culture* (University of Nebraska Press, 2004)
[2] *Oh Boy! Masculinities and Popular Music*, edited by Freya Jarman-Ivens (Routledge,

Presley shook up and shocked America, a gyrating performer who had to be shot from the waist up, just *exuding*. 'When I was young, I knew I was gay when I first saw Elvis,' recalls John Waters, 'this Martian twitching like something that freaked out my parents so much. I so embraced him and, so I now realise, sex.'

Presley sported a substantial quiff that had as much in common with drag as the masculine cuts that most men wore. He also wore mascara – so his dark-blonde eyelashes matched his dyed-black hair – and eyeliner to ensure better black-and-white photographs.[1] 'Before Elvis, you'd only seen that kind of sugar lacquer on the hair and the eye shade on geisha girls,' claims British fashion legend Antony Price. 'He had the campest image ever by that point.'

One less documented aspect of Presley's early success was performing the first chart-topper to refer to men having sex with other men, 'Jailhouse Rock'. Presley had previously distanced himself from the lyric of 'Hound Dog', saying that he was 'putting down' a friend rather than a lover. But he stuck to the script for Jerry Leiber and Mike Stoller's titular track written for Presley's third film, released in 1957. The filmed rendition is hilariously awkward.

Looking anything but a stage natural, Presley slides down a fireman's pole to announce the warden is throwing a party in the county jail. Surrounded by male jailbait, he sings – probably to no one's disbelief at the time – 'Number forty-seven said to number three/You're the cutest jailbird I ever did see/I sure would be delighted with your company/ Come on and do the jailhouse rock with me'. Two male dancers begin jiving together – an act that could have got them slung in a real jail, as it was illegal for men to dance together. One of the men jumps around as if the other had goosed him, or worse.

Similar coded thrills had spiced up the 1953 film musical *Gentlemen Prefer Blondes*, where gay choreographer Jack Cole – who championed

---

2007)
1 One such image captured by James R. Reid image was used for the cover of the Smiths' 1987 single 'Shoplifters of the World Unite'.

modern jazz dance, which still endures – utilised the men's US Olympic team, in flesh-coloured Speedos, to swing around Marilyn Monroe's co-star Jane Russell as she lamented their lack of interest in 'Ain't Anyone Here For Love'. Some viewers knew what kind of love was being flagged up here. In the 1956 film musical *White Christmas*, Bing Crosby and Danny Kaye's mimed drag spot – wearing shirts and trousers but also sporting fascinators and huge feathered fans – notably excluded female co-star Rosemary Clooney from the routine.

Hey, hey, we're the Roc-A-Jets

Outside of the urban strongholds and away from the nightclubs and tent shows that drew a gay crowd, citizens went about their lives without rocking the boat by singing, writing or campaigning about their unfair treatment. They accepted they just weren't meant for these times. Yet when lives are repressed, stuff comes out sideways and eventually has to give. This was even true in Maryland's state capital of Baltimore – not a place to break new ground if you were gay in the mid-fifties, as its famous resident John Waters knew. But where there's a will, there's a way.

'The Roc-A-Jets sported pompadours and they made the ladies swoon . . . but these rockabilly idols weren't guys. We meet musicians Carla Mandley and Jo Kellum of the Roc-a-Jets, a band that trail-blazed the social scene for gay women in fifties' Charm City.' A 2009 Baltimore podcast, The Signal, told their story. Jo Kellum, the band's lead guitarist, by then in her late seventies and still living with her long-term girlfriend Robin, didn't know of any gay or lesbian act that preceded them or any that co-existed at the same time. 'We didn't even think of these things,' she sighs. 'We were just having a good time.'

The young Kellum inherited her uncle's guitar after he was enlisted and joined a high school band, considering herself 'one of the guys'. She still followed the traditional route for a woman of getting married after graduation. 'I knew I was different from a young age – ten or so

– but you just didn't know from what. Today, you'd know, but not then.' Motherhood followed. But Kellum quickly bucked the system. 'Usually the husband went to work and that's how your life began and stayed . . . except for me,' she explains.

Kellum left her marriage and began making blinds in a factory line. On the assembly line she met Jan Morrison, originally from West Virginia. They were both what Kellum calls 'tough, no-frills women who loved music. So we brought our guitars in one lunch break. We sounded pretty good! We lost touch for a while, but we met up again and Jan's band had just broken up. She asked if I want to start another.'

Morrison (who died in 2007 of a blood clot) 'could play rhythm guitar like no one else,' Kellum told The Signal. 'And for an untrained voice, she made Patsy Cline look sad. She was good, very good.'

The pair initially employed male guitarists: 'They were playing bars that weren't at all interested in men but they were happy to play with us because we were earning above-union wages,' says Kellum. 'But soon as they'd made some money, they were gone.' Eventually, Morrison told Kellum she better step up; she agreed, but only if drummer Edie Lippincott – a lesbian friend they'd met on the scene – joined the band, 'to cover my mistakes!' Kellum laughs.

This was no wartime scenario where women filled the empty roles left by enlisted men; this was women doing it for themselves, like having the right to vote.

John Waters, who got to know the Roc-A-Jets in the sixties, fondly recalls this 'butch lesbian rock'n'roll band, the house band at Port in a Storm, one of the toughest gay women's bars in the world! And nobody fucked with Jan. Nobody booed them, that's for sure.'[1]

The Signal's presenter, Aaron Henkin, described a press photo of the Roc-A-Jets comprising 'a young Elvis Presley, a diminutive Buddy Holly and a baby-faced Johnny Cash'. Their trademark stage garb was white shirts and black slacks and out on the street, Kellum said, 'people

---

[1] Waters know this about Port in a Storm 'because they let me in, probably because of my filth credentials!'

would stare or kids would say, "Is that a man or a woman, mommy?" I liked it more when we played in winter, because you'd go out and it was already dark.'

The band quickly found they drew a crowd in other lesbian hangouts such as Mary's, women who were risking everything for the chance to belong, somewhere over the rainbow. 'They were coming out of the woodwork, lines around the block waiting to come in,' Kellum told The Signal. 'They'd leave home dressed [normally] and then go around the corner and get their clothes from over the fence and come down the bar, go into the ladies' room and change into their butch-looking clothes and when they went home, they reversed that. They'd wet their hair down in the bathroom . . . and out they came with their white shirt and black pants.'

The Roc-A-Jets' sound was rooted in rockabilly but encompassed cha-chas, polkas, tangos, and Top 40. 'Whatever you wanted, we did it,' Carla Mantley, the band's second drummer[1], told The Signal. 'We packed the places. People had smiles on their faces, people were dancing. It was a mixed crowd of gay people and straight people, which was a phenomenon for the time.'

Like Kellum, Mantley was married and a mother. Her husband was away a lot in the marines 'and resentment grew in me. I hadn't had much of a life'. Like Kellum, Mantley got divorced 'and I had to make it on my own.'

Sadly, the Roc-A-Jets never released any records; Kellum and Mantley were both single parents, playing shows (regularly six nights a week, plus a weekend matinée) and occasional tours (they once played Nashville's Grand Old Opry). Recording would have tested the patience of all the babysitters they were depending on. But they did have one session, in a Washington DC studio, demoing two Morrison originals, 'Without Love' and 'This Time You Gave Me a Mountain', plus two instrumental

---

1 Lippincott, says Kellum, 'was really thin and smoked too much, so she was often ill, so she and Carla would alternate every other week, right up until when Eydie retired, I think in the late eighties.'

covers, 'Caravan' and 'St Louis Woman'.

An audience recording exists of Lippincott's 'I Wanna Thank You' and country star Kitty Wells' 'Searching For Someone Like You', with Morrison's voice clear and bright, indeed like Patsy Cline. Wells' lyric was tailor-made for the longing that the band and their loyal crowd felt in those days: 'Dreaming, in all my dreams I dream/ That someday I'd find someone like you/Other loves have come my way but they were not for me/Tell me that you're here to stay, don't ever set me free.'

One downside was the men in the band's mixed audience who didn't like what they saw. 'They'd ask girls to dance and that could start a fight,' Kellum says. 'They'd beat the heck out of us and throw us out into the streets.' She and Mantley had to get Morrison out of jail a couple of times: 'Her ribs were all broken after they'd beat her real bad one time.'

The local vice squad also caused trouble by enforcing the gender-appropriate clothing rule. Kellum said that police would hit women in the chest, to check if they were wearing at least three items of women's clothes, while blouses would be torn open 'to check they were wearing bras. I just found out that it wasn't actually the law, it was just something they did to harass you, for fun.'

Being gay, Kellum said, 'was not a happy thing for me'. People would comment about her to her own child. 'In those days, children could be taken away if they could prove you were gay.' It's why she doesn't like being called a lesbian: 'People used that word to get at us, like "lezzie" or "lizie". Once upon a time we were all gay, men and women.'

Kellum lived in permanent fear of being outed at work, but that declined as people accepted her for who she was. But more importantly the band 'made me feel like I was somebody. I had some importance . . . I needed that.'

They never thought of splitting up: 'I don't think any of us felt that,' Kellum told The Signal. 'We felt relief that we finally knew what we were.' As did the band's audience. 'They had a place to go and to able to know who you were. You've no idea how important that was.'

From the mid-fifties to mid-sixties, the Rail Room bar[1] in Kansas hosted an all-female lesbian band called the Rail Runners and Alix Dobkin recalls a lesbian bar in Philadelphia with an all-girl band.

A matter of gender

Other women of the era were less bold, with two taking subterfuge to astonishing lengths. The more famous of the pair, Billy Tipton, born Dorothy Lucille Tipton in 1914, passed as a man for almost sixty years, binding her breasts and padding her pants – various wives were told a car accident had crushed his chest and genitals, ruling out traditional sex. Children were adopted and life rolled on. In 1957, the Billy Tipton Trio released two profile-raising albums of jazz standards (*Sweet Georgia Brown* and *Billy Tipton Plays Hi-Fi on Piano*), but Tipton suddenly abandoned music to work as a booking agent, fearing fame could mean intrusive attention. When Tipton lay dying of a haemorrhaging peptic ulcer, at the age of seventy-four, her secret was finally revealed by paramedics called to the house.[2]

Wilmer M. Broadnax was a similar case; having sung with several gospel groups through the forties and fifties, passing as male, he would be murdered by his girlfriend in 1992, only to have his autopsy reveal his gender.

Despite Christine Jorgensen, the concept of female-to-male gender reassignment didn't exist; these transgender figures were trapped in the wrong body as much as the wrong era.

Others fluctuated with identity in the face of overwhelming

---

1 According to local writer Linda May, the Rail Room was 'frequented by male railway workers during the day. After a certain time of day, a "magic transformation" happened. It was taken over by women and there was a halfway point in the room, unspoken and unmarked, past which no men ventured', *Women in Kansas City's Heritage*, Gay and Lesbian Archive of Mid-America, http://library.umkc.edu/spec-col/glama/pdfs/history/article-may.pdf

2 Tipton would later inspire an opera, a play, a jazz musical, tribute songs and the predominantly female Billy Tipton Memorial Saxophone Quartet.

The Fifties: The Tutti Frutti Revolution

odds. *Recollections of a Part-time Lady*[1], the brief, riveting and hilarious biography of Minette, recalls a life of trials and tribulations interspersed with triumphs and breakthroughs. Born Jacques Minette to French parents but raised in Boston, he was a child performer[2] whose vaudeville impressions included Ethel Waters, Mae West, Eddie Cantor and Maurice Chevalier. Aged fourteen he started singing in clubs and, uncomfortable as a boy, began drag performance in the forties. By 1951, known only by his surname, Minette was working in Boston's popular club, the College Inn. He specialised in song parodies, such as Eddie Cantor's 'Doodle Doo Doo', which he turned into a cross-dressing farce: 'Now mama is butch, her morals are scanty/Papa's turned too and he's an old aunty/ The family's gone mad, they sure got it bad/'Bout doodle doo doodle doo doo.'

Minette was aware of the enforced clothing rule but got away with wearing French high-heeled shoes by claiming they were men's shoes from the time of Louis XIV ('And if they looked in the encyclopaedia, there was something to back me up').

Another drag queen made breasts out of paper serviettes that could be instantly crushed if the police walked in. It didn't stop arrests and Boston's entire drag scene was shut down in the mid-fifties as part of the continuing decimation of gay venues. Minette simply travelled to where he could find work.

On the opposite coast, Ray Bourbon continued working, releasing records on his Under The Counter label while skirting dangerously around the moral majority. At least he'd outlived McCarthyism, which was dead in the water by 1955, its leader censured by his own Republican party under President Eisenhower. But the law didn't need a political figurehead to continue the mission; in 1955, twenty men were arrested

---

1 Flower-Beneath-the-Foot Press, 1979, http://queermusicheritage.com/drag-minette1.html#
2 Information found at A Gender Variance Who's Who, http://zagria.blogspot.co.uk/2010/02/minette-1928-2001-usa.htm1#.VxZIjDHRDzM

in Sioux City, Iowa and incarcerated in a 'sexual psychopath' ward in the local psychiatric hospital.

In his own way, Bourbon was behaving erratically, blowing through his fortune on expensive outfits (often the kind of furs that Liberace would take to extremes) and he got more daring; the cover of his 1956 album *A Girl of the Golden West* featured Bourbon in drag portrayed between a man's spread legs, with a pronounced outline in the crotch of his jeans.

Bourbon was arrested once again and spent a month in prison. His response was to declare – falsely – that he'd had gender reassignment in Mexico. He celebrated in 1957 with the album *Take a Look at my Operation* and now billed himself as Rae Bourbon, pre-empting the crime of female impersonation – unless some police officer was brave enough to check.

Girl power and the USA's first gay record label...

Alix Dobkin recalls the lesbian bar scene of the day, one that 'partied and sometimes vacationed together, successfully loving, then betraying, cherishing and abusing, one another in wracking succession.' She says two of the all-time jazz/blues legends, Billie Holiday and the emerging Nina Simone, were favoured singers, 'tragic icons who touched this hard-boiled, volatile community of lesbians the way Judy Garland affected their gay brothers'. For lighter relief, there was Frances Faye: 'She could be found in the collection of every gay man in Philadelphia,' says Dobkin.

Living through icons was one way to feel less alone, but if anything was going to change, more gay community action was needed. In 1955, a group of female Mattachine Society members formed a splinter group in San Francisco, named the Daughters of Bilitis, after Pierrre de Louys' nineteenth-century poetry cycle *Songs of Bilitis*. It was more social than political, bringing together lesbians who avoided the bar and club scene and providing information that was otherwise unavailable.

Nine long years after Edith Eyde's *Vice Versa*, the US's first nationally distributed lesbian publication was launched, *The Ladder*. The first cover depicted figures approaching a ladder that disappeared into the clouds. A metaphor for continuing to dream?

By October 1957, *The Ladder* only had 400 subscribers. But one of them was Edith Eyde, under the pun-heavy pseudonym of Lisa Ben.[1] She also socialised in the bars and clubs where lesbians congregated for shows by Beverly Shaw and also Chris Connor – the first white female jazz singer signed by major label Atlantic – who oozed urbane cool and was widely felt by lesbian fans to be one of theirs. It was later revealed that Connor had had a long-term relationship with Lori Muscarelle, who later became her manager. The intoxicating 'Moon Ray' from 1956's *A Jazz Date with Chris Connor* had been intended for a man and Connor didn't change the pronoun: 'Let your sweet enchantment find her/Then I shall wake and find her near/In my lonely arms.'

A Beverly Shaw show, at LA's Flamingo club on a Sunday afternoon, prompted Eyde to start writing openly gay songs that couldn't be interpreted any other way. 'As evening wore on, the straight people would wander in just to see how the other half lived,' she later recalled.[2] 'One of the drag queens that night made a terrible remark about Beverly Shaw, her being a butch or something. It was a very offensive joke, and all the straight people laughed at it... I thought, what a stupid thing to do, to play into the hands of these outsiders by demeaning themselves in this way.'

Eyde decided she'd use humour to make her point, and her target was the gay community itself. 'I thought, Well, I'm going to write some gay parodies, and they're going to be gay, but they are not going to be demeaning or filthy. I just presented something else instead, hoping that people would latch onto it and realise they didn't have to talk themselves down to be accepted.'

One parody adopted 'I'm Gonna Sit Right Down and Write Myself

---

1 Eyde had first chosen the pseudonym Ima Spinster, which *The Ladder* rejected.
2 *Making History: The Struggle for Gay and Lesbian Equal Rights, 1945-1990, An Oral History*, Eric Marcus (HarperCollins, 1992)

a Letter', originally sung by Fats Waller, which Eyde changed to, 'I'm going to sit right down and write my butch a letter and ask her won't she please turn femme for me.' Gene Austin's 'Wedding Bells (are Breaking Up That Old Gang of Mine)' became 'The Vice Squad Keeps Breaking Up That Old Gang of Mine'. Edye added original songs too, from the light-hearted 'I'm a Boy Being a Girl' to the sombre 'A Fairer Tomorrow': 'Here's to the days that we yearn for/To give of our hearts as we may/The world cannot dare to deny us/We've been here since centuries past/And you can be sure our ranks will endure as long as this old world will last.'

Lisa Ben's first single, released in 1960 on the DOB (Daughters of Bilitis) label, paired one cover and one original. Her rather shaky, rough-cut version of the traditional folk song 'Frankie and Johnnie' – Frankie catches her man with another woman and shoots him dead – became a stand-off between two men while her own 'Cruising Down the Boulevard' had more mellifluous charm. Finally: an English language song that promoted gay identity, without resorting to code. DOB's advertisement in *One* magazine had the headline, 'The Gayest Songs on Wax', though Ben's single was intended to be a fundraiser rather than a commercial gambit limited to a thousand copies.

There were no male equivalents to Ben's milestone. Instead, a vogue for actors releasing albums was dominated by closeted gay men – Tab Hunter, Antony Perkins and Sal Mineo – Plato to James Dean's Jim Stark in *Rebel Without a Cause*. Hunter was the best-looking and the most popular, his US and UK no. 1, 'Young Love', was an effective tear-jerker. But Perkins had the best voice, a silken croon that glided over jazzy arrangements.[1]

Young, gifted and black – and gay . . .

Not for the first time, the black drag acts led the way to a more honest representation. While Little Richard was tearing up the charts, the rest

---

1 Tab Hunter and Antony Perkins had a long-term affair, though Perkins later married. Hunter managed to maintain a façade without such assistance.

The Fifties: The Tutti Frutti Revolution

of black America, touring the chitlin circuit – the given name to the US venues accepting Afro-American artists – were trying their luck. One leading light was Bobby Marchan, born Oscar James Gibson in Ohio, who ran the Powder Box Revue at New Orleans' Dew Drop Inn. Marchan was also kept busy singing at the R&B venue Club Tijuana and, in 1953, recorded the sturdy R&B ballad 'Have Mercy'. According to blogger Corey Jarrell[1], Marchan – like Dew Drop Inn hostess Petite Swanson – made for a very convincing woman; Ace Records reputedly offered a deal believing he was a she. The relationship prospered initially, starting with the slow, rollicking rock'n'roll of 'Chickee Wah-Wah' but his crowning glory was 'There is Something on Your Mind (Parts One and Two)', a burning-blue soul ballad that predicted Otis Redding's style[2] and topped the R&B charts in 1960, selling a million copies. Blues and gospel were merging into this embryonic style of soul music, but a smoother, harmony-led version had emerged first, christened doo wop. It took its cues from the white crooners and numbers from the Great American Songbook such as Rodgers and Hart's 'Blue Moon'. Like rock'n'roll, doo wop could pick up the pace and turn grittier but with the falsetto at the front and all those creamy harmonies, it was the most feminine of black music genres, though mostly the preserve of male voices.

Doo wop bands tended to name themselves in clusters: there were birds (the Swallows, the Ravens, the Orioles, the Flamingos) and cars (the Edsels, the Cadillacs, the Impalas, Anthony and the Imperials) and a gaggle of Gays – the Gay Knights, the Gay Tunes, the Gay Notes, the all-female Gay Charmers and, yes, the Gay Poppers (their 1961 ballad 'Please Mr Cupid' is epic). Given that doo wop emerged from gospel, it wasn't surprising gay men were part of the tradition.

It seems that the police and the vice squad were more interested in

---

1 http://illkeepyouposted.typepad.com/ill_keep_you_posted/2011/04/bobby-marchan-was-there-something-on-his-mind.html
2 Otis Redding later invited Marchan to record at Stax Records in Memphis, underlining the esteem in which Marchan was held.

the US's Caucasian communities, going by the number of black entertainers who didn't hide their sexuality. These included Charlie and Ray (surnames unknown) on the cusp of R&B and doo wop. One blogger, named Jaymar, saw them perform at Harlem's Rockland Palace and called them 'easily the most unique duo of the fifties and light years ahead of their time' and 'unabashedly gay and black. They presented themselves as not drag queens, which was a popular method at the time, but as straight looking singers with a singular delivery.'[1]

Then there was Frankie Lymon, the diminutive boy soprano lead of New York City quintet the Teenagers, whose 'Why Do Fools Fall in Love' was a giant doo wop smash: no. 6 on the national US chart and topping the UK chart. With fame going to his little head, Lymon went solo, crushing both his and the Teenagers' careers. He would be found dead in 1968, at twenty-five from a heroin overdose, taking his secret with him until Jim Fouratt, who later carved a reputation in both civil rights and the music industry, admitted that he'd had an affair with Lymon.

Rudy Lewis, one of only two men to join the Clara Ward Singers before he replaced Ben E King in the Drifters, also died from a heroin overdose, at twenty-seven, the night before the group recorded one of its signature singles, 'On Broadway'. His voice was described as 'burnished mahogany . . . that could stretch and bend like molten steel'. Again, the truth about Lewis' sexuality only surfaced decades later, in the nineties, when reclaiming gay icons became a political necessity. Another reclaimed icon was Cornell Gunter, one of the founders of the Platters before he joined the Coasters – both doo wop legends. Gunther, as he liked to spell his surname, joined the Coasters just in time for the group's run of comedic classics: no. 1 'Yakety Yak', no. 2 'Charlie Brown' and 'Along Came Jones'. Gunther stood out for his voice that was a match for Rudy Lewis and for his androgyny, with a full, round face topped by pompadour hair that needed no wig to give it height.

---

1 http://home.earthlink.net/~jaymar41/doowopTP.html

The Fifties: The Tutti Frutti Revolution

Fellow Coaster, Carl Gardner, recalled meeting Gunther for the first time. 'He was a very young, flamboyant, big guy with about a nineteen-inch neck. He was built like a prize-fighter. But it was his appearance that gave me my first jolt and prompted me to ask Cornell, "Are you gay or just a big woman?"

'Cornell said, "Now, what makes you think that, honey?"

'I replied, "Because you look like that, sister." We both just fell about laughing.'[1]

As Corey Jarrell notes on his blog[2], Gunther attributed his androgynous style to the first time he saw his idol, Dinah Washington, at a concert in LA when he was eight years old. 'I sold papers so I could buy a ticket but they wouldn't let me in because I was so young. So, I climbed up to the window of her dressing room where I was stopped by security people.

'I said, "Oh, Miss Washington, I can sing just like you."

'She said, "Well, you better sound just like me."

'So I sang and she pulled me through the window and took me out on stage with her... I still had two unsold papers under my arm.'

'I saw the Coasters play and I remember Gunther, with his processes, the big waves in his hair,' says Archbishop Carl Bean. 'They did all their hits, but I screamed the loudest when Cornell did his solo spot imitating Dinah Washington, singing "What a Difference a Day Made". He mimicked her so well! The other Coasters would carry him in their arms, the routine was wonderful. I knew I was like him and he was like me, an effeminate boy.'[3]

Gunther unleashed his Washington impersonation on the Coasters' 'Easy Living', a luxurious ballad with cocktail piano trills. It was a much better showcase for his voice than their novelty hits penned by

---

1 *Yakety Yak I Fought Back: My Life With The Coasters*, (Authorhouse, 2008)
2 http://illkeepyouposted.typepad.com/ill_keep_you_posted/2010/11/cornell-gunter-the-queen-of-doo-wop-and-the-coasters.html
3 Gunther's story turned out as tragic as those of Lewis and Lymon; he was murdered in 1980 by gunshots as he sat in his car in Las Vegas. The gunman was never found, nor the reason why Gunther was shot.

the era's song-writing supremos Leiber and Stoller. Gunther should have tackled 'Love Potion No. 9' – given to the Clovers[1] – about a man seeking help to find love; a gypsy supplies him with an elixir that is so potent that the man starts kissing everything he sees, including a policeman.

For impressionable gay boys such as Richard Dworkin, who would make his career as a brilliant session drummer, the song was a wake-up moment. 'It was still a time you'd hear music on the radio rather than see people performing on TV. So you paid great attention to the words, and something overt like "Love Potion No. 9" with, "When I kiss a cop down on 34th and Vine/he broke my little bottle of love potion no. 9", I was, like, wow, what *is* that?'

Lyrics that evoked feelings of hope, romance and validation became even more crucial now that there were so many boy/girl love songs on the radio. 'I knew I was gay the first time I heard Clarence "Frogman" Henry's "Ain't Got No Home"!' says John Waters. The R&B pianist's debut single, a greasy slice of rock'n'roll from New Orleans, had Henry deliver the chorus in a stratospheric falsetto, and then the bass croak that earned his nickname. 'I was about nine or ten years old and, when he said that he sang like a girl, I was like, Oh, my God! Though when he said that he sung like a frog, I was confused! Maybe I was tri-sexual, or a closet frog fucker.'

The lines, 'I ain't got a man/I ain't got a son/I ain't got a daughter/I ain't got no one/I'm a lonely girl/I ain't got a home,' must have bamboozled Waters. 'It just opened me, it made me think sexual,' he claims. 'When you're gay, you take any clue you can get.'

Jack Doroshow, who ran the Miss Philadelphia drag pageant in his home state in 1959 in his drag persona of Flawless Sabrina or Mother Flawless, was smitten by the mixed race singer Eartha Kitt, whose purring style unfurled like an aural striptease. 'There's no question

---

[1] Or maybe The Clovers' (unreleased) parody of Dixie jazz standard 'Darktown Strutters' Ball', renamed 'The Cocksuckers Ball' – though some claim 'cock' was southern states vernacular for 'vagina'.

that she was a woman,' notes Sabrina, 'but Kitt had some sort of gender-bending aspect, like she was teasing her gender. Johnnie Ray sounded like a woman. Little Richard was brilliant and wonderful. He was a woman in the way his humour was presented, and he was very out about his otherness. And I always found [Billie Holiday's] "Strange Fruit" pertinent.'

The teenage Alix Dobkin was thrilled by 'anyone who seemed they were breaking the rules and getting away with it over the authorities'. She'd inherited her communist beliefs from her card-carrying parents. 'I liked Eartha Kitt; of course, black people were allowed to be overtly sexual more than white people, she had that edge. Tom Lehrer, who wrote wonderful, edgy parodies, was huge for me.'

Lehrer was a New York maths prodigy who specialised in spiky, savage satire, influenced by musical theatre, a subject he began to teach (alongside maths) after moving to California. Students were warned not to enquire about his private life, though Lehrer did admit to a fan who tracked him down in his eighties, that he never married and that he owned a 'Nöel Coward shrine' of books and records. As for Lehrer's subject matter, there's just one song, 'Be Prepared' (from 1953's *Songs by Tom Lehrer*) on the matter of homosexuality, advising, 'If you're out behind the woodshed doing what you'd like to do, just be sure that your companion is a Boy Scout too.'

A Lehrer-style comedy number, 'Homo the Range'[1], by former Bing Crosby associate Bob Peck, got in on the act: 'Now all the girls in Texas were simply mad about Alexis/Till they learnt that nature played some funny trick.'

But songs of longing were much more comforting than those that made fun of nature's 'funny trick'. Back on the range, Doris Day's 1953 film musical *Calamity Jane* included the dreamy ballad 'Secret Love' – another seismic moment for Jack Fritscher, who also clocked Day in cross-dressing cowboy attire, a fillip for impressionable young girls too:

---

1 From *Songs That Never Made the Hymnal*, Jubilee.

'Once I had a secret love/That lived within the heart of me/All too soon my secret love/Became impatient to be free.'

Fritscher also responded to the Jimmie Rogers' doo-wop-style ballad, 'Secretly' from 1958: 'Till we have the right to meet openly/Till we have the right to kiss openly/We'll just have to be content to be in love secretly.'

Ballads of sad young men
Indocrinated with the idea his sexuality – the heart of most teenagers' emerging identities – was wrong, Fritscher would respond to similarly forbidden thrills. He also recalls Lieber and Stoller's 'Black Denim Trousers and Motorcycle Boots', a Top 10 hit for the Cheers in 1955, banned by the priests in the seminary where Fritscher lived as a teenager, believing that God was the answer to his unresolved feelings. The songs that the priests permitted were generally Broadway tunes with redemptive, hymnal qualities, such as 'Somewhere (There's a Place for Us)' from *West Side Story*, which Fritscher imagined 'was about a promised gay Eden'.

West Side Story, the outstanding stage musical of the fifties, debuted in 1957[1] with libretto and lyrics by Stephen Sondheim, conception and choreography by Jerome Robbins and screenplay by Arthur Laurents – all three of them gay. William Shakespeare's concept of *Romeo and Juliet*, argued Laurents, of forbidden love and secretive, anguished desire, was still very relatable: 'That kind of bigotry and prejudice was very much in the air. It's really, "How can love survive in a violent world of prejudice?" That's what it's about.'

Fritscher's yearning, 'imagining the impossible Romeo-Romeo secret love I longed to make possible and public,' also zeroed in on Paul Anka's 'Puppy Love', Tab Hunter's 'Young Love' and Chuck Berry's 'Sweet Little Sixteen', the age of one of his seminary crushes. As for 'Mister Sandman', Fritscher says he was on at a Chicago cocktail party by a man claiming to

---

[1] The film version, released in 1961, was even more influential than the stage play and won ten Academy Awards, including best picture.

have written the song, who told Fritscher his original lyric was, 'Mister Sandman/Bring me a queen'. Instead, Pat Ballard wrote, 'Mister Sandman bring us a dream/Give him a pair of eyes with a come-hither gleam/Give him a lonely heart like Pagliacci/And lots of wavy hair like Liberace'.

New portable transistor radios made it much easier to consume pop, 'especially in the seminary where the tiny plastic radios could be easily hidden inside hollowed-out bibles,' Fritscher says. 'We had a rogue classmate from Philadelphia who kept us literally tuned into Philly doo wop. He smuggled in black hits like the Platters' confessional "The Great Pretender" and Mickey and Sylvia's irresistibly alternative "Love Is Strange".'

Fritscher also eulogises Johnny Mathis's 'Stranger in Paradise', written for the 1953 stage musical *Kismet*. Originally a man-woman duet, it was subsequently taken over by male voices, like Mathis, who Fritscher calls 'the best heir, and antidote to the emotional territory blazed by Johnnie Ray.'

The third best-selling singer of the twentieth century, with over seventy charting albums and 350 million sales, Mathis had the most velvet of croons, melancholic to the core, but the classical and operatic voice coaching in his childhood gave him considerable firepower. The young Texan, though, was unhappy with his gift. 'People told me I sang too high and that I sounded like a girl,' he told writer James Gavin. 'I thought it was a horrible thing God had given me, this strange voice.'[1]

As writer Vincent Stephens saw it, Mathis 'conveyed an ambiguous sexual romanticism with room for heterosexual and homosexual audiences to project their desires onto him without having to engage with his sexuality.[2] 'The plan worked; like Liberace, Mathis had legions of diehard female fans who empathised with his vulnerability. Mathis, who

---

[1] The *New York Times*, 19 December 1993, http://jamesgavin.com/page4/page91/page91.html

[2] *Shaking The Closet: Analysing Johnny Mathis's Sexual Elusiveness, 1956–82* (Routledge, 2010)

finally came out in 1982 (he told *Us* magazine, 'Homosexuality is a way of life that I've grown accustomed to,' apparently believing his comment was off the record), chose songs that tapped his sad, lonely self, such as 'Stranger in Paradise', which he recorded in 1958. He notably didn't change the pronoun, unlike the other male interpreters of the song: 'Don't send me in dark despair from all that I hunger for/But open your angel's arms to this stranger in paradise/And tell him that he need be a stranger no more.'

Another Mathis cover from 1958, 'A Certain Smile', was translated by Fritscher to mean, 'a *certain* kind of love, a *different* kind of love, a gorgeous *transient* love set flaming by the bittersweet rituals of cruising, with a gay provenance that Mathis italicised with innuendo': 'A fleeting glance can say so many lovely things . . . You love awhile and when love goes/You try to hide the tears inside with a cheerful pose/But in the hush of night, exactly like a bittersweet refrain/comes that certain smile to haunt your heart again.'

Mathis sang 'A Certain Smile' in the film of the same name, based on the novel by French teen prodigy Françoise Sagan, who was shocking Catholic France with tales of liberated unmarried sex. Ironically, gay men over twenty-one had been legally allowed to have sex in France since 1942, while British Protestants were still imprisoned by the Victorian morals of the past. The UK's home secretary, Sir David Maxwell Fyfe, had promised 'a new drive against male vice' that would 'rid England of this plague'. Over a thousand men were imprisoned and police raided those gay clubs that had managed to survive. But the 1957 committee on homosexual offences and prostitution – the Wolfenden Report – recommended that 'homosexual behaviour between consenting adults in private should no longer be a criminal offence'.

The catalyst for the Wolfenden Report had been three men imprisoned in 1954 for the crime of gross indecency, the same charge that brought down Oscar Wilde. Peter Wildeblood, the diplomatic correspondent for the *Daily Mail* newspaper, had an affair with RAF corporal Edward McNally. In 1953, the pair visited the politician Lord Montagu of Beaulieu, where they were joined by McNally's RAF friend John Reynolds and Montagu's cousin Michael Pitt-Rivers.

The two airmen gave evidence against their more aristocratic companions, claiming they were victims of the other men's advances. Montagu was sentenced to twelve months, Wildeblood and Pitt-Rivers to eighteen months. Wildeblood's subsequent book about prison life and the victimisation of homosexuals, *Against the Law*, was followed by a second book, *A Way of Life*, which described the lives of twelve homosexuals that Wildeblood knew and showed that homosexuality was common across the sexes, classes and cultures.

Wildeblood had fully admitted to being homosexual at his trial, and he also testified at the Wolfenden enquiry. It was an important signifier, like Kinsey's earlier *Sexuality in the Human Male*, but Wolfenden's finding had no immediate effect; the law would not be repealed for another ten years.

The establishment's deep-set intransigence in the US and UK might explain why black actor Gordon Heath abandoned New York City in 1949 and set up home in Paris, after taking the Broadway production of the daring race-relations play *Deep Are The Roots* to London. Heath and his boyfriend, fellow actor Lee Payant, didn't feel accepted in London, but in Paris, they would own the Left Bank nightclub L'Abbaye for over twenty-five years, performing folk songs, spirituals and jazz standards as part of the entertainment.

The couple were surely better actors than singers: their delivery was stiff and solemn, like medieval troubadours[1], but then folk music was a serious business now, emblematic of the nascent civil rights movement. One review claimed applause during their set wasn't encouraged, but the evening's ritual sounds special: 'A candle is placed on every table, and every table has a right to "its" song. When Gordon Heath and Lee Payant have sung it, the candle is blown out. When all of them are out, it's closing time.'[2]

---

1 Compilation *An Evening At L'Abbaye* (1957) is available on Spotify.
2 R. J.-C., *Une Semaine de Paris*, August, 1953

France had a homosexual milieu in the works of Jean Cocteau and Jean Genet, across books, plays and films that constructed surreal and dream-like fantasies such as Genet's 1943 novel *Our Lady of the Flowers*, 'a hallucinatory tale of drag queens, pimps, murderers and sailors', according to journalist Rupert Smith.[1] Their work had a sizeable impact on American new, 'Beat Generation,' of writers such as Jack Kerouac, William Burroughs and Allen Ginsberg, all based in San Francisco. They were joined there by Rod McKuen, now less known for his beat generation roots than a more sentimental style of writing across poetry and albums. These anti-conformist, free-thinking types experimenting with sex, drugs and eastern philosophy were the next 'nature boys', following in eden ahbez's footsteps.

From Oakland, California, McKuen fled home, aged just eleven, to escape his violent alcoholic stepfather. Living hand-to-mouth (an online biography claims he supported himself as a ranch hand, surveyor, railroad worker, lumberjack, rodeo cowboy, stuntman and radio DJ[2]) and having with no formal education, McKuen's writing nevertheless included a newspaper column and propaganda scripts for the US armed forces during the Korean war. He was an actor and a folk singer with a penchant for the spoken word and even as a young man, he sounded like an aged, husky barfly.

On record, McKuen's simple poems had rudimentary musical backdrops that emphasised the fragility of his words, though he often abandoned poignancy for the realms of earnest and cloying – *Newsweek* called him the 'king of kitsch'. It didn't faze prolific McKuen, who wrote over 1500 songs and sold a hundred million records and sixty million books of poetry before his death in 2015.[3]

It was 1960's *Alone After Dark*, an album of soft, dewy jazz ballads, that first raised the notion that McKuen, like several beat generation

---

1 http://www.theguardian.com/culture/2002/jan/30/artsfeatures
2 http://www.allmusic.com/artist/rod-mckuen-mn0000243803
3 My request for an interview was emailed two months before he died and was never answered

fellows, had a fluid approach to sexuality, though he always refused labelling – stubbornly so, given the evidence. 'I've been to bed with women and men... Does that make me bisexual?' he once said. 'Nope. Heterosexual? Not exclusively. Homosexual? Certainly not by my definition... I can't imagine choosing one sex over the other, that's just too limiting. I can't even honestly say I have a preference.'

McKuen had been quick to cover 'Ballad of the Sad Young Men', a glacially slow, simmering ballad written by composer Tommy Wolf and lyricist Fran Landesman for their 1958 musical *The Nervous Set*, about the beat generation's roots. The song has since become a standard, covered by the likes of Anita Day, Gil Evans and Roberta Flack, though only McKuen embodied the sexual reading of the song: 'All the sad young men seek a certain smile/Someone they can hold, for just a little while/Tired little girl, does the best she can/Trying to be gay, for a sad young man.'

Could the song have been written for Johnny Mathis, given the reference to 'a certain smile'? Mathis waited five years before singing 'All The Sad Young Men', though the arrangement was more syrupy, almost Christmassy and it turned out to be an entirely different song with the same title. This 'All The Sad Young Men' by songwriters Jerry Livingston and Paul Webster[1] was closer to a drinking song, beginning, 'Here's to all the melancholy men/here's to all those who've loved and lost,' and ending, 'Bottoms up to all the sad young men,' which is an image to conjure with.

In between, Mathis sang, 'Don't let true love slip away/gather rosebuds while ye may/gentlemen don't leave those songs unsung/while you're still young and gay'. Lyricist Webster would have known the word's double meaning, especially as he also wrote the words to 'Secret Love' for Doris Day and 'A Certain Smile' for Mathis. Maybe Webster had some special insight into the plight of these sad young men.

The sad young – and older – men and women who campaigned for the Mattachine Society (with chapters now in San Francisco, New York,

---

1 *All The Sad Young Men* is the title of a collection of short stories by F Scott Fitzgerald.

Washington and Chicago), its spin-off ONE Inc and the Daughters of Bilitis, continued to struggle. They were making no leeway, while Liberace – whose UK profile now rivalled his following back home – was, 'crying all the way to the bank', as he told the newspapers after successfully suing the *Daily Mirror* in 1956. Columnist William Connor (who wrote under the byline Cassandra) had described him with a deadly homophobic eye as 'the pinnacle of masculine, feminine and neuter ... a deadly, winking, sniggering, snuggling, chromium-plated, scent-impregnated, luminous, quivering, giggling, fruit-flavoured, mincing, ice-covered heap of mother love.'

Never mind that Liber-*ah*-chee lived in a glass closet and, behind closed doors, had boyfriends and a string of affairs; for him to accept the accusation would be to admit that he was a criminal.[1] Hypocritical or not, he was simply doing what was necessary to survive – and who's to say that his female fans' love for this most pansy of performers didn't help lay the foundations for a greater acceptance of homosexuality?

Another lawsuit was won against the US post office, who in 1954 had decided that *One* magazine was obscene and so could not be distributed. But in 1958, ONE Inc were able to cite a prior landmark First Amendment ruling that, while individual states could prosecute, the federal government could not. Similar legal triumphs were recorded either side of ONE Inc's success, when Allen Ginsberg and William Burroughs' defining gay literary proclamations – respectively the poem *Howl* and the novel *The Naked Lunch* – were also cleared of obscenity, because of their apparent social value. Californian filmmaker Kenneth Anger's experimental short *Fireworks* from 1958 was also made available for purchase, the first publicly available slice of homoerotica on film.

In New York, Frank O'Hara's poems were more overtly homosexual than Walt Whitman's and evoked the elation, sadness and cavalier dimensions of a burgeoning gay underworld. And as with Larry Rivers'

---

[1] In 1957, Liberace settled a case with US magazine *Confidential* (headline: WHY LIBERACE'S THEME SONG SHOULD BE 'MAD ABOUT THE BOY'!).

painting, *Frank O'Hara Nude with Boots*, the censor didn't intervene if the work was considered culturally relevant. Nothing in the direct gaze of the mainstream eye, from Hollywood and Broadway to Manhattan's song-writing industries at the Brill Building[1] and Tin Pan Alley, was equally willing to risk the slightest revelation. Homo music-lovers had to put up with 'He's the Queen of Fire Island', from *For Women Only*, an album of 'spicy songs' ('Oooo Have I Got Hot Nuts for You', 'She Loves Her Peter' etc.) by the lounge singer Saul T. Peter.[2]

British rock'n'roll: a gay makeover

UK art was even more restricted. We'd had no Johnnie Ray, Little Richard, Johnny Mathis or Rod McKuen, no lesbian sirens or even spunky lounge singers playfully peddling gay innuendo. Only Benjamin Britten's operas of homosexual repression had challenged the status quo, though that would have meant little to most participants of what constituted the UK's gay scene, based in London's Soho district.

Britten and Soho had plenty to rail against. In parliament, MP William Shepherd blithely announced 'Incest is a much more natural act than homosexuality,' and the Wolfenden Report actually led to an increase in police harassment. According to writer Haydon Bridge, the police 'rarely made arrests, but intimidated everyone by taking names and addresses. Corrupt cops also took cash and booze from bar owners. Queers took refuge in illegal drinking clubs. Gay activist Claire Andrews remembers, 'They were usually run by black people, who were sympathetic to lesbians and gay men who didn't have a place to go.'[3]

Before the police stepped up their raids, there were a surprisingly healthy number of bars to choose from, though they were mostly tiny basement and attic spaces. One contemporary witness recalled the

---

1 Though the studio's owner, Bob Guy and assistants Lor Crane and Joe Cyr, were all gay; Crane and Cyr were also lovers at one point.
2 It's Peter's only known record, though the record label, Davis Records, released an endless number of similar innuendos; aural burlesque. The fleshy artwork followed suit.
3 http://qxmagazine.com/pdf/features.pdf

line-up: 'The Alibi, the Huntsman, Take 5, the Apple, No. 9, the Casino. You didn't have to go a hundred yards. Some had a juke box and people would dance.' He recalled one night in the Mambo, dancing to Fats Domino's 'Blueberry Hill': 'It was the pits. When they all started jiving, you could see the floor going up and down.'[1]

The sound of Fats Domino and his USA peers had yet to be joined by an equivalent imprint of UK rock'n'roll, until the intervention of one gay businessman. Born and raised in London, Larry Parnes showed entrepreneurial spirit at an early age; he was running a women's clothing store at the age of eighteen and was soon buying a share of the La Caverne bar in Soho. La Caverne was close to a theatre staging *Lady of the House* and he invested in the production. The play had been under-performing until, under Parnes, it was renamed *House of Shame* and re-launched by gay publicist John Kennedy, who persuaded two actresses to stand outside the theatre, dressed as prostitutes. The media furore bumped up sales – tapping into the repressed reserves of Londoners.

Alongside Parnes and Kennedy, Lionel Bart was a third member of this gay entertainment cabal. Bart would write the smash hit musical *Oliver!* in 1960, but was then a jobbing songwriter for a theatre group and for BBC radio's Billy Cotton Band Show. In 1956, Bart had seen Tommy Hicks, a former merchant seaman with an acoustic guitar, play a Soho coffee bar and began to mentor him. Bart quickly persuaded Parnes and Kennedy to see his new charge and the pair started managing Hicks under the stage name Tommy Steele. Bart provided some songs, though Parnes also stuck with the accepted habit of covering American hits for the UK market.

Signed to Decca, Steele was Britain's first home-grown rock'n'roller and Parnes' gateway to become the UK's first modern manager, with a succession of photogenic young men to groom for pop stardom. Parnes already had an eye for fashion; he would now concentrate on the archetype who girls wanted to date and boys wanted to emulate. Bart's next

---

1 Ibid.

discovery, Marty Wilde, established a pattern of new first names with a boy-next-door appeal and surnames that lent a smouldering charisma: Billy Fury, Vince Eager, Dickie Pride, Johnny Gentle, Duffy Power, Lance Fortune, Nelson Keene, Georgie Fame. They were almost always working-class, which might have been Parners' sexual peccadillo, but they were hungry and more open to direction in clothes, haircut and choice of songs. They would also demand smaller wages.

Parnes, according to Georgie Fame, was 'a cold, hard fish, ruthless, intimidating. I was sixteen, he had the monopoly on the scene, it was like, "Anything you say, boss." He actually tried to seduce me and he probably tried to seduce all the other singers. I whacked him across the wrist and got the hell out of there.'[1]

Parnes was driven as much by ambition as libido and he was powerful enough to persuade Jack Good, the producer of Britain's new TV pop show *Oh Boy!*[2] to employ Wilde as its resident singer. But a row between Parnes and Good – who was every bit as powerful as his adversary – saw Wilde replaced by a new face, Cliff Richard (born Harry Webb), whose 1958 debut single, the rhythmic nugget 'Move It', reached UK no. 2.

Taking his new surname from his favourite rocker Little Richard, this new Richard had caused a similar quaking reaction as Elvis Presley; even pop weekly *New Musical Express* thought his, 'violent hip-swinging was revolting', while 'he was wearing so much eye-liner, he looked like [actress] Jayne Mansfield.' But Richard quickly ditched the rebel pose and softened up; in 1959, he had his first number one, the featherlight 'Living Doll', written by Lionel Bart.

The new teenage market was there for the taking; conscription into the armed forces was discontinued in 1959, freeing up British youth for more work, bigger earnings and opportunities for play, with a succession of male pin-ups for the girls to adore and the boys to copy. They seemed easily accessible, unlike those film stars far away in Hollywood.

---
1 Told to Lois Wilson, *MOJO* magazine, November 2015.
2 Good had launched Britain's first pop show, *Six-Five Special*, for the BBC.

Just as crucially, an American pop song released in 1959 created more fertile ground not only for the cult of 'teen', but for gay liberation too. It allowed a new kind of dancing, one that didn't require a partner, and didn't involve touching and synchronised movement, just a hip-swivelling groove. Your feet didn't even need to lift off the floor.

The twist not only allowed people to express themselves from the hips and with a lower centre of gravity, it gave adults permission to dance to teenage music for the first time; boys didn't have to lead and girls didn't need to follow. Gay men and women got the chance to dance together, since they weren't touching and so not breaking the law.

The dance was first popularised at a seductively low-rent gay nightclub in Manhattan's midtown district, the Peppermint Lounge, a Mafia-owned hustler joint festooned with mirrors and a dance floor at the rear. 'The Twist' was originally a B-side by Hank Ballard and the Midnighters, but when turned into an A-side, broke the US Top 30, before Chubby Checker's 1960 cover version topped both the US charts (and again in 1962) and reached UK no. 2. The dance craze helped sow seeds of sexual liberation.

Yet there were occasional signs of resistance. The *New York Times* remarked, 'Cafe society has not gone slumming with such energy since its forays into Harlem in the twenties' – which we know to be a very good sign.

CHAPTER 6

The Sixties: Gay Party Pop and the Rock'n'Roll Closet

> 'From every mountain high/Long may they live and thrive/God save the nelly queens/God save the queens'
> Jose Sarria, from the stage of the Black Cat, San Francisco

In 1960, the Daughters of Bilitis described Lisa Ben as 'the first gay folk singer'. A second gay folk singer was not too much to ask for. Someone brave enough to openly articulate the hopes or even the fears of a maligned people that didn't yet realise it was a community.

The Daughters attempted to address the issue with its first convention, also held in 1960, in San Francisco. Two hundred women attended, alongside the San Francisco police who checked if any members were wearing men's clothes.[1]

Television held the key to visibility. In 1961, an autobiography by *The Tonight Show*'s powerful host Jack Paar – curiously titled *My Saber Is Bent*[2] – vilified Hollywood's gay community in the chapter 'Fairies and Communists'. 'In New York, they are prominent in all of the arts. They cavort in ballet. They flutter on the Broadway stage. And they are everywhere in television. Wherever there is one you will find others. They are highly organised and indefatigable at assisting each other.'

---

1 *Different Daughters: A History of the Daughters of Bilitis and the Rise of the Lesbian Rights Movement*, Marcia Gallo (Carrol & Graf, 2006)
2 Trident Press, 1961

The same year, *The Rejected* became the first televised documentary about homosexuality. It was made by San Francisco station KQED and subsequently rolled out across most of America. Lesbians were excluded – according to writer Steve Capsuto, *The Rejected*'s producer John Reavis felt 'the average viewer would find female homosexuality even more repugnant and off-putting and that the subject was less urgent because lesbians were much fewer in number than gay men.'

Homosexuality, 'however unpleasant in its proportions in nature, does indeed exist,' the documentary's presenter noted. The debate, featuring an anthropologist, psychiatrist, lawyer, bishop, rabbi, three Mattachine members and the director of San Francisco's Bureau for Disease Control, was rational; sympathetic even. The point was raised, as Capsuto saw it, 'whether gay activists should keep claiming that homosexuality was a minor, incurable, essentially harmless mental illness, worthy of pity rather than scorn.'[1]

Location material cut from the final edit had been filmed at San Francisco's Black Cat, which was still battling police raids and the efforts of California's Department of Alcoholic Beverage Control to shut the bar down. The frequency with which drag queens were now being penalised drove its long-standing MC, José Sarria, to pass out labels that read 'I am a boy', which would be pinned to their dresses and gowns.

Sarria didn't want pity, but equality. He also engineered a feeling of pride within the Black Cat's crowd. 'People were living double lives and I didn't understand it. It was persecution,' he said. 'Why be ashamed of who you are?'[2]

In 1960, Sarria recorded an album, *No Camping* – incredibly, it was funded by a member of a black congregation who wanted to promote and raise money for their church. The record was mostly spoken word but featured a lusty version of 'A Good Man is Hard to Find'

---

[1] http://www.stevecap.com/alternatechannels_net/us/notable_broadcasts/19610911_The_Rejected.htm
[2] The *Press-Enterprise*, 2006

with revamped words: 'I said, a good man is hard to find, you usually wind up with a nelly, Los Angeles-style/When you think you got a real he-man/Everybody had him last night at the YMCA can.'

Sarria's repertoire included 'Nobody Loves a Fairy When She's Forty' and 'Sailor Boy' and, for his grand finale, another revamp, during which the audience would join hands and sing, 'God save us nelly queens,' to the tune of the British national anthem 'God Save The Queen'.

'Music always unites people,' he told *Queer Music Heritage*'s JD Doyle and then launched into a verse on air: '"God save us nelly queens/God save the queens/and lesbians, too" – I had to add that in because they got upset,' Sarria added, and carried on: 'From every mountain high/Long may they live and thrive/God save the nelly queens/God save the queens.'[1]

In the 1977 documentary *Word Is Out*, Sarria said, 'It sounds silly, but if you lived at that time and had the oppression coming down from the police department and from society, there was nowhere to turn... and to be able to put your arms around other gay men and to be able to stand up and sing... We were really not saying "God save us nelly queens", we were saying, "We have our rights too."'[2]

Randy Sparks, of the left-leaning folk troupe the New Christie Minstrels, got in on the act in 1961. Even a politically savvy songwriter could contribute to the oppression. His parody 'Big Bad Bruce' (sung by fellow folkie Casey Anderson), based on Jimmy Dean's chart-topping country novelty 'Big Bad John', changed the hero's occupation from miner to hairdresser.

'In those days, of course, most of us were totally ignorant of what is or isn't appropriate,' Sparks told JD Doyle.[3] 'I quickly discovered that most gay men had no problem with laughing at the ditty but any lesbians in my audiences seemed to immediately take offence, so I was careful where I sang it. I didn't want to make anyone uncomfortable.' Sparks

---

1 http://www.queermusicheritage.com/nov2012s.html
2 *Word Is Out: Stories of Some of Our Lives* (Mariposa Film Group, 1977).
3 http://www.queermusicheritage.com/jun2004bj.html

also chose not to record 'Big Bad Bruce' and said he was dismayed to find Anderson had done so without his permission.

Without any pressure from civil rights activists, in January 1962, Illinois became the first US state to repeal its sodomy law and establish an age of consent of eighteen. Though San Francisco and Seattle hadn't followed suit, both states were considered liberal bastions in their approach to prosecution.[1] But that didn't stop San Francisco's Black Cat from closing after fifteen years of continually funding legal battles to stay open.

Sarria estimated that his album had sold close to a thousand copies, meaning it had the same minimal impact as Lisa Ben's single. Despite being a landmark, an album and a sing-song wasn't going to change laws. Taking the fight to the enemy again, in 1961, Sarria became the first openly gay candidate to run for public office in America, on San Francisco's Board of Supervisors. With support across the gay bars and other sympathisers, he came fifth out of thirty-two candidates, another landmark result that proved there was a gay community with real voting power.[2]

Meanwhile, the search for a second gay folk singer to cherish led to Rod McKuen, whose folk music was more beatnik-jazz-ambient than the Lisa Ben or New Christy Minstrels kind. Having covered 'Ballad of the Sad Young Men', McKuen wrote his own paean in 'Eros', about the sad young men who were trying to catch that certain smile while out cruising: 'I have to walk at night and be with many/and give myself to many strangers . . . I don't know why . . . I only know that people smile sometimes.'

The introduction of a quivering flute accentuated the pathos: 'Can you still go home with me/Knowing the way I am in the morning/Might make you sorry that you did?'

---

[1] In 1958, an injunction instructed Seattle's city police not to question customers in gay bars unless there was 'good cause' in connection with an actual investigation.
[2] Sarria later founded the League for Civil Education and the Society for Individual Rights.

'Eros' was the nominal title track of McKuen's album, the snappily titled *In Search of Eros: Loneliness and Love in the Age of Eroticism*, released on major label Columbia's imprint Epic. According to the liner notes, 'People need people now, more than ever'. McKuen hedged his bets with the lyric, 'It's been so long since I've had a woman or a special friend,' but how many women went out at night, hoping to meet strangers? And surely the figurine on the album cover was of two men entwined in a passionate kiss.

Music for gay parties

Independent entrepreneurs began to test the idea of gay men as viable consumers of music, just as they had been targeted by magazines, both literary and pictorial. Three albums took different approaches. The first record, dated to around 1960, was titled *Love, Gay-Style* as recorded by the Hollywood Harlots. A plain-white cardboard sleeve contained an inner sleeve 'of five black-and-white softcore photos of nude, young longhair surfer-types laid-in,' according to an online seller. 'Unknown performers. Not a party-disc. "S&M Party" [A-side] has sounds of torture, screaming, moaning, etc. "Young Lovers" is similar but softer.'

A second album, released in 1962 by the High In-Fidelity label, reversed the concept: an album cover but no record. *Music for Mixed Emotions* contained only a round piece of card that read, 'I bought this album for you as a gift . . . sorry, I couldn't afford the record!' But its existence was enough.

'I bought it because the cover photograph was of two men,' says Jack Fritscher, 'one in a suit, one in loafers and slacks, shot from the waist down, belt buckle to belt buckle, with one loafered foot kicked sole-up behind the knee, satirising the movie-poster cliché of a swooning girl stretching up on tiptoe to kiss her man.'

On the album's rear cover, under 'Suggested titles suitable for enclosure in this album cover,' the list included 'Mad About The Boy', 'He's

Funny That Way', 'The Boy Next Door', 'We Kiss In A Shadow'[1] and 'My Funny Valentine'. *Music For Mixed Emotions* was one of twelve such vinyl-free albums produced by Hi-Infidelity: others included *Songs for Swinging Mothers*, *Music for Half-Assed Friends* and *Music for Casual Affairs*, with ample naked female cover stars[2], this being the age of eroticism, of course.

The same year, *Love is a Drag – For Adult Listeners Only, Sultry Stylings by a Most Unusual Vocalist* went a step further. It actually featured music, and again two men on the cover. The musicians weren't credited, but in 2012, it was revealed that the production team was entirely heterosexual – singer, band, producer, financial backer, even the two cover stars.[3]

The story was that in the early forties, Murray Garrett was working in New York as a photographer when he visited his first Greenwich Village nightclub. 'A really good-looking guy came out on the stage and had marvellous presence,' he said. Garrett was astonished to hear the man sing 'what I would have called girl lyrics. And then I realised, My God, that's what he's doing every song. I was really square. I had no idea what was happening.'

Garrett was, 'just overwhelmed that there are these great things, that were written by people like the Gershwins, that were being performed by either a man or a woman without having the lyrics changed. Somehow or another, that stayed in my mind for years and years and every time I'd hear one of these songs, I'd smile.'

Singer Gene Howard had been working with big band leaders Gene Krupa and Stan Kenton. By 1953, he'd stopped performing and gone into partnership with Murray Garrett, who had the idea to recreate his Village experience. He persuaded Howard – and his wife – that any such

---

1 'We Kiss in a Shadow', another song of 'secret love', came from Rogers and Hammerstein's 1951 musical *The King And I*.
2 https://musiceureka.wordpress.com/2014/10/28/hi-infidelity-records-complete-series
3 Interviewed by JD Doyle at Queer Music Heritage, http://queermusicheritage.com/mar2012s.html

record would be dignified, without any hint of exploitation. 'We figured we had a chance to do something that we felt that we would be proud of and would indeed be constructive and non-offensive to our gay friends.'

Some of the twelve songs overlapped with Hi-Infidelity's joke record – 'He's Funny That Way', 'Mad About The Boy', 'The Boy Next Door'– while adding the likes of 'The Man I Love', 'Stranger In Paradise' and 'Can't Help Lovin' That Man'. The pared-back, jazz-tinged arrangements accompanying Howard's mellifluous croon made it clear this project had empathy for its intended audience.

According to the sleeve notes, 'At long last, a male vocalist with great talent has decided to take the big step – that is, to record the classics using their original lyrics. In doing so, he has broken the barrier which has confronted so many other great singers who, for lack of courage, have not attempted.'

The courage didn't stretch to naming Howard, but then this was 1962. At least a record label executive wanted to support it, namely Jack Ames, a former MGM Records man who was looking for unusual records to launch his own label, Edison International (though the eventual imprint was Lace Records). But no one was sure how to market a record like *Love Is A Drag*. Garrett said that he'd been to San Francisco enough times, 'but I didn't know that you could specifically produce an album, a musical album, for the gay market. And so at no time did it ever occur to me, to go after the so-called gay market, because I really didn't know it existed or really how to reach it.' They decided to let *Love Is A Drag* 'find its own way'.

Garrett recalled that Hollywood's Sid Lederman Record Centre – situated opposite a drive-in theatre with a noticeable percentage of gay employees – reported men buying up to six copies of the album, which alerted Lace to get the record 'into spots where we know that there's heavy gay traffic, like . . . San Francisco and Greenwich Village and wherever else they exist.'

The album sleeve might have guided interested punters to the prize. A body clinch in the style of *Music For Mixed Emotions* would have looked exploitative; instead, two of Garrett and Howard's employees posed in an atmosphere of studied cool, like on a jazz album. But the sexual tension was there if you wanted: the younger of the two men hovered in the background, facing the camera, while the other sat sideways in front, blowing cigarette smoke across the sleeve. Beside the visual pun on 'drag', the image underlined how love was indeed a drag for gay lovers, underlined by the choice of material.

Love Is A Drag underlined that gay passion and consumers existed. Garrett shot the artwork for Liberace's 1962 album *Rhapsody By Candlelight* and he played *Love Is A Drag* during the photo session. At the end and without referring to the record, Garrett recalled, Liberace 'went back into the dressing room, picked up his candelabra and very quietly walked over to the turntable, picked up the record and said, "Ta ta." And he walked out, with the record. And I can't tell you how many times after that, he said, "You know, you guys produced my favourite album."'

There was little in the way of a lesbian equivalent. The 1962 spoken-word *Nights of Love in Lesbos*, subtitled *A Frankly Intimate Description of a Sensuous Young Girl's Lesbian Desires* was a reading of French poet Pierre Louys' *Songs of Bilitis*. Blogger Sara Johnson noted the 'flaccid female vocal talent . . . sapphic sounds with heavy breath and audible smile. A flute-y score plays throughout, accompanied lightly by piano and sometimes a tambourine shake at hot moments.'[1] But this was aimed at heterosexual men, produced by Fax Records, specialists in stag-party entertainment.

A mysterious tale of camp

If *Love Is A Drag* catered to romantics, an advertisement in a 1964 edition of *One* magazine appealed to humour – *Queen Is In The Closet*, with the tagline, 'It's terrific! It's mad! It's gay!' The album was released by Camp Records.

Queen Is In The Closet had only a sole credit, for the publishing

---

1 http://blog.wfmu.org/freeform/2007/06/365-days-177---.html

THE SIXTIES: GAY PARTY POP AND THE ROCK'N'ROLL CLOSET

company, 'Different Music, Hollywood, Calif.' It would have taken a brave soul to own up to writing or recording the likes of 'I'm So Wet', 'The Weekend of a Hairdresser' and 'London Derriere'.[1] Some tracks were re-used for a series of ten Camp singles, bolstered by new tracks such as 'I'd Rather Fight Than Swish' and its B-side 'I'd Rather Swish Than Fight', credited to B. Bubba and 'Homer the Happy Little Homo' with 'Florence of Arabia', credited by Byrd E. Bath and Rodney Dangerfield.[2] The musical trappings mostly mirrored the lyrical settings: 'I'd Rather Fight Than Swish' aped fifties' rockabilly while 'I'd Rather Swish . . .' was campy pop. 'Old-Fashioned Balls' was modelled on a Viennese waltz and 'Rough Trade' was a country ballad concerning a casual pick-up that ended in a mugging, broken jaw and a moral lesson: 'You went out and cruised and you got yourself bruised/You've got no one to blame/You must bear your own shame.'

'Rough Trade' wasn't the only stab of realism among the hilarity. The album track 'Down on the River Drive' revolved around a police sting and a prison sentence. 'A Bar is a Bar is a Bar' turned darker still: 'Oh, the laws are getting rougher/The police are getting tougher/If they raid this bar again we'll have no place to play . . . though we break no laws/We'll have to go away.'

Camp parodied a host of genres: doo wop, Broadway, cabaret, pop, Latin. The intro of 'Mixed Nuts' filched the melody of 'Strangers in Paradise', likewise 'A Naughty Cal-Tale' took off the sea-shanty 'What Shall We Do with the Drunken Sailor?' Gay stereotypes were fair game too, such as 'Stanley The Manly Transvestite'. There was room for one lesbian cliché, 'Lil' Liza Mike', based on the folk-blues standard 'Lil' Liza Jane'; a Lisa Ben-style parody with a snarky sense of humour. Was Camp laughing at or with the homosexuals? Were they empathic like Murray Garrett, or opportunists? As the headline of *Goldmine*

---

1 A play on the Irish folk ballad 'Londonderry Air'.
2 'Rodney Dangerfield' was a commonly used pseudonym for musical projects. The popular US comedian/actor of the same name later denied taking part in any Camp recordings.

magazine's Camp label feature in 2005 put it, 'Straights laugh, gays subvert: early gay records played it both ways.' The sleeve artwork depicting a hand wearing a chunky lavender ring and waving a lavender-coloured handkerchief, provided no clue.

'Just like fart records,' wrote M. H. Braitman, 'gay records allowed unacceptable behaviour to surface in the mainstream – but only as a joke.'[1] He added that his father owned some Camp singles in his collection of 'risqué' records. 'As I lived in Hollywood, gay culture was much more present to me than most people in the rest of the country. I remember seeing ads for Camp records in what were really counter-cultural magazines, like *Playboy* and *The Realist*.' So straight audiences *were* coveted...

Fifty years later, Camp's exaggerated camp, its portraits of the 'happy little homo' may seem cheap and exploitative, just like the lacerating tongues of some misogynistic drag queens, but the records still gave homosexuality a chance to laugh with and at itself. It made a change from the likes of Hitchcock's *Rope* and the first English-language film to feature the 'h' word, *Victim*, about a blackmail plot in which a gay character kills themselves. The central character (played – bravely, given he was closeted – by Dirk Bogarde) is finally reunited with his wife as he tells her he no longer has those kind, of 'urges'.

Camp went on to release a second album, *Mad About The Boy*, which was advertised in a 1965 issue of the Minneapolis-based *Vagabond*,[2 3] a catalogue for the discerning gay man that also advertised pulp fiction, stationery, ornaments, jewellery, nude photo-sets and sex aids: the 'gay

---

1 'The picture sleeve archive: a monthly glance at rare, unusual and plain damn strange 45-rpm picture sleeves', *Goldmine* magazine (December 2005)
2 *Vagabond* was produced by Directory Services, Inc., run by Lloyd Spinar and Conrad Germain, so if they printed their names, why didn't Camp?
3 Another advert in the same issue of *Vagabond* was for an unrelated single, from Faireland Records. Recorded live at the Annex Lounge, Chicago, 'Welcome To Faireland' c/w 'Snow White and the Watch Queen' were 'hilarious' routines by female impersonator Skip Arnold ('alias Mother Goose') – music hall-style skits with piano accompaniment.

lifestyle' consumer had arrived, despite existing laws and harassment. Housed in a variety of *Physique Pictorial*-style poses[1], *Mad About The Boy* emulated *Love Is A Drag* with a set of standards sung about men, by men, for men. Noël Coward's title track re-appeared, alongside 'He Needs Me', 'Make The Man Love Me' and 'Boy Wanted'.

And as with *Love Is A Drag*, Camp justified the record with liner notes: 'Gender should not be the determining factor as to who should sing what. Far too many singers have all too often been frustrated by lyrics not being acceptable from them because of text.' No credits were revealed. 'To those with a discerning ear,' the liner notes continued, 'you will recognise the stylings of some very fine and well known personalities . . . four of the better known Hollywood TV and screen personalities.' One singer was referred to as, 'The Boy': 'Perhaps his name in conjunction with this production will become known.'

Soul brothers, sisters, whatevers . . .

Fifty years on, The Boy and his accomplices remain hidden, alongside every facet of Camp Records.[2] Anonymity was simply too valuable. But not for everyone in the music business. One man had the courage to go public. Troy Walker, born Richard Walker in Arizona, had found work in Hollywood's clubs and bars, drawing on influences from Little Richard to the Platters and carving a reputation for impersonations, including Dinah Washington and Johnnie Ray, that showed the versatility and strength of his voice.

Today, Walker, in his eighties, suffers from ill-health, but he still occasionally performs in his native California. Time has marched on. Fifty years ago, judging by the cover of his 1964 album *Troy Walker Live* (recorded at LA club Crescendo), he looked like Sal Mineo crossed

---

[1] The grid design of the *Mad About The Boy* cover was based on jazz crooner Julie London's 1956 album *Carnival Girl*.
[2] J. D. Doyle says that not even Murray Garrett, the producer of *Love Is A Drag*, had any idea who Camp was and he sat on the West Coast Board of the National Academy of Recording Arts and Sciences.

with Cliff Richard. 'When I got on stage, actually, I started getting, you know, I got whistled at, 'cause it wasn't my fault, I was, for lack of a better way to put it, a little pretty boy,' he told JD Doyle.'[1]

Walker had already recorded a handful of singles, starting in 1961, with the rocking doo wop of 'She's All Right' for the Trans World label. In 1962, he recorded a cover of Gershwin's 'Summertime' that rocked and soulfully rolled, like a prototype version of sixties northern soul. *Troy Walker Live* explored multiple avenues – soul, rock'n'roll, Latin, cabaret, show tunes, versions of Doris Day's 'Everybody Loves a Lover' (which writer Jonny Whiteside in *LA Weekly* reckoned, 'invents the Cher style right before your ears')[2] and 'No Regrets', an English translation of Edith Piaf's 'Non, Je Ne Regrette Rien'. But Walker most notably covered 'Happiness is a Thing Called Joe'. Written by Harold Arlen and Yip Harburg of *Wizard Of Oz* fame, the ballad had first been sung by Harlem blues queen Ethel Walters and popularised by Judy Garland, so it had significant gay kudos. Walker recalled the song 'really stood out on the record' and it also provided a reason for stores to return the album. His record label Hi Fidelity told him, '"We can't have an album with a man singing a love song to another man." I was so sick, because that was a work of real love and it was a desperate time when I really felt beat up.'[3]

Maybe Hi Fidelity couldn't locate the right gay retail hotspots or perhaps purchasers of *Love Is A Drag* wanted a defined masculine presence on the cover rather than a pretty boy. Walker's recording career never recovered, though he continued to perform; in a 1999 interview, he said he had opened for Ella Fitzgerald and Dinah Washington, and met Ethel Merman and Judy Garland.[4] But the LA police were not on

---

1 http://queermusicheritage.com/aug2010s.html
2 *LA Weekly*, 1999, at http://www.laweekly.com/music/ladyboy-2131139
3 Ibid. 204
4 A 2014 feature in *Entertainment Voice* expanded the list of Walker fans to include Elvis Presley and Mae West, while former US president Ronald Reagan 'once hired the singer to perform at Reagan's Santa Barbara ranch.' http://entertainmentvoice.com/2014/10/08/viva-cantina-presents-gender-bending-troy-walker

his side, constantly hassling Walker for wearing what they considered female attire, which he insisted was men's clothes. He was one of the early advocates of breaking the boundaries between the way that the sexes dressed, including the length of his hair. Walker doggedly pursued his androgynous look; in the seventies, *Entertainment Voice* recalled Walker had, 'a most unlikely residency at North Hollywood redneck shrine the Palomino, establishing himself as the world's first and only professional transgender country singer.'[1] A concert flyer from 1981 claimed, with insensitivity typical of the time, 'He is a man . . . he is a woman . . . he is a whatever.'[2]

Original songs such as 'Hello Stranger Would You Like to Spend Tonight with Me' – 'Can you love me like I've never been loved before?' – and 'This Is My Life' – 'I've got my own sin and my own sex/I've got my own pain and it's my way' – were never recorded. 'The industry itself has given me nothing but heartache since I can remember,' he told *Zipper* magazine in 1972. He blamed the demanding contracts that he was offered, but ultimately Walker was too pretty, too flamboyant – too gay.

Jackie Shane would have provoked much the same reaction. This much is clear from the only known footage of Shane, from 1965, singing Rufus Thomas' R&B classic 'Walking The Dog' on the Nashville music show *Music Train*. 'The most private person I have ever known',[3] according to the man who is trying to reissue Shane's music for the first time, the singer is believed to have always presented as a woman. Even in 1965, Shane carried off bouffant hair, eye-shadow and a sequined

---

1 Ibid. 204
2 In later life, Walker would also perform risqué rewrites in the drag-queen tradition. In 1999, *LA Weekly*'s Jonny Whiteside wrote that the chant of 'Ah-wee-mo-way, ah-wee-mo-way,' from popular sixties' hit 'The Lion Sleeps Tonight' became 'my weenie's wet, my weenie's wet'. He also noted the singer's 'wicked vocal impersonations and memorably lewd banter . . . a thoroughly frantic and simply unforgettable presentation'.
3 I couldn't find one published interview with Shane. She didn't take part in a 2011 Canadian radio documentary, *Got Mine: The Story of Jackie Shane*, http://soundcloud.com/elainebanks/the-jackie-shane-story.

top, and threw in a verse from the nursery rhyme 'Mary, Mary, Quite Contrary' while shimmering in front of three dapper backing singers and a horns-blasting band that seemed at ease with this gender-fluid apparition out front. 'Prince meets Little Richard meets Eartha Kitt,' was a later description. 'Judy Garland meets James Brown,' was another.

Where Walker had stalled and never enjoyed any TV exposure, Shane clearly went places. She was forced to relocate – Nashville had R&B and gospel roots but, unlike New Orleans, was deeply conservative and though *Music Train* would later put her on TV, she decided to move to Toronto. Black performers had discovered that Canada was less prejudiced than the US – 'covert rather than overt racism', according to one musician who worked with Shane. There is no evidence to say that Canada had its own androgynous black singer at the time. Shane would have been unique and doubtless stopped audiences in their tracks.

As a teenager, Shane lived for a time with Nashville's blues matriarch Marion James, made the acquaintance of Little Richard and joined the tent-show circuit.[1] In 1962, Shane featured at the Sapphire tavern in Toronto's thriving Yonge Street entertainment district, specialising in Ray Charles and Bobby Bland covers. Her voice was more of a supple, smoky tool than a belting brand of soul and attracted interest from Louisiana-based Sue, the label behind rising stars Ike and Tina Turner.

For Shane's Sue debut, she chose to cover soul singer William Bell's 'Any Other Way', a glowing, dramatic soul ballad. In Bell's original, a woman sends a friend to check on the man she's dumped, who responds: 'Tell her that I'm happy/tell her that I'm gay/tell her that I wouldn't have it any other way.' Shane then twisted the old-fashioned meaning of the word into a statement of defiance; without a girlfriend to reinforce the storyline, consider Shane's lines a statement directed at Mother Earth. She's gay and *can't* have it any other way.

---

[1] One photo from 1964 shows Shane rocking a blonde wig in a tribute show to blues singer Etta James, who as a descendant of the Harlem blues tradition and part of the gospel scene was a proven friend of Dorothy.

'Any Other Way' rose to no. 2 on Toronto's local singles chart, but it was to be Shane's only hit record. Audiences weren't yet ready for her pioneering androgyny. She was apparently a popular live draw in LA and was called back to Nashville when demand for 'Any Other Way' suddenly escalated, but no album followed until 1968's *Jackie Shane Live*, recorded back at the Sapphire tavern. The album reveals a stage act as much drag-queen spiel as song. Take the ten-minute 'Money': 'You know, when I'm walking down Yonge Street, you won't believe this but, you know, some of them funny people have the nerve to point the finger at me and grin and smile and whisper . . . but, you know that don't worry Jackie because I know I look good.'

'Any Other Way' also stretched out to ten minutes, like a soul sermon to all the ladies – and gay fellas – in the house: 'I live the life I love and I love the life I live and I hope you'll do the same. You know, you're supposed to live. As long as you don't force your will and your way on others, forget them baby, you don't need them. Because the mean things people say about you can't make you bad 'cause Jackie can't miss a friend that I've never had.'

Shane apparently moved back to Nashville to live with an aunt but grew agoraphobic in her new gender identity. Putting yourself on stage is an outlet for creativity and an expression of an attention-seeking nature but, once there (especially if your transgressive actions solicit negative as well as positive reactions), stardom road is littered with landmines. Shane perhaps had some sort of crisis, further complicated by racial issues. However, in her first public quote 'since the late sixties', claims her current go-between, Shane is remarkably sanguine about the past: 'I wasn't brave, I was just living life. It was wonderful. I had complete control as I always do.'

In which case, Arthur Conley, from Atlanta, Georgia, was far more a victim of circumstances. Like actor Gordon Heath, he would leave the US for Europe, despite having been mentored by soul legend Otis Redding and his major hit 'Sweet Soul Music' hitting US no. 2 and UK no. 5. Some aficionados reckon Conley's gospel-rousing tenor was even better[1] than Redding's. In blogger Soul Boogie Alex's words, 'Arthur was a mighty fine deep soul singer, able to instil a fragility in his testimonies, an honesty in his ache that was quite rare in the macho world of soul.'[2]

Conley, Alex explained, was, 'a sensitive soul who just wasn't up to the harsh realities and strain the record biz brought. On top of that, Arthur was a homosexual man in the masculine world of soul, something he hid from his peers. After Otis, his rock of Gibraltar, died,[3] Conley left the business.' Via London and Brussels in the seventies, he would settle in Holland and change his name by deed poll to Lee Roberts.

'Nobody knew "Lee Roberts",' wrote rock historian Ed Ward, 'and at last Conley was able to live in peace with a secret he had hidden – or thought he had – for his entire career: he was gay. But nobody in Holland cared.'[4]

In the mainstream, behind the scenes

With relative anonymity and discretion, avoiding the glare of publicity, music industry executives – managers, record label employees, songwriters – lived reasonably active social lives. They could meet similar types at work and – with regular income, especially if successful – they had less need of the clubs and bars and could host gay shindigs at home. But it was a delicate balancing act, asserting one personality at work and then another in business; could the two worlds comfortably fit together?

In the UK, Larry Parnes continued to work his stable of young male

---

1 For proof, try the 1966 B-side 'In The Same Old Way', an exalted slice of heartache, in which Conley tells his ex-lover that he still loves her and holds no bitterness toward her, despite being devastated.
2 http://bosstracks.blogspot.co.uk/2009/02/boss-tracks-arthur-conley-sweet-soul.html
3 Redding was killed aged 26, in a plane crash.
4 Blogger Soul Boogie Alex writes that Conley, 'finally found the love of his life in Amsterdam in 1981, a Dutch carpet weaver, who had no idea who Arthur Conley was and miraculously had never heard "Sweet Soul Music".' http://bosstracks.blogspot.co.uk/

The Sixties: Gay Party Pop and the Rock'n'Roll Closet

hopefuls, but though he had a gift for styling pop singers as if they were a singing menswear catalogue, he depended on others for the songs. Following his initial breakthrough, Parnes proved to be a follower of musical trends rather than an instigator. In this regard, Joe Meek moved ahead of Parnes. He was both a studio owner and producer, a record label boss and all-round control freak who invented his own sound and several landmark chart-toppers.

The Gloucestershire-born Meek was a prodigy with electronics, building his own transmitters as a boy; in the air force he worked as a radar technician and deepened his love of astronomy and science fiction. Moving into audio engineering for the radio industry, Meek opened a studio, making him the UK's first independent record producer. He used his considerable neuroses to fire up both his artists and to wildly experiment with recording techniques, adding to his releases an echoing, dramatic edge missing from his studio rivals except the equally madcap Phil Spector in LA. Meek's genius came with pain and frequent rages. Socially gauche, his only comfortable way of meeting men – outside of the straight musicians he coveted from a distance – was in the public toilets near his north London studio/home.

Like Spector, Meek had very early success, a UK no. 1 with his first home production written by Geoff Goddard, who was also gay and shared the producer's interest in the afterlife. John Leyton's 'Johnny Remember Me' was a vivid slice of gothic kitsch that followed the death of Meek's obsession Buddy Holly. Leyton's manager, Robert Stigwood, was another gay entrepreneur who'd set up shop in the UK after emigrating from Australia in 1954 and first establishing a theatrical agency.

Stigwood had signed a production deal with the head of the major label giant EMI, Joseph Lockwood – also gay. In 1961, another gay businessman, Brian Epstein, who was managing the record department of the NEMS music store in Liverpool, had been so impressed by a local band, the Beatles, he'd started managing the quartet, applying the Larry Parnes approach by remodelling the band with smart suits and tidy hairstyles. He instigated a musical revolution that would knock out Parnes and Lionel Bart too (who retreated to stage musicals).

The Beatles were conversant in rock'n'roll, as fans of fifties Americana, so it could have been either their idea or Epstein's to cover girl-group originators the Shirelles' 'Boy' – 'I'm talkin' 'bout boys/Yeah, yeah, boys!/What a bundle of joy!' The manager also secured a support slot for Little Richard, who had just returned to secular music after getting married in 1959; he subsequently taught Paul McCartney his trademark, 'Ooooh!' Fired up alongside Epstein, Lockwood signed the Beatles to EMI, creating a little gay industry cabal to match those of Hollywood and Broadway.

Before the Beatles could get a firm foothold, Meek's outré approach hit the heights. In 1962, the space-age instrumental 'Telstar'[1] by Billy Fury's backing band, the Tornados, became Meek's second production to top the UK chart and the first record by a UK group to top the US chart. Three more Top 20 Tornados hits followed in the UK but the band was kiboshed by Meek's solo plans for the Tornado he lusted after, Heinz Burt. The producer persuaded him to dye his hair peroxide, like a male Jayne Mansfield.

In 1963, another Meek protégé, Mike Berry, had a hit with 'Tribute To Buddy Holly' and agreed, under duress, to cover the Shirelles' 'Will You Love Me Tomorrow', a blatant way of recasting a man in the woman's clichéd passive position. On Berry's 1963 Top 10 hit, the pro-marriage ditty 'Don't You Think It's Time', Meek's lyrics for the B-side 'Loneliness' even sneaked in a male pronoun: 'Loneliness, wow-wow/ He's got his claws in me . . .'

The year 1963 was good and bad for Meek: more hit records but a criminal record too, for importuning, which opened the door to blackmail – Epstein had been guilty of the same offence in the late fifties. As the Beatles and the subsequent Merseybeat movement of

---

[1] Telstar was the name of the US communications satellite launched into orbit that July. The full (fictionalised) saga of Meek's life can be explored in the 2008 movie *Telstar: The Joe Meek Story*.

fresh-faced bands took over the UK charts, Meek was increasingly sidelined, having his final UK no. 1 in 1964 by new UK quintet the Honeycombs. They were unique for having a female drummer in Ann 'Honey' Lantree but the song Meek paired them with, 'Have I The Right?', was also notable, not only for its stomping beat but the verses that each began with a question: 'Have I the right to hold you? . . . Have I the right to touch you? . . . Have I the right to thrill you? . . . Have I the right to kiss you?'

Ken Howard and Alan Blaikley, BBC employees turned songwriters who managed the Honeycombs, were both gay[1] and intent on expressing their desire using the band as a Trojan horse. 'Have I The Right?' had a euphoric chorus, accentuated by stamping feet, driving its message of forbidden love to US no. 5 as well as the top of the UK chart. But like most of Meek's work, success was temporary. The Honeycombs' follow-up 'That's The Way' made the UK Top 20. Their third single would be tantamount to commercial suicide.

It wasn't the band's fault; Meek gave Howard and Blaikley's haunting ballad 'Eyes' an unusually taut and clammy treatment: 'extremely melodramatic, unpredictable and peculiar-sounding for 1964,' according to blogger David Bryant.[2] Honeycombs' singer Denis D'Ell's performance matched Meek's, with a palpable edge to the way he inhabited the part of a man sitting in a bar, clearly, and desperately, seeking that certain smile: 'Eyes, I've seen in some crowded places/Staring from lonely faces/Wanting someone to want them too . . . Eyes that now we have left behind us/In places you never find us/Where people go 'cause they're alone.' The chorus was positive: 'Now I gaze in the eyes of the one I love/Now no longer alone and afraid', yet 'Eyes' sounded as bleak as its sales figures.

Meek's final act of subversion, in 1966, was his riskiest, hidden on the

---

1 Howard was later involved in publishing Axle Spokes, five booklets on controversial topics commissioned by Blaikley. They included analyses of new wave cinema, pop music, drugs and homosexuality, at a time when it was still a criminal offence in the UK.
2 http://left-and-to-the-back.blogspot.co.uk/2008/09/honeycombs-eyes.html

B-side of the fallen Tornados' final single 'Is That a Ship I Hear?'. The band probably weren't even involved in 'Do You Come Here Often?', the first pop record from a mainstream band (and on Columbia too) with a discernible gay plot: not a cruising anthem or pleading lament but a bitchy conversation buried two-thirds of the way through an uninspiring slice of lounge music:

Man one: 'Wow! These two, coming now. What do you think?'
Man two: 'Mmm. Mine's all right, but I don't like the look of yours.'
Man one: 'Well, I must be off.'
Man two: 'Yes, you're not looking so good.'
Man one: 'I'll see you down the Dilly.'[1]
Man two: 'Not if I see you first, you won't.'[2]

Gay US songwriters were also making inroads into the music business. Budding lyricist Howie Greenfield, who would have the guts to come out in the early sixties, had written words to go with Neil Sedaka's music for 'Stupid Cupid', a 1959 hit for Connie Francis, the biggest female star of the early sixties. It suggested who you fell in love with was out of your control and, if it was wrong, why did Cupid make you feel that way? Francis's bittersweet protest 'My Heart Has A Mind Of Its Own', another Greenfield/Sedaka co-write, followed suit: 'I told this heart of mine/Our love could never be/But then I hear your voice/And something stirs inside of me/Somehow I can't

---

1 Dilly was Piccadilly Circus on the edge of Soho, London's rent-boy district.
2 Perhaps Meek had been encouraged by the debut of Julian and Sandy on the BBC's long-running radio comedy *Round The Horne* a year earlier. The two unemployed and outrageously camp British men, played by two employed and outrageously camp British actors, Hugh Paddick and Kenneth Williams, peddled endless innuendos – playing lawyers set up the genius line, 'We've a criminal practice that takes up most of our time' – and spoke in the coded language of Polari. This dates to the criminals' cant of the eighteenth century, mixing up Romany, Italian, French, Yiddish and rhyming slang. It was most popular in the twentieth century, among gay men of a certain age.

The Sixties: Gay Party Pop and the Rock'n'Roll Closet

dismiss/The memory of your kiss/Guess my heart has a mind of its own.'

One of the pair's biggest hits for Francis was an ultimate song of yearning, 'Where The Boys Are', the title track of a 1960 beach movie, one of the first to handle adolescent sexuality. It was a US and UK Top 5 hit. Squeezing every yearning atom out of the lyric, Francis (who also starred in the film) would later describe the song as 'the gay national anthem': 'Where the boys are, my true love will be/He's walkin' down some street in town and I know he's lookin' there for me.'

Like Greenfield, Francis knew about forbidden love, as her father banned her from seeing the man she wanted, fellow pop idol Bobby Darin. But what of Sedaka, who'd written the music to 'Where The Boys Are'? The rumours have stuck to the married songwriter since the early sixties, after a string of hits[1] without any resolution either way. If not, then Sedaka at least liked gay company, from Greenfield to the owner and the assistants at New York's legendary Brill Building where many of the great songwriters of the day worked and played.

One incontestable gay song-writing partnership was also based in New York, though lovers George Cory (music) and Douglass Cross (lyrics) hailed from California. They had met during World War II and moved to Brooklyn to peddle their songs; Billie Holiday covered their 'Deep Song' ('I only know misery has to be part of me/Never hope to count on love'). Missing the west coast's 'warmth and openness of the people and the beauty,' as Cory put it and finding, 'San Francisco has newness and vitality,' the pair moved, and soon wrote a tribute, 'I Left My Heart In San Francisco' as early as 1954, though it took nine years[2] to reach baritone crooner Tony Bennett. His manager thought the song could help the Brooklyn-born singer sell more records on that side of the country.

---

1 'Breaking Up Is Hard To Do', 'Calendar Girl', 'Oh! Carol', 'Happy Birthday Sweet Sixteen' – the list goes on.
2 Opera singer Claramae Turner was the first to sing it, often as an encore, but she never got around to recording it. It was then turned down by the popular crooner Tennessee Ernie Ford.

If the likes of Cory and Cross were closeted as far as their songs and their public personae were concerned, their evident partnership in romance as well as business was a positive role model for other aspiring songwriters. And their epochal signature song was at least based on a gay-cultural standard. Like 'Somewhere Over The Rainbow', a song Cory and Cross would have been well aware of, the Grammy-winning 'I Left My Heart . . . ' follows the same structure – tranquil mood with swelling climactic orchestration – and imagines a world where everything will be A-OK. The final verse, which begins, 'My love waits there in San Francisco', suggests it was one lover singing to the other, but it's nice to think the love awaiting was San Francisco itself and its liberal attitude toward homosexuality. The song's success – nine months on the chart, and two Grammys – allowed the pair to move back and build their own house just outside of the city.

San Francisco was liberal, but only relatively. 'I knew [Cory and Cross],' says great American songbook expert Peter Mintun. 'I don't think they were ever out. They were still part of the old Tin Pan Alley scene. It would have been: Don't rock the boat, our friends know and that's good enough.'

Having written one of the great standards, one of San Francisco's two official city anthems, Cory and Cross don't appear to have written a single song afterwards. Mintun recalls how they both drank heavily and hosted many parties and, when Cross died at fifty-four after a long illness, even his San Francisco obituary didn't mention Cory, who committed suicide three years later over fears of his own declining health.

The late fifties and early sixties were the domain of teen ballads, from 'Where The Boys Are' to the Everly Brothers' 'Crying In The Rain' (another Greenfield credit). Romance, whether happy or sad, triumphed over dancing, which, despite the twist, was still rooted in ballroom styles. The nuanced melodies and emotional palate of these songs suited the gay bars, which didn't yet have spots for dancing on account of the threat of arrest if boys and girls danced with their own gender.

The significant experimental homoerotic film of the era, Kenneth

The Sixties: Gay Party Pop and the Rock'n'Roll Closet

Anger's 1963 short *Scorpio Rising*, played his visual feast of leather, bikes and brawn against doe-eyed teen ballads, from Peggy March's 'I Will Follow Him' to Bobby Vinton's 'Blue Velvet' (decades before David Lynch appropriated it) to Kris Jensen's 'Torture'. There was female-fronted melodrama in the Crystals' 'He's a Rebel', Angels' 'My Boyfriend's Back' and the sole example of machismo, Elvis Presley's '(You're The) Devil in Disguise'.[1]

Anger could just as easily chosen 'Hurt', Timi Yuro enthralling cover of Roy Hamilton's country ballad from 1954, a staple of gay and lesbian bars into the mid-sixties. Possessing a 'deep, strident, almost masculine voice and the occasional sob,' according to writer Bob Dickinson, Yuro's contralto resembled, uncannily, a black, butch Judy Garland. She gave 'Hurt' her all as her occasional singing partner Johnnie Ray did with 'Cry'[2], never hiding any of the torment that ruled her planet – supposedly the anguish of the closet, through more than one marriage (and one stolen boyfriend Joe, care of Troy Walker).

Another entry in the hypothetical gay hit parade, 'Two Faces Have I' was the second single from Lou Christie, born Lugee Alfredo Giovanni Sacco, who was willing to test the boundaries of sexual propriety more explicitly than even the UK's new blues combo the Rolling Stones. Where Mick Jagger got more androgynous as the decade progressed, Christie turned all Italian stallion, baring the hairiest of chests and packing his jeans at every opportunity, another dogged by those pesky rumours. Christie's trademark was his piercing falsetto, which subverted his chosen image's macho values and encouraged rumours about his sexuality.[3]

---

1 Over on the East coast, in New York, Jack Smith was coincidentally releasing his similarly experimental but far more pan-sexual and pornographic short *Flaming Creatures* in New York. The eclectic soundtrack included opera, classical, country singer Kitty Wells" 'It Wasn't God Who Made Honky Tonk Angels' and the Everly Brothers' 'Be-Bop-A-Lula'.
2 Yuro and Ray united for a near-hysterical version of 'I Believe' in 1961; Yuro also covered 'Cry' but she didn't own it like Ray did.
3 The latest was July 2015, in the *Guardian*, by Bob Stanley: 'Christie was one of the few acts in the sixties who genuinely confused people – was he serious? Was he gay? Why was he urging us to go "back to the days of the Romans?" – without it being any kind of put-on?' www.theguardian.com/music/musicblog/2015/jul/07/cult-heroes-lou-christie-pop

His song-writing partner, flame-haired Twyla Herbert, was an interesting choice; twice Christie's age and once memorably described as, 'a bohemian gypsy, psychic, and former concert pianist gypsy'.[1] Christie referred to his vocal tic as 'the gypsy cry', which became the title of his debut single. Some believe 'Two Faces Have I' addresses bisexuality but, 'I don't want the world to know/I don't want my heart to show, two faces have I' – is more about pretence: underneath it all, he's, 'Mister blue'. But it was all in the power of suggestion.

'I've heard that Lou Christie is gay, but I have no idea to this day if he is,' said John Waters. 'But the idea of him singing "Two Faces Have I" felt gay at the time, even if it wasn't and that's what mattered.'

Waters felt the same about UK singer Ian Whitcomb, whose 1965 hit 'You Turn Me On' was 'a big jam at gay parties', according to writer Stephen Davis. Whitcomb's beatnik ditty was sung in a wobbly falsetto with some orgasmic heavy breathing for a chorus; it wasn't a UK hit but it made the US Top Ten. Together with Whitcomb's follow-up 'N-N-Nervous!', Waters says Whitcomb's songs, 'still make me crazy. I wasn't a child by the sixties and they were the kind of songs that stopped you in your tracks. You had no idea if he was gay, but those songs appealed to my twisted gay sensibility. They were beyond sexual for me.'

Lou Christie only had one true competitor in falsetto – Frankie Valli, one of the Four Seasons. Christie had a gypsy on his side but Valli had Bob Crewe, one of the savviest entrepreneurs of sixties' and seventies' pop. He not only ran his own record label and studio but shared in the lucrative trade of song-writing.

Crewe studied architecture but worked as a US Overseas entertainer and then as a male model with dashing Robert Redford looks – both worlds more accommodating to gay men in the fifties. Crewe's skill set grew to interior decorating (a no-brainer) and the music industry. He turned out to be only an average singer, but much better in business; he

---

[1] The source is unknown

approached song-writing like interior design, fashioning details, 'a harp flourish here, a harmonica part there, a drum roll, a flamenco guitar riff, a weird sound effect, a dramatic pause,' wrote Donny Jacobs.[1] He incorporated global, especially Latin, influences. The result was a flair for 'story-driven lyrics, innovative musical "hooks" and a final lyrical twist that were to become known as Crewe trademarks.'[2]

Crewe's first collaboration, with songwriter Bob Gaudio, was 'Sherry' in 1962, the Four Seasons' first no. 1 single, inspired by Valli's performance one night in New Jersey. As Crewe told writer Joe Smith, 'Frankie did a thing that night that blew me away. He put a bandana over his head, took two maracas and stuck them under his coat, and began singing "I Can't Give You Anything but Love" like Nellie Lecher with that high voice.'[3]

Crewe told Gaudio: 'Go write a song for Frankie with that chi-chi voice and jump it an octave. I don't care if you call it "Bananas", we'll make a record of it, whatever it is.'

'Sherry' was followed by more Four Seasons melodramas, with Crewe's lyrics tapping a different emotional state: 'Pity was the theme of "Rag Doll"; painful longing permeated "Ronnie" and "Silence Is Golden"; wounded pride was the subject of "Walk Like A Man" and "Big Girls Don't Cry" was a catty revenge-fest,' according to Donny Jacobs.'[4]

In 1967, Crewe would produce and write half of *California Nights*, the final commercially successful album by Lesley Gore, whose peak period was 1963 to 1965 and who topped the US chart with the dear-diary drama of her debut single 'It's My Party'. Described as 'the Taylor Swift of her day' after her 2014 death, Gore personified the anguished teenager – 'It's my party and I'll cry if I want to' is one of pop music's

---

1 http://popculturecantina.blogspot.co.uk/search/label/Bob%20Crewe
2 An unattributed comment on Wikipedia.
3 *Off The Record: An Oral History of Popular Music* (Grand Central Publishing, 1989)
4 One lyric Crewe didn't give to Valli was 'Navy Blue', a US no. 6 in 1963 for teenager Diana Ray, about a girl pining for her sailor boyfriend away at sea, followed by the minor hit 'Kiss Me Sailor'.

most iconic phrases. Gore fought back; her follow-up hit, 'Judy's Turn To Cry', turned the tables on her boyfriend-stealing rival, before 'You Don't Own Me' (US no. 2, UK no. 4) became the first feminist teen pop anthem. It was masterfully constructed, a slowly building bolero of hormonal resistance.

Gore admitted that she didn't know her true sexuality until she'd reached her twenties, 'so if [people] knew it, they knew it before I did! You know, maybe someone did think that.' Joy Silver, who later became Gore's PA, thinks that 'You Don't Own Me' 'was a signal, in many ways, about music that was chosen for certain artists. Even if they weren't out, the record company knew and wanted to find songs that fit them. When problems arose, they knew what was going on. Lesley learnt to devise a career to express herself without giving anything away.'[1]

Gore recognised the song – a feminist anthem, a gay anthem of sorts too – was 'very powerful: don't abuse me, don't misuse me. I think the record industry . . . is still totally homophobic; it's always been a man's world . . . and it always puts women not necessarily down but certainly on a lower rung.'[2]

A girl named Dusty

Gore was able to pass on her rebellious DNA to arguably the best white singer of all time. 'You Don't Own Me' was soon covered by Dusty Springfield, born Mary Isobel Catherine Bernadette O'Brien, one of the most incendiary, headstrong and tragic singers of either gender, who fought all attempts to control her. In love with black music (and sounding soulful enough to be mistaken on record for being black), Springfield refused to play before segregated audiences in South Africa before singing to a mixed-race crowd (which got her thrown out of the country), but her sexuality was a closet built by her

---

1 Ironically, 'You Don't Own Me' was written by two men, Philadelphia songwriters John Madara and David White.
2 http://www.afterellen.com/people/43863-interview-with-lesley-gore

The Sixties: Gay Party Pop and the Rock'n'Roll Closet

smothering Catholic upbringing and the over-arching morals of the sixties.

Having left brother Tom's side, who she played with in the Springfields, her joyous solo debut single, 'I Only Want to Be With You', was a UK Top 5 hit and the first UK-produced single of the British invasion era to follow the Beatles into the US Top 20. It pushed Springfield to the front row of UK star singers, but success brought self-doubt that left her with nowhere to hide as the media zeroed in.

'You Don't Have to Say to Say You Love Me' upped the ante. It was her first UK no. 1 and first US Top 5 hit; not bad for a song whose English lyrics (to an Italian melody) were written on the hoof during a ten-minute taxi ride by her friend (and later manager) Vicki Wickham with writer and music business manager Simon Napier-Bell, both gay. Springfield confessed that only performing gave her joy; the stage was her emancipation.

Springfield's sexuality would have to come out in other ways. 'Most of the queer boy bands of contemporary rock music, as well as androgynous or sexually ambiguous women performers such as Annie Lennox, Alison Moyet, Chrissie Hynde and even Madonna, demonstrate the musical, visual or aesthetic influence of Dusty Springfield, one of the very first women in rock who dared to, "to strike a pose",' wrote Patricia Juliana Smith.[1]

With her beehive wig, outsize eyelashes and flamboyant (had any female singers before her deserved that adjective?) hand movements, Springfield had a singularly strong presence. As Smith wrote, the singer, 'created a decidedly queer persona while achieving popular success in a trendy milieu in which lesbianism, lacking the criminal status and thus the glamour of male homosexuality, remained invisible and unfashionable. Utilising the tactics of camp, she adopted more visible (and modish) marginalised identities by "becoming" a gay man in drag (or a female female impersonator) visually and a black woman vocally.'

---

1 *The Queer Sixties* (Routledge, 1999)

Girls rock and heads roll...

Unlike gay men, lesbians didn't have to battle the law, but their straitjacket was society itself, controlled by men. Indeed, any woman driven to make a career out of music would butt heads with male producers and engineers, managers, record companies, agents, et al, and their progress depended on their willingness to compromise. In the fifties, as the Roc-A-Jets had discovered, it was easier to create your own isolated bubble and accept the commercial and creative restrictions. But women still felt they had to kick against the pricks. If you were lesbian, the battle was likely to be insurmountable.

The first all-female band signed to a major label, Goldie and the Gingerbreads were chosen in 1963 by Decca in the UK. The band had been assembled by singer Genya Zelkowitz, the one straight woman of the quartet, after a meeting with Ginger Bianco (another rare female drummer) prompted the idea of women taking every instrumental role in the group.[1] Next to join was organist Margot Lewis and finally guitarist Carol McDonald, who'd released two soulful singles under the name Carol Shaw. That was the easy part.

Their third single 'Can't You Hear My Heartbeat' made the UK Top 30 but was crushed in their own country by Herman's Hermits' version. In 1965, the band had already changed labels, and signed to Atlantic but by 1967 they had begun to fracture. Zelkowitz and Bianco returned home to the US but McDonald and Lewis stayed in London. They occupied one floor of a house in west London while Dusty Springfield and her friend and backing singer, Madeline Bell, a former member of the Alex Bradford Singers[2], also took flats in the house.[3]

Wickham had been the producer of ITV's new weekly pop show

---

[1] Goldie was the name that Ravan's mother gave her after emigrating to the US from Poland. 'Gingerbreads' derived from Ginger Panabianco's first name.

[2] Bell was the only female in US musician Alex Bradford's gospel troupe. After a UK tour in the mid-sixties, Bell stayed on and worked with Springfield. She became the UK's most in-demand session singer, as well as the voice of seventies soul-pop band Blue Mink.

[3] *Dancing With Demons*, Penny Valentine and Vicki Wickham (St. Martin's Press, 2001)

THE SIXTIES: GAY PARTY POP AND THE ROCK'N'ROLL CLOSET

Ready Steady Go!, which had debuted on August 1963, five months before the BBC's *Top of the Pops*.[1] Springfield occasionally presented *RSG!*, as did fellow singer Polly Perkins, who was out in a way that Springfield would never dare. But then Perkins (born Gillian Arnold) had stage performers for parents and had grown up around gay people. She also had the advantage of discovering Frances Faye through her mother's record collection.

'Faye's music was fantastic, I even saw her live in London in the sixties,' Perkins recalls. 'I didn't know she was a lesbian but she was the first strong woman I'd ever seen perform.'

Perkins fancied performing too. At fifteen, she became the youngest woman to join the nude revue at the Windmill theatre, London's low-rent answer to the Folies Bergère and Moulin Rouge. But nudity wasn't a career with longevity or much job satisfaction. Guided by her girlfriend Lena Davis – a rare instance of a female manager, trying to emulate Larry Parnes' style of grooming – Perkins started releasing pop songs, adopting an alias from the music hall song 'Pretty Polly Perkins of Paddington Green'.

Like the Gingerbreads, Perkins signed to Decca. Her debut single 'I Reckon You' had a potentially revealing B-side, 'The Girls Are at It Again'. Was it just a slice of girl power, or more? 'The song was offered to me,' Perkins says. 'It's only now occurred to me that the title's a bit camp! I was a naive seventeen-year-old, but perhaps the publishers or Lena sussed it.' None of Perkin's four sixties singles, even 'You Too Can Be a Beatle', sold well, despite her TV appearances and a fabricated romance with Larry Parnes' pop singer Terry Dene. Perhaps the diminutive Perkin's preferred image, a suit and a cigar, was too challenging?

'They were *women's* clothes,' Perkins maintains. 'I'd wear a cap and a little blazer jacket and little trousers, more like ski pants. But the papers called it a man's suit. On *Ready Steady Go!*, I'd wear dresses, but on my

---

1 Though *Ready Steady Go!* preceded the much more famous *Top of the Pops*, the latter lasted fifty years longer than its rival, which broadcast its final show in 1966.

own shows, being an ex-dancer, I wanted to do things like jump over the drums, which you couldn't do in a Mary Quant dress.'

At *RSG!*, Perkins shared a dressing room with other presenters, including Springfield. 'I knew Dusty was gay, but it wasn't talked about,' Perkins says. 'But that was all right, it wasn't my business.' Perkins was soon eased out of the show. 'I didn't think so at the time, but it probably was because I was gay. I think Vicki was probably nervous about it. I'm frightening to people who weren't out, they're frightened of being outed themselves.'

Like Dusty, Vicki Wickham championed black music, especially that of Detroit-based Motown label, which had been accumulating hits in America since 1959 and had become the first black music label with a sizeable UK profile. When the Tamla Motown[1] Revue toured the UK in 1965 with its lead acts the Supremes, Smokey Robinson and the Miracles, Stevie Wonder and Martha Reeves and the Vandellas, *RSG!* staged a special *The Sound of Motown* that also featured the Temptations and Marvin Gaye.

The sound of young, black America, with its vibrant melodies, plush production, springy rhythm, soulful urgency and soaring voices, began to dominate the gay bars, wiping away years of sad ballads and jubilant, escapist show tunes. It was to the new sounds that the 1970 film version of *Boys in the Band* turned to rather than *Love Is A Drag*, Camp singles or Broadway extravaganzas. It had been the first play (staged off Broadway in 1969) to portray homosexuality as a defined community and the soundtrack for the central birthday party featured Marvin Gaye and Tammi Terrell, Wilson Pickett, Martha Reeves – plus Harper's Bizarre's bubblegum-poppy 'Anything Goes' for the opening credits, presumably for its suggestive title.

This musical shift had begun at clubs like the Peppermint Lounge, while the twist craze persisted through The Starliters' 'Peppermint Twist' (a US no. 1 in January 1962) and Sam Cooke's 'Twistin' the Night Away' which didn't name the Peppermint Lounge, only, 'a place

---

1 As the label was branded in the UK.

somewhere up a New York way/where the people are so gay'. The third verse talked of 'A fella in blue jeans/Dancin' with an older queen/Who's dolled up in her diamond rings and/Twistin' the night away.'[1]

The police invariably turned up, when the boys would still have to turn to face the girls and vice-versa. At the Kandy Lounge in Soho, the manager was taken to court because plainclothes police had witnessed men twisting with each other.[2] Yet, far from shutting down Soho's gay scene, the police did, 'in a strange way,' says manager and writer Simon Napier-Bell, contribute to its growth. 'The London police would have known where every gay club was and demanded money off them all, the gay pubs, the clubs, the coffee bars,' he says. 'There were no gay after-hours drinking places. It was more, "the queers can have their clubs". The police were totally corrupt, but that's why swinging London was able to happen.'

Le Duce was the most famous Soho gay bar, conveniently owned by an ex-policeman and his boyfriend, with a clientele of gay mods and a little dancefloor. One source recalled how, 'working class poofs and straight dolly birds danced to black music'.[3] Le Duce's jukebox was heavily dominated by Motown, peppered with some heftier soul records from Stax, and Jamaican blue beat. It's unconfirmed whether or not Fitzgerald Henry, a calypso musician from Trinidad and Tobago who called himself Mighty Terror, was on the jukebox too. He lived in London in the sixties and produced comedic same-sex ditties such as 'Patricia Gone With Millicent' and 'The Fig Man' (a phallic reference, as fig was another term for banana), in which Henry rebuffs a man's advances without any homophobic reaction, but simply by stating that he wasn't gay himself.

---

1 Sam Cooke also had a hit with 'The Great Pretender', which echoed the old doo wop ballads. Cooke was married three times and there were no gay rumours around him, but he had no problem singing 'gay' again and in a song about pretence: 'Oh, yes, I'm the great pretender/just laughing and gay like a clown/I seem to be what I'm not, you see I'm wearing my heart like a crown/Pretending that you're still around.'
2 http://jackthatcatwasclean.blogspot.co.uk/2008/02/gay-london-at-le-duce.html
3 Ibid. 246

Le Duce's jukebox also had room for Dusty Springfield's 'You Don't Have to Say You Love Me', presumably when people fancied a break from dancing or to warm the evening up. Jukebox memories, however, don't include hypothetical gay hit parade ballads or Frankie Valli's first solo hit, 1967's 'Can't Take My Eyes Off You' – the twentieth century's fifth most-played song on radio. Perhaps the cha-cha rhythm of the chorus was too cheesy for the cool clubbers. If only they'd known then that the lyric was Bob Crewe's love song to his lover, lying beside him in bed.[1]

If Brian Epstein had been a lyricist as well as a manager he might have written something equivalent. Instead, one of his charges wrote something in tribute to his troubled feelings. The Beatles' manager was mindful of his criminal record and was constantly on guard in his private affairs, which made him as much, if not more, of a liability than any member of the band.

The upper-class Epstein sought out rough, working-class types, which made his life that much more unpredictable and lonely. He risked professional estrangement by propositioning both the band's first drummer, Pete Best and then the most vulnerable and complicated Beatle, John Lennon. He recalled his relationship with Epstein was 'intense' and 'almost a love affair, but not consummated'. Lennon knew Epstein was interested in him and perhaps enjoyed the attention and even felt a little curious (his widow, Yoko Ono, confirmed that Lennon had a bisexual side that he never explored) and he agreed to a short break in Spain with Epstein.[2] On their return, Lennon wrote 'You've Got to Hide Your Love Away', which the Beatles recorded for the soundtrack to their 1965 film *Help!*. Lennon's words centred on a woman who had broken his heart and forced his love underground, but by singing 'You've got to hide' rather than 'I've got to hide', he suggested another story altogether.[3]

---

[1] The story was revealed in the stage musical *Jersey Boys*.
[2] By several accounts, Lennon allowed Epstein to give him a handjob.
[3] 'John wasn't a homosexual but he was daft enough to try anything once,' Hunter Davies

THE SIXTIES: GAY PARTY POP AND THE ROCK'N'ROLL CLOSET

Would you let your son marry a Rolling Stone?

The Beatles lacked the raw charisma that Epstein liked in his companions but the Rolling Stones had it in spades. As Simon Napier Bell saw it, 'The Beatles looked like four boys set up by a sugar daddy in a Mayfair penthouse. The Stones looked more like rough trade from the meat rack [the area around street railings used as a pick-up area] behind Piccadilly Circus.'[1]

'The Beatles looked like they were in show business, and that was the important thing,' manager Andrew Loog Oldham told journalist Tim Nudd,[2] 'and the important thing for the Rolling Stones was to look as if they were not.' Having worked in music PR and promotion for the Beatles and Joe Meek (who he found 'frightening'), Oldham set his sights on management, modelling himself after Parnes' and Epstein's aura of sensation. According to author Gordon Thompson, Oldham's 'descriptions of his own sexuality suggest that, while he was predominantly heterosexual, he adopted stereotypically homosexual behaviours in part as a form of social aggression. He found the straight men he encountered in the business to be intimidated by overt gayness.'[3]

None of the Stones were gay either, but Keith Richards conveniently looked like rough trade, Brian Jones was handsome and Mick Jagger had a captivating androgyny, with full rich lips. In the words of celebrated gay British playwright Joe Orton, 'Sex is the only way to infuriate them. Much more fucking and they'll be screaming hysterics in next to no time.'[4] Oldham encouraged the Stones to push boundaries. For the band's 1966 single 'Have You Seen Your Mother, Baby, Standing in the

---

wrote in his autobiography *The Beatles, Football and Me* (Headline Review, 2006).
1 *Black Vinyl White Powder* (Ebury Press, 2007)
2 http://www.adweek.com/news/advertising-branding/what-man-who-invented-rolling-stones-can-teach-you-about-branding-152719
3 *Please Please Me: Sixties British Pop, Inside Out: Sixties British Pop* (Oxford University Press, 2008)
4 Orton, a habitual user of the same North London public toilets as Joe Meek, wrote a script for a proposed Beatles film called *Up Against It*. One reason the band rejected it was that they were expected to all get into bed together.

Shadow?, Oldham dressed up the Stones in drag (as air stewardesses!) for the sleeve. You'd have imagined lead pouter Mick Jagger would have made the most of the shoot, but pictures shows Brian Jones clearly enjoying it most, in a blonde wig, cigarette dangling from a posed hand, while a dowdy Jagger looks almost embarrassed.

The story goes that Jones was up for more larks, suggesting a threesome with Stones guitarist Keith Richards and writing the lithe rocker 'Miss Amanda Jones' for 1967's *Between The Buttons* album. His inspiration was Amanda Lear, a muse of surrealist painter Salvador Dali who was beginning to ingratiate herself with musicians and strongly rumoured to have been born Alain Tapp.[1]

Jones had also reputedly been open to a threesome with his Parisian girlfriend and Dave Davies, the guitarist of the Kinks, 'the queerest of the sixties beat groups,' according to their biographer Jon Savage. The north London quartet were fronted by Dave's older brother Ray, but it was Dave Davies – revealed in his autobiography, *Kink*[2] – who enjoyed 'camping it up' in public. 'It was exciting to watch people's faces, to shock them,' Davies told journalist Peter Doggett.[3] People thought you were different, so they reckoned you knew something that they didn't. It was just provocation – and contempt as well.'

The Kinks' 'See My Friends' – a UK Top 10 hit – was also the first pop song to address bisexuality, albeit in heavy code: 'She is gone and now there's no one left to love/'Cept my friends/Layin' 'cross the river.' Ray Davies said his inspiration was 'a person in this business who is quite normal and good-looking but girls have given him such a rotten time that he becomes a sort of queer.' A 1994 interview with *Gay Times*

---

1 According to *April Ashley's Odyssey*, by Duncan Fallowell (Jonathan Cape, 1982), the transsexual entertainer claimed that she and Tapp worked together in Parisian transvestite revues in the fifties and early sixties.

2 Hachette Books (1997). In an interview with the *Independent* in 2011, Davies said, 'A major thing I discovered, especially from the relationship I had with [TV producer] Michael [Aldred], was that I liked women more. And that guys are sensitive too. I realised it was not wussy to feel sensitive or upset.'

3 *Record Collector*, April 1996

revealed the river represented the gulf between straight and gay: 'I was thinking I have the choice to go there if I want. But I can't analyse other people's analysis. I just suddenly found wonderful things to write about.'

While Ray never chose – or admitted to – crossing the river, Dave was game. In the sixties, as he told journalist Andrew Lynch, 'you could get away with anything if you had the self-confidence to carry it off. It was in that spirit that I experimented sexually. But, honestly, I wouldn't describe myself as bisexual. I was just young and I wanted to try anything and everything, you understand?'[1]

Ray noted Dave's lifestyle and 'David Watts' was a concert promoter who had romantic designs on his brother, which Ray turned into a tale of schoolboy envy: 'He is so gay and fancy free . . . All the girls in the neighbourhood try to go out with David Watts . . . but can't succeed.'

Dave was also the Kinks' more adventurous fashionista, mixing up male and female items of clothing as he did partners in bed and he might have inspired 'Dedicated Follower of Fashion', one of their jauntiest and juiciest of hit singles: 'He thinks he is a flower to be looked at/And when he pulls his frilly nylon panties right up tight/He feels a dedicated follower of fashion'.

Ironically, if the Kinks were the queerest of Britain's pop giants, they were the only ones without a gay manager – or one who acted gay. After all, it was Andrew Loog Oldham who wrote the words to the Rolling Stones' 'I'd Much Rather Be with the Boys', a perfect pastiche of a girl-group archetype (The Shangri-Las, say).[2] Like Oldham, the Who's co-managers Kit Lambert (gay) and Chris Stamp (straight) were arch-schemers, with Lambert the dominant influence on the band's songwriter and guitarist, Pete Townshend and the band's defining anarchic behaviour. Like Brian Epstein, Lambert dressed in suits, exuded money, liked bad boys and would be fatally undone by drugs. He was ramping it up as Epstein faded away.

---

1 Interview by Andrew Lynch, *Trinity News*, 1996
2 'I'd Much Rather Be With The Boys' was only released on the 1975 compilation *Metamorphosis*.

Simon Napier-Bell worked for Epstein as a publicist and fraternised in the same circles: he claimed that Epstein fell in love with him – contrary to the type of young man that the Beatles manager liked most – and addressed his last message to him.[1] The next day, Epstein was found dead from an overdose of sleeping pills. There was no note and few thought it was anything but an accident.

Napier-Bell still had Kit Lambert among his closest friends and described him as 'emotionally volatile, easily bored, sexually ambivalent and irresistibly drawn to self-destruction.' Lambert's excess exceeded that of most musicians. He burned through cash, properties, boys and friendships, chasing every available high, heroin included. Part of an establishment that treated him as a criminal, Lambert's nihilistic energy pushed the Who from tidy mod origins to proto-punk art-rock, smashing their instruments on stage for an unforgettable climax. Lambert also pushed Townshend creatively, suggesting he write a rock opera, the first of its kind.

Townshend, whose appreciation of sex was more fluid than he initially showed, first conceived of *Quads*, set in a future where parents could choose the sex of their children; one couple wanted four girls but instead had three girls and a boy, so they raised him as a girl. Townshend abandoned the story, though the Who released 'I'm A Boy', the first mainstream pop single to tackle cross-dressing and gender confusion: 'I feel lucky if I get trousers to wear/Spend ages taking hairpins from my hair/I'm a boy, I'm a boy/But my ma won't admit it'.

Quads was replaced by *Tommy*, the tale of a deaf, dumb and blind 'pinball wizard' who recovers his senses as the leader of a spiritual cult. It was a huge success on release in 1968 though the only example of any sexual aberration was the paedophilic character Uncle Tommy – Townshend later claimed that therapy revealed this was inspired by childhood abuse by a friend of his grandmother. Ernie fit the overriding UK concept of sexuality, 'that everything was hidden, a bit pervy,

---

[1] *Ta-Ra-Ra-Boom-De-Ay: The Dodgy Business of Pop Music* by Simon Napier-Bell (Unbound Books, 2014)

a bit saucy, with darker undercurrents,' reckons Who biographer Mark Blake. There was a precedent in UK pop: 'Uncle Bert' by the Who's mod peers the Creation: 'Uncle Bert with his trousers hanging down/Well, I spied him lurking deep on Hampstead Heath/Rumour has it Uncle's a tillie'.[1] The Berts and Ernies implied that homosexuals were dangerous, untrustworthy – and Kit Lambert wasn't the greatest role model.

In 1966, Napier-Bell moved into management with the Yardbirds. They featured three of the most definitive guitarists of their generation in Eric Clapton, Jeff Beck and Jimmy Page, though Napier-Bell didn't restyle the Yardbirds as other gay managers had done with their bands. He also seemed much less ambitious than his peers. After discovering Marc Bolan, a pretty, sharp-dressing mod with a unique, bleating style of singing and a complex book of songs, Napier-Bell bailed out very early on.

But other gay managers made major inroads; Robert Stigwood progressed beyond the pop puppet John Leyton and Mike Berry to manage brothers Barry, Robin and Maurice Gibb as the Bee Gees and Eric Clapton's Cream, the first hard rock trio. Signings to Stigwood's new label Reaction included the Who. Tony Stratton-Smith managed the Nice, Ken Pitt had new chart-topper Crispian St Peters and Marc Bolan's friend and rival David Bowie. For their newest charges the Herd, Ken Howard and Alan Blaikley wrote 'Something Strange', about a married man straying while on holiday ('He takes a stroll in the jasmine-scented night/Gay voices beckon to some new delight'), but wisely hid it on the B-side to the no. 5 UK hit, 'I Don't Want Our Loving To Die.'

The new generation were gravitating toward gay managers and with good reason, says Napier-Bell. 'Being gay was illegal so we didn't have much respect for the law – we were more anti-authoritarian and anti-establishment, more naturally subversive. We were more liberal with drugs and we had a different attitude to young people.'

Pete Townshend agreed. 'A lot of my friends from the Goldhawk [the

---

1 London's biggest patch of green is Hampstead Heath, the city's most famous cruising ground. I can't find any supportive evidence, but 'tillie' must be an old-fashioned reference to homosexual.

Who's west London hangout] tried being gay because it was a fashionable thing to do,' he told Mark Blake. 'We thought all the cool people were gay.'[1]

Napier-Bell says there was equally a good reason why gay men had gravitated to the pop industry: 'If you were gay and wanted an open life, let's not pretend, you only had the civil service or the theatre or hairdressing. Everywhere else, you'd have to change your way. But the law wasn't very heavily enforced providing you didn't do it in a public space.'

From camp to exploitation

Slowly, and covertly more than overtly, UK pop and its cabal of gay managers were seeding the idea that some sexual difference or fluidity or androgyny was fascinating, even enjoyable, rather than to be mistrusted or feared. Yet pop still didn't have any pop stars who declared they were gay; it was still against the law. The most blatant gay British record of the era was one of its rarest, a 1967 single released on the Thrust label by the Brothers Butch. The duo was all about innuendo – the songwriter was reputedly Eileen Dover. The song title 'Kay, Why?' was named after the lubricant K-Y Jelly and its lyrics followed the drag queen tradition:

> Queen one: 'Oh, George, isn't it nice having a group backing us?'
> Queen two: 'You always were greedy, Clarence.'[2]

The same spirit of camp and of Camp Records infiltrated the 1966 album *These Are The Hits, You Silly Savage* by another invented male duo, Teddy and Darrel. The US record label responsible was Mira, whose owner Mike Curb was an aspiring record mogul. He would soon form the Mike Curb Congregation, a happy-clappy vocal ensemble and then oversee the Osmonds' formative recordings. In 1978 he would serve as California's lieutenant governor. But in 1966, Curb was working in

---

[1] http://petetownshend.net/news/pete-townshend-an-extended-interview-by-mark-blake
[2] The B-side 'I'm Not Going Camping This Winter', a parody of Victorian music hall, continued in the same fashion.

exploitation movies, low-budget B-grade efforts to sensationalise and shock or to feed the vices of members of the public impervious to outrage. He'd scored the soundtrack for Roger Corman's *The Wild Angels*, the pioneering 'outlaw biker' cash-in, so funding Teddy and Darrel's 'fantastic, freaky, camp interpretations of our biggest hits,'[1] was par for the course.

According to blogger UK Jarry,[2] Darrel was an aspiring songwriter, while Teddy was scriptwriter and actor Theodore Charach. Theirs was at least a contemporary collection of covers rather than another fifties makeover. One song was brand new, Frank Sinatra's US and UK no. 1 'Strangers In The Night',[3] a lush midnight stroll of a song that Teddy and Darel, lisping and sniggering, transformed into the ultimate queeny cruising anthem: 'Strangers in the night, exchanging glances/ Wondering in the night, what were the chances?/We'd be sharing love before the night was through.'

If sexual liberation had truly arrived, Teddy and Darrel's jokes seemed lame and made on the cheap. 'Hanky Panky' was little more than the title endlessly repeated; orgasmic groans propped up Sam and Dave's soul-chugger 'Hold On, I'm Coming'; an invitation to 'make a scene in a bowl of Dick's whipping cream,' punctuated 'Say There'. If any gay party record of the era felt homophobic and exploitative, it was *These Are The Hits* . . . The cover – a man shields his face as he's pursued by a second man brandishing a bullwhip – suggested an outsider's view of gay life; likewise the expression, 'you silly savage.'[4]

---

1 In the words of president of the duo's National Fan Club, which printed its address on Sunset Boulevard.
2 http://ukjarry.blogspot.co.uk/2010/01/356-camp-comedy-cash-in-records.html
3 There is a curious UK connection: Mike Curb organised a release of the track through UK label Surrey International in 1974, credited to Teddy, Harold and Jeremy – the first names of the leaders (Ted Heath, Harold Wilson and Jeremy Thorpe) of the core political parties contesting a general election that year.
4 Curb didn't stop there; as music director of the 1967 'shockumentary' *Mondo Hollywood* (hippies or 'freaks' were as much a source of exploitation as bikers), his soundtrack included a new Teddy and Darrel track, 'Beast of Sunset Strip' and Curb co-wrote 'You're Beautiful', sung by one Darrell (now with two Ls) Dee.

BREAKING DOWN THE WALLS OF HEARTACHE

The album re-emerged through the blogs of record collectors and there were theories that Curb had an agenda. The story J. D. Doyle heard 'is that the album was an effort to track homosexuals. Here's the plan, you release an album and track the sales of it to see where those creatures live... The plan didn't work because record sales were just too spread out.'[1]

Unsurprisingly, Curb's extensive website list of musical, political and sports achievements leaves out *These Are The Hits*... Yet, in political office, he would show a pro-gay attitude despite his Republican beliefs[2] and his 1967 film *Teenage Rebellion* included 'The Gay Teenager', a brief soliloquy that adopted a sensationalist but sympathetic tone. Narrator Burt Topper, who also made exploitation movies, cited the examples of Greece and Rome, Alexander the Great, Julius Caesar, Leonardo de Vinci and Michelangelo, 'some of the names that any homosexual will point to as examples of virility in the defence of his way of life.'

Topper also named the Mattachine Society and the efforts of homosexuals who 'no longer hide in shadows... but rather they have joined together into groups or clubs in an attempt to seek freedom and acceptability for their type of sex inclination. They can be found in all walks of life and down any street in this lonely world, forever searching for whatever it is that drives them on.'

The rock machine turns on

On the other side of the USA, one singer-songwriter was searching for whatever it was that drove him on, despite the fact it had led to a nervous breakdown, electro-shock treatment and an early, reckless fascination with drugs. Born in Brooklyn and raised on Long Island, the teenage Lou Reed, 'possessed a fragile temperament', according to his sister

---

1 http://queermusicheritage.com/qmh101s.html
2 He took charge of a merged Sidewalk with MGM and fired artists that were actively pro-drugs. But Curb worked alongside San Francisco mayor Harvey Milk to defeat the Briggs Initiative that would ban gays and lesbians from working in California's public schools.

Merrill[1] and suffered panic attacks. He was obsessed with rock'n'roll, from doo wop to R&B, and also with literature. After some primitive efforts to form bands, he had begun an English degree at Syracuse University. His studies were interrupted by an episode that led to a course of electro-shock therapy – not to curb his homosexual tendencies, as generally believed, but his 'high anxiety', according to Merrill.

Recovering, Reed went back to Syracuse in 1960. The creative writing course was taken by Delmore Schwartz, once a highly regarded poet and short-story writer, but a victim of his own repressed homosexuality who quickly unravelled in a haze of alcoholism and mental illness; he would be dead by 1966. Graduating with honours, Reed moved to New York City and worked as an in-house songwriter. Inspired by Schwartz and his own alienated and misanthropic outlook, Reed went on to imagine a version of rock'n'roll with the scope of Hubert Selby's 1964 novel *Last Exit To Brooklyn*, a heady diatribe of social breakdown peppered with drugs, violence, homosexuality and transvestism. Falling in with similarly clad-in-black musicians, he formed the Velvet Underground, named after Michael Leigh's pulp novel about one couple's secretive sexual exploits, from husband and wife-swapping to group sex, orgies, homosexuality and sado-masochism.

The Velvets were making slow progress until Andy Warhol saw the band play and offered to be their manager. Warhol was a former graphic designer turned multi-faceted artist, from pop art to photography. His short films included 1964's *Blowjob*, which focuses on a man's face as he enjoys oral sex – Warhol was not backwards in coming forward about sex in general and, specifically, homosexuality. In the Velvets' thrilling and pioneering blend of melody, noise and transgressive attitude, he heard the perfect musical foil to his own thoughts.

The band joined Warhol's live Exploding Plastic Inevitable spectacle and in 1966 recorded a debut album, *The Velvet Underground & Nico*. It was a new strain of rock'n'roll, ranging from exquisite

---

1 https://medium.com/cuepoint/a-family-in-peril-lou-reed-s-sister-sets-the-record-straight-about-his-childhood-20e8399f84a3

145

European-influenced (by way of Nico's Germanic presence) ballads to droning rock, pithy R&B to avant-garde minimalism and iced by Reed's Selby-esque depiction of New York life: drugs, sado-masochism, drug paranoia, Warhol's social scene and more drugs. There was no clear reference to homosexuality aside from Warhol's phallic image on the cover (a peelable yellow banana that revealed a pink interior), though Reed's cast of characters looking for a heroin fix in 'Run Run Run' – Teenage Mary, Margarita Passion, Seasick Sarah and Beardless Harry – sounded like drag queens or a street-level equivalent.

The Velvet Underground's second album, *White Light/White Heat*, did venture into the realm of drag with Rosie and Miss Rayon among the cast of the seventeen-minute volcanic jam 'Sister Ray',[1] a story 'of total debauchery and decay,' Reed explained. 'I like to think of Sister Ray as a transvestite smack dealer. The situation is a bunch of drag queens taking some sailors home with them and shooting up on smack and having this orgy, when the police appear.'[2]

The album's narcoleptic ballad 'Lady Godiva's Operation' described a sex change – the first song to tackle the subject. But the musical and lyrical adventures were ahead of their time and not even Warhol's patronage gave the band decent sales or a profile.

Though Reed and the Velvets weren't to know until a few years later, a copy of their debut album had reached David Bowie, via his manager Ken Pitt, who had met Warhol to discuss representing him in the UK. From south London, the former David Jones had made an early mark as the seventeen-year old founder of the Society for the Prevention of Cruelty to Long-haired Men, who admitted in a BBC interview that he'd been taunted on the street by comments like, 'Hello, darlin',' and 'Can I carry your handbag?'. US band the Barbarians had lampooned this new look, while also modelling it, on their single 'Are You a Boy or

---

[1] Some claim that Reed named 'Sister Ray' after Ray Davies, who the Velvets admired for his storytelling and The Kinks' pioneering aggression with guitars.

[2] Source unknown, but included in *Lou Reed "Talking": Lou Reed in His Own Words*, Nick Johnstone (Omnibus Press, 2005)

a Girl?' ('You're either a girl or you come from Liverpool . . . You can dance like a female monkey but sink like a stone/Yeah, a rolling stone'), but long hair was part of the new youth fashion, breaking down another boundary between men and women.

Jones was also open to breaking boundaries in bed. Simon Napier-Bell recalls the singer's first manager, Ralph Horton, offering the chance to co-manage Jones and as a sweetener, a night with the boy himself (Napier-Bell declined both offers).

By 1966, having gone through R&B and mod phases, the newly christened Bowie was sufficiently smitten by *The Velvet Underground & Nico* to steal lyrics from its S&M anthem 'Venus In Furs' for his own 'Little Toy Soldier' and to impersonate Lou Reed's drawl. Bowie also started to write theatrical narratives of his own. But he didn't share Reed's warped Manhattan worldview and his version was resolutely English, emulating the exaggerated accents and stage-musical settings of actors Anthony Newley and Tommy Steele and creating quaint, rather than debauched, vignettes.

Among his portraits of gravediggers, brass bands and grown men living at home with mother and heavier themes such as sci-fi megalomaniacs and Buddhism were two comic references to homosexuality. One, 'Over The Wall We Go', was passed on by Ken Pitt to Robert Stigwood. He had his new charge Oscar Beuselinck (UK actor Paul Nicholas) cover Bowie's song, inspired by a recent rash of prison breaks and including a clearer reference of prison sex than 'Jailhouse Rock': 'The new lads would ask me if I am a screw/I'll tell them, "Oh, cheeky, not even for you."'

The second, 'She's Got Medals', Bowie recorded for his 1967 self-titled debut album, about a girl who changes her name to Tommy, joins the army and passes the medical ('Don't ask me how it's done') but 'gets very tired of picking up girls/Cleaning her gun and shaving her curls'. Tommy deserts the army, re-emerges as Eileen and settles down.

One committed fan was Lindsay Kemp, a student of the Ballet Rambert who'd created his own mime company and made his mark with a production of Jean Genet's debut novel *Our Lady of the Flowers*, an explicit autobiographical journey through Paris' queer and criminal underworld that the Frenchman had written while in prison. Bowie's debut album, says Kemp, 'was very me. The tone of his voice, the sentiments of songs, absolutely enchanted me.' The pair soon bonded over shared interests: 'the circus, musicals, expressionist art, Berlin cabarets, Brecht,' says Kemp, who mentored Bowie in all things Genet and the other Jean, Cocteau, inspiring his young charge to instill his work with more dramatic, sexual tensions. While Bowie bedded both Kemp and his troupe's set designer Natasha Korniloff, he took the part of Cloud in Kemp's *Pierrot In Turquoise* (also known as *The Looking-Glass Murders*), a three-way gay love tragedy featuring a handful of more sombre and reflective Bowie originals, such as 'The Mirror', with its reference to a 'gay harlequin.'

None of Bowie's records in the first five years of his career sold enough to give him confidence, but he had been left behind by the new, amplified, intensified sound of rock music, personified by the Velvet Underground, Cream, Jimi Hendrix and the Doors all energised by the liberating, intoxicating and unpredictable effects of LSD, marijuana, amphetamine and the muscle relaxant methaqualone (Quaalude in the US, Mandrax in the UK), providing a more suitable soundtrack to the erotic age than fey Rod McKuen.

In this new burgeoning counter-culture, homosexuality was still a strange, unknown identity, fascinating and frightening: but then songwriters preferred to write about love and relationships rather than sex. LA's ambitiously named quintet the United States of America, whose pioneering union of rock and electronics was as radical as the Velvets' avant-garde rock, were another exception that proved the rule: they tackled societal taboos, such as communism, drugs and in 'The American Way Of Love', a parallel between love and prostitution with one unusual image: 'Look around and see what the meat department has today/ And watch the queens do their thing... Late on an indiscreet encounter in the men's room/While you tell yourself that a natural urge prevailed.'

The Sixties: Gay Party Pop and the Rock'n'Roll Closet

If 'queen' was acceptable parlance in a rock song so was 'faggot', when it came from Arlo Guthrie, whose father Woody – godfather of modern folk music – had been introduced to radical politics by Mattachine founder Harry Hay and his actor-boyfriend Will Geer.[1] Arlo had grown up around gay men and the title track of his 1967 debut album *Alice's Restaurant* was an eighteen-minute anti-Vietnam war tract that suggested potential draft dodgers sing his song. What's more, 'if two people do it, in harmony/they may think they're both faggots and/They won't take either of them.'

Sodomy was even acknowledged in the title of a song from *Hair*, the first stage musical to document the new hippie culture. In a story laced with anti-Vietnam protest, drugs, nudity and sexual liberation – all together now: 'Sodomy, fellatio, cunnilingus, pederasty, father/Why do these words sound so nasty?', the character Woof admits he wouldn't kick Mick Jagger out of bed, though with the proviso, 'But, uh, I'm not a homosexual, no.' At least two other male characters in *Hair*, Claude and Berger, share a kiss....

The king and queen of the closet?

Rock music was brimming with rebels and declarations of sexual prowess, but not a single mainstream rock'n'roller had yet admitted to being even bisexual. What a difference it could have made if the revelations gleaned from posthumous biographies had been confessed at the time. Take Texan powerhouse Janis Joplin, who idolised Bessie Smith[2] for her gritty cathartic blues, and emulated the blues legend's attachment to both sexes. Smith expressed her fluidity, but Joplin only ever appeared enslaved to men. 'And when she gets lonely, she's thinking 'bout her man,' in 'A Woman Left Lonely' was

---

1 Geer narrated Woody Guthrie's prose in *Bound for Glory: The Songs and Story of Woody Guthrie*, on the Folkways label. Geer would later play the part of Grandpa on the long-running TV series *The Waltons*.

2 In 1970, shortly before her own death from a heroin overdose, Joplin paid for a headstone for Smith's unmarked grave, which read, 'The greatest blues singer in the world will never stop singing'.

typical, yet Joplin was clearly most affected, and undone, by her female lovers.

Sam Andrew, Joplin's bandmate in Big Brother and the Holding Company, the Kosmic Blues Band and Full Tilt Boogie, reckoned the singer was 'pan-sexual' but in the spirit of the times: 'There was [a] phrase at the time: if it moves, fondle it. That about sums it up.' However, Joplin biographer Alice Nichols[1] reported that five or six of Joplin's key lovers were women, among them Jae Whitaker and Peggy Caserta, who lasted longer than any man Joplin dated. Yet her presence was drastically dialled down in the 2015 Joplin film documentary *Janis: Little Girl Blue*, while a man (David Niehaus) was portrayed as the one who tried to save Janis from problems with alcohol and heroin and to get Caserta out of her system. It doesn't need much deduction to see being with men as Joplin's way of boosting her chronically low levels of self-esteem (when studying at the University of Texas at Austin, a fraternity voted her 'ugliest man on campus') and of being accepted.

Jim Fouratt, who first met Joplin in 1965 before working with her at Columbia Records, recalls, 'Around women, Janis was a very different person, sweet and flirtatious. And then around the guys, she acted like one of the guys.'

Joplin's combustible life was ended in 1970 by a heroin overdose; a year later, Jim Morrison, The Doors' rakish, priapic talisman, the self-appointed magus of LA's psychedelic scene, died the same way. Morrison's bisexuality is harder to prove as no male lover has emerged in the way that Caserta managed with her book *Going Down With Janis*. Jerry Hopkins and former Doors' manager Danny Sugarman's book *No One Gets Out Of Here Alive* (the base for Oliver Stone's film *The Doors*) pointedly avoided the subject, though admits that Morrison adored John Rechy's 1963 gay hustler novel *City Of Night*[2] (the title is

---

1 *Scars of Sweet Paradise: The Life and Times of Janis Joplin* (Metropolitan, 1999)
2 In the introduction to *City Of Night* (Grove Press, 1963), Rechy wrote, 'Before writing, I listened to music: Presley, Chuck Berry, Fats Domino . . . to absorb the dark, moody sexuality of rock.'

regularly repeated in the Doors' 1971 track 'LA Woman'), though the singer's appreciation might only have extended to Rechy's embracing of taboos. But a more recent biography, Stephen Davis's *Jim Morrison: Life, Death, Legend* reports the singer told his attorney Max Fink that 'a male hustler was leaving graphic, blackmailing phone messages that threatened to go public with details of Morrison's midnight ramblings in the gay underworld.'[1]

Davis also recounts a story told by the British singer Ian 'You Turn Me On' Whitcomb, who encountered Morrison in an LA coffee shop, dressed exactly like one of Rechy's hustlers and soaking up the attention.[2] Various girlfriends' claims that Morrison enjoyed anal sex most of all (The Doors covered Willie Dixon's 'Back Door Man') were also noted. Dissectors of his lyrics are generally on shaky ground, though blogger Jeffrey D.[3] cites 'The Soft Parade': 'There's only four ways to get unravelled/One is to love your neighbour 'till his wife gets home'.

It's an artist's prerogative to fantasise and elaborate and Morrison did love to provoke (see also the court case for his apparent cock-waving incident on stage in Miami). But there's always Jim Fouratt's first-hand account that he was hooked up with Morrison by a mutual acquaintance when The Doors first came through New York.[4] Eliott Tiber, who wrote a book about his role in the staging of the Woodstock festival, also said he fooled around with a stoned Morrison. 'Jim Morrison knew how to hide and compartmentalise his friends and didn't really care who sucked his dick as long as someone was sucking it,' wrote Stephen Davis.

Morrison seemed fixated on his penis, writing poems in celebration of it, though it was Seattle's most wanted, Jimi Hendrix, whose penis was immortalised in plaster by the groupie known as Cynthia 'Plaster

---

1 Gotham Press, 2004
2 *Jim Morrison: Life, Death, Legend* by Stephen Davis (Ebury, 2004)
3 http://everydayheterosexism.blogspot.co.uk/2013/10/jim-morrison-bisexual-poet-of-dark-side.html
4 'I was the lead in a play,' Fouratt recalls. The make-up person was this outrageous queen, he said, "You should meet Jim, he'll eat you up." Morrison was fucked up on drugs, alcohol . . . but he was hot in his leather pants and that snake dick of his.'

Caster' Albritton. Hendrix, whose blazing showmanship had been learnt in part from Little Richard (one of his mid-sixties employees), was an advocate of the guitar-as-penis-extension thrust and there is one lone voice – not Jim Fouratt this time, but US guitarist-songwriter Chris Robison – who swears that Hendrix was periodically sleeping with his young protégé Velvert Turner.

Independent of Robison, UK singer-songwriter Tom Robinson, a closeted seventeen-year-old when he saw Hendrix perform his hit single 'Purple Haze' on *Top of the Pops*, had also clocked something. 'There's the famous misheard lyric in "Purple Haze",' Robinson says, '"Acting funny and I don't know why/'Scuse me while I kiss *this guy* [the written lyric is 'the sky']". It's a cliché now – but it was gay folklore that Hendrix did look round at [drummer] Mitch Mitchell as he sang it. It's probably a myth, but then in 1967, gay teenage music fans like us were pretty desperate to find any tiny snippet at all that seemed to reflect and validate our own secret feelings.'[1]

Robinson also felt that even folk music hero Bob Dylan's 'Ballad of a Thin Man', from 1965. was 'a straight man blundering into a gay party': 'Well, the sword swallower, he comes up to you/And then he kneels, he crosses himself/And then he clicks his high heels/And without further notice, he asks you how it feels/And he says, "Here is your throat back/ Thanks for the loan".'

'Illegal drug use was widespread among musicians but could only be referred to obliquely in song,' says Robinson. 'Likewise, queer sexuality was a part of everyday life that artists tended to be coy and covert about, but which you could find if you picked up the signals.'

Desperate times meant desperate measures. Online scholars have found signals in the scantest of circumstances. UK folk-rocker Donovan's 1966 single 'To Try For The Sun' addressed his teenage friendship with sculptor Gyp Mills but, 'We slept on the breeze in the midnight ... And who's going to be the one/To say it was no good what we done?' has been

---

[1] Charles R. Cross's 2005 Hendrix biography *Room Full Of Mirrors* claims that the artist pretended to be gay to get out of the Vietnam draft.

read as sexual congress. Likewise 'I'm Tired' by the UK blues rock band Savoy Brown: 'I'm tired of trying to be something I know ain't me'. Some believe that the title character in Bobby Gentry's dusky country-pop classic 'Ode To Billie Joe' jumped off Tallahatchie bridge (having thrown something unspecified in the song: a wedding ring? An aborted baby?) because of his sexuality. The Beatles' 'Ob-La-Di, Ob-La-Da' had a ring of gender confusion when Desmond, rather than Molly 'stays at home and does his pretty face', though Paul McCartney claimed his line got switched by accident and he liked it that way. John Lennon's lyric for the band's 'Polythene Pam – 'So good-looking but she looks like a man/Well, you should see her in drag dressed in her polythene bag' – seems more like wordplay than an articulated comment on gender.

Like McCartney's explanation, Van Morrison claimed 'Madame George' was originally Madame Joy, but was mysteriously transmogrified when it appeared in 1968 on the Irishman's intense folk-jazz opus *Astral Weeks*. But what of the lyric, 'In the corner playing dominoes in drag/The one and only Madame George'?

Either way, writer Duncan Fallowell detects a queer spirit in the record: 'There's just something about it. Morrison was not part of the macho world, it's about dreaming, your hopes for yourself, about angst and young love.'

Another album from 1968, described online as 'the gay *Astral Weeks*' turns out to have been written by a man who didn't realise he was gay. Aged twenty-eight, Ed Askew, from Connecticut, had come out in late 1967 and met his first boyfriend in 1968, but *Ask The Unicorn* had been written from inside the closet, while Askew was still dating women. 'Perhaps it was unconscious,' he suggests. 'One song, "Peter And David", was about two boys at the school where I'd been teaching, who I thought made interesting characters. Maybe it sounded like they were in a relationship, without meaning to.'[1]

Like Askew, Janis Ian didn't know she was gay either when she wrote 'Society's Child' – but then she was fourteen at the time, 1965, two years

---

1 The one song Askew wrote at the time, regarding his first boyfriend Carl, 'What We Are', wasn't recorded until 2015: at https://edaskew.bandcamp.com/track/what-we-are

before it was a US no. 15 hit: Without realising, Ian's exquisite and brave interracial drama was 'one of these days I'm gonna raise my glistening wings and fly/But that day will have to wait for a while.'

'I got a lot of letters from drag queens after that song,' recalls Ian, who was to come out in the early nineties, 'and strippers, too. But I didn't think about sexuality when I wrote it.'

Sadly, the one song of the era to be unequivocably gay-themed was emerging Brit-folk rocker Al Stewart's 'Pretty Golden Hair'. In BBC footage from 1967, a narrator announces, 'These troubadours sing to win your love, for the outsider, the despised, the rejected. The outsider speaks for the outcast who cannot speak for himself,' leading in to Stewart's cautionary tale, in which a boy often mistaken for a girl moves to London and escapes the poverty trap via prostitution, before his looks and prospects fade: 'Now the living's hard to find/And early friends have vanished in the air/And the gay parties' ease/Changed to public lavatories/Have turned to grey his pretty golden hair.' The song ends with suicide, or as Stewart sang, 'murder by his pretty golden hair'.

If only there had been been the pop or rock equivalent to the nerveless antics of Indiana's modern classical composr Ned Rorem, who had adapted five Walt Whitman poems in 1957. Much more shocking was his 1966 memoir *The Paris Diary of Ned Rorem*[1] (documenting his years between 1951 and 1955), a groundbreaking, candid confession for the era. It included details of relationships with Leonard Bernstein and Noël Coward, whom he outed. His *New York Diary* (1956-1960) was equally unapologetic. Heroic or otherwise, Rorem was forcing people to acknowledge what most everyone else was frantically denying. His publisher Da Capo Press wrote: 'The diaries marked the beginnings of gay liberation, not because Rorem made a special issue of his sexuality, but because he did not; rather, he wrote of his affairs frankly and unashamedly.'

Jazz could have done with a Ned Rorem as well. After being diagnosed

---

1 Da Capo Books

with cancer in 1964, Billy Strayhorn died in 1967,[1] a prisoner of the times and his culture. It wasn't only Dizzy Gillespie who spouted homophobia. Writer James Gavin recalls interviewing a closeted saxophonist, then in his sixties, who summarised the persisting attitude: 'If you are gay you cannot be playing this music that requires you to have a much higher level of testosterone.'

A telling passage in comedian Richard Pryor's autobiography put Gillespie's comments into context. Pryor alleged that in 1968 he'd walked into trumpet supremo Miles Davis' dressing room and found him kissing Gillespie, 'with tongue and shit, which made me wonder what kind of shit he had planned for me.'[2] They wouldn't be the last people to bury their guilt by deflecting it on to others.

Gillespie's claim that there were no gay men in jazz was challenged first by Strayhorn, then pianist Cecil Taylor, who never publicly came out but was never in (though he refuted the label 'homosexual'). Both French jazz violinist Stéphane Grappelli and British composer, trumpeter and bassist Graham Collier, whose ensembles featured the cream of British players,[3] were out all their adult lives. But not in the US, the birthplace of jazz. In the 1971 memoir *The Night People*, written by Strayhorn's gay friend and fellow pianist Ralph Burns, he quotes gay jazz trombonist Dicky Wells regarding the topic of conversation on the Count Basie band tour bus: 'Chicks. What else?' The word 'fag' was a casual insult 'and if they wanted to be funny, they'd lisp. My one fear was that at one time or another they'd turn on me, but luckily they never did.'[4]

---

1 In *Duke Ellington's America*, (University of Chicago Press, 2010), the bandleader was quoted as praising Billie Strayhorn's 'four major moral freedoms': 'freedom from hate, unconditionally; freedom from self-pity (even through all the pain and bad news); freedom from fear of possibly doing something that might possibly help another more than it might himself and freedom from the kind of pride that might make a man think that he was better than his brother or his neighbour.'
2 *Pryor Convictions: And Other Life Sentences* (Pantheon Books, 1995)
3 'Britain's most original jazz talent', according to the *Financial Times*.
4 http://gayinfluence.blogspot.co.uk/2013/06/ralph-burns.html

BREAKING DOWN THE WALLS OF HEARTACHE

In the UK, Collier was joined by jazz and blues singer George Melly who later admitted he enjoyed lean, androgynous creatures of both genders, though his preference for men in his youth[1] gave way to women as he grew older. Like Melly, John William Baldry – known as Long John Baldry on account of his height (six foot seven inches) – never hid his sexuality from family, friends and band mates. Both men appeared at the Eel Pie Island hotel, one of London's most important blues venues (future Rolling Stones were also schooled there), but ten years apart.

Baldry soon had his own blues-rock band, the Hoochie Coochie Men, whose co-singer he'd discovered busking, Rod Stewart. Baldry could spot talent; his next band, Bluesology, featured pianist Reginald Dwight and saxophonist Elton Dean. When Dwight decided to go solo, he took a stage name borrowed from his band mates, Elton John.

In Paul Myers' biography of Baldry, future gay icon and fund-raising activist Sir Elton John admitted that he was so closeted at the time that he didn't even recognise Baldry's homosexuality: 'Looking back on it now,' he said, 'John couldn't have been any more gay than if he'd tried.'[2] By every account, Baldry was at ease with his sexuality, although also a persistent heavy drinker, often a compensation for inner torment. Not that Baldry's first hit single 'Let The Heartaches Begin' was connected. Word that Baldry fancied a stab at a pop song had reached songwriter Tony Maculay, who'd been searching for the kind of powerful, gruff presence that Baldry commanded. Inspired by a bottle of Courvoisier brandy, Baldry soared through the stirring, if syrupy, big ballad and by November he was the first gay artist to have a UK no. 1.

---

1 Jazz/blues chronicler Chris Albertson recalls being taken to an all-night jazz party in 1953. 'We entered a small second-storey flat where shadowy figures lined the dark room. Bruce Turner and Johnny Parker were playing a deadly slow blues while two scantily clad, cigar-smoking ladies performed bizarre movements in and around a dining room chair. Their movements were in sync with a weird narrative from a man who waved his arms in the smoke-filled air as if conducting. It was George Melly, I later learned and when he heard that I was Danish, he looked me up and down. "I bet he has lovely legs," he said. "Danish tennis players have lovely legs."'
2 *It Ain't Easy: Long John Baldry and the Birth of the British Blues* (Greystone Books, 2007)

Breaking down the walls of heartache

By this time the walls of heartache behind which gay British men lived had finally been shaken. In 1964, the North-Western Homosexual Law Reform Committee (whose membership was predominantly heterosexual) and the London-based Homosexual Law Reform Society campaigned for the Wolfenden Report's recommendation to decriminalise sex between men. 1967 was a seismic year for the sexual revolution. The contraceptive pill – prescribed for married women in Britain in 1961 – was finally available for all, abortion was legalised, further freeing up women's choice and, under a Labour (socialist) government, the Sexual Offences Act of July 1967 decriminalised sodomy and the crime of gross indecency between men in England and Wales[1] if both were over the age of twenty-one and they were in private – meaning the freedom was limited to two men at a time.

The heterosexual age of consent was sixteen, so the change in law remained a compromise, but it changed people's lives. Yet the secrecy, battened down by decades of guilt and fear, would mean no sudden defiant statement of pride in line with Nina Simone's 'To Be Young, Gifted and Black' to reinforce the on-going push for civil rights or even a race-related lament such as 'I Wish I Knew How it Would Feel to be Free'.

Long John Baldry wasn't a songwriter and, in any case, he wasn't about to draw attention to the way he was hiding in plain sight by singing about love for a man. His pop star eligibility was also undermined by his lack of – and inability to cultivate – the necessary female fan base. The cover of his 1968 album *Long John Baldry and the Hoochie Coochie Men* tried valiantly on his behalf by surrounding the singer with bikini-clad models: the Sexual Offences Act wasn't going to change anything or anyone overnight.

Where else could the gay music lover turn toward the end of the sixties? Even cabaret was a moribund scene, losing its cachet of cool after the vibrant forties and fifties as the new pop had risen up. But a new

---

[1] Scotland followed in 1980 and Northern Ireland in 1982.

style of cabaret, which mutated with pop, was taking shape and Rod McKuen was one of the key instigators.

The French connection

In part, McKuen was still stuck in the fifties. Like an alternative Liberace, his soft-focus art had a very mainstream and female-based fanbase; not a single gay man canvassed for this book about their musical influences mentioned McKuen. But Frank Sinatra was a fan and commissioned an album of McKuen pieces for his 1969 album *A Man Alone*, where the title track, 'Night' and 'The Beautiful Strangers' prolonged McKuen's lonesome nocturnal tropes. 1970's *Rock Hudson Sings the Songs of Rod McKuen*, the closeted Hollywood actor's first recording since 'Pillow Talk', a 1959 duet with Doris Day and just as camp, confirmed at least one gay man was responding to McKuen.

McKuen's easy-listening brand of introspection didn't mean he lacked ambition and he temporarily moved to France in 1964, drawn by the caustic and lusty stories of Belgian singer-songwriter Jacques Brel, whose French lyrics McKuen began to translate for his own use. He still played it safe, as a mainstream artist might, by avoiding Brel's more sexually charged works, preferring sentimental cliché for 'Seasons In The Sun' and 'If You Go Away', which worked commercially as they became Brel's most-covered songs.

It was left to US lyricist Mort Shulman (formerly half of a dynamite song-writing partnership in fifties rock'n'roll with Doc Pomus) to tackle Brel's provocative side. First came 1968's off-Broadway production *Jacques Brel is Alive and Well and Living in Paris*, which included 'Next' and 'Jackie'. By all accounts, Brel was homophobic but included homosexuals in his cast of society's rejects among the whores, pimps and drunks. In the squalid army life of 'Next', Shulman translated Brel's observations as, 'Now I always will recall/The brothel truck, the flying flags/the queer lieutenant who slapped our asses as if we were fags' – and the reference in the self-referencing 'Jackie' as, 'authentic queers and phony virgins'.

The Sixties: Gay Party Pop and the Rock'n'Roll Closet

Scott Walker, born Scott Engel, the core voice of mid-sixties US giants the Walker Brothers, before going solo in 1967, made it his mission to popularise Brel after Andrew Loog Oldham introduced him. His first three solo albums (*Scott 1, 2* and *3*, released between 1967 and 1969) included nine Brel covers, including 'Next' and 'Jackie'. The latter was even released as a single, though the BBC wouldn't allow its listeners the pleasure of authentic queers and phony virgins. But the rival channel ITV had no issue and Walker sang 'Jackie' on the popular *Frankie Howerd Show*, fronted by the closeted – yet quintessentially camp – comedian, who might have blanched – or been secretly delighted – at the word 'queer' sung loudly on his show.

Walker was equally inspired to write vignettes of the lost and downtrodden, such as the transgender lament 'Big Louise' ('She's a haunted house/And her windows are broken/And the sad young man's gone away') and a rent boy's farewell note to a sugar daddy in 'Thanks for Chicago Mr James'.

There were more converts to the cause; David Bowie – then in his folk-singing phase covered 'Next' as part of a Brel trilogy. Bob Crewe was familiar with Brel through McKuen's work and helped inspire an album that exchanged Crewe's trademark pop acumen for an elaborate folly.

1967's *What Now My Love* was the solo album debut by Mick Ryder, born William S. Levise in Michigan. Ryder fronted Billy Lee and the Rivieras, tapping fifties rock'n'roll and sixties' soul. Like Dusty Springfield, his voice was often mistaken for black. Crewe had signed the band to his new Dyno-Voice label and renamed them Mitch Ryder and the Detroit Wheels; with their dynamic comprising Brit invasion and Motown pop, the band were the first, 'blue-eyed soul' act.

But Crewe saw Ryder as a Las Vegas act, as he had Frankie Valli and created an album of gilded, chocolate-box orchestrations, like an entire record of Long John Baldry's 'Let The Heartache Begin'. Crewe would have recommended Ryder's cover of 'If You Go Away', but it's uncertain who imagined a take on female trio the Jaylettes' 1963 US hit 'Sally

Go 'Round The Roses', which began with Ryder hollering, 'Here it is, almost 1968 and you still ain't straight!'

According to Ryder's 2011 autobiography, he'd been married but was still haunted by an incident in his youth, when the singer was 'made the prey of a soft-spoken and gentle (and older) homosexual', who had led him astray and also must have forced his pen to change the original hook of 'Sally Go 'Round The Roses' from 'The saddest thing in the whole wide world/See your baby with another girl' to 'The saddest thing in the whole wide world/Love a guy who loves another girl.'

Crewe wasn't the only gay producer in pop, just the only one to facilitate a frisson of gay love. The closeted married producer, arranger and occasional bandleader Curt Boettcher, who was largely responsible for the genre known as sunshine pop, sublimated everything in happy harmonies and pocket pop symphonies. Other gay men found employment on the business side of music, such as Jim Fouratt, who'd escaped the intended salvation of seminary life for San Francisco's beatnik boom before moving to New York where he co-founded the counter-cultural Youth International Party (a.k.a. The Yippies), which organised the hippie coming out party, 1967's 'Be-In' gathering in Central Park.

Fouratt also took the chance to work from the inside when Clive Davis, the new head of Columbia, offered him the post of artist liaison, or 'house hippie', as Fourratt calls it. Two similar house hippies at prominent labels, Danny Fields at Elektra and Billy James at Warners, were also gay. Fouratt was responsible for artists as disparate as Janis Joplin, Bob Dylan, Miles Davis, Simon and Garfunkel, the Byrds, Sly Stone and Laura Nyro; but only the last of this epic list was to write a song that lesbians, starved of validation, could finally cling to as one of their own.

Ladies only

Laura Nyro is less of a feted name than Joni Mitchell, who is widely accepted to be the mother of modern singer-songwriters, as Bob Dylan is the father. Yet Mitchell admitted to taking cues from Nyro's arrangements and the latter was every inch her melodic equal. While Mitchell was rooted in California's grassy canyons, Nyro was drawing on the soul, R&B and doo wop of New York, growing up in the multi-cultural Bronx. Born Laura Nigro, of Catholic Italian and Jewish-American descent, Nyro's soaring, plangent voice sounded even more soulful than Dusty Springfield, while her songs embraced Brill Building pop, R&B swing, intoxicating soul, folky introspection, jazzy cadences (years before Mitchell got there) and Broadway-influenced show tunes, saturated with poetic longing. She was groundbreaking and complex, but commercially on the money too, writing hits for The 5th Dimension, Three Dog Night, Blood, Sweat and Tears, Peter, Paul and Mary and Barbra Streisand, while unable to hit the charts with her versions. Nyro was too intense and brooding and her gothic brand of hippie fashion clashed with the bright hippie stylings and patched denim.

Nyro also mined a brand of anguish far removed from her peers. On her 1968 debut for Columbia, *Eli and the Thirteenth Confession*, 'Emmie' was, by all appearances, a love song to another woman. This is disputed by the late Nyro's family, who maintain she believed the lyric addressed 'the cycle of a girl becoming a woman and here, Laura the young woman lyrically coddles and longs for, but ultimately bids goodbye to the fading innocence of her girlhood.' The family cite the photo on the back cover, a silhouette of, 'a mature Laura sweetly kissing the forehead of the representation of Laura the girl.'[1]

At the time, Nyro's boyfriend was her manager, the equally closeted David Geffen, but the prosecution will point to the fact that Nyro lived her last eighteen years with her younger lover, Maria Desiderio and to the lyrics to 'Emmie' such as, 'Touch me, oh, wake me ... Move me, oh, sway me/Emily you ornament the earth for me' and 'Who stole Mama's heart/And cuddled in her garden?' Then there is the Italian concept of *'flamma'* meaning flame or crush; an intimate friendship between an older and younger woman.

'Something about the way she sang "Emmie" and the subject matter

---

1 http://lgbt.wikia.com/wiki/Emmie_%28Laura_Nyro_song%29

and her introspection, it was clearly a love song,' reckons Leslie Ann Jones, director of music recording and scoring at George Lucas' Skywalker Sound. '"Emmie" had such tender and emotional lyrics, she had to have feelings for women,' adds singer-songwriter Marsha Malamet. 'A short time later, mutual friends confirmed it, though for years no one ever said that Laura came out.'

Neither did Malamet come out at first, not until the mid-seventies. In the late sixties, her blend of R&B and Broadway, of Nyro and Streisand, on her debut album for Decca, *Coney Island Winter*, hinted at the perils of the closet; even though the lyrics weren't hers – 'Other people wanted to write for me, I didn't think about it,' she says. She thinks one of the three male lyricists involved, Larry Abelove, tapped into her secret on the album's lead single 'I Don't Dare'. 'I think Larry had a crush on me, that was his underlying excitement,' Malamet recalls. 'But everything he wrote for me was about my life, this bittersweet cry, this need, this dream of being somewhere else other than where I am. Being unhappy colours your world.'

If Nyro, Malamet and Springfield didn't disclose the truth, it was left to the mid-sixties poppet Polly Perkins. She and her manager Lena Davis, who had organised Perkins' pop career and string of singles, openly lived together and, in 1969, Davis wrote most of the lyrics for an album of pastel-shaded, lightly jazzy songs under the title *Pop-Lore According to the Academy*. Perkins took most of the lead vocals, though fellow gay singer Damon J. Hardy also joined in. Davis' Jewish roots inspired the Holocaust saga 'Yellow Star' while two tracks embraced sex and gender: 'Girls In The Mirror' is a late contender for Best Cross-Dressing Song of the Sixties and 'Polly Perkins Loves Georgia Brown' was a clear lesbian love song. Perkins says she's unsure if 'Munching The Candy' also qualified but admits that 'it was written by two dykes'. Case closed.

For the 'L' word to find its way into a twentieth century song, trust a German band to put the word out. As in the UK, the split East and West Germany had only just decriminalised homosexuality (1968 and

1969 respectively) and, judging by the stills, the 1969 film comedy *Engelchen Macht Weiter – Hoppe Hoppe Reiter* (retitled in English *Up The Establishment*) was a sexy romp with both hetero and bi swingers. One track, the pop-psychedelic 'Leave This Lesbian World', written and performed in English by Nuremburg's Improved Sound Ltd, was a baffling addition: 'You suffer from that rape/Girl, blot out the tape/ Leave this lesbian world/Leave the things that break your heart.' Surely the victim would want to *join* the lesbian world and leave the world of men. And how was rape a topic for a comedy?

There's a riot going on

Minette, one of the drag performers of the late forties and early fifties, had lived through it all. After she'd been forced to leave Boston after its drag venues were shut down, Minette resettled in New York. She'd kept busy on stage and writing her own parodies, such as remodelling 'The Lady In Red' as 'The Lezzie In Red' ('The lezzie in red is driving her taxi/When the town should be dead . . . Just like a fairy, she likes her vice versa/She's a pansy without a stem') and acting in experimental films made by cult photographer Avery Willard, short, silent eight-mm dramas alongside a cast of other queens.

It's at this point in her autobiography *Recollections of a Part-Time Lady*[1], that Minette discovered LSD and experienced an epiphany. 'On that trip,' she wrote, 'I said to myself, "Kid, all your life, jobs have been dying out from under you. Burlesque. Vaudeville. Nightclubs. Everything died out." And I said, "Why go to Morocco? Morocco has come to me." See, you'd go over to the *kasbah* – that's what I call the section of Tompkins Square – and you'd think you were in Morocco. All these hippies and these freaky fabulous people. It was the only time I was ever in style – I had always been ten years ahead and twenty years behind.'

Minette continued to write songs and in 1968 released an album for the

---

1 She never had surgery but preferred female clothing and pronouns.

label Collectors Choice. *Come To Me at Tea Time* was the first record by a drag queen that didn't depend on comedy, parody or innuendo. Her louche drawl bore hallmarks of cabaret and lounge style, backed by ragtime-style piano fronting a rickety bar band, but the arrangements bordered on the psychedelic, while several lyrics were clearly lysergic in origin, such as 'Minette's 69th Trip', 'On a Psychedelic Astro-Flight' and 'The Hot Hippie Rag'. But Minette got serious too, as on the Vietnam-inspired 'Hey, Hey, LBJ [a.k.a. President Lyndon B. Johnson], How Many Kids Did You Kill Today?' and 'LBJ, Don't Take My Man Away'. Only 'Hello, Big Boy' and the title track accentuated the camp, but 'Revolutionary Blues' was far more typical.

Come To Me at Tea Time might sound as if it was recorded in a nightclub after the punters had gone home and the entertainers were winding down, but it has its own unique atmosphere with the mixture of political and personal. But as usual, it would have had very limited pressing (one record collectors' site in 2009 claimed only four known copies are in existence, one copy fetching $1272 when sold in 2012[1]), distribution and promotion. It wasn't helped by the album title suggesting it was more of a traditional drag-queen record.

By the time she'd made her album, Minette had also sung in *The Queen*, the 1969 documentary of Flawless Sabrina's travelling drag pageant. Filmed in 1967, its tenth year of competition, the regional competitions culminated in a national final, which was being held in New York. Andy Warhol and Truman Capote were among the judges; Warhol had helped secure funding for the documentary, one of the earliest screen depictions of female impersonators – some of whom identified as gay, others as transgender who couldn't yet afford the necessary operation.

Unsurprisingly, the pageant was staged in secret and the air of glamour in *The Queen* was undercut by its resilience and sadness. The song chosen for Minette to sing as the contestants paraded in their swimsuits was 'Am I Blue', a song she'd mastered as a child when impersonating

---

1 http://collectorsfrenzy.com/details/190307916023/MINETTE_COME_TO_ME_AT_TEATIME_LP_WEIRD_VERY_RARE_PSYCH

Ethel Waters and later popularised by Dinah Washington. This was still not a time to sing of pride or freedom. Bars were still raided and gay lives marginalised. Sabrina lost count of the times she'd been arrested for cross-dressing.

'"Am I Blue" was an indelible signature tune to my spirit,' she says today, forty-seven years after *The Queen* was released. 'Maybe it was a reminder that we are all mortal, lest one be too jovial and campy about stuff, the realisation that it wasn't an easy life. A little taste of bitter weed.'

Revolution

By the time *The Queen* was showing in a very select number of cinemas, the old social and moral order surrounding homosexuality and gender was beginning to wobble as it had in the UK. In 1965, ten people drawn from the Mattachine and Daughters of Bilitis had staged the first gay and lesbian protest outside the White House. In 1966, Mattachine staged a 'Sip-In' protest against the State Liquor Authority's regulation against serving drinks to homosexuals; members were instructed to enter the Greenwich Village gay bar Julius (which had only just been raided), declare they were gay and order a drink. If they were turned away, the bar's owners would be sued.

In 1966 too, Compton's Cafeteria in San Francisco's Tenderloin district was picketed by its transgender and rent boy customers, in the first recorded resistance by what the police called the 'homophile community'. Many were members of Vanguard, the country's first known gay youth organisation. Windows were smashed and policemen tussled with, but there was a positive outcome as bar raids and police harassment declined.

The year 1967 witnessed the opening of New York's Oscar Wilde bookshop, the first in the world dedicated to gay authors; Columbia University's Student Homophile League, the country's first recognised gay student group; San Francisco's earliest organisation for bisexuals, the Sexual Freedom League and Argentina's *Nuestro Mundo* (meaning 'our world'), the first Latino-American homosexual group. Despite all the advances and the Sip-In, gay bars were still harassed and places threatened with closure.

One night – 28 June 1969, to be precise – the police turned up at New York's Stonewall Inn on Christopher Street in the West Village, claiming that liquor was being sold illegally.

Like most of New York's gay venues, the Stonewall was Mafia-owned and its existence dependent on police bribes. The bar had managed to survive where rivals such as the Snake Pit, the Sewer, the Checkerboard and the Tele Star had folded, for reasons probably only recorded in contemporary police files. Unlike its rivals, the Stonewall had a dancefloor, with a prized jukebox and an atmosphere closer to a club than a bar. It also had a mixed-age crowd (according to Martin Duberman's *Stonewall*,[1] from late teens to early thirties, while the mid-thirties crowd drank at Julius) and 'the poorest and most marginalised people in the gay community: drag queens, transgender people, effeminate young men, butch lesbians, male prostitutes and homeless youth' according to another source.[2] It was a potentially volatile mix of people who felt they had little to lose.

Much of what happened that night at the Stonewall is impossible to ratify, including who was there or even the chronology of events as presented in David Carter's authoritative gathering of eyewitness accounts.[3] What is known is that the police had forgotten to give the owners prior warning of a raid, as was usual, which meant a full crowd was in that night. The usual order for patrons to line up and provide identification and for transvestites to undergo 'anatomical inspections' were met with an unusually violent resistance, but what came next? Police officer Gil Weissman's injury? The arrest of the folk-singing political activist Dave Van Ronk, who'd been alerted to the furore? The retreat of the police inside the bar, setting off the crowd that had gathered outside?

---

1 Dutton (1993)
2 https://en.wikipedia.org/wiki/Stonewall_riots
3 *An Analytical Collation of Accounts and Documents Recorded in the Year 1969 Concerning the Stonewall Riots*, www.davidcarterauthor.com

The Sixties: Gay Party Pop and the Rock'n'Roll Closet

It's also impossible to know which song was on the jukebox at the moment that the police waded through. Like London's Le Duce, Motown ruled at the Stonewall, including the most-played song of the moment, Diana Ross and the Supremes' 'No Matter What Sign You Are (You're Gonna Be Mine You Are)' and its dreamy B-side 'The Young Folk'. Substitute the word 'gay' for 'young' and you had a new anthem in the making: 'Here they come, looking so alive/They're here for business but it's all none of your jive/Brighter tomorrows are in their eyes/You'd better make way for the gay folks.'

There was room too for the androgynous tone of Chris Montez's tropical smooch 'The More I See You' and various show tunes for intimate, camp moments – Frank Sinatra's 'My Way', Henry Mancini's 'Theme from *Romeo and Juliet*', Barbra Streisand with Jerry Herman on 'Before The Parade Passes By' from the musical *Hello Dolly!*, but also Harry Nilsson's 'Everybody's Talking', the wistful theme from the acclaimed hustler drama *Midnight Cowboy*, another sombre depiction of troubled lives in New York.

It's believed that the jukebox didn't feature any Judy Garland, whose funeral had been held earlier that day. The singer had died on 22 June, a day of mourning; the recording of Garland's 1963 concert at New York's Carnegie Hall was one album arguably found in any gay man's collection.[1] But that largely white-collar, white fan base wasn't typical of the Stonewall crowd and the theory that Garland's death triggered the fight-back has been widely discounted. Instead, perhaps the trigger point was the police entering as Jerry Butler's 'Only The Strong Survive' was on the jukebox or Sly and the Family Stone's euphoric 'Stand' (he'd yet to write 'There's A Riot Goin' On') with its definitive, defiant message of pride: 'Stand for the things you know are right/It's the truth that the truth makes them so uptight.'

Or 'This Is My Life' sung by Welsh gay favourite Shirley Bassey:

---

[1] John Waters recalls attending a Garland show in the gay haven of Provincetown: 'It was like a gay Beatles concert, like the miracle scene in Fellini's *La Dolce Vita*, people running everywhere and falling down.'

'Today, tomorrow, love will come and find me/But that's the way that I was born to be.'

Sonny Charles and the Checkmates' gorgeous soul ballad 'Black Pearl' would have been perfect for the black drag queens, such as Sylvia Rivera and Marsha P. Johnson, who came to symbolise the strength and community of the resistance: 'Black pearl, pretty little girl/Let me put you back where you belong . . . You've been in the background much too long.' Co-writer Toni Wine said that 'Black Pearl' was inspired by 'the very difficult times. It was disturbing, everything that was going on at that time between people. All of our people. And segregation, differences.'[1]

One woman that everyone knows was present was Stormé DeLarverie, from New Orleans, who had joined the travelling Jewel Box in 1955 and become the revue's singing MC and only male impersonator in the production of *Twenty-five Men And A Girl*. DeLarverie had left the revue only two months earlier, to work, of all things, as a nightclub bodyguard. She was handcuffed and put in the waiting police wagon, only to escape more than once as the action escalated. DeLarverie apparently fuelled the fire by shouting at bystanders, 'Why don't you guys do something?' When one drag queen started rocking a police car so that it began to tip over, the blue touchpaper was lit.

David Carter's findings were summarised in *The Atlantic*[2] magazine: the conflict spilled over the next six nights and 'played out as a very gay variant of a classic New York street rebellion'. There was even a musical soundtrack of sorts. 'It would see fire hoses turned on people in the street, thrown barricades, gay cheerleaders chanting bawdy variants of New York City schoolgirl songs, Rockette-style kick lines in front of the police, the throwing of a firebomb into the bar, a police officer throwing

---

[1] http://www.songfacts.com/detail.php?id=7961. But maybe the songwriter had known of 1968's Black Pearl International Awards, a drag ball of colour held at Washington DC's Hilton hotel.

[2] http://www.theatlantic.com/politics/archive/2013/01/an-amazing-1969-account-of-the-stonewall-uprising/272467/

his gun at the mob, cries of "Occupy – take over, take over", "Fag power", "Liberate the bar!" and "We're the pink panthers!", smashed windows, uprooted parking meters, thrown pennies, frightened policemen, angry policemen, arrested mafiosi, thrown cobblestones, thrown bottles, the singing of "We Shall Overcome" in high camp fashion and a drag queen hitting a police officer on the head with her purse.'

The Rockette-style kick line was to the tune of the old playground chant, rewritten for the occasion: 'We are the Chelsea girls/We wear our hair in curls/we wear our dungarees/above our nelly knees'[1] The sound of defiance and camp celebration was met by reports of rock music, blaring from a burnt-out room inside the Stonewall as it tried to reopen for business.

There's an art riot going on

Coming up from Atlanta, Wayne – later, Jayne – Rogers had also found the Stonewall, hearing the Supremes and The Doors on the jukebox 'and everyone danced the boogaloo and the shingaling, which were the big dances that year,'[2] according to her autobiography. Back home, Rogers had been one of a pack of 'screaming queens who'd enjoy nothing so much as "wrecking" people by catty intimidation.' They'd also gather for 'gay parties' or in bars such as the Catacombs, where they'd don wigs and mime. Rogers recalls choosing Cher, Dusty Springfield and Janis Joplin for his Catacombs debut: 'Most of the younger queens did the Supremes, while the older ones did Judy Garland.' But when some locals started firing pistols at him and his friend Miss Davina Daisy, Rogers got on a Greyhound bus and was gone.

In New York, he discovered, 'a lot of the hippies thought drag queens were cool . . . they just saw you as someone who was experimenting with

---

[1] A later version went: 'We are the Stonewall Girls, we wear our hair in curls/We always dress with flair, we wear clean underwear/We wear our dungarees, above our nelly knees/We ain't no wannabees, we pay our Stonewall fees!'
[2] From *Man Enough to be A Woman*, Jayne County with Rupert Smith (Serpent's Tail, 1995)

different ways of living your life.' He'd got talking to a young man on a Christopher Street stoop, by the name of Leee (with three 'e's) Childers, who offered Rogers the chance to move into his East Village apartment. The pair spent time at the Sewer, a hangout for Charles Ludlam's Ridiculous Theatrical Company, 'the hippest underground group in town and for a lot of drag queens'. Ludlam had started his company after a disagreement with the founders of Playhouse of the Ridiculous, where he worked as a director.

The Playhouse had been inspired by the 'theatre of the ridiculous', a phrase created by Ronald Tavel to describe his own books, after Martin Esslin's Theatre of the Absurd, a theatrical movement based on man's reaction to a world without meaning. It included works by literary heavyweights Samuel Beckett and Harold Pinter. But Tavel – who Warhol had employed as a screenwriter – was keener on another kind of absurdity, parodies of popular culture with limitless opportunities for over-the-top costumes, speeches and themes. A feature of every production was cross-dressing and gender confusion.

Ludlam freely ran with the concept; some productions had musical connotations, such as *Corn*, a country-and-western musical 'for the whole family' or *The Life Of Lady Godiva*, starring Jackie Curtis (born John Curtis Holder), a transgressive vision in ripped dresses, recycled curtains and crudely applied make-up. 'Jackie had to come out and sing hymns,'[1] recalled Rogers, while the Lady Godiva character 'had sex with a wooden horse. I didn't know whether to laugh or scream or what.' In another Ludlam production, *Heaven Grand in Amber Orbit*, 'these characters appeared in the lobby covered in glitter, singing a song called "Thalidomide Baby" . . . We were astounded.'

Minette also joined the Ridiculous Theatre alongside Holly Woodlawn, born Haroldo Danhakl in Puerto Rico. Curtis, Woodlawn

---

[1] Curtis sang in most of her productions but the only evidence of any recordings is four songs from 1968, written by Paul Serrato and from various stage productions featuring Curtis, such as *Vain Victory*. The tracks remained unreleased until a 2004 CD came out entitled *Who Are You?*, on X-Centric Records.

and the similarly transgender figure of Candy Darling (born James Lawrence Slattery) all graduated to Andy Warhol's inner circle as his coterie of 'superstars' in residence at his HQ, the Factory, and they populated his films too, such as *Flesh* and *Trash*. These underground legends-in-the-making made a second home in the invite-only back room of Max's Kansas City. The nightclub and restaurant on Park Avenue and Eighteenth Street was a few blocks from Warhol's second Factory location and away from the Village bars, the Mafia and the police. 'Max's was the place where all the different scenes crossed and merged,' Rogers recalled. 'The gay scene, the drug scene, the theatre scene, the music scene, the art scene.'

Having given New York a wide berth for three years, the Velvet Underground had begun playing at Max's upstairs room. Though Lou Reed had fired Warhol as their manager, the band were still treated as Factory family. The opening song on 1969's self-titled third album was the twilight ballad 'Candy Says', inspired by Candy Darling – 'Candy says I've come to hate my body and all that it requires in this world,' a reference to transgender identity, which the world outside didn't recognise unless surgery was involved. 'Some Kinda Love' was another quest for freedom: 'And some kinds of love, the possibilities are endless/And for me to miss one would seem to be groundless.'

In San Francisco, a similar explosion of gender and sexual fluidity, tied up in an artful bow of theatrical absurdity, was unfolding. Raised in Clearwater Beach, Florida, George Harris had started a children's theatre, the El Dorado Players, with his siblings and after his family moved to New York in 1964, he'd worked as an actor before following his new boyfriend Irving Rosenthal to the Bay area, and the forty-member vegetarian Friends of Perfection commune, based in hippie-central Haight-Ashbury, one of the hundreds of communal spaces that had sprung up as flower power gripped the city. Taking the name Hibiscus, he moved out of the socially-minded Friends of Perfection and started a new commune whose members were keener on dressing up and taking drugs. He'd spend days 'in Golden Gate Park, sitting naked in the trees, singing show tunes,'[1] such as the *Show Boat* standard 'Can't Help Lovin' Dat Man'.

Hibiscus reckoned the commune's members should take to the stage and after being invited to perform at the Nocturnal Dream Show, a showcase of underground films, the commune formed a theatrical troupe, which took the name of the Cockettes, a gay male version of the Rockettes. 'Originally it was nine gay men, four women, and an infant,' says founder member Rumi Missabu (born James Bartlett). 'The ranks swelled to sixty-five.'

The adult founders – 'brought together by Hibiscus' charisma' – raided the storeroom of clothes, transforming the Cockettes into an explosion of vintage dresses (many purchased from MGM Studios' sale clearance), sequins and costume jewellery. Fellow Cockette, Reggie, described bearded Hibiscus as, 'Jesus Christ, with lipstick.'

These 'bearded, transvestite, drug-crazed hippie Communists,' as John Waters described them or, as Missabu recalls, 'The Little Rascals in drag doing Busby Berkeley on acid!', made their stage debut on New Year's Eve 1969, doing a can-can dance to the Rolling Stones' latest single 'Honky Tonk Women'. On the US and UK no. 1, Mick Jagger sung about, 'a gin soaked bar-room queen in Memphis,' but it's likely 99 per cent of its purchasers thought of a Tina Turner type, just as they did of their 1971 single 'Brown Sugar'.

The Cockettes' debut took place just twenty-five days after the Altamont Festival, held roughly fifty-five miles west of San Francisco, where one of the crowd was stabbed to death by a member of the Hell's Angel security team during the Stones' headline set. 'The sixties were over,' was Jim Fouratt's verdict. 'The drug culture had triumphed.'

Heroin had not yet claimed Hendrix, Morrison and Joplin. But the acid-infused Cockettes and the equally trashed Ridiculous happening in New York had showed a spirited and peace-loving surge of creativity on very limited resources, something no police raid or existing law could

---

[1] *The Hidden 1970s: Histories of Radicalism*, Dan Berger, ed. (Rutgers University Press, 2010)

hold back. There was a resurgence of direct action too. Jayne County recalls talking after the Stonewall uprising to 'this very straight hippy' about how 'everyone had been yelling for gay power. "That'll never happen," he said. "Fags can never get organised."' But on the third day of Stonewall, the Gay Liberation Front (GLF) was formed, followed just before Christmas by the Gay Activists Alliance (GAA), started by dissident GLF members, including Sylvia Rivera and Marsha P. Johnson, aiming to 'secure basic human rights, dignity and freedom for all gay people.'[1] The Mattachine model of assimilation had been an essential entry point; now a blunter, defiant model of resistance was called for.

The same month as Stonewall, yet another cover parody of 'Big Bad John' was released by Steve Greenberg, titled after the Country Gentlemen's 1966 version 'Big Bruce'. Sticks and stones wouldn't work anymore; it was time for pride, not shame.

It wasn't going to be easy, not when Dr David Ruben's 1969 manual *Everything You Always Wanted to Know About Sex* (*But Were Afraid to Ask)*, the most popular non-fiction book of its time with over a hundred million copies sold, described gay men as 'pathetic psychopaths who hung out in public restrooms writing lurid notes to each other on toilet paper... If a homosexual who wants to renounce homosexuality finds a psychiatrist who knows how to cure homosexuality, he has every chance of becoming a happy, well-adjusted heterosexual.'

In October, *Time* magazine debated the issue in 'Behaviour – a discussion: are homosexuals sick?' following a public symposium in New York with eight experts, including an anthropologist, sociologist, psychologist and 'two admitted homosexuals'. It had been eight years since the TV documentary *The Rejected* followed the exact same format. The magazine subsequently printed a reader's letter from Zebedy Colt, the stage name of Edward Earle Marsh: 'Sir: I am a homosexual. I am also happy as a homosexual (though this society does not make that very easy), and I reject the implications that I have an "undesirable handicap"

---

1 *The politics of homosexuality: how lesbians and gay men have made themselves a political and social force in modern America*, Toby Marotta (Houghton Mifflin, 1981)

– for it is not my homosexuality, but rather society's insane reaction to it, that is the undesirable handicap. More than a homosexual, I am a person: a person with most of the same goals in life and needs from life that heterosexuals have.' Homosexuality was, Colt argued, 'becoming more and more a part of the mainstream'.

An actor with a bombastic voice that suited ballads, Colt had covered 'Green Carnations' on *Ben Bagley's Nöel Coward Revisited*, one of a series of album tributes organised by theatre producer Bagley. Colt's letter to *Time* was printed just as he'd released his own record, *I'll Sing For You*, which embodied the humane values his letter argued for – love, desire, companionship, equality. Colt's album was that old chestnut, built on standards – Gershwin's 'The Man I Love', Rodgers and Hammerstein's 'I'm In Love with a Wonderful Guy', Billy Strayhorn's 'Lush Life' – sprinkled with originals such as 'Michael' ('he's mine for the taking, I'm so happy at last').

I'll Sing For You was mainstream, smothered in orchestrations to suit Colt's delivery, as if he was standing at the top of a mountain, Julie Andrews-style. But Colt and his label Ecco Productions weren't targeting the Broadway queens. 'The first gay superstar on long playing records,' announced a press advert in both *SCREW* magazine and New York's *Village Voice*, with a carefully cropped pornographic photograph, presumably of Colt.[1] 'Zebedy Colt is for those who love boys, Turkish baths, trade, gang bangs, loners, football games, truck drivers and just plain MASCULINITY . . . Buy it not because it's GAY. Because it's GOOD.'

'I live in the frustration of yesterday, live in the freedom of today and await the promise of tomorrow,' Colt wrote in the liner notes, pinpointing the mood that Stonewall and its aftermath represented. Next to those sixties predecessors *Love Is A Drag* and *Mad About The Boy*, Colt had put his name and face to songs for men, about men and sung by a man; in his letter to *Time*, he gave his address in Stockton, New Jersey.

But in one vital way, Colt was outdated and that was his music; at a

---

1 Colt subsequently took up porn, both acting and directing.

pinch, the counter-culture might have respected a master such as Frank Sinatra but not Colt's brand of grandiosity. Reviewing *I'll Sing For You* in *Gay* magazine, Everett Henderson wrote, 'If there is a new homosexual, then there is also a new music, a music that turns you on, that makes you feel passionate and alive, that makes you want to dance and ball and get stoned and have a great time and it does not depend on sitting around the piano trilling dear old Cole's tunes or Dick and Larry's greatest.'

'I took a big chance,' Colt would tell *Gay* magazine in 1970, after finding it impossible to get any traction for *I'll Sing For You*. 'I hoped that queens everywhere would stand up for their own,' before adding, 'someone hopefully will follow my lead but not admit to being a cocksucker. He'll get outside economic backing, and the machine will pick him up, think it's a fun gag and make him a superstar.'

If Colt had misjudged his musical setting, he was astonishingly right about the future.

CHAPTER 7

The Seventies: Let The Children Boogie

'We're coming out/Out of the closet/Onto the street.'
'Make Up', Lou Reed, 1972

'Sashay out and give your way a try/Whether you tuck in or dangle/ When you hear that glad gay tango/You'll just spread your spangled wings and fly.'
'Lavender Country', Lavender Country, 1973

It is Not The Homosexual Who is Perverse, but the Society in Which He Lives
English title of German director Rosa von Praunheim's 1971 film

By 1970, the Rolling Stones had one more single left on its contract with Decca Records, which they had no intention of honouring. The solution was to record something purposefully offensive so that the label would reject it: hence 'Cocksucker Blues', about a schoolboy who pitches up in London: 'Oh, where can I get my cock sucked?/Where can I get my ass fucked?/I may have no money/But I know where to put it every time.'

Decca had no option but to shelve the track,[1] and the Stones were free. But with cock evidently still in mind, the band's next album, released in 1971, was named *Sticky Fingers*, and housed in Andy Warhol's design – a man's crotch with a pronounced bulge down one side of his jeans and a real metal zipper that could be opened to reveal the cotton underwear

---

[1] 'Cocksucker Blues', also known as 'Schoolboy Blues', finally emerged on the Rolling Stones box set *The Best of the Rest*, released in Germany in 1984

and bulge beneath. But for startling album covers, David Bowie beat them to it with his 1970 album *The Man Who Sold The World*.

When Mercury had signed Bowie, he'd arrived at the 'curly-haired Dylanesque folk rocker' stage. Inspired by the forthcoming Apollo 11 moon landing, Bowie conceived 'Space Oddity' and the topicality helped Bowie to his first UK hit. But Bowie hadn't ever repeated himself and, eight months later, he'd formed a band, the Hype. Using Lindsay Kemp's lessons, he had costumes made for the quartet with aliases: Gangsterman, Hypeman, Cowboyman and, in Bowie's case, Rainbowman, eight years before the rainbow flag became a symbol of gay rights. But Bowie was about to become a symbol in his own right, without the slightest intention.

Costumes and all, the Hype's concert debut at London's Roundhouse made no impression and Bowie immediately retired the concept. But six months later he was gazing out from his album sleeve, draped across a chaise longue in what looked very much like a dress, his hair in long, flowing locks. 'A man's dress,' Bowie later claimed, and cited the influence of nineteenth-century dandy-aesthete Dante Gabriel Rosetti – or, as his new wife Angie put it, 'contemporary inspirations on the theme of garments worn by medieval kings'. Either way, no other singer-songwriter in popular music had risked such an image.

The designer of the dress was Michael Fish, known as Mr Fish of London: 'I tried to break down the frontiers for man,' he once said. Fish was also responsible for the frilly white tunic that Mick Jagger wore in July 1969 at the Rolling Stones' concert in London's Hyde Park. But Jagger's outfit was masculinised by the trousers he wore underneath, while Bowie's dress flowed beneath his knees and his long, tangled hair created the most androgynous of figures.

Rock music had come on in leaps and bounds, but Mercury might have baulked too at the contents of *The Man Who Sold The World*. Not so much its heavy rock settings, inspired by new guitarist Mick Ronson or Bowie's themes of madness, sci-fi dystopia and German philosopher Friedrich Nietzsche's vision of the *Übermensch* or 'homo superior'

– mankind's imagined future – or 'She Shook Me Cold', in which 'She sucked my dormant will', but the opening track.

'The Width Of A Circle' was a surreal, labyrinthine epic which concluded with a homosexual seduction by either God or Satan. Rejecting the bittersweet drift of 'Space Oddity', Bowie had taken heed of Lou Reed's unflinching approach: first he gets 'laid by a young bordello . . . for which my reputation swept back home in drag' and then: 'He swallowed his pride and puckered his lips/And showed me the leather belt round his hips . . . His nebulous body swayed above/His tongue swollen with devil's love/The snake and I, a venom high/I said, "Do it again, do it again".'

Bowie was an avid reader, and one of his new obsessions was the (homosexual) occult practitioner Aleister Crowley, a major influence too on filmmaker Kenneth Anger. Bowie's relationship to homosexuality seemed to be more related to power: according to Bowie's former lover Mary Finnegan, Bowie, 'was more into women than men. [Homosexuality] with him was more opportunistic and contrived.' According to his then manager Kenneth Pitt's book *Bowie: The Pitt Report*[1], the singer seemed to only sleep with men who could advance his career while feeding his insatiable need to experiment.

Either way, Finnegan felt Bowie and Angie were 'living in a fantasy world and they created their bisexual fantasy.'[2] In fact, the pair had first met because, Bowie quipped, they were 'fucking the same man' (Mark Calvin Lee, who worked at Mercury Records). There were tales too of Bowie and Angie bringing home 'guests' from the gay clubs, of both sexes. Bowie told *Jeremy* magazine 'I don't feel the need for conventional relationships.'

In the three years following the repeal of the Sexual Offences Act in England and Wales, gay culture on both sides of the Atlantic had made rapid progress. In 1970, San Francisco had staged its first gay march and 'Gay-in'; in New York, Sylvia Rivera and Marsh P. Johnson formed

---
1 Omnibus Press (1985)
2 *Alias David Bowie: A Biography*, Peter and Leni Gilman (Henry Holt and Co., 1987)

Street Transvestite Action Revolutionaries (STAR), an offshoot of the Gay Liberation Front. In 1971, the first nationwide match for gay rights, in Albany, the state capital of New York, was attended by 3000 people.

From 1970, the UK had its own Gay Liberation Front, which followed the North-West Homosexual Law Reform Committee's name change in 1969 from the Committee (and then Campaign) for Homosexual Equality. British culture was making marginal contributions; the 1971 film *Sunday, Bloody Sunday*, starring high-profile actors Peter Finch and Glenda Jackson, showed a fiery kiss between two men in a romantic relationship, with characters that seemed adjusted to their sexuality rather than sunk in self-loathing. In the USA, the sympathetic television movie, *That Certain Summer* had Martin Sheen in the lead role of a gay dad, while New York's first Gay Pride march had taken place in July. Official GLF offshoots had also opened in Canada, the Homosexual Action West Berlin started up in 1971 and similar groups in France and Italy followed in 1972.

In the UK, *Jeremy* had launched even before Stonewall with the slogan 'The magazine for modern young men', a message that was upgraded to, 'Gay gay power for the gay gay people!' Nightclubs were increasing in number too; one of Bowie's favourite haunts was Yours And Mine in Kensington, London. Another patron was costume designer Freddie Burretti, who Bowie decided could be the singer in a new project he christened Arnold Corns in tribute to Pink Floyd's cross-dressing anti-hero 'Arnold Layne'. Buretti would be called Rudi Valentino.

Buretti and Bowie were the cover stars of the May 1971 edition of *Curious* magazine, 'the sex education magazine for men and women'. Inside, Bowie called Buretti 'the leader of the whole gay scene . . . the next Mick Jagger.'

Buretti said, 'I really want to be a big name and make it in America. I have a single out written by David called "Moonage Daydream" and that's only the beginning. An album, *Looking for Rudi*, will be out very soon.'

The album never materialised. Buretti's problem was his inability to sing and Bowie became too occupied by his own launch. 'Fashion, particularly in the extreme, is always news,' said Kenneth Pitt, who suggested Bowie emulate Oscar Wilde's trip (to promote Gilbert and Sullivan's *Patience*) and take the US by storm, dressed to the nines. Bowie's first ever meaningful US notices included *Rolling Stone*'s description – 'ravishing, almost disconcertingly reminiscent of [actress] Lauren Bacall' – and the news that he'd had a gun pulled on him in Texas. It didn't make him famous, but the US music press now knew who Bowie was.[1]

If homosexuality was just one source of energy for Bowie to siphon, there were *bona fide* homosexuals plotting away in pop. Jonathan King – later a controversial figure after receiving a prison sentence in 2001 for the sexual abuse of teenagers under sixteen during the late sixties and early seventies – took Brian Epstein's advice to try his luck in the music industry, with the immediate result of a Top 5 hit 'Everyone's Gone to the Moon' in 1964. As King moved into production and label management, he released a string of infectious, bubblegum pop songs, often under aliases, such as Shagg and the Piglets[2]. But it was as Jonathan King that he released a cover of Neil Diamond's 'Cherry Cherry' with his own 'Gay Girl' on the B-side, describing a 'high-flying, good-looking, groovy-moving, hippy-flippy, gay girl'. Less groovy and more worrying was King's 1971 B-side 'I Don't Want To Be Gay', which could have voiced the protests of those coerced teenagers: 'You can squeeze me and tease me and please me but I don't want to be gay.'

Arch entrepreneur Simon Napier-Bell was also diversifying, taking on production alongside management, making money from the cash-rich major labels by producing albums for less than the advances paid, often making more money from a flop than a success, and happy to do so. After his friend, Who manager Kit Lambert, talked up the band's

---

[1] Mercury's head office in the US censored Bowie's 'dress' album cover, replacing it with a drawing of a man brandishing a gun (a reference to the album track 'Running Gun Blues').

[2] It's impossible now to hear King's chart-topping 1971 single 'Johnny Reggae', a reggae pop about a baseball player inspired by a boy that he met at a youth club disco and not hear 'and he looks me in the eye when he shoots' in a very different light.

concept album *Tommy*, Napier-Bell conceived his own, *Out Of Borstal*, based on the UK prison system for young offenders. His assembled male trio for the job were named Fresh, who dressed as skinheads, the working-class youth subculture famous for its mod-scene dress sense and love of uplifting West Indian ska and reggae, and then for street violence.

Still, once violent offenders were imprisoned in an all-male environment, the dynamics of power could shift, as referred to by one of the tracks, 'And The Boys Lazed on the Verandah', written to order by the folk/AOR singer Peter Sarstedt. 'The young lad who did the running commentary between tracks spoke quite a bit about the homosexual side of borstal,' says Napier-Bell. 'Many of the more open remand homes were overseen by lustful gay prison governors whose houses – complete with verandas – were open at weekends to the better-behaved – and better-looking – boys in his care.'

Sarstedt jauntily depicted the borstal boys, 'watched by hungry eyes/ Never doubting the attention of their sun-burned thighs/They're not for you little girl/They're much too beautiful for that'. Napier-Bell persuaded RCA – Bowie's future employers – to fund and release *Out Of Borstal*. Fresh denounced the record ('Our development did not represent our style or music,' claimed guitarist Bob Gorman) and the album died, leaving behind only early traces of punk-rock aggro. Yet one person picked up on the record; falsetto king Lou Christie recorded a version of 'And The Boys Lazed on the Verandah' in 1971, though he chose not to release it.[1] Napier-Bell is unsure how Christie discovered the album but thinks it might have been via actor Sal Mineo, who ordered a thousand copies and sent them out as Christmas cards.

It's hard to imagine Napier-Bell thought an album about young offenders was a commercial goer, but then it was hard to know what audiences were ready for; you'd imagine a song that delighted in transvestism and strongly hinted at gay sex wasn't fit for purpose either.

---

[1] Lou Christie's version of 'And The Boys Lazed on the Verandah' went unreleased until 1992's box set *Glory River: The Buddah Years, 1968–1972*.

If the subject could be handled with wit and charm, then you never know.

The Kinks had had nine Top 5 singles over five years, but the last had been in 1967, which meant by 1970 they badly needed another. So 'Lola' was taking a sizeable risk. Ray Davies' song was set 'in a club down in old Soho' where the narrator meets a character who, 'walked like a woman and talked like a man'.

The narrator has only left home a week earlier and has never kissed a girl before, but he is nevertheless hip enough to realise, 'girls will be boys and boys will be girls/It's a mixed-up, muddled-up, shook-up world/Except for Lola.' Lola clearly knows what she wants and, after a night with Lola, so does our man: 'Well, I'm not the world's most masculine man/But I know what I am and I'm glad I'm a man/And so is Lola.'

Davies claimed the story wasn't inspired by his meeting Candy Darling but the night when Kinks manager Robert Wace was dancing in Paris club the Carousel with 'this black woman,' the singer recalled, 'and [Wace] said, "I'm really onto a thing here." And it was OK until we left at six in the morning and then I said, "Have you seen the stubble?" He said, "Yeah," but he was too pissed to care, I think.'[1] Davies later told *Gay Times* that he 'stole her,' from Wace. 'It was back to my place and there was stubble. I'm just not mad about stubble . . . There was a sense that you couldn't write about it.'[2]

Davies played coy in the *Gay Times* interview: 'You didn't think of it as sleeping with men,' he said. 'It's a dangerous thing to answer . . . I think I'm more of a voyeur.' Ultimately, what was important was that Davies approved: 'It really doesn't matter what sex Lola is, I think she's all right.'[3]

Blessed with a typically rakish Kinks melody and an arrangement that began quietly and slowly built the tension to a joyous resolution,

---

1 *The Kinks: The Official Biography*, Jon Savage (Faber and Faber, 1985).
2 *Seduced and Abandoned: Essays On Gay Men and Popular Music*, Richard Smith (Continuum, 1995)
3 *God Save The Kinks: A Biography*, Rob Jovanovic (Aurum Press, 2014).

'Lola' became a worldwide hit: no. 1 in four countries, no. 2 in five more, including the UK, and four more Top 10 showings, including the US. 'It was the first gay rock song,' claimed venerated gay journalist Adam Block. 'The first time I'd ever heard us perverts mentioned, let alone celebrated, on the radio.'[1] The inevitable backlash wasn't damaging: 'Lola' was faded out on some US radio stations before Lola's biological sex was revealed[2] while Australia banned it for 'controversial subject matter'. But the lack of outrage and the song's widespread success indicated that attitudes were beginning to soften. A night out with Lola didn't constitute a crime.

Glam bam, thank you ma'am

The Cockettes were also pursuing the ideal of gender fluidity, though their extreme version would have left none of the confusion that Lola created. After their New Year's Eve stage debut, the troupe embarked on monthly adventures at the Nocturnal Dream Show event at San Francisco's Palace theatre. They were crazed, inspired, LSD-tainted extravaganzas: Rumi Missabu says their influences spanned 'Edith Piaf, Jean Genet, Bertolt Brecht, Jean Cocteau, the Rolling Stones, Janis Joplin, Billie Holiday, Tina Turner, Jayne Mansfield, Walt Disney, old Hollywood glamour and especially Broadway show tunes.' But the execution was more in the vein of low-budget amateur dramatics and no Broadway show would include the bluesy vamp 'Endless Masturbation Blues', one of the periodic breaks in their catalogue of standards written by Cockette pianist Scrumbly Martin. He also penned the Cockettes' most enduring show, *Pearls Over Shanghai*[3].

Janis Joplin was an early fan and friend of the troupe, Missabu says, while Bowie had enquired about them on his first visit to San Francisco, though he didn't get to see them. Mainstream magazines such as *Vogue*,

---

1 *The Rock History Reader*, Theo Cateforis, ed. (Routledge, 2007)
2 Ibid. 328
3 *Pearls Over Shanghai* was based on John Colton's 1926 Broadway play *The Shanghai Gesture*.

Rolling Stone and *Esquire* profiled this radical new style of drag-queenery, far from the attributes of perfection that Flawless Sabrina's pageant aimed for, more what's come to be referred to as 'genderfuck' – a term tailor-made for Hibiscus' crew.

But the Cockettes weren't built to last. An internal row over whether their shows should have a cover charge to allow the members to be paid – Hibiscus said absolutely not – saw their founder dumped from his own troupe; he quickly formed the Angels Of Light, which included some of the Cockettes. Those remaining accepted the offer of a paying gig in New York and flew over in November, 1971 – 'a huge mistake,' claims fellow art-drag pioneer Jimmy Camicia. 'The manager of the event invited the uptown crowd, who just didn't get it. But the downtown crowd were smitten.'[1]

Playing in support during the New York run was Sylvester James, a new addition to the Cockettes, both a very rare black Cockette and a very rare accomplished singer for the troupe. His musical slot was titled 'Sylvester Syncopation'. More interested in drag and performance than consciousness- and hell-raising, Sylvester (he always went by his first name) showed signs of disloyalty, but also realism, when he apologised to the New York audiences for the main act to follow. Back in San Francisco, he left the Cockettes to concentrate on his own career, thus missing out on shows such as *Journey to the Centre of Uranus*, in which a muse of noted underground filmmaker John Waters, Divine, made his Cockettes debut. He sang 'A Crab on Your Anus Means You're Loved' while dressed as a humungous red lobster.

Returning to New York, downtown Ridiculous Theatre/Warhol crowd mingled socially and professionally with the Cockettes. From New Jersey, Jimmy Camicia was an adventurous spirit who'd spent the second half of the sixties in London, working in market research by day and hanging out at bars like Le Duce at night among future legends of gay culture David Hockney and Derek Jarman and BBC London radio

---

1 Andy Warhol, however, was among those who walked out of the Cockettes' New York debut. You'd think that, of all people, Warhol would favour attitude over professionalism.

DJ Pete Myers, Camicia's boyfriend at the time. In New York, Camicia befriended Hibiscus' Angels Of Light, who'd also come out east (to play for free, of course). When Hibiscus went out of town, those Angels got antsy and asked Camicia to write them a new show, which was performed by a mix of performers under the name Hot Peaches.

Camicia was more grounded than most in this art-riot scene and he had a plan. 'I wanted to do gay shows for gay people – and what do queens like? *The Wizard Of Oz*! So I wrote *The Wizard Of Us* and got Jackie Curtis to play Dorothy.' Curtis had some spare time, since he'd finished filming *Women In Revolt*, his last collaboration with Warhol. The filmmaker had arrived at a relative downturn too. Having survived an assassination attempt in 1968, he turned the filmmaking over to his assistant Paul Morrissey and others started creating their own productions; Curtis wrote *Femme Fatale: the Three Faces of Gloria*, which featured the stage debuts of both Jayne Rogers, then calling himself Wayne County,[1] as lesbian prison inmate Georgia Harrison and a young, aspiring poet from Ohio, Patti Smith, 'sporting a three-foot long cock,' County recalls.

County's own play, *World: the Birth of a Nation, the Castration of Man*, was promoted as a 'homosexual fantasy' expressly to shock and offend with every perversion that he could imagine. If these shows played to the converted denizens of downtown NYV, reviewers would readily turn up, ensuring the public got to read about them. Warhol had seen *World: the Birth of a Nation* too and, suitably inspired, imagined turning the hundreds of phone conversations that he'd taped over the years at the Factory into a play. Tony Ingrassia, who had worked with Ridiculous Theatre founder Charles Ludlam and also wrote and directed County's play, had the task of editing Warhol's conversations – by turns mundane, bitchy and vainglorious. Ingrassia also got to direct the play, titled *Andy Warhol's Pork*, populated by caricatures of Factory luminaries; the scene that ate itself.

---

1 Wayne County was part of the state of Michigan; Rogers chose the name because of her fondness for the Michigan proto-punks the Stooges.

Andy Warhol's Pork debuted in 1971 before the cast – including County, Kathleen Dorritie Vanilla, who had appeared in *World*... and was now calling herself Cherry Vanilla, and debutante Tony Zanetta – flew to London for a two-week residency at the Roundhouse, scene of Bowie's failed Hype.

Just as he was transformed by Lindsay Kemp, Bowie was never the same after seeing *Pork*. But the effect would take a few months to filter through. At the time, County recalls accompanying Leee Childers and Cherry Vanilla to a Bowie concert and meeting him. Bowie still had long hair and was wearing yellow, bell-bottom pants and a floppy hat (those men's dresses had been so *very* 1970). The cover of Bowie's next album, *Hunky Dory*, released in December 1971, saw him posed on the cover like a Hollywood actress – very Lauren Bacall, in fact, with long, blond hair swept back to reveal killer cheekbones.

In 'You gotta make way for the Homo superior,' the pay-off to 'Oh! You Pretty Things' – a tune so jaunty that Herman's Hermits frontman Peter Noone covered it as a single – Bowie seemed to fuse gay liberation and Nietzsche. The album's boldest rocker, 'Queen Bitch', Bowie admitted, was a Velvet Underground tribute in which one queen jealously watched his lover, 'trying hard to pull sister Flo... so swishy in her satin and tat/In her frock coat and bipperty-bopperty hat/Oh, God, I could do better than that!'

By the time *Hunky Dory* was released, Bowie had already recorded his next album, and completely revamped his look. When *Melody Maker* journalist Michael Watt met Bowie in January 1972, the singer was wearing a 'skintight pantsuit, big hair, huge, red plastic boots – dazzling,' more of a Cockette or a freak from Andy Warhol's *Pork* than Lauren Bacall. Even more startling was Bowie's brash declaration, primed for outrage: not that he was bisexual, but 'I'm gay and always have been, even when I was David Jones.'[1]

For all the political advances of gay lib organisations, no artist had

---

1 http://www.theguardian.com/music/2006/jan/22/popandrock.davidbowie

ever publically stated that they were gay – though Bowie did have a wife and child to temper the revelation. He also was playing a role. His new album was a concept, based on a sci-fi messiah of sorts, known as Ziggy Stardust, a 'Starman', according to Bowie's forthcoming single, who carried the message, 'let the children boogie'. The pretty things were here, and the future was theirs. The Spiders from Mars, Ziggy's backing band, were spiritually modelled on 'the marauding boy gangs' as Bowie put it, of William Burroughs's dystopian novel *The Wild Boys*, 'with their bowie knives.'

Looking back, it's clear that once Bowie had found fame, he would only single out women[1] and that his 'confession' was part of Ziggy's marketing and was Bowie's contrivance – 'he knew what he was doing', Watt recalled. Bowie's bisexuality was also tempered by the way it could also be incorporated into Ziggy's storyline, as if it was a virus from outer space rather than earthly reality. But it was on the front page of a leading music paper and one of rock music's biggest news stories in years.

In comparison, Dusty Springfield's confession to the daily London newspaper the *Evening Standard* in September 1970 – eighteen months before Bowie – was a done-and-dusted story in what seemed like minutes. While Bowie was rising and looking spectacularly like a Martian, topped with startling, spiky dyed-red hair, contrary to the fashion for long hair, Springfield was on the way down. 'Son Of A Preacher Man' would be her last Top 30 hit for nineteen years and its parent album *Dusty In Memphis* didn't even chart; in the US, it made no. 99. Bowie's news was also backlit by the former criminal status of male homosexuality, while lesbianism lacked – fortunately, of course – the same sensationalist context.

'There's one thing that's always annoyed me – and I'm going to get into something nasty here,' Springfield had told interviewer Ray Connolly, 'but I've got to say it, because so many other people say I'm bent and I've

---

[1] Not a single Bowie biography or interview with those that worked with him has unearthed a male lover in the post-Ziggy years, unless you believe ex-wife Angie's claim that she found him in bed with Mick Jagger.

heard it so many times that I've almost learned to accept it. I don't go leaping around to all the gay clubs but I can be very flattered. Girls run after me a lot and it doesn't upset me. It upsets me when people insinuate things that aren't true. I couldn't stand to be thought of as a big butch lady.'

Springfield was gay and had been living with US singer Norma Tanega for the last five years, but she underlined her apparent bisexuality as a safer halfway house. So Dusty was 'perfectly capable of being swayed by a girl as by a boy. More and more people feel that way and I don't see why I shouldn't. There was someone on television the other night who admitted that he swings either way. I suppose he could afford to say it, but I, being a pop singer, shouldn't even admit that I might think that way.'[1]

Connolly later claimed that Springfield had goaded him into securing a confession: they'd talked about Catholic guilt to sex and promiscuity, 'when Dusty suddenly said: "There's something else you should ask me now. Go on, ask me. I know you've heard the rumours".' Perhaps it was, as Connolly noted at the time, a bid for attention; her latest album was named *A Brand New Me* and it hadn't charted in the UK either (in the US, it reached no. 107). Or maybe she'd had enough and wanted to take back control of her life. It was a better solution than the self-harming that was outwardly expressing her distress.

Connolly did reveal that, 'much of the time', Springfield lived with Tanega, who'd had one hit single herself with 'Walkin' My Cat Named Dog', recorded for Bob Crewe's label New Voice, and had moved to London where she subsumed her own career for writing songs for Dusty. They had a tempestuous time; both had affairs[2] and in 1971, Tanega returned to America where she released the solo album *I Don't Think It Will Hurt If You Smile*, written about their relationship. Springfield,

---

1 www.rayconnolly.co.uk/pages/journalism_01/journalism_01_item.asp?journalism_01ID=78
2 'Ode To Dusty Springfield' – on closeted jazz singer Blossom Dearie's 1970 album *That's Just the Way I Want to Be*, was co-written by Tanega.

feeling too vulnerable in the UK after her confession, moved stateside in 1972, just as Bowie's fame exploded.

Bowie's announcement was only the start of Ziggy's ascendance. As Michael Watt saw it, 'busting taboos stokes the star-maker machinery' and on the tour leading up to the release of *The Rise And Fall Of Ziggy Stardust and the Spiders from Mars*, Bowie was photographed straddling Mick Ronson's guitar, teeth bared, an 'electric blowjob' that Bowie's management turned into a full-page advert. 'Starman' was released in April, with an irresistibly lilting melody and an octave lift in the chorus that mirrored the same device in 'Somewhere Over The Rainbow'. 'It draws on the same emotion – a yearning for escape,' wrote Bowie biographer Paul Trynka.[1]

The performance of 'Starman' on *Top Of The Pops* became intrinsic to Ziggy's legend,[2] as a grinning Bowie slung a campy arm around Ronson's shoulder for the chorus and, in one nonchalant move, made homosexuality seem daring and colourful rather than shameful. 'A moment of epiphany for a generation of teenagers,' Trynka wrote.

It had as profound an effect on heterosexual teenagers. For future Depeche Mode singer Dave Gahan, 'Bowie gave me a hope that there was something else . . . I just thought he wasn't of this Earth.'

Future Echo and the Bunnymen singer Ian McCulloch recalled, 'I'd get girls on the bus saying to me, "Are you a boy or a girl?" Until [Bowie] turned up, it was a nightmare. All my mates at school would say, "Did you see that bloke on *Top Of The Pops*? He's a right faggot, him!" With people like me, it helped forge an identity and a perspective on things, helped us to walk in a different way, metaphorically.'[3]

The story of *Ziggy Stardust* – a very loose narrative in which this messianic alien swinger comes to save Earth, blows everyone's mind and for his pains is martyred by his own fans, while creating what Bowie

---

[1] *Starman* (Little, Brown, 2011).
[2] Exactly forty years later, Dylan Jones wrote a book, *When Ziggy Played Guitar*, inspired by the event.
[3] *Strange Fascination*, David Buckley (Virgin Books, 1999).

called 'the ultimate pop idol' – was celebrated live at London's Rainbow theatre, with choreography by Lindsay Kemp and a set list that included Jacques Brel and Velvet Underground covers. Bowie wore a variety of costumes, including the tight jumpsuit designed by Freddie Buretti for the cover of the album. Bowie, not Buretti, was the new Valentino, the new Jagger.

By cutting an androgynous, unknowable figure – and apparently gay, though married – Bowie was creating a character that could be read as a political statement, but was also totally apolitical. As Bowie fan – and fellow singer-songwriter – Nicholas Currie puts it, 'Bowie has also said that he'd be delighted if his work allowed people to find different characters within themselves. In order to do that, you don't over-determine things. There's a kind of negative capability in not being too intentional, too specific, too narrative. This is artistry on a higher level.'

The Ziggy album only hinted at a gay/bi identity. Among the snapshot images of 'tigers on Vaseline' and the Little Richard-inspired, 'Wham-bam thank-you ma'am!', 'Five Years' (about the revelation that earth was doomed) offered the image, 'A cop knelt and kissed the feet of a priest/And a queer threw up at the sight of that', which didn't sound very sexual to a fourteen-year old at the time. There was a portrait of androgyny in 'Lady Stardust' ('People stared at the make-up on his face, laughed at his long black hair, his animal grace'), written for Marc Bolan, and one possible line in 'Soul Love', 'the church of man love is such a holy place to be' – though there could easily have been a comma between 'man' and 'love'.

There was more encouragement in what was to come; the track that Bowie gave to UK rockers Mott The Hoople, 'All The Young Dudes', was a steely, rousing anthem that suggested the Beatles and Stones were old news, that T. Rex, led by Bolan, was the new. Likewise, the kids that were taking over: 'Now Lucy looks sweet 'cause he dresses like a queen/But he can kick like a mule/It's a real mean team.' And Bowie's first post-Ziggy single was 'John, I'm Only Dancing', which flipped the 'Queen Bitch' scenario of jealous boyfriends to make a woman the object of friction – 'She turns me on, but don't get me wrong/I'm only dancing'.

Paul Trynka's *Starman* points out that Bowie wasn't even the first rock male rocker to publicly adopt bisexuality. Like Bowie, Bolan had got married in 1970, and in 1971, told UK music weekly *Sounds*, 'I'll go and kiss guys if I think they're nice.' His former manager Simon Napier-Bell claims that Bolan's 1966 debut single 'The Wizard' was not inspired by a real magician, as Bolan had said, but a conjuror in Paris that he'd slept with. The first time Napier-Bell had met Bolan, 'We went to dinner and talked for two hours and went back to my place and went to bed. Marc said, "If you're going to take 20 per cent of my income, I want 20 per cent of your brain", and stuck his tongue in my mouth.'[1]

Bolan fans also claim that their man had been first to wear the sparkling make-up that created the term 'glitter rock', though it was swiftly taken over by 'glam rock'. Actually, Trynka notes that Bolan, Bowie and Elton John – who was shifting from a Californian rock sound – with matching beard and plaid shirt – to a glam-inspired pop agenda with a penchant for overblown costumes – had all been guests at parties thrown by fashion editor (and wife of Bolan's manager) Chelita Secunda, who introduced them all to glitter make-up – and cocaine too, which would blight all three of their careers as they struggled to handle immense fame: Bolan had numerous UK no. 1 singles and albums while John achieved the same at home and in the US.

Glam rock was the UK's most tangible musical subculture since the Beatles launched Merseybeat almost a decade earlier. Numerous bands, clearly straight judging by their lack of fashion finesse and animal grace, hitched themselves to the glam bandwagon, including the Sweet, Slade and Mud, with odd band members revelling in sexual ambiguity, but a cartoon version, like a pantomime dame. The one female glam rocker, Suzi Quatro, was also straight, but wore a trademark black leather

---

[1] Marc Bolan's one lyrical contribution to the cause was, 'I know you're shrewd and she's a dude/But all I want is easy action,' in T. Rex's UK no. 1 'Solid Gold Easy Action' (1972).

catsuit, a butch image tempered by the fact she was dating her guitarist. She was still the one decent role model for gay girls.

The glam bands were joined by a new London stage musical, written by *Hair* and *Jesus Christ Superstar* actor Richard O'Brien. *The Rocky Horror Show* debuted in 1973 and would play almost 3000 performances over the next eight years; transvestite pansexual scientist Dr Frank N. Furter was the show's ringmaster and the creator of a muscle-bound 'monster' in tight silver pants. It's the doctor who sleeps with both Brad and Janet, the show's fifties-style innocents, all to a razzed-up soundtrack of kitsch fifties rockers and ballads.[1]

One of glam rock's only unabashed sexual statements came from gay songwriting duo Ken Howard and Alan Blaikley, who wrote 'Do You Like Boys?', a 1973 single for UK duo Starbuck: 'Do you feel strange when you see blue denim and a studded jacket on a masculine frame?' The Sweet were also on topic with 'A.C.D.C.' ('She got girls, girls all over the world/She got men every now and then/But she can't make up her mind').

Glam was a notable event in Australia too; Skyhooks were the most popular act at the time, with gay portraits in 'Toorak Cowboy' and 'Straight in a Gay Gay World'. Canada had Justin Paige, 'king of rock and rouge', whose self-titled album debut in 1974 featured 'Steam Queen', 'Rough Trade' and 'Tea-Room Tramp', with an image suffocated by glitter and make-up. 'Let all the children boogie,' Bowie had sung on 'Starman'. In light of Stonewall and Ziggy's revolutions, the gay children of the western world at least could choose: stay closeted, or boogie, as nature intended.

Of all South American countries, Brazil holds by far the most liberal views on homosexuality, as its annual *Carnaval do Brasil* in Rio de Janeiro illustrates. Following Bahiano's pioneering efforts, Noel Rosa of

---

[1] Jonathan King caught *The Rocky Horror Show*'s second performance and promptly invested in the production for a share of the profits; he quickly recorded his own pansexual glam drama, *Pandora's Box*, which advocated, astutely, 'If you want to get a woman, you gotta be gay.'

the Samba Aces had been responsible, in 1932, for the first samba song to address homosexuality, *'Mulato Bamba'* ('Brave Mulato'), about a mixed race man who 'did not want to fall in love with women', the song referring to being hounded by the police. Rosa was reputedly inspired by Ismael Silva, who co-founded the first samba school. But Brazil's most famous gay samba maestro was Assis Valente – arguably, as researchers have claimed there is no supportive evidence of his homosexuality, though he repeatedly tried to kill himself (and eventually succeeded).[1] His songs were often covered by samba queen Carmen Miranda. In turn, she inspired Brazil's drag queens to mimic her fruity extravagance. The Miranda-Valente partnership's innuendo-laden fare included *'Uva de Caminhão'* ('Truck Grape'): 'They said to me that you've been horsing around/That you've been sucking a lot of grapes/And even been in a truck'.

No Brazilian voice carried the torch through the fifties and sixties the way that Chavela Varga did in Mexico, She sang the stirring *ranchera* ballads that were otherwise the exclusive domain of men, an image she reflected by dressing in suits, chewing cigars and refusing to change the female pronoun of the song.

It was only in the late sixties that Brazil's military dictatorship faced calls for liberation, from the cultural movement known as *tropicalismo*, a cauldron of music, art and literature, whose leading lights, Caetano Veloso and Gilberto Gil, were jailed and temporarily deported.

Given this backdrop, Dzi Croquettes, Brazil's choreographed (by US dancer Lennie Dale) equivalent to the Cockettes (notice the namecheck), were an astounding creation. There was no South Americam precedent for this thirteen-man collective, their glitter beards and headdresses, their miming and dancing, the version of Jacques Brel's *'Ne Me Quittes Pas'* performed in pink wedding gowns and combat boots. Rio's annual carnival was a costumed party but had seen nothing like this.

---

1 Writer Roberto Midlej thinks it was cocaine addiction and debt that undid Valente: http://www.correio24horas.com.br/detalhe/noticia/sambista-baiano-assis-valente-foi-viciado-em-cocaina-e-teve-vida-atormentada-por-boatos-de-homossexualidade/?cHash=c3fbcdd88341250eb603665a87f909e5

'Their performances mixed humour, imitation, pole dancing, Broadway camp, of musical styles from samba to tango to jazz and a lot of sexual innuendo,' says journalist Carmino Rocha. 'They'd dress as nuns, prostitutes, pregnant women and hustlers. All very outrageous for early seventies Brazil.' With success came the regime's censors, who finally checked them out in 1973 when the show was banned. Three Croquettes were sons of military officers so they managed to carry on with a temporary authorisation, but they felt unsafe and decided to take time abroad.

Dzi Croquettes clearly impacted on Ney Matogrosso, the singer of Secos e Molhados (a.k.a. Dry and Wet), whose visual brand of psychedelic glam had carnival DNA in its showy roots. Born Ney de Souza Pereira, Matogrosso and his (heterosexual) bandmates wrote slyly about masculinity and sexuality; his uncanny counter-tenor sounded more female than male and his look included face-paint, tassels and headdresses. He milked Carmen Miranda's 'Bambu Bambu' ('Bamboo Bamboo') for every ounce of campness and even recorded 'Calúnias (Telma Eu Não Sou Gay)' (a.k.a. 'Telma, I'm Not Gay'). Matagrosso escaped the censors because he was more 'carnival' than drag and sold over a million records as a result.

'If I'd waved the flag of homosexuality, I would be labelled and everything about me would have been explained,' he said. 'I want liberty of expression . . . It is all human sexuality anyway.'

Glam vs America

In North America, glam acts weren't selling anywhere near a million. *Ziggy Stardust* had only made no. 75 in the charts and 'Starman' not even that, while after the top ten hit 'Bang A Gong (Get It On)', T. Rex never again reached the Top 50. The brilliantly inventive Roxy Music, styled by gay designer Antony Price to match their fifties-meets-the-future sound, were only lauded in America once they'd ironed out all the kinks for safe, soulful AOR. Price says Roxy's singer Bryan Ferry liked going to gay clubs because of the women he'd meet. The cover girl of Roxy's second album *For Your Pleasure* was Price's friend, the glamorous Amanda Lear, Brian Jones' former pal.

The only successful US band that pursued the bending of gender was Phoenix, Arizona hard-rockers Alice Cooper, whose singer Vince Furnier also called himself Alice. Wayne County recalls their Max's Kansas City show. Alice wore 'false eyelashes, garish make-up, a woman's yellow and pink dress and leather trousers.' Heckled with, 'Queer!', the singer responded, 'Hmm . . . you'd better believe it, honey.' But Alice's aim was shock, not sex; there as only one hint in 'Desperado' – 'I wear lace and I wear black leather' – but the track came from an album named *Killer* and the band's stage act culminated in Alice's execution by the gallows or guillotine.

Yet, with Bowie's assistance, America did make an exception, giving a belated hit to Lou Reed. He'd had enough of the Velvet Underground's lack of success. His final appearances with the band were at Max's Kansas City in 1970, after which the club's upstairs room was locked and shows discontinued. The disconsolate Reed retreated to work at his father's accountancy firm in Long Island; in his absence, the Velvets' manager re-edited songs on their 1970 album *Loaded*, including its finest song 'Sweet Jane', though the song's gender-switching image – 'Jack's in his corset, Jane's in her vest' – stayed.

But after a year, Reed had emerged, released a self-titled solo album in 1971 on RCA, untroubled by gender-switching or any sense of alternate sexuality. In early 1972, he'd been the special guest at a Bowie/Spiders show, and now Bowie was offering to produce Reed's next album. Perhaps bolstered by Bowie's risk-taking or because Reed had finally come to terms with his inner gay or finally wanted to some money off the back of glam, he didn't hold back. 1972's *Transformer* was his most commercial record and gayest – almost at the level of the pansy craze and Minette. And Warhol's Factory was at the heart of it.

Post-Stonewall nightlife in New York had blossomed, with all manner of new clubs and bars, from cabaret to dives. Though Max's was out of commission, the owner made one exception for a new band, the Magic

Tramps, fronted by former Factory acolyte Eric Emerson. From New Jersey, Emerson had made his film debut in Warhol's *Chelsea Girls* and slept with several of the Factory's male alumni, but he had girlfriends too and he became a father while living in Hollywood.

Emerson had also joined a band in LA, the Magic Tramps and persuaded them to move east because they could play Max's. Once in town, Emerson appeared in Jackie Curtis' play *Vain Victory: Vicissitudes of the Damned*, an exercise in pure anarchy that took place over seven hours. Emerson wore glitter from head to toe, which might be where glitter rock was born. The music in *Vain Victory* was based on old-style Broadway/cabaret, in a Cockettes vein, with songs by Lou Reed. He'd already demoed 'Lonely Saturday Night', which became the last track on *Transformer* under a new title, 'Goodnight Ladies', with an arrangement air-lifted out of twenties Berlin, complete with tuba, as if sung by a drag queen, or Jackie Curtis.

Bob Fosse's film of the stage musical *Cabaret* had been released in January 1972, starring Judy Garland's daughter Liza Minnelli, but *Transformer*'s airs of Berlin cabaret seemed more the son of *Andy Warhol's Pork*. The album started with 'Vicious', after Warhol had suggested Reed write a song based on the line, 'Vicious/you hit me with a flower'. 'New York Telephone Conversation' – basically *Pork*'s storyline – was delivered in Reed's conversational sing-song and 'Make Up, another tuba-fronted confection, announced, triumphantly, 'We're coming out/out of the closet/onto the street.'

But the record's trump card was the slinky, hypnotic 'Walk On The Wild Side', which brought the Max's Kansas City backroom to life as the verses detailed an infantry of Warhol acolytes. First was Holly Woodlawn: 'Holly came from Miami FLA . . . plucked her eyebrows on the way/Shaved her legs and then he was a she.' Then Candy Darling: 'Candy came from out on the Island/In the back room she was everybody's darling/But she never lost her head/Even when she was giving head'.

'Little Joe' was actor Joe Dallesandro, who played a male hustler in

Warhol's 1968 film *Flesh*. The 'sugar plum fairy' was Joe Campbell's role in Warhol's earlier film *My Hustler*.[1] Last but not least, Jackie Curtis: 'Jackie was just speeding away/Thought she was James Dean for a day.'

Drugs, male prostitution, cross-dressing, oral sex; that the BBC didn't know the meaning of 'giving head' added to the thrill of hearing 'Walk On The Wild Side' on UK daytime radio, giving Reed his first-ever hit: no. 10 in the UK and then Top 20 in the US. *Transformer* also charted, out-pacing Bowie in America. Its artwork was equally thrilling, less for the front cover of Reed in full pancake make-up but the rear. Styled by Anthony Price, female model Gaia stood framed by a full-length mirror, faced by Reed's über-butch roadie Ernie Thormahlen with a cucumber stuffed down his jeans.

The transformation from boy to girl and vice-versa was clear to see, though Reed was not giving in to temptation yet; after aping Bowie's glam-rock profile, he followed Bowie by getting married, to aspiring actress Bettye Kronstadt. The marriage failed. In 1974, facing the question, 'Why do you write songs about transsexuals? Are you a homosexual or a transsexual?' Reed mumbled, 'Sometimes.'

Both Reed and Bowie never did any fundraising or acted as spokesmen for the homosexual cause. Both Reed and Bowie would never act as spokesmen for the homosexual cause. In 1973, Bowie told *NME* journalist Charles Shaar Murray, 'it's a great puzzle to me, because I don't know whether I am against or for Gay Lib. I understand that they want to have people to be with, so that they're not on their own.' But he advised, 'to put that many people together at once . . . you can be stamped on immediately. To be a guerrilla, to be on your own, is far more rewarding in the end.'

By eschewing a political dimension, Bowie allowed others to climb on board the glam bandwagon – but as flamboyant showmen rather than revolutionaries. Heterosexual musicians, like bricklayers in make-up and drop earrings, were joined by Elton John, who had retired the

---

1 One of Joe Campbell's first boyfriends was Harvey Milk, who later moved to San Francisco and will enter this story in 1977.

denim and plaid and gone overboard with the most elaborate costumes, while staying firmly closeted. The US had its own fair share of pretenders, but if glam had not captivated the US in terms of chart placings, the gay roots of rock'n'roll that influenced Bowie began to produce their own radical flowers before even Ziggy Stardust's arrival.

With Max's Kansas City out of commission for concerts, New York's latest downtown venue of note was the Mercer Arts Center, a decrepit complex of theatres occupying the lower floors of the University hotel. One night in February 1972 was especially memorable, as the Magic Tramps were joined by two new bands: Queen Elizabeth, with lead singer Wayne County, and the New York Dolls. The performers were notable for their varying degrees of drag and bouffant hair while peddling a gnarly blend of sixties' garage rock, the Rolling Stones and the Shangri Las.

'It's a fact that LA soft rock has been stomped on by glittering, lurid, day-glo platform shoes worn by a female impersonating, posturing hard rock singer,' British journalist Miles wrote in *International Times*, after seeing the Mercer triple bill. 'Faggot rock, the music of total drop out.'[1] Miles' tone was simultaneously dismissive and excited. He noted that one Queen Elizabeth song was named 'It Takes a Man Like Me to Fuck a Woman Like Me', but was most taken with County himself: 'A huge Afro-wig sprayed vivid green and pink, a black neck-ribbon and a diamond necklace . . . He totters about on outrageous high platforms being as gratuitously obscene as possible. Triumphant, he straps on an artificial vagina: "I'm ready any time you are!" and goes down on the silver sprayed legs of a mannequin during a song called "Dead Hot Mamma", which concerns someone's incestuous relationship with his mother's corpse.'

'I was determined to take all of my experiences in the Ridiculous shows and all my influences from people like Jackie Curtis and present them in a rock'n'roll format,' said County.

Miles saw the New York Dolls as 'a terrible alter-ego Rolling Stones,

---

1 www.internationaltimes.it/archive/page.php?i=IT_1973-02-23_B-IT-Volume-1_Iss-148_006&view=text

come to haunt Mick'n'Keith and the boys with a direct expression of all that camping on stage. A hard rock, camp, prissy 100 per cent homosexual group in black tights,[1] posturing and imitating all of Mick's stage gestures and leaps. It's terrific!'

Regarding the Magic Tramps, Eric Emerson was 'covered with gold glitter dust and flexes his muscles to make little bits pop off while he gives naughty looks to the boys in the audience. He is a combination witch doctor and Captain America in a white feather head-dress and white tights with a sort of gold lead jock-strap.'

Ziggy Stardust fever had exploded in New York and his management company sought to make him as popular all across the country – though Texas, where Bowie had that gun pulled on him, might have needed some persuasion. The founder of Bowie's management company MainMan, Tony Defries, believed that to make Bowie a superstar you had to treat him as if he already were one, so they hired Pork actors Tony Zanetta and Cherry Vanilla and Jayne County's photographer friend Leee Black Childers to join MainMan and promote Bowie as if he really was the messiah. County's Queen Elizabeth and the Stooges – whose lithe, dynamic lead singer Iggy Pop was as much of an influence on Bowie/Ziggy as Lou Reed – were also signed to MainMan, leaving the New York Dolls to be snapped up by Bowie's old label Mercury.

The Dolls' purposefully tawdry efforts at drag were copied by bands such as the Harlots of 42nd Street and the Berlin Brats, though neither band got signed by majors; the US brand of glam was much rockier and outrageous and druggy and less commercial and careerist than the UK's. But it was the USA that unearthed the first identifiably gay glam pop idol; the self-proclaimed, 'true fairy of rock'. In truth, Wayne County holds that title, though he never tried to write pop songs and ingratiate himself into the mainstream.

At least Jobriath was the first 'true fairy' to sign to a major label and

---

1 Miles was wrong in thinking the Dolls were gay, though guitarist Sylvain Sylvain once said, 'Maybe David [Johansen] tried it. I certainly tried it . . . If I saw a good-looking kid, what the fuck's wrong with that?'

release an album. From Philadelphia, born Bruce Campbell, a gifted pianist as a child, whose teens were blighted by being conscripted into the military. He later absconded and renamed himself Jobriath Salisbury. In 1969, he won the part of gay teenager Woof in the LA production of *Hair*, singing about sex and taboo in 'Sodomy'. Salisbury then fronted Pidgeon, the progressive folk band, before being incarcerated in a psychiatric hospital after the military police tracked him down.

Salisbury was already vulnerable and destitute – homeless, drinking heavily and earning a living partly from prostitution – when Jerry Brandt found him in LA. Brandt was the booking agent who'd brought the Rolling Stones to the USA and his management roster included Chubby Checker and the new singer-songwriter sensation Carly Simon. He'd heard Salisbury's demo in the office of Columbia chief Clive Davis, who had decided the music was 'mad, unstructured and destructive to melody'. Brandt was undeterred and hatched a plan with Jobriath Boone, as he was now rebranded: the real-life gay rocker rather than the one Bowie had only created in a storybook fantasy.

Jobriath – now going only by his first name – signed to Elektra, which had joined the rapidly expanding Warners Bros empire and released his self-titled debut album in 1974, when he was still barely known. But you wouldn't have realised that, given the giant billboards trumpeting the singer, as Brandt deployed the MainMan tactic with Bowie of treating his charge as an instant superstar. Jobriath has his worshippers but it was as much the sound of *Hair* as Ziggy and Jobriath hadn't half of Bowie's song-writing talent: 'Space Clown', 'Earthling' and 'Morning Starship' reflected Bowie's aura without the depth, sharpness and hooks.

Jobriath's gay content wasn't much more pronounced than Bowie's: 'I'm a fragile man . . . light of step and soft of touch/A gentle man . . . You know I could love you/The way a man loves a woman' ('I'Maman') and 'It's very gay to blow away . . . In a space-suit made of Mary Quant I'll blow away/I will/Get your drag and let's go, forget Joe' ('Blow Away') was the extent of it. Where it got really interesting was his proposed live launch. Nothing less than the Paris Opera House would do; Jobriath would be dressed as King Kong, swinging from a rope onto a replica of the Empire State Building, which would turn into a squirting penis complete with stairway and piano. As the singer descended the penis, he'd turn into a Marlene Dietrich lookalike. The budget would be a giddy $200,000.

Furthering the cart-before-the-horse scenario, every outlandish Jobriath quote was reinforced by Brandt's even more far-fetched claims: 'Elvis, the Beatles, Jobriath,' he told the UK trade publication *Music Week*. The 'true fairy of rock' wasn't a lie, but the phrase 'hype of the year' stuck to Jobriath as well. The Paris show never happened; instead, he was launched on US TV's *Midnight Special*, a credible slot and he sounded terrific. But the ballet steps and body-stocking were camper than Ziggy and too Broadway for rock, too rock for Broadway. Six months after his album, a second set, *Creatures Of The Street*, compiled from the same sessions, limped out and both Brandt and Elektra dropped Jobriath like a hot stone.

The singer would announce he was retiring 'Jobriath' in January 1975, only returning as Cole Berlin, a thirties' cabaret throwback playing New York's piano bars. Bowie had already retired Ziggy Stardust in July 1973, on stage at London's Hammersmith Odeon, feeling trapped by his creation; it made sense anyway, as Ziggy's tale was always about the rise and fall and it was a spectacular theatrical coup that reinforced the singer and his alter ego's legend.

While Jobriath managed to emulate Ziggy's rise and fall, even if he'd only risen in his manager's eyes and had fallen before he could make any meaningful mark, Bowie moved on. Before retiring Ziggy, he'd released 'The Jean Genie' – inspired by Iggy Pop, with a slight gay tease ('lives on his back . . . loves chimney stacks') and its parent album *Aladdin Sane*, with only 'Cracked Actor' ('Suck, baby suck, give me your head') suggesting some gay liaison, but it could just as easily be a heterosexual scenario.

Songs for marching

There were different ways to be frank; the parodies of Lisa Ben, the drag performance of Rae Bourbon and Minette, German singer Sonny Costa's 1970 bubblegum pop single 'Homo Joe' – after East and West Germany had legalised homosexual relations between men (respectively 1968 and 1969) – and his compatriot Johnny Delgada's single 'Wir Zwei, Wir Sind Nicht Wie die Anderen' ('We Two, We Are Not Like the Others') and 'Achilles' Klage' ('Achilles' Grief').

Delgada had been recording since the thirties, and his two orchestrated compositions sounded like they'd been pickled in aspic since before the war, as did his patronising, if sincere, explanation for writing them: his 'first encounter with homosexuals', after Delgada realised they were 'a group of cultivated, sensitive people, discriminated against as pariahs. In contrast to the classical period, people treated them like lepers . . . therefore, no one risked singing about their loves. How else, wild and unrestrained, could Achilles mourn his dead friend Patroclus?' The artwork, however, was startlingly current; an image of two naked and cuddling teenage boys, one with pubic hair showing, the other's hand hovering over his partner's groin.

There was still another way, one that had been missing so far, bypassing sci-fi, classical, drag or sexualised imagery, using the unadorned social message and political protest, to become the first songs to fully articulate gay rights since 'Das Lila Lied'.

One of the three thousand marchers who attended the USA's first nationwide match for gay rights, in New York state capital Albany in 1971, was Madeline Davis. In the fifties, she'd sung in various choirs and on the folk music, coffee-house circuit before fronting the jazz/rock/soul ensemble the New Chicago Lunche and her own Madeline Davis Group. But joining Mattachine's Niagara Frontier branch, based in Buffalo, and marching, signalled her growing politicisation. 'I'd never been in a march before, it was scary and it was wonderful at the same time,' she told J. D. Doyle. 'I was so high from that experience that on the way home, I wrote in my notebook the words to

"Stonewall Nation" and also a poem, "From The Steps of the Capitol 1971".'[1]

Davis' poem filled the B-side to her single 'Stonewall Nation', the first English-language gay rights anthem. Mattachine pressed up five hundred copies of the seven-inch record, with Davis' high, clear, folk diction, overlapping harmonies and precise statements all reminiscent of Joan Baez, the queen of folk music activism: 'Sisters take me by the hand/We're going to build our promised land ... You can take your tolerance and stow it/We're going to be ourselves and show it.'

Davis was encouraged to become the first openly lesbian delegate to a national political convention (alongside Jim Foster from San Francisco, the first gay male delegate),[2] where she asked her fellow Democrats to officially defend the civil rights of gay people. That a female delegate from Ohio rebutted Davis' proposal and linked homosexuality with prostitution and paedophilia, proved even some Democrats were Republican in bed[3] and more direct action was necessary. In 1972, she co-founded, and taught, the first US course on lesbianism, at the University of Buffalo, and wouldn't release another record until 1983.

In parallel to 'Stonewall Nation', Maxine Feldman was sketching out an equally defiant manifesto while wielding an acoustic guitar. This self-described 'big, loud, Jewish, butch lesbian' from Brooklyn – who later identified as transgender – wore her emotions much more nakedly. In 1963, she told J. D. Doyle, she'd been 'thrown off the Boston coffeehouse circuit ... for being queer and bringing around the wrong crowd.'[4]

Having been trained in children's theatre Feldman put it to good

---

1 http://queermusicheritage.com/nov2000.html
2 In 1972 too, Nancy Wechsler became the first openly gay or lesbian person in political office in the USA, elected to the Ann Arbor City Council as a member of the Human Rights Party.
3 Davis says the Ohio delegate later apologised, saying that the analogies she drew in her speech were aimed to show the possible ramifications of Davis' proposal and that she was not aware that the speech would imply that homosexuals are child molesters. www.npr.org/2012/09/05/160607418/in-1972-davis-blazed-party-trail-on-gay-rights
4 www.queermusicheritage.com/apr2002s.html

use at Boston's Emerson College before being fired for the same crime. She was told she could return after a course of psychiatric treatment; a doctor prescribed electroshock therapy that Feldman refused, before the cavalry arrived in the form of feminist/lesbian comedy duo Patti Harrison and Robin Tyler. They had met Feldman at Emerson, heard her songs and offered to take her on tour.

One of Feldman's songs was 'Angry Atthis', which dated from 1969. Atthis was both the lover of the Greek poet Sappho and a pun on 'angry at this'. Feldman drew on the sixties, when lesbians bars were Mafia-run and the police insisted on seeing the three 'female' items of clothing. 'I didn't like the way it made me feel – like we were useless and sick,' she told Doyle. 'I felt we were worth a lot more. Stonewall proved I was not alone. It was time for our protests . . . The song just spewed out of me'[1]: 'I hate not being able to hold my lover's hand/'cept under some dimly lit table . . . I hate to tell lies, live in the shadow of fear/We run half of our lives from the damn word "queer!"'

'Angry Atthis' lay unrecorded until Feldman found an outlet through Harrison and Tyler's Productions label. To match her angry lyric, Feldman's delivery performance was closer to the anguished delivery of Native American folk activist Buffy Saint Marie, especially her 'My Country 'Tis of Thy People You're Dying'. By the end of the song, Feldman got angrier and louder and the pace got faster as she hollered, 'It's not your wife that I want, it's not your children I'm after/It's not my choice I want to flaunt/Just want to hear my lover's laughter.' The finale was emphatic, exhilarating: 'Feel like we're animals in cages/And have you seen the lights in the gay bar/Not revealing wrinkles or rages/God forbid we reveal who we are . . . No longer afraid of being a . . . les-BIAN!'

Few got to hear 'Angry Atthis'. In fact, 'We could hardly give the record away,' Feldman told J. D. Doyle. 'People were still so closeted and so, "How could you be so, how could you be like that, all that

---

1 www.queermusicheritage.com/apr2002.html

pride, all the arrgh . . ." I would look at them and say, "How come you're not?"'[1]

Robin Tyler told Doyle that while her and Harrison's 'pro-lesbian humour' was 'somehow acceptable' because they were 'kind of svelte and very Hollywood-looking' Feldman was this – 'and I use it in the kindest terms, big, 'cause she was proud of it, fat, dykey-looking dyke, singing, "I am proud to be a lesbian." It was very, very difficult. And people started going after her and started going after us and cancelling our performances.'[2]

The old problem, a lack of funds for distribution and pressing, meant not even Jim Fouratt, perfectly positioned at the juncture of music and activism, heard either 'Stonewall Nation' or 'Angry Atthis'. There was no distribution channel or commercial outlet for a lesbian-identified item; America's first national gay lifestyle magazine, *The Advocate*, wouldn't launch until 1973.

In the UK, there was still the charge of gross indecency where one man was between sixteen and twenty years old with an *increased* maximum sentence of five years and it was still illegal to even *arrange* sex (for example, exchanging phone numbers) between two consenting adult men if they were in a public space. Resistance was limited, but fervent. The UK wing of the GLF's weekly meetings had up to 300 present and in 1972, 700 people formed the country's first Gay Pride March, from Trafalgar Square to Hyde Park. One of the marchers was Alan Wakeman, who was about to record Britain's first gay protest song.

Until he passed away in 2015, Wakeman lived in the same Central London flat (behind the neon signs of Piccadilly Circus) for nearly fifty years. Surrounded by old copies of the few records he got to make and the books that he wrote (he specialised in English language courses and co-wrote the first ever vegan cookbook), he recalled those good old, bad old days of his closeted youth, early romance, tragic circumstances and, eventually, some peace of mind. It was all contained in his

---

1 http://queermusicheritage.com/apr2002s.html
2 http://queermusicheritage.com/apr2002s.html

autobiography, *Fragments Of Joy And Sorrow*, which was published just two months before the heart attack he suffered at the age of 79. At least the newspaper obituaries recognised his importance in Britain's gay rights movement, while 'A Gay Song' was played at his funeral.

Raised in rural Surrey, Wakeman had done his national service in the army after World War II. Realising he was gay, he'd contemplated suicide after the man he'd fallen for got married and emigrated. Wakeman's reaction was to move abroad too, living in France for three years, taking various part-time jobs before his fluency in French opened up a job back in London setting up language laboratories and publishing the *English Fast* language course that included two seven inch singles, happy songs that helped to educate. But what truly fired Wakeman up was the GLF.

'I threw myself into it as soon as I heard about it,' he said. 'It was a miracle, I was thirty-five and I'd spent my whole life feeling ashamed of myself and hiding. I'd written a lyric, "Motorway Madness", about cars taking over the world and I thought, God, I'm not the only one who wants to save Earth.'

Wakeman was a classical music buff but aware of pop: 'It was all songs about girl-meets-boy, boy-meets-girl. I felt excluded. The most momentous occasion was the Beatles "All You Need Is Love", that was lovely. I felt included.' Having written lyrics and collaborated with musicians for *English Fast*, he decided a humanitarian-based band was the way forward, so he invited friends to jam: 'I called us Everyone Involved, which was shorthand for everyone turning up at mine. I wrote the words and my friend Michael wrote the music but the arrangements were by whoever turned up. It was totally democratic.'

Wakeman named their album *Either/Or*. 'Side one was about the damage we're doing to the planet and side two was the possible solutions. There was a gay song on side one, but it's called "A Sad Song". Side two had "A Gay Song".'

Over a crisp, rollicking rhythm, Wakeman's lyric for 'A Sad Song' imagined an elderly lesbian and gay man who had never come out, reflecting on their lives: 'All the things you wanted to do/All the things

Early 20th century

(far left) The drag king sings; England's immaculately tailored music hall favourite, Vesta Tilley.

(left) 'Hello, Freda!' The black sheep of his family, music hall's first gay idol, Fred Barnes.

(below) Sheet music for '*Das Lila Lied*', a.k.a. 'The Lilac Song', the first gay pride anthem, 1920.

T'aint nobody's business if she does: Bessie Smith, blues queen of the Harlem Renaissance.

'America's greatest sepia piana artist' – lesbian blues legend, Gladys Bentley.

1920s-30s

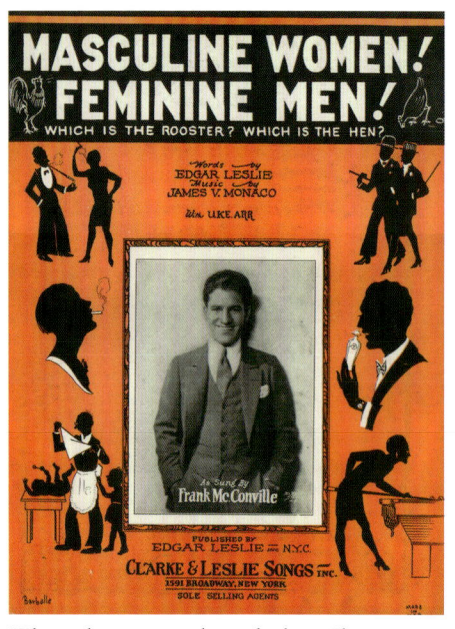

Who is the rooster, who is the hen? Sheet music for 'Masculine Women, Feminine Men', 1926.

Gwen Farrar – cellist, comedienne, friend of Radcliffe Hall and lover of fellow singer, Nora Blaney.

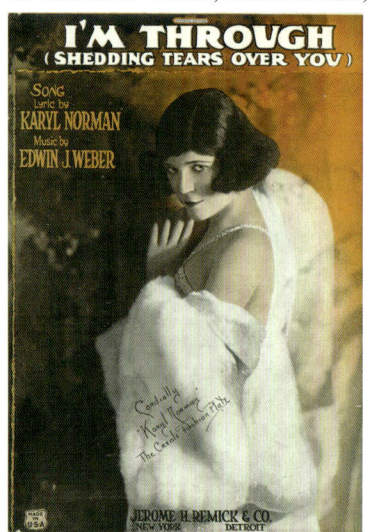

(above left) Sheet music advertising the Pansy Club's singing, songwriting compere, Karyl Norman.

(above right) Call him Gene, or Jean – the mannish, not Spanish, Mr Malin.

(right) Drunk with love: the pansy craze's forgotten boy, Bruz Fletcher.

1940s

(top left) 'Gay, gay, gay, gay, gay; is there any other way? Frances Faye!'

(top right) 'Only God and Infinity deserved capitals' – America's nature boy, eden ahbez.

(above left) The lonely, lush life of Duke Ellington's trusted arranger, Billy Strayhorn.

(above right) The real roots of rock'n'roll: Sister Rosetta Tharpe.

(left) Madame Spivy, the singing hostess with the mostess at New York nightclub Spivy's Roof.

1950s I

'Faggot, sissy, freak, punk' – and rock'n'roll revolutionary Little Richard (centre), and the rivals that time forgot, Billy Wright (left) and Esquerita (right).

Heaven-sent: 1950s lesbian rockabilly trio the Roc-A-Jets (*left to right*: Jan Morrison, Jo Kellum, Edie Lippincott).

1950s II

Mr Emotion, the Nabob of Sob, the Prince of Wails – Johnnie Ray.

The King of Kitsch, and master of cruising ballads: poet/singer Rod McKuen.

Doo wop's gay genie, Cornell Gunter, with The Coasters (*left:* 1950s, second right, and *right:* 1970s, front).

1960s I

(top left) Edith Eyde, founder of the first gay 'zine Vice-Versa, and the first lesbian folksinger as Lisa Ben.

(top right) The lure of the closet – the irrepressible, tragic Dusty Springfield and the more repressible, tragic Liberace.

(above) The cover of *Love Is A Drag – For Adult Listeners Only, Sultry Stylings By A Most Unusual Vocalist* (compilation, 1962).

(right) 'Prince meets Little Richard meets Eartha Kitt' – North American soul treasure, Jackie Shane.

1960s II

Blues belter, pop crooner and Elton's 'Sugar Bear', Long John Baldry.

'Give me a torn dress, a beach and a hit of acid and that's enough': Hibiscus (front) and the Cockettes.

(above) Zebedy Colt, the self-styled 'first gay superstar on long playing records' – if only.

(left) Polly Perkins: Carnaby Street image for Ready Steady Go!

1970s I: glam comes out of the closet

(left) 'A dress – but a man's dress' – David Bowie and protégé Freddi 'Rudi Valentino' Buretti, cover stars of *Curious* magazine (1970).

(above) When he was a Cockette: future disco superstar Sylvester, alongside Cockettes co-founder Rumi Missabu (1971).

The first out gay, and drag, and transgender, rocker, the inimitable Jayne County.

(above) Brazil's gay glam idol, Ney Matogrosso (front), of Secos e Molhados, a.k.a. Dry and Wet (1973).

(left) John 'Smokey' Cordon of US glam duo Smokey, modelling their S&M record label logo (1975).

you never dared to/Because it wasn't natural/Because it wasn't good.' For the responding 'A Gay Song', Wakeman told the GLF meeting that anyone was welcome to sing the chorus – 'and they did! The off-beat clapping is them! It added a sense of reality.' The song's rambling folk charm, as much campfire singsong as pride anthem, was delivered in the most basic terms: 'Gay is natural/Gay is good/Gay is wonderful/Gay people should/All come together/And fight for our rights.'

Wakeman hoped 'A Gay Song' would be sung at Gay Pride events, which never happened, and there would be no comparable song for another three years. The US was comparatively more galvanised into a political response, with the experience of race relations, feminism and gay rights.

The first officially promoted lesbian concert was in May 1972 at Chicago's University of Illinois; the bill featured local singer-songwriter Linda Shear and the Chicago Women's Liberation Rock Band, which had joined forces with the New Haven Women's Liberation Rock Band for a new album, *Mountain Moving Day*. The title track demanded, 'all sleeping women, now wake'. Despite the Chicago faction's presence that May day, the liberation bands both identified as feminist rather than lesbian, though Chicago keyboardist Naomi Weinstein told writer Ruth Rosen, 'Everybody I knew experimented with lesbian relationships.'[1]

In 1973, former *Ready Steady Go!* presenter Polly Perkins was feeling liberated, working the cabaret circuit and releasing *Liberated Woman*, an album of bluesy rock and music-hall turns. Next to her *Pop-Lore According to the Academy* album, Perkins's new record was more circumspect about lesbian themes, 'but they are so when a woman is singing them,' she says, citing 'Cindy' ('she is a pretty girl . . . Cindy, you can have my key'). For Perkins, feminism was more pressing but not the only issue: the liner notes read, 'Liberation for woman means society crumbling, marriage ruined, children left to go their own scenes, men losing their hold on the purse strings and bedclothes, women fancying other women.'

---

1 *The World Split Open: How the Modern Women's Movement Changed Americ*a (Viking Adult, 2000)

The first categorically lesbian-themed album was also released in 1973. *A Few Loving Women* was a recording of an open-mic lesbian talent contest organised by members of the Lesbian Feminist Liberation group, held at the Firehouse in New York's Soho district, a community centre run by the Gay Activist Alliance. Author-poet Margaret Sloan's opening track 'I'd Like to Make Love with You' cut to the chase: 'I'd like to make love with you/because you are a woman and I am too'. Through 'Big Orgasm', 'Funny Lady' and 'People Like Me', the tone was undiluted coffee-house folk, earnest and amateur. Their message was not making any musical claim, but setting their own agenda.

The feminist movement was, in part, fuelled by converts fresh out of consciousness-raising groups. As the daughter of staunch communists in Jewish New York under FBI surveillance, Alix Dobkin says she felt the same passion about politics and justice as her parents: 'That's how I experienced my difference at that time. I was very reserved. Sex meant hetero sex, and I wasn't interested. Well, yes and no.'

Making music was a safer option. Doblin loved her family's Broadway soundtracks, but civil rights equated with folk music. The first song she wrote, with her friend Elliott, was 'Cigarettes, Whiskey and Wild, Wild Women': 'He wrote about whiskey and I wrote about wild women! It was like a warning to young men. I wrote about politics in the form of love songs or that men couldn't satisfy me. My shows became very sexual and challenging.'

It didn't stop Dobkin from getting married. She and husband Sam Hood, who'd been running the Gaslight Café in Greenwich Village, moved to Miami where he opened the Gaslight South, but their heart stayed in New York, so they returned in 1968. Hood later managed Max's Kansas City, where Dobkin saw the all-female rock band Fanny. 'It was great that women were playing rock'n'roll in the consciousness-raising spirit of the times, it was exciting beyond belief,' she says. She soon joined a consciousness-raising group: 'I became a feminist and saw the light. There was no stopping me. My story is not uncommon.'

Freshly divorced, Dobkin was at the Firehouse when she heard flautist Kay Gardner playing upstairs. 'I'd written these lesbian songs and people said I should make a record, so I asked Kay.' Bassist Pat Moschetta, who called herself Patches Attom, completed the trio Lavender Jane, but Dobkin didn't only stop at an all-woman band. She didn't want any men involved in making their album. With recording engineer Marilyn Rees and Dobkin starting her own label Women's Wax Works, *Lavender Jane Loves Women* was 'by, for and about lesbians, which no one had ever done before. You can't change the pronoun for any of the songs to make sense. I was very careful about building that into the songs.'

Dobkin's melodies and Gardner's flute echoed the innocence of children's songs, yet the contents were frank, everything that Frances Faye, Lisa Ben and Dusty Springfield had not articulated: 'Her Precious Love', 'Talking Lesbian' and 'View From Gay Head': 'There are two kinds of people in the world today/One or the other a person must be/ The men are them, the women are we/And they agree it's a pleasure to be/A lesbian in no man's land.'

Beside singing the word 'lesbian' more times than any record before or even after, it's probable that Dobkin was first to sing 'penis' in a song, as in 'View From Gay Head': 'I'll return to the bosom where my journey ends/Where there's no penis between us friends.'

Lavender Jane herself, Dobkin says, was based on three Janes: 'the plain Jane, the "everywoman" aspect, Jane Powell the singer and actress, who I'd been in love with for a long time, and Jane Alpert, who'd written about women and how sexist the left were, like thinking women always had to be available for sex. So I ripped them another asshole.' The album included the Scots folk ballad 'Eppie Morrie', about a successfully resisted rape and forced marriage: 'That song was in my head all summer before I came out.'

Dobkin's independence was necessary given the experiences of other women in the music industry, where even Joni Mitchell had been hung out to dry when *Rolling Stone* voting her 'old lady of the year' for having myriad relationships with men: no man would have received similar treatment. But in the two years since Madeline Davis' single, a better distribution system for lesbian art and media had developed, via feminist bookstores and mail order and the growth in women-only events. 'We pressed a thousand copies and just kept re-pressing,' Dobkin says. 'The response was monumental.'

Around the same time, singer-songwriter Cris Williamson was being interviewed on radio by fellow songwriter Meg Christian and Ginny Berson of Washington DC lesbian collective the Furies. From Deadwood, South Dakota, Williamson had a head start on her lesbian peers, having released three private-press albums of mostly folk-rock covers in the placid mould of Judy Collins before writing her own album, 1971's *Cris Williamson*. Knowing enough about the music industry, she suggested, on air, the idea of a record label that supported lesbians. 'I didn't think of it as revolutionary at the time,' she told writer Andrew Poteet. 'Now I can see that it was, but I just thought, What are they talking about? Let's just go do it.'[1]

'It' became Olivia Records, named after the eponymous heroine of Dorothy Bussey's 1949 novel, who falls in love with her headmistress at a French boarding school. The label launched with a double A-side sold by mail order, featuring Christian's 'Lady' (written by Brill Building duo Carole King and Gerry Goffin) and Wiliamson's own 'If It Weren't For The Music'. The workforce were members of the Furies and its sister DC collective, the Radicalesbians, hardcore separatists who had broken off from the Gay Liberation Front after feeling excluded from the shared gay/lesbian dances at the Firehouse.

According to lesbian writer Alice Echols, 'GLF dances were meant to engender love and acceptance and to create community, which they tried to achieve through hippie-like circle dances. However, GLF dances also featured a mirrorball, go-go boys, and to some radical lesbians a lot of "groping and dry-fucking" among men as well.'[2]

---

1 www.pridesource.com/article.html?article=48493
2 *Hot Stuff: Disco and the Remaking of America* (Norton and Company, 2010)

It was equally felt that gay men would selfishly commandeer the agenda of gay rights, and that heterosexual women – because of their relationships with men – would not commit to ending male supremacy. Hence Radicalesbians' pioneering manifesto *The Woman Identified Woman*, which posited the theory that sexual orientation could be a political choice.

Like Dobkin, every facet of Olivia was to be orchestrated by women, from production to distribution. Olivia reportedly made $12,000 profit from its split single, which funded Christian's debut album *I Know You Know*.

From Lynchburg, Virginia, Christian had moved to Washington in 1969 and worked up a set of feminist songs, though her album consisted mostly of covers such as Williamson's 'Joanna' and Canadian folk singer Ralf Kempf's 'Hello Hooray'. Alice Cooper had covered the song in 1973 as a troop-rallying exercise, though Christian re-traced Kempf's original declaration of 'self-renewal', to which Christian added new lyrics of closet-busting zeal: 'After all these years of crying, self-denying/And lonely waiting and fears and hesitating/Yes, we'll laugh/As we see this thing finally begin.'

Though released first, Dobkin's *Lavender Jane Loves Women* is typically passed over as the record that launched the genre of women's music for Olivia's second album, released in 1973. Cris Williamson's presciently titled *The Changer and the Changed: a Record of the Times* was like striking oil: it sold a hundred thousand copies the first year, and eventually over 250,000 (some claim 500,000, though sales have never been ratified). It was the biggest independent release of its day and a game-changer for Olivia. The album might still be the label's finest, a richer and more rounded effort than her peers, Olivia's Carole King crossover, the lesbian *Tapestry*, more than earnest sixties folk purity. In 2011, looking back at almost fifty years of making music, Williamson told journalist Andrea Poteet, 'I didn't mean to make this big piece. I was making a small piece and it was big because the need was so great.

Necessity is the mother of invention. Women needed it so badly they almost invented it.'[1]

Susan Wiseheart, one of the current organisers of OLOC (Old Lesbians Organising for Change), was twenty-four when she heard Williamson's album. 'Growing up, I was totally brainwashed to be heterosexual,' she recalls. 'It wasn't until the late sixties, in my late twenties, that I figured out who I was as a lesbian and I thought I'd like it a lot if out-lesbians could be heard too. I used to listen for songs that did not use pronouns and I tried to think the women were singing about other women and eventually I heard about Gladys Bentley and other blues women who were lesbians, but I only knew that "Sally Go Round the Roses" might have been a lesbian song. But the first real lesbian performers I knew were Meg Christian and Cris Williamson. And after that, Alix Dobkin, who actually used the word, "lesbian".'

Christian and Williamson, alongside Margie Adam – the pianist on Olivia's first two records – and the more politically charged Holly Near,[2] a former cast member of *Hair* and anti-Vietnam activist – were deemed the big four of the women's music scene and all four linked up for the Women On Wheels tour of 1976. Susan Wiseheart subsequently discovered that Christian and Williamson would also be appearing at the inaugural Michigan Womyn's Music Festival – or Mitchfest, as it was called during its forty-year reign as the pre-eminent annual women's gathering.

'I was at the first Mitchfest and every one after that,' says Wiseheart. 'I learned huge amounts there about what we called "womyn's music" of all genres and at other festivals too and through records that individual artists released and labels like Olivia and Redwood. Holly Near came out at the first Michigan festival, which was a huge thrill because she was a peace movement hero.'

---

1 www.pridesource.com/article.html?article=48493
2 Near would form her own label, Redwood, while Margie Adam would form the Pleiades label, both keeping their identity separate from Olivia. There were other labels run by lesbians, for example Linda Shear's Old Lady Blue Jeans. Alix Dobkin's flautist Kay Gardner started Wise Woman/Urana.

Mitchfest wasn't exclusively lesbian, but it provided a secure, separatist space. Olivia was an equal safe haven – its inclusivity was confirmed when a request from staunch feminist Yoko Ono to make a record for the label was snubbed because she was married to John Lennon. A tightly bound scene, women's music artists guested on each other's records. *The Changer* . . . also featured Margie Adam, Meg Christian and Holly Near. Another name that kept cropping up was guitarist June Millington, a founder member of Fanny, the first all-woman rock band, having recovered from what she calls, 'the boy-defined rock world'.

Women rock, women roll
In 1970, Fanny had also been first all-female band to release an album on a major label, Warner Bros offshoot Reprise. The band's founders, US-Filipino sisters June and (singer-bassist) Jean, had previously formed two all-girl bands – the Svelts at high school and then Wild Honey, who got talent-spotted by producer Richard Perry, searching for just such a line-up. Renamed Fanny after a female spirit rather than any part of the female anatomy, the band would reinforce Janis Joplin's point, that women could rock as well as men, but the odds remained stacked against them. So was June's emerging sexuality. 'I didn't think of sexuality back then,' she says. 'To play music as a girl was much huger than any attraction to boys and girls.'

That was before Millington fell for fellow musician Tret Fure. 'It wasn't, like, all of a sudden, I know I'm a lesbian, I just stopped worrying about it,' she says. 'Sure, I was upset that society was not into [lesbianism], but a woman playing lead guitar wasn't much different in that sense. And racism was the first "ism" that I'd encountered.'

But when Fure left her – 'June was always on tour, I never saw her' she says – Millington fell apart. 'I felt alone,' she says. 'I was so young when I started, I hadn't had enough life experience. I was in the limelight and people wanted Fanny to present as sex kittens. The constant pressure to be beautiful and good all the time. I wasn't allowed an off night. So I had to leave the band. I needed something more spiritual.'[1]

Cris Williamson was a Fanny fan and the pair formed a mutual admiration society, bringing Millington into Olivia's orbit and making her the first musician to bridge the scenes of rock music and women's music. 'Cris' music had a deep, spiritual energy that was a calling for me,' says Millington. 'Within a few months of playing with her, I realised we'd summoned this healing energy, which was way bigger than me. I'd never had that feeling in Fanny.'

Millington wasn't alone in trying to find a place in a boy-defined rock world. LA quartet Birtha – who Millington thinks were all lesbian, with guitarist Shele Pinizzotto and drummer Liver Favela lovers – were more bluesy, Joplin-esque rockers than Fanny. A flyer for their UK tour supporting the Kinks promised 'Birtha has balls'. They certainly had stamina, touring incessantly and supporting prominent rock bands such as Alice Cooper and Fleetwood Mac, but they've been virtually forgotten today.

In 1973, Tret Fure released a self-titled album on major label MCA, a dreamy west coast, singer-songwriter kind of record with Fure's Baez-influenced vocal and a stellar supporting cast, including the album's producer, Little Feat guitarist Lowell George, former employer Spencer Davis (who'd formed the premier British beat-blues combo the Spencer Davis Group) and the Millington sisters. Though she'd never realised she was a lesbian until she met June, Fure felt comfortable enough not to hide it even from her record label. 'But they weren't interested in promoting artists who were lesbian, it was hard enough to get a record deal as a woman,' she recalls. 'MCA dropped me and I did get another deal with United Artists, but then they got out of music and I couldn't resell the album I'd made. I was gay, approaching thirty and, I thought, over the hill, but I held my ground and I became one of the first female studio engineers in LA.'

---

[1] Millington's replacement in Fanny was Patti Quatro, sister of glam-rocker Suzi. The sisters had been members of the Pleasure Seekers, the second all-female band to sign a record deal after Goldie and the Gingerbreads.

The Deadly Nightshade had an even tougher assignment as 'the only all-female band signed to a mainstream major record label that recorded songs with explicit outright feminist content,'[1] as Pam Brandt told J. D. Doyle. Brandt had formed the band in 1972 with Anne Bowen and Helen Hooke, ex-members of late-sixties, all-female quintet Ariel. Feminism had energised them to give it another shot and RCA had signed the trio, possibly hoping they had a three-headed version of Helen Reddy, whose 1971 hit 'I Am Woman' had just reached US no. 1. The Deadly Nightshade had songs of female empowerment such as 'High Flying Woman' and a similarly polished country-MOR sound, but Reddy was a straight woman, a more manageable concept for a record label than three empowered lesbians.

'There was that business of, "Why don't you write regular songs?" They sure didn't want us to write gay songs,' Brandt told J. D. Doyle. 'Sometimes, [RCA] would explicitly throw things in our faces, about Laura Nyro, or "Oh, Dusty Springfield, she came out in *Rolling Stone* as bisexual and it ruined her career." And it wasn't that we had even said, hey, we're going to write a gay song or something.'

A psychoanalyst might think that signing to a major label was like accepting the closet that still surrounded gay musicians. The Deadly Nightshade played gay bars, all-women events, gay pride rallies and benefits while Brandt and Hooke were lovers, but they weren't out to their families. As a band too, Brandt admitted, '[We were] too closeted, closeted enough that I rapidly grew ashamed of it. It was what was done at the time.' Even performers in the women's music community were not out, she claimed. 'This was back in the days when everybody was being like overly considerate of each other and protective about not outing people. The gay community was almost like encouraging artists not to talk about it openly because so many of us in all walks of life were, in some aspects of those lives, in the closet.'

One all-female rock band, Isis, signed to the major-affiliated label

---

1 www.queermusicheritage.com/mar2013s.html

Buddah, managed to get away with a lesbian statement in 'She Loves Me'. The eight-piece Isis had been formed in 1972 by ex-Goldie and the Gingerbreads guitarist Carol MacDonald and drummer Ginger Bianco and were a much tougher proposition, playing powerful, brass-driven rock, blues, funk and soul. And MacDonald was emphatically out. 'I had too many years of being in the closet with the Gingerbreads – it drove me crazy!" MacDonald said. So if Isis were to be photographed naked and sprayed in chrome metallic on the cover of their self-titled album debut, that was their decision.

It got the band noticed, but the battle for all-female bands remained uphill; *Rolling Stone* wrote about Isis' formation, then ignored all three of their albums and disparaged them in a live review. MacDonald finally gave in after the third album, ironically named *Breaking Through*. 'Isis may have made it if I hadn't come out,' she mused. 'Maybe. I don't know that, though. The girls that [joined] the band, they were . . . gonna get a rep as being gay because of me and I would tell them that from the beginning – because most of them weren't [gay].'

'Only Carol was crazy enough to buck the system, you could not hold her back,' says Joy Silver, who played bass in the Isis-style band Lilith. 'Goldie and the Gingerbreads had more or less conformed when [singer] Genya [Raven] was the boss, but once Carol had the reins, she was defiant and so Buddah dropped Isis. Record labels were looking for packages and not musicianship; these girls were great players but not glamour girls by a long shot, which wasn't important to them. People in the industry thought Carol was crazy rather than heroic but she blasted the doors open for all of us to follow.'

Silver had joined the seven-piece Lilith in 1975. 'Scarlet Fever were in New York, and Witch in Boston, we all followed what Isis had laid out, it was the middle of women's liberation and we weren't interested in presenting as straight,' she recalls. 'But none of those bands made the big time because they presented as lesbian.'

An ideological gulf soon opened between the rock and women's music communities, who were enjoying their separatism – take Linda Shear, who had played at the inaugural lesbian concert in Chicago and whose 1974 album was called *A Lesbian Portrait (Lesbian Music For Lesbians Only)*. 'They thought Isis and Lilith, who played rock'n'roll, were copying men, so they'd boycott us,' says Silver. 'We felt we were changing the world by showing up in the mainstream but they felt they were creating a new world. That's not to say you wouldn't put on a Cris Williamson record if you were making love, but I was more interested in blues and funk. I'd listen to Led Zeppelin! And Laura Nyro was our Bob Dylan. We loved "Emmie" and knew that Laura was bisexual. She was just the heart and soul of our music.'

Nyro had made the same choice as June Millington and got out while she could. Her music had gotten more complex and anguished, consumed by man trouble (check out 'Captain Saint Lucifer' and 'Tom Cat Goodbye'). But in the course of her 1971 covers album *Gonna Take A Miracle*, a stunning memory trip that took in her doo wop, R&B and Motown roots, Nyro transformed male quintet the Charts' 1957 single 'Desiree' into a lesbian torch ballad: 'Oh, my darling, Desiree/You make my heart feel so free/And I'd like to know, why do I love you so?'

And with that, Nyro was gone, leaving New York for rural Massachusetts, getting married and having a child. She wouldn't record again until 1976's *Smile*, which eschewed man-crisis blues for a more eco-spiritual brand of awareness without a hint of her sexuality (she wasn't to start living with painter Maria Desiderio until the early eighties). Nyro would have been snubbed by the separatists anyway, who drove a hard bargain. June Millington experienced the hardcore politics of the era when she played guitar on Cris Williamson's 1976 tour. Reaching New York, Millington brought along two former bandmates, both male, to see the show. 'They were standing at the back of the room, in this packed church' Millington recalls, 'and someone started screaming, "There are men!" I was really shocked, and Cris was really embarrassed.'

'That was us,' Alix Dobkin admits. 'I'd been staying with friends, who were super-separatists; they called men "mutants". They were talking about how hard it was to have women-only concerts and I'd played at the church where Cris was playing and I felt it was my space – though someone else saw the men and shouted, "Throw out the pricks!", which people then started chanting. Kay [Gardner] and her spiritual crowd were chanting, "The goddess is alive, the magic is afoot!" These poor men; one half of me wanted to take care of them, the other half was saying, "*Get these pricks out of here*!" I felt that if even one man entered a room of women, everything changed. They interfered with women being together and acknowledged and valued.'

It's understandable that lesbians felt the need for self-protection. As Janis Ian recalls, she was outed in 1976, by gay journalist Cliff Jahr in the *Village Voice*: 'He'd come on tour with me and my band and he felt it was his duty,' says Ian. 'I freaked for a day, because everyone in the music industry knew; my girlfriend came to every event of mine, including the Grammies. Fortunately, no one else picked up on it which was very kind because it would have destroyed my career. Any venue that needed a liquor license had a morals clause so they could technically break your contract or not hire you or you could lose your union membership. I was working in pop and folk and they were not bastions of openness.'

Ian did write one 'love song to a woman' called 'Maria', which featured on her 1976 album *Miracle Row*, and which, she says, was pretty overt: '"Eyes are like a demon lover's child/and lips of velvet issue invitation/ every time you smile", but so few people picked up on it that it wasn't an issue, which just goes to show you how little most folks listen to lyrics.'

Women's music fans would have been listening but, as Ian says, 'Olivia's audience wouldn't be caught dead at one of my shows. I recognised there were women who felt safer in that environment, but fortunately the men I have worked with, I can't think of one that wasn't accepting.'

Separatism was not confined to the USA; in West Berlin, Germany, the six-piece Flying Lesbians formed to provide live music at a party that was showing a documentary about abortion that a TV station had pulled from the schedule. According to their 'Mission, Vision, Values' statement, men, 'used their instruments like sexual organs,' and treated live performance, 'like a violent sexual act and as a submission ritual: "Under my thumb . . .", sang the Rolling Stones. We disliked the ego-trippers, sex maniacs with their groupie system, their fantasies of almightiness, and how they let the puppets dance.'

Their website quotes Italian author Meri Franco Lao: 'As women, you must make totally different music; you must not use any instrument from the patriarchal orchestras or built by a patriarch; you must not use their musical forms. You must not perform their rituals. You shall play witches' music and reconstruct and recreate their musical forms.'

You wouldn't expect, with that attitude, that the Flying Lesbians had discovered, 'It was not too difficult to agree that we would play mainly blues and rock patterns.' At least they didn't *rock* but they did *roll*; the piano-driven 'I'm A Lesbian, How About You?' was a subtle, shaky brand of boogie-woogie.

Regarding positive action, the Flying Lesbians vowed 'to be amateurs instead of professionals. We wanted less distance to the public. We wanted the other women to say, "Hey, we could do that, too!"' The band's lyrics would align with the slogans of the lesbian and women's movements, 'mirroring the euphoric, rebellious, Amazonian and optimistic mood in those early years . . . We were singing about battered wives, love (between women), about disappointments caused by women in power, on bisexuality which was "in" at that time, on girl junkies and female unemployment and about matriarchy – "We are one million years old, but what did we learn?"'

Having handled being Germany's first all-female band as well as the country's only lesbian band, the Flying Lesbians were still forced to face facts that weren't exclusive to sexuality or gender – the dynamics of band life. Especially a collective-style band with no profit motive nor the will to widen their appeal. The band split up after three years, citing exhaustion and 'different personal, political and musical developments'. On top, 'the euphoric wave of the women's movement, which had carried our band, wore off. The surprise factor, the flair and the sensation of the first years and women's parties turned into routine for us.'

While Germany had just the Flying Lesbians, the UK had a small, but committed, scene. In 1971, a faction of the Gay Liberation Front supporters involved in London's Women's Liberation Workshop formed the London Women's Liberation Rock Band (LWLRB). The band's inspirations were eclectic, from women rock singers such as Carol Grimes, Maggie Bell and Elkie Brooks to the Velvet Underground, Bowie and the Chicago and New Haven Women's Liberation Rock Bands, but the emphasis was more on that commitment than musicianship: at their early rehearsals, 'our instruments were acoustic and I was drumming on saucepans with chopsticks,' says Frankie Green, who now runs the Women's Liberation Music Archive, a comprehensive online guide to the UK and Ireland's feminist music scene of the seventies and eighties.[1]

LWLRB members mostly lived in squats around north London, though rehearsals extended to pub rooms, council flats and community centres. Life was busy and never dull. 'Music-making was entwined with the rest of our lives,' Green recalls, 'which involved communal houses, frequent political meetings, campaigns, demonstrations and marches, running women's centres, consciousness-raising, spray-painting excursions, producing leaflets, dealing with various court cases arising from being arrested while squatting or demonstrating, being evicted and moving frequently. The band didn't make any money and apart from an initial donation, it was self-funded. Most of us were in low-paid jobs or on the dole [social security].'

LWLRB songs included 'Body Squat', entwining 'the taking over of houses with control of our physical selves for ourselves, asserting our right to bodily integrity, reproductive and sexual rights, an end to alienation from our bodies and their objectification,' They would also alter lyrics of existing songs, like changing the gender of the Rolling Stones' 'Street Fighting Man', 'which got us involved in discussion about women playing "cock-rock",' says Green.

---

[1] http://womensliberationmusicarchive.co.uk

There was a Northern Women's Liberation Rock Band (NWLRB), who played covers that suited their cause, from racism (Jimmy Cliff's 'You Can Get It If You Really Want') to feminism (Laura Lee's 'Stand Up and Fight for Your Love Rights'). Original songs such as 'Blue Blood Blues' critiqued capitalism but also referenced to sexuality: 'I didn't want to marry/I'm one of the Gateways[1] kind/But Mummy said I ought to/Just to perpetuate the family line.'

There were even bands whose names showed a little imagination. Named after the east London borough where they squatted, the Stepney Sisters' frontline of Caroline Gilfillan, Marion Lees and Ruthie Smith had started out as the backing singers of the soul band Xpensive – before that, Gilfillan and Lees 'used to wear hotpants and sing in a band called Tilly Teeth and the Braces,' said Smith. Feminism would transform them and trigger relationships between band members. On the WLM archive, guitarist Nona Ardill wrote, 'The four who still identified as "straight", felt confused and threatened, not so much because of their lesbian sisters in the band but of assumptions now being made by other people (both men and women) that we were a lesbian band ... In a bid to redress the balance, we made a decision to have a few "pro-men" songs in our set – to make it clear that we did not wish to exclude men altogether.'[2]

Jam Today were the most prominent of Britain's feminist bands, the only representatives profiled in a feature on all-women bands in the December 1976 issue of the rock music weekly *Sounds*, under the headline 'The new other wave'. The other bands were feminist simply by nature of forming all-women bands, but weren't using their music to make a political stand. Frankie Green formed the eight-piece band after advertising for members.

In the mid-sixties, Green had 'briefly played drums in a band known by that demeaning term "all-girl group", which was set up by a male

---

1 Gateways was the most legendary of all London lesbian clubs, having opened in Chelsea in 1931, becoming women-only in 1967 and running all the way through to 1985.
2 https://womensliberationmusicarchive.files.wordpress.com/2010/10/nony-on-the-stepney-sisters.pdf

manager as a gimmick,' she says. Now she had the chance to turn the gimmick into a model of self-sufficiency.

'We played rock of a funky kind,' she says. 'We included lyrics about women uniting and breaking free, being in control of our own lives, love and friendship between women and criticising romantic pop songs.' The collective mirrored Olivia's self-sufficiency by starting to their own label, Stroppy Cow, so-called because 'a man aggressively yelled, "Stroppy cows!" at us in a recording studio when we failed to pay him the attention he felt he was due.'

Ova were a duo who put out records on Stroppy Cow, the only exclusively lesbian band of the time, comprising lovers Rosemary Schonfeld and Jana (formerly Jane) Runnalls. As a member of folk-rockers Rockwood, singer-songwriter Schonfeld had been closeted: 'Being lesbian was a tough choice, I'd heard the horror stories, we knew what happened to Dusty [Springfield] and Joan Armatrading had never come out. Friends said I could learn to find feelings for men, I tried but I never did. And then I met Jana."

Schonfeld and Runnalls – also British, but then living in Paris – met when they were independently visiting friends in a north London squat. They subsequently moved in to the squat but were attacked by an alcoholic who lived a floor below them; told 'We'd got what we deserved' by their fellow squatters, the couple moved to a south London gay squat known as the Brixton Faeries. 'The incident really politicised us,' says Schonfeld, 'what with all the homophobia and misogyny. We started writing songs about our experiences, and found there was an audience.'

Ova were unusual in two regards: they were early practitioners of ethnic instruments, and they were more forceful than other women's music bands, with songs such as 'Self-Defence' – 'One day I'm going to kill a man in self-defence' and 'Lesbian Fighting Song': 'You humiliate our minds/You violate us all/We don't care what you call us/We will scream our rage/We will fight all our lives and more/We may die but our culture will stay!'

'Many women musicians at that time had horror stories of being threatened by male musicians,' says Schonfeld. 'I'd been in a band where the men would simply turn down my amp while I was performing. Terry Quay, a percussionist, was threatened by a male drummer that he would break her wrists.' To take back complete control, Schonfeld and Runnalls founded Ova Music Studio in 1983, funded by the left-wing Greater London Council. They had their own PA system and sound engineer and ran music singing, drumming and recording workshops. 'We were virulently opposed to the music industry because of the sexism and politics, they exploited everyone,' says Schonfeld. 'So we were passionate about being in control of our creative output. A big part of what we did was how we did it . . . It was all about getting our hands on the technology.'

The forces of opposition to gay and lesbian rights continued to put up a fight. In 1984, Ova were interviewed on the BBC World Service strand *Inside London*. Referring to their songs, the interviewer said, 'They're not only political, they could be described as, I don't know, dangerous, couldn't they? Also, 'Let's put it bluntly, there's a strong lesbian leaning there, words like, "I want her to stay the night, hold each other on and on with kisses that go far beyond the dawn", to hear a woman sing a song like that might make some people feel uncomfortable.'

'Yes, it might, and it's about time that it becomes a bit more commonplace doing that kind of thing,' Schonfeld and Runnalls responded. 'I get really annoyed still, there are so many gay people at the top of the tree, musically, men and women. The most you get is an ambiguous, "you," in "I love you".'

Rock'n'roll, meet gay politics

The politicised campaigners of women's music contrasted starkly with the role-playing approach of men, who stoked fantasies and liberated stifled emotions via decadent thrills, sci-fi fantasy and coded messages.

The only song of the early seventies that didn't require de-coding was, perhaps unsurprisingly, from the more liberated mainland Europe. Charles Aznavour, a former protégé of Edith Piaf, had already scandalised France with the post-coital bliss of 'After Love' and he wanted to break boundaries again: 'French *chanson*, indeed the *chanson* all over the world, had insipid lyrics,' he told writer Jody Rosen. 'I wanted to do something new, more truthful and far more to the point.'[1]

Aznavour considered *'Comme Ils Disent'* ('What Makes A Man')[2] to be the first song about homosexuality in France – not so, given Robert Rocca's 'Ils En Sont Tous'. Given Rocca's rarity and Aznavour's huge popularity, it would have been the country's first mainstream gay song and the first to include the word 'gay', in this interior monologue of a drag queen: 'So many times we have to pay/For having fun and being gay . . . Nobody has the right to be the judge of what is right for me/Tell me if you can. What makes a man a man?'

'I wanted to write about the specific problems my gay friends faced,' Aznavour explained. 'I could see things were different for them, that they were marginalised. I always wrote about things that others might not have written about. We don't mind frank language in books, the theatre or cinema, but for some reason still to sing about such things is seen as odd.'

Patrick O'Haggerty felt the same. To lay down a valuable marker of gay identity in popular song and across an entire long-playing record rather than a one-off, it took a man with a sense of nothing to lose, having chosen a genre that was antithetical to any progressive ideology, let alone fledging gay rights – country music, the domain of rural, conservative USA.

By 1973, the gay/country affair had been restricted to the old homophobic chestnut 'Lavender Cowboy' (the latest version had come from South African raconteur Paddy Roberts, in 1959, who also named his 1964 album *Songs For Gay Dogs*), the Sweet Violet Boys, Billy Brigg's 'The Sissy Song', Howard Barnes' 'Helluva World' ('You can't tell the women from the men') and Johnny Cash's 'A Boy Named Sue', in which

---

1 http://www.salon.com/1999/07/15/aznavour/
2 Released on his album *Idiote Je T'Aime* and in English on *Aznavour Sings Aznavour Vol. 3*, both 1972.

a man is ridiculed by his birth name to ensure he is tough enough to stand on his own two feet.

Country music's one unrepentant out (to the music industry) singer, had gone unreported – Wilma Burgess, previously a physical education teacher. Producer Owen Bradley decided she had a similarly strong voice to take the place of his charge Patsy Cline, who had died in a plane crash. Cline's classic tragic songs, detailing the men who did her wrong, ensured she was the one country singer to develop a gay and lesbian following (her premature death and larger-than-life fashion sense, only reinforced her status). Burgess took it further by only recording gender-specific lyrics if she was especially fond of the song. But her sexuality was known by her friends and label associates, though not publicised, not in a city like country music capital Nashville, not in the mid-sixties or even the early seventies.

One country song, Freddy Weller's 'Betty Ann And Shirley Cole', was a non-judgemental tale of a lesbian couple but it still wasn't the articulate fighting talk of Lavender Country and Patrick Haggerty.

Growing up on a dairy farm in Washington state, Haggerty had bucked the trend even as a boy. At fourteen, he won a cooking contest (the only boy among three hundred girls) and another contest for cheerleading; he even organised a small pageant and wore a ballerina costume for the occasion. He was extraordinarily blessed to have a father – a farmer, remember and from Irish Catholic stock – who, Heggerty recalled, told his son, 'If you spend your life sneaking around, it means you think you're doing the wrong thing . . . with a dad like that, it's not surprising I wrote the first gay country music album.'[1]

Haggerty joined the Peace Corps in his teens but remained open about his sexuality and got discharged. He survived a spell in a psychiatric ward and didn't back down: 'I didn't want to be a closet homosexual – I didn't want to sneak . . . So when Stonewall hit, I really gravitated to it immediately . . . I belonged to the open.'

---

1 All Haggerty quotes are from the 2014 reissue of the *Lavender Country* album, on the Paradise of Bachelors label.

Haggerty joined a more suitable peace corps: a hippie commune in Seattle and the city's Gay Liberation Front. Seattle's progressive social policies matched San Francisco: the city's Counselling Service For Homosexuals predated Stonewall. But Haggerty felt he needed to do something himself, to do with music. His early heroes were country stars Patsy Cline and Hank Williams, but also Connie Francis and Frankie Avalon and though he felt he was 'closest, politically and sexually,' to David Bowie, 'I wasn't comfortable in that genre, it's just not who I was . . . I cut my teeth in the fifties, in terms of what was ingrained in me musically.'

Neither was Bowie 'hitting the nail on the head when it came to gay rights. He wasn't saying it, but rather pretending like he might say it in the next song. But he never did. I'm not faulting him – he was brave for what he did – but that's not what Lavender Country was.'

The band was three-quarters gay – Haggerty (vocals, guitar), Michael Carr (keyboards) and Eve Morris (fiddle, vocals) – plus token heterosexual Robert Hammerstrom (guitar): 'He was just down for the struggle,' Haggerty said. Their inspiration was 'the issues that were on the mind of the community . . . having sex with young people, ending up in prison, being in psychiatric institutions, having really lonely sexual lives, crossdressing – just being proud of who we were.'

Lavender Country was funded and released by Seattle's Gay Community Social Services – with bonus funding and connections from a crusading Jewish drag queen John F. Singer, who had just changed his name to Faygele ben Miriam.[1] Singer had filed one of the first gay marriage lawsuits in US history after being denied a marriage license in 1971 and was in the process of winning his case against the equal employment opportunity commission, which had fired him in 1972 for being gay. This resulted in the commission enforcing prohibitions against discrimination on the basis of sexual preference.

Having co-founded the Gay Community Social Services of Seattle,

---

1 *Faygele* is Yiddish for 'little bird' or 'faggot'.

Miriam knew the band were an important landmark but he wasn't to know how powerful and poetic a statement Haggerty would make. *Lavender Country* was, by turns, angry, anguished, disheartening and hilarious, sometimes simultaneously. Being sexy and political was a hard balance to pull off but Haggerty managed it. He wrote some great poetry too. 'Georgie Pie', one of the album's folkier counterparts, was a lament for a closeted friend: 'A prodigy of bluffing/A master of rebuffing . . . So dig your trench and wear the stench/Of shadows if you will.'

Haggerty could be equally prosaic: the album's first line was, 'Wakin' up to say hip, hip, hooray/I'm glad I'm gay,' before a glorious celebration of sex over a sawing fiddle and pumped piano: 'There's milk and honey flowing/When you're blowing Gabriel's horn.' 'Waltzing Will Trilogy' was upbeat, too, despite Haggerty's memory of the psychiatric ward: 'They call it mental hygiene/But I call it psychic rape!'

'Back In The Closet Again' was a notable rewrite of singing cowboy Gene Autry's 'Back In The Saddle Again' that castigated the Democrats' inability to get behind gay rights, but 'Cryin' These Cocksucking Tears' always took centre stage because of its title. 'I'm fighting for when there won't be no straight men/'Cause you all have a common disease,' hit the target, with Eve Morris belting out the song's title refrain as if she was on stage at the Grand Ole Opry, Nashville's premier venue. But just as the album had started with a positive message, so it ended with one, a shout out to anyone who fancied being a Cockette: 'Sashay out and give your way a try/Whether you tuck in or dangle/When you hear that glad gay tango/You'll just spread your spangled wings and fly.'

Denying *Lavender Country* even the chance to get off the ground was its availability. Only a thousand copies were pressed, sold only by mail order and word of mouth: Haggerty said he intended to press more but never had the finances. The album was reissued in 1999 after the *Journal of Country Music* published an article on gay country musicians, but though 'Cryin' These Cocksucking Tears' was included on the 2012 compilation *Strong Love: Songs of Gay Liberation 1972-1981*, it wasn't until the album's 2014 reissue that Lavender County finally won appreciation and validation, with a spread of Haggerty interviews.[1] What still hasn't been noted was that Lavender Country were the first band with gay *and* lesbian musicians and songs of both persuasions too, given the tranquil 'To A Woman', written and sung by Morris in a Cris Williamson style: 'Gentle lady, in my life/Do you know what you see?/ Tell me you want to be with me.'

'Anybody who was seeking information about gay rights wanted a Lavender Country, 'cause it was information that they couldn't get anywhere else, that we were all desperately seeking. "Yes, someone understands me!"' Haggerty said. 'It was like a beacon, like "Yoo-hoo!" You have to remember, the information at the time was completely lacking . . . if you were trying to figure out why you were gay and someone gave you a Lavender Country, it'd really be quite a relief.'

Haggerty knew he wasn't setting himself up for a long-term career. 'I certainly never had any illusions that it was going to catch on with a mainstream audience,' he told journalist Brandon Stosuy.[2] 'I couldn't have a career anywhere in music because I wrote it. But I knew that when I made it and I've never regretted that decision. But I had a whole life to lead and I lived it.'

The validation he offered reached Richard Dworkin, who had started playing drums, and moved to San Francisco in time to play a couple of shows with the Cockettes. The city was like a gay Mecca or the land over the rainbow. 'You did have very few legal rights, but San Francisco was still incredible, you could mostly be around gay people all the time if you wanted,' Dworkin recalls. 'I'd heard Lavender Country and I saw them play this drag ball night at Gay Pride . . . "Crying Those Cocksucking Tears" was amazing! And then I found

---

[1] Perhaps Haggerty did too many interviews. Despite numerous attempts to reach him, Haggerty surprisingly never got in touch to contribute to this book. Or perhaps the documentary, forthcoming at the time of writing, on the band meant he hadn't the time or wanted to reserve his thoughts for it.

[2] www.pitchfork.com/features/interviews/9373-lavender-country

the Michael Cohen album, which was great. I was desperate to find stuff like that.'

In the only interview on record with Michael Cohen,[1] the singer-songwriter said how much he'd craved the validation that his own album had given Dworkin. 'If, when I was fourteen or fifteen and I could have heard someone I respect who was gay, sing love songs, hate songs, anything, it would have meant something,' he told *In Touch* magazine in 1974. 'I'd like to think that somehow those kids out there will be able to identify with my material and maybe benefit from it a little.'

The post-Stonewall swell, where artists such as Haggerty and Cohen could express their gay spirit and reach a visible community, was a cause for optimism. Even the doo wop/soul singer Jewel Akens (who'd made the US Top 3 with "The Birds and the Bees" in 1965) was willing to change the words to his co-written song so that 'He's Good For Me' could be marketed in the new *Advocate* magazine as 'The first gay rock 45!' But it was still too early for some to feel emancipated. In 1973 too, a consortium of the Catholic church, a Democratic politician *and* the firemen in Cohen's home city of New York were in the process of successfully defeating a gay civil rights bill.

Like Haggerty, Cohen had endured psychiatric evaluation but while the former had come out on top, the latter had taken an extended bout of aversion therapy. Though Cohen eventually decided 'I was a human being, I should be allowed to have feelings and express them,' he admitted that he'd over-compensated: 'I got heavily into drugs. Heavily into the bible. Almost became a Jesus freak.'

Cohen managed to channel it all into confessional songs: if you want to comprehend the pain and shame of the pre-Stonewall era, here's your man. Cohen initially found support from *Out Of The Slough*, a pioneering gay radio show on New York's WBAI; the DJ, Charles Pitts, engineered Cohen's recordings and convinced him to

---

1 www.queermusicheritage.com/jun2005mc.html

reject an offer from one record label and go the non-profit route with WBAI marketing the album. One wonders which record label would have taken a chance on *Mike Cohen*, released in 1973, a haunting and compelling document that would have made for unsettling listening, including a pensive folk piece, 'Evil And Lusty': 'Now with a mark on my forehead and sperm on my tongue/And enraged with a fever of a man who's been numbed/Now I close your holy book and demand back the time that you took/I'll sing it out loud/I'm gay and I'm proud.'

Folkways, Moses Asch's non-profit label, were assembling a library of folk records that documented everyday experience with a left-wing bias, but they didn't have one from a gay perspective. Cohen subsequently re-recorded five songs from his debut and added new songs to create a new version of his debut, which Folkways released only months after his first, renamed *What Did You Expect? Songs About the Experiences of Being Gay.*

While Lavender Country's album opened with a celebration of gayness, Cohen's began, 'My mother said the day I came out to her/She said, "You don't want to be the last angry young man"/I said, "I don't know, I got so much inside that ain't ever come out".'

If Cris Williamson was the lesbian Carole King, then Mike Cohen was the gay Leonard Cohen or the gay Nick Drake, beautifully stark and solemn. His namesake's poem was the base for 'Bitterfeast', an exquisitely sad, and bitter, portrait of gay relationships, but not even his namesake Leonard could tap the reserves of 'self-hatred and self-denial', as Mike Cohen told *In Touch* magazine. Religious bigotry shaped 'Pray To Your God', with talk of needles, veins and promiscuity and 'Orion' tackled sex in a way that no fellow songwriter was willing, like exorcism: 'I've been digging up the ruins from all my high school years/the gym locker fantasies and the mad masturbatory fears.'

With the album's subtitle advertising the gay content within and Cohen looking as haunted on the cover as his lyrics, staring down any potential buyer, the album had a limited appeal but for those, like Dworkin, seeking that validation, it was priceless. Let's not forget, Nick Drake sold little in his lifetime, his music too sad and real for the masses. But his reputation was rehabilitated, to the point that his song soundtracked a Volkswagen advert, while Mike Cohen's profile remains as low as it ever was. But then Drake had recorded for a mainstream label with heavyweight musical pals and his story was compelling – dead at twenty-six, of an apparent overdose, an accidental suicide – with no controversial political dimension. Cohen had no PR – Folkways' non-profit initiative also meant non-marketing muscle – and no tragic demise in the public eye.[1]

Still, you wonder how Olivia could sell so many Cris Williamson albums but Folkways barely shifted any: where were all the gay men such as Dworkin, craving something they could call their own? Where were they when US singer-songwriter Paul Wagner released his debut album, *To Be A Man* in 1973, with its acoustic folk songs about falling for straight friends and trying to find 'The One'?

Another gay songwriter living in New York, Chris Robison, might have the answer. He recalls hearing Michael Cohen's album, 'but I didn't get very far, all that self-pity and morbidity. You, know, *boo-hoo*. His whole attitude was different from mine.' The difference between Lavender Country's 'yoo-hoo!' and Cohen's 'boo-hoo' was clearly crucial. Compared to his gay peers of 1973, the Boston-raised Robison was a rock'n'roller and, like Haggerty, not feeling shamed by his sexuality. He recalls reading Rolling Stone Brian Jones 'saying he wants to stand up for homo rights. I had the inkling that I wasn't alone in having feelings for my own sex. I played on the same bill as the Stones when I was at high school.'

---

[1] There was one more Cohen album, 1976's *Some Of Us Have To Live*, also on Folkways. It's a relatively lighter experience and Cohen was smiling on the sleeve. Queer Music Heritage reported one listener who'd managed to locate Cohen in 1984: 'We didn't talk long – he sounded very sad and it was awkward. I told him I'd just discovered his albums and how much I enjoyed them and he said he was glad to hear the music was still alive and touching people, something like that. I realised I couldn't delve deeper, he just sounded too sad and I didn't want to intrude.' Cohen died in 1997.

BREAKING DOWN THE WALLS OF HEARTACHE

A guitarist, Robison had joined the touring version of Steam, a studio session band at the time of their 1969 US no. 1, 'Na Na Hey Hey Kiss Him Goodbye'. He then joined the heavier rock band Elephant's Memory, who had backed John Lennon in New York after the Beatles had split. 'I was wild when I was younger, I didn't give a fuck what people thought,' says Robison. 'To their credit, every band I played with didn't care at all about me being gay.'

Glam rock was perfect timing. 'A lot of bands were acting gay,' Robison says. 'Not just Lou Reed but guys like Edgar Winter on the cover of *They Only Come Out At Night*. But these guys were posers, playing peek-a-boo. I wanted to show them real gay rock, for kids who feel closeted. I had this manager, married with kids, who had a crush on me, who said, "You have all these songs that you sing for me, record an album."'

Edgar Winter, a former blues rocker inspired to loosen things up, had topped the US chart with the rock-tronic hybrid 'Frankenstein' and appeared on his album cover with a brushed-back mane offset by shovels of foundation, ruby-red lipstick and a huge sparkling necklace. Philadelphia soulsters Daryl Hall and John Oates, the most successful US duo of all time, had turned to make-up artist Pierre LaRoche, who had worked with Bowie and Ziggy Stardust, for the cover of their self-titled album (1973) with a pull-out that had Oates naked and Hall looking just as awkward in glam threads. Singer-songwriter Todd Rundgren, who produced the New York Dolls' self-titled album debut in 1973, disdained this manoeuvre with 'You Don't Have to Camp Around': 'Save the satin undies, don't pluck out your eyebrows/Stow the mincey lisping, you don't have to camp around.' But Robison wasn't planning on camping around, only on being himself. He almost got lucky.

'RCA wanted to sign me,' he sighs. 'I did an audition, I sang "Jimmy Row", where I'm asking a kid to come out and to "bring your love on out to me". But my manager later said that RCA had Lou Reed and Bowie, they didn't want a third fag.'

Robison eventually released the *Chris Robison and his Many Hand*

Band album himself. Plumbed into the rock scene, he could get further than Cohen, Grossman and Haggerty and it wasn't obvious that 'Doctor Doctor' was about the traumatic world of gay shock therapy Robison himself had agreed to psychiatrist evaluation for 'a break with reality, a manic episode, when I'd quit school'. But even here, it's a happy ending, as the patient abandons his treatment and spends the cash instead on a man date). Of the album's surprising crop of delicate ballads, 'Mocha Almond Boy' and 'Italian Boy' lusted after the same neighbourhood crush. Neither song was sexualised enough to make waves, unlike 'Looking For A Boy Tonight': 'I know to some of you out there it may not seem quite right/but I am not the only one to know your own sex can be fun.'

To soundtrack his cruising anthem, he took a leaf out of Lavender Country's book (not that he'd heard their album) with a country arrangement. 'Steam were touring down south, it was all shotguns and confederate flags. People would stare at you when you went in anywhere,' Robison recalls. 'In one saloon, I put Merle Haggert's "The Fightin' Side of Me" on the jukebox – I just thought it would be hilarious to record a song in that style.'

But Robison's eclectic touch and libidinous lyrics crossed a line with the Caribbean-flavoured 'Down In New York', sung by Robison in the mock accent equivalent of blackface, with the words, 'Looking for a chicken, can't find none . . . Well, I found me one and his name is Tony/ he's a little boy, about fourteen.'

'When the album was reissued,'[1] Robison says, 'some people said it was paedophilia. I originally wanted to call the album *Chicken-Bone Fagan*, about a fictitious guy who took care of gay runaways but I recycled that into the rest of the album. When people write about murder, it doesn't mean they're murderers.'

Not a single reviewer in 1973 picked up on the track: but why would they, when groupies of that era were often fourteen and few in the pop

---

1 Chapter Music, 2014

and rock world considered the matter of underage sex a crime?[1] Instead, with his contacts in the rock business, Robison's album was well received; better still, after placing an advert in *After Dark* magazine, 'Suddenly people started calling. I was even on the cover of *Gay News* in England! It was unreal. The first pressing was maybe four thousand copies and it went to a third pressing.'

Robison played New York's Gay Pride in 1973 'to thousands of people'. But his follow-up album, *Man Child* – Robison, bare-chested and in sawn-off denims, looked about fourteen himself on the cover – didn't take off. 'Record company executives weren't ready for a gay album by an artist who is really a musician first and not some kind of flamboyant performer who titillates, you know, like the bearded lady,' Robison reflects. 'They weren't ready for just plain music.'

Steven Grossman would have agreed with Robison. He was the first openly gay man to release an openly gay-themed album on a major label, Mercury, though Jimmie Spheeris would have got there first if his similarly soft-rocking debut album, *Isle Of View*, released by Columbia in 1971, hadn't veiled his sexuality behind oblique poetry ('White flame of love burns on your breath . . . oh, my wings are so ripe' and song titles such as 'I Am The Mercury'). But Grossman was willing to ditch the metaphors. His album's opening words were, 'Austin, you got that gypsy in your eye/We have four good months behind us . . .'

Grossman was another New Yorker; he'd worked in childcare, garbage collecting and market research and planned to be an actor but was writing songs too. He'd seen a listing placed by two record producers, Lonnie Lambert and Bobby Flax, for a singer-songwriter who wrote about the 'gay experience'. Grossman had first slept with a man after they'd bonded over Laura Nyro,[2] though he said his main influence was Joni Mitchell. Yet he was much more the gay Cat Stevens, folk-sweet and tender, wholly lacking Michael Cohen's tortured edge. The cover

---

1 Iggy Pop sang in his 1996 track 'Look Away', 'I slept with Sable when she was thirteen.'
2 Grossman adored Laura Nyro but Jimmie Spheeris actually shared an apartment with her in the early seventies.

of Grossman's debut album *Caravan Tonight* was pastoral, a painting of the singer gazing out at a Tolkien-esque landscape, a horse and cart alongside a man and a young girl playing a tambourine.

A psychologist might interpret the image as a gay man looking longingly at the happy life he's been denied, but it mirrored the title track's storyline, comparing his departing lover Austin to a roving gypsy and his caravan. The four months that Grossman and the seventeen-year old Austin had been together wasn't much, but it was the singer's first relationship and, like Michael Cohen, he wanted true romance rather than play the field. On 'Christopher's Blues', named after New York street where much of the city's cruising took place, Grossman pleaded: 'And I don't want no hit-and-run cruiser/I don't want to waste my days . . . Trying to catch the eye on each corner/There must be a better way.'

The song documented Grossman's first time cruising, post-Austin. His eventual pick-up that night 'was into an incredible butch trip, he said, "I'm going to rape you, baby."' Grossman managed to escape; the moral was, as his song concluded, 'You're a fool to give candy to a stranger.' The sentiment, he told *In Touch*, 'has upset a lot of people. And the writers from the gay magazines, they say, "What's wrong with giving candy to a stranger?"'

On the album's lengthy finale 'Dry Dock Dreaming', Grossman was plainly willing to offer candy himself: 'I'm turning to stone/I'm anxious and angry and want to go home/But please, not alone.'

Caravan Tonight was not a cheaply made record; horns and strings decorated some songs and the deluxe gatefold sleeve suggested Mercury believed strongly in Grossman. They also supported his frank stance, billing him – a bit apologetically – as 'a young singer who happens to be gay.' *The Advocate* – now printing 40,000 copies a month – accepted the advert, but *After Dark*, a closeted gay magazine that purported to simply cover nightlife, refused because of the word 'gay'.

Rolling Stone's view of *Caravan Tonight* was fully supportive: 'His communication of intense compassion, honesty and tenderness so eclipses the imperfections inevitable in the work of such a young artist

'... one of the most auspicious singer-songwriter debuts of the seventies'. The *New York Times* thought Grossman's songs were 'of a quality that enables them to transcend narrow categorisations and to appeal to an audience beyond their specific sub-culture.' But Mercury reported sales were between 5,000-6,000 – where 50,000 was the minimum the label expected.

It wasn't Grossman's fault; it was more an implicit failing in the bond between the rock gene and the gay gene. As gay journalist Adam Block argued, 'Rock's strongest appeals have always been more implied than overt: sly promises in a shared, secret language – ambiguous in the same way that sexual ambivalence can be. Forthright celebrations and denunciations were folkie tools that often preached to the converted. Rock was more shadowy and subversive; the walk often was the talk.'[1]

Though UK model-turned-singer Twiggy had a Top 20 UK hit with a cover of 'Caravan Tonight', Grossman said he was told, 'my songs had no hooks or Top 40 potential and that they were simply too esoteric' and that, 'You're a good songwriter, but you have to change those pronouns to "she".' Given his album track 'Out' concluded, 'You know it's OK/ Nothing wrong with being gay,' this was unlikely to happen.

Grossman didn't help his cause by rarely playing live, denying him any following that could snowball into something tangibly like a career. It was as if he didn't believe he deserved it or could handle it. Mercury dropped him and Grossman would soon move to San Francisco and stop recording.

Grossman soon made friends with Richard Dworkin. 'I knew *Caravan Tonight* before we met, I thought it was incredible,' Dworkin says. 'I remember Jim Fouratt and I went to see Cris Williamson play, before *Changer and the Changed*, in San Francisco – we must have been the only men in the room, like nothing I'd ever experienced, such a tight and loving community. Many gay men involved in seventies music would ask, Why can't gay men do this?'

---

1 *The Rock History Reader*, Theo Cateforis, ed. (Routledge, 2012)

The Seventies: Let The Children Boogie

On an online forum[1] about gay and lesbian folk music, Goldie01 posted the comment, 'Someone once said that gay men want to be entertained and lesbian women want to be "validated". That's pretty general but I think there's a germ of truth in it.'

There's more than a germ of truth in how Cohen and Grossman's angst were too uncomfortable a reminder of the closet; few wanted to go back in there, even through the medium of music. But even when the sound of sexual liberation and celebration were heard and the joys of cruising and sex was in the ether, there was little payback.

Thirty-five years after their last record, Smokey's profile finally amounted to something when their rare recordings were compiled as *How Far Can You Go? The S&M Recordings 1974-1980*. This was Australian independent Chapter Music's latest valiant effort to rehabilitate some of rock's gay artists, following its Chris Robison reissue and the compilation *Strong Love: Songs of Gay Liberation 1972-1981*. 'Strong Love' was Smokey's tune, written and performed by singer John Cordon and studio wiz EJ Emmons, who were lovers for the duration of the band. They had met via The Doors' (gay) road manager Vince Traynor, who had invited Cordon to go on tour while employing Emmons as a roadie.

Cordon, whose nickname was Smokey, had been living in Baltimore where, even as a teenager, he'd fallen in with John Waters' wild crowd and was a regular habitué of leather bars. 'It was tough on my folks,' Cordon says. 'I wore stuff like tight pants and crop tops, with long hair that I curled, make-up, platform boots and about forty bracelets. We partied all night, slept all day.'

The 1970 documentary *Groupies* showed there were some male admirers of travelling bands, who would compete for their attention; having moved to LA, Cordon admits there was plenty of, 'Hey, let's do this,' from some artists, 'but quietly, it was very underground.'

Chuck E. Starr, the house DJ at Rodney Bingenheimer's English

---

1 mudcat.org

Disco in LA, recognised the same scene. 'Although very few rock stars admitted to being gay, they all admitted to being bisexual whether they were or not,' Starr says. 'I was the original club kid, I was also a groupie and I can say in those days I really did not sleep with rock stars but I sucked a hell of a lot of dick in the men's room at the Rainbow [club].'

From California, Bingenheimer – who Sal Mineo called, 'The mayor of the Sunset Strip' – was a music publicist who'd met Bowie in 1970 on the 'man's dress' promo tour. Encouraged by Bowie, Bingenheimer opened a rock club in LA in October 1972, attracting teenage hordes and musicians such as Marc Bolan and the Who's drummer Keith Moon. The place was a launching pad for glam; Bowie was as popular in LA as in New York. The Smokey duo found instant acceptance at the English Disco; their debut single 'Leather' (with its drag-queen tribute 'Miss Ray' on the B-side), the first in a run of brazen gay themes, was on the club's jukebox and although the venue was only occasionally used for live shows, Smokey were as close to the English Disco house band as any.

You'd think that might have counted when Smokey tried to get a record deal. Cordon was 'devastatingly beautiful', his former partner says and Emmons' studio nous ensured everything sounded great. But Cordon recalls one label executive saying, 'We can't put this out, it's a fucking gay record, what's the matter with you? It's really good though.'

So 'Leather' and every Smokey single that followed, appeared on their own S&M label; the logo was a muscled arm wearing a leather cuff with the hand curled up into a fist. Compromise was not on their agenda. 'I'm not very commercially minded,' says Emmons. 'I just wanted to be honest. I told Smokey, "Write about what you know."'

'People said, "Sing a ballad, do this and that,"' says Cordon. 'But, fuck you, we're not going to sell out. The music wouldn't grow if we don't push the boundaries.' He wasn't willing either to curtail his lifestyle so he could have a stab at success. 'I was out of control, outrageous, just sex and drugs and rock'n'roll. I wouldn't have been able to go on tour. And if we ever did play outside LA, audiences were stunned. They didn't know what to think.'

The Seventies: Let the Children Boogie

At one show, Smokey played with future heavy metal icons Van Halen: 'They just looked at us like we were aliens,' says Cordon. 'And then, that night, we were pushing our big song, "DNTA" – which stands for "Dance the Night Away". Van Halen – who are a heavy metal band, right? – later come out with their own song called "Dance the Night Away" and had their first hit. Stuff like that is why I eventually walked away.'

'DNTA' was Smokey's fourth single, a double A-side coupled with 'Strong Love'.[1] Both tracks sounded more muscular and rhythmic than glam rock; the movement had peaked and David Bowie knew it better than most.

Having killed off Ziggy, Bowie was plotting his next move; in 1973, he'd previewed a new song, '1984', rooted in a much funkier black sound than any previous Bowie track, which he recorded for his next album, *Diamond Dogs*. Inspired by George Orwell's dystopian vision in his novel *1984*, the record became a goldmine of decadence within Bowie's imaginary Hunger City. But glam magic was apparent in the album's lead single 'Rebel Rebel', right down to the line, 'You got your mother in a whirl/she's not sure if you're a boy or a girl.' But the overall tone was much darker, especially 'Sweet Thing-Candidate-Sweet Thing (reprise)', a brilliantly cinematic, seedy hustler's anthem inspired not by Orwell but novelist William Burrough's homosexual spin in dystopia, *The Wild Boys*: 'It's safe in the city to love in a doorway/Wrangle some screams from the dawn/And isn't it me, putting pain in a stranger? . . . '

Still, Bowie's future lay in '1984', with a rhythm guitar straight out of Isaac Hayes' 'Theme From Shaft', topped by swirling strings. Bowie had been spending most of his time in the US, where he began living after touring *Diamond Dogs*. He knew very well which way the wind was blowing; from the dancefloor with a soundtrack of funk, soul and disco, lauded and supported by the emerging gay culture that he was partly responsible for liberating.

---

1 *Strong Love* became the title track of Chapter Music's compilation, subtitled *Songs of Gay Liberation 1972-1981*

CHAPTER 8

The Seventies II: Disco, Punk and Out Come the Freaks

'When the sun goes down they hit the streets in the bars to try and meet/Some other stranger to ease the pain/Of living alone till it drives them insane/The woodwork squeaks and out come the freaks.'

'Out Come the Freaks', Was (Not Was), 1981

'Georgie boy was gay I guess/nothin' more or nothin' less.'

'The Killing Of Georgie', Rod Stewart, 1976

What kind of New York City did Peter Grudzien inhabit in the early seventies? 'With pimps and prostitutes populating the streets, an economic collapse and a crime-filled subway system, the streets of Manhattan were a gritty and dark place,' the *New York Daily News* recalled. 'While the city was on the verge of bankruptcy, many New Yorkers were out of jobs.' According to the scant evidence online,[1] he grew up in Queens, protected for the time being from central Manhattan's pimps, prostitutes, drug dealers and drunks. He had been playing classical music until, at a precocious age, he experienced an epiphany after a trip down south and switched to country music. At sixteen, he was writing lyrics for bluegrass hillbillies the Pell Brothers but after discovering LSD and peyote, began creating a brand of frazzled, fragile and electronically tweaked version of country in the Greenwich Village's more

---

1 There doesn't appear to have been an interview conducted with Grudzien and there is no indication of his current whereabouts.

open-minded venues. In 1974, he tried to sell the five hundred albums he'd pressed up of his primitively home-recorded album *The Unicorn*, with very little return.

Musically, Grudzien was a one-off, an acid casualty in a world where cocaine was the new drug of choice and at a time when the only recognised cosmic country cowboy, Gram Parsons, had died the previous year. Grudzien believed he'd been cloned by the government, and wasn't sure if he was the original or the copy. One or the other is believed to have been at the Stonewall Inn that legendary night in 1969, though his track 'Stonewall'[1] was left off *The Unicorn*. Instead, any purchaser would have heard 'White Trash Hillbilly Trick' and the outer limits of its haunting and compelling appeal in the loping title track, which concludes 'Night turns to day/The whole world is gay/Angels descend from the sky.'

'A beautiful song whose lyrics recast the early seventies New York gay demi-monde in terms of a barren, zombie-filled wasteland which will be reborn when the titular unicorn is found by the queen,' suggests blogger Kári Tulinius.[2]

Most of the city's gay demi-monde at the time wasn't living in a wasteland, even if parts of the city were decrepit and some citizens looked deathly pale when morning rolled around and they were leaving their club of choice. The potential audience for Grudzien and all his gay singer-songwriter peers were too busy, too engrossed in a more sensual, upbeat, rhythmic soundtrack. Music to dance the night away.

Smokey had cottoned on to the change: 'DNTA' and 'Strong Love' were both informed as much by funk as glam. But the duo's fusion was ahead of the game and they didn't have the profile, finances or influence to change their situation. According to Smokey, Elton John bought

---

[1] Grudzien's 'Stonewall' explained the cloning scenario, and claimed, 'Everyone takes credit for what happened on that night/And all of them seem happy while I'm drugged to be uptight.'

[2] www.metafilter.com/97807/Peter-Grudzien-is-the-original-New-York-gay-country-musician

copies of their early singles but he wasn't in the habit of talking up unapologetically gay rockers. Neither did the most unapologetic album yet, advertised as the 'first gaysexrock lp', Mickey 7's 1975 album *Rocket to Stardom*, stand a chance. The cover was already pushing it, with a cut-out of the quartet, legs straddling a phallus-shaped microphone, but the songs – 'Stroke My Spoke', 'Uranus (Space Butt Hole)' – gleefully went for broke, only pausing for a cover of the enigmatic 'Nature Boy'.

If it wasn't for the music's competent swagger, you'd think Mickey's 7 was some privately pressed Camp-style novelty item. But the producer, Roy C. Ames, had plenty of experience in southern blues and soul, and he used the liner notes to plead his case: 'Lenny Bruce once parodied an amateur talent show and called it *Ricket to Stardom* . . . Well, this album's no parody and Mickey's no amateur but it's spirit is dedicated to people like Lenny Bruce – people who believed in sexual freedom for everybody, straight – gay – or whatever.'[1]

There's not a shred of evidence that *Rocket to Stardom* got played in any bars or clubs in that era; maybe it would have stood more chance in the earlier seventies, when pop and rock still held sway. A Californian now living in New York, Kristian Hoffman recalls dancing to John Lennon's 'Instant Karma' at New York gay club the Church 'and the floor was absolutely packed with gyrating fags'. But from gyrating to any peculiar thing the DJ might play, like Bryan Ferry, T. Rex or Bowie's 'John I'm Only Dancing', suddenly they were growing those Marlboro man moustaches and saying, 'Rock music is OK but you can't dance to it.'

The new, in-demand sound was called disco, derived from *discothèque*, the French for 'library of phonograph records' but used to describe nightclubs before the word was shortened. Radio presenters

---

1 Ames's concept of 'whatever' turned out to be freedom for paedophiles; by the time *Rocket To Stardom* was released, two counts of sexual abuse of a minor had been filed against Ames. They were eventually dismissed due to the difficulty in securing testimonies and issues with search warrants, but he still served prison time after pleading guilty to distributing child porn by mail.

were known as disc jockeys, or DJs. Disco came to stand for music that fused soul, funk, pop and Hispanic, with a groove and rich arrangements, swirling strings and horns. 'Funk with a bow tie,' one of James Brown's musicians described it.

Though it lacked disco's signature frills, a proto-disco track reached out to the gay audience. Harrison Kennedy was straight but he was the first black performer since Troy Walker to make a stand against the closet.

Motown's former in-house songwriters Holland-Dozier-Holland had started their own labels Invictus and Hot Wax; among their signings were Detroit soul vocal quartet Chairmen of the Board. A year after their 1971 hit single 'Give Me Just a Little More Time', each member was given a shot at a solo album. the Board's Canadian member, Harrison Kennedy, made the album *Hypnotic Music*, which included the empathic 'Closet Queen': 'Gay is nothing but good if it don't kill, steal or lie . . . Accept what is you and live the way you want to . . . God created you . . . Is it the different ways we love that hurts, or the different ways we hate?'

'Edward Holland encouraged me to speak my mind in musical terms,' says Kennedy. 'I had grown up around straight and gay people and one of my close guy buddies had a sex change. Respect was natural with me. If I didn't like anyone, it wasn't because of their sexual orientation. It pissed me off to see anyone hurting because of hate, so I wrote about it. We are one grand species!'

Standing in stark opposition to Kennedy's empathy was black poet Gil Scott-Heron, whose progressive politics and proto-rap fusions were to become hugely influential and revered. But in 1970, he nailed the homophobia of even right-on thinkers with 'The Subject Was Faggots' from his 1970 debut album *A New Black Poet – Small Talk At 125th and Lenox*, written about an evening in New York when Scott-Heron went to a 'dance house' where a 'faggot dance' was being held in one half of the space, and he got 'confused' . . . 'Ain't nothing happening but faggots and dope . . . Giggling and grinning and prancing and shit/Trying their best to see the misses and miseries and miscellaneous misfits . . . Balling,

balling, ball-less, faggots/Cutie, cootie and snootie faggots . . . Had there been no sign on the door saying "Faggot ball"/I might have entered/And God only knows just what would have happened.'

For all Scott Heron's political nous and fight for civil rights, his poem remains one of the nastiest pieces written about an individual's right to their sexuality – and he never apologised for it. By comparison, former doo wop singer Young Jessie, who'd reverted to his real name for Obie Jessie and Seeds For Freedom suffered a mild case of confusion, with a streak of transphobia, in the undisputedly funky 'Who's To Blame': 'Somebody please tell me what kind of world are we living in/Where boys want to be girls, good God/And woman, she want to be man/Who's to blame?'

Fortunately, the dominant forces within the black music industry were more open-minded. After Motown had ruled through the sixties, with some competition from the Memphis's funk/soul powerhouse Stax, both labels had to quickly cede ground in the new decade to Philadelphia International Records (PIR), run by songwriters Kenny Gamble and Leon Huff. They specialised in a lush, touchy-feely brand of soul such as The O'Jays, Harold Melvin and the Bluenotes, the Stylistics, Billy Paul and the Three Degrees, a soundtrack for a more sensual and social age. Motown had its own brand of smooth in the Commodores and Lionel Richie, but their most Philly, soul-related response was an unusual political act for the label; a vocal quintet with an openly gay frontman.

Motown had supported social commentary, from one of the first interracial dramas, 'Does Your Mama Know About Me' (by Bobby Taylor and the Vancouvers) to Marvin Gaye's epochal album *What's Going On* and spoken-word albums that included gay Harlem legend Langston Hughes and also bisexual poet-activist Leroi Jones. But Washington DC's Dynamic Superiors were the first black act with such a pronounced androgynous frontman since the Coasters' Cornell Gunther and that was in the closeted era: now people would zero in on it. Lead singer Tony – or Toni, as he liked to spell it – Washington was the first openly black gay artist on a major label and no one was trying to tone it down. In a 1977 interview with *New Gay Life*,[1] Toni's brother and band-mate Maurice said of his brother's gayness, 'It was always there, we just brought it out. He never did hide it. I said, "Maybe we got something."'

Washington told *The Advocate* he appreciated fans saying he was an inspiration. 'I guess I was trying to push the clock ahead, though I wasn't that flamboyant in the beginning,' he said. Gay liberation had been his salvation 'and all the gay people in the entertainment industry ... though a lot of them still play the closet role.'[2]

The story was that another Superior was gay: on stage, Toni said, 'I hope you don't think I'm the only one up here.' The rumour was Maurice, though he told *New Gay Life* that he'd tell the closeted member, 'A day in the closet is a day without sunshine.' Either way, Toni just *exuded* sunshine. His costumes were more feminine than the other four; he wore false eyelashes and his hair was often coiffed in permed waves. When they performed their first hit, the dreamy ballad 'Shoe Shine Boy' (it made the US Top 75) on the popular TV show *Soul Train*, their dance routine was extraordinary: at one point, two of the backing four singers fell back into the arms of the other pair as Washington pouted (no other word for it) out front.

The cover of the Dynamic Superiors' self-titled debut album was all pink colours, butterflies and a band painting with a bare-chested Toni, hands on hips. On stage, they'd cover PIR label soul man Billy Paul's chart-topping ballad 'Me And Mrs Jones' with the chorus changed to 'Me and Mister Jones'. On record, they were more circumspect; it should have been them and not their better known soundalikes the Stylistics, who got to sing 'Children Of The Night' ('So I go into the darkness of the night/All alone I walk the streets until I find/Someone who is just like me/Looking for some company').

For their second album, 1975's *Pure Pleasure*, Motown assigned them the brilliant (married) songwriting team of Nick Ashford and

---

1 http://queermusicheritage.com/aug2006ds.html
2 Ibid. 389

BREAKING DOWN THE WALLS OF HEARTACHE

Valerie Simpson. One of their songs was 'Nobody's Going To Change Me', one of the less recognised pride anthems. The steady four-on-the-floor beat was decorated with strings, horns, a little flute and that chakka-chakka 'Shaft' guitar: silky like Philly soul, danceable like Motown. Washington used his falsetto to full effect and if you can't hear the roots of the Bee Gees' *Saturday Night Fever* soundtrack, then you don't know disco.

In sound and vision, disco fused those communities that had been most under attack in white American society: black, Latin, gay – minorities that were slowly restoring their pride and independence.

In New York, the Peppermint Lounge had only lasted until 1965, but other clubs had taken its place, such as the Electric Circus. But the Stonewall effect was palpable; New York state law had finally been revised to permit men to dance with each other and gay clubs had multiplied. Some didn't last long, but there were so many: the outrageous but short-lived (because of arson) Tamburlaine, the mixed after-hours Sanctuary, the Tenth Floor, West 12, Le Jardin, the Flamingo, the Haven, Limelight and the all-male sex clubs the Anvil and the Mineshaft, plus the Sandpiper and Ice Palace out on the burgeoning gay hotspot Fire Island. There was even a disco within the complex of the Continental, the city's favourite bathhouse.

The Mineshaft took another approach. The club's founder/manager Wally Wallace made his own tapes: 'At the beginning,' he told Jack Fritscher, 'it was electronic variations on classic themes. Ella Fitzgerald. Jazz. We tried to avoid basic disco, references to females, references to "Let's dance", things like that. We were about kink.'[1,2]

Fritscher remembers 'a blend of classical music, jazz, energetic beats and S&M-themed lyrics,' citing one favourite: the great Tim Buckley's

---

1 http://www.jackfritscher.com/PDF/Drummer/Vol%201/33_Mineshaft_Mar2008_PWeb.pdf

2 According to Wallace, he turned away Mick Jagger, while a bouncer turned away the world's most famous ballet dancer Rudolph Nureyev. But Judy Garland's ex-husband Vincente Minelli and Rock Hudson were both allowed in.

The Seventies II: Disco, Punk and Out Come the Freaks

rock/soul slowburner 'Sweet Surrender': 'more seductive than poppers for fisting'.

Buckley, through his folk, jazz, funk and soul phrases, was resolutely filed under rock, a style of music that gay men generally didn't respond to, not on the Stonewall jukebox or in the clubs. Or so the cliché goes. As the older gay generation were stereotypically loyal to Broadway tunes, so the seventies' gay man plumped for the soundtrack suited to their nocturnal pursuits, fed by a steady diet of releases by PIR, Motown and – now that disco was a fashion – the major labels.

Yet the consensus says the first record to be classified as disco and written up in the first magazine feature on 'dance music' by (gay) journalist Vince Aletti for *Rolling Stone*, came out of nowhere, on a French label, made by a Cameroon saxophonist. Manu Dibango's 'Soul Makossa' was broken on air by DJ Frankie Crocker at New York station WBLS-FM before it was re-released by Atlantic and carried into the Top 40.

It was a private party hosted by David Mancuso at his loft – handily known as the Loft – where Crocker first heard the Afro-rock classic. The Loft had been going since 1970; by the time of Vince Aletti's *Rolling Stone* scoop, 'gay men had been dancing in discos for three years!' wrote disco historian Alice Echols.[1] Mancuso was a new breed of DJ, not broadcasting from a radio but standing in front of his audience.

'The DJs became the stars, because the records came and went,' said Aletti. 'The DJs were the ones who found a way to mix all this very disparate stuff and create a whole evening.'[2]

Gay men not only created the market for disco, they then consumed it, eager for the chance to let go, to be lost in music. 'Accustomed to being surveilled and harassed on the dancefloor and arrested during bar raids, this was a revolution,' wrote Echols. 'Denied the opportunity of uninterrupted dancing with other men, gay men took to disco like a drug.'

Aletti's feature described 'private lofts open on weekends to members

---

1 *Hot Stuff: Disco And The Remaking Of American Culture* (Norton and Co., 2010)
2 www.vanityfair.com/culture/2010/02/oral-history-of-disco-201002

only', but the one of note was Mancuso's Broadway home. He'd had a variety of jobs (including washing dishes, typing and selling antiques)[1] before discovering the joy of expensive hi-fi equipment. He first launched a non-profit 'listening' party in the late sixties before stepping up to a more dance-inspired event in 1970 called Love Saves The Day, after LSD. The party's reputation spread; in 1972, PIR's in-house session team MFSB[2] released the Gamble and Huff-penned instrumental 'Love Saves The Day', a sumptuous disco beauty with brass and woodwind solos that would have sounded incredible on Mancuso's hi-tech stereo system.

In 1975, Mancuso moved his operation to another loft, in Prince Street, Soho. 'The original Loft was very gay, with a sprinkling of straights,' the space's manager Judy Weinstein explained.[3] 'The Prince Street Loft was more mixed – black and Spanish gay boys and girls. The white gay boys went to the Tenth Floor.'

One Marlboro Man – literally, a model for the cigarette company – was instrumental in giving disco its own unique identity. In 1971, Tom Moulton, who also worked in record promotions, had created a mix tape for Fire Island's bar-restaurant the Sandpiper, but had overlapped the songs to create a flowing forty-five-minute sequence. This smoothed the transition between records so that people wouldn't leave the dance-floor between tracks.

For time-saving reasons, to make a longer mix, Moulton extended each track rather than increase the number of tracks on his tape. By reintroducing the mid-section beat from Don Downing's 'Dream World' at the end of the song, Moulton created the first 'disco break'.

The next revolution was more of an accident. When Moulton's mix for (Ron's brother) Al Downing's 'I'll Be Holding On' was ready, the vinyl pressing plant ran out of seven-inch blanks for the promotional

---

[1] Information sourced from *Love Saves the Day: A History of American Dance Music Culture, 1970-1979*, Tim Laurence (Duke University Press, 2004)
[2] MFSB either stood for Mother Father Sister Brother or Motherfucking Sons Of Bitches.
[3] Ibid. 396

The Seventies II: Disco, Punk and Out Come the Freaks

versions and had to use an album-sized twelve-inch, which spread out the grooves and made it louder. Moulton could tell it was better quality and he insisted all his mixes be pressed on twelve-inch. The new format was both a novelty and a step forward, giving dance music its own distinctive hardware.

Disco was the first music to be tailor-made for dancing, which was suddenly part of a lifestyle rather than being a discrete hobby or sport. For UK DJ and writer Alan Jones, 'disco was family. It was a shared understanding of everything that celebrated life, celebrated existing and celebrated the wonder of getting up from a major hustle workout the night before, still with the mirrorball reflections in your eyes. Disco made me feel good and positive and literally did embellish everything I did.'[1]

Lesbians had their club culture but, just as women didn't go cruising or create a billion-dollar porn industry, their preferred haven was the heart-song of Women's Music. There was one lesbian DJ who made a mark, Bert Lockett, the self-styled, 'dyke on the mic', the resident weekend DJ at the lesbian club Bonnie And Clyde and then the black, gay hotspot Better Days but, as she discovered, 'women disc jockeys weren't respected, not even by women.'[2]

But one thing disco failed to do was address gay sexuality, nor the race (black or Hispanic) of its other core constituents. The words to disco songs typically referred to love and heartache and surviving whatever life had thrown at you, but most of the popular disco songs were sung by women, through which gay men could imagine the full extent of their feelings. It's why tragic Judy Garland was a gay idol and not cucumber-cool Tony Bennett. Why spoil a blissful night out with any realism?

In the lexicon of great female voices working in disco, sixties survivors Diana Ross and Gladys Knight would make their mark, but the

---

[1] http://thequietus.com/articles/04198-disco-discharge-essay-alan-jones-gay-disco
[2] from *Love Saves the Day: A History of American Dance Music Culture, 1970-1979* by Tim Lawrence (Duke University Press, 2004)

first to be truly synonymous with the genre and earn the sobriquet 'disco diva' was New Jersey's Gloria Gaynor, who hit the US Top 10 and reached UK no. 2 in 1975 with a disco remake of the Jackson 5's 1971 single 'Never Can Say Goodbye'. The club DJ's power was evident in the way her single sold 20,000 copies a week in New York without radio play. Tom Moulton later created the first continuously segued side of an album: three two-and-a-half-minute songs stretched out to nineteen minutes for Gaynor's debut, also titled *Never Can Say Goodbye*.

The first continuous mix in the clubs was made by Francis Grasso at the Sanctuary, the first public gay club with a DJ rather than a jukebox, though he was mixing between genres as Mancuso had: acid rock, hard rock, Afro-rock, Motown. It would be Nicky Siano who would create the intense, sweaty disco vibe that still pervades club culture.

Siano is still busy working, flying between DJ gigs across Europe and the USA. Born in New York, of Italian extraction, Siano was fourteen when he hung out at the Stonewall Inn the night after the uprising. He'd seen the effects of gay lib: 'Women were the ones that usually flipped,' he says, 'but even straight men were having gay sex – even if it was, "I really want a blowjob tonight and I don't care who it's by."'

Siano loved the Firehouse dances, where he heard tracks such as Barbara Acklin's sweet 'I'll Bake Me A Man' and then discovered the Loft. In 1971, he'd landed his first DJ gig, aged just sixteen; in 1973, he'd opened the Gallery in partnership with his first girlfriend, Robin Lord and his older brother Joe. When Mancuso started winding down, the Gallery assumed the mantle of NYC's hottest underground spot.

Siano was first to beat-match, on twin turntables, a live version of Tom Moulton's mixtapes that kept everyone on the dancefloor as one syncopated rhythm bled into the next. He'd have two copies of the same song, repeating snippets of one before introducing the second deck. Siano was also first to add a third turntable to play sound effects. 'But the beat-matching wasn't the point,' he vouches, 'it was always the music.' And Siano didn't go for disco when it broke out. 'The Gallery was basically gay but black and gay, we had much funkier music, it wasn't so campy,

The Seventies II: Disco, Punk and Out Come the Freaks

that was more 12 West, the white gay crowd – what I'd call uptempo faggy music, though not in a negative way. I'd go dancing at 12 West many Sundays. The closest I came to play something "gay" was Diana Ross' 'Sweet Surrender", that was the gay national anthem when I came out.'

Getting the music on to the dancefloor became much easier once the first record pool (consortium) had been launched by Mancuso, Vince Aletti and emerging DJ/producer Steve D'Aquisto in order to provide exclusive new tracks for DJs. But you couldn't keep the opportunists out and the biggest disco hits were the novelties made by outsiders – Carl Douglas' 'Kung Fu Fighting' was one in the summer of 1974. Straight UK clubs helped popularise the number, which had no airplay until it charted, rising to no. 1 in eleven more countries, including the US.

Neither was Siano likely to play 'Get Dancin'' by Disco Tex and the Sex-O-Lettes, a UK Top 10 hit first in December 1974 and then in the US – the first disco hit by a gay man, that even inferred he was gay. And behind it was wily pop merchant Bob Crewe.

Born to a Puerto Rican family in the Bronx, Joseph Montanez, Jr was celebrity hairdresser Mr Monti before he was Disco Tex. Talking from Las Vegas, where the 78-year old conducts weddings (he's an ordained minister) and pens a celebrity gossip column, the man who now calls himself Sir Monti Rock III has enjoyed and endured a drama-packed ride with troughs as well as peaks. The first battle was with a very strict, religious household: 'My parents thought they could beat the faggot out of me and they threw me out of the house when I was fifteen. But I never had any guilt. So I went to Manhattan.'

His tenure as a rent boy was brief as he soon found his niche: 'I was a rebel with a comb, the youngest hairdresser to take over at Antoine [de Paris]. I became the city's top hairdresser.' But that wasn't enough, so he moved to Paris, France, for two years. 'I realised I could be anything, a noble queen if I wanted, so I returned to New York and joined café society. I thought, if I'm going to be gay, I'll be the gayest fucker in the world. I was the most outrageous faggot of my time. I went into fashion – the press wrote about the "He-She" man. And this was still the late fifties.'

Monti loved his lady singers – Dinah Washington, Judy Garland, Sarah Vaughan, Mabel Mercer. 'I had a pretty good voice, I sounded like Chet Baker with a vibrator!' he vouches. 'But gays didn't like me because I pushed it up front. I wore costumes before Liberace. Johnny Carson and *The Tonight Show* came calling around 1962. I was the first openly gay man on television. I sang at Caesars Palace in Las Vegas in 1968, where I tried to emulate Marlene Dietrich and a very young Barbra Streisand. Though I had no clue, really. It took me ten years for me to get a record deal. They didn't know what to do with me. I was neither black nor white.'

Monti first met Bob Crewe outside the producer's triplex on 50th Street. 'I was still this little boy, I wouldn't get in the car with these men. I didn't know Bob was watching me. He was an outrageous queen too, he wanted me to be his friend. When my lover stole my money, Bob gave me a home and he recorded "Get Dancin'".[1] This was 1973 'but the single didn't chart for eighteen months, until Frankie Crocker said, "This isn't R&B or pop, it's disco," so I was the first disco artist. I hold that dearly, darling.'

The exuberance of 'Get Dancin'' can't be denied, with disco's formula given a roaring twenties jitterbug twist with Monti/Disco Tex's hysterical (in both senses of the word) rap: 'I'm your fairy disc jockey tryin' to tell ya, it's time to get dancing/You can't think of all the wrong in the world . . . of all the bad things you do . . . put it out of your mind and be happy . . . What a ride!'

'Nothing was written down,' he says, 'it was off the top of my head after a glass of brandy and a line of coke. The only thing we changed was adding the line, 'My chiffon is wet, my wig is wet.' Bob was so emotional after!'

In live PAs and on promotional videos, Monti out-did Liberace in

---

[1] In another interview, from 2010, Monti claimed, 'I left New York in 1972 and went to Hollywood to become a night club act. I was drinking a lot and ended up crashing my car and Bob Crewe took me in and told me that I could have a hit record.' http://www.zeitgeistworld.com/?p=10853+

chiffon, furs, feather boas and glittery make-up. But it was hard work: 'It took seven months of visiting every disco in America to break it. I sold my soul to the devil for a hit record.'

The party went on, through the 1975 hit 'I Wanna Dance Wit' Choo (Doo Dat Dance)' and other recordings, but the Disco Tex franchise was now steered not by Crewe but 'Get Dancin'' co-writer/producer (and Sex-O-Lette backing singer) Kenny Nolan. Monti claims that he and Nolan fell out over pay, 'so I left. I moved to Miami and went back to hairdressing. And became a gay gigolo for ten years.'

Throughout his brief reign, even the most outrageous faggot of his time didn't refer to himself in public as gay, only bisexual. 'I'm your fairy disc jockey,' was as far as it went.

'I loved women at one point, but I've always been tri-sexual – a man whose sexuality has always been his power,' is his defence. Small wonder, when the media climate was routinely cruel; even the apparently switched-on UK music weekly *New Musical Express*, who had lauded Bowie and Reed to the heavens, reviewed an English show in 1975 and reported, 'Monti Rock III minced on stage . . . Initially, he was fairly funny in the outrageous poove style of comedy so popular these days.'

Bob Crewe was also involved in another 'classic', co-writing with Kenny Nolan 'Lady Marmalade', a US and UK no. 1 hit for Labelle. The band were originally known as Patti Labelle and the Bluebelles, a black vocal troupe as popular among gay men as the Supremes: when Bluebelle Cindy Birdsong left to join the latter, the remaining trio eventually changed names, and toughened up their sound and image. Of the three women, only Nona Hendryx identified as bi: 'I first fell in love with a boy, but I played around a bit,' she recalls, 'and in my twenties, I had girlfriends but today I don't have a preference.' (Hendryx's long-time partner is former UK TV producer and Dusty Springfield manager Vicki Wickham.)

Labelle's first record was shared with Laura Nyro, introduced to them by Wickham, who started managing the trio as well. One gig Wickham secured was supporting Bette Midler at New York's Continental Baths and their new, future-glam costumes were created by gay designers Larry Legaspi and Richard Eyker, who ran the New York design studio Moonstone. They went with Hendryx's erotically and politically charged songs, as she took over Labelle's direction – the first black female group to be so bold, in their songs and their image.

'I wrote about sexuality, not gay or bi sex,' Hendryx maintains, 'just as people didn't talk about being gay or bi, it was people being free, kissing each other, stoned out of their minds. Like "Going Down Makes Me Shiver" is about oral sex, but it wasn't male or female.' However, the song's lyric, 'going down to your river', undeniably was a more female image.

'Lady Marmalade', Labelle's funk-disco hybrid was an unquestionably straight song in that she was a (New Orleans) prostitute, but the, '*Voulez-vous coucher avec moi ce soir?*' ('Would you like to sleep with me tonight?') hook was, as Hendryx says, 'cutting-edge and people living on the edge. We weren't like any girl group that had been, it was more like a guy group. We didn't draw any lines as to who we wanted to be or be known.'

Labelle weren't the only group styled by the Moonstone boys; there was the rising heavy metal band KISS, who wore thick, disguising face paint and George Clinton's twin-headed band known as Parliament *and* Funkadelic, who'd made a similar transition (from doo wop troupe the Parliaments) as Labelle and whose space-age outfits were very post-Labelle. The crazier Funkadelic half of Clinton's brain also threw in a gender-bender, namely 'Jimmy's Got a Little Bit of Bitch in Him', a sly, jazz-funk groove, which sounded homophobic on the surface but not deep down, with reference to 'the angle of the dangle . . . the heat of the meat' and the tongue-twisting 'Jimmy's got a little bit of she in he/But when he pee, he see.'

A similarly objective take was 'Ain't Nobody Straight in LA' by the Miracles, Motown king Smokey Robinson's former accomplices, found on the vocal troupe's 1975 concept album *City Of Angels* about a man from 'Anytown, USA', who follows his estranged girlfriend out west.

Reflecting on what he found there, 'Homosexuality is a part of society/ well, I guess that they need a bit more variety.'

'Some of the finest women are in gay bars,' one Miracle enthused in the song's spoken coda over a swishy samba beat.

'Hey, but dig, how you know they women?' another replied.

'Gay people are nice people too, man!' they concluded.

Indeed, many of them were nice, but mostly too busy dancing to make time for consciousness-raising: whatever emancipation they had would do for now. David Mancuso believed, 'dancing and politics were on the same wavelength,'[1] but it would take a heterosexual woman to combine the two strands. As Bunny Jones told *The Advocate*, 'Monti Rock said his chiffon was wet, but that didn't say he was gay.'[2]

The politics of dancing

Like Monti, Jones had roots in hairdressing, owning a chain of beauty salons in Harlem, which had mainly gay employees. 'I began to feel that gays were more suppressed than blacks,' she said. 'You hear of great designers or hairdressers, but that's as about as far as society will allow gays to go.'

The success of Jones' salons allowed her to freelance in the music business: she co-wrote a handful of singles, such as the Millionaires' 'Cherry Baby' in 1965, released on her Bunny label. Jones had the lyric to 'I Was Born This Way' years before she found the right person to add the music, written by her friend Chris Spierer. Jones still needed the right vocalist and, in line with the message, he or she needed to be gay.

Born in Alabama and raised in New York, Charles Valentino Harris was fond of ballet, singing and dancing, 'even as a child,' he told John Abbey of *Blues and Soul* magazine. He graduated to performing on Broadway and the Australian version of *Hair* and Bunny Jones became his manager. Valentino created the vocal melody for Spierer's music

---

1 *Love Saves the Day: A History of American Dance Music 1970-1979*, Tim Lawrence (Duke University Press, 2004)
2 http://queermusicheritage.com/jun2002v.html

and Jones' words, with a clear message (including Jones and Spierer's 'Liberation' on the B-side): 'I'm walking through life in nature's disguise/You laugh at me and you criticise/'Cause I'm happy, carefree and gay/I was born this way.'

Valentino (going by the singular name for the release), never said he was bisexual, only gay. 'The song isn't telling people to be gay – it simply says that . . . to quote the song. . . "so be happy, be carefree," because I was born that way and there really isn't anything wrong with that,' he said.

Jones had connections at Motown and she managed to get Stevie Wonder, of all Motown greats, to play the drums on the recording. The next step was a record label, which she named Gaiee: 'I wanted to give gay people a [record] label they could call home,' she said. Frankie Crocker again broke the single, catching Jones by surprise; she coped with demand by selling it from the back of her car and shifted 15,000 copies before Motown boss Berry Gordy decided it was a hit and took over the distribution.

'I Was Born This Way' sold respectably but it never charted. Made by relative novices in disco, it lacked the gloss and syncopation of the best disco and, in any case, the message was still too strong for anyone who didn't want to have such an identifiable record in their record collection. Dave Godin – an early British advocate for black music, Motown's UK rep and a journalist himself – told writer Jon Savage that he worked 'I Was Born This Way' without any success 'and I was advised by a staff writer at *Blues and Soul* not to review that record because, if I did, everyone would think I was queer. I thought, Well, everyone thinks I'm queer anyway, what's the odds? And it was a bloody good record.'[1]

Even Tom Moulton, in his weekly disco column for the US trade weekly *Billboard*, hesitated to offer unconditional support: 'Most controversial record this week is "I Was Born This Way" by Valentino on Gaiee Records, on which a young man sings about his homosexuality,

---

1 https://web.archive.org/web/20110613015803/http://www.jonsavage.com/compilations/godin-1/

The Seventies II: Disco, Punk and Out Come the Freaks

how happy he is and how others put him down because they don't understand. Feelings on the disc are mixed, as some think it offensive, others think it is a great cut.'

'I never played it, but "I Was Born This Way" was huge in the gay clubs,' says Nicky Siano.

When Valentino was promoting the record in straight clubs, he noticed the point where he sang 'I'm gay' was where people stopped dancing. But it wasn't the reason why there was no follow-up: he told *The Advocate*, 'I don't want to cash in on making gay records just for the sake of it because that would detract from the point I've made.'[1]

Political disco was almost an oxymoron. Even if the lyrics embraced heartache, these were songs intended for the unabashed celebration of love, sex and dancing. The simpler the message, the better. Mainland Europe, not known for its black music traditions, got on board with the simplest of formulae. Italian producer Giorgio Moroder and Boston singer Donna Summer, who were both living in Germany, created 1975's first electronic disco record, 'Love To Love You Baby' (US no. 2, UK no. 4), prolonged over seventeen minutes on the twelve-inch version.

Andrea True Connection's 1976 hit 'More More More' (US no. 4, UK no. 5) was more traditional disco fronted by a real porn star, Andrea Marie Truden. The track had originally been written by Flawless Mother Sabrina's half-brother Gregg Diamond for a porn film, though Truden's performance was wooden and lacked heart and passion.[2]

Disco producers could be guilty of writing to order and peddling clichés to maximise their chances, but Motown boss Berry Gordy wasn't one of them. He still believed in 'I Was Born This Way' and

---

1 Neither Valentino nor Gaiee would release another record.
2 Gregg Diamond had been a member of Jobriath's band. 'After working with Jobriath,' Sabrina recalls, 'Gregg found the easiest way to raise money was a film and the easiest film to raise money was porn. So we made *More More More*, which had gay sex and straight sex. Gregg had the music rights to the title song and when it went to no. 1 [actually, only in Canada, but US and UK Top 5], we pulled the film so as not to stand in the way of Gregg and the record.'

in 1977 resuscitated the song by commissioning an in-house version, with a singer that gospel legend Mahalia Jackson christened 'Baby Boy'.

Carl Bean is a unique soul. It's not every day an archbishop picks up the phone with the greeting, 'Hey darlin'!' But then few archbishops have recorded 'I Was Born This Way' and decide to forego music so he could serve the gay black community and later form the Unity Fellowship Church Movement to administer to the gay, lesbian and transgender black community's religious needs.

Raised in Baltimore, Bean 'never had a need to be a straight guy, I was always surrounded by gay people. Gay bars and restaurants were out in the open, not with bricked-up windows. And if you were a member of the community, you were protected. I was fortunate too, as my church was steeped less in religion than a broad-based spirituality and social justice.'

In 1960, Bean took the prized second-voice position in the Alex Bradford Singers before he moved to New York, to sing more gospel. By the end of the sixties, 'gospel didn't feel satisfying anymore. I wanted to sing about people, not the Bible and history.' He didn't want to sing R&B either but then he heard the Staple Singers' 'I Know A Place, I'll Take You There'. 'They later called it message music, like Marvin Gaye's *What's Going On*,' says Bean. 'That's what I wanted to do.'

Bean moved to LA in 1972 and formed the vocal troupe Universal Love, which released the 1974 album *All We Need Is Love* for ABC Records. Label head Lee Young moved on to Motown and, after Berry Gordy heard Bean's voice, the singer followed. 'Motown knew I was openly gay, they knew I was the right guy when they wanted a new version of "I Was Born This Way",' Bean says. 'I thought the Valentino version was Broadway-ish, I knew it had to have more soul. But I didn't want Motown's sound, I wanted my friends, the Sweet Inspirations, to sing back up in the old gospel tradition. That's why it came up so powerful.'

Everything about the new version was more soulful and syncopated, audibly invested with the spiritual uplift Bean had imported from gospel. 'I'd never heard sermons about a hateful god, or homos going to hell in the Book of Romans; I never thought I wasn't valuable,' he says. 'We were all one.'

'I Was Born This Way' was again broken by Frankie Crocker at WLIB, but also this time in the clubs, reaching no. 15 on *Billboard*'s club play singles chart. 'You didn't have to worry about radio, the power was in the hands of gay men,' says Bean. But again, there wasn't enough traction to put a gay pride anthem into the national charts. Bean says his message was still the more palatable of two options, 'I was singing about social justice and freedom, which is a much easier message than "I love him".'

Knocking on Rock's Closet Door

David Bowie and Elton John had both caught disco fever by 1975, the year of Bowie's first US no. 1 single 'Fame' and its parent album *Young Americans* and Elton's single 'Philadelphia Freedom', his fourth US no. 1. The song was written as a favour for Elton's friend, tennis star Billie Jean King, who was part of the Philadelphia Freedoms pro tennis team (and one of the first tennis players to admit to having lesbian relationships). But Elton's lyrics were all written by his (straight) friend Bernie Taupin and there was no context whatsoever to the song, just the request, 'Philadelphia Freedom, shine on me.'

Taupin had written a couple of lyrics with gay characters for Elton's 1973 album *Goodbye Yellow Brick Road*. 'All The Girls Love Alice' was a twisted little vignette: 'Getting your kicks in another girl's bed/And it was only last Tuesday they found you in the subway dead.' The title track was more optimistic, as the song's hustler chooses to end his soulless occupation – 'I'm not a present for your friend to open' – and tells his sugar daddy, 'Maybe you'll get a replacement/There's plenty like me to be found/Mongrels who ain't got a penny/Sniffing for tidbits like you on the ground.'

There was relief too in 'Someone Saved My Life Tonight' from 1975's autobiographical *Captain Fantastic and the Dirt Brown Cowboy*[1], the story of how Long John Baldry – the 'sugar bear' in the lyric – convinced Elton not to marry his girlfriend, Linda Woodrow. But Elton stayed closeted, unwilling to jeopardise his incredible level of fame. He had good reason. In 1976, he was interviewed by Cliff Jahr for a *Rolling Stone* cover feature headlined *Elton's Frank Talk: the Lonely Love Life of a Superstar*. As Jahr described the singer's New York show – one of seven at Madison Square Garden – 'with its dancing bananas and flying trousers' and his 'spangles and feathers' – Elton said that he'd gone dancing at the gay disco 12 West – 'great fun' – and that underground film legend Divine had taken him to the bar Crisco Disco (they couldn't get in because Elton was wearing a striped jacket). He talked about Bowie's admission that he'd called Elton 'the Liberace, the token queen of rock'. And as Jahr asked him to get personal, Elton came out with it.

'I'd rather fall in love with a woman eventually because I think a woman probably lasts much longer than a man,' he said. 'I've never talked about this before. Ha, ha. But I'm not going to turn off the tape.' Asked if he was bisexual, Elton replied, 'There's nothing wrong with going to bed with somebody of your own sex. It's not a bad thing to be,' adding, 'I would have said something all along,' he told Jahr. 'Nobody's had the balls to ask me about it before.'[2]

In the aftermath, Elton gave up live performance for a while and his sales suffered; after a string of no. 1 albums, he wouldn't have another US Top 10 album until 1992. Talking to NBC's *Today* host Matt Lauer in 2012 Elton said, 'I honestly didn't [think it would hurt my career]. And, to be honest with you, it did a little bit. In America, people burned my records for a second and radio stations didn't play me.'

The art of keeping quiet was expertly practised by a newcomer to rock's top tier, arguably the most blatantly camp frontman rock had ever seen, Freddie Mercury. He never once discussed his sexuality, and

---

1 Elton's album was the first to debut at US no. 1.
2 www.rollingstone.com/music/news/elton-john-lonely-at-the-top-rolling-stones-1976-cover-story-20110202

such was the power of the don't-ask-don't-tell mentality of the time that people were shocked when they realised the truth about the frontman of a band named Queen.

Mercury's upbringing had built a tough closet. Born in the island sultanate of Zanzibar, off Tanzania, to a family of Paris (followers of the Iranian prophet Zoroaster), the boy born Farrokh Bulsara eventually moved to the outskirts of London with his family. At college he studied art and design, sold second-hand clothes with his girlfriend Mary Austin and joined a rock band, Smile, which he renamed Queen, while giving himself a new identity too.[1] Though the idea behind Queen was 'to be regal and majestic', he knew its other meaning well. When a journalist finally asked if the singer was gay, Mercury replied, 'as gay as a daffodil, dear.'

'Freddie was screamingly camp on stage, almost like a double bluff,' says Mark Blake, author of *Is This the Real Life?: The Untold Story of Queen*.[2] 'People just didn't join the dots.'

The whole charade was so typically showbiz: being gay was still a stigma because no mainstream performer would own it. Mercury's closest friend through the years, former *Hair* musical star Peter Straker, had come close with his homoerotic nakedness on his album sleeves (1972's *Private Parts* and 1978's *Changeling*); arguably restricted by being outnumbered by three straight bandmates, or simply too self-conscious. Mercury was much coyer, like a music hall act flirting with innuendo. Queen's songs regularly dropped hints, such as 'My Fairy King', coated in layers of falsetto shrieks or 'Killer Queen', as much Nöel Coward as Bowie or Jagger, with the offhand comment, 'if you're that way inclined'. 'Good Old-Fashioned Lover Boy' made it clear that Mercury and the object of his affection were both the lover boy. The cast of 'The Fairy Feller's Master-Stroke' – named after a nineteenth-century painting – included, 'The nymph in yellow/ What a quaere fellow.'

---

1 Queen's arrival forced Britain's only glam-punk band in the New York Dolls tradition, the Queen, to change their name to the Hollywood Brats.
2 Aurum Press, 2010

If any musical genre's lyrics were open to interpretation, it was progressive rock, riddled with elaborate musicianship and escapist theatrical fantasies, but there wasn't a single gay man (and no woman of any sexual orientation) among the most popular bands. The only song on offer was Emerson, Lake and Palmer's tepid 'Jeremy Bender', about a man 'who decided to become a nun'.

But then progressive rock wasn't remotely interested in sexuality or any personal matters, including the fans: 'They tended to be failed geography teachers,' says the one gay infiltrator of prog, Robert John Godfrey of the cult band the Enid. 'Everyone's lyrics were allegorical, ours included – they could be read any way you wanted. I wasn't interested in gay politics.'

That didn't mean that Godfrey shied away from gay life. Raised in the fifties, he spent his teenage years at Finchden Manor, 'a therapeutic community for adolescents', according to its founder, for boys at odds with authority. Godfrey emerged with his sanity intact and dived into Soho's gay underworld. He'd hang out at Le Duce and also the famous rock showcase the Marquee, 'a gay mafia', Godfrey claims, whose venue's manager, Jack Barrie, had previously run La Chasse, a small, gay drinking den. 'Jack was a sweetheart, but others were nasty and predatory,' Godfrey contends. 'I knew lots of people back then – if their private lives had been known... The classical world was overrunning with poofs! Every family had one or knew one.'

Godfrey maintains that Britain's legal crackdown against homosexuality was a smokescreen 'to distract attention from what was going on in the establishment, to protect certain politicians and others. It was against the public interest for men to have relationships with each other. I was one of those who said, "Fuck it" and never sought to hide it, which didn't do me any favours.'

A change is gonna come

Robert Godfrey's experience encapsulated life for British gay men and women in the fifties and sixties, but another Finchden schoolboy would

The Seventies II: Disco, Punk and Out Come the Freaks

show how much life had changed, making gay politics the centre of his music. From Cambridge, Tom Robinson was thirteen when he fell in love with a boy at school; in 1963, this wasn't advisable and his shock and shame led to an attempted suicide and a place at Finchden.

Encouraged by the community of outsiders, Robinson decided to take his chances in London and enjoy his sexuality rather than fear it. In 1972, Robinson had read about Bowie, though he couldn't relate to Ziggy, 'freakishly dressed, the painted nails, all that stuff'. But at his first London GLF disco, Robinson was picked up by a British Rail guard. 'The next morning, he brought in breakfast – he had a log fire going – and he put *Hunky Dory* on. "Put another log on the fire for me, I made some breakfast and coffee" [from "Oh! You Pretty Things"]. It was really happening to me! I was reading Homo superior as "homo", yes! Song after song resonated with my life – I was one of these pretty things, "Queen Bitch" was explicit and "The Bewlay Brothers", this dark, mysterious, romantic story of two boys roaming through London at night. Connecting my secret queer life with world-class music – which had all been boy-and-girl before – blew my mind. Even if Bowie later retracted it, that he was only pretending, his impact can't be over-estimated. I knew I wanted to do for others what was done to me.'

Robinson went to GLF discos in London, dancing to early disco, Bowie and a slow smooch to The Beach Boys' 'God Only Knows' to end the night. 'Happy days,' he says. 'The GLF did so much at that time, though it would splinter quickly, into *Gay News*, [theatre group] Gay Sweatshop and the Campaign for Homosexual Equality [CHE].'

When Robert Campbell – 'the only other out musician I knew' – wrote and performed the music for Gay Sweatshop's production of Edward Bond's play *Stone*, Robinson played bass, as he did for Jimmy Camicia's Hot Peaches, touring Europe with a run of shows at London's Oval Space. As with Ziggy Stardust, Robinson was unsure of this freakish strain of gay. 'New York radical drag with glittery platform heels, stuff scavenged from thrift stores, I didn't think I liked that sort of thing. But seeing Hot Peaches, the scales fell from my eyes. As Jimmy wrote about Stonewall in *The Divas of Sheridan Square*, it was the drag queens who fought the cops, so for me – straight-looking – to denounce the queens was so tacky. And the coy, ambiguous imagery of Bowie's *Hunky Dory* just paled by comparison. Hot Peaches radicalised me, like, "Wise up, you suckers, this is what's been done to you, this is your enemy, they not fucking about and you shouldn't either," which stayed with me when I wrote "Glad To Be Gay". "Put down the queens and tell anti-queer jokes".'

Hot Peaches was also the main inspiration for a London-based theatre troupe, Bloolips, formed by Bette (*née* Peter) Bourne, an actor and GLF activist who had joined Jimmy Camicia's troupe for tours of Europe. Bourne would return to form Bloolips, with shows such as *Ugly Duckling*, *Lust In Space* and *Get-Hur*, some featuring songs such as sissy anthem 'Let's Scream Our Tits Off' and anti-machismo ode 'Daddy Is Dangerous.' The policy, said Bourne, 'wasn't about being women, it was about being gay men in frocks. We were looking for a new kind of gay man.'[1]

While volunteering for the phone counselling service Gay Switchboard, Robinson felt the absence of 'out-and-out unambiguously queer music to be heard in the UK.' When CHE were allowed to host its annual conference at Sheffield City Hall, making it the biggest official gay event yet in the UK, Robinson wrote 'Glad To Be Gay' as a form of recruitment for the campaigners. A record label, CHEBEL, pressed up three hundred copies of a four-track EP, released as Tom, Rose and Annie, with Robinson's A-side joined by the lesbian duo's[2] song 'Schizophrenia' on the B-side.

Musically, 'Glad To be Gay' was an oddity, fusing glam with a calypso beat, buoyed by handclaps because they couldn't afford a drummer. Robinson's lyric began in the prosaic, positive mode of Everyone Involved's 'A Gay Song' and Lavender Country's 'Come Out Singing": 'We all come together 'cause we're happy to say/It's a

---

1 www.unfinishedhistories.com/history/companies/bloolips
2 Robinson says he never knew Rose and Annie's surnames at the time and lost contact with them soon after. There is no further trace of the pair online.

natural fact that it's good to be gay.' But then Robinson came on all Maxine Feldman: 'We've been analysed, ridiculed and driven away/By our elders and betters just for growing up gay/They trampled on our feelings till we hid them for shame/Well, now "glad to be gay" is the name of the game.'

Robinson decided music was his vocation, and became one third of the acoustic trio Café Society. Ray Davies' Konk label signed them but Robinson says the gay factor wasn't on Davies' radar; Robinson wasn't the lead singer or songwriter, more the arranger. But Robinson managed to persuade the other members to add 'The Gay Switchboard Jingle' – one of the four tracks on his EP – to Café Society's live set. In a later *New Music Express* cover feature,[1] Phil McNeil wrote that audiences for the headline acts, such as the Kinks, 'would blink with amazement when the three guys strumming guitars would suddenly gather at the mic and croon: "If you're down in London town and happen to be gay/There's a great information service open every day/It will tell you who and where and when and how and why and more/One eight-three-double-seven-three-two-four."'

It didn't take long for Robinson to leave, 'the well-behaved and uncontroversial,' Café Society and go solo. He then staged what the December 1975 edition of *Street Life* magazine called 'Britain's first-ever gay concert' in a feature headlined 'Gay music: dancing out of the closet'. At the London show, Robinson sang 'Glad To Be Gay', but concentrated on covers that he felt spoke to gay people, no matter how veiled the lyric: The Beatles' 'You've Got to Hide Your Love Away', Bob Dylan's 'Ballad of a Thin Man', even Paul Simon's 'Me and Julio Down by the Schoolyard: 'The song is actually about three boys – "You, me and Julio", who have broken a law, although it's not stated in the song,' he says.[2]

---

1 *NME*, February 1978, www.tomrobinson.com/OLD/press/pressabout/tomrob.htm
2 'I have no idea what [the crime] is,' Simon told writer Jon Landau. 'Something sexual is what I imagine, but when I say "something", I never bothered to figure out what it was. Didn't make any difference to me.' 'Or perhaps it did,' Robinson thinks, 'which was why he didn't want to spell it out.'

BREAKING DOWN THE WALLS OF HEARTACHE

Robinson talked to *Street Life* about 'three categories of songs about homosexuals'. The first was songs 'from the outside'. Secondly, there were 'songs about homosexuality, but the main trouble is, they're apologies.' Third, 'songs about the homosexual situation, which mainly churn out the standard situation with changed pronouns, which is a cop-out because the homosexual situation is a different way of relating.'

For the 'outside' category, Robinson cited 'a dreadful opus by Shirley Bassey and another by Loudon Wainwright.' The cherished Welsh singer Bassey had covered 'Ballad of the Sad Young Men'. In 1959, the song was sympathetic to its subject, but in 1975 Robinson only heard 'a gay icon with a huge gay following' who 'reinforced the old school, fatalistic, doomed "nobody loves a fairy when she's forty" mindset – the diametric opposite of everything that the GLF was fighting for at the time.'

Worse was Wainwright's 'Hardy Boys at the Y', which was named 'Untitled' on his new album *Unrequited*, because of copyright fears over using the name of the children's book heroes. In his song, Wainwright sent the Hardys to the Young Men's Christian Organisation (YMCA) – founded in 1844 for the purposes of developing a healthy 'body, mind, and spirit' and a favourite social hub for gay men – for a work-out at the gym and then another in the showers. Wainwright claimed he'd witnessed men openly cruising while using the YMCA's athletics track to justify why a singer-songwriter known for his freewheeling satires had turned moral guardian: 'Back inside, a dad tied sneakers for his six-year-old young son/And around and around the indoor track a pretty girl did run' – like the Hardy boys had turned into paedophiles. Decades after the 'Big Bad John' and 'Lavender Cowboys', Wainwright turned in the first homophobic song of the post-Stonewall era. 'Don't underestimate the power of the cheap shot,' he said in his defence. 'What's so serious about anything? You don't think I'm serious about the love relationship between men and women? I certainly don't treat that with kid gloves. I suppose I do put on a phony gay accent on that track, which is maybe going for the easy laugh, but again that's something I'm always doing. It's not gonna stop me though.'[1]

'From his standpoint, Wainwright was only having a bit of fun and rips the piss out of pretty much everybody, including himself,' says Robinson. 'But back in that time when there were almost no positive songs about and role models for gay kids, the Hardy Boys song struck me as deeply unhelpful.'

In the same feature, Robinson talked enthusiastically about a band that he'd discovered, named Handbag: 'They've been banned everywhere they've been on,' he claimed. 'People can't see them.' So it turns out that the UK did have an openly gay glam rock band, which wrote out-and-out unambiguously queer songs – but Robinson's quote was Handbag's only sliver of publicity outside of the (still nascent) gay press.

'It was too painful,' recalls Handbag's singer and songwriter Paul Southwell, who eventually left music in 1982 for academia, lecturing in anatomy and physiology. 'It felt like bashing your head against a brick wall. But maybe I didn't have the talent.'

Handbag's zest and panache refutes that suggestion, but the band's name didn't help.

Southwell and his fellow gay bandmates, Dave Jenkins (guitar) and Allan Jordan (drums), even considered Whore's Handbag before deciding it was a step too far. But Southwell wasn't willing to compromise the content of his songs.

From Lancashire, Southwell had moved to London in his early twenties and swiftly come out. 'I'd not found one gay role model when I was growing up and I was practically a virgin when I got to London, but I had to be true to myself,' he says. 'Gay lib had started so I joined in with a vengeance. Handbag started by playing Bowie and Lou Reed covers but my own songs too. I was going on marches, and going to the [London pub] Coleherne and [underground disco] the Catacombs. That was my life, so I wrote about it.'

---

1 Interview in *New Musical Express*, 29 September 1979

Handbag had seen *The Rocky Horror Picture Show* and read about San Francisco's new sensations the Tubes, whose wild stage act included singer Fee Waybill in leather bondage gear for their S&M satire 'Mondo Bondage', so Handbag ramped up the theatre: 'We'd dress outrageously, wear make-up and mess about, like we'd kiss each other and bite on blood capsules or simulate buggery, whatever a song warranted.'

Paralleling Smokey in LA, Southwell wrote 'Leather Boys', documenting the Coleherne's clientele. There was 'Closet Queen' while 'Will the World Ever Change for the Better' was written for a short film, *David Is A Homosexual*, produced by the south London branch of CHE.

Jet Records, home of Electric Light Orchestra, offered Handbag a deal. 'I don't think anyone at Jet had met any gay people,' Southwell says. '[Label MD] Don Arden once described us as a novelty, but Jet were serious about the band. The album must have cost them an arm and a leg. The gatefold sleeve was in the form of a handbag and inside was everything you could find in a handbag, like a condom and maybe a dildo if I remember rightly.'

In a music trade press interview, Jet's A&R man David Arden, son of Don, sounded enthusiastic, even if he reflected the general perception of homosexuality: 'Handbag are, well, queers! Queens! Call them homosexuals and they'll hit you with their handbags! I'm sure gay rock will be the next big thing. Now that gay is open, they need their own music and their bands to follow, just like everyone else. And why not?'

When Jet suddenly dropped Handbag, Southwell was shocked. 'I could never found out why. They just stopped returning my calls. I couldn't get my songs back either. And being dropped was the kiss of death, no one else would touch us. One label said, "Change your gimmick and get another." Of course, it wasn't a gimmick, but I thought, Maybe I do need to change.'

Robinson was changing too – not in the subject of his songs, but in the commitment to the cause. He'd read 'fascist editorials' in the Conservative Party-supporting newspapers concerning the so-called 'Buggers' Charter of 1967' and the regular inference that homosexuals were paedophiles in disguise. A friend at Gay Switchboard had been attacked and facially scarred. A British man, Peter Wells, was given two years in prison for sex with a consenting eighteen-year-old. 'At eighteen, you're meant to be an adult,' Robinson told *NME*. 'You're allowed to vote, kill, buy a house, get a mortgage – you can do anything except go to bed with another guy.'

Fuck sex, let's punk

Fed by anger and injustice and the bravery of Hot Peaches and Handbag, Robinson was further stoked by the new sound of punk rock, similarly fed by fury and frustration towards Britain's political and social conservatism and the economic downturn of the mid-seventies. Musically, bands such as the Sex Pistols and the Clash drew on the mania and simplicity of Iggy and the Stooges, the New York Dolls and a new wave of mainly New York-based bands who had been similarly inspired, such as the Ramones.

The embryonic punk scene was all over the UK's music papers by 1976; it was time, says Robinson, 'to wear your heart on your sleeve and do something, anything, because the world was going to end soon anyway. Or, at least, that's how it felt. If you did something authentic and interesting, even if it was controversial, audiences and the music press would want to know. At grassroots level. And I had nothing to lose – people like Bowie and Elton were operating in an entirely different universe from the likes of Hot Peaches and me.'

In the seventeenth century, a 'punk' was a prostitute, but by the twentieth century, it was a catch-all term for a juvenile delinquent and a gay hustler. The louder, more abrasive rock bands of the sixties were referred to as 'garage rock' but also punks. 'Punk rock' was only adopted after a fanzine was launched in New York to cover the city's scene centred on two clubs, a resurgent Max's Kansas City and the new CBGB, while two gay bars Mothers and the 82 also staged punk shows as an alternative to the ruling duopoly.

Punk also took musical cues from the Velvet Underground, where passion and attitude ruled over musicianship. Perhaps this necessary antidote to mid-seventies musical conservatism – staid singer-songwriters, overblown stage shows and concept albums, a paucity of rock'n'roll's original fighting spirit – would incorporate a new openness to homosexuality, rather than just 'chic' bisexuality.

It helped that this grassroots insurgence in New York had been witnessed by Malcolm McLaren, an expert entrepreneur working in fashion with a shop on the King's Road in London, selling fifties-style rock'n'roll clothes. He'd been in New York to begin managing the New York Dolls, photographing them in red leather and sticking a communist flag behind them, the kind of situationist art prank he remained fond of after he'd found four young men back in London for a new band that he named the Sex Pistols.

By now, he and his partner Vivienne Westwood had changed tack and were selling more fetish-friendly fashion out of their boutique SEX – rubber, leather, bondage and sexual images such as the 'Naked Cowboys' T-shirt lifted from Jim French's drawing for the gay porn studio Colt (found in the French magazine *Manpower!*).[1] SEX also began to sell what became the punk uniform – ripped clothing held together with safety pins, clothes with provocative slogans, stressing the anarchic and anti-royalist beliefs of the movement. As the Queen's silver jubilee anniversary approached in 1977 and the punk movement swelled, Robinson found a conduit for his own protest, fuelled further by the police's blunt style of peace-keeping.

'Cops were arresting and beating up gays in London, with the SUS [Stop and Search] laws[2] used indiscriminately to harass black youth,' he recalls. 'When I sang "Glad To Be Gay" at Gay Pride in 1976, the police outnumbered the marchers. They were intimidating, ringing the stage and the crowd. Halfway through singing it, a message came from the police, that if I didn't shut up I'd be arrested, so I had to stop

---

1 Information found at www.paulgormanis.com/?p=2935
2 The SUS law permitted the police to stop, search and potentially arrest people on suspicion of them breaching section four of the Vagrancy Act, 1824.

mid-song. But "(Sing If You're) Glad To Be Gay" wasn't the most pro-police song.'

'(Sing If You're) Glad to be Gay' was Robinson's second stab[1] at a gay pride anthem, but an angrier version. The four verses, separated by a rousing chorus, targeted police harassment, hypocrisy (*Gay News* would get prosecuted for obscenity, yet porn magazines and the *Sun* newspaper's topless page three models were allowed free rein), homophobia. It came to a cynical conclusion: 'So sit back and watch as they close all our clubs/Arrest us for meeting and raid all our pubs/Make sure your boyfriend's at least twenty-one/So only your friends and your brothers get done/Lie to your workmates, lie to your folks/Put down the queens and tell anti-queer jokes/Gay lib's ridiculous, join their laughter/"The buggers are legal now/What more are they after?"'

The song joined the set list of the new Tom Robinson Band (TRB), a proper rock band that followed the milder musical settings Robinson had plied before. 'Long Hot Summer' recalled London's socially volatile heat wave of that year and Hot Peaches' own run-ins with New York police. 'Better Decide Which Side You're On' declared, 'Too bad for the gay revolution/This is as far as you get/And if you think you're free, well, listen to me/You ain't seen nothing yet'.

'Right On Sister' was a worthy shout-out to feminism, which encouraged some lesbians from the local GLF to storm the stage at a TRB show, accusing Robinson of patronising them. 'It's cool,' was his response. 'I stopped playing "Right On Sister" at once. It was written as a statement of solidarity with those women and if they don't want it, I'm just gonna play the next number.'

Seeing the way that the wind was blowing, the major labels were signing punk bands. EMI had got the ball rolling by signing the Sex Pistols, but had dropped them after their debut single, 'Anarchy In The UK', due to the rising media furore orchestrated by McLaren. The label subsequently took on the TRB, one of the bands that favoured more of

---

[1] Robinson later changed the title of the original 'Glad To Be Gay' to 'Good To Be Gay' to differentiate between the two versions.

a melodic, two-chord-based template, which were being described as 'new wave'. But punk and new wave didn't mean that all other forms of music suddenly fell away; bands such as the Eagles, Fleetwood Mac and Led Zeppelin – as well as Bowie and Elton John – remained hugely popular and out of the very centre of the mainstream, before the TRB could release a record, a song from the 'outside' category that Robinson had described to *Street Life* became a shock UK hit single.

Long John Baldry's discovery and former bandmate, Rod Stewart, had long cultivated a carousing, womanising image, but he was gay-friendly too. His manager Billy Gaff and his assistant/publicist, Tony Toon, who Stewart called Fag-Ash Lil,[1] were gay and he was mates with Elton John: the pair used Baldry's nicknames for each other – Stewart was Phyllis, Elton was Sharon. 'Everybody around me was gay,' Stewart told *GQ* magazine. 'I don't know why that is. Do I attract gays? I don't know. It doesn't worry me at all.'[2]

Stewart's 1976 single, 'Tonight's the Night', a love ballad to girlfriend and actress Britt Ekland, had become his second US no. 1, but the follow-up was an equally devoted ballad with a very different theme. In 1974, Stewart had heard his gay friend had been murdered, inspiring 'The Killing Of Georgie'.

A year earlier, the Rubettes, a pop band on the edge of glam known for their fifties retro style, had changed tack to tell the empathic tale 'Under One Roof', about a gay man who was disowned and later murdered by his father; but between those two events, he'd found some happiness: 'One kind guy with the painted eyes picked him up and bailed him out . . . for the first time in his life Billy found out what it felt like to be loved.'

'Under One Roof' was the first pop song to address homophobia and although a downbeat tale in a downbeat acoustic setting, the single

---

1 In the seventies, a story circulated that Stewart, married three times with eight children, had to have his stomach pumped after an encounter with sailors at a gay bar in San Diego. Stewart said that Toon fed the story to the press as revenge for being fired. 'This story has stayed with me ever since,' Stewart wrote. 'And – God rest his soul – but he was good at his job.'
2 http://www.gq-magazine.co.uk/article/rod-stewart-interview

reached the UK Top 40. Openness about homosexuality didn't have to mean public indifference. Testifying both to Rod Stewart's popularity and the elegance of 'The Killing Of Georgie', the single climbed to no. 2, and made the US Top 30 as well. Stewart's lyric deftly moved from empathy – 'Georgie boy was gay I guess/Nothin' more or nothin' less' – to shock – 'Pa said, "There must be a mistake/How can my son not be straight?"' – to relief – 'Georgie went to New York town where he quickly settled down' – to horror – 'A leather kid, a switchblade knife/ He did not intend to take his life' – to end at sorrow – 'Georgie, please stay, you take our breath away.'

'I think it was a brave step, but it wasn't a risk,' Stewart told *MOJO* in 1995. 'You can't write a song like that unless you've experienced it. But it was a subject that no one had approached before.'

Tom Robinson loved 'The Killing Of Georgie', 'though I know people from a right-on political spectrum who thought it was patronising. Really, what do you want? Let's take what we can get!' He covered the song during a run of shows he called Robinson Cruising, alongside covers of Hot Peaches and 'Closing The Door' by the Canadian singer-songwriter Lewis Furey. 'You wanted music to validate your life and people like Furey and Robert Campbell made it all right.'

Robinson's Gay Sweatshop mate Robert Campbell was also openly gay. His 1977 album debut *Living in the Shadows of a Downtown Movie Show* was more of a late glam-rock statement, with Jacques Brel, Kurt Weill and *Transformer* influences to the likes of 'Dreamboy': ('Making love with my dreamboy in the hall/Writing our love on the prison walls') though his record label Decca, one of the more conservative major labels, had asked Campbell to change 'Dreamboy' to 'Dreamgirl'.

Montreal's Lewis Furey – a married man who has never made his sexuality clear – was similarly indebted to those chroniclers of decadence. Furey had worked as a busboy at Max's Kansas City: 'I was fascinated with life in New York with male hustling,' he says, writing 'Hustler's Tango', a hit single in Canada and 'Late Night': 'I'm a tourist in town picking up boys/Faking a love and then just letting them down.'

Robinson's favourite, 'Closing The Door', addressed the jealous side of gay relationships – 'Maybe you need more than one man/Probably a legion, everyone a fan.'

If Furey seemed more enraptured by the transgressive side of gay life than the actual taking part, Lou Reed couldn't make his mind up. His marriage hadn't lasted and he'd taken up with an ambiguous figure known as Rachel, who was either transgender or transsexual – Reed wouldn't say and she never gave interviews. As the title track of Reed's 1976 album *Coney Island Baby* put it, 'Remember that the city is a funny place/Something like a circus or a sewer/And just remember, different people have peculiar tastes.'

Lou Reed had eulogised the Factory crowd's trans beauties, but he seemed a bystander, coolly detached, as opposed to the narrator in 'He's A Woman, She's A Man' from Germany's heavy metal band Scorpions: 'Cool like a cat and like a crazy dream/I'm looking twice again and can't believe/It turned around and then it looked at me . . . I'm feeling hypnotised, I have to stay.' Maybe her name was Lola . . .

Glad to be gay?

These tales of decadence, murder, romance and intrigue were all life-saving antidotes to boy/girl orthodoxy, but Tom Robinson felt the times demanded direct action. EMI were unwilling to launch the TRB with '(Sing If You're) Glad To Be Gay', so Robinson compromised with '2-4-6-8 Motorway', a catchy, crunchy pop ode to the joys of travel, though the chorus was based on the gay lib chant, 'two-four-six-eight, gay is twice as good as straight/Three-five-seven-nine, lesbians are mighty fine,' while Robinson felt the name-check of Bowie's 'Lady Stardust' certified the hitchhiker's sexuality.

Perfect for radio, the TRB's debut single reached no. 5, and off its back EMI pushed '(Sing If You're) Glad To Be Gay' as the lead track of the four-track EP *Rising Free*, recorded live at London's Lyceum in November 1977.

On stage, Robinson introduced the song: 'This song is dedicated to the World Health Organisation. It's a medical song and it concerns a disease...' *Rising Free* made the UK Top 20 in February 1978: listeners to London radio station Capital had voted the song its favourite song for six weeks, but the BBC wouldn't play '(Sing If You're) Glad To Be Gay' during daytime hours, claiming, disingenuously, that the decision was based on the music, not the words. Robinson says even 'the gay mafia inside the music business' didn't want to be associated with his band. 'It took ages to get a gig at the Marquee, for example and Rod Stewart's management weren't interested in us. Gay radio producers said they'd love to help, but couldn't be tarred with that brush either, though it was balanced out by sympathetic heterosexuals taking a brave stance.'

Fan support was broad enough to push the TRB's debut album *Power In The Darkness* into the UK Top 5. Robinson now had the uncanny experience of hearing predominantly straight audiences singing his gay anthem. On a website that Robinson created to tell its detailed history, he recalled how he'd carefully position the song in the band's set.

'Before you got to "Glad To Be Gay", there would have been [bromance anthem] "Martin", delivered as a laddish, boozy singalong to try and get the laddish, boozy element on your side . . . Then would come more up-tempo militant songs like "Long Hot Summer" with lyrics like, "Hey, fag, you're just a drag," starting to broach the idea. Subliminally, you hoped, it was all going in.

'And then ["Glad To be Gay"] started off with "The British police are the best in the world, I don't believe one of these stories I've heard" and people would go, "Yeah, right, all coppers are bastards" and you'd get right to the end of that verse with people on your side before you hit the chorus and they'd go, "WHAT?" But usually by then, they'd already bought into it a bit.'[1]

When the TRB sold out two nights at London's prestigious Hammersmith Odeon, 4,000 people a night sang along. Robinson felt 'the world hadn't changed this much in twelve months, so I stopped

---

1 http://gladtobegay.net/interview-tom-robinson/

the song and went over to [keyboardist] Ian Parker and kissed him on the lips. It was like a shock wave of *"eurgh!"*, an almost tangible shockwave of revulsion. The audience was seeing the reality as opposed to the theory for the first time. A friend said he heard two beer boys at the back of a hall, who'd been singing along and waving their hands around and when I kissed Ian, one said to the other, "I think these geezers are bent!"'

Another of Robinson's inspirations, Dead Fingers Talk, would also confuse audiences. From Yorkshire, the quartet had moved to London and exchanged their glam image for something consciously new wave. According to guitarist Jeff Parsons, lead singer Bobo Phoenix had 'kind of flirted with his sexuality', while the band shared 'a sense of relating to those who were out of society's norm'. Homosexuality was 'a powerful and, in those days still quite shocking, subject and we felt we tapped into something in the minds of our audience who could relate to that.'[1]

For 'Harry', Phoenix would adopt 'this persona of a redneck avenger to wipe out all the queers ... and on the word "queer" it all burst into this huge punk thing. It was a comment on the anti-gay attitude.' Live, Phoenix would isolate members of the audience with a spotlight, as if he was outing them or exposing their homophobia. The trouble with satire, said Parsons, is that audiences and journalists alike 'thought we were advocating queer-bashing'.[2]

'Harry' was never recorded but another Dead Fingers Talk satire did make their only album, 1978's *Storm The Reality Studios*. The Velvets-y grit of 'Nobody Loves You When You're Old And Gay' tackled 'how gay people were represented in the media and in people's attitudes,' said Parsons.

'I don't think music changes the world, that's down to audiences,' Robinson concludes. 'But music is the soundtrack that makes you feel

---

1 In an interview with *Record Mirror*.
2 Interview with Paul Marko, http://www.punk77.co.uk/groups/dead_fingers_talk_history.htm

you're not alone, that you have a sense of solidarity in the world. Gay people who had been isolated and the people who'd never met a gay person until now . . . the music reflects back an audience's own prejudices. But that happens on a one-to-one basis.'

Given punk's aesthetic – anarchic, anti-establishment and taboo-breaking – and the fact many of the UK's scene founders grew up in the glam era and were huge Bowie and Velvet Underground fans, you might imagine that it was a haven for gay men. Think again. Not only did punk largely avoid sexuality, but no one would declare they were gay and even the bisexuals kept a low profile. This was even more surprising given that punk was partly cultivated in Soho's gay clubs as the only places that would tolerate another minority daring to be different and dressing provocatively. The teenage mob christened the Bromley Contingent (after the south London suburb where they lived), which included members of the Sex Pistols, the Clash, Siouxsie and the Banshees and the Slits, favoured Soho's lesbian/mixed Club Louise; Gene October, the lead singer of Chelsea, hung out at Soho's gay/mixed Chaguaramas.

It was October who had suggested to Chaguaramas' owner, who was hoping to sell his unprofitable business, that he turn the club into a punk venue. The Roxy would be as identified with punk as in the UK as CBGB was in New York. But by opening night, October had been abandoned by bandmates Billy Idol and Tony James, whose new band, Generation X, became the first to play the Roxy, while October's new Chelsea would follow a political direction – their debut single was called 'Right To Work'. You wonder how October was affected by being outed and being taunted as 'former full-frontal flesh-fodder for homosexual skin rags' by the *NME*'s punk faction Julie Burchill and Tony Parsons – who, incidentally, were very vocal in their support of Tom Robinson because of his politics.

Only one identifiable punk was content to admit he was bisexual: born in Leigh outside Manchester, Peter Shelley of Buzzcocks might have shared the love of Bolan, Bowie and the Velvet Underground, but he stood outside London's competitive punk crowd and believed more in the scene's political dimensions: 'I was involved in student politics,' he says, 'and the words "liberation" and "equality" were seen as a good thing.'

Shelley was attracted equally to boys and girls, but mindful that 'love songs could be used for any occasion, to work on more levels, I took great pains not to be gender-specific. It was my mental state I was trying to put into a song, to write about the turmoil of being in love, without having to pin it down.' The result came in the shape of songs such as 'Orgasm Addict' (initially inspired by the 'mad rush in gay bars, at the end of the night, so you didn't go home alone') or 'Ever Fallen in Love (with Someone You Shouldn't have Fallen in Love with)' – written about his ex-boyfriend Francis, who would later get married. Shelley still made statements by wearing a plastic badge on his guitar strap that read 'I like boys' and another on his jacket lapel, 'How dare you presume I'm heterosexual?' [1]

'It didn't seem strange at the time that there was nobody else [admitting to being gay or bi] but, looking back, I can see it was,' says Shelley. 'But I found that people were accepting. It was a tolerant time.'

Reports of periodically wasted Pistols bassist Sid Vicious offering blowjobs and questioning his sexuality circulated years later, when books documented the punk era. By the time Siouxsie Sioux mentioned she enjoyed women as well as men in 2007, it wasn't newsworthy.[2] In the late seventies, however, all we had beside Robinson and Shelley was Pistols singer Johnny Rotten sneering 'Ya poor little faggot' at the New York Dolls and the Heartbreakers, formed by two ex-Dolls, who had played the Roxy and stayed on in London.

---

1 Only in a 1994 interview with *Outpunk* fanzine did Peter Shelley confirm that he and co-guitarist Steve Diggle were occasionally more than just bandmates: 'We used to share hotel rooms,' Shelley says.

2 Siouxsie told the *Independent* journalist Hermione Eyre, 'I've never particularly said I'm hetero or I'm a lesbian. I know there are people who are definitely one way, but not really me. I suppose if I am attracted to men then they usually have more feminine qualities.' https://web.archive.org/web/20090108132132/http://arts.independent.co.uk/music/features/article2904327.ece

Rotten also famously described sex as a few minutes of 'squelching noises'. Like all clichés, Britain's image as a nation of repressed sexual tension has a grain of truth and many of the first wave of punks were young and inexperienced and none of the bands had gay managers who might steer their charges or educate them. Using Joe Orton's prophetic words, Malcolm McLaren employed sex to get a reaction, from the 'Naked Cowboys' to another T-shirt, of a gay orgy,[1] that he bought at the LA sex shop the Pleasure Chest and doctored with tattoos and spiky and Mohican punk hairstyles.

Despite Tom Robinson's efforts, gay identity was still seen as something transgressive and subterranean. And for all punk rock's challenge to conformity, it was mostly puritanical, as if writing about sex was inherently sexist, a throwback to the cock-rock of the Rolling Stones and Led Zeppelin or the theatrical flamboyance of glam.

The exception were the Stranglers, older and with broader musical influences than the Bromley Contingent, who embraced sex, though mostly with an ugly streak of misogyny, treating sex as power or a cursory exchange of bodily fluids and sometimes cash. But the thrilling jab of 'Hanging Around' name-checked the Coleherne: 'I'm moving in the Coleheme/With the leather all around me/And the sweat is getting steamy . . .'[2]

Punk Americana – and rock's first trans warrior

The Heartbreakers weren't the only US punk band to base themselves in London; Wayne County also came to town and wouldn't leave Europe for a decade. The Heartbreakers' manager was his friend Leee Black Childers, who suggested that County could make something of the new

---

1 Information found at http://www.paulgormanis.com/?p=17578#more-17578
2 Tom Robinson recalls that 'one or two' musicians on the punk scene 'took me aside to say they had affairs with boys as well.' Jean-Jacques Burnel wasn't one of them, though he told John Robb of Louder Than War that, in the late seventies, young Welsh fan Steve Strange had engineered sleeping in the same bed as the Stranglers bassist: 'I shagged the arse off him, literally and it was great from what I remember. I didn't make a habit of it. But it was there so I took it . . . it had a pulse I shagged it, it's as simple as that.'

punk scene, which was more style-led than its dressed-down counterpart in America.

County had little to lose. He'd exchanged Queen Elizabeth for the Backstreet Boys, his backing band for the theatrical show *Wayne County at the Trucks*, which he named after the vehicle containers down by the Greenwich Village piers where most of the outdoor gay sex happened in the city. County's management MainMan sat in on the recording and then shelved it and dumped County, too, without securing a record deal in the three years he'd been with the company. Adding insult to injury, County says, MainMan's mainman David Bowie ripped off both his *Truckers* show for the *Diamond Dogs* tour and his is-s/he-a-boy-or-girl track 'Queenage Baby' for 'Rebel Rebel'.

Crushed by the experience, County started to question his identity: 'I wasn't happy with the identity of a drag queen or a female impersonator any more . . . it was not so much a desire to be female as a feeling that I already was female.' After counselling regarding transitioning to a woman, he started taking female hormones and wrote 'Man Enough To Be A Woman' about her gender identity. County was rock'n'roll's first openly gay male performer; now she was the first transgender performer. Before she'd started taking hormones, County finally made it onto record in 1976 with three tracks on the compilation *Max's Kansas City: New York New Wave*. She felt London was worth trying out; her act would be even more outrageous, unique and fresh in the UK.

County had visited Chagueramas when she was in London during the *Andy Warhol's Pork* run, so the Roxy was a familiar space. She found it accepting of gays and lesbians and reckoned the punk scene's lack of interest in sex was down to their drug of choice, amphetamine. That didn't stop various messy encounters in the Roxy bathroom and she went down a storm on her Roxy debut, in full OTT drag. But County figured that record labels wouldn't be interested unless she reined in the drag so she began to dress more as a male punk and stopped taking the female hormones, losing her newly budding breasts. She also subsumed her solo identity within a new band name, the Electric Chairs.

The Seventies II: Disco, Punk and Out Come the Freaks

County's popularity and that of the other mainstays at the Roxy soon transferred to bigger venues. When the rent wasn't paid on time, the original Roxy managers were ousted and the keys given to Kevin St John, a gay man who decided to widen the Roxy's musical remit. He included a gay night which took place every Thursday night through the spring of 1978. Handbag were his chosen headline band. In songs and stage act, the trio had toned down the gayness and theatre, so you might not know 'Lovers' was written for Southwell's boyfriend or that 'You Are My Destiny' recalled an earlier fling with a university student who would front a globally successful rock band and start a family.

Both songs were included on Handbag's 1977 album *Snatchin'*, which at least had a cover that looked unequivocally gay, all three members combining make-up and moustaches.[1] But the joy of finally getting a deal was short-lived. The record label behind them was, bizarrely, a small independent reggae label, City International.

'I thought they'd be interesting, plus it was run by a punk guy,' says Southwell. Interest turned to anger when City International sold what were only Handbag demos to an Italian label, who released them as *Snatchin'*. Resigned to their fate, the trio kept playing shows, including the Roxy run; Southwell says he has no idea if their support acts or audiences were in any part gay.

When punk and new wave became a commercial juggernaut, the Italian label re-promoted *Snatchin'* as *The Aggressive Style Punk Rock* with a new cover of a young punk in a jean jacket with a Union Jack flag sewn on the back.[2] 'Enough was enough,' says Southwell. 'The music business was run by sharks.' The band changed their name to Dino Daz and the Machine, and played shows during 1978's Gay Pride week, but split up soon after.[3]

---

1 It was shot by Mick Rock, of *Transformers* cover and Bowie/Ronson's guitar-fellatio fame.
2 The model is supposedly a young Eros Ramazzotti, who became a hugely popular pop pin-up in Italy.
3 In 1980, Southwell self-released the solo single 'The Anthem' – 'the message was, "Don't persecute us, understand us"' – before quitting music for good. He says he still plays for fun.

Handbag's frustration with record labels mirrored that of Wayne County, who'd also toned down her image. Five years after signing to MainMan, County finally released her own record, *The Electric Chairs 1977* EP and *The Electric Chairs* album. County's excessive outrage had been reined in too: 'The idea was to keep the album clean and promote it as a mainstream rock album,' she says, and all 'the really dirty stuff' was saved for the next EP, *Blatantly Offenzive*. County's signature song, '(If You Don't Wanna Fuck Me, Baby) Fuck Off!' led the way, a ballsy amalgam of rock, blues and punk with a burlesque-style finale. The EP included one of her earlier 'classics', 'Toilet Love': 'I make it with you/It gives me a rush/You stick your head in the toilet/And I give it a flush.'

County saved 'Man Enough To Be A Woman' for the second Electric Chairs album *Storm The Gates Of Heaven*, by which point she was back on female hormones and wearing her hair long and blonde: 'I got a transsexual feeling/It's hard to be true to the one that's really you/I got a scandalous feeling/ . . . Conditioned to portraying the mask of masculinity/Another blend of different shading/I am what I am/I don't give a damn.'

Soon after, County moved on to Berlin, got a nose job and embraced the transgender life, as Jayne County. 'I was dressing much more like a woman on stage,' she said. 'I had tits again and I was wearing wigs and see-through dresses . . . It made people nervous. There was the danger that I might actually start turning the boys on. Underneath that liberal exterior, a lot of punk fans were really straight-down-the-line conservatives and they hated the fact that I was actually living out the implications of my songs.'

County's move to Europe had deprived New York of its most brazen gay and trans rocker. She left behind a scene with noticeably queer roots where ambiguity still ruled. Even the three gay brothers in the Fast, one of the less-celebrated CBGB bands, defined themselves as bi throughout their teens and into their twenties, according to Paul Zone, on behalf of his late brothers Armand (known as Mandy) and Miki: 'We didn't go to gay clubs, we went where the musicians went, like Mercer's, Max's,

CBGB,' he says. 'Everyone we hung out with had bi lifestyles too, everyone experimented. Drugs had a lot to do with it. I had many homo encounters in Max's backroom, I was fourteen, fifteen, but I didn't think much of it. I had encounters with girls too.'

Published in 2015, his photo-based story *Paul Zone's Playground: Growing Up in the New York Underground* confirms that Paul knew almost everybody on the Max's and CBGB scenes. The Fast had begun with Miki (guitar, songs) and Mandy (keyboards); as the youngest, Paul handled clothes and make-up, 'like painting one big black heart over one eye, the kind of thing Kiss started doing after'. Debbie Harry of Blondie suggested Paul – the prettiest Zone, with Bolan-style curls – become lead singer: 'As soon as I joined, Miki started writing songs that could be taken both ways,' says Paul. 'Like "Boys Will Be Boys", "Jack Is A Jock" and "Wet And Wild". "Black Leather Jacket" was about cruising, but women were out on the street too. Miki wanted us to be ambiguous.'

Ambiguity and bisexuality ruled; Debbie Harry would later reflect on her wild youth as a Max's Kansas City waitress, go-go-dancer, Playboy bunny, folk singer and member of girl group revivalists the Stilettos before she was transformed into Blondie's iconic figurehead and confirmed that she slept with women. She is still chiefly known as one half of the most solid relationship of the punk era, with Blondie guitarist Chris Stein. CBGB's other legendary female, Patti Smith, combining poetry and garage rock, had only been once with a woman, but she looked far more gender-fluid. 'Female, female, feel male,' she told *Time Out* in 1976. 'Ever since I felt the need to choose, I'd choose male. I felt boy rhythms when I was in knee pants.'

The Patti Smith Group's *Horses* isn't only one of the all-time great album debuts; the photo by her best friend, former lover and future gay icon Robert Mapplethorpe was one of the all-time great album covers, with Smith in crisp white shirt and black jacket slung over her shoulder, a classic drag king pose. The record opened with a version of Them's libidinous rocker 'Gloria', given a lesbian twist as Smith eulogised the song's heroine while singing of 'humpin' on the parking meter'.

'Redondo Beach', although inspired by a row with her sister, was named after the beach popular with gay men and women. Smith would introduce it on stage with, 'Redondo Beach is a beach where women ... love ... other ... women!'

'I always enjoyed doing transgender songs,' she told writer Simon Reynolds in 2005. 'That's something I learnt from Joan Baez, who often sang songs that had a male point of view. No, my work does not reflect my sexual preferences, it reflects the fact that I feel total freedom as an artist. On *Horses*, that's why the sleevenote has that statement about being "beyond gender".'[1]

Smith admitted that the only time she'd 'tried to make it with a chick ... she was too soft. I like hardness. I like to feel a male chest. I like bone. I like muscle.'[2] In this way, she seemed to combine the sensibilities of a gay man and a straight woman. This gender conundrum was shared by Camille O'Grady, also based in New York, who also crossed poetry with rock'n'roll and claimed she played CBGB before Smith. O'Grady was more notably the only woman allowed into the Mineshaft's otherwise all-male domain, where she also sang on the sex club's first anniversary. With her band Leather Secrets, O'Grady 'wrote all of her songs from a gay man's point of view,' claims Jack Fritscher, such as 'Toilet Kiss', the perfect (if unrecorded) companion to County's 'Toilet Love'.

The first of the iconic CBGB bands to get a record deal, the Ramones – managed by former Elektra label homo 'house hippie' Danny Fields – sung about '53rd and 3rd', the midtown rent boy district where guitarist Dee Dee Ramone hustled in order to fund his heroin habit, while the band's uniform of jeans ripped at the knees was apparent rent-boy code for a willingness to give blowjobs. On the opposite coast, Black Randy and the Metrosquad's single 'Trouble At The Cup' was another hustler

---

[1] *The Observer*, www.theguardian.com/music/2005/may/22/popandrock1
[2] From *Please Kill Me: The Uncensored Oral History of Punk*, Legs McNeil and Gillian McCain (SOS Free Stock, 1996), in which Smith also recalls, "Allen Ginsberg thought I was a cute boy and he tried to pick me up, so I said, "LOOK AT THE TITS, ALLEN! NOTICE THE TITS!"'

song ('School and factories make me sick/I'd rather stand here and sell my dick'), located at LA's Golden Cup Café, one of the city's two rent-boy HQs. But punks actually being gay? It still didn't wash with the record labels.

Take the case of the Runaways, the all-girl band that straddled glam and punk. Evelyn McDonnell's 2013 biography *Queens Of Noise: The Real Story of the Runaways* reports that several members – vocalist Cherie Currie, drummer Sandy West and guitarist Joan Jett – slept with other girls and each other. In her own memoir, *Neon Angel*, Currie wrote that she'd experimented with Jett and West, but just that those were the times. 'Elton John, David Bowie, people were coming out of the closet,' she told Hitfix. 'It was just right in that time when the experimental factor kicked in.'[1] Jett seemed much more committed: she told McDonell, 'I think I'm being pretty blatant. I think anybody who wants to know who I am, all they have to do is listen to the music,' though her lyrics – rather than the 'dykes rule' sticker on Jett's guitar in more recent times – revealed nothing about her sexuality. And not a word was leaked to the press at the time, as the Runaways were packaged as jailbait for their predominantly male fans.

Take also the Mumps. They had multiple, enviable pop hooks and mouthy, charismatic singer Lance Loud, who'd already reached a level of national fame as the gay son on the PBS documentary *American Family*, the first reality TV show, drawing ten million viewers. By the time the show had aired in 1973, Loud had relocated from Santa Barbara, California, to New York, in search of his idols, having become penpals and phone chums with Andy Warhol. Loud had been followed by his best friend Kristian Hoffman, also gay and together they formed a band.

Like the Fast, The Mumps were one of the poppiest of CGBG bands, but the one crucial difference was that three of the five Mumps – Loud, Hoffman and bassist Kevin Kiely – were openly gay. US talk-show host

---

1 www.hitfix.com/blogs/the-beat-goes-on/posts/cherie-currie-sets-the-record-straight-on-the-runaways

BREAKING DOWN THE WALLS OF HEARTACHE

Dick Cavett's *American Family* special included a live performance of the band's 'Muscleboys', a racy power-pop ode to the beach boys back in California: 'I could sit on this beach forever thinking how great it would taste/If someone big and strong would kick some sand in my face!'

Still, Hoffman was uncomfortable with Mumps being seen as a gay band. 'I wanted to be in a rock band and not a gay band,' he says. 'Gay was a cul de sac, a ghetto. If that's gay shame, so be it. I was a newbie at the time!' Major record labels seemed to agree. 'Our managers said we were passed over by A&M in favour of the Dickies,' Hoffman recalls. 'Even though we were slightly more popular than they were at that fleeting moment, they were the "straight" band.'

Gay shame would have been amplified by the lack of other gay musicians besides Mumps. 'I wouldn't say the punk milieu was gay-hostile,' says Hoffman. 'I even had a boyfriend, Bradley Field, from [NY punk band] Teenage Jesus and The Jerks; we were seen all over town as a couple. But it was definitely not a gay-friendly moment. It was sort of a detente. I did feel I could stand in the front row at CBGB and know I was perhaps the only out gay person there besides, say, Bill Arning.'

Sixteen-year-old Arning was the president of the Mumps' fan club when he started playing keyboards for the Student Teachers, but the band split after one EP: for every success in the nascent punk scene there were as many false starts and dead ends. Mumps themselves lasted just two singles. Gay shame ruled, as their best song, 'Muscleboys', was stuck away on a B-side.

Take the case of the tall, gangly UK new waver Joe Jackson, whose 1999 autobiography revealed he'd fancied both sexes as a teenager. 'People were always calling me a poof or a queer,' he told writer Joe Jackson (no relation). 'I was somewhat effeminate, but not a pretty boy. Rather, I was awkwardly androgynous and wouldn't have minded being a poof if it meant I could be a sexual being . . . I think I was always bisexual.'[1]

---

[1] *A Cure For Gravity: A Musical Pilgrimage* (Public Affairs, 1999)

The Seventies II: Disco, Punk and Out Come the Freaks

The trouble was, Jackson's signature songs, 'Is She Really Going Out With Him' and 'It's Different For Girls', were heterosexual narratives, while he didn't address the same-sex side of his psyche until 1982's 'Real Men', not a relationship song but an attack on gay culture's machismo: 'Sure, they're all straight/Straight as a line/All the gays are macho/Can't you see the leather shine?' Even the line 'Don't call me a faggot unless you are a friend' didn't sound like he was on side. 'I guess what I'm saying... is that I almost prefer the older stereotype, this sort of Oscar Wilde/Quentin Crisp gay stereotype,' he said in 2003.[1] It would have to wait until his book for Jackson to out himself.[2]

Disco goes mainstream, disco goes gay

There was one gay singer at CBGB who escaped Kristian Hoffman's recollection, though Jimi Lalumia is less remembered for the music of his 1977 single 'Death To Disco' than its message, supplemented by the 'Death to disco shit' badges and bumper stickers that he sold around town.

Lalumia had borrowed the headline of a short editorial rant in the first issue of *Punk* magazine by its editor John Holmstrom, who had concluded, 'The epitome of all that's wrong with western civilisation is disco.' From punk and new wave's vantage point, disco was just another facet of music's bloated corporate complacency, the sound of mass-produced, formulaic, hyped-up romance, scarred by cover versions, endlessly similar remixes and superficial sentiments. The battle lines had been drawn, just as rock and disco had not been considered compatible.

Of course, the two genres weren't mutually exclusive; there were quasi-disco elements to new wave songs and the more experimentally diverse sound that was christened post-punk had electronic elements boosting the beats. This blend was the soundtrack of New York clubs

---

1 www.puremusic.com/joejackson3.html
2 Jackon agreed to be interviewed for this book via email, but after receiving the questions, he changed his mind. No reason was forthcoming.

such as Hurrah, which opened in 1976, managed by gay rights activist and former Columbia homo house hippie Jim Fouratt. The Mudd Club opened in 1977, where UK writer Chris Sullivan[1] recalled 'one might see punks, rockabillies, the New York literati, artists, transvestites, strippers, Bronx beat boys and Wall Street bankers all shaking a leg to DJ Anita Sarko's seductive mix of raw funk, Latin, fifties' rock'n'roll and show tunes.'[2]

Hurrah and the Mudd Club drew both straight and gay crowds, but two new clubs that opened in 1977 were specifically gay. Mel Cheren, who ran the premier disco label West End Records and his partner Michael Brody launched the Paradise Garage: resident DJ Larry Levan had earned his spurs at the Continental Baths and the Gallery (he and Siano were former boyfriends). Paradise Garage was modelled on the Loft, with private membership, no alcohol and an eclectic playlist. Like Siano, Levan seamlessly fused genres using three turntables, while adding more percussive breaks to create an updated model of dance, christened garage after the club.

Levan's good friend Frankie Knuckles (born Francis Nicholls), who had also DJed at the Continental and Gallery, followed the same path in Chicago, at the Warehouse, which also lent itself its name to a similar musical blend, house.

The most infamous and eulogised club in the US was Studio 54, which also opened in 1977 and closed when owners Steve Rubell and Ian Schrager went to prison for tax evasion in 1980. It wasn't the music that made Studio 54, but the cocaine-fuelled crowd, with a high celebrity count including Mick and Bianca Jagger, Andy Warhol, Liza Minnelli, Grace Jones and Truman Capote. The weekday DJ was Nicky Siano – whose drug addiction had led to his brother shutting down the Gallery – and at the weekend, Richie Kaczor. His legacy was breaking Gloria

---

1 Sullivan became a writer after he formed the band Blue Rondo à la Turk during the new romantic era of the early eighties.
2 http://sabotagetimes.com/music/chris-sullivans-memories-of-new-york-clubland-in-the-70s-and-80s

Gaynor's 'I Will Survive' after a cloth-eared A&R man had hidden the track on a B-side.

'I Will Survive' achieved the kind of success that 'I Was Born This Way' could only dream of, topping the US and UK charts in October 1978. But then the singer was female and the message apolitical, though it was adopted as a gay anthem. Disco was becoming ever more popular the straighter it got. The peak was Robert Stigwood's charges the Bee Gees – who'd paralleled Bowie's shift into dance music – supplying the songs for *Saturday Night Fever*, a film revolving around one man's love affair with a disco in an Italian quarter of Brooklyn. The film's soundtrack also topped the US and UK charts, for a respective 24 and 18 consecutive weeks.

Disco was now in a very different place. In *Dixie Lullaby: A Story of Music, Race, and New Beginnings*, author Mark Kemp's gay friend Jeff Brown discovered that, in Atlanta, 'Disco was not the music of gay liberation or black power. It was the music of the high school elite. Disco didn't make me feel empowered as a gay man ... because the people who listened to disco made me feel bad about who I was.'[1]

Even the disco stars that might have been gay presented as straight. Luxuriously moustached New Haven singer David Charles, who called himself DC La Rue, had a major club hit with 'Ca-the-drals' in 1976.[2] According to disco historian Alan Jones, the track 'was written as a result of a breakup between LaRue and a girlfriend and the personal antagonism he felt at the time toward the promiscuity of disco culture.' At the same time, the track's 'pumping bass and shimmering sexy vocals only emphasised the picture of sexually dominant lifestyles.'[3] 'Where have the numbers gone that marched across my bed/The faces after faces still inside my head/No words of love, the hollow sound/Of hungry

---

1 University of Georgia Press (2006)
2 'Ca-the-drals' topped *Billboard*'s dance music/club play singles chart. LaRue was also the first white male to top the UK R&B/soul chart.
3 *Saturday Night Forever: The Story of Disco*, Alan Jones and Jussi Kantonen (Mainstream, 1999)

people in the night/Oh, can heaven tell me/Where they are now/They could fill cathedrals.'

Was 'Ca-the-drals' based on LaRue's own heterosexual experience or a comment on the gay bacchanalia that he witnessed at close hand? And wasn't the track's B-side 'Deep Dark Delicious Night' suggesting all was good with the sex on tap? And what sort of a name for a straight man was DC LaRue? The title of his 1974 debut single 'Honey Bear (The Good Time's Right Here)' didn't suggest a lady was the object of his affections. His 1977 album *Tea Dance* came with images of male/female couples dancing in evening dress in the twenties, but more likely, it was named after the popular afternoon sessions in gay getaways such as Fire Island, Provincetown and the Russian River. LaRue also enlisted Lou Christie[1] to duet on a Bee Gees-pillorying disco track 'Don't Keep It in the Shadows', a title equally rich in possibilities.

LaRue's productions were among the era's swishiest, but 'Ca-the-drals' was his highest national chart single, at no. 94. Gay men adored their disco divas, not their male counterparts. The openly gay Keith Barrow, a much stronger singer than LaRue – on a par with the creamy tones of Dynamic Superior Toni Washington – would get no higher than no. 26 on the R&B chart – reaching the Top 30 with his supreme Philly soul ballad 'You Know You Want to be Loved'. The Dynamic Superiors, meanwhile, never made the Top 100 again after 'Shoe Shine Boy'.[2]

It's fun to stay at the YMCA

The idea of a group of male singers, assembled in the same mercenary fashion as a boy band and dressed in novelty costumes, might have appeared to have no commercial mileage. Yet the Village People would

---

1 Not even his psychic gypsy pal Twyla Herbert could have predicted that Lou Christie would abandon music in the seventies for manual labour. He moved to London where he married a winner of the Miss United Kingdom beauty pageant, Francesca Winfield before returning to music for a country-and-western album.

2 The cover of Barrow's 1978 album *Physical Attraction* is intriguing, to say the least. A woman holds Barrow, romantically, around his waist though another man is in the background, as if he's cruising the singer. Mixed message ahoy!

sell a hundred million records and senior citizens' workouts would one day include the hand movements of 'YMCA', a song that celebrated recreational sex in the confines of an all-male hostelry. As a bonus, 'You can get yourself clean, you can have a good meal/You can do whatever you feel . . . '

The idea of a gay vocal troupe had taken shape when two Frenchmen, producer Henri Belolo and songwriter/arranger Jacque Morali, were trawling the bars in Greenwich Village. 'Jacques was gay, I was not,' said Belolo, 'but we were very good friends and had a lot of gay friends. I was talking to the gay community about what they liked and their lifestyle, what they wanted to listen to musically and what were their dream, their fantasy.'

Morali had seen, 'a [Native American] Indian walking down the street . . . We followed him into a bar. He was a bartender, he was serving and also dancing on the bar. And while we were watching . . . we saw a cowboy watching him dance. And Jacques and I suddenly had the same idea, we said, "My God, look at those characters." So we started to fantasise on what were the characters of America. The mix, you know, of the American man. But also a song of the turbulent gender that trigger the attention of the gay community.'[1]

The Native American Indian was not considered a gay man's fantasy, unlike the cowboy, leather biker, New York cop, construction worker and soldier that made up the remaining Village People, but Felipe Rose was good-looking, athletic and wore a loincloth – all good qualifiers. If the troupe's brand of music was based on canvassing gay men's opinions about the music they liked, you got what you deserved.

Morali already had his lead singer, Victor Willis, who had been part of Broadway's adaption of *The Wizard Of Oz*, restyled as *The Wiz*. Only some of the chosen Village People identified as gay, such as Rose; Willis was straight but he saw the Village People as a potential big break, since Morali already had a deal with Casablanca Records, home of Donna

---

1 http://www.disco-disco.com/tributes/henri.shtml

Summer. The Village People's debut single 'San Francisco (You Got Me)' was not silken disco with swirling strings, but a steroid gym track with pumped-up brass and a message for the real life Greenwich Village people: 'Freedom, freedom is in the air, yeah/Searching for what we all treasure: pleasure'.

The single didn't chart in the US but reached UK no. 45. Felipe Rose aside, the dancers chosen for the promo video were more comical than sexy: unrehearsed and in the short, thin 'leather man', the polar opposite of butch. This changed after Morali's trade press ad: 'Macho types wanted: must dance and have a moustache' and the iconic Village People line-up. Given beefy leather-clad Glenn Hughes's thick handlebar moustache, they clearly meant business. Yet the next single 'I Am What I Am' didn't chart anywhere: messages of gay self-determination still weren't hit material. So back to the gym for 'Macho Man', which broke the US Top 30. The aesthetic of Bob Mizer's *Physique Pictorial* was now all over national TV in a Village People music video. And straight society bought into it.

Casablanca Records had already gone for the gay male dollar; check the title of Summer producer Giorgio Moroder's 1976 solo album *Knights In White Satin* and the artwork, with Moroder surrounded by moustached admirers. Female trio the Ritchie Family would be similarly surrounded by macho men on the cover of 1979's *Bad Reputation*. If these images didn't further any political advances, they were a form of coming out, alongside the 'Macho Man' video, putting gay iconography in the mainstream's eye. Casablanca wasn't alone. The cover of Italian disco band Easy Going's debut album comprised two men who only shared one motorcycle cap and one leather vest between them.

Sensitive poet Rod McKuen was the instigator of an album with even more graphic artwork. The gatefold sleeve of the 1977 album *Slide . . . Easy In* featured the extended hairy forearm of gay porn star Bruno, his fist filled with the shortening Crisco – the lubricant of choice for the sexual practise of fisting – scooped out of a can labelled 'Disco'. The album's lead single, 'Amor Amor' – the name of the album when

The Seventies II: Disco, Punk and Out Come the Freaks

released in an unusually prudish Europe – was an instrumental overlaid with male groans to match Donna Summer's 'Love To Love You Baby'.

This sweaty budget version of disco suggested the work of outsiders, as it lacked disco's swishy sophistication. By 1970, McKuen had, finally, put his name to a record squarely aimed at the gay male market, providing jazz-lite arrangements behind actor Jess Pearson for *The Body Electric-2: Walt Whitman's Timeless Words Set to Music*, released on his own label, Discus, with a bare-chested man on the cover – the first (intentionally) homoerotic album sleeve, beating the Rolling Stones' *Sticky Fingers*.[1] McKuen and Discus moved with the times, though he claimed *Slide . . . Easy In* was only a satire of what he called the '"put a disco beat behind it and it will sell" movement'.

For their seventeen-minute cover of the Spencer Davis Group's sixties hit 'I'm A Man', which made the US dance chart Top 10, another Italian disco project, Macho, also chose two men. The pair were dressed but the smouldering gaze and body language of the white T-shirt guy and the leather-jacket hunk was obvious – but only to people who knew the gay look, which couldn't have been many in the light of the Village People's astonishing crossover success.

While the Italians and McKuen were pushing sex, Morali was positioning the Village People as a light-hearted novelty with cartoon innuendo. Their first two albums, 1977's *Village People* and 1978's *Macho Man*, had primarily worked as holiday brochures, celebrating gay destinations from San Francisco, Hollywood, Fire Island and Key West to 'Sodom And Gomorrah'. For their third album *Cruisin'*, they pitched up at the YMCA: 'They have everything for you men to enjoy/ You can hang out with all the boys.'

Charged by horns and a chorus that could be sung by sports fans, 'YMCA' hit the jackpot; US no. 2 (beaten only by Rod Stewart's disco single 'Da Ya Think I'm Sexy') and no. 1 in the UK and fourteen other countries. The Village People's fourth album *Go West* quickly followed

---

[1] I don't count Bowie's *The Man Who Sold The World*, which was a study in androgyny rather than anything sexual.

and the title track was released as a single. It only reached UK no. 15 and US no. 45: covert messages of fun in the showers were preferable to the promise of freedom in the sun, ringed with melancholy rather than frothy celebration. Morali quickly picked another album cut, 'In The Navy', which reverted to joyous camp and another venerated gay institution.

Its success (Top 3 in seven countries) was enriched by the way that many fans had no idea who and what the Village People stood for. In an interview, Willis, who wrote the lyrics to Belolo's storylines and Morali's tunes, had claimed his inspiration for 'YMCA' was the urban black youth playing sports at the Y. Sure, and 'In The Navy' was a recruitment campaign. And that was exactly how the US Navy heard the track – 'In the navy, can't you see we need a hand?/In the navy, come on, protect the motherland' – and requested its use for a series of TV/radio adverts. Permission was granted on the condition that the Village People could film their promo video on board ship. The ad campaign was cancelled in the end, but only because of concerns about the use of taxpayer money for a music video rather than the fact that the navy were sponsoring a section of society that had been considered a mental disorder only six years earlier. The American Psychiatric Association finally declassified homosexuality as a mental disorder in 1973, followed in 1975 by the American Psychological Association Council of Representatives.

Morali and Belolo expanded their empire of gay disco singers. For the Swiss-born Patrick Juvet, who overplayed his role of a ladies' man, they wrote 'I Love America' and 'Where Is My Woman'. 'The Gay Paris' – as the city was once called, using the original meaning – from his 1979 album *Lady Night* was as far as they'd go.

New Yorker Dennis Posa went much further but then he was a (straight and gay) porn actor under the name Wade Nicols, though it was as Dennis Parker[1] that Morali and Belolo penned the hyper-swirling 'New York At Night', which painted the city as one big endless avenue of cruising pleasure: 'Bushes in the park, shadows moving dark/Fast

---

1 Dennis Parker was also his name for his role as a police chief on the TV soap *The Edge Of Night*.

romance, furtive glance . . . On 53rd and 3rd, a dollar is the word/"You better hurry, kid, turn that trick!"'

Regionally, New York had grabbed all the glory, from the clubs to the records, but the next figurehead was a San Francisco cult, a former Cockette who would lead the charge toward a new disco blueprint; a faster, sexier, electronic sound for the age.

From Watts in LA, Sylvester had learnt his trade in the church, adopted drag and joined the Disquotays, a party crowd of black cross-dressers and transgender women, before he created a show, *Women of the Blues*, in which he'd embodied the spirits of Billie Holiday, Ma Rainey, Bessie Smith and Lena Horne, calling himself Ruby Blue. After leaving the Cockettes, Sylvester was offered a chance to record demos by an unlikely benefactor, Jann Wenner, the editor of rock music's *Rolling Stone* magazine, who called the singer a 'beautiful black androgyne'. A&M financed the session but decided against staying involved. Two Sylvester tracks were included on the KSAN station compilation *Lights Out San Francisco*, released on the Blue Thumb label, one a cover of Leonard Cohen's 'Hey, That's No Way to Say Goodbye' and his own 'Why Was I Born', backed by Oakland vocal trio the Pointer Sisters.

Sylvester, with his new all-white, all-straight the Hot Band plus the Pointer Sisters, appeared in drag for the cover of *Sylvester and the Hot Band*, released on Blue Thumb. The blues/funk/soul stew was heavy on cover versions, including Bessie Smith's 'Gimme A Pigfoot (and a Bottle of Beer)' and Billie Holiday's 'God Bless The Child', but few bought into this first effort. As the Pointer Sisters established their own career, Sylvester returned to the source and hired black drag queens for his vocal back-up, but it was the same old story. To be more widely accepted, he surrendered the female drag for male drag, though nothing could hide his queenly disposition. His new backing singers were a pair of plus-size ladies, Two Tons O'Fun, which proved more acceptable as Motown producer Harvey Fuqua offered Sylvester a contract with the Fantasy label, who released *Sylvester* in 1977.

BREAKING DOWN THE WALLS OF HEARTACHE

The conservative suit he was wearing on the cover was part of Sylvester's upgraded appearance for the disco marketplace, as *Saturday Night Fever*'s hero had never looked sweaty even when dashing around the dancefloor. But disco suited Sylvester's vocal sophistication and 'Down, Down, Down' made the US dance Top 20. Enter Patrick Cowley.

From upstate New York, Cowley was, in the words of his best friend and collaborator Jorge Socarras, 'one of the thousands of young men arriving from all over the country and overseas, somehow knowing that San Francisco was the place to create this new gay culture.' They'd met at City College; Cowley and Socarras were respectively studying electronic music and performance art and they'd started playing each other their favourite music. 'Patrick's tastes were so eclectic,' Socarras recalls. 'He loved the Eagles, Stravinsky, Nina Rota, Walter Carlos . . . I turned him on to Roxy Music, Bowie, Lou Reed, Eno.'

Cowley had already mastered the new breed of synthesisers as well as guitar and drums and, while playing in a local funk band Short Circuit, he was making dark electronic instrumentals purpose-fit for San Francisco's bathhouses and backrooms, 'generally seedy, gritty, intentionally dimly lit places,' according to his instrumental accomplice, Maurice Tati. 'Not truly dangerous, but the vibe was hot, sweaty and dirty. Patrick plunged into this world as it grew and it became a major part of his life. The soundtrack to places like the infamous Barracks bathhouse was generally R&B dance music. Naturally, Pat was inspired to do his own signature take on sex music.'[1]

When the pioneering gay porn studio Fox asked Cowley to use some of his music, they acquired titles such as 'Somebody To Love Tonight', 'Deep Inside You' and 'Nightcrawler'. Cowley was also making adventurous music – 'electronic, punk, new wave, disco and experimental,' says Socarras, who added vocals and co-wrote the songs. 'Patrick was an explorer of sound, a creative chameleon.'

---

1 *Getting Deep Inside Patrick Cowley, the Greatest Gay Pornography Soundtracker of all Time*, Daniel Dylan Wray, https://thump.vice.com/en_uk/article/getting-deep-inside-patrick-cowley-the-greatest-gay-pornography-soundtracker-of-all-time

The Seventies II: Disco, Punk and Out Come the Freaks

The Socarras material was sidelined after Cowley was recommended to Sylvester, who was playing a piano bar in the Castro, San Francisco's newly exploding gay district. 'I don't know if Patrick was the single catalyst for Sylvester's new sound, but he was definitely the facilitator,' Socarras claims. 'Sylvester recognised something in Pat's electronic sound and rhythm, which was much faster than the music I was used to dancing to.'

Cowley worked on Sylvester's next album, *Step II*. The first single 'Dance (Disco Heat)' reached US no. 19. At last, a bona fide hit. It was a halfway house, a streamlined, pulsing disco sound with an old-school funky clavinet break and the Two Tons O'Fun's gospel backdrop. Two other tracks on the album were even Philly soul ballads. But one song Cowley truly made his own, 'You Make Me Feel (Mighty Real)', as he transformed Sylvester's original ballad into a Moroder-style throbber,[1] but even more hypnotic and feverish; it was soulful and humanistic, a new alliance between man and machine. And the gays finally accepted a gay disco hero.

Cowley was even more involved in Sylvester's following album, 1979's *Stars*, writing and arranging half the album, the title track and the stunning 'I Need Somebody To Love Tonight'. The four tracks averaged out at nine minutes each (Sylvester labelled 'Body Strong' 'muscle disco') and reintroduced the twelve-inch remix to the album format.

In the promo videos and the TV appearances over the course of both albums, Sylvester had reverted some way back to his former self, wearing long, billowing tops, make-up and hair – grown out or braided – to match. But it was no matter that Sylvester wasn't wearing full drag; he was singing drag. And if he didn't sing specifically about gender or sexuality, 'his very presence was iconoclastic,' says Socarras. 'He was putting himself in the league of great female soul singers.'

'You Make Me Feel (Mighty Real)' was thrilling new disco, and

---

[1] In 1982, Cowley would create a brilliant fifteen-minute version of Donna Summer's 'I Feel Love'.

reached a respectable US no. 40; maybe Sylvester's androgynous appeal and the new electronic sound were too progressive to sit alongside the Bee Gees and Village People at disco's top table. But in the UK at least, his single reached no. 8 and, on a promotional tour, the singer joked about, 'being the next Queen of England'. He was a local hero too, selling out San Francisco's War Memorial Opera House while 11 March 1979 was proclaimed 'Sylvester Day' and he was given the keys to the city.

Harvey Milk and the death of disco

It was a good time for gay San Francisco. The city's (straight) mayor George Moscone had broken ground by appointing minorities – women, gays, lesbians, people of colour – to the city's commissions and advisory boards. In 1978, Harvey Milk was voted onto San Francisco's legislative board of supervisors, the first openly gay man to hold public office in California. Sylvester performed at Milk's birthday party. It seemed the start of a golden age.

San Francisco had also given birth to Buena Vista, the country's first openly gay band.[1] In an earlier time, the vocal frontline of Terry Hutchison, Michael Gomes and Kenny Ross might have been solo acts, but like several lesbian bands – the Flying Lesbians, Isis, Lilith – there was safety in numbers, in the spirit of a community. Though Buena Vista started out as a smaller group of choir members and pianist from the liberal Glide Memorial church, the band soon numbered nine, including a rhythm section and horns. 'We were once described as a gay rock-gospel-soul band,' says drummer Richard Dworkin. It was as if the Stonewall jukebox had come to life.

Buena Vista's frontline trio modelled themselves after Labelle; their set covered Motown and Philly soul (including Ashford and Simpson's inspirational 'I Need Your Light': 'If we let nothing get in our way/We will make it to a brighter day') and disco, such as a cover of Brainstorm's

---

[1] Well, eighth-ninths gay, which is good enough.

'Lovin' Is Really My Game': 'I can't catch no man/Hangin' out at a discotheque.'

But Buena Vista had a risqué side: they named themselves after San Francisco's cruisiest park, while 'Hot Magazine', the B-side of their debut single, was the first musical tribute to porn. The A-side 'It's OK' was a love song, written by Charles Ashmore, another of those men who had been magnetically drawn to San Francisco.

Born in Buffalo, New York, Ashmore had been thrown out of the navy after a shipmate had informed the authorities of his colleague's sexuality. Going on to study music at the University of Arizona, he'd made a decision 'to make conscious gay music. I'd sung with this hard-rock blues trio Gunther Quint and one song of mine was "Frenchie", about a boy I liked: "Oh, Frenchie, I really love you so, tell me you'll never let me go/Please take me in your arms/Please Frenchie, show me all your charms." I think that was pretty blatant!'

Now calling himself Blackberri, a name that couldn't be defined by gender, he'd moved out west and met Steven Grossman. The pair recorded *Two Songmakers*, the first openly gay music programme, for San Francisco station KQED. 'People on the street, mostly black gay men, would tell me they liked it,' Blackberri recalls. But his audience was restricted to the coffeehouse circuit. 'I've found that gay men tend to let women do all their emotional work, especially white gay men,' he says. 'You'll find black women artists in their record collections, all the divas, but never one black male singer. Black men weren't considered attractive. When I toured, women were the large part of my audience.'

Blackberri's experience was later ratified when *The Advocate*'s music writer, Adam Block, wrote 'Men's music: tuning up with music of our own making' in 1981. 'Trying to survey "gay men's music" is a bit like heading out on safari after Bigfoot,' Block claimed. 'Who knows what the creature looks like? Well, a lot of true-believers claim to – and most disagree.'

Block's 'first candidate for perusal' was the compilation album *Walls* to Roses: Songs of Changing Men, released in 1978, a full three years before The Advocate included it. The album was released by Folkways, still honouring socialist and minority causes,[1] in this case a collective of seventeen musicians that had met through pro-feminist/gay conferences under the title of Men and Masculinity. Charlie Murphy's 'A Gay Spirit' set the tone: 'When we were born they tried to put us in a cage and tell our bodies what to feel/We have chosen to feel all the truth, that our bodies do reveal... There's a gay spirit singing in our hearts, leading us through these troubled times.'

'I took the record over to my friend Larry's,' Block wrote. 'He's black, thirty-two and a disco savant, a self-styled keeper of the faith. I mentioned this article. "These are my gay records," he announced grandly and began flipping discs. "Garland, Streisand, Midler, Diana, Donna, Grace, Jane Olivor, Bernadette Peters, the Bette Davis, the Mae West."' Block gave Walls To Roses to Larry. 'He squinted, then eyed me suspiciously. "That's one of those lesbian/folkie records. Isn't it?"'

'No, they're all men, half of them gay,' Block said. Larry responded: 'Folkways Records. Darling, don't you know that gays are not folks?'

Block then took Walls To Roses to his young punk rock-loving friend, Eric, who said, 'It sounds like a hootenanny at a halfway house... it sounds like they're real afraid that people won't get the point – so they have to say it all real stiff.' Block asked for Eric's idea of gay music; he replied, 'Something tough, like "Let's Face It, the Boy Can't Make It with Girls",' referring to the new single by UK punks 999.

Next, Adam Block tried out Walls To Roses on Jay, a veteran of men's groups. 'These artists have been willing to de-masculinise themselves, to uncover soft places where disco and punk avoid,' Jay reckoned. In the

---

1 Earlier in 1978, it had released Songs of Fire: Songs of a Lesbian Anarchist, by Philadelphia singer-songwriter Kathy Fire. She'd failed to find support from a single women's music label, presumably because sentiments such as 'You're long overdue for your hour of castration,' from 'Mother Rage' – inspired by the rape and murder of Fire's younger sister and Fire's claim that she was abducted and beaten up by the FBI for her political work – were too extreme.

The Seventies II: Disco, Punk and Out Come the Freaks

liner notes where each songwriter got to say their piece, Chris Tanner agreed, writing that he'd been waiting, impatiently, for the kind of men's music that spoke to men as women's music had to women. He'd had to write it himself: 'His name was Jeff, only twenty-three/All he wanted was to be touched by a man/Oh, so gently/But we made him afraid of the pain/And so he chose to die' ('Brother').

'Sure, [*Walls To Roses*] sounds awkward,' Jay continued, 'but coming out was awkward and it reminds me of the pain I felt then.' But, he added, 'I do wish these guys could move me like Springsteen, make me want to cry and dance at the same time.'

Buena Vista were expressly the kind of band that could fulfil that need. 'Our three shows at the Stud were some of the best gigs I've ever played,' recalls Dworkin. 'It was music by and for and of a community. One time, we played a rally in front of city hall to forty or fifty thousand people. Harvey Milk has been elected. It was an incredible feeling, to be playing that music at that space.'

But as Blackberri had discovered, only a select number of gay men wanted the experience of being sung to by gay men. Lacking a disco beat, Buena Vista's 'He's OK' got little radio support, even in San Francisco. The coast of travel outside of the Bay Area for a nine-piece band was also prohibitive and eventually lead singer Terry Hutchison left because of his desire to earn a living from music.[1]

'Our sole purpose was to be a gay band for gay people and when it started trying to be something besides that, that's when it stopped working,' says Dworkin. 'Our moment had passed anyway. The gay clubs were playing disco, they didn't want a band and the straight clubs were playing punk. And we were neither.'

Buena Vista hadn't lasted more than two years, but they were another vital landmark. As founder member Andrew Brown put it, the band 'presented an image of having a good time and not being brought down

---

1 Hutchison would move to New York, and find that not even gay club owners wanted to hire gay male singers. As he told *The Advocate* in 1981, 'Do I have to put on a wig and a dress for an audience to take me seriously?'

by the pressures of being out and gay . . . its legacy is about that, in spite of the pressures of the time of people coming down on gay people and their image and Harvey Milk being murdered . . . '[1]

Milk had been in office for only eleven months when he and mayor Moscone were assassinated by Dan White, who had sat alongside Milk on the board of supervisors. It was the gay community's President Kennedy or Martin Luther King moment, a figurehead for a brave new era chopped down by the old reactionary guard, fearful of change.

White's intervention was the most violent part of a backlash that had been building for a year, since Dade County in Miami passed a gay anti-discrimination law in 1977 that was quickly overturned by a campaign orchestrated by Anita Bryant. The former beauty queen and pop singer was the national spokesperson for the Florida Citrus Commission and the Save Our Children organisation, which based its beliefs on the idea that childless homosexuals would naturally respond to recruitment and abuse. 'God puts homosexuals in the same category as murderers,' she vouched.

Bryant went on a promotional tour to spread her gospel, supported by fellow Christian fundamentalists.[2] Gay and lesbian artists rallied in response; J. D. Doyle counted more than thirty-five 35 protests including Olivia Records' compilation *Concentrate*, singles such as the International Gay Society's 'Stand Up for Your Rights' – written by soul music veteran Bobby Sanders – and Rod McKuen's disco-fied 'Don't Drink The Orange Juice' ('it will lead to all kinds of bigotry').

Word Is Out, the first film documentary about gay and lesbian lives premiered in December 1977 at San Francisco's Castro Theater. It was another direct response, based on twenty-six interviews (plus music clips from Buena Vista and Olivia signing Trish Nugent) to stress the normality of gay and lesbian lives without any need for child molestation.

---

1 www.queermusicheritage.com/jun2010s.html
2 Rod McKuen actively campaigned against Bryant, playing benefits for gay rights groups, and taking out full page ads in *Variety* to protest.

The Seventies II: Disco, Punk and Out Come the Freaks

The temperature continued to rise as Republican state legislator John Briggs tried to ban homosexuals from working in California's public schools. He failed, but civil rights ordinances were overturned by voters in Saint Paul, Minnesota, Wichita, Kansas, Eugene, Oregon and even New York City. Briggs had also been accused of whipping up homophobia in San Francisco by calling the city 'a sexual garbage heap'. A week later, Robert Hillsborough, a gardener employed by the city, was fatally stabbed as his murderers chanted 'faggot', an incident mayor Moscone blamed on Briggs.

The responding San Francisco Gay Freedom Day Parade in June drew 250,000 people, the largest such gathering to date, at which Milk announced his candidacy. The Gay Freedom Day Marching Band and Twirling Corps, the first openly gay music group in the US,[1] formed by choir conductor and music teacher Jon Reed Simm, made their debut, marching behind Milk's convertible.

Five months later, Dan White, a self-appointed 'defender of the home, the family and religious life against homosexuals, pot smokers and cynics', resigned after the passing of San Francisco's gay rights legislation. Two weeks later, having asked for his job back without success, he climbed through a city hall window, walked calmly through the building and shot Milk and Moscone.

On the night of the twin assassination, the San Francisco Gay Men's Chorus – also started by Jon Reed Sims – the first openly gay US choir, made an unscheduled debut on the steps of San Francisco city hall. A year later, despite his premeditated actions, White was convicted of manslaughter rather than murder.

Songs inspired by the egregious verdict told the story: Art Peterson's cheery bluegrass ditty 'Twinkie Insanity' referred to White's defence; that he'd not only suffered from depression after being fired, but from the judgement-impairing effect of sugary junk food. MonDellos' punky

---

1 They soon changed their name to the San Francisco Lesbian/Gay Freedom Band. They were joined in 1978 by LA's Great American Yankee Freedom Band and New York's Lesbian and Gay Big Apple Corps.

'White Riot Night' referenced disturbances outside city hall once the verdict had been announced.[1] Holly Near wrote 'Singing for Our Lives', 'so that something can be built rather than something destroyed, so it's become kind of a peace anthem, a gay and lesbian anthem and an anthem that allies and gay people can sing together.'[2]

As if the gay community hadn't suffered enough, another organised offensive took shape on the night of 12 July 1979 at Comisky Park in Chicago – a figurative assassination. The city's White Sox baseball team were hosting the Detroit Tigers on what was billed as Disco Demolition Night by local DJ Steve Dahl. He invited fans to bring along their unwanted disco records, for which they'd gain entry to the match for 98 cents. Seventy thousand people showed up to a 55,000-capacity stadium and, when the pile of records in the centre of the field were exploded with dynamite, the riot inside and outside the ground saw the match abandoned.

Dahl's stunt, undertaken in cahoots with programming consultants Lee Abrams and Kent Burkhart, was an effort to spur on other genres – Top 40, AOR, country – that disco had seemingly killed off. Just three months earlier, in April 1979, Donna Summer had appeared on *Newsweek*'s cover as part of the story 'Disco Takes Over'. The movement seemed unstoppable, given *Saturday Night Fever*, another disco-themed mainstream movie *Thank God It's Friday* (soundtrack by Giorgio Moroder) and a jukebox of hits – Abba's 'Gimme Gimme Gimme (A Man After Midnight)', Chic's 'Le Freak', Sister Sledge's 'We Are Family', Chaka Khan's 'I'm Every Woman', Grace Jones' 'I Need A Man' and Alicia Bridges' 'I Love The Nightlife'.

But the day immediately after Disco Demolition Night, 'Chicago's dedicated disco station WLUP played Donna Summer's "Last Dance" for twenty-four hours straight, then pronounced disco dead and started

---

1 Brain Damage's 'Kill Dan White' spoke for many people. White was to do them the honour himself in October 1985. Less than two years after he left prison, he shut himself in his garage and turned on the engine.
2 www.queermusicheritage.com/jun2010s.html

spinning Top 40 rock songs,' wrote disco historian Alice Nicols.[1] She quoted West End's Mel Cheren as saying, 'Disco was so officially over that the word itself ceased being used by the mainstream media except as a pejorative.'

Disco's demise can be read as a homophobic and racist attack on disco's core communities. Nicols also blames America's self-image for the incident in Chicago – crushed by its loss in Vietnam, the oil crisis and the associated economic downturn. In any case, any genre that had capitulated to an identikit, profit-driven factory-line production was bound at some point to reach critical mass before imploding.

'I Like The Nightlife', the first disco smash from an openly lesbian singer, was a typical case. From North Carolina, Alicia Bridges specialised in bluesy, ballsy rock of the Janis Joplin variety, while as open about her sexuality as Joplin was closed. Given the freedom by record label owner/producer Bill Lowery to, 'just write it all, girl, write it all,' Bridges responded with a safer theme: 'One day, I said, "Let's write a song that has the word 'disco'" . . . It was kind of a lark.'[2] 'I Love The Nightlife' was a memorably lithe, opportunistic million-seller. But Bridges wasn't up for milking the lark, veering off into a vaguely new wave rock/dance hybrid.

Disco was full of opportunism and quality control could go awry. *Can't Stop The Music*, a pseudo-biopic of the Village People released in June 1980, stands as the zenith of disco's sell-out, a tacky, glitzy and hammy car crash in which the band played straight. 'A stupid gay movie for stupid straight people,' reckoned Arthur Bell of Gay Activists Alliance.[3] In other words, disco *did* suck.

As things tanked, it worked in disco's favour: the opportunists moved

---

1 *Hot Stuff: Disco and the Remaking of America* (Norton and Company, 2010)
2 http://queermusicheritage.com/mar2008.html
3 *Can't Stop The Music* did have one great gay episode: the choreographed 'YMCA' sequence employed a team of underdressed, buff athletes that echoed the Speedo-wearing Olympic squad in *Gentlemen Prefer Blondes*.

on and the diehards strove to be more creative and less generic, helping to fuel the interwoven sound of house and garage music that was lighting up the clubs like Paradise Garage and Warehouse. Both were predominantly black and Hispanic spaces that returned disco to its roots, rejuvenated.

Boys keep swinging, boys – and girls – will work it out

Among Brazil's black and Hispanic populations, the biggest cities – Rio and São Paulo – had thriving gay populations. One of the former's most popular cruising zones, the 'Alaska gallery', inspired Agnaldo Timóteo to write and sing the passionate ballad 'The Gallery of Love'. He didn't write about the cruisers, transvestites and other perceived rejects of society but, poignantly, 'an area of freedom, warm and pleasant,' wrote gay historian Rita Colaço.[1]

Timóteo recalled that his record label, EMI-Odeon were anxious about the song. 'I said, "This is a reality. We must talk about it. There are millions of people living in this way."' He'd already recorded *'Amor Proibido'* ('Forbidden Love'), arguably the first lesbian song of Brazil's social revolution, written by veteran singer Dora Lopes (alongside *tropicalismo* icon Chico Buarque's 'Barbara') and returned to the subject of cruising in 1976 with *'Perdido Na Noite'* ('Lost In The Night'). He went further with the tango-style *'Eu Pecador'* ('I, Sinner'), the first Brazilian song to highlight the conflict between homosexuality and religion.

Timóteo said he wasn't afraid of the censors: unlike others, he noted, 'I'm crude; I am angry; I'm tough. So I put out there.'[2] He was also unafraid because he said he wasn't gay, but had experimented with his cousins, as boys did. Similarly, one of *tropicalismo*'s two figureheads, Caetano Veloso – one of the 'gentler' singers that Timóteo had com-

---

[1] http://memoriamhb.blogspot.co.uk/2012/06/trilogia-homossexual-de-agnaldo-timoteo.html
[2] From *Eu Não Sou Cachorro Não* (*I Am Not a Dog*), Paulo Cesar Araújo (Editora Record, 2002).

pared himself to – insisted he wasn't gay, but confessed he had identified equally with women as men since childhood. On stage, he regularly wore skirts and kissed band members on the lips, and wrote *'Ele Me Deu Um Beijo Na Boca'* ('He Kissed Me on the Mouth') and *'Menino Do Rio'* ('River Boy), 'an ode to male beauty,' Colaç wrote, one with a palpable erotic charge, like a homoerotic 'Girl From Ipanema'. Tropicalismo's other god, Gilberto Gil, wrote *'Corações a Mil'* and *'Logunedé'*, which both celebrated bisexuality, while *'SuperHomem'* ('Superman') celebrated the feminine spirit: 'The women's side of me . . . is the best side I have in me now/It's the one that makes me live').

Lesbian singer Marina Lima also recorded *'Corações a Mil'* and, according to blogger César Braga-Pinto, 'everybody in Brazil knew, or at least assumed that some of the greatest Brazilian singers, such as Maria Bethânia, Gal Costa[1], Simone, Angela Rô Rô, Cassia Eller, Adriana Calcanhoto, Ana Carolina and many others were lesbians. Many of their songs were interpreted indeed as love songs addressed to other women.' Leci Brandão was the first Brazilian singer to come out in 1978, alongside her song *'Ombro Amigo'* ('Shoulder Friend'), about the closet and the 'ghettos' of gay and lesbian clubs – though Rio's annual carnival increasingly brought the exuberance of those closed spaces into the open.

The equivalent of Caeteno Veloso and Gil Gilberto in seventies bisexual glam rock, David Bowie and Lou Reed, were fast abandoning the musical and lyrical traits of those heady days. Yet Bowie made one last connection to those roots after leaving the US in 1977 for Europe, where he recorded his so-called Berlin trilogy, namely *Low*, *Heroes*, and *Lodger*.

While living in Berlin with his friend Iggy Pop, Bowie had formed a friendship – supposedly sexual – with Dutch transsexual Romy Haag. He owned a nightclub famous for drag acts who'd tear off their wigs and smear their make-up at the end of their set. Working on 1979's

---

1 As famous as Caeteno Veloso and Gilberto Gil, Tropicalismo's female supremo Gal Costa has been outed by another singer, but she's been married three times and never confessed to any lesbian leanings.

Lodger, Bowie wrote 'Boys Keep Swinging', an ode to a free'n'easy life that wasn't really gay. The 'other boys check you out' line was arguably more an homage to fashion envy than locker-room jealousy–but the video stole the Haag routine to underline how boys can swing equally as girls.

Lou Reed, meanwhile, had separated from his trans partner Rachel and was metaphorically tearing off his wig: 'No more bullshit, no more dyed hair, faggot junkie trip,' he said and would remain true to his word until his death in 2014. Bowie himself wouldn't address the subject again until 1997. Nothing else matched the bravery of Rod Stewart's 'The Killing Of Georgie', Tom Robinson's '(Sing If You're) Glad To Be Gay' or the first acknowledged German rock band, Warmer Südwind, whose Danish member, Bent Jacobsen, had released his own album *Bøsse* – slang for homosexual – in 1975, his country's first musical foray into homosexuality and gender roles. Warner Südwind's 1977 album *Schwul* – again, slang for homosexual – similarly took route one with tracks such as 'The Gay Market' and 'Turn Around, Black Leather Man' with two entwined naked men on the cover and an explicit collage-based poster insert. No British all-gay band emerged to match them, or Buena Vista, nor a singular black presence like Blackberri. And if gay characters and themes were to figure in the UK, the job would have to fall to straight musicians.

In the punk and new wave sphere, besides 999's charged 'The Boy Can't Make It With Girls', the Drug Addix released 'Gay Boys In Bondage', an effective Lou Reed parody. Elton Motello's stamping pop-punk single 'Jet Boy Jet Girl' was sung from the standpoint of a teenager who discovers his older boyfriend also sleeps with women. But then the hookline, 'He gives me head' and the claim, 'I'm gonna make you penetrate/I'm gonna make you be a girl,' sounded like the confused bisexual lover had taken control of the song.[1]

---

[1] Six years after 'Walk On The Wild Side', the BBC had cottoned on to the meaning of 'giving head', banning 'Jet Boy Jet Girl'. Just a few months later, the same backing track with new lyrics and title – '*Ca Plane Pour Moi*' – was a Top 10 hit across Europe for Plastic Bertrand, a pseudonym for Elton Motello's drummer Roger Jouret.

Shifting sexual identities remained a rich subject and only Bowie and Reed muddied the waters as much as Kinks frontman Ray Davies. But it still took him seven years after 'Lola'. 1977's 'On the Outside' was a sympathetic plea to 'a closet queen' with more transparency than Davies' typical approach: 'Don't hide your troubles inside/You should be glad in the gay/Nobody cares anyway on the outside.'

Davies had worked with Tom Robinson's old band, Café Society and 'On The Outside' made a direct, and positive, reference to 'Glad To Be Gay'. But Davies shelved 'On The Outside', and instead released 'Prince Of The Punks' as a Kinks B-side, a negative portrait of a mercenary rocker reputedly inspired by Robinson, with the swipe, 'He thinks he's a stud but I think he looks more like a queen.'

The reference to a 'closet queen' also made it onto a Kinks record, this time a plea on behalf of a Lola-esque figure, 'A chick called Dick . . . He's not a pansy, he's only being what he wants to be' – as if being gay/a pansy would undermine his cross-dressing cause. Meanwhile, the effect on Dick's wife was interesting: 'She wears the trousers and smokes a pipe . . . '

Frank Zappa was equally opaque when it came to taking responsibility for his creations. Having steered the Mothers of Invention through merciless satires, of both the establishment and society's alternatives, including the counter-culture that bought his records, Zappa's seventies output focused on the US sexual revolution with graphic glee. In 1979's 'Bobby Brown Goes Down', a boy-next-door is turned gay by sleeping with a lesbian feminist and develops a taste for S&M: 'Oh, God, I am the American dream/With a spindle up my butt 'till it makes me scream.' Had women's liberation emasculated men? Or was white, straight male privilege finally getting its comeuppance? Or was Zappa just a bigot with a license to offend?

In 1978, the Rolling Stones wrote 'a straight gay song', as Mick Jagger labelled the hustler saga of 'When the Whip Comes Down' ('I go to 53rd Street and they spit in my face/But I'm learning the ropes, yeah, I'm learning a trade'), though he told *Rolling Stone* he had 'no idea why I wrote it. Maybe I came out of the closet!'

In the US, Mitch Ryder was, like Jagger a believer in R&B/rock crossover but, unlike Jagger, a bisexual dabbler.'[1] 1978's *How I Spent My Vacation* – his first solo album since 1966's Bob Crewe-produced debut *What Now My Love* – featured his own songs for a change, audibly indebted to Lou Reed.[2] There were songs of sexual experimentation co-written with Ryder's wife, including the blue-eyed soul power-trip 'Cherry Poppin': 'Roll over a bit and let me stick it in/Nothing's queer, just the loss of fear/Cherry poppin', love is grand/Cherry poppin', I hold it in my hand/Cherry poppin', poppa stick it, uhh.'

Two fellow sixties survivors had come through the more permissive seventies. Dusty Springfield had discovered women's music. In 1974, she had been making a new album, *Longing* and had covered the exquisite 'Beautiful Soul', written by Margie Adams,[3] who could have had Springfield in mind for her portrait of a woman still in denial: 'I wonder what you're thinking, beautiful woman/It seems like fog is settling in within your eyes/And the weight of something is pulling your shoulders down . . . So you're hammering at a door that will not open/And your beautiful soul is weeping.'

Springfield's old demons remained. Feeling neglected by her new record label, she abandoned the sessions and 'Beautiful Soul' would only be released posthumously, on a box set in 2000. But in 1978, she released 'Closet Man': 'There's nothing new at all under the sun/You've got company/You're not the only one/Why, it's older than religion/And, quite honestly, more fun.'

If Springfield could not take her own advice, at least Long John Baldry, who had moved to Canada, had stuck by his convictions with

---

1 *Devils and Blue Dresses: My Wild Ride as a Rock'n'Roll Legend*, Cool Titles (2011). In his book, Ryder said he'd been married, had gay and extra-marital heterosexual experiences but that he was presently committed 'to a heterosexual relationship. I'm free to choose anything I want. Anybody on the planet is.'
2 In 1971, Mitch Ryder's band Detroit covered the Velvet Underground's 1970 track 'Rock And Roll'.
3 Adams' own version (on her *Songwriter* album) counted Meg Christian and Cris Williamson among the backing vocalists.

the winking title of his album *Baldry's Out*. The title track referred to his recovery after leaving hospital following a nervous breakdown, but the record's true closet-buster was 'A Thrill's A Thrill', written by Ontario's Bill Amesbury, a Casablanca signing whose own version from 1976 documented his sojourn in downtown New York: 'Now the young boys are all hanging out in the bars/Old men they don't have to cruise all night in cars . . . Oh, I will try anything if it makes my head go round/ Leather whips and fingertips/I know a boy who is growing tits.'[1]

Baldry's old friend Elton John had even committed to a new level of boldness by asking Tom Robinson to write some lyrics for a forthcoming album, doubtless knowing that he wouldn't shirk from the opportunity. 'Sartorial Eloquence' (renamed in the US 'Don't Ya Wanna Play This Game No More?' after its chorus) suggested a man hiding the truth behind stage costumes: 'Oh, your lifestyle shows in the clothes you chose/Sitting pretty in the masquerade.'

A sparse emotive ballad, 'Elton's Song' removed all traces of masquerade and metaphor as Robinson drew on the memory of the teenage crush that had precipitated his suicide attempt: 'They think I'm mad, they say it isn't real/But I know what I feel and I love you/But I would give my life for a single night beside you.'

Robinson's own songs had abandoned gay themes, judging by 1979's *TRB2* album, and the band had split up. But his job had been done. 'Somebody told me at the time they'd been on the top deck of a crowded number twenty-seven bus when the conductor tried to throw off two blokes who were holding hands or had kissed each other or something,' he recalled in 2009. 'Apparently, pretty much everyone sitting on the top of the bus started singing "(Sing If You're) Glad To Be Gay" at the conductor, who backed down and left the blokes alone. A fantastic moment of validation for the song.'[2]

Having seen the attendees at London's Gay Pride 1976 almost

---

1 Amesbury claimed 'A Thrill's A Thrill' wasn't autobiographical, but later transitioned to Barbara Amesbury.
2 http://gladtobegay.net/interview-tom-robinson/part-3

outnumbered by police, Robinson would have been validated by 1979's summer event, which he compered. But he was disappointed to see a faction of the 10,000 in attendance turn against one of their own – and one of the braver pioneer at that. Polly Perkins sang 'Superdyke' and recalls 'being heckled by dykes, for wearing make-up and not big boots.'[1]

Robinson knew that the gay community were as varied as the colours on the rainbow flag that had been recently been adopted for the cause. The variety was mirrored by his latest gay-themed show, Cabaret 79, to mark Stonewall's tenth anniversary; he sang both versions of 'Glad To Be Gay', 'Gay Switchboard Jingle' and 'Sartorial Eloquence'. He resuscitated Lewis Furey's 'Closing The Door' from his last event and added Noël Coward's 'Mad About The Boy', plus 'Stand Together' – a GLF song that Robinson had witnessed 'sung by an angry gay crowd confronting two police officers in 1975'.

US punk: still not glad to be gay?

By 1979, when Robinson was done with new wave, punk in its original form seemed to die in 1978 with the messy end of the Sex Pistols in San Francisco.

UK new wave was now much more likely to chart than punk's diehard sound, especially if it incorporated synthesisers and drum machines. There was another new style of alternative, post-punk, which upped the experimental elements, including the electronics. But the original punk sound was late arriving in the US and though there were small stirrings in 1977, California's punk scene – centred in LA – only exploded in 1979.

LA punk had little time for the UK's melody/hook model, preferring

---

1 Might Pride's lesbian hardcore have jeered the all-female Wicked Lady as they did Perkins? On the cover of their 1979 single 'Girls Love Girls', their look was leather catsuits: the music was pure glam too. Like Perkins, Wicked Lady found it hard to find an audience, but they chose to live in Amsterdam and find work across Europe. Singer/guitarist Sue Exley recalls the negative reactions to their lesbian anthem from the military bases on the live circuit; soldiers who expected a little leather-clad raunch would have been surprised to find Wicked Lady didn't return their affections.

The Seventies II: Disco, Punk and Out Come the Freaks

a more caustic, flat-out energy that became known as hardcore. Early adopters were the Screamers, co-founded in 1975 by David Harrigan, a former Cockette who now called himself Tomata du Plenty. He'd led the drag-inspired lip-syncing comedy troupe Ze Whiz Kidz and then formed the Tupperwares with drag artist Melba Toast before the Screamers came to life.

The band were early adopters in using synthesisers rather than guitars to make their punk roar. But just like UK gay punk, LA's brand was unwilling to sing its name, not even when it was a former Cockette. Jon Savage, who interviewed the Screamers in 1979 for the UK music weekly *Sounds*, recalled, 'Two of them were gay, as I was, but nobody mentioned it, not a single word. But at the time, there was no touchy-feely culture, not even in America. Sex still wasn't something you talked about.'[1]

In her dissertation on LA's punk scene, Mary Montgomery Wolf quoted Brendan Mullen, manager of the LA club the Masque and frontman of the punk band Arthur J. and the Gold Cups, which took its name from one of the city's downtown rent-boy hangouts. Mullen estimated the gays accounted for 20-35 per cent of his crowd, 'a mostly closeted, but considerably large, don't-ask-don't-tell homo costituency.'[2]

Wolf also quoted Screamers' drummer KK Barrett: 'It was a time of gay fear and there were a lot of gays in the scene ... but it was all hidden, 'cause there was a lot of homophobia.' Looking back from 2005, the Germs' manager Nicole Olivieri said, 'I saw a video of [The Screamers] a couple of years ago and I was struck by how flamingly gay they were, something that went right by me back then.'

One bystander thought women had greater freedom to experiment

---

1 Jorge Socarras had another view. Fronting a new band, Indoor Life, he was interviewed by *The Advocate*: 'They kept asking me to say I was gay, as my songs were all gender-ambiguous, I was the only gay member and I saw no reason to say it to someone interviewing me about my music!'

2 *We Accept You, One of Us?: Punk Rock, Community and Individualism in an Uncertain Era*, Mary Montgomery Wolf (2007), https://cdr.lib.unc.edu/indexablecontent/uuid:9da5d840-fe83-4988-82ac-5f78a9e73c84

313

with sexuality as there would be less chance of triggering a violent reaction that more typified relationships between the men. The scene's most infamous figure was Darby Crash (born Jan Paul Beahm), singer of the Germs, who were first known as Sophistifuck and the Revlon Spam Queens. Crash was petrified that the obsessive ring of fans he'd cultivated would desert him if the truth of his sexuality was circulated. In Penelope Spheeris'[1] documentary on the LA punk scene, *The Decline of Western Civilisation*, Crash invented a girlfriend for cosy domestic shots in his kitchen, but he didn't need to keep the pretence for long; his five-year plan[2] – to form a band, create a stir, release one great album and commit suicide to secure said legend – was perfectly executed and he went out with a heroin overdose in 1980.[3] His suicide note read, 'My life, my leather, my love goes to Bosco,' namely David 'Bosco' Danford, the bassist of the short-lived Darby Crash Band. The fictionalised film biography of Crash's life of 2007 was aptly named after the Germs track, 'What We Do Is Secret'.

The Germs had been the support band for the first advertised show by the Zeros, whose guitarist Robert Lopez was openly gay – not that he was ever asked about sexuality in an interview, he says. There were other odd gay and lesbian representatives, such as Phranc, the co-founder of synth-punks Nervous Gender, who one reviewer described as looking like 'a fourteen-year-old runaway from a boys' reform school'.

At seventeen, Phranc, born Susan Gottlieb, had attended the Lesbian History Exploration summer camp, where Alix Dobkin sang and lectured. There, she discovered a new, butch name and that she belonged more among the punks than the lesbian separatists. 'I was always trying to pull the dykes and the punks together, which was such a futile dream,'

---

1 Spheeris' gay brother, Jimmy, a musician with roots in early seventies Californian rock, finally showed his own colours by posing on the cover of 1977's *Ports of the Heart* floating on a lilo, tanned and slim, wearing just Speedos.
2 Darby Crash's allocated time span was based on his idol David Bowie's *Ziggy Stardust* song 'Five Years'.
3 Crash's five-year plan couldn't have foreseen that one day after his suicide the news would be overshadowed by John Lennon's murder.

she told Adam Block. 'The one time I did, Nervous Gender played this benefit for a women's video center and they pulled the plug on us! Apparently, to the women's community, punk rock was the epitome of violence against women. Anyone with different coloured hair or a different look was violence against women! What really upset me . . . for lesbians to read all this gnarly stuff about punks and *believe* it.'[1]

Phranc's preference for the punks led her to join the Velvets-y rockers Catholic Discipline[2] alongside Robert Lopez and fellow gay musician Craig Lee of the Bags. Though singer Claude Bessy was straight and wrote the lyrics, this was still the most out band of the era. Karla Duplantier, known as Mad Dog, was also out and was the planet's first black lesbian drummer.

And then there were two.

Up in San Francisco, Tony Hotel was rhythmic half of female duo Noh Mercy (motto: 'No boys and guitars'). The Bay Area scene was more experimental and diverse than the one in LA:[3] the Offs were unusual in America for aping the politicised punk/ska/reggae meld of the UK's the Clash, while Offs vocalist Don Vinyl was 'the first openly gay front man on the punk scene,' according to filmmakers Emily Armstrong and Pat Ivers, who documented both east and west coast punk. The Offs' second single 'Everyone's A Bigot', the most exhilarating offensive against homophobia yet recorded, claimed that bigotry knew no colour or race.[4]

San Francisco had a band with two gay members and two straight – and one bisexual. Tuxedomoon were also the most experimental and

---

1 For *The Advocate*, www.monkeychicken.com/AdamBlock/1986_7_22phranc.pdf
2 Joining Catholic Discipline in the broader, new wave camp were boyfriends Michael Ely (vocals) and Spider Taylor (guitar) of Hey Taxi!
3 From Sacramento, nearer in distance and also spirit to San Francisco, the Twinkeyz's debut single 'Aliens In Our Midst' was a compulsively droning oddity that – for no thematic purpose – threw in a verse about a cross-dressing boy who, 'grew up OK/And made his way to junior high . . . and gave his ring to another guy'.
4 Sadly, the Offs made little headway, undone by personnel changes and drug issues: Vinyl died of a heroin overdose in the early eighties.

the longest-lasting. Founder member Steven Brown had been a member of Hibiscus' Angels Of Light, but his new outfit was a long way from a glittery mess of show-tune lovers, rooted as it was in a style of stark electronic cabaret, like a descendant of Bowie's Berlin trilogy. What Tuxedomoon wrote about Harvey Milk, '(Special Treatment For The) Family Man' (referring to Dan White), resembled a funeral march.

In New York, the experimental post-punk trend coalesced into 'no wave', which incorporated a jazz-minded blast that featured saxophone skronk and piercing electronics as agitated guitars. Four bands spearheaded the scene, as captured on 1978's compilation *No New York*: DNA and Mars played their part but the iconic bands were Contortions and Teenage Jesus and the Jerks. The former had lesbians Pat Place (guitar) and Adele Bertei (keyboards) while the Jerks' drummer was Bradley Field, boyfriend of former Mump Kristian Hoffman. Singer Lydia Lunch felt to claim she was bisexual 'doesn't say enough. No, trisexual, because I will try anything.'[1]

Hoffman also played with Contortions and it was the band's manager who suggested he team up with Klaus Nomi, the most individual and outlandish gay artist of New York's downtown scene. But it was David Bowie who had the nous to introduce this bewitching alien soprano on live television. At every point through the seventies, Bowie had remained a talisman, influential with every musical and visual turn and his last stage appearance of the seventies was no less arresting. He had a big audience too, US comedy staple *Saturday Night Live*. Starting with 1970's 'The Man Who Sold The World', Bowie wore a kind of moulded papier mâché tuxedo in which he was carried to the microphone by his backing singers, both in flowing androgynous outfits; one was Joey Arias, the other Nomi.

For 'TVC15', Bowie finally let America know he could still toy with gender by wearing a long skirt, in keeping with Arias and Nomi. For 'Boys Keep Swinging', green-screen technology gave Bowie a puppet's

---

1 www.thescavenger.net/arts-sp-431/arts/102-rebel-with-a-cause-lydia-lunch.html

body. Unbelievably, someone felt it prudent to bleep out the 'other boys check you out' line – even in the late hours of Saturday night in progressive New York – though the producers missed the flash of the puppet's thrusting erection at end of Bowie's performance.[1]

For the last thirty-five years, Joey Arias has been something of a Zelig, but with more fabulous legs than Zelig's creator Woody Allen and a stellar Billie Holiday tribute show, among other compelling configurations. Part-Mexican and part-German, Arias was raised in LA where he'd befriended a young Sylvester, who he recalls was 'a screaming queen. We'd all be running around and my mother would say, "Who are these freaks?"'

In Arias' teens, he'd infiltrated LA's rock groupie scene, where he got close to Steve Marriott, the UK singer of the Small Faces and Humble Pie. 'He'd ask me to drop by his hotel room,' Arias recalls. 'We'd have drinks, we'd kiss ... I don't know if he was gay but he was *very* chummy. But then, on Quaaludes, people were very loving.'

In 1976, Arias moved on to New York 'to rediscover and reinvent myself, to find a different Joey.' Within a week, he'd met Nomi, born Klaus Sperber in Germany, who had worked as an usher at a Berlin opera house while singing arias at the city's gay disco Kleist Casino. In 1972, he'd also come to New York and was working as a pastry chef. 'Klaus was wearing chinos, a fedora, aviator sunglasses and a pin-striped shirt ... though he liked punk, like the Ramones,' Arias recalls. 'One day, at this big art show, he walked in, in leather pants, chains, black lipstick, he looked incredible. We became instant friends.'

That outfit was trumped by Nomi's outfit for his New York stage debut, backed by Kristian Hoffman. On *American Family*, Mumps singer Lance Loud had claimed he didn't have the talent or patience to see

---

1 And they say the British are repressed about sex! In comparison, on UK TV, Bowie sang 'Boys Keep Swinging' on *The Kenny Everett Show*. At the end, the host – a radio DJ turned all-round entertainer, who later came out – approached Bowie in costume, a city-gent suit at the front cut to reveal bra and panties at the back. He began sniping at the singer's 'type,' before begging Bowie to chase and molest him – which he does. *That's how it should be done!*

projects through and he'd quit music for journalism[1], leaving Hoffman to find alternate employment. At the East Village art event New Wave Vaudeville, he'd seen Sperber – now calling himself Klaus Nomi after his favourite sci-fi magazine *OMNI* – wearing a spacesuit with a clear plastic cape, singing the aria *'Mon Cœur S'Ouvre À Ta Voix'* ('My Heart Opens To Your Voice') from Camille Saint-Saëns' opera *Samson et Dalila*. Nomi had pitch-perfect soprano and with strobe lights, smoke bombs and electronic FX, he'd gotten everyone's attention.

'It was like Klaus was from a different planet and his parents were calling him home,' Hoffman recalls. 'When the smoke cleared, he was gone. The place went bananas.'

Adapting Bowie's wide tuxedo costume by adding black leggings, Nomi perfected his alien identity with deathly white make-up and a receding fin of hair. Hoffman wrote his songs – 'Bowie and Jobriath were in my mind right from the beginning' – and chose covers such as Lou Christie's 'Lightning Strikes'. Nomi appeared at the Mudd Club, where Bowie first saw him perform and also Hurrah: both staged live shows where the diverse acts drew on rock and disco, electronics and guitars and world rhythms such as Latin and afrobeat.

Another Hurrah booking was Skafish, a new wave band from Chicago fronted by a man calling himself Jim Skafish, one of the most singular singers of any era: 'He appears to be in transition between man and woman ... dressed androgynously, hair in [sic] a pageboy ... [he] strips down to a woman's bathing suit and nervously applies lipstick to the face,' according to *Billboard*.

The decade's end; winner and losers

Nomi was influential enough to have a film documentary made about his life, while Skafish is one of those names you'll only find by scouring

---

1 Loud wrote columns for several magazines, including *Rock Scene*, *The Advocate*, *Details*, *Interview* and *Creem*. Two retrospective Mumps compilations have been released: *Fatal Charm* (Eggbert Records, 1994) and the double *How I Saved The World* (Sympathy for the Record Industry, 2005).

The Seventies II: Disco, Punk and Out Come the Freaks

the internet. Talent, timing, fortune: all these factors could determine the outcome, but it was also a question of attitude, such as what compromises could and could not be made with the people funding and shaping your mission.

By the end of the seventies, singer and archbishop Carl Bean says Motown was strongly encouraging him to follow 'I Was Born This Way' with love songs – to women. 'Not even Sylvester sang boy-to-boy love,' he points out, 'and his record company tried to tone down his effeminacy.' Indeed, the promo video for Sylvester's follow-up to ' . . . Mighty Real', a cover of 'I (Who Have Nothing)' had the singer back in a suit, perched at a bar and singing to a woman sitting opposite him. She couldn't have looked less bored, while Sylvester, a coat over his suit-clad shoulders and waving a cigarette, could not have looked any less straight.

The idea that mainstream gay had to resemble the Village People, to reinforce all the gender stereotypes, was reinforced by the 'YMCA' rip-off that was 'Men Of Montrose' by the Houston quartet Montrose Men and another Casablanca label strategy to milk the market. LA's Skatt Brothers were a butch crew: luxurious moustaches proliferated. The creative Brother was Sean Delaney, who had helped hard rockers KISS with their on-stage theatrical antics and the occasional co-write. He knew about outrage, and while his sexuality is unconfirmed[1], he was willing to go where the Village People never did, into real sleaze. He started with the dubious band name and continued with the Skatts' first single 'Walk The Night', a stomping rock take on muscular disco:[2] 'Upon his lips the taste of pain/Venom kiss of love insane/He's got a rod beneath his coat/He's gonna ram right down your throat.'

Even without a video and with lyrics that must have restricted

---

1 The only reference I can find is on Wikipedia, where there is the comment about Delaney being 'room-mates' between 1969-1980 with the late KISS manager Bill Ancoin, who definitely was gay.
2 'Walk The Night', which didn't have a promo video, can be seen on YouTube with footage taken from William Friedkin's infamous *Cruising*.

BREAKING DOWN THE WALLS OF HEARTACHE

airplay, 'Walk The Night' was a mind-boggling US Top 10 hit. Was mainstream America suddenly turning on? A video was made by the band's Australian licensees for the Skatts' follow-up single, 'Life At The Outpost', set in a rodeo bar. Unable to use the band, the video-makers used hired hands, whose lame choreographed steps recalled a prototype Village People – if they'd crossed square dancing with a fitness workout.[1] Meanwhile, a female stooge clambered on board a rodeo, presumably to suggest these men were, in fact, straight, rather than secretly fond of each other. Some viewers would be in on the joke, but why alienate those and anyone who thought 'In The Navy' was a recruitment song?

The clone – 'tache, white T-shirt, jeans, leather optional – was the gay community's most ubiquitous look; even pop's most flamboyant frontman, Freddie Mercury, had abandoned the flowing locks and costumes and grown a luxurious slug over his lip to go with his new butch threads. He didn't go the full hog, like Rob Halford of UK heavy metal band Judas Priest, who'd taken to head-to-toe leather, including peaked cap and studded cuffs. But his band's songs weren't going as far as Mercury; in Queen's 'Don't Stop Me Now', released as a single in 1979, Mercury claimed: 'I wanna make a supersonic man out of you . . . I am a sex machine ready to reload.'

The addition of 'I wanna make a supersonic woman out of you' wouldn't render Mercury's lyric any less gay than the Skatt Brothers' cowgirl. If the sixties had been closeted and the Seventies were all about the halfway house of bisexuality – the door kicked open but no one walking through – the Eighties were about to destroy the closet. At the same time, the battle for equality – even for survival – had only just begun.

---

[1] The Skatt Brothers couldn't keep up the joke for long. 'Life At The Outpost' wasn't a hit, and a second Skatt album was only released in Australia, where luxurious moustaches had been proliferating at an alarming rate.

CHAPTER 9

The Eighties: All The Nice Boys Love Sea Men – Pop Comes Out

'I'm coming out/I want the world to know/Got to let it show.'
'I'm Coming Out', Diana Ross, 1980

'Relax/Don't do it/When you want to come.'
'Relax', Frankie Goes To Hollywood, 1983

The androgyny that underpinned much of popular music's key seventies trends – glam, disco, punk, new wave, no wave – had only a tiny amount of trans-genderism: Jayne County and Bowie and Lou Reed's friendships with Romy Haag and Rachel respectively. One breakthrough at the end of the decade promised much for the new decade.

Rhode Island pianist and electronic musician Wendy Carlos had released *Switched-On Bach* in 1968, an inventive and hugely successful take on the German's classical genius using the Moog synthesiser technology. The income enabled Carlos to consider a more crucial transformation, to fully confront the gender dysphoria she'd endured since childhood. The former Walter Carlos had begun hormone replacement even before the album was released, but in public (live shows, a meeting with director Stanley Kubrick about writing the soundtrack to *Clockwork Orange*, even the Dick Cavett Show), she disguised herself with fake sideburns, a wig and drawn-on facial hair.

In 1972, Carlos had sex reassignment surgery, but still released albums as Walter Carlos and shunned the outside world. She avoided even musical enquiries from Stevie Wonder and George Harrison, convinced her career would suffer if the truth got out. In 1979, 'the charade' was finally over when Carlos told her story to *Playboy*: the magazine had, she explained, 'always been concerned with liberation and [I was] anxious to liberate myself. The climate has changed, and the time is right.'

Her fears, that she might never again be taken seriously as a musician[1] and the public reaction, were unfounded. People 'turned out to be amazingly tolerant or, if you wish, indifferent . . . it had proven a monstrous waste of years of my life.'[2] But she considered herself always to have been Wendy and shut down all enquiries into her transition, insisting she should be only treated as an artist rather than a medical or social phenomenon. She very rarely gave interviews and so again disappeared from view rather than provide a focal point for the 'normality' of transsexualism in popular culture.

The public was always going to be more comfortable with a choice of sex (lifestyle) rather than one of gender (surgery). They still had to get used to gay and lesbian identity. As David Bowie had noted, boys will be boys and gay men and their nightlife, dominated the agenda at the expense of lesbian visibility. By the start of the eighties, London's Heaven nightclub had become the focal point for a new standard in gay clubs and, in New York, the expensive redevelopment of the old Fillmore East rock venue into the Saint, the biggest gay club space so far, set the bar higher. It had futuristic design and a ceiling planetarium of stars, which was unveiled to the sound of Donna Summer's 'Could It Be Magic'.

With a members-only policy that only allowed in very few women, the Saint was like a giant coming-out party for the city's gay culture, a place to dance and also cruise (the third floor balcony was treated like a giant darkroom). The club was funded by the same team behind the city's newest and largest gay bathhouse, St Marks Baths. Across the country, from San Francisco to New York, gay men celebrated their freedom, a world without guilt or fear.

---

1 Carlos wrote notable soundtracks to *The Shining* (1980) and *Tron* (1982)
2 www.people.com/people/archive/article/0, , 20091206,00.html

The Eighties: Pop Comes Out

The message was carried in former Supreme Diana Ross' 1980 single 'I'm Coming Out', written for her by Chic's Nile Rodgers and Bernard Edwards. The duo, the most gifted of the disco/funk alliances and more successful across the board than the Village People team, were part of the new freedom, partaking in Studio 54's bacchanalia. Rodgers got the idea for the lyric from seeing how drag queens loved to impersonate Ross. Once he'd convinced Ross that the song wasn't about gay culture, they had a worldwide hit on their hands.

'I'm Coming Out' was a sleek and supple brand of disco in the Chic fashion. It was part of an update on traditional disco, evident in two singles released on Mel Cheren's West End label – Barbara Mason's story of her cheating bisexual boyfriend on 1983's 'Another Man' and the nine-minute 'Is It All Over My Face?' by Loose Joints, a front for songwriter Arthur Russell and club DJ Steve D'Acquisto.

From Iowa, Arthur Russell was a maverick, a student of cello, piano, North Indian classical music, electronic music and linguistics. It gave him a different outlook to other disco lovers. Russell found his way to the Gallery and, with Siano producing, released the lean disco workout 'Kiss Me Again' under the moniker Dinosaur, fronted by the soulfully wailing Myriam Valle. It was the first disco release by Sire, better known for its new wave (in fact, Sire founder Seymour Stein had come up with the term 'new wave' to give the more melodic alternative bands a chance at being heard since 'punk rock' was a negative term in many minds). But Dinosaur was a one-off, and it took another three years for Russell to return, with 'Is It All Over My Face?', a gloriously lean example of post-disco, built on a gloriously slippery bass line, sultry percussion and slurred male voices. Russell's lyric tapped the communal spirit of both cruising and dancing: 'You caught me love dancing/Is it all over my face?'

Russell's progressive sound wasn't slick enough for the Saint, whose pricey membership fees ensured that the clientele was mostly white and white collar with conservative musical tastes. 'Is It All Over My Face' was championed by Larry Levan at Paradise Garage, after Levan had remixed the track using the female vocal that Russell had discarded for his final version. Not even post-disco could so easily discard the accepted rules of what made a great disco record.

If Russell's approach was post-disco, or 'mutant disco', as it got labelled, Patrick Cowley's rippling, pulsing synthesiser music represented another future – and one that suited the Saint's demographic. Cowley's sleek amalgam of synthesisers and female vocal became known as Hi-NRG after Donna Summer had described her 1977 (Moroder-piloted) smash 'I Feel Love' as having 'a high-energy vibe'.[1]

Cowley was working overtime with music on the soundtrack of the 1980 gay porn film *School Daze*, that fifteen-minute remix of 'I Feel Love' and the launching of his record label, Megatron. The debut release, his own 'Menergy' leant heavily on the bass synth pulse of Giorgio Moroder's 'The Chase' but added joyous horns, 'Mighty Real'-style rushes and a combination of male-robotic and female-gospel voices for a boost of testosterone bliss: 'The boys in the back-room laughin' it up, shootin' off energy/The boys in the bedroom, lovin' it up, shootin' off energy.'

'Patrick was very libidinously driven, to feed that erotic frenzy, to work the shirtless guys in the room,' says Jorge Socarras. 'This is what gay men wanted and what he wanted.'

'Menergy' topped the US dance chart in 1981, the most successful of Cowley's four Top 10 dance chart hits. But for graphic 'menergy', Cowley was outflanked by another San Francisco operation. Using the name Boystown Gang, local DJ Bill Motley looked back to two Ashford and Simpson songs, 'Remember Me' and 'Ain't No Mountain High Enough' made famous by Diana Ross, for a fifteen-minute medley and, for the B-side, wrote 'Cruisin' The Streets': 'the *Deep Throat* of disco,' reckoned journalist Alan Jones.[2]

This was no gay porn soundtrack but gay porn itself, once the music

---

[1] *Saturday Night Forever: The Story of Disco*, Alan Jones and Jussi Kantonen (Mainstream, 1999)
[2] Ibid. 482

had coursed through seven-and-a-half minutes of classic disco. As the music kept pumping, an unspecified number of male characters talked various shades of dirty before one pair got down to it, at which point a female hooker said, 'You guys mind if I watch? It really turns me on to watch two hot studs,' before two policemen turn up at the scene:

First cop: 'What do you think we should do with them?'

Second cop: 'I know exactly what to do with them. Up against the wall, you asshole . . . .'

Cue collective groans as the two cops join in. In 1962, music had come right out with *Love Is A Drag*. Now love was the drug – or not even love.

In Jamaican reggae, the lewd, vulgar lyric was referred to as 'slack', as in slack morals: an early example was Johnny Ringo's 'Two Lesbians Hitch' – the B-side was 'Clitoris In Spanish Town', credited to Rhythm Rulers. Writer Carol Cooper explained the song 'retold a Jamaican newspaper story about a bizarre sexual accident involving two nude women and an unintentionally fatal hormone shot.' But Ringo's saga was only modest slackness next to the filth of 1980's *Sleeze Attack*,[1] by a duo with the slack name of Canya Phuckem and Howe.

Echoing *Love Is A Drag*, the album's liner notes thanked 'the very talented musicians and singers of San Francisco who performed on this album but prefer to remain anonymous,'[2] even though the lyrics were no worse than Boystown Gang's. Still, *Sleeze Attack* resembled the diary of a San Francisco BDSM fan. The record started with 'One Sir, Thank You, Sir' and 'In A Sling', then embraced water sports ('Warm Wet Feeling'), piercing ('Rings') – surely the first lyrical reference to a foreskin) and handkerchief codes ('Left Pocket, Right Pocket'). The odd song out was the romantic – and pun-heavy – 'This Guy's The Limit'. The other surprise was CP and H's music, a hybrid of new wave and

---

[1] The cover of *Sleeze Attack* was charming: a drawing of a pair of legs with a fist aimed at the rear and a jet of – presumably – Crisco ejaculating across the sleeve.
[2] Found at the Terminal Boredom forum, 2008: 'I've searched for information on the record for about five years, asking people who know SF punk and gay punk history and no one has any info.' http://terminal-boredom.com/forums/index.php?topic=11865.0

sixties Merseybeat, plus a country rocker in 'Woof, Woof, Oink, Oink' that would have made Lavender Country blush: 'All the doggies and piggies beg for more/They woof, they oink, they grovel and beg/They never get enough/"Is it in yet?" is often heard.'

The early eighties proffered less gleeful graphic exposition. In 1980, Peter Allen, the Australian TV and cabaret singer who had come out after divorcing Liza Minnelli, fresh from the success of writing hit songs for a succession of women singers, had released the album *Bi-Coastal*. It used the metaphor of choosing to live in New York or LA for the conundrum facing closeted artists, career or happiness: 'Do you like your love in the dark/Or laid out in the sun?/When you can't make up your mind/Don't you know what you've become?' Allen's conclusion: 'Why do you have to pick one?'

In 1981, the San Francisco Gay Men's Chorus' self-titled debut album included 'We Kiss In A Shadow', the old chestnut from *The King And I*, a throwback to the closet. That wasn't enough for two members of the chorus, pianist Karl Brown and vocalist Matthew McQueen, who'd written a punk rock parody for one of the choir's weekend retreats. Greeted with whoops and cheers for songs such as 'Prelude To A Quaalude' and 'Sit On My Face', the pair turned the concept into a working band. Its name, Automatic Pilot, derived from psychiatrist George Solomon's evidence in the trial of Dan White that he was 'sort of on automatic pilot,' when he assassinated Milk and Moscone, thus exonerating him.

Automatic Pilot were nevertheless less concerned with politicised rage than confronting audiences with the likes of 'Bobbing for Apples' (water sports) and 'Rimmin' At The Baths' (the perils of catching amoebic dysentery and hepatitis), served up in a jittery style the band called 'erotic jazz wave'.

It ain't what you say, it's where you say it . . .

By the early eighties, the bravery of making statements about gay identity had shifted from the act itself to where the act was taking place. Given Lavender Country's pioneering efforts, Texas singer-songwriter

Ned Sublette wasn't breaking wholly new ground with his 1981 single 'Cowboys Are Frequently, Secretly Fond of Each Other', an affectionate parody inspired by gay bar Boots and Saddles next to the New York apartment he shared with his wife[1], but Lavender Country were already a forgotten relic. The suggestion that cowboys could be gay was novel. Though not as novel as a gay pride anthem turning up in the nascent world of hip hop.

Hip hop's battling rap rhymes mixed boasting with slackness and politicised verse over dry, primitive electronic beats – the polar opposite to the lush, swaying climes of disco and soul. Hip hop had gone mainstream with virtually its first release, the Sugarhill Gang's 1979 single 'Rapper's Delight' while Blondie had crossed it over with their US no. 1 'Rapture' in 1981, followed by Grandmaster Flash's 'The Message', another defining hip hop cornerstone. Yet both 'Rapper's Delight' (rapping about Superman: 'I said, "He's a fairy, I do suppose/Flyin' through the air in pantyhose"') and 'The Message' (references to fag-hags, maytags[2] and, 'an undercover fag') puffed up their chests by zeroing in on another equally marginalised community.

Alongside Gil Scott-Heron's poem, factions of the black community had lost touch with the tolerance shown by gospel and disco. So for John Callahan to suggest that he and his friend David Hughes, two white middle-class guys, write a gay rap was either brave, or foolhardy.

In his only known interview, the late Callahan said that he'd moved from the east coast to LA in 1980, and, to make friends, visited the gay community centre where he stumbled on Hughes' seminar on contemporary music. They argued about disco and then made friends. Callahan, who was ten years older than his co-rapper and much more aware of gay rights, suggested Hughes include rap in his forthcoming

---

1 In 1982, Britain's 4AD label released the EP *Presages*; among the art-rock gloom was 'Hunk Of A Punk' a daft homoerotic ('he's a hunk of a punk and you know that he's my kind of man') country song by Red Atkins, a.k.a. home studio enthusiast Frank Duckett.
2 Prison term for a young inmate who performs sexual favours in exchange for protection.

Sound and Vision series: he told Hughes, 'We can put in the politics that we want and we can communicate with people and so out of that came the "Fight Back Rap".'[1]

'Fight Back' (originally titled 'Rupture' in response to Blondie's 'Rapture', which Callahan called 'mindless'), released under the name Age Of Consent, began by emulating rap's origins in machismo: 'I am the knight of the might/When evenin' comes I spread delight... When you feel that right in your face/Rock, rock, don't stop, rock, rock.'

But Age Of Consent also created their own rap. Said Callahan, 'We wrote about each of our kind of personalities at the time, where David used to go to this dark sort of leather bar, where they had sort of avant garde European music. And I was more promiscuous, to be honest, and so we decided, let's play off of that': 'Well, I've had it with Levi's, disco, lifting weights/Alligator shirts and going on dates/The size of this, the size of that/No blacks, no freaks, no fems, no fats.'

'But we wanted also to end it with a very strong message as to what the hell should happen if someone hassles you,' Callahan concluded, 'which is you have to fight back': 'If you're wonderin' the point of this rap/The message is easy, you don't need no map/When some straight mother hassles you/There's only one thing left to do, you fight back.'

Another Age Of Consent track, 'History Rap' was the first song to look back at Stonewall, 'a story of faggots, a story of dykes/A story of incredible sights'. The track ended with an update of where gay America stood in 1981, naming the US Republican president Ronald Reagan, old foe Anita Bryant and black music's newly risen genius Prince.

From Minneapolis, Prince Rogers Nelson hadn't only sung, written and produced 1978's debut album *For You*; he'd recorded every note (playing over twenty different instruments) of his genre-splicing R&B, funk, pop, disco and guitar jams, equal parts flamboyance and grit. 'Soft And Wet' wasn't the only sign he was sex-positive; his whole demeanour suggested the Little Richard gene was alive and kicking. The request on

---

[1] http://queermusicheritage.com/apr2007s.html

'I Wanna Be Your Lover' (from 1979's *Prince*), to be his lover's mother and sister too, pricked up many ears, but this was little compared to 1980's *Dirty Mind*. Prince was bare-chested on the cover, and wearing bikini briefs and – out of shot – thigh-high boots, while he acknowledged the hint of homo in 'Uptown': 'She said, "Are you gay?" . . . "No, are you?"'

Prince acknowledged the reaction by naming his next album *Controversy*: 'Just can't believe all the things people say . . . Am I black or white, am I straight or gay? . . . I wish there were no rules.'

Relishing his role, Prince pushed on: 'Sister' toyed with incest, but also 'she's the reason for my bisexuality'. 'When You Were Mine' went further: 'When he was there sleeping in between the two of us . . . Now I spend my time following him whenever he's with you.'

Prince never again addressed bisexuality, but he continued to question gender, such as, 'I'm not a woman, I'm not a man/I am something that you'll never understand' ('I Would Die For U' from 1984's *Purple Rain*). But like Bowie, this ladies' man defied expectation and categorisation and legitimised self-determination, especially for people of colour. As one prominent fan, Frank Ocean, wrote when Prince died in April 2016, 'He made me feel more comfortable with how I identify sexually simply by his display of freedom from and irreverence for obviously archaic ideas like gender conformity.'

Prince's impact had yet to play out through the eighties, so when Age Of Consent wrote 'History Rap', there was a note of warning, reminding gay culture of what still lay ahead: 'Now that the nation has swung to the right/And you know damn well they're gonna spring Dan White/Murder and muggings and a lot more fights/Sex and discos instead of rights.'

Adding a female rapper Thea Other – who provided a feminist, though not a lesbian perspective – Age Of Consent played shows on the gay circuit of benefits, festivals and radio shows before splitting up in 1983 without releasing any further tracks.

There was one more gay rapper, Jon Sugar, who founded the Gay

Artists and Writers Kollective (GAWK), but though he recorded 'Gay Type Thang' in 1981 and again in 1984, it wasn't commercially available until 2006. Gay raps lacked the basics: finance and an audience. Sugarhill Gang and Grandmaster Flash fans would doubtless have baulked at Sugar's comedy rap: 'I'm a bastard Jew boy in the promised land/With a big, hairy butt and a pocket full of sand/With the nuts to butts, asshole to belly/Puttin' krazy glue in my KY jelly.'

Would rock fans appreciate a confessional from one of their guitar and songwriting heroes? Pete Townshend of the Who was an unexpected contributor to the cause when his 1980 solo album debut *Empty Glass* included autobiographical songs that he knew that the band's singer Roger Daltrey would never sing. Townshend promoted the jagged rocker 'Rough Boys' even further by releasing it as a single: 'Tough boys come over here/I wanna bite and kiss you/Gonna get inside you/Gonna get inside your bitter mind . . . We can't be seen together.'

In 1989, Townshend described 'Rough Boys' as 'a coming out, an acknowledgment of the fact that I'd had a gay life and that I understood what gay sex was about. I know how it feels to be a woman because I am a woman.' In his 2012 autobiography *Who I Am*,[1] he admitted that the only man he 'ever seriously wanted to fuck' was Mick Jagger, describing the Stones singer's penis as 'long and plump' and 'extremely tasty'. Another album track, the teeming 'And I Moved', sounded like Townsend fantasied about being fucked himself: 'And I moved/And his hands felt like ice exciting/As he laid me back just like an empty dress.'

If Townshend was coming out as bisexual, Elton John was going back in. Having declared his bisexuality and released 'Elton's Song' on his 1981 album *The Fox*, Elton began dating German sound engineer Renate Blauel in 1983. He married her on Valentine's Day, 1984; with Long John Baldry now settled in Canada, Elton's sugar bear was unable to intervene a second time.

---

[1] HarperCollins (2012)

Townshend would never talk of acting out his fantasies, while Elton's future role as gay royalty is well documented. But if bisexuality was the default mainstream position for prevaricators, even those in the punk scene had felt there was too much to lose by being open.

In the US, punk was turning increasingly more hardcore – faster, angrier, showcasing more extreme left and right wing views, increasing the threat of violence and homophobia. And down in rednecksville Texas, the tension would have been magnified – which provides the context for Gary Floyd of the Dicks and Randy 'Biscuit' Turner of Big Boys' brand of confrontational.

At least both the Dicks and the Big Boys bands hailed from the relatively liberal city of Austin, but it was still Texas, in 1981. Both men seemed totally at ease with their lives. 'Even as a child, I always knew the day was coming that everything would be OK and my dream man would come along,' says Floyd. 'I knew nothing was wrong with me.'

Floyd and Turner were large men, if not Divine size then still the polar opposite of the typical waifs that fronted punk bands. If anyone thought they were conspicuous targets, both singers ramped it up with costumes. Floyd might occasionally wear a nurse's uniform, but Turner regularly raided the dresser, like a surrealist Cockette – a tutu, a string of Christmas lights, a suit of bagged-up sandwiches, even a Klansman outfit to mock some of the more traditional Texan citizens. 'I loved to dress up back then and the idea of making a punk crowd feel uneasy was always a wonderful way to spend the evening,' said Floyd.[1]

Big Boys were the more diverse of the two bands, more post-punk (and sometimes punk-funk) than the hardcore fury of the Dicks. Turner also felt that his sexuality didn't define him[2] and so avoided gay-specific lyrics. He preferred to question gender roles; at one show at LA's Whiskey A Go-Go, he wore 'a plain white jumpsuit which I'd pull off a few songs in to reveal a huge ballerina outfit on underneath. And all

---

[1] www.terminal-boredom.com/garyfloyd.html
[2] Said Turner, 'It doesn't make any difference if I'm gay or not, I'm a human being and my sexual preference doesn't play into my lifestyle,' *Flipside* issue 32, August 1982.

these people in LA would be going, "What the fuck?" But, you know, they'd like us because of the attitude. The barriers were completely broken down between audience and performer.'[1]

'Randy was a great model to look up to in punk rock or any music, as a gay singer and artist,' says Floyd. 'He was loud and proud and never a pushy bitch.' Floyd himself was willing to be pushier, and unsettling with his lyrics, such as 'Off-Duty Sailor', 'Young Boys' Feet' and especially 'Saturday Night At The Bookstore': 'Out at the bookstore/It looks like every fuckin' piece of trash in town blew in . . . I don't give a fuck what your name is!/I think I done fuckin' fell in love with a glory hole/I think I fuckin' fell in love with a nameless creep.'

'David Bowie and Lou Reed gave rock'n'roll a big shot in the arm and made it possible for me to play loud rock and dress like a queer,' says Floyd. 'As soon as the Dicks started, I was very openly gay and very *out*. For "Saturday Night At The Bookstore", I just made up the words at first but it turned into a class war against the rich guys who came and got blow jobs, but if you ever saw one of these creeps on the street, they acted like, "Faggot, stop looking at me!". That was a pretty gay and open song and we went on to have many.'[2]

One incident showed how tensions between factions could polarise opinions and turn bands against each other. During the Austin stopover of 1982's Rock Against Reagan tour, Randy Turner had given Washington DC's Bad Brains – hardcore's only black band, and hugely admired – a place to stay and lent them money to buy pot. But after finding out that Big Boys' singer was gay, Bad Brains vocalist and Rastafarian, HR, refused to settle the loan and left a note to the effect of, 'Thanks for the herb, too bad about the money. Fire burn all bloodclot faggots!'[3] according to writer Nathan Leigh. Bad Brains subsequently left the tour. The

---

[1] www.austinchronicle.com/music/2005-08-26/28664/

[2] 'Off-Duty Sailor' was another Dicks classic: 'Me and a friend we're full of gin, the park is blurry/I smell a cop, my gun is cocked, my tongue is furry/I'm in a dress, oh, what a mess.'

[3] http://www.afropunk.com/profiles/blogs/big-boys-more-than-just-a-bad

incident, wrote Leigh, 'left Bad Brains perpetually plagued by accusations of homophobia, forever tarnishing their reputation'.

You'd think a band taking the name the Queers (from New Hampshire) were making a political point, but they were more emblematic of one faction of hardcore's penchant for political incorrectness and fratboy humour. Over time, bands would be called the Fags, Faggz, Homo Picnic, Teenage Queers, Homo Stupids, Billy Bob Faggots, Queenie and the Gaylords, Bobby Sox and the Teenage Queers, Dadfag, Epitaphed Queers, Faggot, Homosexual Death Drive, Humoursexual and Gay Cowboys In Bondage (and their album *We're Not Gay But The Music Is!*). The Queers sang 'Night Of The Livid Queers'; The Meatman sang 'Tooling For Anus' and 'Lesbian Death Dirge'.

'To me, gay people are like anybody else – you've got open-minded gays and you've got conservative gays who can't take a joke,' vouched Meatmen singer Tesco Vee. '"Tooling for Anus" was aimed for the conservative gays; the open-minded gays loved it. They understood it.'[1]

But which way should the Descendents' 'I'm Not A Loser' be taken? ('Your pants are too tight, you fucking homos/You suck, Mr Buttfuck, you don't belong here/Go away, you fucking gay, I'm not a loser!') The California punks later apologised for the words.

The risk was that tracks such as Aryan Disgrace's 'Faggot In The Family', Mighty Sphincter's 'Fag Bar' and Angry Samoans' 'Homo-sexual' ('Homosexual, up the ass/Homosexual, make it last/Homosexual, jerk me off/Homosexual, go get lost!') might stoke the homophobia they were satirising. The New York hardcore band Ism were serious in writing, 'When you're white, straight and male, you take a lot of crap' on their 1983 album *Man-Boy Love Sickie*.

Karen Allman might argue that a queer, half-Japanese woman fronting a hardcore band might take a lot more crap. Taking the name K Nurse – she was head psychiatric nurse at the public hospital in Tucson, Arizona – the singer of Conflict was 'a tough one', according to the

---

[1] www.collegian.psu.edu/arts_and_entertainment/article_0ead7214-94d9-5536-a93f-093e0e0035be.html

band's guitarist Bill C., 'an outspoken feminist... There weren't a whole lot of women fronting hardcore bands in those days. Karen used to get a lot of shit and I remember some gnarly guy slamming her pretty hard in Denver one night. The punks paid a lot of lip service to equality but when it came down to it a lot of them were macho assholes who could not handle having a woman on stage singing to them their atrocities.'

With what she called the 'ambiguous lesbian content of some of my lyrics', Allman had chosen the path of most resistance. 'Some of my most infamous lyrics . . . were a reaction to the asshole "rape is funny" mentality of some segments of the scene,' she said. 'It was an incredibly sexist environment . . . I was really lonely for the company of other women at the time.'

The slam-dancing at hardcore shows and the mentality of some of the bands made for a hard place for all women and for gay men. As shown in the documentary *The Decline of Western Civilisation*, the singer of California's Fear, Lee Ving, baited the audience with, 'How many queers are here tonight? I can see there are a bunch of fags out there' – hilarious if you weren't a fag, less so if you were and thought someone in the crowd might start throwing their weight around.

'It was strictly a joke, a confrontational tack to get these big, boneheaded jocks all riled up,' said Lee Ving, who pointed out that guitarist Philo Cramer would wear a dress on stage. 'We thought it was our job to throw these bozos into a state of mass heterosexual panic . . . we were never putting out hate messages against homosexuals at all.'[1] Ving was an equal-opportunities shit-stirrer: 'I'm not at all homophobic, but they got no sense of humour, and that eggs me on. If they weren't so uptight, I'd stop.'[2]

Fear was also associated with a pop song that had the word 'queer' in not only its lyric but its title. Another unexpected landmark, but Josie

---

1 *We Got the Neutron Bomb: the Untold Story of LA Punk*, Marc Spitz and Brendan Mullen (Three Rivers Press, 2001)
2 *Visual Vitriol: The Street Art and Subcultures of the Punk and Hardcore Generation*, David A. Ensminger (University Press of Mississippi, 2011)

Cotton's 'Johnny, Are You Queer?' was attacked by both the gay and mainstream press for using a traditionally insulting term. Before Fear turned into a hardcore band, they wrote a much catchier new wave-style song, 'Fetch Me One More Beer', which included the line, 'Fetch me one more beer, boy/You're a fucking queer, boy.' The song was only demoed and when sibling songwriters Bobby and Larson Paine heard it, the song was either donated or bought and rewritten as 'Johnny, Are You Queer?' about a boy that just can't seem to make it with girls.

The song had first been given to The Go-Gos, a new LA-based all-female band that the Paines were mentoring, fronted by former Germs drummer Belinda Carlisle. But the band and the Paines had fallen out and the song was given to Cotton.

In its new form, a bouncy, new-wave update of the sixties girl-group sound, 'Johnny, Are You Queer?' was first released in 1981 by the independent label Bomp, before Warners offshoot Elektra picked it up in 1982. The track reached no. 38 on the club play singles chart: not an overwhelming success, but the contentious word in its title limited radio play. It would have a second life on the soundtrack to the popular 1983 film *Valley Girl*, but what kept the single in the headlines was the media reaction.

'There were protests at LA radio station KROQ, there were counter-protests, there were fake protests[1] and fake counter-protests,' said Cotton. On TV she saw the cover 'held up to the camera by a lady evangelist with pink hair. They were playing "Johnny, Are You Queer?" at half-speed . . . The televangelist said there was no Josie Cotton. I didn't even exist. What I hadn't known was that I was actually a gay man trying to convert unsuspecting straight men to my homosexual lifestyle.

'For the record,' Cotton added, 'it was my supreme honour to be the girl who got to stick it in the eye of all the small-minded morons of the world. They owned the word "queer" back then. They kept it in the back

---

1 For example, the invented Parents Against Decency, who mock-picketed KROQ radio in LA and made the evening news.

of their pickups or in the locker room, to haul out when someone just didn't look right. Where I grew up, if a guy looked the slightest bit interesting, he was often called a queer. Even if they didn't say it out loud, there was this look they gave; you could see the pure hate in their eyes.'

Cotton's question to Johnny was less an accusation that a plea; if he was queer, you'd imagine she would have accepted it and they'd become friends. But the gay press were understandably trying to forge ahead from the bad old days and *The Advocate* called her a homophobe. New York's *Village Voice* chipped in with the headline, 'Josie, are you a bitch?'

Cotton later claimed people had told her the song helped them come out. 'It had so many different levels of interpretation,' she told *Out* magazine. 'It was just all out in the open. Someone had said the word [queer] and expressed a reality that I imagine people aren't really comfortable talking about. At the time, people were shocked, either in a good way or they were insulted.'

And *was* Johnny queer? 'He was flamin',' Cotton reckoned.[1]

The girls want to be with the girls

If Josie wanted to be with the boys, there were girls who just wanted to be with the girls, as the 1978 song by CGBGs favourites Talking Heads put it ('Well there is just no love/When there's boys and girls,' they claimed). But to express it in a rock song and be accepted by a rock audience wasn't so easy. That didn't stop the more risk-averse songwriters from making their point. In 1981, one of Britain's best, and most feminist of post-punk bands, Au Pairs, released their debut album, *Playing With A Different Sex*, dealt with police harassment and the political unrest in Northern Ireland but mostly the politics of relationships, from women's submissive roles to domestic violence and

---

[1] The first song to address the purported psychological condition of 'gay panic' also debuted in 1981 with 'Valerie' by Portland, Oregon's AOR rockers Quarterflash, written by singer Rindy Ross and her husband Marv Ross: 'I never suspected your intentions/ When you showed unusual affection . . . That moment just made no sense I lost my nerve and innocence/I turned and ran away/I'll never understand that day.'

rape, from male sexual inadequacy to a rare statement of lesbian desire in 'Dear John', dismissing said John for a different sex: 'There's only room for one, here she comes, here she comes.' The B-side 'Pretty Boys' also admitted, 'I like pretty girls...' 'Instant Touch' (from 1982's album *Sense and Sensuality*) went further, describing the female orgasm and the image, 'coat her in olive oil from Marseilles.'

'I don't object to being called a lesbian, but I identify as bisexual,' says Au Pairs singer and co-guitarist Lesley Woods. 'But it's been so long since I had a relationship, I'd say I was asexual!' Still, Woods' most meaningful relationships have been with women, while her post-Au Pairs band, the Darlings, rose out of London's lesbian scene.

When younger, Woods had actively searched for female role models 'who sang in a non-feminine-pretty way,' which led to Janis Joplin and Patti Smith. Au Pairs may have constituted two women and two men, but the band's male half supported Woods' efforts to 'challenge all those norms about conforming to female stereotypes,' she says. On top, Woods was got asked about being gay 'by every interviewer. I remember a lot of bands that had women were very defensive when they got asked, so I said, 'Yes,' even though I wasn't strictly. *Playing With A Different Sex* referred to homophobia and to acknowledge other possibilities in terms of sexuality and gender too. I felt very strongly that the laws and societal attitude toward gay people was absolutely wrong. It was not just unfair, it was madness.'

In the course of Au Pairs' travels, the band played a women's music festival in Berlin in 1981 where they ran into the Bloods. 'They were so exciting, oh, wow, a band of American gay women, really attractive and exciting,' Woods says. 'I'd met women in British bands but I'd never met any women who were happy to identify as gay women. I'd just read *Surpassing The Love Of Men*.[1] I was ripe for it.'

The Bloods vocalist Adele Bertei had played drums and keyboards for No Wave contenders Contortions: of the five members of her new

---

[1] To give the book its full titled, *Surpassing the Love of Men: Romantic Friendship and Love Between Women from the Renaissance to the Present*, Lillian Faderman (William Morrow and Company, 1981)

band, Bertei had the most prominent profile, until she walked away from music in the early nineties after a job as backing vocalist 'for a closeted performer' turned nasty. 'The manager threatened me, almost physically and said I should quit the tour. I had to sign a confidentiality agreement not to talk about their personal life, because I had encouraged them to come out.'

From Cleveland, Ohio, Bertei says she was always drawn to tomboys on film, while the 'homosexual panic films of the sixties piqued my curiosity, like *The Children's Hour*, *The Fox* and *The Killing Of Sister George*. They'd all ended in tragedy.' She had no inkling that Dusty Springfield or Lesley Gore were gay, but then Bertei says she identified more with men. After falling for the Beatles and Stones, seeing Bowie in concert 'was life-changing, that the world could be fluid, not one thing or another. He exploded all stereotypes. Labelle blew my head off too. And Laura Nyro seemed very lesbian-onic. I was aware of the lesbian separatist music scene, but I wasn't a fan of the music. Then Patti Smith gave me the feeling there was another creature doing rock'n'roll who didn't fit in, this glam femme, she also exploded stereotypes.'

Bertei's first band was Peter and the Wolves, formed with fellow Clevelander and Patti Smith fanatic Peter Laughner. 'I wrote out lyrics, like one about my girlfriend in reform school and we co-wrote "Everything I Saw Goes Right Through her Heart". Peter's whole demeanour was androgynous and accepted me as a gay woman and encouraged me to celebrate it, which meant the world. I was devastated when he died [of complications relating to alcoholism].'[1]

Bertei moved to New York, and joined Contortions: 'I dated [Contortions frontman] James Chances' girlfriend, Anya Phillips, before he did! When she started managing the band, it got tense and I'd always wanted to do an all-girl band.'

A *Village Voice* ad attracted Anderson (formely Annie) Toone (keyboards), who was about to stage the cabaret revue *Sex, Drag and*

---

1 At the time of writing, Bertei is preparing to publish *NO NEW YORK: Adventures in the Town of Empty*, a memoir of her time with Laughner and in New York.

Rock'n'Roll at 1980's inaugural WOW (Women's One World), a lesbian-oriented women's theatre festival with her and WOW co-founder Jordy Mark playing both male and female roles – the drag king was back.

At WOW, they met Kathleen Campbell (drums). Brenda Alderman (bass) and Kathy Rey (guitar) were also lesbian. Which meant the Bloods weren't just the first all-girl rock band, but the first all-lesbian rock band. 'We didn't particularly want it to be all-lesbian,' says Bertei, 'It just ended up that way. We were all pretty much out.'

Bertei says they soon got an offer to release a single independently: 'the guy there got off on the fact we were lesbian until we didn't do what he said.' The other problem was that the Bloods weren't actually 'pretty much out' at first, as Bertei claims.

'We were technically out on paper,' she says, 'but then *New York Rocker* [magazine] outed us and when everyone knew we were a gay band, no way we were going to get a record deal. In those days, if you weren't signed to a big label, you didn't have a chance at a career in rock'n'roll. The indie avenues we have today didn't exist then, nor did any out gay females. So we were touring Europe for about two years and our attitude was, let's just embrace sex and drugs and rock'n'roll, it was like, "Lock up your daughters and one of your sons too, the Bloods are coming to town!" We had the ladies running after us, no doubt! Groupies galore.'

At that German women's festival when they ran into Au Pairs, Bertei and Lesley Woods started dating and one time did a cabaret-style show at the Mudd Club dressed in tuxedos. The Bloods' debut single, the punk-funky 'Button Up', was released on Au Pairs' label Exit; the artwork, like Bertei's lyric, had a S&M-tinged butch-femme theme.

Relationships in the Bloods began to take on a similarly sadistic edge: 'We weren't a good mix,' Bertei says. 'There was lead-singer envy and other arguments. Anderson was very domineering.' Bertei's time in reform school suggest a wild streak and she admits she was drinking heavily those days and a wild card: 'I'd hang out at the Mudd Club to dance and if some guy hit on me or one of my girlfriends, I'd slug them and I'm five foot tall! I had a bit of a reputation.'

The Bloods quickly imploded. 'Our lifestyle was self-destructive to individuals, and the band,' says Bertei.' They'd only lasted the one single.[1] Bertei thinks the band 'didn't have a chance, because we were out and up against so much homophobia. We paid dearly for our bravery and our bravery has never been acknowledged. The homophobia against gay women at the time contributed greatly to our implosion. Being banned from your own authenticity in the public sphere is a death knell for artists. But I have been known to resurrect on occasion. There may be surprises in store! We did what gay people had always done; you internalise and it becomes self-destructive, which had a lot to do with why we chose the darker path.'

Bertei stayed on the same path while working as a DJ in an Amsterdam lesbian bar but, after six months, she returned to New York, determined to start again. Co-writing with former Blood Brenda Alderman, Bertei turned to R&B 'and freely singing about "she", not disguising my gayness or gender.' She soon attracted the attention of the newly formed Geffen label, formed by Laura Nyro's ex-manager/boyfriend David Geffen, who had had huge success in the seventies with his Asylum label. But it was the label's A&R man, Danny Keeps, who signed Bertei 'and, as soon as I did, he said I couldn't work with Brenda, the songs were too gay and had to pursue another path.'

Bertei was introduced to English singer, songwriter and synth whizkid Thomas Dolby but more interference from Keeps, she says, nixed the chance of Dolby producing her album[2] and, when she eventually recorded the record in the UK, she got into a fist fight with the producer (who she claims was wasting time and drinking the budget) and Geffen dropped her. 'Everything pointed to me as the lesbian hellion. It was very easy for them to blame me. Back then, female performers couldn't

---

1 There was also a Bloods track ('Underwater Nation') on the soundtrack of the feminist sci-fi film *Born In Flames*, directed by Lizzie Borden. More tracks can be heard at Anderson Toone's website, www.andersontoone.com/mp3gallery/index.html
2 Bertei is the prominently featured backing singer on Thomas Dolby's hit single 'Hyperactive'.

be too wild and certainly not outspokenly gay, even a little. Defying the rules had its consequences.'

Women's music: where was it now?

Even in a women-only music industry, there were consequences. By 1983, Olivia Records had discovered that their focus on acoustic music and their non-mainstream distribution system was having diminishing returns. Linda Tillery, who had produced Olivia's third album release by the smooth-soul quartet BeBe K'Roche, had sung with San Francisco's the Loading Zone in the late sixties, raising comparisons to Janis Joplin. CBS released her soulfully blazing album debut *Sweet Linda Divine* in 1971, produced and arranged by the venerated Al Kooper. With this form, you might think her own (self-titled) album on Olivia would find some favour, somewhere, but not even the label could get much traction among its considerable fanbase – and no label comfortably survives when it releases one album a year, as happened in 1979. Olivia hadn't found the next Cris Williamson either, while Meg Christian was about to retire from music.

In 1981, *Heartsong* by former Fanny guitarist June Millington was released by Olivia on a subsidiary label, Fabulous, an entity that blossomed into a more permanent offshoot label, Second Wave. This broadened the musical range and allowed the artists to work with male musicians. One of the first beneficiaries was Tret Fure, Millington's former girlfriend, who released *Terminal Hold*, her first album since veering into studio engineering following her 1973 album debut. Given the fact she was openly gay, Olivia was a natural fit for her work. Before she accepted, she'd been offered another contract, 'but the guy wanted to dress me in leather and to sing his songs. Lowell [George, of Little Feat] taught me not to compromise integrity; I may have suffered for it financially, but not career-wise. It's my art, under my terms.'

As an engineer too, 'I had to prove myself to every client – they'd visibly blanche [at seeing a woman] when they arrived,' Fure recalls. In tandem with her three albums for Second Wave, Fure became Olivia's in-house engineer, including the recording of *Meg and Cris at Carnegie Hall*, 'a landmark record in women's music,' Fure says. 'To play to over five and a half thousand lesbians over two nights, in 1984, was incredible, magical.'[1]

It was clear that Williamson and Christian were still the big favourites and that lesbian singers and songwriters weren't limiting themselves to the heart-singing acoustic music that had sold so well in the seventies. For all the issues that the male-dominated record industry had with lesbians, the greater cultural visibility of lesbians and gay men gave others the confidence to take their chance. Perhaps it was the novelty of being the only sexually provocative woman artist in the Canadian music industry that allowed Carole Pope to make headway.

Pope is still doing what she does; in 2015, she released the EP *Music For Lesbians*; the lead, 'Lesbians In A Forest', took on the sacred ground of women's music festivals. 'Some lesbians and feminists don't have a sense of humour,' Pope declares, 'so I wanted to write about the funny, tragic things about being with another woman.'

Born in northern England but raised in Canada from the age of five, Pope had gravitated towards 'aggressive' singers such as Janis Joplin, and also sixties' soul singer Jackie Shane: 'I'd heard "Any Other Way" and couldn't believe people didn't know what he was singing. But then straight audiences often don't get it.'

Pope experienced a similar reaction with 'High School Confidential', a Top 20 hit in Canada in 1981 for Rough Trade. She'd met Kevan Staples in 1968 at an audition for a band that neither joined, forming their own band, O, and then a duo, invitingly named the Bullwhip Brothers, which morphed into the quartet Rough Trade, an equivalent term for male prostitution. 'I was influenced by gay men and their image, the leather and fetish wear,' Pope says. 'I mean, where were the lesbians? It took a lot longer to find them.'

It didn't take the gays long to find Rough Trade; 'the art crowd and

---

[1] Cris Williamson and Tret Fure went on to be a couple for the following nineteen years; Fure produced many of Williamson's records while they recorded three albums together.

the crazy showbiz people' came along too. Pope and Staples also worked with Divine in *Restless Underwear*, a 'massive gay' musical revue they staged in Toronto: 'I wore a bondage suit, we had a guy on a leash and all these insane songs. I was obsessed with sexuality and how sexually repressed North America was, so I wrote about it because nobody else was. To me, it was parody, but people interpreted it different ways. Some even got turned on!'

Rough Trade played New York a handful of times and were asked to write for William Friedkin's *Cruising*, a murder mystery set in New York's gay leather/BDSM community. The film not only lost to the Village People's *Can't Stop The Music* in the worst film category at the inaugural Golden Raspberries awards, but it engineered furious protests for giving a nihilistic impression of gay men, as sadistic and perverted, in whose company investigating cop Al Pacino appears to become a killer himself.

With its taut, prowling, sultry mood, 'High School Confidential' would have fit *Cruising* like a fist in a glove but it wasn't used in the film, so Rough Trade released it themselves in 1981: it's arguably still the most sexually explicit record to have graced Canada's Top 20: 'She's a cool, blonde, scheming bitch/She makes my body twitch/Walking down the corridor/You can hear her stilettos click . . . It makes me cream my jeans when she comes my way.'

'"Cream my jeans", you can't say that, it's too risqué!' people told Pope. 'The record company was happy but a radio chain asked us to change it, so I sang, "She makes me order Chinese food . . ." They ended up bleeping it out.' More infamously, when Rough Trade performed it at Juno Awards, a ceremony honouring Canadian industry's best albums, Pope grabbed her crotch during the rehearsal 'and they asked me not to do it live. So, of course, I did. I was the one that invented the crotch-grab, before Michael Jackson and Madonna! Jim Fouratt told me Madonna saw me do it at Danceteria[1] before she was famous.'

---

1 Fouratt was the first band booker at New York's Danceteria after Hurrah closed down.

Pope would also sing about a gay male couple on another of Rough Trade's Top 20 singles, 'Crime Of Passion': 'Their tanned bodies bathed in sweat/They looked like two young gods/Writhing in the throes of ecstasy.'

Pope's autobiography, *Anti-Diva*,[1] was equally frank and charged, especially about her intense, and eventually doomed, relationship with Dusty Springfield through the first half of the eighties. They'd met through their mutual manager Vicki Wickham and even collaborated; Springfield contributed backing vocals to Rough Trade's 1982 album *Shaking The Foundation*, while she covered two of Pope's songs on *White Heat*, the Casablanca label's doomed effort to make Springfield relevant again with a composite of disco, AOR and ballads.

Pope's songs were the most interesting. 'I Am Curious' didn't state the singer's sexuality but it was revealing to hear Springfield sing, 'I'm addicted to lethal sexuality/I live life on the edge of ecstasy/Need to be desired/Nothing else fulfils me.' 'Soft Core' was Pope's song about living with an alcoholic. 'Dusty was a whole book on her own,' she says. 'It was a rollercoaster having a relationship with her, she was drinking and drugging and cutting [herself]. But she was also a very funny and brilliant woman.'

Away from Pope – and. with due respect, Canada was not as influential as the US and UK markets – lesbians in the mainstream remained closeted. It would be 2004 before folk icon Joan Baez would talk about the lesbian relationships of her twenties, while the rumours surrounding Joan Armatrading were never addressed by the singer, who only made it plain when she married girlfriend Maggie Butler in 2011.

When Armatrading released 'Drop The Pilot' as a single in 1983, fans were convinced that she had finally let out a lesbian lyric, about persuading a woman to ditch her man and switch sides. Armatrading agreed with the theme – 'Forget him and get with me,' she elaborated – but wouldn't commit to singing to a man or a woman. 'People read all kinds

---

[1] Random House (2011)

of things into that song,' she said. Alongside 'Drop The Pilot' on *The Key* was 'Tell Tale': 'I saw ya kissing all the boys and I saw ya kissing all the girls/but you got obsessed with the boys/So when you're telling all your lies about me/Think awhile before your story ends/'Cause I've seen you in the parks and alleys/Now I got things that I can tell your friends.'

The Dutch singer Matilde Santing broke the mould when she released a self-titled album in 1982 that set the scene for her exquisitely crooning style, like an update of the sophisticated jazz/cabaret singer (Ray Charles is her favourite singer) and included a cover of 'I've Grown Accustomed To Her Face' from the 1956 musical *My Fair Lady*, without changing the gender. She also did a swinging cover of Jimi Hendrix's 'Hey Joe' as 'Hey Joan' and sung Sinatra's 'One For My Baby' in the style of Marilyn Monroe, for a song set in a bar at 4 am when women are not meant to be hanging around. But Santing maintains that she's always been bisexual. 'I know a lot of gay people have a bad relationship with bisexuality, because it's a word to hide being gay,' she says, 'but I really am.'

Apart from citing four long-term relationships in her life, split between the two sexes, Santing explains that her breakthrough album *Water Under The Bridge*, released in 1983 by Warner Bros, was co-written with her then boyfriend, but she was in a relationship with a woman when the album came out and the album cover and publicity photos showed Santing with a very short haircut and suit.

'The first time I did TV,' she explains, the make-up girl started dressing me as a butch, I didn't realise what was happening or what it would mean – there were no lesbian singers around. For a time, I was seen as a role model for dykes, which I was a bit offended with at the time, because music is much bigger than sexuality for me and I was more dedicated to improving my voice than the image. But I looked great in a male suit. I still do! And I feel more comfortable with a more masculine look. But I'd rather be respected as a singer and a mad woman!'

And the boys want to be with the boys

Joining Mathilde Santing in the division of 'butch' was pop's first drag king, heterosexual woman Annie Lennox, the singing half of UK duo Eurythmics. US and UK no. 2 'Sweet Dreams (Are Made Of This)' was a terrific combination of sultry and haughty and came with a terrific promo video. Lennox was distinctly Bowie-like in close-cropped burnt-orange hair and a suit. Their next hit, 'Love Is A Stranger', had Lennox tearing off a Dusty-style bouffant wig to reveal her crew cut, confusing some US commentators who suggested Eurythmics were fronted by a transvestite. In the video for their third hit, 'Who's That's Girl', Lennon – in another blonde wig – was seen kissing a man, also played by Lennox, looking like Elvis. 'You cannot define me through my sex, I'm more malleable than that,' Lennox said.

Bowie was himself wearing a suit through all the promo for his 1983 album *Let's Dance*, easily his biggest selling record and his least radical and most classically heterosexual persona of his three decades of music. In the absence of the old, fluid Bowie, his children were making amends, in the biggest musical and fashion movement since punk, something very much in Bowie's image.

In fact, the seeds of the new romantic scene lay in the 'Bowie nights' held at Billy's, as Gossips nightclub in London's Soho had been christened for three months in 1978. The instigators were Stephen Harrington – who called himself Steve Strange – and Rusty Egan, the drummer of new-wavers the Rich Kids. Those who wanted the glory dressing-up days of glam with a frisson of punk and new wave had found their niche. The outfits were far more adventurous and more home-made than the glam look. Before long, the crowd at Strange and Egan's next Soho club, the Blitz, were being called 'the new dandies', 'romantic rebels', 'peacock punks' and the 'Blitz kids'. The description that stuck was 'new romantics'. Soon, members of the crowd began creating their own music, centred in the electronic dance sound. Brothers Martin and Gary Kemp assembled the five-piece Spandau Ballet; Blitz cloakroom attendant George O'Dowd

The Eighties: Pop Comes Out

– Boy George – fronted Culture Club; Strange and Egan were the core of Visage.

It had been Strange who, as a teenager in the late seventies, engineered sleeping with the Stranglers' none-more-macho Jean-Jacques Burnel, as the bassist surprisingly revealed in 2011. Though Strange was a typical new romantic Blitz kid, androgynous and asexual; it was all down to fashion and make-up to say it for the bands.

Scene outsiders Depeche Mode and Soft Cell first radiated a gay sensibility; even if all four Mode boys were straight, the chorus to their 1981 album track 'Boys Say Go' was a bold update of Bowie's 'Boys Keep Swinging': 'Boys meet boys get together/Boys meet boys, live forever/Don't say, "No"/Boys say, "Go".' They also sometimes wore black leather, including the occasional peaked leather cap. The same year, Soft Cell's Marc Almond favoured all-black garb, too, with studded leather cuffs and heavy eyeliner for the duo's *Top Of The Pops* performance of their UK no. 1 'Tainted Love'. Gay British fans of this generation clutched at it in the same way that a previous generation had Bowie's 'Starman' performance, nine years earlier.

From Leeds, in the north of England, two hundred miles from new romanticism's London HQ, Marc – then Peter – Almond plotted his escape. He'd had to contend with homophobia from his alcoholic father and at school. 'It was fearful to be gay,' he recalls. 'It was a hard thing to break out of the mould and come out.' He kept quiet about his sexuality but slowly transformed himself, starting by changing his first name to Marc after his teenage idol Marc Bolan and equally looking to Bowie: 'They showed me another world, so I could express myself in a different way.'

After studying performance art – one exam show featured Almond naked except for black boots, thong, mirror and razor – he finally made the move south: 'I was a misfit and felt only a city like London could offer acceptance.' With his innate gift for drama matched by his former college friend Dave Ball's artful way around synthesisers, Soft Cell was formed. They attracted a sharp manager Steve 'Stevo' Pearce, who set about securing major label deals for his charges. The only hitch in the duo's rapid rise was the failure of their debut single 'Memorabilia'. But their following cover of an obscure sixties soul track, 'Tainted Love'[1] became the country's best-selling single of 1981. It also experienced an epic climb through the US charts to break the Top 10 in October 1982, as the new music channel MTV spread the news about this new-fangled electronic pop.

'Tainted Love' was a UK no. 1 despite its terrible promo video, with Almond in a toga that resembled a little skirt while a towering black slave fanned him from behind. The US didn't get the full force of Almond in Soft Cell's TV performances, with hand movements and thick eyeliner cribbed from Dusty Springfield, his arms ringed by bangles (cribbed, says Almond, from twenties' socialite Nancy Cunard). He defied his record label's request to tone it down for his *Top Of The Pops* debut: 'I went on defiantly being myself, but nervous as hell! It was a vision to people in their living rooms, a sexuality that young men could recognise, in the same way I recognised people's sexuality when I was watching.'

The BBC received numerous complaints, but it only reinforced Almond's resolve. 'By my third *Top Of the Pops*,' he says, 'I was wearing a leather cap and outfit and gigantic false eyelashes! I was so shocked at myself, at how far out that was at the time – even though I was still having girlfriends created for me by the record company and I had thousands of young girl fans. I had this ambiguous image, which was my way of getting into people's homes and making a statement.'

But again, the look had to carry the message. Decades later, talking to writer Nigel Farndale, Almond admitted that the worst aspect of the era was having to lie about his sexuality. 'In the early eighties, if you said you were gay, it was a career-destroyer. Pop stars were never really openly gay. It was always that bisexuality thing. A cop out.'[2]

Instead, the content of Soft Cell songs would have to suffice. Thinking many of his eighties peers were dishonest in their 'glossier depiction of life' during Britain's economic recession, he wanted 'to show what we

---

1 Almond knew 'Tainted Love' because the original had been sung by Gloria Jones, who became Marc Bolan's second wife in the mid-seventies.
2 www.nigelfarndale.com/2013/06/marc-almond/

felt Britain was really like, its sleazier reality and what went on behind closed doors.' Namely, 'the criminals, drag queens, hustlers and prostitutes' he'd discovered through Jean Genet and John Rechy, Andy Warhol and John Waters and in Soho's red light district where Almond had first worked during college breaks to pay his way through art college.

No chart act, Bowie included, had been so upfront about sleaze and audiences hadn't witnessed such brazen camp since Bowie either. That said, Almond only rarely hinted at a gay perspective, such as 1981's 'Secret Life' – 'My secret life/Living life on a knife edge of life/Tell my wife/And she's just had a breakdown' – and 1982's 'Sex Dwarf' – 'Sex dwarf in a gold Rolls/Making it with the dumb chauffeur.'[1] 1983's hustler saga 'Numbers' was only queer if you knew Almond's fondness for John Rechy's novel of the same name. But in a roundabout fashion, people must have known. In the January 1982 issue of *The Face* magazine, Almond started talking freely to interviewer Jon Savage about the body fascism of gay porn.

'Well, when they look through *Honcho* and *Him*,' he said, 'they're reading about muscles... huge... wonderful... glistening... torso... I sometimes think there must be some poor little gay bloke lost in his little attic saying I can't stand it anymore.'

But when Savage asked Almond if he was gay, the reaction was both a coming out and a running in. 'I'm... experimental,' Almond replied. 'I don't think... I'm not... OK, so I'm not into politics or making stands, you know, right? I've had girlfriends, permanent girlfriends and maybe other things as well... and also, living in Leeds, in a place like that you don't go and make stands like that if you want to go on living there... a lot of the time it is very much more sort of survival than it is in London. I enjoy going out to the clubs and pubs and I want to sort of keep my face intact. It's not that I'm chickening out, and saying I refuse to... do you understand?'

---

1 The original – and subsequently banned – fetish-friendly video for 'Sex Dwarf' was filmed for the duo's video collection *Non-Stop Exotic Video Show*. Complete with chainsaw, meat carcasses and blood-soaked orgiastic finale.

'A friend told me off for asking Marc if he was gay,' says Savage. 'Would I like someone to do that to me? he said. No, I wouldn't. So I didn't ask anyone again. And I understand the idea of fluidity, that if you define things too closely, it takes away the magic. There is a fine line between honesty and keeping the fluidity and if an artist comes out, you do, to some extent, lose your audience.'

'I didn't say in print that I was gay until around 1997,' says Almond, 'when a journalist was at my house and pulled out a Judy Garland album [laughs] and asked me outright. But everyone knew, it was obvious. I loved the mischief, actually, that I could be as outrageous as I wanted and people didn't know for sure. It was liberating when I did finally say it, though I was afraid too, because I didn't want to be boxed up as a "gay" artist, in that you only appeal to gay people. I wanted to appeal to everyone and that way I could break down barriers. I'm sometimes camp or macho, feminine or masculine, theatrical or introspective; songs come from all aspects of my life. But I've probably been more homoerotic than most artists have, which people haven't always latched on to. That's been great, to be very subversive.'

Boy George would radiate the same confusion, simultaneously uncomfortable with the public gaze while revelling in the ambiguity and hiding his real sexuality while broadcasting it via his entire public persona, wearing flowing tresses with long hair and immaculate make-up: 'Heavy kohl eyes and heavier make up, like Divine,' says George.

When he first progressed from the Blitz cloakroom it was to sing with Bow Wow Wow, a band assembled by former Sex Pistols' manager Malcolm McLaren. He was pushed out after only a few weeks. Undeterred, George soon had Culture Club. Having had an affair with a musician, Kirk Brandon of Theatre Of Hate, who identified as straight, he then began another, with Culture Club's drummer Jon Moss.

'Each time you saw George, you didn't know if he was the same bloke or woman,' Moss recalls. 'I ended up having a crush on him, which was very weird – me, a nice, straight Jewish boy. I wasn't attracted to men but with George, I didn't have any choice.'

1970s II: politics comes out of the closet

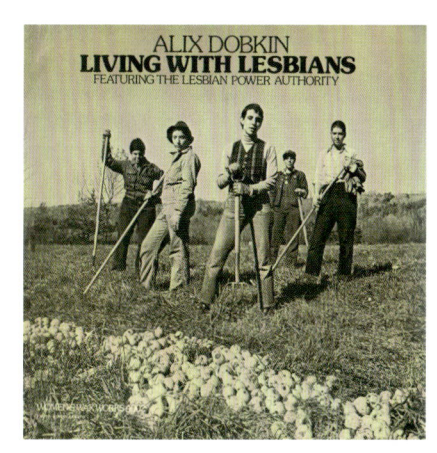

(left) The album *Living With Lesbians* by Alix Dobkin.

(above) The only known photo of country music's first queer alliance (1974).

(above left) 'Sing if you're glad to be gay' – Tom Robinson, writer of the gay national anthem.

(above right) Britain's pioneering lesbian roots duo Ova: Jana Runnalls (left) and Rosemary Schonfeld (right).

(left) 'Gay Music Spring Night', New York, 1976, with Blackberri (singing), Steven Grossman (second left) and Gwen Avery of *Lesbian Concentrate* fame (centre).

1970s III

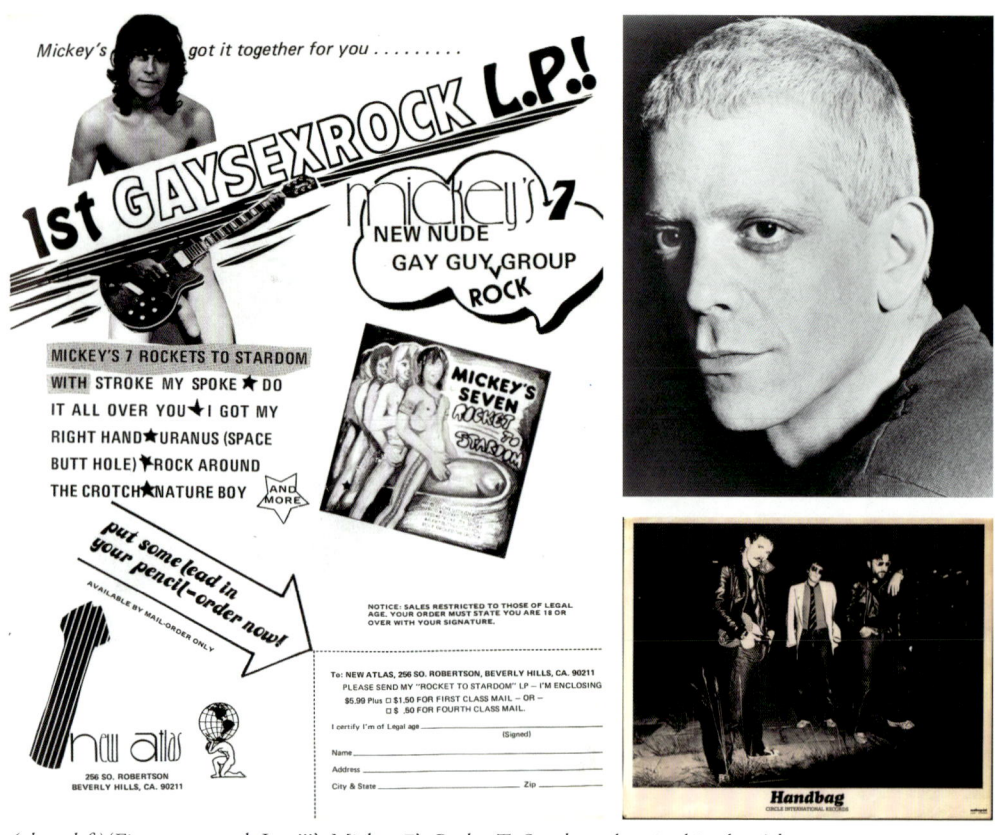

(above left) 'First gaysexrock L.p.!!!': Mickey 7's *Rocket To Stardom* advertised in the *Advocate* magazine.
(top right) Lou Reed, after taking a walk on the wild side.
(above right) The album cover for *Snatchin'* by Handbag.
(below) Jobriath Salisbury, before and after the space-alien makeover.

1980s: the girls want to be with the girls

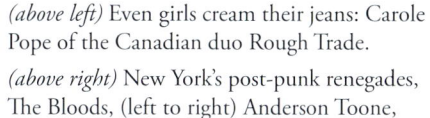

(above left) Even girls cream their jeans: Carole Pope of the Canadian duo Rough Trade.

(above right) New York's post-punk renegades, The Bloods, (left to right) Anderson Toone, Kathy Rey, Adele Bertei, Kathleen Campbell. (Brenda Alderman not pictured).

(right) Toronto's post-punk renegades, Fifth Column, (left to right) Michelle Breslin, Torry Colichio, Beverly Breckenridge, Caroline Azar, GB Jones.

(below right) The self-styled 'all-American Jewish lesbian folk-singer' – Phranc.

(below left) Three nice girls, actually: Texan nu-country trio Two Nice Girls, 1990, (left to right) Laurie Freelove, Kathryn Korniloff, Gretchen Phillips.

1980s: the boys want to be with the boys

(top left) Germany's outer-space soprano, Klaus Nomi, one of the first performers to die of AIDS.

(top right) New romantics, new androgyny: Culture Club's Boy George (centre) with friend/rival Marilyn (right).

(above left) San Francisco's Castro district hits number one in the UK: Frankie Goes To Hollywood's Holly Johnson dines out at Paul Rutherford's crotch.

(above right) Committed to the cause, and each other: Michael Callen and Richard Dworkin.

(left) 'Arguably the most enduring LGBT anthem ever released' – 'Smalltown Boy' by Bronski Beat. Steve Bronski (back), Jimmy Somerville (middle), Larry Steinbachek (front).

1980s: record sleeves

'Johnny Are You Queer?' by Josie Cotton (single, 1981).

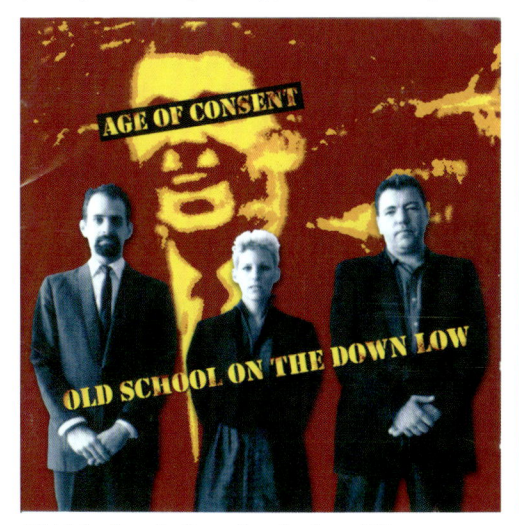

Old School on the Down Low by Age of Consent (album, 1981).

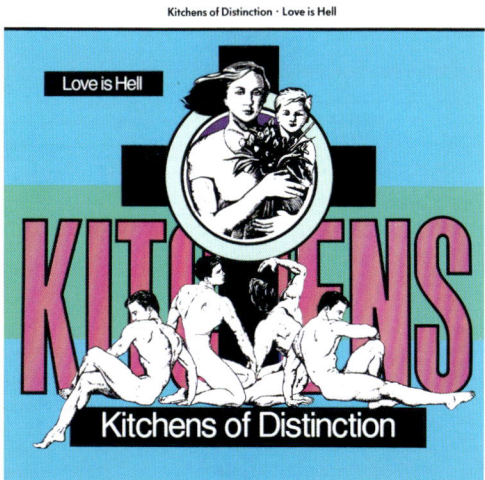

Love Is Hell by Kitchens Of Distinction (album, 1989).

1990s

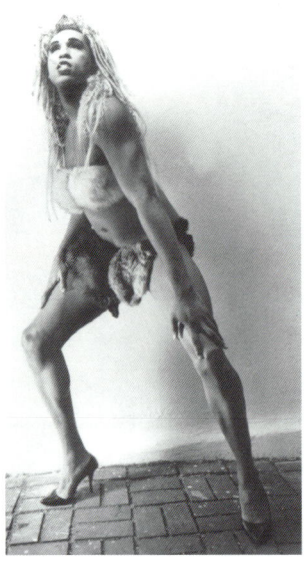

(left) 'Too gay for the punks and too punk for the gays' – queercore icon Vaginal Creme Davis.

(right) Young, gifted, black and gay: Britpop maverick David McAlmont.

(above left) 'I am a L-L-L-L-Lopez fan!' – the first lesbian superstar, k.d. lang, 1993.

(above right) Heavy metal machismo, gay style: Judas Priest singer Rob Halford.

(right) Queers can rap too: Rainbow Flava, (left to right) Dutchboy, Juba Kalamka, DJ Monkey, N. I. Double K. I. Photo by Phat Family Records.

1990s: record sleeves

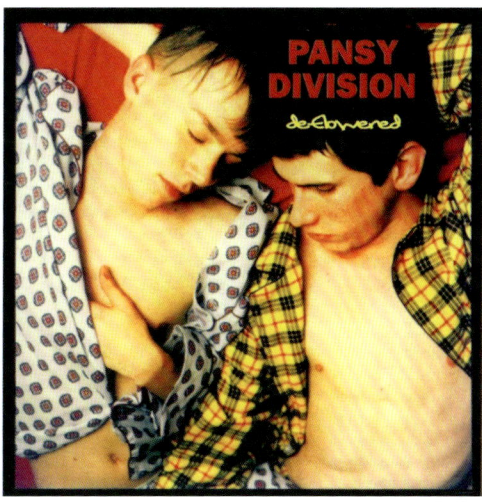

Deflowered by Pansy Division (album, 1994).

V/A *Join The Queercorps* (compilation EP, 1998).

The original planned cover for Antony & The Johnsons (album, 1998) before it was placed on the back.

21st century

(above left) Heaven-sent: all-black, all-queer, all-hip hop – Deep Dickollective, (left to right) Jeree Brown, Tim'm West, Juba Kalamka.

(above right) The age of trans: FTM rapper Rocco 'Katastrophe' Kayatios.

(left) The age of trans: MTF rock singer Mina Caputo of Life of Agony.

(below) Against all odds: two anonymous members of Rainbow Riots Uganda.

'Even then, I saw it as a nail in the coffin, that there were going to be problems,' says Culture Club bassist Mikey Craig. 'But, in a way, their relationship was the life of the band too. It gelled everything together.'

It was Kirk Brandon who had inspired George to write Culture Club's third single, the reggae-light 'Do You Really Want to Hurt Me', 'but I'd had a succession of boyfriends who said they were straight,' says George. 'Pretty soon into the relationship, Jon slept with a girl so the song was really about all those kind of boys.'

Culture Club's US record label, Epic, marketed the first single in a white sleeve, 'so audiences were 90 per cent black at first,' says Moss. 'They thought George sung like Smoky Robinson, then they thought George was a woman and by the time they found out he wasn't and that he was white, it was too late. How we got away with it, I don't know.' 'Do You Really Want to Hurt Me' topped the UK charts and reached US no. 2.

Soft Cell had arguably paved the way for this UK sensation, but Marc Almond was too subversive, too *gay*, for the US and the duo never again broke the US Top 100. George's less threatening presence and Culture Club's savvy soul took 'Time (Clock of the Heart)' to US no. 2 and 'I'll Tumble 4 Ya' into the Top 10; the first time since the Beatles that a British band's debut album (*Kissing To Be Clever*) contained three US Top 10 hits. And 1983's no. 1 'Karma Chameleon' was still to come.

George's public persona was toned down; as part of his way of handling attention, he told the UK press he'd 'rather have a cup of tea' than bother with sex. Mikey Craig recalls the band were touring Scotland; stopping at a dairy shop 'in the middle of nowhere', when the band were recognised by 'an old granny, who went round the back and pulled out the single. That's when we could see the enormity of what was going on.'[1]

It wasn't just grannies, either. On stage, George recalls, 'These little girls were throwing dolls and teddy bears, with the hair and the ribbons

---

1 Another new pop band, Kajagoogoo, were similarly caught in a trap with the band's UK no. 1 single 'Too Shy'. 'I wasn't embarrassed about being gay," singer Limahl later said, 'but my pop star role had to be more enigmatic. I didn't want to start talking about gay sex in 1983 when most of our following was teenage girls.'

and the hats. I used to be much more outrageous but it was suggested I use a make-up artist for the cover of the album, who really toned me down, like, "Ooh, I'm really pretty, like a girl.' I looked like a girl anyway, but I looked like a wholesome, Brooke Shields-type of girl. That picture was pivotal in turning me into this cutesy, doll-like figure. It was weird but you don't question who it is who's screaming at you. We lapped it up.'

But in private George was mouthy, unpredictable and even violent; Moss admits he twice broke a finger in fights with the singer, acting like 'a raving queen' and who also knocked Moss unconscious with a bottle. At the same time, says George, 'My misery fuelled my creativity.'

Gay sex at No. 1

Great chunks of the new romantic movement were straight, from pretty boys Duran Duran to rugged types Spandau Ballet, but Culture Club outsold them all. Even better, as *Attitude*'s editor Pas Paschali wrote in 1994, 'We were in love with the idea of a trannie at no. 1. The mere thought was revolutionary.' But revolution needed its revolutionaries to stay onside. As Paschali added, 'George gave an interview to the press in which he went on and on about, "poofs". Well, we in the gay community were outraged. He was clearly a traitor and was challenged as such when he tried to get into London's premier alternative gay nightspot of the time, the Pied Bull in Islington, home of the politically correct. The doorman immediately entered into a wrangle with George. "Someone in your position should support gay rights. I'll have you know I've been beaten up for wearing a gay pride badge." . . . We weren't quick to forgive.'[1]

Other bold statements were being drafted further north. From Manchester, Buzzcocks' Pete Shelley had gone solo and released the synth-driven 'Homosapien', which the BBC banned, ludicrously, for 'explicit reference to gay sex' though Shelley says, 'Homo superior/in

---

1 www.zttaat.com/article.php?title=480

my interior' was only a reference to David Bowie's 'Oh! You Pretty Things'. Over in Liverpool, something far more explicit and worthy of a ban was a song called 'Relax'. If Culture Club's anodyne androgyne presence brushed sex under the carpet, frontmen Holly Johnson and Paul Rutherford of Frankie Goes To Hollywood put sex on the table. And on TV.

Born in 1960, William Johnson was another of Bolan and Bowie's children who, like Marc Almond, overcame domestic homophobia: 'What have I done to deserve a walking freakshow for a son?' his father said, according to Johnson's autobiography.[1] The camp comedy stereotypes on UK TV through the seventies – entertainers such as Larry Grayson and John Inman – 'were our worst nightmare . . . Bowie was a more appealing stereotype to relate to,' Johnson told journalist Richard Smith. 'The bisexual act was helpful, but it was bad in a way because those artists that did come out as bisexual in the seventies were still colluding with the closet. It would have been easier if Elton or David Bowie had just said, "I am gay." Pete Shelley of the Buzzcocks was the only musician that I met that showed any sympathy for gay men.'[2]

Through Bowie, Johnson found 'Andy Warhol and Lou Reed and Holly Woodlawn and Candy Darling . . . the stars in my imagination' and he started calling himself Holly in tribute. After visiting Earl's Court's 'home of the clones', the Coleherne, Johnson adopted leather, a risky manoeuvre once back in Liverpool, but a necessary statement. '[Gay porn artist] Tom of Finland was quite a big influence . . . there's a kind of beauty and an inner happiness with his figures and that comfort with who you are was an extremely attractive trait. Perhaps it was the first glimmer of sexual happiness that I ever saw in the homosexual world.'

By 1978, Johnson was playing bass for new-wavers Big In Japan (alongside future members of the KLF, the Lightning Seeds and Siouxsie and the Banshees), but after clashing egos ensured a swift exit, he found solace with three staunchly heterosexual teens that he'd met while

---

1 *Bone In My Flute* (Century, 1994)
2 www.zttaat.com/article.php?title=475

record-shopping and formed Frankie Goes To Hollywood.[1] At an early show, Holly's gay pal, Paul Rutherford, was excited enough to jump on stage to dance and became Frankie's backing vocalist and joint agent provocateur.

More than a Sex Pistol wearing the 'two cowboys' T-shirt, or Freddie Mercury with his clone look, Johnson and Rutherford dressed to stress the homo in sexuality, also 'to attract record company interest in London. The only way you could do it was by thrusting not only flamboyant or ferocious homosexuality but the whole lifestyle that went with it in people's faces. That was the kind of thing it needed to get A&R men to sit up and notice.'[2]

After FGTH recorded two songs, 'Relax' and 'Two Tribes', they created a film to seduce the record companies. 'We had really gone to town on the bondage look,' Johnson wrote, listing his attire: leather knickers, an old Seditionaries[3] cropped T-shirt, with unzipped nipple holes and shoulder pads made from bike tyres. Rutherford wore 'leather thigh guards that strapped at the back which left his arse completely bare. We dressed the boys in denim shorts with the odd bit of leather. The Leather Pets [backing dancers] were there in studded-leather mini-dresses and suspenders holding up laddered stockings; we chained them to the scaffolding.'

The video – 'very seedy and tacky', even by Johnson's reckoning – was too outrageous for *The Tube*, the flagship music series of Channel 4, the UK's adventurous new TV network, but the show's producers decided to make their own film of 'Relax'. Johnson and Rutherford's outfits were toned down but still featured skin-tight leather vests, harnesses, codpieces and caps, worn with tight cycle shorts. The straight FGTH backline were kitted out too, while the Leather Pets gyrated and brandished whips.

---

1 Johnson found the name Frankie Goes To Hollywood from artist Guy Peellaert's book *Rock Dreams*, inspired by Frank Sinatra.
2 Ibid. 515
3 Malcolm McLaren's shop in the mid-seventies before it was renamed SEX.

354

The Eighties: Pop Comes Out

It worked; Trevor Horn, one half of the Buggles, whose UK no. 1 'Video Killed The Radio Star' had launched MTV, was looking to start a new record label, Zang Tuum Tumb (ZTT) and spotted in 'Relax' an insistent vocal hook and very funky bassline and a readily marketable image. With *NME* journalist Paul Morley pulling ZTT's ideological strings, the track's phallic thrust – 'When you want to suck it to it/ Relax don't do it/When you want to come' – was bound to create a fuss.

The mega-charged version of 'Relax' that Horn produced was unrecognisable from FGTH's tinny original and sounded brilliant in the clubs and on the radio. Morley scripted a teaser ad campaign with images of Johnson (shaved head and rubber gloves) and Rutherford (sailor cap, leather vest) and the tag line 'All the nice boys love sea men' and declared, 'Frankie Goes to Hollywood are coming . . . making Duran Duran lick the shit off their shoes . . . nineteen inches[1] that must be taken always.'

What truly ignited 'Relax' was the BBC ban. The single was released in November 1983 and didn't enter the charts for two months, but eventually FGTH played 'Relax' on *Top Of The Pops*, appearing in dialled-down leather trousers and jackets. Just eight days later, BBC Radio 1 DJ Mike Reid was reading the lyrics while the single was on air and took it off halfway through, suddenly unable to handle the apparent obscenity. What did people think the song's promo was all about? It remained the most sexually explicit video for years, staged like a Busby Berkeley production in a gay S&M club, with preening leathermen, drag queens, simulated buggery and a Roman emperor figure whose fleshy groin was covered only by a flimsy piece of cloth. To cap it all off, firing water cannons signified both water sports and ejaculation, supporting the line 'But shoot it in the right direction', aided by Trevor Horn's liquefied 'cum' sound on the record.

Once again, Joe Orton's epochal statement about inciting British society with sex comes to mind. The ban of both song and video propelled 'Relax' to UK no. 1 and the biggest *cause celebre* since the Sex Pistols'

---

1 'Nineteen inches' meant the seven- and twelve-inch versions of 'Relax' combined.

equally censored 'God Save The Queen'. Ban or no ban, the barriers were coming down.

'Gay sex, kinky sex, SM sex – they rammed it down our throats and we wanted more,' wrote Paschali. 'When they went to no. 1, we were over the moon. 'Relax' reflected a barometer swing in gay politics; Frankie represented a new archetype.'

'Relax' topped the UK charts for five weeks and when FGTH's second single, 'Two Tribes', topped the charts in June 1984, 'Relax' climbed back up to no. 2 behind its successor.[1] 'Two Tribes' would stay at the top for nine weeks and held the record for the longest run for the next thirteen years. FGTH's debut album, *Welcome To The Pleasuredome*, had advance orders of one million, ensuring the joys of fisting that was 'Krisco Kisses' entered many homes: 'Let's take it to the top/with a fist way past the rest/You fit me like a glove, my love . . . you can take it up, up and up.' Canya Phuckem and Howe, indeed.

In 1994, when writer Richard Smith congratulated Johnson for 'putting the sex back into homosexuality', the singer admitted that this wasn't his intention. 'Nothing so worthy,' he said. 'I'm not going to pretend that the position I was in then was anything but selfish. My view of "gay libbers", as we called them then, was that they were just ugly queens who couldn't get laid. Between the ages of fourteen and twenty-four, all I was interested in was having a fabulous time, taking drugs and having sex and going to Amsterdam.'[2]

Frankie's boldness was too much for some, including Boy George, who wrote to UK music weekly *Record Mirror*, claiming the 'Relax' video 'gave gay people a bad name' and that the song was 'not educating people, only telling them being gay is like a four-letter word sprayed on a toilet wall — cheap, disgusting and very childish.'

---

[1] 'Relax' eventually sold around two million copies in the UK alone, making it the seventh best-selling single in UK history. When FGTH's third single, 'The Power Of Love', went to no. 1, FGTH became only the second act in UK chart history to reach the top with their first three singles, after Beatles contemporaries Gerry and The Pacemakers.
[2] www.zttaat.com/article.php?title=475

Richard Smith said that George later admitted it was the likes of Frankie that made him 'stop faffing around and come out, but that he'd felt threatened at the time.'

'OK, so in the past I didn't go round saying, "I'm homosexual,"' George told writer Paul Burston in 1994. 'But surely I made it clear through all the visual statements. What else did I have to do for people to actually say, "There's a queen"? Hop, skip and jump across Red Square in a fucking tutu? But I suppose since then, I've realised I was mentally closeted in a way, even though it was blatantly obvious.'[1]

The revenge of the teenage perverts

If Tom Robinson opened the closet door and Frankie pulled off its hinges, Bronski Beat ensured the closet remained wide open, with an appeal from the heart. Following the TRB and FGTH mixed gay/straight line-ups, Bronski Beat were the first all-gay pop band. Their debut single was as political as 'Relax' was hedonistic and the narrative of the song's promo video was even more daring than 'Relax'. It showed the reality of same-sex attraction rather than the fantasy – and the violence, social stigma and familial tension associated with homophobia.

In 1982, the London-based Lesbian and Gay Youth Video Project made a forty-five-minute documentary. *Framed Youth: Revenge of the Teenage Perverts* was the first time that British gay and lesbian youth had been given a public platform and it was shown on Channel 4. Among its enshrined testimonials and vox pops ('How would you feel if your daughter was a lesbian?') was another first; two minutes of music, called 'Screaming' – Jimmy Somerville's public debut.

It wasn't just the tone of this young Glaswegian's uncanny countertenor, but the haunted folk-blues spiritual he was singing. 'My lying, my deceiving ... my physical abuse .... my loneliness, my aching brain ... . my tempting to destroy ... my confusion disillusion ... my wanting just to scream.'

---

1 www.zttaat.com/article.php?title=475

Like Almond and Johnson, Somerville had suffered horribly for his effeminacy. 'Most of my youth, I was traumatised and bullied,' he says. 'I was red-headed, short, very sensitive and obviously gay. I was always mistaken for a girl.' And like Almond and Johnson, it gave him a resilient streak, though Somerville was more reckless: he drank heavily and 'did things most boys my age didn't, in the bus station toilets.' But he wasn't a lost cause. Attending Glasgow's new Gay Centre – the UK's first such social initiative, open since 1977 – he'd read *Gay News*, which sparked a political awaking. 'I was always moved by the injustice and difference,' he says.

Somerville also 'always felt I had to get away, which saved my life.' In 1979, aged eighteen, he took a train to London (he didn't tell his parents where he was for three months), taking various jobs to survive, including a spell as a rent boy. He found himself part of a new underground gay scene in north London's alternative gay pub scene, first at the Carved Red Lion pub – 'Saturday nights in the basement bar, a club called Movements'– and then the Pied Bull, whose doorman had harangued Boy George.

Somerville forged an identity beyond the pleasure-seeking clone. 'Heaven [nightclub] was trying to mirror the San Francisco idea of gay, but a bunch of us didn't fit in. We loved Talking Heads and Lou Reed as well as Donna Summer,' Somerville says. 'That's when I crossed over from this wandering, lost little soul boy into politics. I met my boyfriend Lawrence, he had a PhD in history, economics and politics; he was quite a Trotskyite. Suddenly I was part of something rather than just reading about it. I'd finally found my tribe.'

He also found his voice in the Framed Youth project – and Steve Bronski and Larry Steinbachek, through mutual friends. He moved into their south London squat crammed with keyboards, synths and drum machines. Here the trio kickstarted Bronski Beat and were quickly signed to major label offshoot London. 'Screaming' became part of their set but 'Smalltown Boy', a heartfelt and vulnerable ballad that doubled as a dance track, was chosen for their debut single.

Glasgow was more a big city than a small town but Somerville was singing for any and every gay or lesbian youth rejected at home who craved safety and validation in numbers: 'You leave in the morning/ With everything you own/In a little black case/Alone on a platform/ The wind and the rain/On a sad and lonely face.' The chorus was simple: 'run away, turn away, to your soul.'

'The song tried to evoke the romantic notion of this journey and a positive outcome, so the music has that pulsing feel and, for me, my cry is almost like the whistle of a train,' says Somerville. 'But again, it's sad. I didn't want to leave Glasgow, but circumstances drove me away.'

'Smalltown Boy' was a UK no. 3 hit, aided by its equally pioneering video. At a swimming baths, Somerville cruises a swimmer who grins back at him before subsequently rounding up his friends to attack. Bloodied and beaten, he goes home, to the visible horror of his father and takes a train to London. Bronski and Steinbachek join the young lad as the train is about to depart and their exchange of grins as it moved off suggests a world of promise.

'We wanted an antidote to the Duran blockbuster video,' Somerville explains. 'It was important to get this unashamed sexuality in there. And there's no distraction, it's a guy looking at a guy in Speedos at a swimming pool.' The video proved too contentious. 'MTV unofficially banned it for ten years, because it was obviously someone cruising' recalls Somerville. 'It was a man's domain back then and the homophobic discriminatory response was to not show it. Sadly, some of those men were closets. There's nothing worse than a closet in fear.'

Pop music's first insight to the young gay experience has lost none of its power and relevance: digital magazine Queerty recently called 'Smalltown Boy' 'arguably the most enduring LGBT anthem ever released.'[1]

'The notion that three gay people could actually be in the same space laughing and supporting one another was revelatory to me,' Shaun

---

1 www.queerty.com/jimmy-somerville-reveals-what-inspired-his-new-disco-album-why-he-terrified-boy-george-and-the-impact-of-smalltown-boy-20141028

Dellenty, the founder of the anti-homophobia campaign Inclusion For All, remembers from his closeted youth. 'Perhaps there was a place for me on planet Earth after all.'

'It's not throwaway, it's a very important moment in pop and gay political history,' Somerville agrees. 'There had been gay singers before but not this kind of evocative, emotional plea. We didn't or drown the song in ambiguity; we didn't disguise it or who Bronski Beat were.'

Tom Robinson would have been proud of the single's artwork, which featured a very large pink triangle. 'The first book I'd read about gay politics was about why men wore the pink triangle, to mark them out in the concentration camps,' says Somerville. 'We wanted to use imagery that would get people curious. When we did interviews, we'd mention it and automatically you're on to gay politics.'

Bronski Beat's second single, 'Why', was more political, dynamic and angry: 'Contempt in your eyes as I turn to kiss his lips/Broken I lie, all my feelings denied/Blood on your fist, can you tell me why?' The track started with the sound of breaking glass and ended with Somerville's falsetto shrieks.

With Bronski Beat's newfound fame thrown into the mix, the tension was rising for the band. After Somerville was arrested for having sex in London's Hyde Park, the trio went on to record their debut album in New York – 'for someone driven by sex and clubbing and alcohol and danger, you can imagine I was on fire there!' recalls Somerville. But they retained their political clout by naming the record *The Age Of Consent*, to draw attention to the inequalities between heterosexual and homosexual ages, across the world – though the statistics on the cover were removed from the US version.

The trio also headlined the Pits And Perverts benefit concert for the UK's striking miners, held in London in December 1984, taking its name from a headline in the *Sun*.

Tempering their image, Bronski Beat's next two singles were cover versions, but still made a point. First, 'It Ain't Necessarily So', from the Gershwin brothers' opera *Porgy And Bess*, which questioned the authenticity of Biblical tales. This was followed by a medley of Donna Summer's 'Love To Love You Baby' and 'I Feel Love' with John Leyton's 'Johnny Remember Me'[1] with co-vocalist Marc Almond. The video camped it up and it seemed that enough of the public had voted on Gay = Good: the single reached the UK top three.

But there was an underlying, graver tone to the choice of the Donna Summer covers, released in 1985, as a new virus has begun to work its way through the gay community. Summer had become a controversial figure after airing apparent homophobic comments in 1983 from the stage in Atlantic City; now a reborn Christian, she peddled the 'Adam and Eve, not Adam and Steve' line. As *Advocate* writer Adam Block wrote, 'When questioned about gay rights, she is reported to have responded, "I've seen the evil homosexuality come out of you people . . . AIDS is your sin," finally closing, "Now, don't get me wrong; God loves you. But not the way you are now."'

Silence = death . . . so music sings out

The origins of the human immunodeficiency virus (HIV) that lay behind AIDS (Acquired Immunodeficiency Syndrome) can't be ratified, but it could have originated as early as 1930; the earliest known infection of an identified human being dates back to 1959, in what is now known as the Democratic Republic of the Congo and the first known case in the US dates to 1969. But HIV wasn't medically classified, and it wasn't until May 1981 that the first journalist, Lawrence Mass, wrote about the epidemic, in the gay newspaper *New York Native*, about rumours of a number of gay men being treated for a virulent strain of pneumonia. A *New York Times* headline, RARE CANCER SEEN IN FORTY-ONE HOMO-SEXUALS, soon followed.

In San Francisco, Patrick Cowley had been hospitalised with

---

[1] Produced by Joe Meek, Leyton's original 'Johnny Remember Me' 'is a haunting melody of wanting,' says Somerville. 'I thought it'd be great to have this three-way with me and Marc – and who is this Johnny? It's also a nod to those early stirrings we all had at cowboy films on TV.'

pneumonia. According to Joshua Gamson's biography *The Fabulous Sylvester*,[1] 'Patrick was screaming that he wanted to be unplugged and his parents were considering the request. Then Sylvester walked in.' Cowley's friend had been instructed to give the patient hope and now the singer demanded they make more music together. Cowley responded by leaving hospital and at his home studio, the pair came up with the joyous, sexed-up 'Do You Wanna Funk' and had a hit record across the UK and mainland Europe.

Cowley was inspired enough to complete an album of his own, *Mind Warp*, released in 1982. Gamson wrote that Cowley directed proceedings 'while reclining on a couch in the studio. People propped him up by the synthesizer so he could work.' With hindsight, *Mind Warp* can be read as a man trying and failing to keep hope alive. 'Invasion' and the title track tapped the same vibrancy that drove 'Menergy' and 'Megatron Man' but the overall mood was darker, enervated, markedly warped.

Brad Gooch's 2015 memoir *Smash Cut*[2] chronicled his experience of the early onset of AIDS when his boyfriend, filmmaker Howard Brookner, fell ill. Gooch characterised that time as, 'This sort of science fiction disease going on . . . For a while, people thought it was the air conditioning system in clubs in San Francisco and New York . . . It seemed like science fiction, but it was happening.'

Mind Warp is the 'science fiction' AIDS record. The opening track 'Tech-No-Logical World', which pitched up between Giorgio Moroder, Hi-NRG and synth-pop, was sung by Cowley collaborator Paul Parker and set the tone: 'Mankind's splendour spread out far and wide/but the flags of doom unfurl.' 'They Came At Night' linked to the theme of 'Invasion': 'They changed their shape/They made their move on a human race/Uh-oh! Beware of darkness.' The finale, 'Going Home" – 'leaving our troubles far behind' – had no audible trace of hope. Cowley died in November, aged thirty-two.

By then, elements of the gay community had rallied round after the

---

1 Henry Holt and Co., 2005
2 Harper, 2015

first cases of what was originally called GRID (Gay-Related Immune Deficiency) until July 1982, when doctors realised sufferers weren't only gay. The first fundraiser in August, 1981 had been organised by Larry Kramer, author of the 1978 novel *Faggots*, which had controversially criticised a culture for exchanging its roots in liberation, in men *loving* men, for a revolution rooted in sex. The thousands of dollars raised were enough to set up the Gay Men's Health Crisis. A benefit at Paradise Garage in April 1982 subsequently raised over $50,000 and the fight was on.

In LA, Carl Bean also saw the writing on the wall. He'd not only rejected Motown's request to sing straight love songs but a career in music and instead established a visitors centre for the black gay community. 'I'd had kids calling from London and Paris, on the phone for two hours, asking me about being gay, so why would I sing, "Oh, girl, I love you"?' Bean says. 'Getting involved in the gay community meant more than getting on stage to hear people clapping. And then AIDS hit. I knew guys who'd screw other guys and then sleep with women; I felt I had to educate men and women, no matter how they identified. I could either pursue music and make excuses or get involved with the AIDS crisis and my heart said to choose AIDS.'

After Cowley, Klaus Nomi was the next musician to fall. Another symptom of AIDS, Kaposi's sarcoma, was the 'rare cancer' of the headlines that created lesions on the skin. Nomi stopped wearing his tuxedo and adopted a more formal outfit with a ruff collar to hide the lesions. His repertoire changed too, with more opera (such as 'Cold Genius' from Henry Purcell's *King Arthur*) as his illness gripped. In a tragically ironic episode, Nomi's creative provider Kristian Hoffman thought 'it might be funny to cover Donna Summer's "I Feel Love" but change the words to "I Feel Sick". It had no prescience about the soon-to-come GRID, I was just sick of disco. But the joke was too bald, and not that funny and we only did it a couple of times.'

Nomi also guested on New York DJ/producer Man Parrish's 1982 debut album *Hip Hop Bee Bop*, as an operatic counterpoint to the robotic voice on 'Six Simple Synthesizers'. Parrish had been asked to write music for a new porn film, *Heatstroke*; a pirated copy of the music – inspired by Patrick Cowley, says Parrish – was played at the Anvil in New York. He traced it back to a record label, which led to getting a deal for *Heatstroke* and also his debut album, which exemplified hip hop's original electro roots.

'I visited Klaus in hospital. We had to wear paper aprons and face masks and gloves because they didn't know if it was airborne or by touch and the doctors didn't know what to give him,' says Parrish. 'It was the beginning . . . people began dropping like flies.'

In response, the 1983 Fighting For Our Lives march was one of the first public AIDS demonstrations. And in another response, to Donna Summer's comments, a Trash Donna campaign in the Disco Sucks tradition didn't go as far as burning her records, but settled for a boycott and for urging fans to return their Summer records to her record company. Ian Levine at London's Heaven club was one of many DJs to comply. Meanwhile, Bronski Beat were criticised for contributing to her royalties, but Somerville says the covers were a response to the 'outrage and shock' regarding Summer's 'retribution' comments.

'She was misquoted, possibly but I was twenty-four and "in yer face". I didn't take homophobia on my knees, just homos!' Somerville says. 'And I wanted to sing those tracks as an openly gay man because I'd spent my youth miming them on the dance floor.'

Summer later claimed that journalist Jim Feldman, reviewing her born-again Atlantic City comeback concert in *Village Voice*, made up the comments: 'I think he was angry at me for accepting God,' she told *The Advocate*.[1] But Summer didn't help her cause by delaying a response (although she claimed her manager had shielded her from the controversy), but in 1985, she released a statement to *Village Voice* and *The Advocate*. 'This was not a retraction, but an apology,' Block wrote.

'It is very difficult for me to believe this terrible misunderstanding

---

1 www.donna-tribute.com/articles/80/advocate.html

continues,' Summer began. 'Since the very beginning of my career, I have had tremendous support and friendship from many in the gay community. It is a source of great concern to me that anything I may have said has cast me as homophobic . . . my true feelings have been misrepresented. As a Christian, I have nothing but love for everyone and I recognise it is not my place to judge others. I believe with all my heart and soul that AIDS is a tragedy for all humankind. A cure must be found and all of us have to do whatever we can to help.'

Summer's statement didn't extinguish the fire and New York's ACT UP (AIDS Coalition To Unleash Power, formed in 1987) would picket her shows.[1] AIDS was too heightened a crisis to put up with equivocal views, especially after the first celebrity had died of AIDS, Hollywood star Rock Hudson, in October 1985. This increased the press coverage and public awareness moved from sympathy to outrage.

Throughout the eighties, musical responses to AIDS would parallel activism. The first had been written as early as 1981: teacher and massage therapist John Calvi wrote 'The Ones Who Aren't Here', which Meg Christian and Cris Williamson sang at their 1982 Carnegie Hall show, an early sign that lesbians were supporting gay men at a time of crisis. 'Thousands left the lesbian community to take care of the dying,' recalls Alix Dobkin. Craig Carnahan's choral work *I Loved You* and, later, lesbian comedian Lynn Lavner's cabaret ballad 'Such Fine Young Men' were similarly empathic. But there was room for gallows humour. In 1984, Matthew McQueen and Karl Brown of Automatic Pilot produced a musical, *The AIDS Show: Artists Involved with Death and Survival*. The duo wrote 'Safe Livin' In Dangerous Times' and 'Vaccine Day', but they also updated the band's 'health crisis' parody, 'Rimmin' At The Baths', adding: 'So, don't be seduced

---

[1] In 1989, Summer wrote again, to ACT UP: 'I have made numerous replies and spoken openly to try and clear up this misunderstanding. I cannot force you to believe what I tell you, so if you choose to continue on with this fighting and arguing, that's up to you. I did not say God is punishing gays with AIDS, I did not sit with ill intentions in judgement over your lives. I haven't stopped talking to my friends who are gay, nor have I ever chosen my friends by their sexual preferences.'

by that sweet aroma/Think twice before you dive into that ass/You might even get Kaposi's Sarcoma/From rimmin' at the baths.'

Back in the land of empathy, Dionne Warwick's cover of 'That's What Friends Are For'[1] was recorded for the American Foundation for AIDS Research, with guest vocalists singers Gladys Knight, Elton John and Stevie Wonder. The single topped the US chart and outsold every other single in 1985. This was a public vote of support, as Ronald Reagan's government maintained a wall of silence; the president would only publically address AIDS for the first time in 1987.

Other responses were as grave as the subject. In 1984, US-Greek avant-garde singer/composer Diamanda Galas released *the Plague Mass*, and the operatic trilogy *Masque of the Red Death* (1986-88), inspired by her brother's Philip-Dimitri's sickness and subsequent death. In 1985, UK duo John Balance and Peter Christopherson, a.k.a. electronic experimentalists Coil, recorded a new cover of 'Tainted Love' as a benefit for the Terence Higgins Trust, the charity named after one of Britain's first AIDS casualties. Next to Soft Cell's perky touch, Coil's version was funereal, with a matching video of flies trapped in honey; a man in a hospital bed who suddenly disappears; a closing shot of a gravestone.

Michael Callen's 'Living In Wartime' equally used metaphors for a grim reality. His song of embattlement was chosen to open and close Larry Kramer's off-Broadway play *The Normal Heart* – about the early days of the AIDS epidemic, the public protests and the government indifference – and for the 1987 video documentary of AIDS activism, *Testing The Limits*.

Callen, like Marc Almond, Jimmy Somerville and Holly Johnson, epitomised the triumph of the diminutive sissy. Raised in Hamilton, Ohio, he found himself increasingly drawn to the valiant voices of resilient women – Barbra Streisand, Julie Andrews and Bette Midler. Gifted with his own dramatic voice, Callen won a music scholarship to Boston

---

[1] The original 'That's What Friends Are For', written by Burt Bacharach and Carole Bayer Sager, was sung by Rod Stewart for the 1982 romantic comedy *Night Shift*.

University and moved to New York in 1977, singing in cabarets and, later, the New York City Gay Men's Chorus.

In 1982, Callen was one of the first to be diagnosed with GRID. Only a few weeks later, he was called by Richard Dworkin, who had left San Francisco for New York, looking to further his musical career and again seeking out other gay musicians. He'd responded to Callen's advert for 'male, female and out-front queer'. In a 1987 interview with Dr David Schmidt, Callen said, 'In our culture, the experiences of an estimated twenty-one million Americans is [sic] never alluded to. We are made invisible in this culture. And I guess I got tired of waiting around for somebody else to take the step of singing their own truth, being courageous and saying, "This is my experience" and putting it out there.'[1]

Dworkin went to Callen's apartment; Pam Brandt, bassist of the now disbanded lesbian trio the Deadly Nightshade, was also there, She'd felt that lesbians and gay men should 'focus on our similarities and not our differences'. After Brandt left, Dworkin stayed over, despite Callen's protestations that he had this new illness.

'The first night I met him,' Dworkin told AIDS historian, Matt Jones, 'he said, "Have you heard about this thing?", meaning GRID ... it was still so new. I don't know if I'd had a serious discussion about GRID with anyone at that point. I think it's hard for anyone to understand how vague things were from this vantage point.'

Callen and Dworkin became boyfriends and, with Brandt, formed Lowlife. They were briefly a quartet, with Janet Cleary, but Dworkin says the band were held back by their 'eternal search for a good lesbian guitarist'. They persisted as a trio, playing small clubs and benefits, from covers of Connie Francis' 'Where The Boys Are'[2] to originals

---

[1] 'How to Make Music In An Epidemic: Hearing AIDS, 1981-1996', Matt Jones, http://libra.virginia.edu/catalog/libra-oa:6951

[2] Says Brandt, '"Where The Boys Are" was also a vehicle for Michael ... he had had a life-long musical goal of holding a note as long as the longest note that Barbra Streisand ever held on a recording. So at the end of the song that's exactly what he does. He holds, "Someone waits" and then he holds "for" ... you know, before "me" and he holds that "for" for three seconds longer than the longest note that Barbra Streisand ever recorded.'

such as 'Living in Wartime': 'Conspiracy of silence/The enemy within/ Complacency and arrogance/Make us think we cannot win.'

'That was the difference between Michael or Steven Grossman and people like Jobriath,' says Dworkin. 'Michael was laying it all out there and it's serious – this is love, this is not screwing around, high on coke at the disco, this is for real and he's not afraid to write intelligently and seriously about it and in front of thousands of people.'

Both songs were demoed, but Lowlife never got a record deal: 'I don't know if I would have given us a record deal,' says Dworkin. 'Maybe we weren't good enough.' Maybe there were other reasons to not sign a band whose singer was theoretically living on borrowed time and who, Dworkin says, 'could never pass as a rocker and he couldn't write songs that way. But Michael had an amazing voice, and could have pursued music at a pretty high level if not for being gay, being a sissy and having AIDS.'

Callen was also diverted by his extraordinary commitment to activism, which rivalled Larry Kramer's efforts to drive the GMHC and ACT UP. In 1983, Callen wrote *How To Have Sex in an Epidemic: One Approach* in conjunction with his doctor, Joseph Sonnabend, Dworkin and former rent boy Richard Berkowitz; it was the first manifesto to recommend 'safe sex'. The same year, Callen helped win the first AIDS discrimination lawsuit, when Sonnabend fought eviction from a Greenwich Village co-op for treating people with AIDS. Callen co-founded the Lesbian and Gay Community Services Centre, the People With AIDS Coalition and the Community Research Initiative – a group of AIDS patients and doctors who conducted their own drug trials. This led to editing *Surviving and Thriving With AIDS: Hints for the Newly Diagnosed* in 1987.

By 1987, Callen had survived living with AIDS for five years, 'two years longer than medical research suggested that he would have under the best circumstances,' wrote Matt Jones.[1] Dworkin says that some

---

[1] Callen had the good fortune to be prescribed Bactrim at the start of his diagnosis, which helped prevent the pneumonia that was the biggest killer among AIDS patients.

critics claimed Callen was surviving because he wasn't actually ill, that he was using AIDS to further his career. In which case, he was taking his time about it – it was 1986 and he still hadn't recorded an album. And the illness was not guaranteed to boost your sales.

Without a record label, finances were an issue. Callen wanted to emulate the production values of Streisand or Midler, but Dworkin introduced Callen to the stripped-back beauty of *Nina Simone and Piano*. Callen agreed that 'emotion first' was the key. So Dworkin tracked down Fred Hersch, one of the very few prominent gay men playing jazz, a genre still in the dark ages regarding proportional representation. Hersch had just been diagnosed HIV-positive, too, so there was a sense of repayment for the work Callen had done.

Callen named his album *Purple Heart*, 'referring to the military honour given for wounds or death sustained in battle,' Matt Jones wrote. Purple – or lavender – also referenced the lavender resistance. The album was split into 'top' (up-tempo) and 'bottom' (ballads) sides; it started with Lowlife's version of 'Where The Boys Are', a timeless evocation of the teenage hope of finding love and happiness and ended with a multi-tracked Callen on the spiritual 'I'd Like To Be (Home)'. It was as if the dream was over and reality had set in.

Between the two were 'Life During Wartime' and 'How To Have Sex' (the first 'safe sex' ditty: 'Use a rubber, find a lover/In time you will discover/It's OK to get laid'), both synthy AOR. 'Me And Dickie D' (about boyfriend Dworkin) aped fifties' rock'n'roll. A cover of Elton John's 'Talking Old Soldiers', dedicated to Dr Sonnabend, was typical of side two's quivering piano ballads, which fit the theme of battle (you wonder what Elton made of it, or had even heard it during his marriage).[1] And there was 'Love Don't Need A Reason'.

---

1 Callen's liner notes to *Purple Heart* thanked four artists 'who have profoundly influenced my music and my life': Tom Robinson, Elton John, Bette Midler and Barbra Streisand. 'These days,' he concluded, 'I have two main goals in life: to live long enough to be eligible for membership in SAGE (Senior Action in a Gay Environment) and to help make the world safe for queers. I thought maybe music was a good place to begin.'

The song that would become the unofficial AIDS anthem actually preceded *Purple Heart*. The impetus had come from Barbra Streisand, who intended to make a film of *The Normal Heart*. Playwright Larry Kramer had asked Callen to write a song and he then called on Marsha Malamet, who he'd first met at Reno Sweeney's bar in Greenwich Village.

'Michael loved women and he always worked to get more lesbians into the movement,' Malamet recalls. She hadn't released an album since 1969's *Coney Island Winter*, but had come out in 1974, and was writing for musical theatre, where she claims to have been the first openly lesbian songwriter. One collaborator was Liza Minnelli's ex, Peter Allen, who had been diagnosed HIV-positive after his boyfriend Gregory Connell had died of AIDS in 1984. Malamet suggested Allen join her and Callen to write a song: this homosexual trinity came up with 'Love Don't Need A Reason' 'in two hours: voila!' says Malamet. 'Peter sung it at the first AIDS walk in New York and we were off to the races. Everyone started singing and recording it. I think there are twenty-five versions out there. And we must have performed it at ten AIDS walkathons. Michael would sing and I'd play piano.'

Their song dispensed with poetic metaphor and went straight to the heart: 'Love don't need a reason/Love don't always rhyme/And love is all we have for now/What we don't have is time.'

Matt Jones heard a similar tone to that of Dionne Warwick's 'That's What Friends Are For'. 'However, "Love Don't Need a Reason" acknowledges that time is running out for someone with AIDS; thus, its sentiments are buttressed by urgency and a kind of desperation in the face of death.'

Purple Heart was named 'the most remarkable gay independent release of the past decade,' by *The Advocate*'s pop and rock editor Adam Block, who had often criticised 'men's music' as too earnest and cloying. Dworkin says the album sold around ten thousand copies, hardly the numbers of Olivia's heyday: gay men *still* evidently wouldn't respond to music sung by openly gay men, or maybe it was Callen's subject matter.

Marches, benefits and conferences were fine, but the album was not required listening in the comfort of home.

David Lasley shared the same fate. From Detroit, he was a white gay man singing the kind of music gay men seemed to love – authentic, Philly-style soul, in a creamy falsetto, on a vocal par with the great Daryl Hall with production and songs to match. His extensive CV included co-writing credits with Dionne Warwick, Patti LaBelle, Whitney Houston, Chaka Khan and Aretha Franklin; he'd sung backup on records by the likes of Chic, Melissa Manchester, James Taylor and also Luther Vandross, the premier soul singer, who Bowie had let loose on his soul opus *Young Americans* before he progressed to a notable solo career. But Vandross remained in the closet – and Lasley had a problem with those kind of artists.

When he was signed to make his own albums, his 1982 debut, *Missing Twenty Grand*, contained 'Looking For Love On Broadway' and specified his kind of love. 'If I Had My Wish Tonight' reached the US Top 40 and prominent US magazines put his stellar, blue-eyed soul collection – as good as any Vandross record – in their end-of-year Top 10. Lasley's *Raindance* album ended up in *The Face* magazine's Top 20 albums of 1984, alongside Prince's *Purple Rain* and Madonna's *Like A Virgin*. Lasley joined Smokey Robinson as one of the music industry's five top falsetto singers as nominated by *Esquire*. The net result? Spotify has a total of four Lasley tracks and few recall the man. In 1985, Lasley already felt he knew why.

'It is *not* hip to be gay,' he told Adam Block. 'And it's not hip to be white and sing black – sing soul songs. Look at Hall and Oates – there are like ten soulful white guys in the whole world. I'm talking about *serious* – there is something about white cats who come almost from the woman's side, who listen to women and girl artists – and often they're going to be gay singers. And it *ain't* hip to be gay.'[1]

---

1 http://adamblockmemorial.blogspot.co.uk/2008/02/from-dr-jay-lalezari.html

America – the backlash

The USA as a whole didn't seem overly fond of gay singers. The lead story of the January 1985 edition of *Life* magazine was 'Gender Benders: The Year of Living Androgynously' and it really was just a year, for the Brit-gay invasion turned out to be short-lived. Frankie's 'Relax' had made the US Top 10, but 'Two Tribes' didn't make the Top 40 and their third UK no. 1, The Power Of Love, didn't even dent the Top 100. Frankie's Hollywood dream was over.

Bronski Beat's 'Smalltown Boy' reached the Top 50 but, like Soft Cell, they never had another US hit. Britain's cross-dressing predecessor to Boy George, Pete Burns, the frontman of Liverpool's Dead Or Alive since 1980, finally broke through in 1985 with their UK no. 1 'You Spin Me Round (Like a Record)', a US no. 11. They took the similarly Hi-NRG-sounding 'Brand New Lover' to US no.15, but that was their last hit.

Of the original gay incumbents, only Culture Club had persistent American success, probably because their music was more soulful than dance – but then quality control wobbled and George's anti-drugs approach collapsed in a blur of ecstasy, coke and finally heroin. Additionally, he was finally coming out.

'George had played a very clever game with the tabloids, allowing them loads of access and feeding them stories, but they turned against him when he was seen out with his friend Trannie Paul, who was dressed in a black rubber swimsuit,' says Culture Club backing singer Helen Terry. 'He'd maintained the "cuddly George" thing and the "abstaining sex" thing and this tipped the balance. It was a free-for-all in the press after that.'

'Politically, things had changed,' George says. 'You had Bronski Beat and Frankie Goes To Hollywood. Things became more aggressive and I didn't fit in to that category. The first time I heard "Smalltown Boy", I felt very lightweight. I thought it was really amazing and brave and I thought I had to get tough but, because it didn't come from the heart, it didn't work. Plus Frankie had the sound of the moment.'

Marc Almond had also decided to change tack. 'I experienced all kinds of homophobia and violent threats which made me realise what other people have to deal with every day and made me more determined,' he says. 'Though the first person who was really honest about their sexuality was Jimmy Somerville, who was responsible for dragging me into a more public arena of open sexuality.'

Soft Cell split up with the 1984 album *Last Night In Sodom*; Almond's ode to a transgender hooker, 'L'Esqualita', pointed the way to his new project, Marc and the Mambas. It was packed with homoerotic melodrama and Lou Reed and Jacques Brel covers and similarly charged solo albums followed, such as *Mother Fist and her Five Daughters*, a reference to the art of masturbation.

'I had a really straight audience at first, which was very strange and scary,' Almond told journalist Joe Morgan. 'It felt like I was still being stared at in the playground so I formed Marc and the Mambas as a way of moving from pop music and challenging my audience. Are you with me or against me? Some fans departed, but many stayed, including a lot of straight ones, surprisingly unfazed by how homoerotic and subversive my lyrics can be.'[1]

Almond also guested on several Coil albums, while some of his solo videos were directed by Coil's Peter Christopherson. 'We loved to see how subversive we could be without alarming the major labels, using homoerotic signs and symbols and, of course, good-looking lads as extras,' he told journalist Luke Turner.[2]

As the UK's increasingly uncompromising gay pop stars disappeared off the US map, the Pet Shop Boys took their place, initially disguised as two very dressed-down and normal individuals who wrote in the old-fashioned ways of code, albeit in a rich, sharp and nuanced fashion – but still code. From Newcastle in Tyne and Wear, Neil Tennant had been a staff writer for the pop magazine *Smash*

---

[1] www.gaystarnews.com/article/soft-cell-singer-marc-almond-growing-gay200912/#gs.OQvqsIQ
[2] http://thequietus.com/articles/10721-marc-almond-desertshore-interview

Hits before he met Chris Lowe, from Blackpool in Lancashire. Lowe was the all-purpose musician to Tennant's keening vocal. They'd made their first record in 1983 after contacting a favourite producer, Hi-NRG hit factory Bobby 'O' Orlando. The original, more definitively disco version of the PSB's 'West End Girls' was a US club hit, but after falling out with the controlling Orlando, they signed to the UK major EMI. Their re-recorded version topped both UK and US charts in 1985, establishing a template for the most successful duo in UK pop history.

Due to the urban myth centring on actor Richard Gere and referring to the sexual practice of inserting a small rodent (in conditions that would satisfy health and safety) into the anal passage, Pet Shop Boys were dogged by the controversy over the origins of their name. They claimed it was derived from their friend's workplace. What kept the story running was the persistent aura of gay identity in the duo's work, though they remained tight-lipped. 'We've never said anything about our sex lives to the newspapers or the magazines,' Neil Tennant told *NME* in 1986, 'and we don't intend to.'

Instead, their songs played with nuance and ambiguity. For starters, did 'Which do you choose, a hard or soft option?' from 'West End Girls' mean the choice between men and women? Boston university professor Aaron Lecklider claims Pet Shop Boys' second album *Actually*, 'employs a full throttle queer aesthetic, exploring such indicatively gay subjects as rent boys, AIDS, religious condemnation, camp, consumption, dancing and other gay pop musicians.'

The video for the Catholic confessional of 1987 UK no. 1, 'It's A Sin', was directed by gay filmmaker Derek Jarman and populated with choirboys, but the video to a later UK no. 1 that year, 'Heart', depicted Tennant about to marry a woman: they had it both ways. So too the intervening UK no. 2 'What Have I Done to Deserve This?' It featured a newly sober Dusty Springfield making – at last! – her comeback on guest vocals, but this knowing revival of a cherished gay icon was only facilitated because of her peerless vocal.

The Eighties: Pop Comes Out

There would be two Pet Shop Boys singles inspired by AIDS: 'Domino Dancing' (1988) – 'I've watched you dance with danger still wanting more/Add another number to the score' – and 'Being Boring' (1990). Tennant later revealed it was about a friend 'and so it's about our lives when we were teenagers and how we moved to London and I suppose me becoming successful and him becoming ill.'

'The acute sense of longing, the droll and sometimes acerbic view of relationships, and the social observation . . . are, I believe, unmistakeably queer,' wrote journalist John Gill. 'It is unlikely that a heterosexual listener would glean this information, nor are the Pet Shop Boys about to draw their attention to it.'[1]

Tennant wrote more about AIDS: 'It Couldn't Happen Here' when his friend died and 'My Funny Uncle' about the funeral. But he never clarified, preferring mood and mystery and letting fans work out the meaning. Militant as ever, Jimmy Somerville accused the duo of exploiting gay culture for career purposes. 'We didn't come along to be politicians or to be positive role models,' Tennant retaliated when he came out to *Attitude* magazine in 1994. 'Having said that, we have supported the fight for gay rights.'

AIDS began to decimate gay artists, who were promiscuous by association. Still, people were widely misinformed about the disease and scare-mongering was rife. Most deaths of musicians were in the world of musical theatre, but pop was also affected. Jobriath died in 1983, at thirty-seven; then Ricky Wilson, guitarist of Athens, Georgia new-wavers B-52s, in 1985, aged thirty-two, and Miki Zone of the Fast at thirty-one. Liberace died in 1987, the year Sylvester announced he had AIDS; he would himself die by the following year, six years after his dear friend Patrick Cowley.

Perhaps unsurprisingly, the rock industry was lacking in similar empathy. After all, AIDS was considered a gay condition, and 'gay music' was perceived as contained within dance music. Frank Zappa of the Mothers of

---

1 *Queer Noise: Male and Female Homosexuality in Twentieth-Century Music* (University Of Minnesota Press, 1995)

Invention, who had already written the questionably homophobic 'Bobby Brown Goes Down', made AIDS a key plotline of his 1984 concept album *Thing-Fish*, in which a racist theatre critic manufactures the virus to get rid of the Afro-Americans and gays, as the US authorities actually had with syphilis on black convicts. But with a track such as 'He's So Gay' conflating homosexuality with a panoply of fetishes (rubber, spanking, leather, water sports) – and a camp delivery of the line 'do you really want to hurt me?', it's highly likely that the majority of Zappa's audience would have felt their own prejudices confirmed.

AIDS was a huge scare not only for the gay community but the straight community, who saw their own comfortable world threatened by the idea of a killer disease, and gay men were again turned into pariahs. It's why Queen fell out of favour – not because Freddie Mercury was perfecting his clone look with each record or because his 1984 solo single 'Love Kills' could have been read as a comment on AIDS, but for the crime of dressing in drag for the video of 1984's 'I Want To Break Free'.

The single was written by bassist John Deacon but Mercury seized on the title for the full transgressive treatment. For years, Mercury had avoided taking risks but finally put himself out there, even if he persisted with music hall values. In fact, the whole of Queen dressed up but Mercury took it the furthest: he kept his moustache but wore a bouffant wig, leather mini-skirt and high heels. MTV banned the clip and the band's US audience halved overnight, unable to handle the concept. In the UK, Mercury even donned the wig and false breasts on stage, though when he wore it at 1985's Rock In Rio festival, the crowd threw bottles and cans at the stage. It turned out that South America had treated 'I Want To Break Free' as an anthem of liberation and Mercury was cruelly mocking their beliefs.

US rocker Billy Squier was similarly undone by a video, for his biggest career hit, 'Rock Me Tonite'. Squier was evidently a Queen fan; he'd shared vocals with Mercury and Taylor on the title track of his 1982 album *Emotions In Motion* and appeared as the opening act on Queen's North American tour. 1984's *Signs Of Life* was his third consecutive platinum album, but 'Rock Me Tonite' was saddled with a video in which Squier out Freddie-d Mercury, flouncing around a bedroom in a pink, ripped T-shirt. Like Queen, his sales nose-dived under the weight of ridicule, of simply appearing 'gay'.[1]

The evidence for staying in the closet mounted up. The Supreme Court, in the Bowers vs Hardwick case, ruled that it was constitutional for individual states to criminalise gay sexual behaviour. In 1987, there was a nearly unanimous senate ban on federal funding for gay AIDS education. 'The election of Ronald Reagan on an anti-ERA [Equal Rights Amendment], family values platform,' wrote author and historian John Loughery, 'validated a yearning in America, a wish to return to a more ordered world where deviance and disruption were supposedly non-existent or invisible.'[2]

According to Aaron Lecklider, Frankie's 'Relax' was 'encouraging Americans to talk openly about sexuality and offering a hopeful vision for gay men beginning to feel the tragic effects of AIDS in their lives.'[3] That this was wish-fulfilment was underlined by Lecklider himself, who pointed out that *Time* magazine journalist Jay Cocks described Holly Johnson as 'the archetypal Brit pop poofter, waving a salmon-coloured silk scarf as he wafts his way through Springsteen's "Born to Run".' *Rolling Stone*'s equally homophobic reviewer claimed Frankie's debut album was 'dedicated to the elevation of hip agitprop and homo-erotic self-absorption' – as if the charge of self-absorption had ever been levelled at heterosexuals.

Alternative rock on the downlow

Heavy metal had a strange relationship to gay culture. The most popular strain was hair or glam metal, as bands such as Hanoi Rocks, Mötley

---

1 To add insult to injury, a cross-section of four hundred people voted 'Rock Me Tonite' the worst music video of all time in the book *I Want My MTV* (Craig Marks and Rob Tannenbaum, Dutton Penguin, 2011).
2 *The Other Side Of Silence: Men's Lives and Gay Identities: A Twentieth-Century Cultural History* (Henry Holt and Co, 1998)
3 *Between Decadence and Denial: Two Studies in Gay Male Politics and 1980s Pop Music*: www.umb.edu/academics/cla/faculty/aaron_lecklider

Crüe, Poison and Cinderella stressed their macho values while dressing curiously femme: huge hair and blouses, make-up and tight jeans. Manowar dressed like a gay fantasy of *Game Of Thrones*: muscles, leather, little leather loincloths. Judas Priest's Rob Halford had the most leather-clad image of all, complete with peaked cap, like he'd stepped out of the film *Cruising*. But trust the Germans to go all out, in the title of Accept's album, *Balls To The Wall*.

Housed in the image of a muscled thigh, leather shorts and a clenched fist – just another day at the metal office – the Cologne band's 1983 album was rife with supportive evidence. Different band members gave different explanations: guitarist Wolf Hoffman claimed that 'London Leatherboys' referred to bikers. But what about 'Head Over Heels'? 'Down on my knees, help me please/Don't know who's there in the dark/I'm starved for breath, can't feel my hands/Clutching at the sound of people making love.'

'Love Child' also painted a scene of confusion: 'Don't know what I am, a woman or man . . . Feeling the power of lust when the guy's passing by.'

'We just wanted to be controversial and different and touch on these touchy subjects, because it gave us good press and it worked fabulously, you know,' said Hoffman.[1] It turned out that the lyricist was Hoffman's wife, Gaby, who claimed, 'Certain lyrics are mind games and pure interpretation from outsiders. This is a band who has as individuals . . . absolutely nothing in particular with anything but being *very* straight.'[2]

Drummer Stefan Kaufmann contradicted the Hoffmans when he considered the album's homosexual bent: 'This is a phenomenon of society that needs to be taken as such. For a long time, gay people have been considered as sick or insane. And yet, it's time to respect these people, open our minds which are often closed.'[3]

This was easy enough for *very* straight musicians but what about *very*

---

1 www.fullinbloommusic.com/wolfhoffman.html
2 web.archive.org/web/20041229182735/http://www.schlared.com/gaby.html
3 france.metal.museum.free.fr/revues/enfer_magazine/07/page_09.htm

gay musicians or those who identified outside of that defined band of sexuality, who really follow Frankie's advice and 'Relax'?

In 2011, Michael Stipe, the singer of Athens, Georgia's R.E.M., gave a speech on *Trailblazers*, a TV series on US cable channel Logo, to commemorate the first anniversary of the over-ruling of the Defence of Marriage Act, which defined marriage (for federal purposes) as the union of one man and one woman and allowed states to refuse to recognise same-sex marriages granted by other states, denying the financial benefits that heterosexual unions enjoyed. Introducing Ugandan gay rights activist John Abdallah Wambere, Stipe talked about the era when, 'as a twenty-two-year-old queer man living during the Reagan-Bush administration, I was afraid to get tested for HIV for fear of quarantine, the threat of internment camps and having my basic civil rights stripped away. I waited five years to get my first anonymous test.'

Active between 1980 and 2011, R.E.M. were the most successful of all so-called 'alternative' US bands, and were immediately successful[1] with their debut album *Murmur* going Top 40. Given that Stipe once referred to his public persona as 'quiet, difficult, enigmatic, paralysingly shy' and that he'd been nicknamed Mumbles for his barely decipherable lyrics (something the title *Murmur* played into), the level of attention was going to be an issue.

Back near the start, in August 1981, R.E.M. had played in North Carolina at what was billed as the 'first gay new wave disco and costume party' in Charlotte, a fundraiser for gay and lesbian charities. It wasn't that Stipe kept his sexuality secret from friends, family and – as he pointed out – those he slept with, but as he began to be increasingly vocal about other topics such as politics and the environment, AIDS entered the equation and the backlash had begun before gays and lesbians were even accepted.

'I had to grapple with a lot of contradictions back in the eighties,' he told journalist Sean O'Hagan in 2011. 'I would look out from the stage

---

1 R.E.M.'s debut album *Murmur* reached US no. 36. It was *Rolling Stone*'s best album of 1983, beating Michael Jackson, the Police and U2.

at the Reagan youth. That was when R.E.M. went beyond the freaks, the fags, the fat girls, the art students and the indie music fanatics. Suddenly we had an audience that included people who would have sooner kicked me on the street than let me walk by unperturbed. I'm exaggerating to make a point but it was certainly an audience that, in the main, did not share my political leanings or affiliations and did not like how flamboyant I was as a performer or indeed a sexual creature. They probably held lots of my world views in great disregard and I had to look out on that and think, well, what do I do with this?'[1]

Stipe kept quiet and let his oblique lyricism take over. Years later, he revealed that 1984's 'Seven Chinese Brothers' addressed 'breaking up a couple before dating both of them . . . a terrible thing to do. But I was young and stupid.' Yet the lyric – 'This mellow, sweet, short-haired, boy/woman offers to pull up a chair/Take in one symphony now/I guess we lost that battle' – wasn't going to betray his actions. 'Pretty Persuasion' was only slightly less coded: 'He's got pretty persuasion/She's got pretty persuasion/Goddamn your confusion.'

Again, a straight musician, Paul Westerberg of Minnesota's the Replacements could openly reflect, 'Same hair, revolution/Unisex, evolution/Tomorrow who's gonna fuss,' in 'Androgynous'. But Bob Mould, of fellow Minnesotans Hüsker Dü, would only address his sexuality in one song across six albums, and then still obliquely, in 'The Biggest Lie': 'Back to your hometown/Back to your day job/Back to your girlfriend/The biggest lie.'

Like Michael Stipe, Tommy Keane was out to his inner circle, though he had no issue advertising the fact. That was the problem. He recalled 'an A&R guy at Geffen coming up to me, out of the blue and saying, "Now, Tommy, it's OK to be bisexual . . . it's not OK to be homosexual."'

Even the three gay men in the quintet B-52s, Athens' most popular band until R.E.M. took the crown, stayed deeply closeted, though guitarist Ricky Wilson and drummer Keith Strickland had sometimes

---

1 www.theguardian.com/music/2011/mar/06/michael-stipe-rem-collapse-interview

walked to school in lipstick and wigs. The situation didn't change when Wilson died of AIDS: that probably nailed their closet door shut.

It was a symptom of the decade that the two most talismanic figures of alternative rock, Stipe and Steven Morrissey of Manchester quartet the Smiths, would never address their sexuality at the time. The latter still hasn't, as if putting a name to it meant he'd lost the battle to stay enigmatic or unclassifiable. 'Obviously any kind of tag, I'll dodge,' he told *Rolling Stone*. 'I'm not embarrassed by the word "gay" but it's not in the least bit relevant. I'm beyond that, frankly.'

Morrissey finally provided some evidence, in his twenty-sixth year of published lyrics, on 2009's solo song 'Please God Please Help Me': 'When he motions to me with his hand on my knee/Dear God, did this kind of thing happen to you? . . . Now I'm spreading your legs with mine in between. . . '

Even then, he wouldn't be drawn on the subject. Did artists need to come out? Didn't their work speak for them? Morrissey always discussed the matter of sex – or lack of it – and gender, as in being a different species. He talked of 'the fourth sex' – not male or female, nor presumably androgyny, which he claimed 'has been tried out, but it failed. I want something different. I'm bored with women and men.' The fourth state was asexuality or celibacy, since Smiths lyrics would point invariably to frustrated, embarrassing and failed fumbles.

The teenage Morrissey's obsessions were certainly gender-fluid, such as the New York Dolls: 'I tried to get them as much press attention as possible by writing to letters pages, radio stations,' he told the Dolls' biographer Nina Antonia.[1] Morrissey also held a candle for Jobriath, who he wanted to be his support act in 1992 before discovering the American had died nine years earlier. Morrissey was equally indebted to Bolan and Bowie and sixties girl-group pop. The earliest Smiths recording, on a demo never meant to be heard, was a snippet of them covering the Cookies' 'I Want A Boy For My Birthday'. Initial Smiths concerts

---

1 http://louderthanwar.com/interview-morrissey-on-glam-rock-and-the-new-york-dolls

featured Morrissey's (much more openly gay) friend James Maker as the band's on-stage dancer, in stilettos: Morrissey's song-writing foil, Johnny Marr, admitted that in the planning stages, the Smiths 'were going to be a gay band'.

Probably Morrissey's intention was more 'to cleanse the world of sexual stereotypes, because they can be extremely dangerous'. But the first Smiths record sleeve supported Marr's comment. Only John Lennon had put a naked man (himself, alongside wife Yoko Ono) on the cover of a record, in 1968, but *Unfinished Music No. 1: Two Virgins* was sold in a brown wrapper and, in any case, the intent was anything but homoerotic. So Morrissey was the first to create that frisson with the Smiths' debut single 'Hand In Glove', housed in a photo (taken by Lou Thomas of the gay porn studio Target) from Margaret Walter's book *The Nude Male*, of a man whose curved buttocks commanded the attention. Nudity, Walter had claimed, signified both liberation and 'a licentiousness which threatens traditional moral standards,' which were Morrissey's core themes – romanticism, shock, vulnerability, confrontation.

The B-side 'Handsome Devil' pushed those particular envelopes harder: 'A boy in the bush is worth two in the hand/I think I can help you get through your exams,' was enough to have the tabloid press accuse Morrissey of paedophilia. The fuss died down, though not the homoeroticism, as The Smiths' second single 'This Charming Man' detailed the charged moment that the anonymous 'charming man' offers a ride home after the narrator's bicycle wheel is punctured,[1] But when the opening words of the Smiths' self-titled debut album (from 'Reel Around The Fountain') were 'It's time the tale was told/Of how you took a child and you made him old', the paedophilic charges doubled, and Morrissey would never return to any such point of homoeroticism or use such a provocative image on record.

---

1 Morrissey lifted the 'A jumped-up pantry boy who never knew his place' in 'This Charming Man' from the 1972 film adaptation of Anthony Shaffer's 1970 play *Sleuth*, one of the very few UK productions centred on a homoerotic relationship.

The Eighties: Pop Comes Out

As a fan of American underground culture – before The Smiths, he wrote two short books, on James Dean and the New York Dolls – Morrissey was also enthralled by Warhol's superstars. A still of handsome hustler Joe Dallesandro from (Warhol assistant) Paul Morrissey's 1968 film *Flesh* adorned the cover of the Smiths' self-titled debut album, while Candy Darling, from Paul Morrissey's 1971 film *Women In Revolt*, was chosen for the band's single 'Sheila Take A Bow', an ode to female independence with the observation, 'I'm a girl and you're a boy'. Let's not forget the double meaning of the album title *The Queen Is Dead*, and Morrissey's tribute to fifties' icon Johnny Ray – wearing a hearing aid.

It was ironic that rock's first advocate for celibacy was the only one in alternative rock addressing sexuality; otherwise, the new wave of guitar bands that followed in the wake of post-punk on both sides of the Atlantic dug deep into sixties-influenced sound and fashion, with the emphasis on druggy escapism and none on the original era's political acumen. R.E.M. managed to break away from the herd as the band became more successful by addressing their country's political and ecological woes, but the AIDS crisis' impact on Michael Stipe ensured that that sex was still off the singer's agenda.

The odd lyric emerged to clutch on to, however obscure, such as 'Vicky's Box' from Rhode Island quartet Throwing Muses, written by the band's female singer and guitarist Kristin Hersh: 'He won't ride in cars anymore/It reminds him of blowjobs/That he's a queer.' At the same time, three alternative (or 'indie', as it became known) bands were fronted by gay men and openly so: Mark Dumais of New York's Crash, Mark Eitzel of San Francisco's American Music Club and James Maker (Morrissey's chum) of Manchester's Raymonde. Yet none of the trio's songs clarified their singers' sexuality, though a Raymonde B-side, 'Eulogy To Harvey Milk', was a rare acknowledgement of an identifiably political figure for the more informed fan. But a more accurate portrait of the scene was Eitzel's memory of coming out in an interview with *Genre* magazine in 1985 and then no interviewer asking him about his sexuality for almost ten years.

Homocore: queer punk comes of age

The two-pronged spearhead of gay-meets-hardcore that was the Dicks and Big Boys had not lasted; in 1983, Gary Floyd left Austin for San Francisco and in 1986 he started the more bluesy, apolitical Sister Double Happiness with the Dicks' female drummer Lynn Perko. Randy Turner was political more by action than content and concentrated as much on theatre performance and spoken word as music. The gay underground resistance was at an all-time low – except for a small cell in Toronto that came of age in the early eighties.

In 1980, Caroline Azar had high hopes to be an actor (she now works as a playwright) – but after seeing the all-female trio Second Unit at a house party, she was impelled to take another direction. 'I was well acquainted with the punk and pop girl music of the day, like the Slits, but Second Unit – a queer, baby dyke trio – were the most explosive, wonderful, addictive sound, better than any other high,' she recalls. 'It was ... bullets, flowers, colour, form, sex, anger, power – it was all there. Because they only had three songs, they played them again twenty minutes later but I wished they played them ten, twenty times.'

Second Unit decided to move on, to find a new singer and, on finding Azar, to change band names: 'Caroline brought so much to the band – her singing, her amazing lyrics and keyboard playing. It was like a new group,' says Jones. They chose Fifth Column, a term first used in the Spanish civil war that became synonymous with any group that wanted to undermine a larger group. 'Provoked by mutual pals to audition' for the role of singer, Azar was alarmed to be chosen: 'I was only seventeen at the time and the real dark horse. I couldn't play and I had never sung live.' But attitude was everything in punk and, armed with a Casio keyboard (the band told her to find an instrument), Azar set to work.

'I know about psychedelia, soul and folk but not so much about R&B, except for its political aspect that spiritually rescued black people,' she says. 'But for me, punk is my rescue music, more than protest folk, because it referred to our time where the neo-con movement of [UK prime minister Margaret] Thatcher and [Canadian prime minister Brian]

Mulroney was sprouting a first-time, absurdist and inhumane presence over the people. And I always wanted to rescue kids, I couldn't stand the tyranny of adults. Fifth Column couldn't just critique a lack of justice and equity, we needed to describe it, as viscerally and compassionately, with teen anguish, as possible. We had no other reference of this type of expression, so we had to make it ourselves.'

As teenagers lacking 'dyke' role models, Fifth Column were more in touch with feminism over sexuality: for example, they only gave their initials when talking to any interviewers rather than their surnames passed down from their fathers. Azar and G.B. Jones (drums, guitar) became a couple, but were closeted to the outside world. For starters, says Azar, 'Lesbians didn't know about style, punk, history, there was no glamour or drama there, they were luddites!' On top of that, 'the only way to be recorded and booked for shows was to be in cahoots with men and they weren't comfortable with lesbian or even bisexuals and, if they were, it would be only to eroticise it. We were young and pretty and we'd get called slutty; that we were starting a band to get laid. It was like catch-22; we were too punk to be gay and too queer to be punk. Outside of Canada, I think it would have been different.'

Azar's lyrics, if they referenced sexuality at all, were coded, such as Fifth Column's debut single, the woozy, broody 'Boy, Girl': 'It was a modern joke about gender, about when you see a man and woman, you assume they're partners but it could be a dyke and a fag.' Other coded songs were written, 'Like this hidden eroticism for girls who we hoped would pick up on it and come to our shows, because it was guys otherwise, or girls drunk on their arms and yelling at us to get off the stage. I had no idea so many people were threatened by what we did, but I thought, If they don't like it that much, we should keep doing it, and it doesn't get more punk than that!'

Azar and Jones would still date men, 'but unique men, men with nice personalities, who were comfortable with who we were. But we were all in love with each other first.' The couple split but stayed friends; other women joined (sometimes dating each other) and left the band

and, over time, they grew more confident about being out and in their songs. 'Fairview Mall Story' from 1985's debut album *To Sir With Hate* was based on the true story of thirty-two men arrested for having sex in a men's bathroom in St Catherines, Ontario, whose names were ruthlessly spilled to the media.

'An old man very close to me,' Azar says, 'he was abused as a child in a monastery. Boys reared to become a patriarchy, yet betrayed by their patriarchy, the tyranny from adult males to child males was horrid. He was a very complex individual and I wrote it for him. He could have been one of those poor men caught.'

Fifth Column were also active in other areas; Jones and Azar with a third, Candy Parker, published five issues of a fanzine, *HideZine*; starting with the second issue, it came with cassette compilations with Fifth Column tracks alongside other post-punk bands such as Boulder, Colorado punks Anti-Scrunti Faction (ASF). Fifth Column also appeared in the pages of another fanzine, *J.D.s*, which Jones and film student/journalist Bruce LaBruce launched in 1986 that aimed to put the nascent gay punk scene on the map. Jones says, 'Caroline asked him to dance with the band and then we stuck Bruce into "Fairview Mall Story". That was really the beginnings of homocore.'

LaBruce – born Justin Stewart or Bryan Bruce depending which source you trust – is one of the most lauded and controversial of queer filmmakers, from his skinhead romance *No Skin Off My Ass* (1993) to his zombie film *Otto; Or Up with Dead People* (2008) and the comedy *Gerontophilia* (2013), about sexual attraction to senior citizens. In 1986, LaBruce was still a frustrated film graduate with eclectic taste in music across hard, glam and folk, soul, disco, Peggy Lee and Barbra Streisand. Rough Trade also 'blew my mind. Elton John's *Goodbye Yellow Brick Road* was an eye-opener too. Songs about suicidal lesbian runaways, hustlers, sexually ambiguous glam rock stars and tragic Hollywood icons revered by gays really informed my emergent sexual identity.'

G. B. Jones begun totting up those punk songs with queer references such as the Dicks, Bad Boys, Angry Samoans and Nip Drivers'

'Quentin' (a tribute to Britain's self-described 'stately homo', Quentin Crisp)[1] and stuck them on a cassette for friends. Inspired, she imagined the concept of 'Homocore' and thought of a fanzine with the same focus and asked LaBruce to co-publish it. *J.D.s* stood for Juvenile Delinquents but also the rebels James Dean and J. D. Salinger.

'It was a dirty little gay-punk fanzine, which we started out of boredom and frustration with Toronto and the gay scene, which was notoriously dull,' LaBruce says. 'We wanted to stir the pot. Our strategy was to create the illusion that there was a full-blown, wild, and subversive queer punk scene going on here, when actually it was just me and a couple of our dyke and faggot friends hanging out, taking photos and movies of each other and producing fanzines.'

As Jones saw it, 'It was like they took the finale of the ultra-queer *Rocky Horror Picture Show* to heart, when everyone sings, "Don't dream it, be it".'[2]

J.D.s was as much a reaction to the hardcore scene. 'Queers were not exactly welcome,' LaBruce recalls. 'I was beaten or threatened a couple of times at shows. I was very obviously an effeminate homo-punk. So we got our revenge with *J.D.s*. It not only gave Toronto the international reputation of being a hotbed of queer punk activism, but we also criticised these macho mosh-pit punks for claiming to be radical, yet actually being sexist and homophobic and quite conventional and homo-normative when it came to sexual and social relations. We'd sometimes invite over straight punk boys and get them drunk, have them take their clothes off and photograph them in compromising positions for our little fanzines.'

Over in LA, two 'beautiful black militant drag queen love goddesses'

---

[1] Crisp was, after Oscar Wilde, the most pioneering homo of them all, dying his hair purple and wearing make-up as early as the thirties. In 1968, he wrote an autobiography, *The Naked Civil Servant* (Jonathan Cape) which was turned into a film for TV. Crisp had a new career, as a writer and raconteur, mostly in the US after he moved to New York in 1981. He died in 1999.

[2] http://shamelessmag.com/blog/entry/the-greatest-band-youve-never-heard-of-fifth-colu

– according to *J.D.s* – were already publishing their own queer zine: one had taken the name Fertile LaToya Jackson, which was also the fanzine's name; the other was Vaginal Crème Davis.

'There was no coming out process for someone like me; I was hatched from an egg complete with false eyelashes and pumps,' claims Davis, born Clarence Sanders in LA, and now resident in Berlin, working in performance art and music. She started calling herself Vaginal Davis at thirteen: 'From middle school on, I came to class wearing outrageous outfits, many made by my mother, who had been part of a radical lesbian separatist feminist collective. So floating around from her side was womyns' music like Holly Near and Cris Williamson. And because of my cousin Carla [Duplantier, lesbian drummer of LA punks the Controllers], I felt much more comfortable in a bull dagger and bull dyke scene then a gay male scene.'

Davis' pioneering transgender/punk sensibility flowered on their fanzine, 'an underground rag that featured SoCal punk scene gossip,[1] photos of hot Huntington Beach surfers and wistful musings by Miss Davis herself,' says LaBruce.

The two fanzines shared the same target audience: 'Lonely, isolated queer kids who were bullied or had no social life because they dressed alternatively, baby butches, femme faggots, outcasts, exiled sexual outlaws,' says LaBruce. 'We were very idealistic in that regard.'

J.D.s combined soft (visual) and hard (written) porn with punk-style collages, Jones' *Tomgirl* drawings (lesbian erotica inspired by Tom of Finland), guest contributors like Vaginal Crème Davis and aspiring author Dennis Cooper. LaBruce and Jones also provided playlists of queer-themed songs: one was Beefeater's 'Fred's Song', 'a love ballad dedicated to a skinhead!' says LaBruce. The song triggered *No Skin Off My Ass*, which almost single-handedly launched a new wave of queer indie cinema.

---

[1] The gossip included 'outing rock and punk rock stars,' says Davis. Though she proceeds to list numerous musicians whose 'fluid sexualities' she had written about, including pieces in her two syndicated columns 'Yes Ms Davis' and 'Because I Said So' for the *LA Weekly*; it's best not to spread unsubstantiated material.

The playlists included the occasional UK record, but there was only one British punk band with identifiably gay members – singer Andy Martin and guitarist Dave Fannning of London-based the Apostles. Like their US counterparts, the band risked accusations of homophobia when they wrote satires such as 'Kill Or Cure' and 'Fucking Queer', one of punk's greatest subversive songs, sung from a viewpoint of a violent homophobe, who concludes: 'For one day I awoke, my thoughts no longer dim/I met this strange young lad and fell in love with him/So I realise while I'm lying here/The truth that I despise that I'm a fucking queer.'

Both Martin and Fanning officially came out in 1986, which Martin says halved their correspondence from fans, and lost them 40 per cent of their sales. 'Coincidence? I doubt it,' he wrote.

'Punks and anarchists are notoriously conservative,' Martin told *Homocore* fanzine in 1989, just before the Apostles became Academy 23 and adopted a more melodic post-punk style.

J.D.s' other UK recommendations were similarly eclectic, such as Coil's electronic dirge 'The Anal Staircase' and Shock Headed Peters' unique 'I, Bloodbrother Be', which paired wonky jazz-swing with the memorable lines, 'I want to walk through Sodom with a boy on my arm . . . nothing out of our loins, sweetie, will ever see the light of day' – written and sung by heterosexual sympathiser Karl Blake.

The UK lacked a comparable queer music fanzine, while the US sprouted a 'zine scene, with the likes of *Boysville USA*, *My Comrade*, *AQUA*, *F Plus F* and *Chainsaw*, while the San Francisco-based *Homocore* took the artform to a more professional level.

One of *Homocore* two co-founders, Tom Jennings admits he was more driven by the culture: 'The phenomenon of punk was great, the music not always so!' Even aspects of the community didn't impress him: 'A lot of San Fran queer folk were a mess and a handful quite ruinous,' he claims, singling out the Hags, an amphetamine-gobbling crew of 'scary young dykes.' On the plus side, Michael Joseph Collins, his band the Popstitutes and his club Klubstitute 'were deeply important.

They spawned all sorts of hilarious and bizarro stuff. The more male, macho default punk stuff was secondary.'

Jennings' personality was different to the other fanzine editors, as a skilled software programmer and pioneering inventor of the online 'bulletin board' FidoNet. He used the profits from selling software to the military to restore a warehouse that was used for skateboarding, live shows, living space and publishing. Jennings secured international distribution for *Homocore* and the contents reflected his politically and community-minded interests. He also staged guerrilla-style concerts around San Francisco which the police would invariably close down, but legitimate ventures too. He compiled bills that included hardcore's most popular band Fugazi, whose efforts to rid hardcore of its macho identity included supporting queer bands. The band also headlined shows for San Francisco's Positive Force, political activists who provided social care and AIDS counselling for the city's lesbian, gay and transgender youth.

One Positive Force show took a stand against anti-sodomy laws with Broken Siren and Bad Pieces, both outfits including gay and lesbian members. But the homocore scene was still tiny compared to hardcore's sprawling reach and, in an attempt to further stir the pot, LaBruce and Jones succeeded in having the country's biggest zine, *Maximum Rocknroll*, publish their manifesto 'Don't be Gay or, How I Learned to Stop Worrying and Fuck Punk Up the Ass'. It began by explaining the original meanings of 'punk' and 'faggot' – 'dried wood used for tinder. Homosexuals, witches, criminals, all denounced as enemies of the state, were once burned at the stake. It's no accident that "punk" and "faggot" have a similar root. Whaddyaknow. Punks are fags, too. Better start worrying now.'

The argument moved on to how 'punk' was also a term used in jail for those inmates 'recruited to serve other prisoners' sexual desires ... these original punks, many of them delinquent minors imprisoned for breaking society's rules, became, on the inside, sexual outlaws as well.' Punk also meant CBGB and Max's Kansas City 'and rejecting social norms'.

The hardcore scene was annihilated: 'Let's face it. Going to most punk shows today is a lot like going to the average fag bar (MIGHTY SPHINCTER notwithstanding): all you see is big macho "dudes" in leather jackets and jeans parading around the dance floor/pit, manhandling each other's sweaty bodies in proud display. The only difference is that at the fag bar, females have been almost completely banished, while at the punk club they've just been relegated to the periphery, but allowed a pretense [sic] of participation (i.e., girlfriend, groupie, go-fer or post-show pussy).'

Meanwhile, back on the dancefloor . . .

Though Bruce LaBruce's early loves also included Gloria Gaynor and Donna Summer, his list didn't embrace the Hi-NRG scene, which had fallen into the same creative trap as disco by churning out identikit tracks for an unquestioning target market. Hazel Dean's 'Searchin' (I Gotta Find a Man)', Miquel Brown's 'So Many Men, So Little Time', Eartha Kitt's 'Where Is My Man', Gloria Gaynor's old-school cover of 'I Am What I Am', the signature song from the first Broadway smash with a gay storyline, *La Cage Aux Folles*[1], US duo Modern Rocketry's plainly named 'Homosexuality', whose video featured pop's first screened kiss between two men . . . All had their supporters, but surely only 'It's Raining Men', by Sylvester's former backing singers Two Tons O'Fun, reborn as the Weather Girls, could be considered a timeless classic.

Divine had also forged a new career outside of John Waters films, making Hi-NRG tracks with producer Bobby Orlando such as 'Shoot Your Shot', switching to the UK team of Stock, Aitken and Waterman (SAW) for the tongue-lashing camp of 'You Think You're A Man', a UK Top 20 hit which Divine performed on *Top Of The Pops*. The show

---

[1] *La Cages Aux Folles* was a French stage comedy from 1975 about a gay male couple who have to convince their adopted son's prospective in-laws that they are both straight. It became a very successful film in 1978 and subsequently a stage musical, written by Jerry Herman, the gay composer behind the scores for *Mame* and *Hello Dolly!*, earlier iconic favourites among Broadway's adoring gay fanbase.

had never featured a drag queen or a 'monster' as John Waters lovingly referred to her – 'Divine never wanted to pass as a woman.'

Another Hi-NRG UK hit, 'Male Stripper', was the work of Man2Man. With eldest brother Mandy leaving the nest, Paul and Miki Zone had finally released albums as the Fast, *The Fast For Sale* (1980) and *Leather Boys From The Asphalt Jungle* (1981), before reinventing themselves as a synth-pop duo. Paul also decided 'to wise up and stop having hetero encounters! Miki agreed that I should be our spokesman and to gear things toward homo activities. We felt we could anything with that musical style, though it wasn't called Hi-NRG yet.'

The Zones had also tried out Bobby Orlando for the last Fast single 'At The Gym', before adopting the name Man's Favourite Sport and finally Man2Man, whose look crossed dressy new romantic and gay clone fashion. The duo recorded a Hi-NRG version of the Four Seasons' 'Walk Like A Man' but Divine copied it and his more lascivious vocal and SAW's classier production snared the UK Top 30 hit. But Man2Man persevered, releasing the *Malenergy* album in 1986, co-produced and scored by Man Parrish.

The collaboration hit the jackpot, starting in Mexico where 'Hottest Of The Hot' was a no. 1 single before 'Male Stripper' became the UK's no. 1 club/dance record of 1986. Any joy was quickly annulled by Miki Zone's AIDS-related death on the last day of the year (Mandy would succumb ten years later). When 'Male Stripper' was re-released in early 1987 and broke into the UK Top 5, Paul was the only Zone left to mime on *Top Of The Pops*. He was accompanied by two flexing, twirling and stripping dancers, a mutant collision of Frankie meets Village People meets Boystown Gang.[1] If the US didn't care for gay dance music, the UK seemed to enjoy its party-hard mood.

For 'Male Stripper', Zone used the band name Man2Man Meet Man Parrish: 'We asked if he would not mind using the title. We thought it

---

1 After Miki's death, Paul Zone renamed the act Man To Man and recorded a follow-up single, a cover of Grace Jones' 'I Need A Man', a UK no. 43 hit and his last record to chart.

was like the Wolfman meets the Mummy or Godzilla meets King Kong,' says Zone. Parrish, however, says the first he knew about it was when he was told he had a Top 10 record in the UK. He says he was never paid: 'Paul bought a condo apartment off that record and I was penniless.'

Parrish found compensatory employment as the tour manager of a resuscitated Village People. The troupe – with a new police officer and construction worker, the first in a long line of revamps – had ditched Jacques Morali once they'd discovered they'd never transcend the status of hired dancers to share in the profits. They had a new romantic makeover (it flopped) before returning to the classic image, making them the first seventies revivalists of the eighties. 1985's 'comeback' album, *Sex Over The Phone*, was a stronger statement than before and an ironic comment on AIDS. The video went further, showing one of the troupe climbing into bed for a hot solo session, but a succession of women waiting at the other end of the phone. Who were they kidding?

The Village People tried gamely to keep up with the trends; new wave, funk, Hi-NRG, even early hip hop, but they could never replicate the commercial punch of their hits and never managed to tap the house and gospel-influenced (and female-fronted) garage sound that was now reshaping dance music.

Larry Levan's Paradise Garage in New York and Frankie Knuckles' Warehouse in Chicago were still ruling, as well as Knuckle's own club, the Power Plant, after the Warehouse doubled its prices and tried to attract more than its initial gay black crowd. Knuckles had also bought his first drum machine and started making records[1] and, sensing that the club scene had peaked, closed the Power Plant down in 1986. The Paradise Garage closed a year later when co-owner Michael Brody died of AIDS and Levan – addicted to heroin – couldn't find another residency.

Ron Hardy, who replaced Knuckles at the Warehouse – soon rebranded Muzic Box – was equally visionary. He would open his DJ

---

1 Knuckles' 1987 single 'Your Love' was voted best house track by *Mixmag*.

stints with the title track of Frankie Goes To Hollywood's *Welcome To The Pleasuredome*, but he made his mark by securing rhythm tracks from a cache of Chicago house producers such as Marshall Jefferson and Phuture's DJ Pierre, the man behind the twelve-minute 'Acid Tracks', built around the squelching sound of the Roland TB-303 bass synth. The track was exported to the clubs in Europe's Balearic Islands, especially Ibiza, which played soulful house music alongside a minimalist, electronic version of dance. This emanated from Detroit and was christened techno, spearheaded by schoolfriends Derrick May, Kevin Saunderson and Juan Atkins, the straight fraternity to house's gay brotherhood.

As Knuckles found a new lease of life in London, with a four-month residency at Delirium in 1987, UK DJs began to import the Balearic mix back to the UK, but 'Acid Tracks' was the defining, influential sound and the resulting array of tracks led to a new term, acid house, just as the MDMA drug derivative ecstasy was breaking through. Not only was UK club culture irrevocably altered, so was youth culture. The immersive experience of the formative discos and the latterday gay clubs, was now felt in straight clubs and helped foster a mood of acceptance. Any unease around the mix of gay and straight on the dancefloor melted away.

Britain – the backlash

Just as it seemed acceptance was within grasp, arch homophobe Margaret Thatcher's Conservative government in the UK cracked down on the acid house 'rave' scene and its accelerated drug use and on homosexuality, as if it was a similar social threat. In May 1988, Section 28 of the Local Government Act instigated a ban on any 'promotion' of homosexuality as an acceptable alternative lifestyle. Section 28 had a galvanising effect on the UK's gay resistance, prompting the creation of Stonewall, a grassroots organisation. It had visible, recognisable patrons, such as actor Ian McKellen and soap opera actor Michael Cashmore.

Tom Robinson was still making music but, after his biggest hit single, 'War Baby', hit UK no. 6 in 1982, he'd settled into a steady, if unspectacular, pattern of records with a more generic mix of quasi-funk and ballads. He averaged five songs per album through the decade that reflected his homosexuality and even updated '(Sing If You're) Glad To Be Gay', in 1987 and in 1989, to reflect the right-wing press' sensationalist reporting, from Boy George's heroin addiction to AIDS: 'And now there's a nightmare they blame on the gays/It's brutal and lethal and slowly invades/The medical facts are ignored or forgot/By the bigots who think it's the judgement of God.'

'Five or ten years down the line, you have to start changing the words because the external situation has altered,' Robinson reasons. 'The arrival of AIDS and then Section 28, for instance. I never wanted it to become a fossilised museum piece about ancient injustices. It was always intended more as journalism than poetry.'[1]

Robinson's charting days were over but Jimmy Somerville had remained in touch and, after burning out after fame, and falling out with his Bronski Beat bandmates, he'd formed the Communards with pianist Richard Coles, an old friend from the *Framed Youth* era. Named after the nineteenth-century French revolutionaries, the modern-day Communards would be better known for their cover versions of disco classics than for providing music for climbing the barricades.

The Communards first reclaimed 'Don't Leave Me This Way' from

---

[1] The media were a constant target of derision in every version, 'the gutterpress dailies' as Robinson sang. He wasn't just inspired by the *Sun*, the UK's best-selling tabloid newspaper, famed for its lies, celebrity focus, xenophobia and all-round low-brow appeal, but the reporting of a new phase in his life: living with a woman, and parenthood. He'd met his partner Sue – who identified as lesbian – at a Gay Switchboard benefit. When Robinson talked to both *Capital Gay* and the *Pink Paper* newspapers, 'their reactions were, so you're bisexual? Big deal. Non-story.' It took the *Sunday People* tabloid two years to pick up the story, headlined STARS WHO GO STRAIGHT – 'which was damaging and inaccurate, as I've never claimed to be straight,' says Robinson. 'I've always liked men.' He thinks the hospital tipped off the paper when their first baby was born and, to ward off another negative story, agreed to publish their own baby pictures, which were sent to the *People*'s rivals, 'these scummy rags, with our most intimate moment. The result was the LGBT community see me apparently bragging about my "new-found heterosexuality" with the inevitable "Glad to be Dad" headline. It caused a lot of misunderstanding that no amount of rebuttal and clarification managed to redress.'

Philly soul kings Harold Melvin and the Blue Notes, by way of Thelma Houston's 1977 disco version. Theirs was a UK no. 1 and 1986's best-selling UK single and also made the US top 40, while Houston's own version was adopted as an unofficial theme song for the AIDS epidemic. An update of Gloria Gaynor's 'Never Can Say Goodbye' was a UK no. 4. They released original singles too, but only 1988's 'For A Friend' was among their best recorded work, a piercing ballad about Somerville's oldest friend, Mark Ashton[1], who had died only twelve days after his HIV-positive diagnosis.

Still the AIDS-inspired songs mounted up. In Somerville's absence, Bronski Beat released an AIDS-inspired single, 'Dr John' ('Loving is different, so full of fear/Can't love you right, until the cure is here'). San Franciscan gay couple (Ron) Romanovsky and (Paul) Phillips, who had been recording comedy songs since 1984, released 'Living With AIDS' and 'Be On The Safe Side' on their 1988 album *Emotional Rollercoaster*.

Across the country, in New York, the Flirtations – billed as 'the world's first openly gay, politically-correct doo wop singing a cappella group' – compromised six gay men, including Michael Callen, who was still campaigning and singing, at AIDS demonstrations, ACT UP rallies and gay pride events.

But songs and demonstrations alone weren't going to swing public opinion. Another group of six gay men, mostly graphic designers, but also including Jorge Socarras, Patrick Cowley's close friend (and collaborator), gathered together to hash out a solution.

Despite living openly through his life, Socarras had always 'resisted easy labelling, musically or sexually' by the media. But times had changed. 'Disillusioned by the pressure of commercialisation and the dissolute calibre of many music industry people and increasingly upset by the growing number of friends succumbing to AIDS, I'd quit music,'

---

1 Mark Ashton is the gay rights activist at the centre of the 2014 film *Pride*, about the LGBT activists who raised money to help families affected by the British coal miners' strike in 1984. Both communities were united by their opposition to Thatcher's Conservative government.

he recalls. By the end of the sextet's gathering in 1987, they had a logo – the pink triangle – combined with a slogan, 'Silence = Death'.

The 'slogo' was plastered anonymously around New York, supported by the statement, 'Silence about the oppression and annihilation of gay people, then and now, must be broken as a matter of our survival.' Simultaneously, the sextet heard of the emergency meeting at the LGBT Center – named after the new coalition of lesbian, gay, bisexual and transgender communities, to emphasise diverse sexual and gender identities – which gave birth to ACT UP. The slogo was offered to ACT UP to use 'and the rest is history,' says Socarras.

The ballroom scene

The battle for survival and pride was on, once again. From the formation of the GLF to that of ACT UP, there had been no new political gains and much more was at stake because of AIDS and it was here that ACT UP had their most telling success. In 1989, seven members invaded New York's stock exchange and chained themselves to a balcony to protest the high price of the only approved AIDS drug, AZT, produced by the pharmaceutical company Burroughs Wellcome. Days later, the price came down from approximately ten thousand dollars per patient per year to $6,400.

In New York, the community most vulnerable to AIDS needed all the help it could get, as the one with the least opportunities for education and welfare – the same predominantly poor, black, gay and transgender community that had lit the fuse at Stonewall and had been subsequently marginalised as the pink dollar – and pound – were lavished on having a good time.

The gay black community was long used to providing for its own. Serving a social function as well as providing an expression of identity, drag balls had been held since the Harlem Renaissance and then driven deep underground, though echoes had resonated through the Jewel Box Revue and amateur drag night at Harlem's Apollo Theatre. There was also Flawless Mother Sabrina's travelling pageant, which mixed black and white contestants. In the sixties, the first drag balls of colour were staged in Harlem and other major cities with prominent black populations, resulting in events such as 1968's Black Pearl International Awards at Washington's Hilton hotel.

What the drag balls couldn't provide was security, but in the early seventies, contestants who had shown well at the drag balls began to gather their own followers. They were grouped in a 'house' overseen by a 'den mother' – or both a mother and father figure, who offered assistance and support and sometimes a place to stay. Their children were gay and transgender youths rejected by their biological families or who felt constricted at home. The earliest house is thought to have been started in 1970 by Pepper LeBeija, followed by Mother Dorian and Father Chipper's House of Corey. The Houses of Dior and Chanel, spins on the perfumery brands, followed. Most houses took on their founder's drag name, such as the Houses of Wong, Dupree, Omni, Ebony, Xtravaganza, Pendavis, Ninja – there were twenty-seven in New York alone by the end of the eighties.

The first drag ball hosted by a house was given by Crystal LaBeija in 1972. In 1966, she'd won the New York regional of Mother Sabrina's pageant, as featured on *The Queen* documentary, but when she won third place in the nationals the camera caught her scowling. As the winner – Miss Philadelphia – was about to be announced, LeBeija walked off the stage.

'Crystal, where are you going?' said Sabrina. 'This is not the time to be showing temperament.' The camera also caught a full-scale row as LeBeija claimed racism had undermined her rightful win.[1] By hosting her own drag pageant, LeBeija reasoned, justice would be done.

LeBeija's drag ball unwittingly triggered a trend, as each house

---

1 Tim Lawrence's excellent feature 'Listen, and You Will Hear all the Houses that Walked There Before: a History of Drag Balls, Houses and the Culture of Voguing', claims LeBeija was 'one of the few black queens to be awarded a queen of the ball title at a white-organised ball,' though often, 'black queens were expected to "whiten up" their faces if they wanted to have a chance of winning the contests.' www.timlawrence.info/articles2/2013/7/16/listen-and-you-will-hear-all-the-houses-that-walked-there-before-a-history-of-drag-balls-houses-and-the-culture-of-voguing

decided to host their own. The competitive edge grew as members began to catwalk to win trophies, based on skills, costumes, appearance and attitude. It was as if street gangs were created to be fabulous and fashionable rather than criminal. If the contestants were not having to sashay and lip-sync for their lives, at least they had felt valued and rewarded.

'It's like crossing over into the looking glass,' said a member of the House of Xtravaganza in Jenny Livingston's *Paris Is Burning*, the 1990 documentary that brought international attention to the 'ballroom' scene. 'You feel a hundred per cent right, being gay.' Another member talked about contestants having the opportunity to experience fame or glamour, like a celebrity might. But there was a rough side; once ballroom was established, houses sometimes didn't accept new members unless they could ably compete and win trophies. Even here, it was survival of the fittest.

Paris Dupree, who had founded her house in 1975 and whose annual drag ball gave *Paris Is Burning* its title, is believed to have invented the categories for competition. Contests were held for butch queens, femme queens, butch queens in drag, butches (masculine lesbians), women (or female), men and OTA (Open To All). It meant all chosen gender expressions and even sexualities – you didn't have to be gay or lesbian – or of colour (the House of Field was white) to take part; you just had to compete for 'realness' in your chosen category. There were sub-categories too, such as 'town and country', 'girl going to school' and 'executive realness', 'body', 'runway/model effect' and 'bizarre'. But ballroom's most famous contest was the hand-based dance style of voguing.

In Tim Lawrence's liner notes for the 2012 compilation *Voguing and the House Ballroom Scene of New York City 1989-92*[1], DJ David DePino claims that voguing began at the New York club Footsteps. 'Paris Dupree was there and a bunch of these black queens were throwing shade [insults] at each other,' DePino recalled. 'Paris had a *Vogue* magazine in her bag and, while she was dancing, she took it out, opened

---

1 www.timlawrence.info/articles2/2013/7/2/voguing-and-the-house-ballroom-scene-of-new-york-city-1989-92-soul-jazz

it up to a page where a model was posing and then stopped in that pose on the beat.' One of Dupree's rivals copied her, only for Paris to strike another pose. 'At first they called it posing and then, because it started from *Vogue* magazine, they called it voguing,' DePino concluded.

Voguing quickly added a flurry of hand movements to its athletic poses, but it didn't require a costume. The trend spread to other clubs, first at the Paradise Garage (DJ Larry Levan belonged to the House of Wong) and also Tracks, presided over by DePino and the newest mixed temple of house, the Sound Factory, with DJ Junior Vasquez and later Frankie Knuckles.

The ballroom scene typically used house as its soundtrack, though there was room too for seventies soul, such as MSFB's 'Love Is The Message', Diana Ross' 'Love Hangover', plus Sylvester's 'You Make Me Feel (Mighty Real)', Loose Joints 'Is It All Over My Face?', Man Parrish's 'Hip Hop Be Bop' and 'Just an Illusion', the 1982 smash by UK trio Imagination, whose frontman Leee John was the queeniest frontman since Sylvester. Any track that encapsulated an extreme of emotion, or featured beats for dramatic voguing, was perfect for ballroom's grand gestures.

When the public got to see voguing, ballroom had a real chance for fame and glamour in a much more public arena. In 1987, UK soul singer Jody Watley featured voguing among the dance routines in the video for 'Still A Thrill' and the scene crossed over in 1989 when crafty opportunist Malcolm McLaren released 'Deep In Vogue', using samples from the still-unreleased *Paris Is Burning*[1] with Willi Ninja and Aldonna and Adrian Xtravaganza voguing in the video. In 1989 too, David Ian Xtravaganza released 'Elements Of Vogue' but its effect was negligible compared to that of *Paris Is Burning* (den mothers Pepper Lebeija, Dorian Corey and Willie Ninja were guests on Joan Rivers' TV talk show) and the world's best-selling single of 1990, Madonna's 'Vogue'.

None-more-canny Madonna was no stranger to nightclub trends.

---

1 McLaren had been sent an early tape of *Paris Is Burning* in the hope that he could raise the finance needed for Jenny Livingston to complete her film.

Having discovered voguing at New York's Love Ball of 1989, the Design Industry Foundation Fighting Aids (DIFFA) fundraiser modelled on a Harlem drag ball, Madonna had visited Tracks and the Sound Factory clubs to do more research. A team of dancers – foremost Luis and Jose Xtravaganza – were recruited for the 'Vogue' video, while the track's arrangement adopted elements of 'Elements Of Vogue'.[1]

Madonna was criticised for exploiting ballroom before moving on, and for reducing the scene's complexities to a soundbite: 'Strike a pose/ There's nothing to it.' Yet Madonna helped make voguing and ballroom part of a new lexicon of dance choreography, and employed Luis and Jose Xtravaganza for her Blonde Ambition world tour, captured in the 1990 film documentary *In Bed With Madonna* (in the US, *Madonna: Truth Or Dare*). Prince was a notable influence too, but no one bankrolled such a shift in sexual consciousness, across homosexuality, gender and female empowerment, more than 'Madge'.

Salim Gauwloos recalled the impact of a passionate kiss with fellow back-up dancer Gabriel Trupin in the documentary: 'I still get letters about that!' he said. 'Now everyone is kissing, but at the time people didn't think it was cool. We were just being ourselves. But it inspired a lot of people just to be yourself and express yourself.'

Fuck dance, let's art

Downtown as well, New York's arts scene was experiencing its own response to AIDS. Watching friends die, with funding restricted and – lest we forget – the unchanging inequality in civil rights, artists responded with anger and humour, costumes and scripts, across music, spoken word and theatre. The centre of the city's eccentric talents was the Pyramid club in the East Village: 'It was gay, it was straight, it was punk, it was rock'n'roll, it was drag . . . not just female drag, it was all sorts of drag,'[2]

---

1 According to Tim Lawrence, 'Vogue' also took the bass line from MFSB's 'Love Is The Message'.
2 *Nightclubbing: New York City's Pyramid Club*, http://daily.redbullmusicacademy.com/2014/03/nightclubbing-pyramid

recalled performance artist John Kelly, whose range of 'character studies' included painter Michelangelo Caravaggio, dramatist Antonin Artaud, Jean Cocteau and Joni Mitchell – not your typical drag act.

The Pyramid had opened in 1981; one of its earliest moves was to fund a mini-album, *No Motive*, by the post-punk-funk band 3 Teens Kill 4, formed by Brian Butterick, Jesse Hultberg and David Wojnarowicz, who'd all worked as busboys at Danceteria in 1980. *No Motive* was both angry (a cover of Chaka Kahn's 'Tell Me Something Good' included material from the newscast of the attempted assassination of President Reagan in 1981) and humorous – 'Bean Song' included the lines, 'We must, we must, we must improve our bust/The bigger the better, the tighter the sweater/The boys depend on us.'

Ultimately, 3 Teens Kill 4s' members are better known for what they did after; Wojnarowicz forged a reputation as a challenging mixed-media artist, motivated by AIDS; Butterick was better known as drag act Hattie Hathaway and as co-founder – with Jon Ingle, better known as the Lady Bunny – of the drag festival Wigstock, which would be an annual event from 1994 for all but one of the next twenty years. As the Pyramid's music promoter, Butterick also showcased acts such as the Red Hot Chili Peppers, Madonna and RuPaul, who made his New York debut at the club in 1982.

Like Lady Bunny, RuPaul Charles originally came from Atlanta, though he'd first moved to San Diego, California, at the age of fifteen to study performing arts. Using only his first name, RuPaul worked in both underground film and music, combining them for 1986's low-budget short *Star Booty*, in the lo-fi spirit of John Waters, with an accompanying soundtrack of songs. He also fronted a band, Wee Wee Pole, a brave, oddball collision between scratchy new wave and soul that played at the Pyramid. Butterick recalled RuPaul at that point was an 'androgynous punk', wearing a mohawk (or mohican) cut, with only 'a little nod to drag in there'.[1]

---

[1] http://daily.redbullmusicacademy.com/2014/03/nightclubbing-pyramid

The advent of cable TV and cheaper hand-held video cameras explains the surfeit of footage of the young RuPaul, from Wee Wee Pole to the 1987 Pyramid show, where he sang backing vocals alongside Vaginal Crème Davis for Glen Meadmore. Meadmore was a very tall Canadian musician with a penchant for drag and a punky hillbilly style inspired by the old hymns he'd heard his grandmother sing. His 1985 album *Chicken and Biscuits* and 1987's *Squaw Bread* albums sent up country music with 'I'll Teach You To Steal My Man' and 'Cornhole'.

Any queer musician who didn't make concessions for commercial advantage had room to roam. The experimental side of electronica, known as industrial music or industrial techno, after UK pioneers Throbbing Gristle's record label, had a fascination with sexual taboo and transgression, from leather and rubber fetish to homoerotica. This manifested in band names such as Surgical Penis Klinik[1], Revolting Cocks and Meat Beat Manifesto, though none of the line-ups had gay members.

Revolting Cocks was a side project involving members of two prominent industrial bands, Ministry (from the US) and Front 242 (from Belgium). They called their 1990 album *Beers, Steers + Queers*[2], released by Wax Trax!, a Chicago label run by gay couple Jim Nash and Dennie Flesher. They also released Divine's early records. But they didn't sign those industrial bands that showed a stronger gay aesthetic, such as Düsseldorf duo Deutsch Amerikanische Freundschaft (DAF), fronted by the openly bisexual Gabi Delgado[3] or the UK duo Nitzer Ebb, whose homoerotic video for Hi-NRG/techno hybrid 'Let Your Body Learn' dwelt on a glistening male gymnast. At least the UK's Test Department, who used sheets of metal, drills and chainsaws to create their fearsome

---

1 SPK was driven by New Zealander Graham Revell and the outfit was also variously known as SoliPsiK, SepPuKu, System Planning Korporation and Sozialistisches Patienten Kollektiv.
2 The album took its title from Stanley Kubrick's Vietnam-inspired film *Full Metal Jacket*: 'Only steers and queers come from Texas, Private Cowboy. And you don't look much like a steer to me so that kinda narrows it down.'
3 Delago was that rare case, a bisexual who decided to be straight, admitting that he stopped sleeping with men in 1982.

percussive din, had gay and straight members, but their aesthetic exuded physicality more than sexuality.

The band with the most to lose, given their commercial success, was Depeche Mode. They'd bravely abandoned perky synth-pop origins for a doomier, industrialised electronic dance that ironically turned them into one of the eighties' biggest acts, complete with gay and S&M imagery, especially from main songwriter Martin Gore. 'It wasn't so much the miniskirt over the leather pants with boots – that had a punky thing about it,' said singer Dave Gahan. 'But when Martin wore the full-length maxi with the cowboy hat – that was beyond gay.'

Playing arenas now, Depeche Mode helped popularise a freer view of gender and sexuality for the pop/teen market, as Bowie had fifteen years earlier. At the opposite end of the commercial scale, playing few shows and constructing artful videos to represent them, was the one industrial band formed by gay men, Coil.[1] Even before writing 'The Anal Staircase', their EP, *How To Destroy Angels*, was 'ritual music for the accumulation of male sexual energy'. The duo also wrote the soundtrack to Derek Jarman's 1985 film *The Angelic Conversation*, a homoerotic reading of Shakespeare's sonnets.[2]

The gay/experimental axis in America wasn't any *J.D.s* or *Homocore*-approved band, but the Frogs, formed by Milwaukee, Wisconsin, brothers Jimmy and Dennis Flemion. Their independent record label Matador smirked they were leaders of a 'new gay supremacy movement', delivered by lo-fi folky parodies such as 'Dykes Are We', 'Been A Month Since I Had A Man' and 'Hot Cock Annie' ('She's the one with cock and vagina combined'), all from their 1989 debut album *It's Only Right and Natural*. (But when the Frogs delivered their next album, *Racially Yours*, Matador felt a line had been crossed and refused to release it.)

---

1 Peter Christopherson was also one of Throbbing Gristle's four founding members.
2 Coil also contributed to the soundtrack of *Blue*, Jarman's last film, released in 1993, a year before he died of AIDS and to Julian Cole's 1986 film short *Ostia (The Death Of Pasolini)*. Jarman played the title role. He also directed a three-part video – impressionistic and homoerotic – for the Smiths on the release of their 1986 album *The Queen Is Dead*.

Presumably by 2012, when the Frogs released 'The Day I Got AIDS' ('Don't wait by the mailbox/This is my last letter/The day I got AIDS/ This is the happiest day of my life'), the brothers reckoned everyone could appreciate the humour. AIDS was no longer a death sentence. No doubt anyone not laughing deserved, as Fear vocalist Lee Ving thought, to be mocked. But in 1989, the omnipresent spectres of homophobia and AIDS made it hard for LGBT communities to see the Frogs' joke and not feel demeaned.

The backlash against the backlash

The British alternative rock scene continued along its day-dreamy, escapist, druggy path, following acid house on the dancefloor but, like the cavalry, a couple of knights led the charge.

Arguably, the first song with an openly gay subject in Irish history was written by Philip Chevron, former frontman of the Radiators From Space, one of Ireland's most beloved punk bands. They grew into the more melodic Radiators, before splitting in 1981. Chevron moved to London, and joined rowdy folk-revivalists the Pogues in time for their 1985 album *Rum, Sodomy and the Lash*. The album title referred to an unattributed quote about the British navy's favourite pursuits while 'The Old Main Drag' was an accordion-led waltz about Soho's gay scene, from rent boys ('In the dark of an alley you'd work for a fiver/For a swift one off the wrist') to nightlife ('The he-males and the she-males paraded in style').

When the Radiators reformed in 1987 for an AIDS benefit in Dublin – still the capital of a homophobic Catholic country – Chevron took the opportunity for a narrative of his own, though the exquisite 'Under Clery's Clock'[1], was far less salty and lurid. It was more an almost unbearably poignant lament about two teenage boys who arrange a rendezvous under the Dublin landmark of the title: 'Strange as it seems/ All I want is to embrace/By the street light/Just like other lovers do without disgrace... Long, lonely nights just imagining his face/Only in

---

1 'Under Clery's Clock' was released as a one-off single in 1989.

dreams do I kiss him and embrace/Cold morning light, he's gone with only shame to take his place.'

'Being gay and growing up in Ireland in the 1970s was a terrifying experience for any young man,' Chevron said. 'I decided to come out when I was in the Pogues because I thought, Well, here's an-all drinking, all-rousing, all-shagging, all stay-up-all-night sort of macho band which has me, too. With Bronski Beat and Frankie, it was very obvious, but I guess I wanted to show a more ordinary side to it.'[1]

'Under Clery's Clock' was timely, but it was also a one-off single by a band that no longer existed. The Smiths were gone too, with Morrissey going solo and abandoning his 'fourth sex' androgyny for a tougher image, fascinated by boxers and skinheads and attracting legions of adoring boy fans along the way. Could an openly gay frontman in indie rock be similarly appreciated?

The Smiths had been an important influence on Patrick Fitzgerald, growing up in the eighties on the outskirts of Manchester, 'in middle-class hell, friendless and isolated,' he says. 'I didn't properly realise I was queer until I was twenty. I was ashamed of my sexuality until that point, but I'd always looked for clues in music. Like Elton John's *Captain Fantastic* album, especially "Someone Saved My Life Tonight". Even though I was only ten, it felt like there were secrets in there, like in a few R.E.M. songs, trying to find kindred spirits in a world I didn't understand. Staring at the cover of Bowie's *Young Americans*, this androgynous person, not quite understanding and Queen – what a funny old name for a band, why not call themselves King? And the man's bum on the cover of the Smiths' "Hand In Glove". Hello, what's this? And Morrissey's lyrics, like, 'Shove me on the patio, I'll take it slowly,' how could people not realise how explicit it was? But he was still fudging it, it was still more cloaks, screens and closets. And wisely so, because it was a hostile [music] industry.'

Moving to London to study medicine, Fitzgerald was soon making

---

1 https://sites.google.com/site/cultureandireland/philip-chevron-artist-and-writer-radiator-and-pogue

music after meeting guitarist Julian Swales and drummer Dan Goodwin. As the archly named Kitchens Of Distinction, with Fitzgerald on vocals and bass, the trio's melodic wall of sound typified alternative rock at that time, but Fitzgerald's lyrics scythed through with an articulation at odds with the competition's asexual abstraction. KOD's single 'Prize' was a case in point, triggered by a documentary on Jean Genet – 'he was outspoken about his homosexuality' says Fitzgerald – and a pub conversation in which he was quizzed about the first time he'd had sex with a man.

'It seemed such a stupid question,' he recalls. 'To me, it was a jokey, suspicious way of asking and you know he wouldn't have asked a straight man the first time he got fucked – it's just not important. I was already bored of people commenting on gay life and with AIDS being such a killer at the time I felt the implication was, If you're having sex, you'll get AIDS. In 1984, the head of the surgical team said, "Well, if that's what they do, that's what they deserve." It was one of the reasons why I left medicine, though I'd wanted to make music.'

'Hammer', the maelstrom that closed KOD's 1989 album debut *Love Is Hell* – the three words that Fitzgerald's boyfriend wrote on the singer's toilet wall before walking out – was also inspired by AIDS: 'I wanted to hammer the point home, that anyone could get AIDS, that it wasn't a gay disease. There was this unrecognised horror of the disease among people and the universal nature of it and the idea of being an evil person. The idea was even floated that people with AIDS should be rounded up and put on some island – it wasn't far from a concentration camp mentality. "In A Cave" was the first song I wrote about not belonging, about jumping up to the moon and taking your lover with you. The only way to get the love you wanted was to leave this world.'

Fitzgerald was openly gay in the band's first interview, in the *NME*. 'I thought the rules had already broken by the late eighties,' he says. 'There'd been so much negativity around AIDS and Section 28, the whole gay thing had become so upfront and you'd had Jimmy Somerville and Morrissey, in his own way. It seemed so obvious to be out. I didn't realise it would be a problem.'

It began with the *NME* quoting Fitzgerald as saying, 'Our songs are usually about sex with men,' but didn't specify that he was the only gay man in the band. 'I didn't like the moniker of us being a "gay band", because it misrepresented Julian and Dan and it insinuated our music was different to what it was. At the time, there were no gay men out in rock and if you *were* gay, you obviously made silly dance music. It belittled what we were which was, basically, drunken men with guitars. It put us in a certain category of inaccessibility, along with the awful band name, which we chose because we were so dismissive of playing the game, of not taking ourselves seriously, except in my lyrics.'

Fitzgerald's two bandmates supported his openness and the painting of a (full-frontal) naked man on the cover of 'Prize'. 'It was extreme politics to them, so it fulfilled their ideas of nihilism, so that was allowed,' Fitzgerald explains, 'but Julian got really annoyed by being labelled a gay band and our American record label A&M said, Could we tone it down a bit? So I did, purposefully, I started putting "she" as well as "he" in lyrics . . . We'd got so much negativity from everyone around and it's weird to say it now, but playing music was more important to me than politics. I remember writing "Drive That Fast" which to me was about nothing and it became our most popular song! It wasn't the stuff of politics and sex and anger, which I wrote *Love Is Hell* about.'

Even the words to 'Gorgeous Love', about his boyfriend Paul ('I can feel the waves of your gorgeous love/And it hurts to think that this is seen as wrong'), from 1991's *Strange Free World* were more circumspect, avoiding gender. But by 1993's *The Death Of Cool*, Fitzgerald was again unapologetic, tackling homophobia after violent attacks on both himself and Paul on 'Breathing Fear' and 'the AIDS death song', 'When In Heaven'. Fitzgerald used it to admonish God for AIDS – 'and me saying I won't end up in hell, I'll be in heaven, as Marilyn Monroe, so fuck you! I was so angry about having our youth fucked around with . . . the hatred was really difficult to deal with.'

Packaging anger in black humour, the band dragged up for a video centred on a dazed drag Marilyn Monroe wandering the streets. Among the indie bands of the era, KOD were unique for their combination of weightiness and frivolousness, as only Fitzgerald had something so serious to kick against. But it could only carry them so far: 'Breathing Fear' was a US college radio hit and (just) made the UK Top 75 but, sadly, cool never dies and KOD, it seems, just weren't cool enough, or their words vague enough, to rise higher.

AIDS vs hip hop and rock

By 1989, songs about AIDS were commonplace, as antidotes and cures were sought, people kept dying and sides were taken. In 1987, Panama's salsa superstar Ruben Blades, releasing his first English language album *Nothing But The Truth*, included a moving paean to a dying friend in 'The Letter': 'I went to my home and sat and waited for tears to come/ But suddenly I changed my mind/Got up and played my favourite songs/I wanted to show myself that death could not take my heart.'

The same year, Prince's 'Sign O' The Times' was a very rare admission that AIDS was not an exclusive gay male disease: 'In France, a skinny man died of a big disease with a little name/By chance his girlfriend came across a needle and soon she did the same.'

Yet still the worlds of rock and rap stirred up homophobic currents, and worse, several of the messengers were huge stars. UK rock band Dire Straits' 1985 single 'Money For Nothing', a US no.1 taken from the 15-million-selling album Brothers In Arms (no.1 in eighteen countries), 'was a satire of a working man's jealousy of the rock stars he sees on MTV,' explained its frontman Mark Knopfler, but the lines 'The little faggot with the earring and the make-up . . . That little faggot, he's a millionaire,' would have had the same effect as Frank Zappa's similarly risky satire 'He's So Gay'.

Knopfler's gambit paled next to New York trio 1986 the Beastie Boys' debut album *License To Ill*, originally titled *Don't Be A Faggo*t until their record label Columbia intervened. The lyrics still included homophobic slurs and similar comments were made in interviews. Sales for the first crossover white rap band were to exceed ten million. The same figures were posted in 1988 by *G N' R Lies*, the third album from the most popular hard rock band of the day, Guns N' Roses. The closing track 'One In A Million' managed to be doubly offensive: 'Immigrants and faggots/They make no sense to me/They come to our country/And think they'll do as they please/Like start some mini-Iran or spread some fuckin' disease.'

Frontman Axl Rose insisted he was neither racist or homophobe, in the latter case pointing to his admiration for Freddie Mercury and Elton John. The real reasons, Rose said, were his 'bad experiences' with 'immigrants' and an attempted rape while hitchhiking to LA in his teens: but was Rose anti-homosexual, asked *Rolling Stone*'s Del James?

'I'm pro-heterosexual,' the singer replied. 'I can't get enough of women and I don't see the same thing that other men can see in men. I'm not into gay or bisexual experiences. But that's hypocritical of me, because I'd rather see two women together than just about anything else.'

Some observers held David Geffen, the head of Guns N' Roses' record label, responsible. In 1994, Geffen would tell journalist David Sheff that, 'I don't believe Axl Rose is homophobic. I know him,' though Geffen also felt the negative reaction that 'One In A Million' received 'was certainly deserved'. Yet Geffen Records also distributed albums by the label Def American, whose roster included the comedian Andrew Dice Clay, who made many homophobic remarks (for example, 'In Hollywood, they have herpes, AIDS and fag-it-is') in the name of entertainment.

Geffen, who had privately conceded that he was bisexual, had then attempted to go straight by exclusively dating women, including Cher. But the furore over Guns N' Roses and Clay inspired journalist Michelangelo Signorile of US news magazine *OutWeek* – co-founded by session musician and ACT UP member Gabriel Rotello – to challenge Geffen's sexuality, as part of the first wave of 'outing' celebrities who activists felt were harming the LGBT community by staying silent in the closet while their power and privilege facilitated homophobia.

The controversy of outing was to rage for years, though in Geffen's case, it had the desired effect; he severed ties with Def American, and came out as bisexual in a Vanity Fair interview. But the damage had been done. Hatred was manifest in thrash metal band M.O.D.'s 'A.I.D.S' which, in their song, stood for 'anally inflicted death sentence/That's what you get for having a penis up your ass.' They passed it off as humour, inspired by a Andrew Dice Clay sketch. In 1989, the debut album from Guns N' Roses wannabes Skid Row included 'Sweet Little Sister', whose friend was 'doin' time for kickin' ass on a queer'. Soon after, frontman Sebastian Bach was photographed on stage wearing a T-shirt with the slogan, 'AIDS kills fags dead'.

'I understand it's not cool to make fun of death,' Bach said, claiming he'd put the T-shirt on without looking after a fan had thrown it on stage. 'I guess nobody gets my jokes. But let me just state this – I do not know, condone, comprehend or understand homosexuality in any way, shape, form or [laughs] size.'

Hip hop was another pit of vipers, such as LA crew N.W.A.'s three-million-selling *Straight Outta Compton* album, which defined the emerging sub-genre of gangsta rap in 1988. Facing down social emasculation and police oppression, hip hop's need to prove its self-worth deployed the language of braggadocio and putdowns. MCs battled with their rhymes to take the opposition down, in the process habitually picking on similarly ostracised people – women and homosexuals. For example, the rollicking 'Gansta Gangsta': 'But she keep cryin', "I got a boyfriend"/Bitch, stop lyin'/Dumb-ass hooker ain't nothin' but a dyke.'

On his solo album, *Eazy-Duz-It*, N.W.A. member Eazy-E added for good measure, 'Put the gat [gun] to his legs, all the way up his skirt/ because this is one faggot that I had to hurt.'

In 1989, Biz Markie's 'A Thing Named Kim' mistook a woman in a bar: 'Had hair on her chest longer than King Spade/Even though I got a band, I don't need the AIDS.'

Coming out: the musical

Against this flow of poison, Elton John's eventual declaration was an antidote, after *Rolling Stone*'s Cliff Jahr finally popped the question. 'I've been waiting for people to ask me this,' the recently divorced singer replied. 'It's not exactly a secret. I live with my manager. I'm openly gay outside. I just thought it was common knowledge.'

But still Freddie Mercury was keeping quiet – perhaps, like Elton, he'd have been more vocal at this stage of his career had the Queen singer not had another secret: an HIV-positive diagnosis. Was this the reason why he wrote 'Who Wants To Live Forever', a Queen single in 1986? Was it why he also recorded the Platter's doo wop classic 'The Great Pretender' for a solo single in 1987?

Had Mercury come out on both accounts, he might have had the same impact as Agenor Miranda Araújo Neto. The Brazilian artist, known as Cazuza, confessed he had AIDS in 1989 in a country with a paradoxical relationship to homosexuality. There was both widespread tolerance (Rio's gay pride parade is one of the largest) and homophobic violence, two attitudes that were inextricably linked. A superstar in Brazil, Cazuza was the kind of spirit guide who could humanise AIDS and help shift public perceptions and attitudes about HIV/AIDS prevention and treatment – not just in Brazil, but in all South America.

Brazil emerged from more than two decades of fascist dictatorship and Cazuza's 1988 track 'Brasil' declared *'Brasil, mostra sua cara'* – 'Brazil, show your face'. According to the online companion to Thomas E. Skidmore's *Brazil: Five Centuries of Change*, Cazuza was demanding that, 'Brazil be absolutely forthcoming and truthful, about everything from politics to sex.'

Cazuza didn't quite meet his own demands. Having been diagnosed HIV-positive in 1985, he only admitted it publically in 1989, but his lyrics addressed his struggle with illness and the rumours, which only made him more popular. It helped that Cazuza claimed to be bisexual: 'He made easy references to kissing girls and having girlfriends, but he neither ascribed to being gay per se, nor denied his interest in men. He would be able to defy the notion that AIDS was purely a gay man's disease; though he slept with men, he was not necessarily identified, by himself or others, as gay.'[1]

Cazuza would die in 1990, having set the wheels in motion and the equally popular Renato Russo could have continued the forward roll. The frontman of the rock band Legião Urbana (Urban Legion), Russo was regarded as the Brazilian Morrissey, bookish and poetic and Brazilian rock's most important songwriter. But he was gay rather than bisexual and after being diagnosed HIV-positive in 1989, his band released *'Meninos E Meninas'* ('Boys And Girls'), which concluded, '*E eu gosto de meninos e meninas*' – 'and I like boys and girls'.

In a 1992 interview, Russo flatly denied being HIV-positive, which he maintained all the way through to his death in 1996. 'Russo's outburst,' Skidmore wrote, 'perpetuated an attitude of disgust and fear around AIDS, speaking to the deep complexities of sexuality and public discourse that marked his music and public persona.'

Role models might help in the long term, but in the short term, the communities had to look after themselves. The public discourse on AIDS in North America was similarly conflicted, but the scale of the crisis engineered a practical framework of fundraising and health care. In 1989, the Gay Men's Health Crisis came together with the world of ballroom to create the House of Latex, an operation to distribute condoms at house balls and to help educate the younger members.[2]

Furthermore, the public grieving for AIDS victims in the US had served to humanise a community 'commonly depicted as soulless narcissists', as journalist Alex Ross wrote. A Gallup poll hints at the persuasive power of ACT UP and of the AIDS Quilt, called 'the premier symbol of the AIDS pandemic, our greatest HIV prevention education

---

1 http://library.brown.edu/fivecenturiesofchange/chapters/chapter-8/aids/cazuza-brazils-first-public-face-of-aids/
2 Not all ballroom's problems were related to AIDS. For all the statements of pride, resilience and fabulousness in *Paris Is Burning*, there was a shocking denouement to the documentary, when the young, petite, trans female Venus Xtravaganza was found strangled, her body stored under a bed.

tool and the largest ongoing piece of community folk art in the world,' which was displayed on the Washington Mall in 1987 and then began touring the country.[1] In 1988, 57 per cent thought that gay sex should be illegal; in a single year, the number dropped to 36 per cent.'

The message of loss persisted through an unexpected return by Lou Reed – to form, to great storytelling and to the city that he so unnervingly described. Inspired by his love for a city in political and social crisis, his 1989 album *New York* included the profound lament 'Halloween Parade' that began, 'There's a downtown fairy singing out "Proud Mary" as she cruises Christopher Street/And some southern queen is acting loud and mean where the docks and the badlands meet/This Halloween is something to be sure/Especially to be here without you.'

That same year *Longtime Companion* became the second film to address AIDS, after 1986's *Parting Glances*. The party scene, in which Village People's 'YMCA' is rendered by a string quartet, is wry and comical; the closing scene, in which the friends lost to AIDS during the film's eight-year timespan reappear alongside the living, is still devastating.

The one pop artist still getting into the charts using male pronouns was Jimmy Somerville, who was increasingly driven by the AIDS crisis. After the joyous synth-pop of 'There's More to Love than Boy Meets Girl', the Communards had split[2] and, for his solo debut, Somerville had released a cover of French singer Françoise Hardy's '*Comment Te Dire Adieu*' ('How To Say Goodbye To You'), once 'an independent, feminist woman, but now she's supposedly right-wing and makes anti-gay comments, like AIDS is the fault of homosexuals. I wanted to take a song she was famous for and make it accessible to a new audience who'd think it was mine and for all French-speaking gays.'

The song opened *Read My Lips*, released in November 1989.

---

[1] Today, the AIDS Memorial Quilt weighs 54 tons and is composed of more than 48,000 panels dedicated to more than 94,000 lost individuals. www.aidsquilt.org/about

[2] Somerville and Coles fell out when the latter falsely claimed that he'd become HIV-positive.

Somerville's next single was a cover of the recently departed Sylvester's 'You Make Me Feel (Mighty Real)', with all royalties going to gay and AIDS charities. Somerville wore his ACT UP T-shirt on the *Terry Wogan Show* in front of an audience of 12 million, and again for the video of his third solo single, 'Read My Lips (Enough Is Enough)': 'We'll shout as loud as we can/And we'll shout 'til they hear our demands/Money is what we need, not complacency.'

The video ended with a shot of a poster that read, 'Action = Life' ('Silence = Death' would have been a tough sell for a pop single). 'I didn't want the video to be morbid and depressing, I wanted people to think they could do something, that this was the energy we had and this is how we could use our power,' Somerville declares. 'But the video couldn't be fun without content, it had to be strong and angry and upfront, even quite crude, which is what the song was also saying. I was fed up with subtleties, especially as far as AIDS politics were concerned. The time that some people had left to live and the way the political climate was changing because of AIDS, didn't allow for subtlety.'

Somerville talked of his label, London Records, trying to edit out footage of Harvey Milk from the 'Read My Lips' video. 'What a ridiculous contradiction! Milk was an identifiable gay man, so what was I? Probably the country's most famous queer and they were worried about two seconds of Milk? What planet were these people on? Bronski Beat were originally signed because London realised they could market gay culture, gay sensibilities and gay ideas, anything that was sellable. Now they were trying to hide all that. It was a real sign of the times and a constant uphill struggle.'

Somerville knew that the situation had to change. 'Someone like [Australian actor and pop star] Jason Donovan, with his boy-next-door image, was far more of a threat to normality than me. I'd been doing this so long, it was almost accepted that this was what I was like.'

Somerville had enough peers, from Marc Almond and the post-Frankie Goes To Hollywood Holly Johnson to Andy Bell, the singer chosen by Depeche Mode founder Vince Clarke to front his new synth-pop duo

Erasure. They would mine a rich vein of camp with Bell's stage outfits (tutu included) and cover Abba's 'Gimme Gimme Gimme (A Man After Midnight' and so push an overt, positive version of 'homopop'. 'I'd had enough of being bullied, so I thought I'd put myself out there, as outrageous as I could be, so there was nothing more that people could say,' Bell told journalist Dave Simpson.[1]

Yet Erasure never wrote a 'Relax' or a 'Smalltown Boy' and none of these frontmen were willing to fight the way Somerville did. 'The kind of audience who'd buy my singles or read *Smash Hits* were going to be schoolkids and they were the people you had to reach,' he says. 'There was propaganda from the state and the church, so I had to get my propaganda to them too, to represent a positive image to people, to be what you are instead of having to be moulded by someone else.'

Silence = death; action = life. Could music make gay = normal, acceptable, *equal*? In 1989, UK TV's Channel 4 played its part by launching *Out On Tuesday*, a weekly show about lesbian and gay life on national TV. It was made by Abseil, a production company staffed by gays and lesbians and named after the act of the lesbians who'd abseiled into the Houses of Parliament to protest against Section 28. Music played its part; Jon Savage and Liz Naylor contributed to one edition and Patrick Fitzgerald was interviewed alongside Lynn Sangster of the mixed-sex Liverpool band Kit, a 'country folk postpunk indie' band according to singer/guitarist Sangster. 'We saw being completely open about our sexuality as being authentic, the only way to be,' she recalls. 'We wrote "I Love Her Like Mad" because [fellow all-male Liverpool peers] the LAs wouldn't think twice about singing about girls so we thought, why can't we? I like the first line of that song: "I said don't worry about those sleeping pills and social ills/ Don't worry about her, come to me with a promise of fun." We talked about it in interviews but we didn't get that many! It was still a very homophobic music industry.'

---

1 www.theguardian.com/culture/2014/jul/30/andy-bell-erasure-hiv-cocaine-interview

The likeable lesbians

The music industry gave female artists less credence than their male counterparts, so how could lesbian performers carve a successful career with their integrity intact? Musical guile, an identifiable image and a sense of humour seemed to serve Phranc, a member of jittery US punks Nervous Gender and Catholic Discipline in the late seventies, who had subsequently pursued a solo career armed with an acoustic guitar to better get across her newly politicised messages such as 'Take Off Your Swastika' – addressed to the misguided punks she'd grown up alongside. Advertised as the 'All-American Jewish lesbian folk-singer', with her flat-top haircut and her workclothes, Phranc's 1985 album *Folksinger* connected both to her Jewish folk roots and the women's music scene, while the album cover – a moody B&W shot of the singer and a vintage microphone – was a cheeky nod to the fifties' male crooners. But though she particularly liked Alix Dobkin's habitual use of the word 'lesbian', and felt many of women's music artists, 'beat about the bush a lot,'[1] Phranc's wry, sharp satires eschewed the L word – though her odes to female sexuality were the most sexualised of any lesbian singer-songwriter to date, such as 'Carolyn' ('I am crazy about you, because no one else I know has muscles like you ... you make me want to be a gym teacher') and 'Amazons'.

The music industry may have homophobic roots but Phranc's unique sound and image – as the first butch lesbian icon – snared the media, and major label offshoot Island Records, which released her 1989 follow-up *I Enjoy Being A Girl*, named after her stereotype-busting cover of the outdated Rodgers and Hammerstein song, even as Phranc remained a beloved peer of the punk and post-punk scenes. Leaving behind the separatists, Phranc muscled into the mainstream while showing lesbians could still be uncompromising and political – to wit, her race drama 'Bloodbath' next to her ode to tennis heroine 'M-A-R-T-I-N-A' Navratilova.

---

1 www.monkeychicken.com/AdamBlock/1986_7_22phranc.pdf

In Austin, Texas, three lesbians by the name of Two Nice Girls were pushing similar propaganda. One of the trio, Gretchen Phillips, was driven by a vision. 'I believed lesbian visibility would change hearts and minds at a time of widespread homophobia because of AIDS, when guys wore "AIDS kills fags dead" T-shirts,' she says. 'If people couldn't say "I don't even know a lesbian", there could be a lesbian they could perhaps even like.'

Phillips knew there had to be a strategy. 'Two Nice Girls especially was a conscious decision to not be a punk band, but to couch queer ideas in pretty harmonies and music that would go down more easily. A lesbianism that was fun and knowable but still transgressive within that melodic genre, which hadn't been done before.'

From Galveston, Texas, Phillips experienced no internal strife over her emerging sexuality and, after her parents divorced and she came out, aged fifteen, in 1978, she left her disapproving mother and moved in with her accepting father. The same year, she attended a performing arts high school in Houston, meeting 'plenty of queers – we'd see the *Rocky Horror Show* at weekends.'

She also admired Janis Ian, 'wearing those three-piece suits, looking so dykey! She came out as bi in *Village Voice*, which we subscribed to. I'd read up everything I could on bisexuality, as no one was homosexual then. But it was clear that Joan Jett [of The Runaways] was a lez and was singing about it. And Joan Armatrading was cryptic but everyone made out to her. But it was Dory Previn's level of honesty about her schizophrenia; I thought, let me be that honest about being lesbian. But I wanted to write like Buffy Saint Marie, tackling love songs *and* political songs. Let's name it and we can move on. Or have a conversation. Or if I'm interviewed about my songs, some straight journalist with a modicum of power can write something that a teenage lesbian can read and realise she's not the only one.'

After moving to Austin, she discovered that it was 'the only city where punk was dominated by the fags! It was exhilarating to be a part of that. I was frightened of being targeted, but it was worth the risk in order to try to change things. I'd enjoyed woman-only spaces like the Michigan festival, but my dream was the normalisation of lesbianism, to sing about sexual politics with straight guys in the band and, if it was possible, to do that in straight clubs.'

Phillips progressed through Meat Joy (drummer Teresa Taylor[1] was Phillips' lover) to Girls In The Nose, which handled her 'rocking, trashy side', with songs such as 'Chant To The Full Moon, Oh Ye Sisters' and 'Honorary Heterosexual Lesbian', while Two Nice Girls addressed her 'trained, meticulous' side. Openly lesbian songs from an openly lesbian band in a mainstream fashion: at last!

Two Nice Girls began as a duo with Laurie Freelove; they kept the name even when Kathy Korniloff joined, giving Two Nice Girls exquisite three-part harmonies and fuller arrangements. The trio's *pièce de résistance* was a tender medley of Lou Reed's ambisexual classic 'Sweet Jane' and Joan Armatrading's 'Love And Affection' that won the popular vote at a 'Sweet Jane' covers night.

The medley kicked off Two Nice Girls' show at Hole In The Wall, part of Austin's South By Southwest (SXSW) festival. Jim Fouratt was in the audience and bowled over. He offered to manage them, and secured a deal with UK record label Rough Trade, where the Smiths had resided. Phillips and Freelove were the principal writers but while the latter – who identified as bisexual – didn't write same-sex lyrics, Phillips made it central to hers, from the dreamy 'Goons' ('Now she's in the motel bed with me ... Arms and mouth that bring me home') to the frolicking 'My Heart Crawls Off' ('Just forget it Gretchen/'Cause she loves someone else') to the merciless country parody 'I Spent My Last $10.00 (on Birth Control and Beer)': 'When I was a young girl, like normal girls do/I looked to a woman's love to help get me through ... My life was so much simpler when I was sober and queer/but the love of a strong, hairy man has turned my head, I fear.'

---

[1] Taylor joined Texas' now-legendary acid-crazed troupe the Butthole Surfers, making them surely the only band that not only had two gay drummers (King Coffey was also gay), but had them at the same time.

'At the song's heart,' Phillips says, 'a woman has given herself to a man and loses herself, like [Tammy Wynette's] "Stand By Your Man". It's extremely critical of hetero relationships.'

Jim Fouratt asked if the trio wanted to be the biggest lesbian band in the world or the biggest band in the world. 'I knew I couldn't go back in any closet,' Phillips says. 'In fact, we had to make a choice how far to go and I went queer, queer, queer.'

In the end, Two Nice Girls weren't waylaid by sexual politics but bad luck. Their album was delayed when the studio they were using was shut down for non-payment of taxes and, while they searched for a replacement, Canada's Cowboy Junkies beat them to market with a similarly slow, seductive cover of 'Sweet Jane'. Different musical agendas saw Freelove leave after their self-titled debut was released at the end of 1989, but they found a replacement, a drummer and acclaim. 'People loved us, straight clubs included, and we had worldwide distribution, fan-mail from across the world, tons of press and very little that was bad,' says Phillips. 'And then Rough Trade went bankrupt and our records just languished in a warehouse.'

It was enough bad luck to fuel a country song. But nevertheless, they had laid down a marker. Despite the AIDS panic, public opinion was favourably turning and if you had the charisma, nerve and talent, there was no need for any closet.

In 1988, at London's Piccadilly theatre, an evening devised by the Stonewall Organisation's Michael Cashman and Ian McKellen to counter the effects of Section 28 raised money for the Organisation For Lesbian And Gay Action. The comedy and stage musical and opera numbers were notable for every word and note written by lesbians and gay men; Tchaikovsky, Tennessee Williams, Sappho, Dame Ethel Smyth ('March Of The Women'), Joe Orton, Noël Coward, Pet Shop Boys, Cole Porter, Leonard Bernstein, Benjamin Britten. As Two Nice Girls Gretchen Phillips might say, 'We're here, we're queer, queer, queer, get used to it.'

CHAPTER 10

The Nineties: Rock'n'Roll – Queer to the Core

'Shock the middle class, take it up your punk rock ass... Why don't you admit that you don't have the balls to be a queer?'
'I Don't Want To Be A Homosexual', Screeching Weasel, 1992

Pop stars generally weren't pro-active campaigners. But having worn his ACT UP T-shirt on TV and in a music video, Jimmy Somerville ushered in a new decade by being arrested for lying down in the road and obstructing a public highway outside the Australian Embassy in London, where ACT UP were protesting against the country's proposed introduction of HIV testing for immigrants. The day after, he lent support to the protest outside the Wellcome shareholders' meeting, the company behind the anti-AIDS serum AZT. ACT UP had bought shares so that they could put across their point of view.

AZT was controversial. 'Wellcome seem to think they're doing something good by bringing the price of AZT down, but they're unnecessarily administering double the dose, so they're still charging too much,' Somerville argued. 'It's out of most people's price range too, £5000 a year. People need to do more.'

Somerville thought that those of his gay pop peers who lacked politic initiative or weren't even openly gay were 'totally unacceptable. Of course it takes courage and it's not the easiest thing to do, but if more did there wouldn't be the same controversy around it. It's fine that people give private donations from their big bank balances but that's not going to help some sixteen-year-old kid who's so traumatised by his sexuality that it could even lead to suicide or being mentally scarred for life. People don't seem to grasp that the idea, "It's our private life," is towing the line because it's acceptable behind closed doors.'

In New York, John Carlin was also feeling that lack of effort. A former art critic for *Paper* magazine, he'd gone into teaching and curating art shows, but a drop in wages led him to move into entertainment law. 'So the AIDS issue hit me on the head,' he says. 'Close friends of mine got sick, like [artists and activists] Keith Haring and David Wojnarowicz. I'd imagine it was like the sixties in America with the Vietnam war, when someone you went to high school with didn't come home. People I went to parties with . . . three months later – just gone.'

One of Carlin's clients organised an AIDS fundraiser after which the money promised from celebrities didn't arrive. 'It was like a moral nuclear bomb went off in my head, which gave me the idea for Red Hot.' Released in 1990, *Red Hot + Blue* rounded up artists such as U2, Sinéad O'Connor, Annie Lennox[1], David Byrne, Erasure, Jimmy Somerville, Debbie Harry and Iggy Pop for an album of Cole Porter covers; while Noël Coward's haughty theatricality preserved his songs in a thirties aspic, the former's greater melodic range has lasted much better. At heart, Coward belonged to those 'naughty nineties', while Porter felt ahead of his time. The compilation's success ensured over a million dollars was donated to AIDS charities and Red Hot released compilations every year through the nineties, supported by club nights around the world.

Another compilation, *Feeding the Flame: Songs by Men to End AIDS*, was also released in 1990. Funding for a cure remained a major cause. 1991 alone would bring down Village People founder Jacques Morali, Michael Callen's bandmate T. J. Myers in the Flirtations[2] and his one-time co-songwriter (of 'Love Don't Need A Reason') Peter Allen, UK singer Vaughan Toulouse of the British band Department S, Joe Bracco

---

1 The video for Annie Lennox's 'Every Time We Say Goodbye' was shot by Derek Jarman.
2 The Flirtations released three albums, *The Flirtations* (1990), *Live: Out On The Road* (1994) and *Three* (1996).

(whose condom-inspired song 'Friends In My Pocket' was used in the GMHC's Say Yes to Safer Sex campaign) and Steven Grossman, at the age of thirty-nine.

In the seventeen years since he'd released *Caravan Tonight*, Grossman had mostly been living in San Francisco without a record deal. Though he worked in accountancy by day, by night he was bar and club-hopping and taking drugs – the lifestyle that his album had taken a stand against. Toward the end of his life, he'd befriended Richard Dworkin, who helped him record his stockpile of songs. Like Patrick Cowley, Grossman created his last will and testament while he was dying.

One of the final songs he committed to tape was 'Last Pioneers', a riposte to those industry figures who'd wanted him to write 'she' instead of 'he': 'From the brothers who can't disguise it/even in men's clothing and the sisters who just do not pass/Comes the spirit of my people, of courage over fear/Comes the only trust I'll find when the enemies are clear/If the other struggles were over we would still be here/the last pioneer.'

Grossman passed without anyone in the music industry noticing while 1991's most prominent loss had a world stage. Questions and eyebrows had been raised about Freddie Mercury since his drawn and muted appearance was noted when Queen attended 1990's annual BRITS music awards to pick up their lifetime achievement statue. From that point, the band's publicist Roxy Meade recalls, 'the tabloids incessantly tried to get confirmation of his illness, but nothing got printed' – just paparazzi snaps of the singer, looking unrecognisably gaunt. Queen's single 'These Are The Days Of Our Lives', released in September, was another Mercury lyric ripe for interpretation: 'When we were kids, when we were young/Things seemed so perfect – you know?'

In November 1991, it was made official. 'The time had come,' a statement read, 'for my friends and fans around the world to know the truth.' There was barely any time to register shock – that came a day later, when Mercury died. Perhaps the announcement had set the singer free. In some respects, it was another Rock Hudson moment, without the sense of astonishment; most people had connected the dots by now.

The hope embedded in the posthumous single 'The Show Must Go On' was supported by the video, using footage of Mercury in his feisty prime, like he'd stepping back out of the looking-glass. The one positive was that, in death, Mercury further humanised the AIDS crisis; he was an untouchable rock star but he drew massive affection, so the public – or at least a couple of generations of music fans – finally experienced the loss of a loved one.

The Freddie Mercury Tribute Concert for AIDS Awareness was staged at London's Wembley Stadium in April 1992. The crowd numbered 72,000, with a TV audience of one billion worldwide. The remaining members of Queen were joined by David Bowie, the Who's Roger Daltrey, Annie Lennox and Elton John – the last of whom joined forces with Axl Rose (potentially angling to shed his reputation for homophobia) on 'Bohemian Rhapsody'.[1]

Immediately after Mercury's death, Bob Caviano – the former manager of Grace Jones and Village People – wrote an impassioned letter to *Billboard*, warning that if the music industry didn't act fast, AIDS threatened not only a loss of life but a creative vacuum. In 1992, the LIFEbeat foundation was launched, just months before Caviano died, with a series of industry and artist-related fundraisers.

Few expected a response from Nashville, but in 1993 Country Music AIDS Awareness was launched after singer Kathy Mattea wore a red ribbon to 1992's Country Music Association Awards. Prominent artists such as Tammy Wynette, Wynonna Judd, George Jones, Dolly Parton and Willie Nelson fronted the multimedia campaign *Break The Silence*.

Arthur Russell was the next musician to die, in 1992. In December 1993, Richard Dworkin experienced the loss of another 'last pioneer' when his lover Michael Callen died, aged thirty-eight, eleven years

---

1 Rose had only just defended his use of 'faggot' in 'One In A Million'. 'I had just heard a story about a man who was released out of the LA county jail with AIDS and he was hooking [being a hooker],' Rose told Kim Neely at *Rolling Stone*. 'I've had my share of dealings with aggressive gays and I was bothered by it.'

after becoming HIV-positive – final damning proof to his detractors who thought he'd invented the diagnosis to advance his career. One of Callen's last appearances had been on film, when the Flirtations appeared in Jonathan Demme's *Philadelphia*. The controversial storyline – Tom Hank's lawyer discovers he has AIDS and, in desperation, turns to a straight attorney after he'd been fired because of his illness, as evidently there was no support from the gay community – raised consciousness levels as Freddie Mercury had.

As he had with Grossman, Dworkin helped Callen record his last stack of songs, released as *Legacy* in 1996. The singer's true legacy was his tireless activism, his commanding voice and his role as the co-writer of 'Love Don't Need A Reason' and other gay anthems such as 'A Love Worth Fighting For' and 'The Healing Power Of Love'. These heartfelt, hard-won sentiments were catnip to Broadway fans but they didn't register with the pop and rock audience. Callen had begun writing a column in *Spin* magazine about AIDS issues, but the music industry was still in denial. Jim Fouratt came up against it when he arranged for Callen to join the closing panel at New York's annual new music seminar in 1990, alongside Lou Reed, country singer Nancy Griffith and (Dworkin recalls) Henry Rollins.

'Several thousand people, all of them involved on the left-leaning edge of the music industry, were in attendance,' Dworkin says. 'Michael was talking about being an out musician with AIDS, that he couldn't hide who he was and couldn't change the pronouns of his songs and how he could have had a more serious career if he had. He said, "I'm just wondering if, at this moment, if anyone or everyone who's gay, could just stand up", so he wouldn't feel so alone, and maybe one or two people got up. That's among all the people in bands and record labels, majors and indies and distributors. And that was 1990.'

You don't have to be a Trini Lopez fan

Artists who cherished their gay fanbases, such as Bette Midler and Cyndi 'Girls Just Want To Have Fun' Lauper, also staged AIDS benefits.

Madonna continued to make it her duty to celebrate sexual fluidity – in the video to her 1990 single 'Justify My Love', in which she grappled with both sexes with her 1992 album *Erotica* and book of photographs, *Sex*, which included gay porn star Joey Stefano among the models. But while Madonna was supporting the gay male community and reinforcing bisexual chic, the lesbians had to do it for themselves. Two Nice Girls and Phranc played their part, while the popular, Grammy-winning, acoustic folk-singer Tracey Chapman was the Joan Armatrading of her day, exuding 'lesbian' but never saying a word in her songs or in public. Folky singer-songwriter Michelle Shocked was more open about her bisexuality but didn't write about it; that task was grasped by fellow folky Ani DiFranco.

From Buffalo, New York, DiFranco had made her recording debut in 1990, a throwback to the seventies in the Holly Near mould: folk singer, civil rights activist, record label owner (Righteous Babe), bisexual: 'Some days the line I walk turns out to be straight/other days the line tends to deviate,' she sang on 1992's 'In And Out'. But she didn't write love songs to women and DiFranco was even accused of marketing herself as bisexual to sell records – which really would have been a sign of the times. Either way, Jim Fouratt points out the irony of her winning female artist of the year at 1999's Gay and Lesbian American Music Awards[1], the year after her first marriage.

Bisexuality was an undisputedly valid and necessary branch of the LGBT diaspora, of the fight to love and lust after your own gender. But figures of unequivocal homosexuality were vital too, in the eye of the mainstream media – and not just in Canada, where Carole Pope of

---

[1] The Glamas were launched by musicians Tom McCormack and Michael Mitchell in 1996, starting with seven competitive categories and growing to twenty-seven by 2000, its final year, when the necessary funds to keep it going at that size dried up. Two special recognition awards were given each year: the Michael Callen achievement award, for 'an individual, group, organisation or business committed to the courageous and important work or engendering, nurturing and furthering gay/lesbian music' and the out-music award, 'to a recording artist, group or songwriter who has advanced gay/lesbian music through their work as an out musician.'

Rough Trade was still the only out lesbian rocker signed to a major label. And then came Sheena McDonald, the woman known as Horse.

As a teenager in Fife, Scotland, McDonald 'identified with boys or, rather, in my mind's eye, that's what I was.' She adopted the nickname Horse when she was twelve: 'I was trying to get away from who I was at the time,' she says. 'By the treatment meted out to me, being lesbian was something to be hidden and ashamed of.'

Seeing Joan Armatrading on *Top Of The Pops* was McDonald's Bowie/'Starman' moment: 'Her voice stopped me in my tracks. I didn't always know she was a lesbian, although I unconsciously knew, like I did with Nona Hendryx.' Jimmy Somerville, gay and Scottish, was another inspiration, likewise androgynous Annie Lennox and Patti Smith, 'though unlike me, they could morph and flirt with that look. They could walk away from that dangerous place.'

Being a big, butch gal – the name Horse implies it – McDonald had to stay where she was, but her gutsy, husky voice – 'like folds of very rich chocolate,' reckoned novelist Iain Banks – was her ticket to a better place. 'People are attracted to singing and, if people liked me, all would be well in my world,' she says. 'Music has saved my life when I've been lost.' She calls 'Careful' – her highest charting UK single at no. 42 – 'my signature song. There's such sadness there, so although it's a love song. It also says, "I'm vulnerable" and appearances can be deceptive as to how strong you actually are.'

Horse says EMI knew what they were signing in 1987, though it was her voice the label wanted. Four months later, Section 28 sanctioned homophobia. 'I did begin to worry, she says. 'It was acceptable for gay men to be like Boy George or like pantomime dames, but there was something about women that people wouldn't accept – no woman was out in this country, no one was looking like me. I was often mistaken for a man. I was always wary of the, "Is it a man or a woman?" conversation.'

Guitarist (and lesbian) Angela McAlinden was Bernie Taupin to Horse's Elton John. 'I wrote some words, but Angela was such an amazing lyricist, she could say so much in so few words. She did put a couple of "she's" in there, but we wanted the songs to speak for everyone. We didn't try to be lesbian, we tried to be the best songwriters we could be. But by having your head above the parapet, you're visible and an example. Fans say I've made a difference.'

No thanks to the BBC TV executive who saw the video to 'Careful' – Horse handsome and androgynous, in a suit and open bow tie – and told EMI they couldn't show it because children would be watching. 'I was devastated, and to think they showed the [dance craze] "Lambada" video, with this little girl dancing provocatively with older men.'

Horse had more success than others – four Top 50 singles, two Top 50 albums – and is still performing but she didn't have the one killer tune that fired Sophie B Hawkins toward the top.

The New Yorker was a percussionist by trade but a singer-songwriter too, which got her a deal with Columbia. She publicly identifies with being 'omnisexual' – 'just because I sing about women doesn't mean I'm gay. Just because I sing about guys doesn't mean I'm straight'[1] – yet Hawkins was in a relationship with writer-director Gigi Gaston for over ten years and 'Damn, I Wish I Was Your Lover' made its gender preferences plain: 'And I lay by the ocean making love to her with visions clear.'

In an act of subtle homophobia, MTV banned the single's video for Hawkins' semi-naked bedroom poses, despite Madonna already setting the benchmark higher. A dowdier replacement did the trick; the song went US Top 5 and she was Grammy-nominated for best new artist. But either because of her image – long, curly hair, soft features, casual jeans and T-shirt non-image – or that no other Hawkins song at the time used female pronouns, she was simply another bisexual artist. The US needed its Horse, an unequivocal wall-breaking statement of intent. And, like Horse, it came from places of isolation and prejudice, where the struggle was acute.

Atlanta has its drag scene and its pockets of gay culture, but it still

---

1 Source unknown

was the deep south and in the young mind of Amy Ray 'the word "gay" meant the worst thing in the world, like bestiality.' She'd imbibed the significant sixties freedom fighters (Hendrix, Joplin, Jefferson Airplane) and the seventies balladeers (Elton John, James Taylor). She was late in discovering punk, but Patti Smith led the way. 'I recognised the underdog, the outsider,' Ray says. 'I was attracted to artists that sang about inequality.' At seventeen, she fell in love with a woman, 'but I didn't have the language for it.'

At college, Ray discovered the women's music scene, especially the Toronto singer-songwriter Ferron (born Deborah Foisy), who was spearheading the second wave with her own label, Lucy Records, featuring lesbian singer-songwriters with a rockier folk sound. Joining forces with her college friend Emily Salliers as the Indigo Girls, Ray found a niche at the gay Little Five Points pub, 'a meeting ground for poets and drag queens,' Ray recalls. 'I had a girlfriend all through college, but Emily was still sorting things out and dating guys.'

Salliers grew up in New Haven, Connecticut, the daughter of a university professor, living in government-sponsored housing in a predominantly black neighbourhood, 'a volatile environment,' she recalls. She loved the R&B, soul, funk and gospel soundtrack that spilled out of the windows. Her family moved to Atlanta when she was ten: Joni Mitchell was her next love and then women's music, after a student of her father's introduced her to Ferron – 'I was blown away, She was as good as Joni, with an incredible turn of phrase. Cris Williamson was equally pivotal.'

Salliers 'had these feelings inside, but I didn't know what they were. It was almost like, "Don't get too close to those records, they'll burn you". It was fear and attraction mixed.' When Amy Ray came out to her, 'I was envious. But I knew gay people were hated, which was very hurtful. I was terrified, but it didn't take me long not to be.'

Little Five Points provided community and other lesbian-identifying bands such as Scallion Sisters and Paper Dolls. But Indigo Girls wanted to go their own way. 'We liked the punk philosophy,' says Ray. 'We didn't want to be pinned as a submissive female acoustic duo. It meant you were doing something mediocre, that's how narrow-minded people were in the media. You know, the lesbian kiss of death, which was incredibly derogatory, but it was our own homophobia and we just didn't want to be boxed in, we wanted to expand.'

Following in Tracey Chapman's slipstream, Indigo Girls were signed by Columbia/Epic in 1987 and the following year's self-titled second album almost made the US Top 20, its progress unimpaired by any pronounced lesbian themes. 'I didn't use male pronouns and pretend to be straight,' says Ray. 'We sang about love and relationships, but not the struggle of being gay. We weren't Cris or Meg [Christian], more a Ferron, who wasn't trying to proselytise in her songs. You can relate if you're straight or gay.'

Still, their sexuality wasn't a guarded secret. After beating the Indigo Girls, Tracy Chapman and Phranc for album of the year at 1989's New Music Awards, Michelle Shocked joked that the category should be renamed 'They Might Be Lesbians'. A journalist friend soon pressed Ray about doing an interview that discussed being gay. 'A big outing felt more about celebrity and exploitative.' Instead, Ray was low-key, talking to a couple of fanzines and getting used to the idea of a bigger platform. 'I would have said something sooner but I had to wait for Emily to feel comfortable.'

In the end, it was Salliers who took the lead, to Ray's surprise, at a college press conference in 1991. 'I was afraid that we'd be pigeonholed and we were,' says Salliers. 'We still are. You think Indigo Girls, you think, "lesbian". But it didn't matter. It was more important to be part of queer civil rights and to state our validity and belonging. And once we were out, we didn't look back. We had to put up with shit from the male programmers and DJs at pop radio. We weren't part of their paradigm, but we weren't women who kotowed to their power. But as you get older, you stop caring so much what other people think.'

All that was needed now was someone who could infiltrate the mainstream on a different level or, as k.d. lang once joked on national TV, the role of the first, 'dy-con' or 'ce-lesbian'.

From Consort, Alberta, Katherine Dawn Lang grew up on the Canadian prairies. 'I knew I was into girls,' she says, 'and I knew it wasn't accepted. But on another level, I didn't feel different to anyone else.' It helped that, of her three siblings, Lang had a gay brother and a gay sister. 'We weren't out to each other at that time but, personally and culturally, we understood each other.'

Having devoured the dulcet voices of Maria von Trapp, Anne Murray, Linda Ronstadt and Karen Carpenter, Lang started entering small town talent contests in her mid-teens. Like Horse, Lang knew she 'looked different. I was a big girl. The odds were I wouldn't have a big chance at music but I still knew it was my chance.'

At college, Lang studied music and the music business, but only after performance art and punk phrases did she fall for country music. Calling herself k.d. lang – the lower-case spelling was a hangover from her performance art days – she had a band, the Reclines, in which she played another role, the reincarnation of Nashville country legend Patsy Cline.

'I was a different kind of musician – a singer who likes to croon,' she says. 'I found there was nothing to struggle against with performance art, no borders. In country, there was. I loved the idea of contrasts and country music was easy fodder for punking. I loved the kitschy aspect and I understood the mindset because I grew up in it, but I honestly loved the music too.'

As a tomboy buckaroo on stage and with songs such as 'Big Boned Gal', 'I didn't try and hide anything, to be cryptic. I'd change the gender of a song that wasn't right, but I wasn't trying to be blatant either, just natural and matter of fact.' Canada embraced lang: she was lifestyle magazine *Chatelaine*'s woman of 1988 and word spread when Roy Orbison chose lang to duet on his re-recording of his signature classic 'Crying' and to sing on his TV comeback special.

Yet lang was 'held at arm's length' by country music radio, despite 1989's *Absolute Torch And Twang* album winning the Grammy for best female country vocal performance and the Nashvillian overtones of her solo debut, *Shadowland*, produced by Patsy Cline's producer Owen Bradley. Country may have agreed to take a stand on AIDS, but a butch crooner was clearly a concession too far. 'I heard at my record company that advertisers had said, "If you play k.d. lang, we'll pull our advertising,"' she says. 'I was too Nashville for punk and not traditional enough for Nashville.'

It could also have been a backlash against lang's stand for animal rights, what with Alberta being prime cattle-ranching territory. She fronted a 'Meat Stinks' campaign (organised by People for the Ethical Treatment of Animals, PETA) in 1990: lang was banned from more than thirty Alberta radio stations and other meaty sympathisers.

But she would soon no longer need the approval of country music or Alberta. Cole Porter's 'So in Love' for the *Red Hot + Blue* compilation was the start of a shift from twang to torch, culminating in 1992's solo album *Ingénue*, an exercise in pure sultry crooning or, as lang hears it, 'Post-nuclear cabaret, dark and slow and different'. The album was also inspired by her first serious infatuation, with a married woman who didn't return her love, leaving lang in a state of 'Constant Craving' – the album's lead single, her first international hit (and second Grammy).

Ingénue avoided specifying gender but, in every other case, lang didn't duck the question. In 1991 she'd made her acting debut in Percy Adlon's film *Salmonberries*, playing a woman working as a (male) oil-rigger in Alaska who falls for a German widow. Three months after *Ingénue* was released in March, lang came out to *The Advocate*.

Lang told writer Brendan Lemon that she'd been reticent before to protect her mother. 'The beef controversy hurt my mom quite a bit and it freaked me out about controversy. You think, is your job as an artist more important than the love between a mother and daughter? Or is lying to protect your mother the biggest sin of all? It was an ongoing question.'

Lang says she pushed herself to come out not because of *Ingénue* but AIDS: 'Not just the horror, but the homophobia. And with the gay press outing people, it felt like warfare. The best way to protect myself and to do the most chivalrous act was to come out and try to stop the negative momentum and lay it all down. But it was bittersweet. For me, the cryptic nature of sexuality is one of its beautiful assets so I had to sacrifice the ambiguity and mystery of it all. But it was the right thing in the long run.'

In the short term, Lang had fun; on stage at London's Hammersmith Odeon after *Ingénue* was released, she announced, 'There's been a lot of speculation in the press' [cue shrieks] and I've decided it's time for me to come out of the closet [dramatic pause]. Yes, it's true. I am a . . . L-L-L-L-opez fan! [cue mass screams],' referring to the very popular Tex-Mex country singer Trini Lopez.

In 1994, Lang delivered the *coup de grâce*, wearing a suit and sitting in a barber chair, being mock-shaved by supermodel Cindy Crawford for the cover of *Vanity Fair*. 'I'm super-proud of that, because it was a nice piece of art,' she says, though eventually the media attention was exhausting. 'In terms of people's interest, in my sex and my clothes and who my girlfriend was. My music was at the tail end.'

Lang's disheartenment shaped her next album, 1995's *All You Can Eat*: 'I wanted to go to the core of the disposable and material aspect of the life of pop music – and then I was pissed that it didn't sell as well! But mission accomplished. I've been happier being low-profile. And it was more important for me to do a duet with Tony Bennett and normalise being gay as quickly as possible, than being super-political.'

Lang's example would have encouraged Melissa Etheridge, who had come out in January 1993 at the Triangle Ball for the inauguration of Bill Clinton, the first Democrat president in twelve years. Lang and Janis Ian were alongside her. From Leavenworth, Kansas, Etheridge had played in various country music bands before moving to Boston to attend the Berklee College of Music, but had bailed before graduation to kickstart a career in LA as a fully-fledged rock musician.

Even before she came out, Etheridge hadn't hidden her sexuality; in 1985, she'd sent her demo to Olivia Records, which turned her down, unwilling to be associated with a rock singer. By 1987, Etheridge had signed to Island Records. Label boss Chris Blackwell had seen her play in a lesbian bar. 'He looked at me and said, "I don't ever want you to lie," and then added, "but maybe don't flag wave."'

1988's self-titled debut album was a US no. 22 hit and its lead single 'Bring Me Some Water' – Etheridge later admitted it was inspired by the pain of agreeing to an open relationship with her girlfriend – was Grammy-nominated for best female rock vocal performance. 'I'd always been careful to say "my lover" or "my partner" and one guy just took it upon himself to say I was talking about my boyfriend,' she told journalist Laurence Watts. 'I was worried people would think I was some kind of liar because a lot of people knew, they knew I'd come from the bars. So it was really important for me to come out officially.'[1]

Etheridge won her first Grammy in 1993 for the single 'Ain't It Heavy', taken from her 1992 album *Never Enough* and, after the Triangle Ball, Etheridge released her fourth title, pointedly named *Yes I Am*. The lead single 'I'm the Only One' identified her lover as female. The album went Top 15 and was six-times-platinum. The single went Top 10, irrefutable proof that coming out didn't harm sales; if anything, honesty was now being rewarded.

Rock'n'roll is homosexual too

In 1990, Michael Stipe was still dealing with the ramifications of AIDS and having been in the closet through the eighties. He'd laid clues for the cognoscenti, such as the references to Derek Jarman's films on reclaimed gay icons Saint Sebastian and Caravaggio in the video of the band's biggest hit, 'Losing My Religion' and wearing a cap with 'White House Stop AIDS' at both the BRITS and Grammy awards. His reward was rumours that he'd got AIDS, stoked by the themes of death and transition on R.E.M.'s 1992 album *Automatic For The People*, his typically

---

1 www.pinknews.co.uk/2011/11/10/interview-melissa-etheridge-on-ellen-the-oscars-and-rock-and-roll

sallow appearance and his decision not to give any press interviews as he backed away from the circus.

U2 followed up their *Red Hot + Blue* contribution with 'One', a single taken from their 1991 album *Achtung Baby*. All royalties were donated to AIDS research[1], while it was widely speculated – but never confirmed – that the song described a conversation between a father and his gay HIV-positive son. The cover photo of buffaloes tumbling off a cliff, after having been chased by Native American hunters, was taken by David Wojnarowicz, himself terminally ill with AIDS[2]. The liner notes – unusual for a single – claimed the photographer 'identifies himself and ourselves with the buffalo, pushed into the unknown by forces we cannot control or even understand.'

U2 also wore drag for the promotional clip, but director Anton Corbijn recalls the band 'became nervous that the drag element in the video might link AIDS to the homosexual community in a negative way. So they dropped the video and got someone else to film something. They replaced it with a video of Bono in a bar surrounded by models, which I particularly didn't like. But once the song had died in the charts ... they got MTV to start running my video instead.'

Manic Street Preachers, a new, young Welsh band much taken to fusing glam and punk imagery, also dragged up for the video of their single 'You Love Us', with bassist Nicky Wire[3] and guitarist Richey Edwards pushing the blouses and eyeliner to the max. The quartet, who often stencilled lyrics on their clothes, came up with the slogan 'Rock'n'roll is homosexual' for T-shirts that they sold at concerts. 'I remember Richey talking about self-love being such an essential part of

---

1 'The band feels that [AIDS] is the most pressing issue of the day and we really have to focus people's attention to the AIDS plague that has been with us for ten years,' said U2's manager Paul McGuinness. The band also sold condoms inscribed 'Achtung Baby' on their global Zoo TV Tour that year.
2 Wojnarowicz died in 1992.
3 In a later Manic Street Preachers tour programme, Wire admitted that his school nicknames included Gay Lord and Shirley. 'I thought that I looked like a stonking woman,' he added.

rock'n'roll,' recalled Wire. 'That seemed to be his twist. It fitted into a lot of what we believed in: narcissism, nihilism, self-love, self-delusion. All those things made for thrilling rock'n'roll.'[1]

When the indie-rock band the Lemonheads released the country-ish ballad 'Big Gay Heart' as a single, it also felt significant that 'gay' was no big deal. But the most powerful statement came from the totemic rock figure of the era, Kurt Cobain, who wore an outlandish canary yellow ballgown when he and Nirvana bandmate Kris Novoselic appeared on MTV's *Headbangers Ball*.

The show was MTV's window on the world of hard rock and heavy metal, dominated by the hair and glam-metal bands. Guns N' Roses would appear, with Axl Rose sometimes rocking a 53rd and 3rd rent-boy look, bare-chested with tight cycling shorts and boots. Bon Jovi, supported by Manic Street Preachers on tour (and selling their 'Rock'n'roll is homosexual' merchandise), also had the glam-drag look down pat. The fact that a plaid-shirt-and-jeans bunch like Nirvana were *Headbanger Ball* guests showed the changing of the guard. The band's second album, *Nevermind*, was reaching Guns N' Roses levels of popularity and the music known as grunge – as much punk as metal – was the Next Big Thing. One way to celebrate was for the trio to don ragged dresses for the video of their single 'In Bloom'.

From Aberdeen, Washington state, Cobain had been another of the those geeky-weedy boys bullied at school but he readily inflamed the situation, as he told journalist Kevin Allman. 'I used to pretend I was gay just to fuck with people. I've had the reputation of being a homosexual every since I was fourteen. It was really cool, because I found a couple of gay friends in Aberdeen which is almost impossible . . . Once I got the gay tag, it gave me the freedom to be able to be a freak and let people know that they should just stay away from me.'[2]

Cobain spray-painted 'God is gay' on the side of trucks to wind up

---

1 www.theguardian.com/music/2012/feb/28/how-pop-lost-gay-edge
2 *Cobain on Cobain: Interviews and Encounters*, edited by Nick Soulsby (Chicago Review Press, 2016)

local rednecks. In 1985, he and Novoselic had been arrested for daubing 'Homosexual sex rules' on the side of a bank. But Cobain also admitted that, when push came to shove, he was attracted to women. One of his girlfriends was Tobi Vail, a key figure in a new feminist punk scene, called 'riot grrrl', after a phrase she used in her fanzine, *Jigsaw*.

Jigsaw reader Kathleen Hanna and Vail formed the all-female quartet Bikini Kill (Hanna sang, Vail drummed), the most significant of all riot grrrl bands, just ahead of their peers Heavens To Betsy and Bratmobile. Hanna sprayed 'Kurt smells like Teen Spirit' (a brand of deodorant) on his bedroom wall, inspiring Cobain to write the similarly named single, 'Smells Like Teen Spirit', that sent Nirvana stratospheric.

Cobain loved gay in many of its manifestations, including flagrant parodists the Frogs, San Francisco's squalling rockers Bomb – whose singer Michael W. Dean would dress in ripped dresses or nothing at all (Mark Eitzel says Dean, 'pretended to be gay, and told me that he wished he *was* gay')[1] – and Rupaul, who joined Nirvana for photos at the MTV Awards.

RuPaul had left Atlanta in 1984 for New York, where he moved into the basement of the Pyramid club. He joined Vaginal Crème Davis for country parodist Glen Meadmore's performance – Davis and Meadmore performed as Pedro, Muriel and Esther, wearing lingerie for the cover of their debut single 'Anna-Ee'. Davis's spoken word intro could have come from a John Waters film: 'Her sexy hustler boyfriend was killed last year . . . Now she has a new hustler boyfriend and he's even cuter than the dead one/She's a real fine chick/She's got tits and a dick!'

Rupaul, however, had come out the other side of his John Waters phrase and was aiming for something classier. He told New York's cable show *The American Music Show*, 'I wanna go further, I want to take my RuPaul message to the world. I feel like I'm going to take off, like a stick of dynamite.'

Rupaul had to wait until 1992 to achieve lift-off, by which point he'd

---

1 Bomb's only obvious song with a gay theme was 'B/E/A/F/A/G' from 1990's *Lucy In The Sky With Desi* compilation.

blossomed into a stunning drag queen, seen all over MTV with his debut single. 'Supermodel (You Better Work)' – ballroom's belief manifesto turned into a slice of chorus-led house music. The company responsible, amazingly, was rap label Tommy Boy. The single even charted – US no. 45, UK no. 39 – with Rupaul's TV appearances including Arsenio Hall's talk show and then an album (again on Tommy Boy), *Supermodel Of The World*. As a cultural force, ballroom may have been too disparate and competitive to maintain its momentum, but a one-man, one-drag-queen mission had been much more likely to succeed.

Britpop and gayglam roots

While US metal and grunge bands tussled for domination, the alternative wing of early nineties Britain had its rival factions. In the late eighties, acid house carried along a raft of rock bands, most notably Manchester spearheads, the Stone Roses and the Happy Mondays. The Roses were the more politically minded while the Mondays proudly talked up taking drugs, and selling drugs. When a joke that lead singer Shaun Ryder had also earned his keep as a rent boy was taken seriously by the tabloid press, Ryder told the *NME*, 'I ain't a fucking faggot and that's it.'

His bandmate Bez added, 'I hate faggots. Anyone who is straight finds them disgusting.'

Fortunately, it wasn't only Manic Street Preachers than embraced the faggot. Simon Gilbert, the drummer of the London-based quartet dubbed 'the best new band in Britain' on the cover of *Melody Maker* in April 1992 was one (an openly gay drummer: that was a first); androgynous singer and agenda-setter Brett Anderson was not so much impersonating one as, inspired by David Bowie and Morrissey, projecting gender and sexual fluidity. Anderson – also a Prince fan – was also willing, going against the grain of alternative UK rock, to address sex and not just identity, but the details, too. As Anderson put it, 'We're talking about the used condom as opposed to the beautiful bed.'

Suede's debut single 'The Drowners' was not only a brilliant, edgy song but the lyrical snippet, 'We kiss in his room to a popular tune', was a tonic thrill for anyone gay who felt starved of being addressed in a rock song (Manic Street Preachers songs didn't delve into sexuality the way their T-shirts did). But it was Suede's third single, the thuggish stomper 'Animal Nitrate', that upped the ante, named in honour of the gay party drug 'aroma' amyl nitrite (or nitrate): 'He said he'd show you his bed/And the delights of his chemical smile.' The track was equally defined by its reference to the homosexual age of consent: 'What does it take to turn you on/Now he has gone?/Now you're over twenty-one?'

To show Anderson's agenda wasn't phallocentric, the cover of 1993's debut album *Suede* was Tee Corinne's photo of two women – one wheelchair-bound, with matching androgynous haircuts – in a passionate kiss, which Anderson had found in the book *Stolen Glances: Lesbians Take Photographs*. Suede compromised by cropping out the wheelchair, but the statement about sexuality stayed intact. 'It's one of the most beautiful pictures I'd ever seen,' Anderson says, 'and it said a lot to me about Suede, the beauty of being under the heel and the high life within you.'

Anderson's efforts were mocked and the singer accused of play-acting after he told one interviewer he 'felt like a bisexual man who's never had a homosexual experience'. Yet Anderson's viewpoint was no different to that of Kurt Cobain or a cross-section of Morrissey fans who would routinely invade the stage to hug and molest the singer.

'Our songs were not intended to be reflections of exact happenings in my life, more of sides of my personality expressed through real-life situations,' says Anderson. 'I wanted to express sexual feelings in myself, but it's more about varying degrees of femininity and masculinity in my body, rather than the idea of homo- and hetero-sexuality . . . I was trying to broaden the horizons.'

As their debut album was released, Suede headlined a Red Hot AIDS benefit hosted by Derek Jarman, whose video projections for Pet Shop Boys' 1989 tour opened the show. More footage by Jarman formed Suede's chosen backdrop. Jarman made a speech referring to the UK's age of consent, which had remained at twenty-one for the past twenty-six years and the news that three men under twenty-one were taking the Conservative government to the European Court of Human Rights. In 1994, a legal amendment to lower the age to be equal to heterosexuals – sixteen years old – was defeated. An amendment compromised at eighteen.

After record label mogul David Geffen finally came out as gay in November 1992, with widespread support from his industry peers, he began to donate sizeable amounts of money to the AIDS cause, alongside Elton John. The demographic of record labels was changing, too. They were now staffed by enthusiasts who'd grown up during glam and punk and had no truck with homophobia. In 1993, the UK's first young gay black singer was allowed to express his inner beauty and truth without any warning or censorship from his major label, Virgin Records. David McAlmont was out from the very start of his career.

Before him, Labi Siffre was that rare case, a black British gay man in seventies pop, who started recording in 1970, six years after he met his long-term boyfriend. In 2014, he told the BBC that his 1987 song 'Something Inside So Strong' was inspired by growing up gay and in apartheid-era South Africa, 'the societal abuse of being told that as a black man and as a homosexual, I was a wicked, evil, disgusting pervert.' But while Siffre understandably took his time to come out,[1] McAlmont took a different path – despite being told he also was morally corrupt.

Born in south London to a Guyanese mother and Nigerian father, David McAlmont was just six when his father walked out and eleven when his mother relocated the family to Guyana, South America's most culturally Caribbean country. Before they'd left, he'd imbibed from her albums of crooners (Crosby, Bennett, Como) and Disney's *Greatest Hits* and seen Bolan, Bowie and Queen on *Top Of The Pops*. But in Guyana, he got the bullying treatment: 'I got called "anti-man" and "Daphne" at school. It was vicious and a real headfuck.'

By the age of thirteen, McAlmont had 'accepted Christ as my spiritual saviour, but pretty soon after, I became aware of my sexuality.' He

---

[1] Labi Siffre declined to be interviewed for this book, for reasons not forthcoming.

confided in a friend at church who immediately shipped him off to be cured by a faith healer. McAlmont also prayed and fasted in order to be saved.

Guyana treated pop 'as the devil's music', but he also absorbed the *Saturday Night Fever* soundtrack, George Michael, Culture Club, Michael Jackson and, especially Prince: 'He got me through high school. He didn't sound like any down-the-line R&B or soul singer. Even though he was ragingly heterosexual, something about Prince spoke of an alternative sexuality; that you could be black and not conform to the Christian norm.'

By 1987, McAlmont was back in the UK, 'To become a star, but in musical theatre or dancing. I didn't know I had a voice. But I couldn't act or count [steps] and I was told I had an amazing voice.' He did – powerful and rangy, with one of the best falsettos in the business.

In 1990, he answered an ad placed by guitarist Saul Freeman: 'Male/female/black/white/gay/straight singer'. 'I knew it was meant for me,' he says. The duo formed Thieves, got signed and recorded a debut album of passionate dream-pop, though Freeman left before it was released. When it was, the record was titled *McAlmont*. David's outfits were as colourful as the music: ethnic clothes, women's clothes, scarves, dangly earrings... 'Emerging from that born-again Christian situation, I can't underestimate the fact that I was like a bottled gay man, so it was like I popped the cork and came out, screaming.'

Lyrically, Freeman's wish to be a vaguer, dreamy proposition – 'more phonetics than meaning' – limited McAlmont's openness, but 'How About You' was about cruising and 'My Grey Boy' was inspired by a friend's AIDS diagnosis. 'I was buying into the fear then,' he says, 'and my friend was upset because he didn't want to be condemned to death.'

Once solo, though, McAlmont could go to town. The pinnacle of his flamboyance was the video for the David Arnold revamp of Shirley Bassey's sixties' *Bond* theme 'Diamonds Are Forever'. McAlmont wanders into a dressing room wearing a long, grey overcoat and caresses a poster of Bassey before emerging on stage in a white catsuit with feather-boa trim, drop diamante earrings and choker and high heels. Later, he slinks across a piano and then the floor. This was up-front and dazzling – black, flamboyant gay men were only ever seen on the drag circuit. 'I thought, I can't do this any better,' says McAlmont, 'and I'd gotten it out of my system. So from then on I wore more male clothes, but I still wear big, sparkly broaches and brightly coloured suits.'

He returned to the subject of cruising on 'Prowling', providing the vocal and lyric for a Patrick Fitzgerald album that didn't have to take into account any straight bandmate. Under the name Fruit, the Kitchens Of Distinction bassist had released a single, 'Queen Of Compton Street' in 1994 – 'He fucks, fucks, fucks, from dusk till dawn/E'd out of his head and his condom swinging'. The album *Hark At Her*, released in 1997, was equally candid, roaming over love and lust, homophobia and AIDS with a savage, poetic eye.

Hark At Her would have been the queerest album that the UK had produced if it wasn't for Spud Jones, one of the young actors who had featured in Derek Jarman's 1990 film *The Garden*. As the vocal half of Tongue Man, Jones was committed to a vision that was more Kenneth Anger and Jean Genet than Derek Jarman – all sailors, leathermen and biker struggles, on the duo's industrial-dance rackets *Hot Angel* (1990) and *Joys Of A Meatmaster* (1991).

'Everything I sing about is a challenge to society's homophobia,' Jones told London's *Time Out*, defending songs such as 'Swingin' On His Bouquet' and lines such as, 'The existential, big-dicked cowboy.' 'The best way I know how to do that is to glorify homosexual love and sex. A lot of so-called gay bands seem to have forgotten what gay sex is. There is a lot more sex than love in my songs, but that's because sex and lust play such a large part in many gay men's lives.'

Jones died of AIDS in 1994, but Tongue Man's furious dynamic was anyway too ahead of its time. Likewise, Minty, the London-based band fronted by the sensationally outlandish Australian performance artist, model and club promoter Leigh Bowery, though the band's debut single 'Useless Man' was an attack on the macho stereotype that had persisted all the way since the disco clone: 'Boot lickin', piss-drinkin', finger-friggin', tit-tweakin', love bitin', arse-lickin', shit-stabbin', mother fuckin', spunk-lovin', ball-bustin', cock-suckin', fist-fuckin', lip-smackin', thirst-quenchin', cool-livin', ever-givin useless man.'

Queer to the Core

A new band in San Francisco, Pansy Division, were equally inspired to put gay sex on the agenda and had more success with their simple, power-pop melodies. They also took on Nirvana's signature classic and turned out 'Smells Like Queer Spirit', which formed part of the trio's 1992 debut single alongside 'Fem In A Black Leather Jacket' and 'Homo Christmas'.

'Queer' had entered common parlance, reclaimed as a show of defiance and in order to denote a broad sexual and gender fluidity outside of the standard binary systems of male and female, heterosexual and homosexual, gay and lesbian. Pansy Division were all queer in spirit, as well as – almost – the first all-gay rock band. The best they managed was three-quarters.

Pansy Division's lead singer and guitarist Jon Ginoli currently works as a legal assistant for the city's attorney office, having devoted the previous twenty years to the band full time. Growing up in rural Illinois, he recalls loving the Beatles and the Stones at the age of five, but also the Supremes: 'I'd see women singing and I wanted to be them. I knew I was gay from that time as well. I later found out about Little Richard – what could be fruitier than "Tutti Frutti"? At fifteen, Patti Smith blew my mind. She was clearly not trying to do anything that she didn't want to – which put me on a direction I knew I could follow.'

Ginoli tracked down Buzzcocks and Tom Robinson records, 'but I hadn't come out then. When I did, I found gay people were antagonistic toward music I liked, such as the Clash and the Ramones, even New Order. If being gay means liking terrible music, count me out.'

At the University of Illinois Urbana-Champaign, Ginoli had started a punk band, the Outnumbered, though he was the sole gay bandmate. 'A friend said that if I came out, we'd be known as "that gay band". Later on, I thought, I *will* be that gay band!' He got the chance after moving to San Francisco in the late eighties. 'It had rankled that I'd had to choose between a musical life or a gay life, so I sold my guitars and amps. But in San Francisco I realised I could have both, if I could find gay people who into my kind of music. I found Chris [Freeman, bassist] right away, but it took five years to find a gay drummer – though when Luis [Illades] joined, we also got a second guitarist, Patrick, who was straight!'

Lyrically, Pansy Division were a hundred per cent homo and mostly humorous. 'Bill And Ted's Homosexual Adventure' and 'James Bondage' were singles; the debut album *Undressed* included 'The Cocksucker Club' and 'Rock'n'Roll Queer Bar'. 'We wanted Pansy Division to be as free as possible, to be blunt and not apologetic or to be assimilators – like, we're gay and nice, give us a few crumbs. Could we really call a song "The Cocksucker Club"? Yeah, let's keep pushing. I wanted us to be funny too. We could have written angry, bitter songs but I didn't want to hear that or play them night after night. I wanted something more out of life and to lift up the audience.'

In turn, every Pansy Division record sleeve was soft pornography. 'Some stores got in trouble for displaying our stuff, but our thought was, the penis is given all this power by being hidden, let's just put it out there. These songs are sexy and horny, let's have sexy and horny images. *Undressed* had a picture of a naked guy on the front, but it's an image of beauty.'

Pansy Division's Nirvana cover helped spread the word, but going on tour with their former Lookout label colleagues, Green Day, magnified their audience. Green Day's 1994 album *Dookie* was on its way to selling twenty million and they were playing to audiences of 15,000. 'We were the first exposure to anything gay for many Green Day fans,' reckons Ginoli. 'We'd grown up listening to songs about heterosexual relationships and could relate to them, so we figured some people could make that leap with us. We weren't going to win over everyone, but maybe we could get through to a certain percentage. And Green Day were so gay-friendly.

Taking us on tour said something about their values and I thought we used the pulpit for something exciting and potentially important.'

Green Day frontman Billie Joe Armstrong was throwing out his own signs: 'I went to a whore/He said my life's a bore' ('Basket Case') and 'Secrets collecting dust but never forget/Skeletons come to life in my closet/I found out what it takes to be a man/Now Mom and Dad will never understand' ('Coming Clean').

'I think I've always been bisexual,' Armstrong told journalist Judy Wieder. 'I mean, it's something that I've always been interested in. I think people are born bisexual and it's just that our parents and society kind of veer us off into this feeling of, "Oh, I can't." They say it's taboo. It's ingrained in our heads that it's bad, when it's not bad at all. It's a very beautiful thing.'[1]

Pansy Division attracted those rock fans who liked Armstrong's openness: 'I was surprised,' Ginoli says, 'because I thought we'd be too frank for them. But we also had songs about how treacherous it was being gay in high school and how to hang on.'

In 1994, Pansy Division threw out a lifeline of sorts to Bob Mould, formerly of Hüsker Dü by covering his song 'The Biggest Lie': 'Back to your hometown/Back to your day job/Back to your girlfriend/The biggest lie'. The hardcore trio had been the first alt.rock band to sign to a major label (Warner Bros), setting the groundwork for the likes of R.E.M., Nirvana and Green Day and Mould was reaping the benefits with his new band Sugar.

That year, Mould finally told his biggest truth to *Spin*. The magazine said it was sending gay novelist – and homocore fan – Dennis Cooper to interview Mould and asked if would he like to discuss his sexuality, as Cooper was going to write about it either way?

'It was the Reagan years, our culture was bad and I was a young, confused homosexual living in a country that refused to acknowledge

---

[1] *The Advocate* magazine, January 1995. The relevant excerpt can be found at www.greendaycommunity.org/topic/76730-billie-joes-sexuality-referenced-in-advocate-article/?page=7

me as a human,' was Mould's defence of his long-held silence.[1] 'So had I been out, I don't know if I would have been a very good spokesperson, especially like Jimmy Somerville was. I may have done more harm than good personally. The flip side is it might have given gay people at the time an example, allowed them to feel more comfortable. In terms of our stuff, I always wanted the songs to stay gender-neutral because music is supposed to be universal.'[2]

1994 seemed to be the watershed year for 'alternative' singers to come out. His 1985 outing having been ignored, American Music Club's Mark Eitzel talked about it again to *The Advocate*, while Stephin Merritt of the Magnetic Fields was never in (his publishing company was called Gay And Loud). With two albums out that year (*The Charm Of The Highway Strip* and *Holiday*) Merritt talked about writing them while sitting all day in gay bars. And Michael Stipe announced he was, 'an equal opportunities lech'. But there was a proviso; he said he didn't define himself as 'gay, straight, or bisexual'.

Though Stipe was on the cover of *Out* magazine in 1995, he still represented the kind of prevarication that the homocore fringe wouldn't tolerate. Only transparency would do, taking militancy from ACT UP and an ACT UP faction, Queer Nation, who didn't have an issue with outing people if they thought their subject was harming the cause. 'A lot of people were reacting to what they see as mainstream values in the gay community, like sexism, racism, conformity, assimilation and self-hatred' recalls Matt Wobensmith, who launched a fanzine and record label in 1992, both named Outpunk.

Outpunk was, 'primarily to fight overwhelming loneliness as a gay, twenty-year-old music fan in the pre-internet era,' says Wobensmith. 'I don't know how I would have survived otherwise. But what started as a social support mechanism became much larger. I realised the potential

---

[1] http://www.spin.com/2008/02/spin-interview-bob-mould. As it turned out, Hüsker Dü drummer Grant Hart was also gay, though he's never formally talked about it.
[2] www.gq.com/story/bob-mould-interview-see-little-light-memoir

impact I could make by promoting LGBT visibility via music, promoting radical ideas that young people would normally never be exposed to, and to further the progress of LGBT culture and art.'

Based in San Francisco, Wobensmith started an indie label, Shred Of Dignity,[1] in 1991. They released the *Pervo-Devo* EP from (heterosexual) Chicago punks Screeching Weasel, which included 'I Wanna Be A Homosexual', written for Bruce LaBruce (that's him talking at the start), denouncing punk for its fear of queer: 'Shock the middle class, take it up your punk rock ass . . . Why don't you admit that you don't have the balls to be a queer?'[2]

The rise of 'queer' saw queercore replace homocore, a much broader, less male-centric designation. And women, suddenly, were thriving, everywhere except that last bastion of machismo, heavy metal. 'There'd been so few women doing rock'n'roll and then suddenly in 1991 alone, you've got Bikini Kill, PJ Harvey, Liz Phair, the doors just flew open,' says Wobensmith. 'With gay bands like us, riot grrrl and other women bands, it was fantastic, and long overdue. The other band in tandem with us was Tribe 8. They played at our second-ever show. They were hysterically funny and they were scary.'

No all-lesbian band – from the Roc-A-Jets to the Bloods – had quite the presence and impact of San Francisco's Tribe 8. Like Jon Ginoli, Lynn Breedlove no longer plays music full time; she writes (books and stand-up comedy) and runs Homobiles, a non-profit car service for LGBTQ elders, which she proudly says has inspired similar ventures. 'Every time the rest of the world catches up with the concept we want

---

1 Wobensmith took the name Shred Of Dignity from the warehouse renovated by Tom Jennings.
2 Screeching Weasels' track had been inspired by 'I Don't Wanna Be A Homosexual' by Indianapolis punks Sloppy Seconds, which had opened with sampled dialogue from John Waters' 1974 film *Female Trouble*. 'Queers are just better,' Aunt Ida tells her nephew. 'I'd be so proud if you was a fag and had a nice beautician boyfriend. I'd never have to worry.' To ensure Sloppy Seconds' intentions weren't mistaken, they wrote on the sleeve of 'I Don't Want To be A Homosexual', 'This song is not intended to hurt or insult homosexuals. If anything, it shows how absurd homophobia is. However, we do not advocate men fucking each other! (yuck!)'

them to embrace, then our job is over, we're obsolete,' she says. 'Like Tribe 8. There are queer bands everywhere now, everyone's bought the theories we were talking about, so let's all move on.'

But back in the early nineties, a bunch of funny, scary butch femmes was radical. 'We were turning gender over and over on its head; it was just disrespectful and stupid to think that gender fit any kind of a box,' Breedlove says. 'I tried to walk people through our monosyllabic, three-chord couplets, simple punk rock, taking some other smart chick's ideas from [American feminist/gender theorist] Judith Butler's class. How can this help me and other people like me? Please explain, so I can pass it on. That's been my job.'

Born in Oakland, California, Breedlove – who identifies as male – recalls Elton John records and 'wondering if he and Bernie Taupin were getting it on, and "All The Young Girls Love Alice". I was butch but I didn't know what that meant. The Kinks' "Lola", Bowie, Lou Reed, all the songs about gender . . . I liked chicks and that was wrong. What do I do about that? Bette Midler was singing to gay guys, which I was sure would make her gay, so I was disappointed when she got married and had a baby. We knew Freddie Mercury was gay! The first time I saw Janis Ian in a three-piece suit she wasn't out – but what a dyke, singing about being trapped by marriage! Then Patti Smith and if you didn't get Sylvester, there was something wrong with you.'

Breedlove spent her eighties waylaid by amphetamines, marijuana and alcohol, acting out a Janis Joplin fantasy while dressing 'like a Castro clone. I said to a friend, "Make me look like the lovechild of Jim Morrison and Patti Smith . . ." I loved those egomaniac poets, but it took me ten years to figure out I was a punk and I could write love songs to another chick, with female pronouns.'

By 1990, Breedlove was sober and writing songs, which she debuted at a birthday party with guitarist Flipper and drummer Jen Schwartz. The trio added a second guitarist, Lesley Mah (formerly of Anti-Scrunti Faction) and bassist Lynn 'Tantrum' Payne to form Tribe 8, named from the practice of tribadism, a non-penetrative form of sex between women.

Flipper – Silas Howard, after transitioning in 2007 – grew up in Vermont, the daughter of sixties' idealists 'who thought music was a radical act, that it could change the world'. But as 'a young queer in a rural town, not a cute look!', Howard had to leave to find his own tribe; in San Francisco he co-founded the Red Dora's Bearded Lady café, a queer space that staged spoken word and music. He met Breedlove in a lesbian bar. 'There'd been so little of any gay and lesbian representation and AIDS was still a death sentence then, so we needed to be loud and get in people's faces and make trouble and to find a community.'

'People started booking us because there were no out punk-dyke bands, our whole reason for being,' says Breedlove. 'And we were going to yell about it.' The yelling was heavily imbued with a dark streak of humour. 'If the audience is laughing, they're listening and they want to hear more, because laughing is like coming, it's the bait,' says Breedlove. 'And if some people aren't laughing, they see those who *are*, so they try to understand more so they *can* laugh. About ninety-eight per cent of our songs used humour.' How much audiences laughed when Breedlove wore a strap-on dildo before mutilating it with a knife might have been determined by their gender. That would be the scary part that Ginoli referred to.

Tribe 8 would spoof not only the hair-metal bands, but their own community – 'Like lesbian spoken word,' Breedlove says. 'Stuff like, "Wave after crashing wave after crashing wave," about those dykes who think orgasms are edgy. And about the butch-femme relationships we were having.'

'Neanderthal Dyke', 'Femme Bitch Top' and 'Butch In The Streets' (from Tribe 8's 1995 debut *Fist City*) were tailor-made for the cause. Other songs took another tack, such as Howard's lyric for 'Wrong Bathroom': 'Sometimes on tour, in a small town, I'd visit the bathroom and women in there wouldn't believe I was female and I'd be asked to leave,' he recalls.

'Behind everything, the subtext was anger,' says Breedlove. 'Dudes in the audience might still not understand that sex with a chick who was maybe asleep or drunk – which means she can't say, "Yes" – is rape. So we explained consent and rape by making a big joke out of it. Nobody wants a bunch of lesbians wagging fingers at you, all preachy, everybody wants to jump up and down and yell, "Castrate!" and then check who they didn't get a "Yes" from in the past and maybe change their behaviour.'

Invited to play the Michigan Womyn's Music Festival in 1994, Tribe 8 described itself in the directory as 'San Francisco's own all-dyke, all-out, in-your-face, blade-brandishing, gang-castrating, dildo-swingin', bullshit-detecting, aurally pornographic, Neanderthal-pervert band of patriarch-smashing snatch-lickers.' They didn't expect that some of the Michigan crowd would label the band misogynists, symbolising the persisting distrust between lesbians and punk.

When Wobensmith launched his Outpunk record label with the all-female *There's A Dyke In The Pit*, it included Tribe 8's 'Manipulate' alongside Bikini Kill, Lucy Stoners and 7 Year Bitch. It wasn't a hundred per cent dyke line-up but it also wasn't far short. 1994's all-queer *Outpunk Dance Party* compilation confirmed how the movement was mushrooming, featuring not just Tribe 8 and Pansy Division but debuts from Randy 'Biscuit' Turner's new band Swine King, Sta-Prest, Mukilteo Fairies and, from the UK, Sister George, whose album *Drag King* was also released by Outpunk.

In the UK, Liz Naylor – formerly one half of Manchester's Gay Animals – released *Drag King* on her record label Catcall, which she named after the radical feminist newspaper. Having abandoned the music industry – 'I was disillusioned because I felt so powerless' – Naylor had lived in Portugal for a year before returning to London and discovering riot grrrl and queercore. Catcall started with a split album between Bikini Kill's *Yeah Yeah Yeah* and *Our Troubled Youth* by Huggy Bear, the UK's first (split-gender) riot grrrl band.

At a Huggy Bear show, Ellyott Dragon, an Israeli based in London who had drummed in former Au Pair Lesley Woods' band the Darlings, approached Naylor. 'She said, "We're a band, we're queer." I said,

"Great!"' Naylor recalls. 'There weren't any other queercore bands in Britain. When *NME* interviewed Sister George, they mentioned other queercore bands, but they'd made them up.'

The US, however, was spoilt for choice. Outpunk and Rough Trade were among a handful of labels that released records by New York's God Is My Co-Pilot, fronted by the novel concept of a gender-fluid married couple, Sharon Topper (vocals) and Craig Flanagin (guitar). The north-west corner of the USA, beside Seattle's grunge scene, was particularly prolific for queercore bands. In Portland, Oregon, Donna Dresch, a former *J.D.s* and *Homocore* zine contributor, was one of queercore's great instigators with her own zine and label, Chainsaw and the band Team Dresch. Their debut album *Personal Best*[1], released in 1995 on both Chainsaw and singer/guitarist Jody Bleyle's label Candy Ass, is one of the smartest of queercore records (The lyrics of 'Music Fanzine' include the lines 'Queer sex is great, it's fun as shit/ Don't worry, Jesus is dead and God don't exist') and 'I'm Illegal' was the first rock song to reference same-sex marriage: 'I was eleven, I said, "Girls can't get married to each other"/I remember thinking how fucked up that was/You say you have a ban on affection/Did I hear you right?'

Dresch, who counted Tuscon's Conflict as an important influence, also penned the raucous tribute 'Uncle Phranc' for the mother of all butch punks. Phranc had continued her journey into accessible folk and pop but she remained forceful and lesbian-onic: 1991's *Positively Phranc* album included odes to Gertrude Stein and forgotten trans jazz pianist Billy Tipton, while her *Goofyfoot* EP proposed a new dance, the 'Bulldagger Swagger'. Team Dresch members played on the EP while Phranc was a guest on their *Captain My Captain* album. Phranc released one last album in 1998, *Milkman*, before beginning to focus her energies into making paper art and – yes, really – Tupperware sales.

---

1 Named after one of the first mainstream lesbian-themed films, starring Mariel Hemingway, which went against the grain of other such films by not having the central character die tragically.

The torch had been passed, at a time when Phranc herself couldn't have believed so much was going on. Dresch's Chainsaw also released records by Sleater-Kinney, formed by Corin Tucker – the guitar/vocal half of Heavens To Betsy – with Carrie Brownstein of Excuse 17.[1] There was even a queercore equivalent to Olivia, Mr Lady Records, formed by Team Dresch co-guitarist Jaia Wilson (who later started a band, the Butchies) and academic/writer Tammy Rae Carland: 'We do consider ourselves a feminist business and part of that involves prioritising work made by women,' said Carland.[2]

Outside of queercore, the drag king scene was alive and kicking, with former Bloods member Anderson Toone at the centre. According to a timeline that Toone created,[3] she stayed in Europe after the Bloods ended, forming Idiosavant with drummer Leroi Pink, with both passing as men and then joined the UK's lesbian-dominated country band the Well-Oiled Sisters.

In 1990, Leigh Crow debuted as the lip-syncing Elvis Herselvis at San Francisco's lesbian club Female Trouble – which also gave birth to Tribe 8 and 4 Non Blondes[4] – and made her live singing debut a year later, with Toone in the crowd. By 1992, Toone had moved back to San Francisco, forming the 'dyke-a-billy' band the Bucktooth Varmints before teaming up with Crow in 1995 to stage the one-off drag king event, Queer Ole Opry and the drag king rock'n'roll musical *Hillbillies On The Moon* in 1996. It wasn't a threat to Nashville, but there was one intrusion, as Toone wrote. 'Elvis Herselvis and The Straight White Males tour the south and get national press coverage when she appears at the second Annual Elvis Presley Conference at the University of Mississippi. Graceland

---

1 In 1997, filmmaker Lucy Thane would document the crossover riot grrrl/queercore scenes with *She's Real (Worse Than Queer)*, interviewing the likes of Phranc, Lynn Breedlove, Leslie Mah, G. B. Jones and Donna Dresch and featuring live performances by many of the luminaries.
2 *Grrrl Power*, Kelley Robert (The Chronicle, Duke Student Publishing Company, 2015)
3 www.andersontoone.com/timeline/dktimeline.html
4 4 Non Blondes were fronted by openly gay singer and songwriter Linda Perry and had one huge hit single, 'What's Up?' in 1992.

The Nineties: Rock'n'Roll – Queer to the Core

withdraws their support when they find out she's a Lezzzbian Drag King! Controversy ensues.'[1]

As queercore and the drag king scene were firing up, Olivia was winding down. The label had begun to scale back in the early eighties, focusing on Cris Williamson and Meg Christian releases, alongside Montreal singer-songwriter Lucie Blue Tremblay – classic gentle Olivia. The label was more about a community and an ideology than a commercial operation and, having released just three albums in the nineties (ending with Williamson and girlfriend Tret Fure's *Postcards From Paradise*), Olivia the label shut down in 1994. Olivia the cruise-ship holiday company, launched in 1988, is still in business today. The separatist movement was a social and political necessity of its time, but unsustainable in the long term; Olivia knew as much from the creation of the Second Wave label. And even then, the label had turned down Melissa Etheridge.

In the UK, where the queercore scene was tiny, lesbian and bisexual artists multiplied in the indie universe, from the dramatically shaven-headed, bisexual singer Skin of hard-rockers Skunk Anansie to Echobelly bassist Debbie Smith, from Gene's bisexual frontman Martin Rossiter[2], to Gary Cosby of London-based quartet Lick. Their debut single, 'Come' (c/w 'Shirtlifter'), was the most overtly gay – and undiscovered – gay anthem of the period.

Rock'n'roll was finally doing a good job of supporting Manic Street Preachers' evidence.

Scotland's Belle and Sebastian, led by the straight – 'to the point of boring myself' – singer Stuart Murdoch, embraced sexual ambiguity and numerous gay characters. Multi-national trio Placebo, led by

---

1 www.andersontoone.com/timeline/dktimeline3.html
2 'I wasn't remotely interested in a game of hide and seek with the media. I'd have considered that to be a betrayal of the people who'd gone before me and fought for gay rights. I couldn't be doing with some long running "Is he or isn't he?" debate because that would have been profoundly boring. I didn't want to be Michael Stipe or Morrissey. Admitting that I was bisexual didn't harm me in the slightest. In the main, my sexuality was irrelevant to the songs.' http://sabotagetimes.com/music/genes-martin-rossiter-interviewed-pulp-and-blur-can-fck-off-to-butlins

bisexual vocalist/guitarist Brian Molko and gay bassist Stefan Olsdal, released their sauciest track, 'Nancy Boy', as a single (marking the first time the word 'lube' got into the UK Top 5). There was another Nancy Boy, the US band fronted by Donovan Leitch (son of sixties folk icon Donovan). He told the press, 'I'm the closest thing to gay you could ever be without doing the deed itself,' while (straight) music journalist Cliff Jones named his band Gay Dad. Their early demos were funded by former Rolling Stones manager Andrew Loog Oldham.

Homophobia: alive and kicking

In the UK, Section 28 continued to hang over any celebration and incidents of homophobic violence were enough to warrant former anarcho-punks-turned-pop-infiltrators Chumbawumba's electro-pop single 'Homophobia'. The band had shown support before; in 1992, they'd printed up the 'Jason Donovan – queer as fuck' T-shirts when the Australian soap actor-turned-singer successfully sued *The Face* magazine for claiming he was lying by denying he was gay. Donovan's popularity took years to recover, showing how public opinion had shifted.

In comparison with the relatively minor furore over Axl Rose's homophobia in 1987, Public Enemy's offences (in two songs from 1990 and 1991[1]) were widely criticised, along with their support of openly homophobic Nation of Islam Supreme Minister Louis Farrakhan.

In the backlash against Jamaica's homophobic reggae community, careers were being threatened. In Jamaica, where sex between men at the time of writing still carries a sentence of up to ten years with hard labour, reggae singers have long been the weathervanes for the Caribbean island's social and political movements. Roots reggae, dub and the ballads known as lover's rock once ruled the airwaves, but tastes had shifted toward the aggression of dancehall and its speedier, digitalised cousin,

---

[1] The Public Enemy songs were 'Meet The G That Killed Me' ('Man to man/I don't know if they can/From what I know/The parts don't fit') and 'A Letter To The *New York Post*' ('It only brings agony, ask James Cagney/He beat up on a guy when he found he was a fagney'.)

raga, the country's equivalent to hip hop. 'Batty boy', after the Jamaican slang for 'bottom' became their version of 'faggot'.

Singer Buju Banton adopted the term for 'Boom Bye Bye', which not only advocated murdering homosexuals by shotgun but torching them too: 'Boom bye bye, in a batty bwoy head'. Banton claimed to have recorded 'Boom Bye Bye' in 1988, when he was fifteen, and claimed that the track had been reissued without permission in 1992.

It wasn't reggae's first homophobic lyric: in 1978, King Sounds and the Israelites' 'Spend One Night In A Babylan' was a fire-and-brimstone dispatch written after King Sounds had spent time in London nightclub Columbo's, according to Jamaican academic Cecil Gutzmore.[1] He also points out that Lloyd Lovindeer's 1980 song 'Don't Bend Down' linked homosexuality to paedophilia – probably the first time this shock tactic had been put into a song, but not the last. In Papa San's 'Sorry', a judge apologises to the offender he has just convicted, as he will be abused by predators in prison.

If Banton was dancehall's prince, the king was Shabba Ranks. The Jamaican had predated Banton with 1988's 'Can't Drop Off A Shape', which recommended 'gun shot' for a 'maama man'. Ranks was a guest of the UK TV series *The Word* where he defended free speech and, as a religious man, said that gays deserved to be crucified because they did not 'multiply'. Presenter Mark Lamarr told Ranks he was 'talking crap and you know it' and shut down the interview.

Given the laws against homosexuality and the fervent homophobia in Jamaica, Banton wondered what he had really done wrong. But the media reaction outside the country put the brakes on both Ranks and Banton's careers. Both men eventually apologised and Banton even recorded 'Wanna Be Loved (*Desea Ser Amado*)' for 1996's benefit album *Silencio = Muerte* [Silence = Death]: *Red Hot + Latin*, which raised money for AIDS patients.

---

[1] *Casting the First Stone! Policing of Homo/Sexuality in Jamaican Popular Culture*, https://docs.google.com/file/d/0By4cLpa4myuqRF9uTEM0c0c2Mkk/preview

The art of coming out

For every one homophobic lyric, another gay or lesbian artist came out. Suddenly, the surprise was less the coming out, but who was speaking up. David Williams talked to *The Advocate* in 1993[1], as one half of the Williams Brothers, the twin nephews of legendary crooner Andy Williams.

Janis Ian also finally came out, in 1995, some years after she'd moved to Nashville, although she wasn't a country artist. It was more the city's broader song-writing community that attracted her. On her first day visiting, she 'instantly felt at home, I can't explain why.' But it wasn't New York. 'There's a tradition in Nashville, "No need to be ugly,"' Ian says. 'There was high tolerance for the two little ladies growing tomatoes down the street, but to be different, particularly if you were a woman, was difficult. But I've been with my partner [Pat, now Ian's wife] since 1989 and I always introduce her as my spouse.'

Ian didn't feel the need to express herself in her songs – 'I try to reach for the universal, so I don't write as someone who is gay or Jewish or American,' she says. But she wanted to be more visible and she attended the Triangle Ball celebration of President Bill Clinton. It was the first time a gay organisation had been linked to a president and Ian says they all 'believed Clinton would usher in a new era of gay rights, but he fucked it up. We didn't expect him to create DOMA [the Defence of Marriage Act]!'

The AIDS epidemic had raised issues of inheritance and death duties between male partners, but the Republican opposition succeeded in pushing through legislation that defined marriage as the union of one man and one woman; DOMA allowed states to refuse to recognise

---

1 'I was tired of avoiding questions in interviews about my personal life and I was not ashamed of my sexuality,' David Williams says. 'I was living with a beautiful young man in a committed relationship.' For anyone who wants some relevant Williams Brothers material, David wrote 'Can't Cry Hard Enough' 'in response to a lover's death of a drug overdose, while 'Don't Look Now' addressed 'the bigotry surrounding the AIDS crisis.'

same-sex marriages granted under the laws of other states. This followed another controversial Clinton manoeuvre, 1994's 'Don't ask, don't tell' (DADT) policy. This prohibited military personnel from discriminating against or harassing closeted homosexual or bisexual service members or applicants, while barring openly gay, lesbian, or bisexual persons from military service. Ian hadn't intended to make a statement because of her disillusionment.

'I'd met Pat in 1989 and I was out in the Nashville community, I was happy where I was,' says Ian. 'Then the head of the National Gay Liberation Task Force took me and Pat out to lunch and said I needed to [come out] when I had an album out, to make the biggest political statement. I said I wasn't interested, and she said, "Did you have any role models grow up who were gay?" Yeah, Radclyffe Hall's *Well Of Loneliness*, and I didn't want to be gay. "Didn't I think young gay people, knowing the writer and singer of 'At Seventeen', would take heart from that?" Everything I did in terms of coming out grew out of that lunch. And when I put out *Revenge* in 1995, I made some noise.'

Rock'n'roll is homosexual (metal edition)

Janis Ian was a part of Nashville, but not identified as a country singer; there would be many years before someone at the heart of the country industry would come out. But slowly, the walls were crumbling in other genres. In 1993, one year before the rash of alternative rockers, the hard rock and metal scene finally had a gay man in its midst – Roddy Bottum.

Bottum played keyboards for Faith No More, a band with many strings to their bow: hard rock, heavy metal, funk rock, trash metal, warped AOR. They weren't a traditional hair-metal band nor part of the grunge response, though Bottum had briefly dated Kurt Cobain's future wife, Courtney Love. His sympathies were more with the open-minded than the reactionary wing of rock.

Born in LA, Bottum grew up with Bowie and Lou Reed – the usual suspects – but he mentions Klaus Nomi: 'Weird trumped sexuality and weird was encouraged then,' he recalls. 'Sexuality only came into it later.' At eighteen Bottum moved to San Francisco in 1981 and came out shortly after. 'Anything went at the time, so politically I didn't feel the need to declare anything,' he says. 'But all of a sudden, there was this crazy, chauvinistic camp, like Guns N' Roses. It spurred my need to go on the record. I couldn't take part in this circus of macho dudes and not wave a flag of my own.'

Bottum says that he'd tried to connect with Bob Mould and Michael Stipe, 'but I got the sense this was not an OK place to go. The door was shut, even in the openly minded independent scene. Even with [Hole's lesbian drummer] Patty Schemel, Courtney was acting hush-hush and Patty didn't want to discuss it in open forum terms. But I get why, because of AIDS and homophobia. It was a crazy time and I wasn't upfront either.'

Bottum's interviewer at *The Advocate* was former Mumps and *An American Family* alumni-turned-journalist Lance Loud. 'I'd like to say that I'm totally together about it,' Bottum told Loud, 'but it does kinda freak me out. From now on, any time my name will be brought up, my sexual preference will be one of the first things discussed. It's a way of categorising people that seems kind of creepy to me. How many aspects of a personality are there? So many.'

That didn't stop Bottum from leaving Faith No More and forming a band, Imperial Teen, with a clear queer outlook. He'd already written 'Be Aggressive' (for Faith No More's 1992 album *Angel Dust*), with a top/bottom role-playing lyric for straight frontman Mike Patton to sing, 'Malnutrition, my submission/You're the master and I take it on my knees/Ejaculation, tribulation/I swallow!'

Imperial Teen were more playful, indie-punk, an alt.rock Abba given the quartet's gender split, including gay frontman Will Schwartz and drummer Lynn Perko, who had played with Gary Floyd's Dicks and Sister Double Happiness. Imperial Teen's 1996 album debut *Seasick*, released on major-label affiliate Slash, included 'Butch' – 'The gun was loaded it never came/I pulled the trigger ignored the strain' – and

'You're One' (partly Bottum's lament for Kurt Cobain[1], who had committed suicide in 1994) in which Schwartz sang, 'You take it like a man, boy/You kiss me like a man, boy.'

Bottum says Slash suggested 'You're One' as the album's lead single. 'To me, it was just sexy, rather than stirring up controversy or making a loud gay sentiment. Word came back that radio in the big markets was resistant, that it was just *too gay*. Even our manager said, "It's fine you're gay, but don't put it out there!"'

Typically, some straight boys loved to put it out there. Limp Bizkit, the most popular of the new rap-metal hybrids, took their name from a game of masturbation among teenage boys. Guitarist Wes Borland wore many gender-fluid costumes, 'just to make people mad' and the band's first three album titles all alluded to homosexuality: *Three Dollar Bills, Y'all* (as in, 'as queer as a three-dollar bill'), *Significant Other* (a subtler reference, in this case meaning same-sex partner) and *Chocolate Starfish and the Hot Dog Flavored Water* ('chocolate starfish' being slang for anus, while the jury's out on hot-dog flavoured water[2]).

On the other side, if you were really gay, then you had to act as straight as you could. Rob Halford, Judas Priest frontman, had – like Roddy Bottum – persistently been advised not to 'put it out there'. On one level, he ignored the advice; though his bandmates were classic glam-rock drag, Halford wore head-to-toe leather, accessorised with chains, studded leather chaps, belt and armbands and even a body harness, alongside the occasional whip. And a peaked cap to finish it off. The Village People cop was a sissy by comparison.

From England's Midlands region, home of much UK heavy metal, Halford was unusual in being a gay teen drawn to emulate the powerhouse voices such as Janis Joplin and Led Zeppelin's Robert Plant. But at

---

1 'I don't think there was a gay bone in Kurt's body,' Bottum says, 'but he was very sweet about it, as a champion of human rights. He pushed that on an audience of people who were open-minded but also had a narrow vision where sexuality was concerned.'
2 According to guitarist Wes Borland, *Hot Dog Flavored Water* came from Borland seeing bottles of Crystal Geyser water and joking about having meat or hot dog flavours.

least heavy metal gave him the chance to dress up, though he didn't get it right at the start. There were his 'flamboyant saggy pants,' as he told *The Advocate* when he came out in 1998. 'It was very extroverted and fluffy in its visual tone, but I didn't feel right. I've got great videos of me wearing outfits that I stole out of my sister's closet. How do I dress with the music that sounds this way?'

As Judas Priest released their 1978 album *Killing Machine*, remarkably renamed *Hell Bent For Leather* (after one of its tracks) for the US market, Halford found his biker/BDSM niche. 'For the first time I felt like, God this feels so good. This feels so right,' he recalled. 'Nobody seemed to have a problem with it and everybody was crazy for it, so we kept doing it.'

Halford had also sneaked on some wonderfully flagrant lyrics, especially the astonishing 'Raw Deal' (from 1977's *Sin After Sin*): 'I made the Spike about nine o'clock on a Saturday/All eyes hit me as I walked into the bar . . . the guys were fooling with the denim dudes/A couple cards played rough stuff, New York, Fire Island.' As Janis Ian said, it showed how few people listened to the lyrics. Or rather, it showed that no Judas Priest fan had a clue about gay life.

But he stayed closeted. Tom Robinson recalls Halford coming out to him in 1978, while Roddy Bottum recalls meeting Halford in the mid-nineties, at the Rock In Rio festival: 'He was looking sexy in his Speedos by the pool, hanging out with handsome gay men. It was very clear he was gay too. But we didn't discuss it.'

Neither did Judas Priest's management encourage talk, for fear of damaging their nest egg – the band's albums sold in millions. Halford said he didn't experience homophobia from his bandmates or deny himself the freedom to have what his bandmates were having – to take a lover on tour or to enjoy a one-night stand, on the odd occasion that Halford's 'gaydar would go off'. But as the sole gay man in metal, it was 'a very isolated, lonely kind of existence'. Freddie Mercury – the only other gay man in UK rock mainstream – never became a chum, even after they met in an Athens gay bar.

'I think it's true, when you become successful in the music world, you probably go more in the closet,' Halford said, 'because of the phobia that still exists in rock music. You could lose a record deal, a fan base.' He also felt protective of his bandmates' livelihood. And the longer he stayed in the closet, the harder it was to escape what he called, 'self-imposed negative fear.'[1]

Eventually, Halford left Judas Priest, in 1991, after his request to be allowed to record a solo album was denied. More likely, it was his escape from responsibilities to his bandmates. It took him another seven years to come out publicly.

For Halford, *A Small Deadly Space*, by his next band, Fight, was a belated response to AIDS, but no one thought to ask. Halford then fronted 2wo, a more industrial rock din that encouraged a more open-minded fan base[2]. Halford went as far as performing Judas Priest's 'Breakin' the Law' with Pansy Division at San Diego's Gay Pride Festival without media comment. But when he outed himself on MTV's *Superrock* series, the media was all over it. 'I was constantly held back, I allowed myself to be intimidated, I allowed myself to do certain things and one of them was not to step forward and come out as a gay person,' Halford claimed at the time, inferring his management were to blame.[3] Halford also suggested metal fans that had a problem with him being gay should, 'seek help and find out why they have a problem with it.'[4]

---

1 http://www.pressofatlanticcity.com/attheshore/headliners/metal-gods-judas-priest-make-a-c-debut-at-harrah/article_1bca6b16-4f0e-11e4-9bac-c731be7471a9.html
2 Champion of the new industrial-influenced bands was Marilyn Manson – both band and the singer it was named after (Brian Warner to his mum) promoted androgyny, fetish wear and all the pervy points in between – they recorded a cover of 'Tainted Love' to make their point.
3 Halford's management are still trying to limit him; over the course of a year, I was told he had no time to talk for this book, despite being very vocal about his sexuality whenever he got the chance. In 2014, the band's record label also told the Guardian not to ask him about his sexuality – though the subject was first raised that day by Halford.
4 Though Halford wasn't to test Judas Priest's fan base until he rejoined the band in 2003. He enjoyed his new-found freedom, hiring gay porn director Chi Chi Larue to direct the video for 2wo's debut single 'I Am a Pig'.

Even the marketing department is gay

One record company decided that gay was good and they could make money out of it. Epic/Sony had contemplated opening a marketing department devoted to gay artists after 1994's Gay Games and the Stonewall 25 Civil Rights march, which drew a million attendees. It was the Warner Bros offshoot Atlantic that went ahead in 1996, putting journalist Peter Galvin in charge of a groundbreaking initiative that would advertise the label's artists to gay music fans and sign openly gay artists to Atlantic.

Massachusetts-born singer-songwriter Melissa Ferrick, a folk-AOR type half way between Ani DiFranco and Melissa Etheridge, just missed the boat; *Massive Blur*, her 1991 debut album for Atlantic, preceded k.d. lang and Melissa Etheridge's breakthroughs, but even with 1995's *Willing to Wait*, the label trod carefully. 'Melissa was never closeted until she signed to a major,' claims Jim Fouratt. 'I was her friend, and journalists would ask me, "Can we say she's a lesbian?" I said, "Ask her!" Atlantic wanted to do a whispering campaign.'

By 1996, Ferrick had left Atlantic, but now the label was now promoting openness. The first to benefit were Extra Fancy, a grungy rock band from LA whose frontman Brian Grillo was openly gay and openly HIV. Atlantic knew what they were getting, as the band's debut album *Sinnerman* had first been released independently before being picked up as the flagship release for Galvin's department.

Grillo's openness extended across the likes of 'Seven Years Ago': 'You set me up, I fell for you, infected me 'bout seven years ago/Punch-drunk, I fell in love, no warning/You should've have told me'.

'I won't tell my man I love him . . . Somebody might be listening,' Grillo sang in 'What I Have'. With Grillo's naked body and the 'Male burlesque' sign in the artwork, Extra Fancy were more out than any other mainstream rock band.

A September 1995 feature in the *LA Times* underlined Atlantic's support for this brave new venture. Journalist Steve Hochman wrote: 'While [Galvin] applauds such artists as Elton John, k.d. lang and

Melissa Etheridge for coming out of the closet, he points out that they still tend to leave their songs non-specific when it comes to sexual orientation.' Galvin was quoted as saying, 'It would be nice if gay people were exposed to more rock'n'roll that spoke directly to the experience of being gay, whatever that means.'[1]

This wasn't the case with Atlantic's first four campaigns: new albums by Bette Midler, jazz-pop newcomer Steven Kowalczyk, Bruce Roberts – who'd most famously written Donna Summer and Barbra Streisand's 'No More Tears (Enough Is Enough)' and had penned hits for Cher, Celine Dion and Dusty Springfield among others – and a *Greatest Hits* from disco favourite Laura Branigan. The next campaign was Extra Fancy, to be followed by Pet Shop Boys, who had just joined Atlantic, apparently intrigued by the idea of their marketing division. Neil Tennant had also come out in 1994, the *annus mirabilis* for gay male singers.

Having responded to Jimmy Somerville's criticism of Pet Shop Boys – 'I reject any notion of being a positive role models to anyone' – Tennant told *Attitude*'s Paul Burston that the duo had supported gay rights (such as the Organisation For Lesbian and Gay Action 1988 fundraiser, for which every piece of work had been created by gay men and lesbians) and had contributed 'rather a lot to what you might call gay culture . . . What I'm actually saying is, I am gay and I have written songs from that point of view.'

Those who cared enough to decipher Tennant's lyrics might ascertain they had traces of gay DNA, though no one needed to work out the purpose of their stirring cover – and huge global hit – of the Village People's 'Go West'. PSB added a male choir and a more melancholic understanding of what had been lost since the original in 1979. They included an extra verse with a poignant note of hope: 'Here, where the air is free/ We'll be what we want to be/Now if we make a stand/We'll find our promised land.'

---

1 http://articles.latimes.com/1995-09-17/entertainment/ca-46767_1_gay-music

BREAKING DOWN THE WALLS OF HEARTACHE

In the US, 'Go West' was a dance chart no. 1, but only reached no. 106 in the national chart. Yet Atlantic might still have had high hopes for Pet Shop Boys' seventh album *Bilingual*, with its Latin rhythms primed for the US vote. Except – eight weeks after Extra Fancy's *Sinnerman* was released and four weeks before *Bilingual*'s release – the label pulled the plug on its gay marketing. Extra Fancy were let go – victims, the label announced, of a restructuring that media reports claimed had cost the lives of up to ten bands.

In the aftermath, *Bilingual* just scraped into the US Top 40. Had the duo simply peaked? The album went UK Top 5, but had the bubble of mystery around Pet Shops Boys burst by Tennant coming out? Were they now, 'a gay band'? Perhaps Pet Shop Boys weren't so enamoured of Atlantic's marketing to the gay community. In a 2012 interview on NPR, Tennant said, 'I've always had a very ambivalent relationship with the idea of gay culture, because I think it's often been used to marginalise people,' he said. 'In the United States, it was used to marginalise the Pet Shop Boys . . . and I sort of resent the idea that being gay means you liked a certain kind of music, which maybe includes the Pet Shop Boys.'[1]

Lacking the solid fan base of PSB, Extra Fancy struggled much more; they started up their own label, Butch Ditties, but would only release one more EP before splitting up. Too gay for rock, too rock for gay – despite Grillo's evident star quality.

In *Billboard*'s June 1998 cover story 'Gay artists making business strides', senior talent editor Larry Flick wrote, 'Some gay and lesbian artists find the highest degree of homophobia they face actually comes from the queer community,' citing the experience of Karel Bouley, a journalist and publicist turned recording artist. His self-released debut album *Dance . . . Or Else* and his single – a cover of Madonna's 'Live To Tell' – had earned a deal with DJ/remixer Jellybean Benitez's label.

'I do believe that my being out has hurt my success in the gay

---

[1] www.npr.org/2012/09/09/160750906/pet-shop-boys-leave-west-end-to-explore-elysium

community,' Karel said. 'Musically, if you're not a black woman with a large voice, a seven-foot drag queen or a chiselled boy with 2 per cent body fat where [having a great voice] isn't an issue, the community really doesn't know what to do with you.'

Karel was white and big-boned, while pretty boys regimented into formulaic boy-band packages fell off the factory line – Bay City Rollers, New Edition, New Kids On The Block, Bros, appealing to female and male fans. The nineties breed was different, starting with Manchester quintet Take That, assembled by gay manager Nigel Martin-Smith; in one early publicity shot, they resembled a teen Frankie Goes To Hollywood, in another, they wore only thongs with the band letters stuck to their bare arses. Louis Walsh, also rumoured to be gay (though he has never confirmed this) launched Boyzone with the same sort of gay image while Tom Watkins – gay and former manager of Pet Shop Boys – put together East 17, though their image was more hip hop and the clothes stayed on.

In response, the US came up with Backstreet Boys – their name alone inferring a gay sexuality – and *NSYNC; both sold millions. This was how you courted the gay market rather than with gay artists, something that one anonymous major A&R executive interviewed by *Billboard* felt would never happen. 'You can be gay and have a hit – if your record is soft and you're a platinum seller like Elton John. But we're years and years away from the day when a gay artist can be broken out of the box. I hate to say it, but gay people are just too frightening to too many people in the straight world.'

It's largely forgotten – though not to the artist – that when Rufus Wainwright, the son of singer-songwriters Loudon Wainwright and Kate McGarrigle, released his self-titled debut album on David Geffen's new label Dreamworks in 1996, his subsequent audience was predominantly straight. He was marketed as a singer-songwriter, despite his obvious Broadway affectations and piano ballads such as 'Danny Boy' and 'Matinee Idol'. In 1998, Wainwright was *Rolling Stone*'s best new artist of the year – but he won the same accolade at the GLAMAS, where he was also nominated in best album, pop recording and video categories. But it didn't translate into a gay audience.

'I did resent it, that all the people waiting backstage were fourteen year-old girls,' Wainwright says. 'I was angry and I'd certainly go out and do drugs, to gain some entry into that [gay] world, but I'd end up most times in a straight bar to get feedback on what I was doing, because no one knew who I was at the disco. I was just resigned to it, to not fitting in and being like everyone else.'

In a 2014 interview with *The Times*, Wainwright was more vitriolic; he was glad he didn't have a large LGBT following back at the start, because gay men have 'terrible taste in music.' He also claimed 'being gay hurt my career' and said he'd have been more popular in the US if he were 'asexual or bisexual'.

Ironically, Wainwright knew that it was his ambitious stage reincarnation of Judy Garland's 1961 double album *Judy At Carnegie Hall* that 'nudged back [gay fans], like, don't forget where you come from. We were all spawned from the loins of Judy!'

Don't stop me now: the floodgates open

Ricky Martin, the late-nineties Latin superstar who crossed over to the rest of the planet, was widely rumoured to be spawned from Judy's loins. But he would stay in the closet, where his companion would have continued to be George Michael had the latter not made himself the centre of the biggest outing news story since Freddie Mercury – though with a far happier ending.

The former singer with Wham!, one of the most popular male duos of the new romantic era, had moved on to solo superstardom via albums such as *Faith* and *Listen Without Prejudice Vol. 1*. At Live Aid in 1985 and again at his own show, Michael had joined forces with Elton John on the latter's 'Don't Let The Sun Go Down On Me' but the duets only seem revealing with hindsight. He was never caught on camera with a boyfriend, nor did he give out clear signals. The video for 1986's US and UK Top 3 'I Want Your Sex' prominently featured celebrity make-up artist Kathy Jeung in lingerie and yet industry gossip created a web of rumours. Looking back, Michael said he never had a moral problem with being gay and added he'd fallen in love with a woman a couple of times, but then fell in love with a man and realised that 'none of those things had been love'. He kept it quiet, he said, because of his concerns for his Greek orthodox family. In the end, it didn't kill them when Michael was arrested in April 1998 for 'engaging in a lewd act' by an undercover policeman in the public restroom in a Beverly Hills park.

On the BBC's *Desert Island Discs*, Michael explained that he'd been out to his sister, and close friends, since he was nineteen, but 'AIDS was the predominant feature of being gay in the 1980s and early nineties, as far as any parent was concerned. My mother was still alive and every single day would have been a nightmare for her thinking what I might have been subjected to.' Looking back on his decision, 'I was too immature to know I was sacrificing as much as I was.'

In 1993 his lover Anselmo Feleppa died of an AIDS-related illness, which Michael could only address in a coded tribute, 'Jesus to a Child'. But once he'd been forced out (a year after his mother had died), the singer's response was as barefaced as his former life had been concealed. Michael never specified gender in the lyric extoling the pleasures of having sex 'in the sunshine', but the video for 'Outside' was a spectacular riposte: a cavalcade of couplings – sailors, construction workers, policemen and heterosexuals too – as a helicopter swooped over, the sex police doing their pointless surveillance work. A men's public toilet turned into a disco, with Michael disco-dancing in police drag. In the closing image, the helicopter flew past the sign 'Jesus saves' and a message flashed up 'all of us'.

As a self-mocking PR coup, Michael couldn't have done better and the response was affirming: Top 20 in thirteen countries –notably not the USA, though MTV aired the video intact. By 1998, a palpable sense of change had pervaded every aspect of the western world. That year, the annual kitschy Eurovision Song Contest was won with 'Diva', by Israeli singer Dana International. The former Yaron (now Sharon) Cohen had worked as a drag queen before transitioning and making dance music. Her victory made Dana the most widely publicised trans female since Christine Jorgensen.

Swedish trio Army Of Lovers had widespread success with a pronounced gay image, as ultra-camp as the documentary from which they had taken their name – Rosa von Praunheim's *Armee der Liebenden oder Revolte der Perversen* (*Army of Lovers or Revolt of the Perverts*) about US gay activism after Stonewall, which argued that sexual promiscuity was harming the gay rights movement.

By 1998, most US bathhouses (though not those in Europe) had been shut down, the concept of safe sex widely adopted and, in 1995, the combination medical treatment, the 'AIDS cocktail', began to have dramatic results in the life expectancy of HIV/AIDS patients. According to figures in a report by the gay and lesbian study group of the American Musicology Society,[1] deaths peaked at twenty-two and fourteen musicians in 1993 and 1995 respectively, before falling to twenty over the following seven years.

Mainstream country star Reba McEntire was one of a diverse group of singers – Elton John, Tori Amos, Patti Smith[2], Indigo Girls and Janet Jackson among them – who kept songs about AIDS in the public consciousness. One of Broadway's success stories of the nineties, *Rent*, wove a strong AIDS storyline around artists grappling with the condition and with homelessness in the East Village[3]. Creator Jonathan Larson admitted the influence of Giacomo Puccini's opera *La Bohème*, but *Rent* also had alarming similarities to Sarah Schulman's 1992 novel *People In Trouble*, sharing a central plot (female artist leaves artist boyfriend for lesbian activist; her subsequent performance piece targets a landlord trying to evict people with AIDS, which creates a riot and the

---

[1] https://static1.squarespace.com/static/5209277fe4b0f89d3271cc3a/t/520cd764e4b06b11 62428a1d/1376573284239/N28.pdf

[2] Patti Smith's 'Death Singing' was inspired by Benjamin, lead singer of the Atlanta bands Smoke and Opal Foxx Quartet, named after his drag alias, who died of AIDS in 1999.

[3] For the full story, read Schulman's book *Stagestruck: Theater, AIDS and the Marketing of Gay America* (Duke University Press, 1998).

landlord's downfall) and supporting storyline (an interracial couple, one an AIDS activist and the other a drag queen, both HIV-positive). The difference was that Schulman's hero is the female artist; in *Rent*, it's the jilted (heterosexual) boyfriend, creating a similarly palatable outcome for mainstream audiences as was seen in Oscar-winning *Philadelphia*.

Rent was similarly rewarded, with a Pulitzer Prize and Tony Award for best musical. It ran for over 5000 performances across twelve years, its hetero-saves-the-day scenario offset by a high-profile denouncement of homophobia: respect trumps ostracism. But a more honest, accurate and satisfying portrait of LGBTQ[1] life was found in two uncompromising off-Broadway pieces: 1995's *Harvey Milk* the opera and the following year's *Hedwig and the Angry Inch*.

New York: A city in transition

New York's Pyramid club was still thriving in the nineties, as the city's queer underground scene launched a new weekly club night in 1994. Squeezebox combined drag performance with glam and punk rock standards, with star turns from the likes of Debbie Harry, Joey Ramone and the scene's godmother, Jayne County. Squeezebox also saw the debut of its musical director Stephen Trask's concept of Hedwig, who was played by actor John Cameron Mitchell, who sang in front of Trask's band, also called The Angry Inch.

Hedwig was formerly Hansel from East Berlin – 'a slip of a girly boy,' according to Mitchell – who undergoes a sex change so she can escape communist East Germany as the bride of an American GI. But the operation is botched, leaving her with the 'angry inch' of the title.

Squeezebox was also home to trans rocker and activist Chloe Dzubilo, with her band the Transsisters. They were Pyramid regulars too, where Dzubilo was an occasional contributor to Blacklips, a performance art troupe co-founded by her close friend Anohni, the artist formerly known as Antony.

---

1 The shift from LGBT to LGBTQ – Lesbian, Gay, Bisexual, Transgender and Queer – has been dated to 1996.

Growing up in the English town of Chichester, Anohni was seven when she first saw the video for Kate Bush's 'Wuthering Heights – 'I'd do her slow-motion cartwheel from the video for all the gawking neighbourhood boys' – before Marc Almond, Alison Moyet and Boy George entered her life, 'those androgynous, soulful voices. Seeing a photo of George when I was twelve was the first time I'd recognised myself in anyone else, a profound sense of androgyny. I thought, OK, that's what people like us do; we become singers.'

Anohni's family had moved to California when she was young, before going on alone to Manhattan after seeing the film documentary *Mondo New York* about the city's underground cabaret scene.

She was particularly taken with Joey Arias' mesmeric Billie Holiday act, while Blacklips reflected much of the Cockettes' spontaneous combustion, though Anohni named them after Bette Bourne's British troupe Bloolips. But while the latter approached AIDS with the song-and-dance humour of 'Tap Your Troubles Away', Blacklips found another way. Shows at New York's Pyramid Club included *The Birth of Anne Frank* and *Miracle Now*, in which Anohni's friend Page – 'the Candy Darling of my generation' – sang 'What Can I Do' in the character of 'the last dolphin on earth, in a rubbery outfit with no arms, singing in a high-pitched voice as I played piano.'

Anohni, who often took the name Fiona Blue for performances, remembers Blacklips as 'blood bags and beauty theatre. There was a lot of offal thrown on stage, and at the end of each show, I'd sing a love song. It was a theatre of extremes, and we'd end in a pile of squealing corpses. It was the time of AIDS and that's how we responded. We'd call Manhattan "Leper Island", where America's disenfranchised all fled to be free.'

Her band of musicians, the Johnsons, were named after Stonewall pioneer and trans activist Marsha P. Johnson, whose body had been found in the Hudson river off the West Village piers shortly after 1992's Pride march: Antony and the Johnsons' self-titled debut album, released in 2000, paid further tribute with 'River Of Sorrow'[1], one of the album's tremulous torch songs.

Another album track, 'Cripple and The Starfish', had debuted as the theme song for a 'post-apocalyptic musical' of the same name which Anohni staged in 1991, but it first reappeared on 1996's *God Shave the Queen*, the first compilation of original material by singers identifying as drag or trans. Tracks included Joey Arias' 'No One Knows'. Anohni, as pictured in the CD booklet, resembled Klaus Nomi, with short black hair, black suit and thick white make-up, making her a strange fit, visually and musically. Two years later, going by *Antony And The Johnsons*, she had begun to radiate an otherworldly androgyny beyond that of Nomi or Ziggy. Vocally, Anohni equally located an uncanny, soulful androgyny, with deep-trawling notes of Nina Simone, which reinforced her unique charisma.[2]

Hip hop homophobia, won't stop

Adam Horowitz, the Beastie Boy who had been dating riot grrrl lynchpin Kathleen Hanna since 1996, publicly apologised in *Time Out* 'to the entire gay and lesbian community for the shitty and ignorant things we said on our first record, 1986's *Licensed To Ill*. There are no excuses. But time has healed our stupidity.'

Time had healed the Beastie Boys, but there were plenty of hip hop replacement with attitudes rooted in the Neanderthal age. Most prominently, given his millions of sales, was Detroit's Marshall Mathers

---

1 Police ruled Johnson's death a suicide though her friends contested the verdict. In 2012, the case was reopened as a possible homicide. Shortly after her death, Anohni appeared in a production about her life, staged by Hot Peaches.
2 The era's other extraordinary androgynous figure was Genesis P. Orridge (born Neil Andrew Megson), the founder member of the UK's industrial music pioneers Throbbing Gristle. In 1993, he and new wife Lady Jaye (born Jacqueline Breyer), initiated the Pandrogeny Project, undergoing body modification, including breast implants and hormone therapy. 'Pandrogeny is not about gender, it's about union,' he told his former bandmate Douglas Rushkoff. www.believermag.com/exclusives/?read=interview_p-orridge_rushkoff

– Eminem – a scintillating rapper and a master of homophobic and misogynistic slurs through his supposed alter ego Slim Shady.

Mathers was the protégé of Dr Dre, who had left NWA for a solo career, his own record label and production duties. In Dre's world, homosexuality was presumably OK if it took place in prison, in the dynamic of dominance and submission, such as his 1992 track 'Fuck Wit Dre Day': 'Gap teeth in your mouth so my dick's got's to fit/with my nuts on your tonsils.' Dre's fellow enlightened Compton hip hopper DJ Quik's 'Dollaz + Sense' included, 'Now, I never had my dick sucked by a man befo/But you gon be the first you little trick ass ho/Then you can tell me just how it taste/But before I nut, I shoot some piss in your face.'

Eminem took the violence up a notch. His 1999 single 'My Name Is . . .' originally featured the line, 'Raping lesbians while they're screaming, "Let's be friends!"'. Labi Siffre – whose song 'I Got The . . . ' had been chosen by Dre to provide the track's main sample – objected. 'Attacking two of the usual scapegoats, women and gays, is lazy writing,' Siffre said. 'If you want to do battle, attack the aggressors, not the victims.'

Eminem changed the line to, 'Extraterrestrial runnin' over pedestrians/In a space ship while they screaming at me, "Let's just be friends!"' but Eminem did battle anyway with the victims on 'Ken Kaniff (skit)', a character created by the rapper Aristotle that linked homosexuality with rape and paedophilia.

Even the 'conscious' rappers, a more spiritual bunch, were offenders, such as Common, Mos Def and Goodie Mob – yet all would record tracks for *Red Hot* compilations. Sen Dog of Latino trio Cypress Hill once told the *NME*, 'I don't get fags . . . how can you not love pussy?' Even KRS-One, of Boogie Down Productions, who'd recorded a rap for R.E.M.'s 1990 single 'Radio Song', felt the need to join the fun with 'Ya Strugglin'': 'Where, oh, where are all the real men/The feminine look seems to be the trend/You got eyeliner on, chillin' and maxin'/See you're a man with a spine extraction.'

Of the emerging female rappers, some might have been inclined to agree with Sen Dog about pussy. Queen Latifah (born Dana Elaine Owens) had launched her pioneering feminist rap agenda in 1989 with her single 'Ladies First' and had graduated to TV and film roles, including a lesbian character in the 1996 drama *Set It Off*, suggesting she had no truck with the rumours about her off-screen preference. Newcomers Missy Elliott and Da Brat were quickly surrounded by similar stories. For all hip hop's 'keep it real' manifesto, being open about your homosexuality was the same as that of sixties' rock: career suicide.

Still, one contender was willing to risk it – but only in a teasing, don't label-me manner that skirted with bisexuality. From Brooklyn, Queen Pen (born Lynise Walter) released a single, 'Girlfriend', which turned around a key hip hop's brag about stealing a rival's girlfriend. The thief here was a woman – and openly bisexual singer-songwriter MeShell Ndegéocello added bass and vocals to the track, which was based on her own 'Boyfriend'.

Ndegéocello knew about provocation – she'd released a single in 1996 under the title 'Leviticus: Faggot', about a gay man rejected by family and church. But though she incorporated spoken word in her work, Ndegéocello wasn't identified as a rapper and Pen's brand of lesbianism suggested a matter of conquest more than genuine desire or that the rapper's girlfriend was the instigator: 'She slid by me four or five times/ Wantin' me to notice the rhythm of her thighs/Girls are just so funny to me.'

"I'm black. I'm a female rapper. I couldn't even go out of my way to pick up a new form of discrimination,' she told Laura Jamison. 'People are waiting for this hip hop Ellen[1] to come out of the closet. I'd rather be a mystery for a minute . . . Even if I sat here and said, "I'm straight," I could be lying. If I said, "I'm gay," it could be a publicity stunt.'[2] When Jamison asked if Pen dated women, the rapper asked how big the article

---

1 In 1997, comedian Ellen DeGeneres had become the first openly gay character on primetime US TV in her sitcom *Ellen*.
2 www.nytimes.com/1998/01/18/arts/pop-jazz-a-feisty-female-rapper-breaks-a-hip hop-taboo.html

was going to be. 'A little later,' Jamison wrote, 'she said that she would talk only "in depth" about her sexuality for a front-page article.'

It only needed one brave and brash individual to consider being an openly gay rapper. Not in the fashion of Age Of Consent, whose interest in hip hop was more cultural and pop-referential, nor electro-rapping 'Chickenhawk' by Cunts With Attitude with its chorus, 'Boy, I fucked your girlfriend . . . she is done with boys', nor the hip hop remix of '(I'm A) Boy Watcher'[1] by Brothers About Living Loving Sensuality (as in BALLS) as an AIDS fundraiser, nor the joke of 'I'm Da Beastie Gay' from comedian Gay Boy Ric[2]. Queer rap needed someone to be serious about the art form. Someone, in short, like Carole Wolfe, who called herself Cyryus – pronounced, 'Serious'.

Today Wolfe is a councillor at a methadone clinic in Columbus, Georgia; her music – producing backing tracks ('hip hop-soul, neo-soul, hip hop, chillout and ambient') – is a secondary vocation. Her only rap in recent years was one rhyme on 'All Figured Out', the lead single – 'a female-to-female break-up song' – from the *Something From Nothing* album that Wolfe produced for neo-soul singer Nesrin Asli. 'It was too good for me to stay off the track,' says Wolfe, 'but I'd got disillusioned with hip hop. There wasn't much comradery, everything was a competition. It was all about ego.'

In the seventies, Wolfe grew up in Philadelphia, loving her soul music before the Sugarhill Gang's 'Rapper's Delight' 'opened a new world. I wrote my first rhyme at twelve. I started drumming too.' She had no concept that being gay was wrong, 'until kids started telling gay fag jokes, I went right into the closet.'

Wolfe found the Indigo Girls and k.d. lang, 'but it wasn't the music I'd have made. I was more inspired by Public Enemy. I identified with their struggle and message about being black in a white society and me being gay in a straight society. I know they had anti-gay lyrics – it was

---

1 '(I'm A) Boy Watcher' was a remake of the O'Kaysions' 1968 hit 'Girl Watcher'.
2 Gay Boy Ric, a.k.a. Ricardo H. Garcia, also served the cause with a documentary about Eminem's homophobia and the now defunct website www.fuckeminem.com

love-hate with them. I hated all rap about bitches and hoes and shooting up everything.'

Wolfe came out when she was eighteen, after moving to LA to study hairdressing: 'Being gay there was no big deal and the gay guys I met were well-adjusted. They introduced me to their lesbian friends.' But she was a lone Wolfe when venturing to south central LA's hip hop clubs, where she found the MCs 'were virtuosos, the hip hop equivalent of Mozart, just mind-blowing.' By 1993, Wolfe had joined in, as one half of an alliance with Lacresha Collins, a black lesbian rapper calling herself Tay-Tae. Their chosen name, One In Ten, put their lesbian status right up front.

The duo rapped live, over their own beats, often on the talent show circuit. 'One place had a boxing ring and the MCs would battle,' Wolfe explains. 'We got really good. We'd completely annihilate someone, physically drop the mic and then just walk out, that was our thing.' The battle extended to the judges. 'It was our very first talent show. Part of the contest was talking to the judges, to show you're professional. One judge asked what our name meant and we said, "It's the ratio of gay to straight." After, we found out a judge had thought that was completely unprofessional, like, "Why would you say that? That's none of anyone's business." But everybody's song on the radio was about their personal business. But that's OK because they're straight.'

The discrimination continued. 'People would say, "You guys look too butch, soften it up, wear some make-up." Tay looked like LL Cool J and I looked like a Beastie Boy. One producer said, "You guys are the MC's MC but you need a party track, dumb it down a little, you make people think too much."'

One In Ten still managed to get a meeting with Michael Jackson's MJ label. 'The A&R guy heard promise in our demos and he didn't have a problem with us being lesbians, or rapping about it. But Tay wasn't sure she wanted to do it fulltime and the guy wouldn't wait. Nine months later, he signed a black and white male rap duo.'

No other record label bit, until Matt Wobensmith got in touch. 'After five years of running Outpunk,' he says, 'I didn't want to do what was expected of me. I wanted to keep pushing boundaries and use the revolutionary power of music to promote LGBT visibility. It was hard to get excited about something [punk rock] whose premise was determined well over five years ago. I wanted to try to recreate the same scenes in hip hop and electronic music.'

Wobensmith launched new label Queercorps with the electronic compilation EP *Join The Queercorps*[1] before he 'caught a glimpse of LGBT activity in the hip hop world'. He approached One In Ten about staging shows and being interviewed for his fanzine before proposing to release their album. By this point, One In Ten had made friends with an all-black female rap crew Da 5 Footaz. One of their affiliates didn't like Wolfe; she says, 'it might have been racial – I was the only white rapper for a mile and some didn't like the fact a white girl was good at hip hop.'

The day One In Ten were to fly to San Francisco to meet Wobensmith, 'Tay said she couldn't trust me anymore. We'd been best friends for four years and now, overnight, this. It was sabotage, divide and conquer, and it worked. I never wanted to do it alone and, as a white, lesbian, female MC, I might as well be left-handed too! But the anger and hurt motivated me and I was a musician anyway, so I could make my own tracks.'

Cyryus' 1998 debut album *The Lyricist* was that of a smart-spirited wordsmith who could rival Eminem for riddles and rhymes. One track, 'The Immaculate Conception', featured a sample of a sermon by archbishop Carl Bean but the content was more spiritual than homosexual. 'The album was all about being gay in the music industry, but I wrote in riddles and tried not to use the word "gay", not because I was afraid but I wanted to trick people. To hear hip hop homophobes rave about my music was great! They'd think it's just a battle rhyme. It was those guys that motivated me.'

The album's guest stars included black lesbian rapper N. I. Double K. I – a.k.a. Deshelia 'Nikki' Mixon – and Judge Muscat, a.k.a. Dutchboy,

---

[1] Of *Join The Queercorps*' four tracks, two were remixes of queercore bands Team Dresch and the Mukilteo Fairies.

who added acoustic guitar in place of his usual rapping. Wobensmith had introduced both to Cyryus and all of them featured in *Outpunk* fanzine's last issue in 'the first comprehensive overview of the state of LGBT hip hop,' says Wobensmith.

Like Cyryus, Dutchboy embraced hip hop when he was young, through a breakdancing older brother who'd bring home Run DMC records. As a white teenager in San Francisco, he'd seen hip hop culture explode at a distance, 'but after seeing quite a few 14-year-old white kids in my neighbourhood wearing baggy jeans and NWA T-shirts, the idea of my participation started to seem less and less ridiculous,' he told the Daily Xtra.[1]

In 1996, he started Rainbow Flava, a loose affiliate of gay, lesbian and bisexual hip hop fans, inspired by the same blend of outsider status and music. 'Hip hop is predominantly a culture of angry young men, many of whom have never felt truly included in society,' said Dutchboy. 'Anyone wishing to be accepted into its inner circle has to be prepared to kick and scream and face dismissal and criticism. It's something women and other minorities in hip hop have struggled with from the beginning, so it's no surprise that LGBT artists should face the same treatment.'

By 1998, Rainbow Flava comprised Dutchboy, Reh-Shawn and Kevin Cruze (a.k.a. DJ Monkey), with a band website and an umbrella organisation christened Phat Family that disseminated information about their operations, queer hip hop events such as Dutchboy's weekly hip hop/house party Freaky and a Yahoo discussion group. As word got out, Dutchboy told *SF Weekly*, 'I started getting these bizarre messages from people all over the planet saying, "I'm in Houston and I'm a gay MC," "I'm a lesbian in New York and I DJ," or "I'm gay and I collect hip hop records." I became aware that even if there weren't a lot of people doing this, there were an awful lot of people wondering the same things I was. Like, "Why hasn't it happened yet?" and "Where [can I] find it?"'[2]

One email had come from Schönheitsfehler, an Austrian hip hop

---

1 www.dailyxtra.com/toronto/homo-homies-56130
2 www.sfweekly.com/sanfrancisco/peace-out/Content?oid=2140637

trio organising an event to raise awareness about homophobia. They offered to fly Rainbow Flava to Vienna, which motivated the troupe to create something they could sell, namely their debut CD *Rainbow Flava Soundsystem*.

But equally, as word got out, hate mail – even death threats – followed. 'One of the things that drew me to hip hop as a vehicle for confronting issues of homophobia and sexual diversity is the fact that it's one of the few areas of American popular culture that is not averse to conflict,' said Dutchboy. 'Differences in beliefs are expressed and verbalised openly . . . Even the most extreme positions can receive a fair hearing when voiced by a talented and credible speaker.'[1] Or so he liked to think. But if this exchange was going to happen anywhere in the US, it would be the Bay Area. With Dutchboy identifying as bisexual and DJ Monkey and Reh-Shawn as gay, their rainbow did have some flavour, but they needed more performers – black and female – to be authentic. Rainbow Flava steadily expanded with two black men, Tori Fixx, who DJed at parties for Prince at Paisley Park Studios before leaving Minneapolis for San Francisco and Juba Kalamka, fresh to the Bay Area from Chicago and adopted the name Pointfivefag.

New Orleans was another traditionally liberal zone. The local, party-orientated brand of hip hop was known as bounce, after its rhythmic momentum typified by call-and-response vocals and explicit lyrics. Bobby Marchan, whose Powder Box Revue had ruled at the city's Dew Drop Inn as he'd once ruled the R&B charts, promoted early bounce artists via his record label and production company, Manicure. But it was another local record label, Take Fo, that released 'Melpomene Block Party' by Katey Red, a towering drag queen MC from New Orleans' central Melpomene housing projects.

The east coast had an emerging home rap duo, Morplay – white gay male Cazwell and white lesbian Crasta Yo – who had got their start in Boston before moving to New York and appearing at the city's

---

1 www.dailyxtra.com/toronto/homo-homies-56130

Gay Pride in 1999. As Luke 'Cazwell' Caswell said in an interview on Mother Jones, 'The first ten rows of people were black and the woman that introduced us, introduced us as hip hop. And when you think hip hop, you don't think a white fag and a white dyke ... there were at least ten people in the front row who were like, "Oh, no. We wanted real hip hop." I think the longer we played, we got a little bit more respect.'[1]

Morplay's agenda differed to that of Rainbow Flava, as they bypassed the hip hop scene for New York's downtown clubs like the Pyramid or CBGB's Homocorps night, where hip hop was just another flavour. Rufus Wainwright might be on stage or boy-band parody the Back Door Boys, drag acts and electronic acts. Morplay's albums *Morplay* and *Thesaurus Metamorphosis* weren't old-school hip hop either, but a blend of techno, jungle, drum'n'bass and electro breakbeats, with help from New York producers such as Larry Tee, who co-wrote RuPaul's 'Supermodel (You Better Work)'.

Queen Pen's *New York Times* interview concluded with the rapper saying, 'Two or three years from now, people will say Queen Pen was the first female to bring the lesbian life to light on wax. It's reality. What's the problem?' In the event, Pen never returned to the subject and nor did she come out (if she had reason to) after 'Girlfriend'. Cyrus's album crept out without promotion or attention and she has not recorded another.

More walls come tumbling down

Even genres in which LGBTQ visibility had been virtually non-existent now had their torch-bearers. From San Francisco, Doug Stevens, with his Outband, was country music's first openly gay artist since Lavender Country and, directly inspired by their example, founded the Lesbian and Gay Country Music Association in 1998. Both sets of Stevens's grandparents were country musicians and his parents regularly sang but, as he grew older, he saw 'bad things in the culture ... wife abuse, alcoholism and poverty. I wanted to get as far away from

---

1 www.motherjones.com/politics/2000/03/homie-sexualz

it as I could.' He became a classical music singer but, in 1990, he tested positive for HIV, his lover left him, and he spiralled into depression – the kind of emotional havoc that underpins the classic country music narrative.

Remembering Tammy Wynette's comment about writing a song to overcome her depression, Stevens did likewise. 'It made me feel much better, so I wrote another one, then another one,' he told Stonewall Society. 'The songs that came out of me were country songs. It didn't take me long to start going to gay [country and western] dance bars. I learned how to two-step dance and made a whole new group of friends. I saw that gay people didn't have country music about our lives, even though we bought a lot of music. So, I decided to form a country band to perform the music that I was writing about my life and experiences as a gay country man, living in the big city.'

Stevens and the Outband's debut album, *Out In The Country*, was self-released in 1993: the singer said that Atlantic Records had been interested in signing him, 'but only if we would change our lyrics. We refused.' Similar gay country artists followed in Steven's footsteps by sounding more authentically Nashville than alternative, including Sid Spencer (who died of AIDS in 1996) and Mark Weigle. They also had to take a DIY route, but they found an audience.

Even jazz, which had expressed its homophobia from within rather than experiencing it from its audience, went through change. Pianist Fred Hersch came out in 1993, twice-married vibraphonist Gary Burton in 1994 and silken crooner Andy Bey in 1996. Singer-songwriter-pianist Patricia Barber wrapped Paul Anka's 'She's a Lady' in a dreamy fug of nightclub smoke on her 1998 album *Modern Cool*.

Following Rob Halford, heavy metal's next gay confessor surfaced in 1998: Doug Pinnick, bassist, songwriter and co-lead vocalist for the US band King's X. His statement was made more daring by the fact the band were part of the burgeoning Christian rock movement.

There was even a victory in the way that MTV's metal-loving cartoon characters Beavis and Butthead didn't taunt, but rather made affectionate fun of, gay songwriter Tom Wilson Weinberg's 1979 track 'Lesbian Seagull' in the 1996 film *Beavis And Butt-head Do America*.

There was also a significant shift in the way that nineteen-year-old Canadian twins Tegan and Sara Quin came out from the start, with their debut album *Under Feet Like Ours*. They weren't the first lesbian twins – New Zealand's Topp Twins Jools and Lynda had been a singing, comedy sketch-writing team since 1982 – though the modern-folky Tegan and Sara were the first to face the merciless media eye.

Tegan recalled, 'All people ever focused upon was that we were twins or that we were lesbians or women'[1] – and spokespeople for all, at an age where they had barely yet formed opinions. 'We were tasked with explaining to straight journalists how anyone who wasn't a gay woman could relate to our music,' Sara wrote on the twins' blog.[2]

Luckily, the Quins had the freedom to talk about their work and their lives. If they'd been partial to rapping they'd have been effectively self-censored and if they were breakout stars of Jamaican dancehall, they might be in fear of their lives. After a short lull following the Shabba Ranks and Buju Banton episodes, a swarm of batty-bashers had gathered by the end of the nineties: Capleton, Sizzla, Elephant Man, Beenie Man, T.O.K., Bounty Killer.

A return to the life-threatening days that had last affected homosexual men – and women – in the nineteenth century was a sobering thought. Yet Jamaica was one island, no one identifying as LGBTQ had actually been murdered and entire continents were feeling liberated, even from the spectre of AIDS. Not all rock'n'roll was homosexual, but it seemed to accept those that were. Could dancehall, hip hop and mainstream country climb on board?

---

1 http://exclaim.ca/music/article/tegan_sara-sisters_of_mercy
2 http://teganandsara.com/post-tour-reflections-lgbtq/

CHAPTER 11

Twenty-first Century: A Rainbow Riot

'Keeping with it real with the new sex appeal/in your face, I'm taking your girl/You never made your lady come with your dick/I made your lady come in less than a minute.'
　　　　　　　　　　　　　　'Oh Shit', God-des and She, 2004

'We are different/But love is love/And it is no different.'
　　　　　　　　　　　　　　'Unmask', Uganda Rainbow Riot, 2016

On 26 April 2000, Howard Deen, the governor of Vermont, signed the USA's first civil unions bill into law, after the state's supreme court ruled that its marriage laws unconstitutionally excluded same-sex couples. The backlash was so fierce that Deen had to start wearing a bulletproof vest.

The following weekend – twenty years and six months after the first gay march on Washington – the Millennium March saw over 700,000[1] gather at the US government's seat of power. The organisers, the Human Rights Campaign (HRC), had been launched in 1980 as a gay and lesbian political action committee to provide financial support to candidates who would support gay civil rights legislation. They could now reap what had been sewn, though grassroots campaigners thought a LGBTQ march that didn't even have 'LGBTQ' in its official title was selling out the movement, and that people were in Washington for the party more than the politics.

---

[1] The usual discrepancy in estimates of public gatherings afflicted the Millennium March: some claimed it was as low as 200,000, while the organisers said between 700,000 and one million.

Food and merchandise stalls and corporate sponsorship (from United Airlines to the Showtime TV network), underlined the Millennium March's commercial foundations. The Equality Rocks concert staged the same weekend in the city's RFK stadium catered to both partygoers and activists. The A-list gay line-up of George Michael, Melissa Etheridge, k.d. lang, Pet Shop Boys[1] and Rufus Wainwright was expanded with honourary heterosexuals; country superstar Garth Brooks and soul legend Chaka Khan, while the live speakers included politicians and comedian Ellen DeGeneres, who had come out in real life as well as on her sitcom *Ellen* in 1997.

President Bill Clinton, who had one more year left in office, declined to attend the rally, choosing to be present by video; it was damage limitation, given he had infuriated LGBT Democrats with 'Don't Ask Don't Tell' and DOMA. The right to marry was part of HRC's manifesto, alongside the repeal of DADT, the provision of lesbian health care, more affordable AIDS/HIV treatment and legislation against employment discrimination and hate crime. Equality Rocks' most emotional moment was the appearance of Judy and Dennis Shepard, whose son Matthew had been beaten, tortured, and left to die on a rural road in Wyoming in 1998, the most widely publicised homophobic incident since Harvey Milk's assassination.

Etheridge performed her Matthew Shepard tribute, 'Scarecrow', the name coming from the words of the passer-by who found Shepard and at first thought the 22-year-old's badly damaged body was a scarecrow. As Etheridge recalled in her autobiography[2], 'in my little cocoon, with my alternative family, I had been thinking I was a big gay rock star actually doing something to change the world.'

The very public debate on homophobia had some ramifications. In 2001, in the wake of another multi-platinum album *The Marshall Mathers LP*, Eminem won Grammys for best rap solo performance, best

---

1 Pet Shop Boy's performance included a cover of 'Homosexuality', a 1985 cult disco track by US duo Modern Rocketry.
2 *The Truth Is... My Life in Love and Music*, with Layra Morton (Villard, 2001)

rap performance by a duo or group (with Dr Dre) and best rap album: this for an album that included 'Criminal', 'My words are like a dagger with a jagged edge/That'll stab you in the head whether you're a fag or lez/Or the homosex, hermaph or a trans-a-vest/Pants or dress – hate fags? The answer's, "Yes."'

In a move that could have been intended as conciliatory, Elton John took the part of (female singer) Dido's chorus for stalker anthem 'Stan' during the televised award ceremony. In statements that seemed to give both an excuse, Elton claimed that Eminem mostly wrote in character, thus giving his homophobia artistic license, while on MTV news in 2004, Eminem disingenuously claimed that he didn't know at the time they sang together that Elton John was gay. 'But being that he was gay and he had my back,' the rapper declared, 'I think it made a statement in itself, saying that he understood where I was coming from.'[1]

Just as disingenuously, Eminem argued that 'faggot' was a term of abuse that had 'nothing to do with sexual preference. I meant something more like assholes or dickheads.' *Advocate* editor Dave White claimed on his behalf, 'If [Eminem] has gay-bashed you or me, then it logically follows that he has also raped his own mother, killed his wife and murdered his producer, Dr Dre. If he's to be taken literally, then so is Britney Spears' invitation to "Hit me, baby, one more time".'[2]

After their performance, Eminem and Elton shared a manly, back-slapping hug and arched their clasped hands in the air as if they'd built a bridge of rapprochement between the aggressor and the victim. Maybe this media-fabricated event would have further ramifications, such as Eminem dialling down the homophobic violence and rap following his lead. But a gay rapper – with more presence than Cyrus and Rainbow Flava could muster in the earliest days of the internet – would make as much, if not more, of a statement. An all-queer, all-black crew of rappers; that would be news.

---

1 www.mtv.com/news/1629030/eminem-talks-about-his-friendship-with-elton-john
2 *The Advocate*, 4 July 2000, http://self.gutenberg.org/articles/the_marshall_mathers_lp

FruitGangsta

One of the key members of Deep Dickollective, Juba Kalamka, a.k.a. Pointfivefag, had been part of Dutchboy's Rainbow Flava collective. Today, Kalamka works in as the HIV co-ordinator for San Francisco's St James Infirmary, America's only occupational health clinic for sex workers and their partners. In the seventies, he was growing up in Chicago with a mother who introduced him to strong female voices such as Nina Simone and Joan Armatrading. To them he added Philly soul, soaking up the falsetto voices and flamboyant performances, alongside Gil Scott-Heron's black nationalism and poetry.

Jalamka was, he says, 'a precocious, smart, artistic kid. I can't recall a time I wasn't called a fag.' Anne Rice's vampire novels was his introduction to the word 'bisexual', describing how he felt inside, but he denied his same-sex side even when clubbing at Frankie Knuckles' Warehouse. Hip hop was equally impactful: sure, 'Rapper's Delight' took aim at what Jalamka calls, 'the indictment of the sissy as the spectacle, a cartoon,' but early hip hop satisfied his progressive ideals, the fashion sense – 'super-flamboyant costumes, the leather and the furs'. Its musical roots were 'in new wave and disco, in Man Parrish and the early graffiti artists like Basquiat, all the stuff nobody talks about. What *wasn't* gay about hip hop?'

By 1991, Kalamka was one fourth of the hip hop crew He Who Walks Three Ways but remained closeted. In 1995, he gave up performing: 'I knew I was going to come out and I didn't feel safe freestyling, as I knew I'd out myself.' He decided he needed to leave Chicago, 'to deal with being out the way I wanted to be. The Bay Area was viable because of its history toward sexuality and Oakland's radical history with the Black Panthers.'

Kalamka had also discovered *Anything That Moves*, a magazine for bisexuals published out of San Francisco; he vowed that if he ever moved west, he'd work for it (he became a staff writer and illustrator) and was determined to track down Rainbow Flava after reading about them in the magazine. After sending spoken word pieces to Dutchboy, Kalamka appeared on Rainbow Flava's 2000 album *Digital Dope*. Jalamka next teamed up with Tim'm West, who he'd met in 1999 at a screening of *Tongues Untied*, Marlon Riggs' 1989 film documentary about the hitherto undocumented world of black gay identity.

After the screening, West read a poem, 'Quickie', 'about trying to negotiate affections or connections with other men,' Jalamka recalls. 'Hearing that dynamic expressed by an openly black gay man, who was unapologetically B-Boy at the same time, I'd never met anyone like that.'

The son of a preacher in Little Rock, Arkansas, West had been denied secular music until he could tune in to the eighties AM radio that schooled him in Madonna, Culture Club and Prince, 'a free-spirited expressive and transgressive space,' he recalls. Delving into house music reminded him of gospel, 'and it was affirming to discover gay and queer people had a major impact.'

Taking a BA in philosophy at Duke University in Durham, North Carolina, West's next crucial discovery was Riggs' *Tongues Untied*. 'I went in closeted and left an out man,' he says. 'To see black gay and bisexual men represented as strong gave me hope.' When West was outed at college, 'I wasn't prepared, but I didn't deny it.' His fellow rappers in the campus hip hop collective Duke's Enlightened Nubians 'had no reference for a masculine, basketball-playing hip hop queer man.[1] But they accepted me, so I felt affirmed in a hip hop space.'

Further affirmation was found in the nimble psychedelic rap of Del La Soul, 'three nerdy, bohemian black guys,' West recalls, and female trailblazers Queen Latifah and MC Lyte. 'In my mind, if women could embrace hip hop and find a space, maybe a queer person could eventually do so too.'

West's studies took him to New York in 1996, where he attended open-mic spoken word and poetry sessions. Here, he discovered gay poet (and occasional singer-songwriter) Essex Hemphill, but he still found the space uncomfortable: 'There was more openness there than

---

1 West identifies as queer: 'I've dated men, women, trans men and trans women. "Gay" dishonours the vastness of my desire.'

in hip hop, but most queer poets, save a few women, were not out.'[1] Like Jalamka, West thought that out west was best, with San Francisco a convergence of 'ACT UP and the Black Panthers, black and conscious' – despite the fact that black nationalism saw being gay as 'counter-revolutionary, because you're not producing children for the revolution'.

West's union of black and queer pride came through 'Quickie', affirming same-sex love in a hip hop context, about two guys who can't be out but express their love for each other through gestures and code. West's motivations also changed while studying for his PhD after he was diagnosed HIV-positive: 'The most important thing became the legacy I wanted to leave behind.' He and Jalamka joined forces with West's campus pal, Philip Goff, 'in a room with a piano,' West recalls, 'like a healing ritual. We just made up songs, and then became the basis for the first Deep Dickollective album.'

BourgieBohoPostPomoAfroHomo, released in 2000 on Kalamka's own Sugartruck label – 'we didn't want anyone telling us what to do' – inaugurated the first politically motivated black queer band as well as hip hop's first black queer crew, a musical breakthrough to match *Tongues Untied*.

'People didn't know what to make of us,' says West. 'They thought, as queer men making hip hop, we were a parody or a gimmick, or people didn't believe we were queer and that it was a way to draw attention. We were such a far stretch for their imagination.'

Kalamka had another take on hip hop's relationship with LGBTQ. 'Homophobia did not exist in a cultural vacuum, separate from the world culture we live in, where so much is stridently racist and classist,' he says. 'Rap didn't create "Don't ask don't tell" or DOMA, that was white folks. Anyone who wants a real conversation about institutionalised discrimination, privilege and about popular music, period,

---

[1] In 2004, West launched the Front Porch, 'an attempt to create an open mic and feature space . . . where all kinds of poetry, spoken word, hip hop, acoustic and soul music could be welcomed by people of diverse racial and sexual orientations.' www.reddirt.biz/thefront porch.htm_

and the way homophobia manifested in mainstream hip hop, then I was interested.'

Like Rainbow Flava, D/DC (as they were often called) were a fluctuating collective; Goff left after the first album to concentrate on his psychology PhD and, by the time the collective split in 2008, another nine members had come and gone. They included the black trans poet, Marcus René Van, who had attended the first PeaceOUT (World) Homo Hop Festival that Kalamka organised in 2001 as part of Pride in Oakland, East Bay. Reviews of the event referred to a scene called homohop, after West's own throwaway description. 'Tim'm said that he could have called it FruitGangsta and it would have stuck,' says Kalamka.

Whatever title the movement merited, it thrived, with enough rappers to populate an annual PeaceOUT festival and three rapid compilations on Dutchboy's Phat Family imprint.[1] Besides Rainbow Flava and Dutchboy, the two constants on Phat Family's compilations were lesbian rappers Montrea Bailey (known as Miss Money and based in Houston) and Alicia Smith, known as God-Des, from Ann Arbor, Michigan. Smith had begun rapping even before Cyrus –who she hadn't heard of, confirming the disconnection in the homohop scene.

Smith was playing cello aged three, violin at seven and drums at ten. 'Rhythm led me to hip hop,' she says. Once there, her experience was similar to that of Cyrus. 'Being a tomboy, I felt ostracised from the other girls, so I could understand the struggle in hip hop even though I wasn't living the same life.'

Without lesbian hip hop precedents, Smith had looked to female rappers Salt N Pepa, 'these powerful women who used hip hop as men did and were as respected. I thought, Maybe someday I could do this.' First, Smith was the drummer of her high school punk band Hector Delatori, but the most applauded part of their live shows was when Smith came out front to rap the track that later became 'Oh Shit': 'Keeping with it real with the new sex appeal/in your face, I'm taking your girl/You

---

[1] *Volume 1: The Dozens* (2002), *Volume 2: Down 4 The Swerve* (2002), *Volume 3: Freaks Come Out* (2003).

never made your lady come with your dick/I made your lady come in less than a minute'.

'These emo kids would go crazy!' she laughs. 'It gave me the confidence to carry on.'

Feeling confident and acting in line with hip hop's credo of self-promotion, Smith adopted the name God-des in 1996 and started creating tracks with Hector Delatori guitarist Aaron, a trained opera singer who added melodic counterpoints to her raps. God-Des felt his loss when he moved to Boston to attend graduate school, but then she started studying in Madison, Wisconsin. There she chanced on the blazing R&B voice of Tina Glassen.

As God-des and She, the duo played a women's showcase at a hip hop conference in Madison. 'After the show, this guy from Nation of Islam said, "I normally wouldn't be about this shit, but you're out of the closet, you're honest and vulnerable, I cannot hate on you." To me, that's some bridge we were crossing. That's how change begins, by somebody that doesn't understand your perspective starts to open their mind and heart and then, if they meet someone else, they think, "Maybe I don't hate gay people."'

God-des was further buoyed when the duo moved to New York in time to be captured in a short documentary, *Hip Hop Homos*, released in 2004. One thing in God-des's favour was that she and the mainstream hip hop audience liked the same thing: women. As she explained in *Hip Hop Homos*, the duo usually played 'political or feminist' hip hop events, but at one show they'd faced a crowd of two hundred 'dudes'. God-des decided to kick off their show by shouting, '"How many of y'all love pussy?" The crowd was like, "Great!" "'Cause we do too!"'

Hip Hop Homos' other featured artist had the harder task – Joseph Thomas Lee and the same crowd of dudes did not share the same tastes. At the same time, the man calling himself Deadlee looked *exactly* like a gangsta rapper, down to the shaved head and bandana. In the documentary, he talked about being 'the faggot superhero, without the cape,' for his decision to stay true to himself and so also embody hip hop's cardinal rule of 'keeping it real.'

His 2002 debut album, *7 Deadlee Sins*, gave 'signs of my sexuality, but I was very Prince-like – I left you guessing,' he told *LA Weekly*. On 2004's *Assault With A Deadlee Weapon*, 'I don't hold back . . . I hit you right off with "Suck Muh Gun". My gun is my voice, my cock. Or you can take it literally, as a weapon. I'm taking the whole gangster image and flipping it. I'm a strong gay man and I'm challenging all these motherfucks to *try* and challenge my manhood. I use my sexuality as a plus, treat straight fucks like they've treated and disrespected women and gays all these years. I'm one faggot you can't fuck with. I break out of the stereotype. I just keep pushing my agenda to show other Latinos and blacks that you can be open with your shit and still be strong.'[1]

7 Deadlee Sins was self-released, but *Assault With A Deadlee Weapon* was released on Matt Wobensmith's new label A.C.R.O.N.Y.M., named with reference 'to the growing complexity of labels our community had attached to itself – we were now at LGBTQ,' he says. Wobensmith had closed Queercorps after releasing just one EP and Cyryus' album: 'I hadn't convinced the queercore scene that they should care [about hip hop] and I ran out of money and energy,' he explains. But after taking time out and earning enough money to pay off debts, Wobensmith 'wandered into the first PeaceOUT and was blown away at the talent and energy of homohop and wanted to be a part of it again.'

A.C.R.O.N.Y.M. also released Tori Fixx's album *Marry Me* in 2004, with DOMA at the front of his agenda. The former Rainbow Flava member had started releasing solo albums in 1998 and *Marry Me* was his fifth. It was proving very hard to create any momentum in gay hip hop, especially in the wake of the saga of hoax gay rapper Caushun.

Brooklyn-raised Jason Herndon – a real person – had, seemingly, outed himself on the Star and Buc Wild morning show on New York's WWPR-FM. Going by the name 'Caushun', he was quickly picked up

---

1 www.laweekly.com/music/suck-his-gun-2138705

by Washington's LGBT magazine *Metro Weekly*. This 'hairdresser for the stars by day' was being managed and produced by Ivan Matias, 'one of the biggest names in the industry, having worked with Toni Braxton, Outkast and Monica.' One verse was quoted from Caushun's track 'Gay Rapper's D-Lite': 'I'm the gayest of all time/I can show you who's greater/Suck that dick 'till it swell up to the size of a skyscraper.'

'Heterosexual men specifically are very intrigued by the homosexual mind, but they don't want to ask about it,' Caushun told the magazine. 'When I perform, their reaction is usually something like, "I'm not into that gay shit, but I feel you for keeping it real." That's their way of saying that I've opened their eyes to an area that they might not have otherwise known about.'[1]

Things went up a notch when the *New York Times* did an interview that read like a caricature of some hip hop Liberace: 'He's a B-Boy with a poodle named Wesley and an apartment with ornate pillows with silk flowers on them and beautiful vases filled with giant lilies.'[2]

Caushun confirmed his debut album was due on Baby Phat, a major label offshoot run by Kimora Lee Simmons, the wife of hip hop mogul Russell Simmons. His Def Jam label had released Public Enemy and Beastie Boys records and one thrash metal band, Slayer, whose singer Kerry King was voted 'most homophobic performer' in a 2012 poll by the Queer F* Heavy Metal blog.[3] The warning signs were all there and the album duly never materialised, but MTV, BET, VH1, *Newsweek* and *Interview* magazine all picked up on Caushun. By the time artists such as Deadlee and D/DC were vying for similar coverage, 'the media people said, "We've already written about gay rap and what it means,"' recalls Alex Hilton, the director of the full-length film documentary *Pick Up The Mic*, released in 2006.

Hilton had begun making five-minute shorts for the Queer As TV website, 'sharing stories of people you didn't hear about through the

1 www.metroweekly.com/2002/05/words-of-caushun
2 www.nytimes.com/2003/04/20/arts/gay-rappers-too-real-for-hip-hop.html
3 https://qfheavymetal.wordpress.com/2012/08/15/homophobia

mainstream gay media, centred around day-to-day life.' He began filming in 2002 after discovering D/DC and PeaceOUT, but when he saw how the scene was mushrooming, he assembled a ninety-minute cut. The title came from the film's promotional sell: 'If you are gay and a fan of hip hop, why would you even consider staring down the mountain of homophobic lyrics that litter the airwaves and dare to pick up the mic?'

Pic Up The Mic profiled the likes of Dutchboy, Miss Money, Deadlee, God-des and She and Tori Fixx. Hilton wanted to include Caushun, 'but he gave us the runaround and when we sniffed around too much, he didn't want to participate. In the end, everyone knew he was a phony.'

Eventually, in 2007, talking to the website Allhiphop, Caushun's 'manager', Ivan Matias. revealed he was behind the prank. Hairdresser Jason Herndon had been recruited to play the rapper's role in public, endlessly repeating the only two verses that he'd learnt. 'I think a part of this project was good because it showed that hip hop is not as homophobic as it projects,' Matias claimed. 'Out of everyone else who could have popularised something as trivial as the colour pink, it took a masculine culture like hip hop to popularise that on men. This showed a good side of hip hop, that it's open and diverse.'[1]

Pick Up The Mic may not have accelerated careers but it pulled in great reviews as it toured the film festival circuit, a document of an authentic movement. At the same time, mainstream hip hop artists acknowledged that homophobia wasn't clever or funny and apologies came from Common and the new hip hop god, Kanye West, on his way to 100 million digital downloads and 21 Grammy awards. As West told MTV news in 2005, one of his favourite cousins was gay and he'd been wrong to have homophobic rhymes. 'Everybody in hip hop discriminates against gay people,' he said. 'You play a record and if it's wack, "That's gay, dog!" And I wanna just come on TV and just tell my rappers, just tell my friends, "Yo, stop it fam".'[2]

---

1 http://allhiphop.com/2007/05/06/ivan-matias-hip-hops-secret-trapped-in-the-closet, Kimora Simmons' label Baby Phat never got off the ground either.
2 www.mtv.com/news/2247128/kanye-west-mtv-interview-2005-sway-homophobia

Trans rap comes of age

Pic Up The Mic found a new wave of queer rappers – all white, but diverse, including gritty lesbian wordsmith KenRo, the salacious Johnny Dangerous, the bear-like Aggracyst, the first gay UK rapper – QBoy – and Katastrophe, the first trans male rapper.

Rocco Kayiatos or Katastrophe, as he used to call himself (it's now Rocco Katastrophe), works as a video education specialist for the website Buzzfeed, but he's also co-founded *Original Plumbing*, the first magazine for trans men. 'Part of *Original Plumbing* was altruistic. I wanted a large reach, for young trans kids to connect with me,' he says. 'But also, it's a sign the trans world has exploded. The struggle I had does not exist for young people, they don't have to search in the back of *Maximum Rockandroll* to find one person like you, now you use Google.'

As a teenage lesbian, Kayiatos' teenage soundtrack was grunge and the 'conscious' rappers: 'Nothing that was telling me I was valueless.' Despite growing issues with gender and sexuality, Kayiatos didn't respond to riot grrrl: 'It was too abrasive and I couldn't understand what they were saying,' unlike the clarity of the spoken word. At a poetry slam organised by Youth Speaks, Kayiatos came second – 'Me and the winner were the only gay kids involved' – and went on to win the event in 1998, leading to poems on four spoken word compilation CDs and to joining San Francisco's lesbian-feminist spoken-word collective Sister Spit.

Kayiatos had rapped a little at high school and, in 2001, was part of the queer rap trio End Of The World, while deciding to transition. 'We were dark, campy hip hop. We'd rap about Armageddon, but it was a bit jokey too,' he recalls. 'We'd dress in suits and capes. Hype Man [a.k.a. Ricky Lee], this butch lesbian, would spew fake blood over the audience. We did one tour but I decided I didn't want to make joke music anymore so I did my own thing.'

Kayiatos once described himself as, 'indecisive and riddled with insecurity, whereas Katastrophe is a ladies' man who's able to figure things out that Rocco can only solve in therapy.'[1] The dichotomy was explored on 2004's solo album debut *Let's Fuck, Then Talk About My Problems*, released on Juba Kalamka's Sugartruck label.[2]

Kayiatos found other dichotomies, such as his new identity with what he calls, 'a transgender brain'. His lyrics included, 'I'm my own worst enemy, I'm my own hate crime/With no one defending me, but I'll be just fine sitting/with my bad feelings.'

Another dichotomy was the importance of carving out a space for queer and trans rappers, 'but calling it homohop alienated us from being seen as viable hip hop artists. It immediately turned off people,' he says. 'When *Pick Up The Mic* premiered at the Toronto Film Festival, both nights sold out and artists were getting excited, like, we're going to be mainstream! I said, I don't think so, it's like riot grrrl, it's getting a lot of attention, but no one in that crowd knew what riot grrrl was. People's expectations were short-sighted and slightly delusional. Nobody who started back then have been truly successful, not even God-des when she was on *The L Word*. It exploded her career but there wasn't a wave left that she could ride.'

The lesbian-onic TV drama *The L Word* had been on air since 2004 while the gay TV channel Logo launched in 2005. God-des had sent Logo the video for the duo's 'Love You Better' and viewers kept voting for it to be shown. She was bartending when a customer told her, 'Your stuff is really touching, have you ever thought of being on *The L Word*? I know the music producer.' The season three finale, set at a bachelor(ette) party, featured God-des & She's 'Lick It', a handy guide to cunnilingus.

'When it ran, we got something like twenty thousand emails,' she says. 'I quit my job and we started touring full time.'

As God-des and She were gaining momentum in 2007, both Deep

---

[1] www.eastbayexpress.com/oakland/trans-cendent/Content?oid=1076745
[2] The only release on the label except D/DC's own work. Kalamka: 'Katastrophe supplied the artwork and I got it manufactured, but I wasn't interested in running a record label and I couldn't support him.'

Dickollective and the PeaceOUT event were winding up. The collective had shared bills with straight hip hop acts and a readers' poll in the *San Francisco Bay Guardian* had voted them best hip hop group. 'But if you wanted a mainstream career, you wouldn't be in a group like D/DC,' Jalamka says. Pressure from fellow D/DC members to step up commercially was one reason behind his decision to quit. 'Fame didn't appeal to me. I knew tons of people with record deals, throwing parties and events. They even had relative success, but they were all broke! And I describe D/DC as like herding cats.'

The mic was picked up by the HomoRevolution, a national hip hop tour headlined by Deadlee, who got media mileage (including NPR coverage and both Tyra Banks and Howard Stern shows) from an interview with *Allhiphop*, shaming Eminem and fellow rap giants 50 Cent and DMX for their persistent homophobia. The *HomoRevolution* CD compilation showed how the scene was expanding, with fifteen names that hadn't featured in *Pick Up The Mic*. One was Foxxjazell, the first trans female rapper.

Born Dwight Eric Jackson Jr in Birmingham, Alabama, Foxxjazell – now her legal name[1] – had seen Prince interviewed by Oprah: 'He said he'd discovered a woman living inside of him and that's how I felt. But I wasn't aware of the word, "trans".' Following two suicide attempts, she started transitioning at sixteen; a year later, she was living in LA. 'My biggest influence was Madonna and I knew her story of leaving Detroit for New York with just $125. I flipped a coin between New York and LA and I moved with $45 in my pocket.' Foxxjazell survived as a sex worker and drug dealer while failing to get work as an actor. Having started rapping in Birmingham, she and a friend formed a hip hop quartet, One20five.

'I was the only female but only my friend knew about me. The other two, both cisgender males, didn't. I think they started to work it out, but they never asked.'

---

[1] Says Foxxjazzell, 'I''ve always felt uncannily related to the fox. It's an outcast like me and Jazell is a play on gazelle, tall and graceful.'

With no deal forthcoming and finances depleted, One20five ended, as did 'the heavy partying. I got my act together and realised I needed to be an openly transgender artist and to go solo.' One of HomoRevolution's organisers was tipped off about her. 'He thought a transgender rapper would be great for opening the show.' The independent label Pretty Boy Entertainment offered to release singles.

Foxxjazell's raps often openly addressed trans issues, although her first single, 2007's 'Feel The Vibe' was 'a party song, me taking a page from Madonna's book, not just talking about one thing but pulling in the biggest audience.' Following 2008's album debut *Introducing . . . Foxxjazell*, 'Pretty Boy wanted me to become the trans Lil Kim, grittier and sexual, and I wanted to be more pop, rapping over dance beats, like Nicky Minaj does now. But radio programmers didn't like that then. They wanted me to keep singing. And they couldn't work me out from my voice, was I male or female? They concentrated on that more than the music.'

Becoming the first transgender artist profiled in hip hop bible *XXL* was 'monumental', she says. But a move to New York and the 2010 album *Boy, Girl, Whateva* on her own FKJ label didn't pay off. Weighing in online to an argument over claims that rapper Chingy had an affair with a transsexual model didn't help: 'I made decisions that I regret now but I was angry at the world and the industry and those people who refused to help me, but sought my services at night and then played it off that they didn't know me.'

Foxxjazell found her live shows were getting limited to Pride events.

'That annoyed me too, because I wanted to cross lines, beyond a single spectrum. There still isn't a LBGTQ hip hop artist signed to a major label and rap doesn't get the support it needs from the LGBT community. The clubs didn't want rappers. They wanted us to do drag shows and lipsync. One guy said, who are you going to be tonight; Beyoncé? And rolled his eyes when I said I was doing my own music. I don't want to come across as bitter but if you want something to change, you have to support it. They support Nicky Minaj and Lil Kim, both of whom have huge gay followings.'[1]

The sound of electroclash

Alongside HomoRevolution, a second national tour with LGBTQ appeal crossed the US in 2007. *True Colors* featured headliner Cyndi Lauper with a supporting cast that included Debbie Harry, Rufus Wainwright, Indigo Girls and lesbian comedian Rosie O'Donnell, to benefit the Human Rights Campaign and LGBTQ charities PFLAG (Parents, Families and Friends of Lesbians and Gays) and the Matthew Shepard Foundation. Toward the bottom of the bill was Cazwell, who had been briefly seen in *Pick Up The Mic*[2] but not interviewed. 'Cazwell would perform with other homohop artists, but he didn't associate with them,' Alex Hilton recalls. 'He was much more interested in the New York club scene, which was rolled up into the whole electroclash sound.'

Following romo, an unsuccessful British revival of new romantic pop in the mid-mineties, electroclash was the latest attempt to resuscitate eighties' synth-pop with a tougher sound mix befitting the early noughties. The initial impetus was Fischerspooner, comprising openly gay frontman Warren Fischer and quietly bisexual studio bod Casey Spooner, though electroclash's true star was Ontario's outrageous and overtly (bi)sexual Merrill Beth Nisker, known as Peaches.

Peaches' 2002 album debut *The Teaches Of Peaches* had the most blatantly sexual image for eons, a close-up of transparent latex hot pants showing off underwear as skimpy as it was tight. Peaches lived in Berlin and was signed to the city's Kitty-Yo label, who didn't have the same commercial reservations about the artwork as the US labels fearful of their distributors baulking at provocation. The video for the album's

---

[1] Foxxjazzell has since moved into management and co-hosts the trans web series *T-Time with the Gurlz*: 'I'm the Barbara Walters of the show. I'm not naïve. I won't be a struggling artist at the age of forty, wanting to be a pop star. I feel I've accomplished a lot anyway and now I wanted to excel at other things, and help the next trans artists coming up.'

[2] Cazwell was included in the extended scenes on the DVD version of *Pick Up The Mic*.

lead single 'Lovertits' centred suggestively on two teenage girls fetishing their bicycles: 'Cum Undun', 'Diddle My Skittle' and 'Suck And Let Go' further staked out her role as a sex-positive priestess for the new queer generation.

Cazwell had been doing his bit too, sharing in the filthiest set of lyrics since Canya Phuckem and Howe. 2003's 'The Sex That I Need' was a collaboration with electroclash duo Avenue D, protégés of Larry Tee, the man behind Rupaul's 'Supermodel' who'd coined the word electroclash.

In 2006, five years after going solo, Cazwell finally released a debut album, *Get Into It*, released by Mel Cheron's West End label which included an update of the label's classic 'Is It All Over My Face' by Arthur Russell. The new version typified the generational shift; Russell only implied the suggestive aspect of the lyric, while Cazwell went explicit: 'I came too close in your direction/DNA on your complexion'. His video was teeming with hordes of buff topless boys and transgender girls (most notably fashion and nightlife celebrity Amanda Lepore), ending in a crowded club of partying pansexual patrons.

Three years earlier, Detroit, Michigan's Electric 6 had had a UK Top 5 hit with the ridiculously silly and gratifying rocker 'Gay Bar'. The line, 'I've got something to put in you, at the gay bar,' was heard all over MTV, with a video of pole-dancing, gym-attending and spandex-clad Abraham Lincoln lookalikes (most of them singer Tyler Spencer). Oh, and a gerbil running through a tube.

In 2007, Sam Norman, from Greenville, South Carolina, calling himself Samwell, had a viral video smash with 'What What (In The Butt)', a very camp slice of neo-disco that he licensed to Comedy Central's *South Park*. 'Let's do it in the butt. OK!' he enthused.

In 2012, Britain's gay lifestyle magazine *Attitude* published an 'evolution of rock'n'roll'. The entries for the twenty-first century read:

2003: Toronto collective the Hidden Cameras release its debut album *The Smell Of Our Own*, with the world's first piss anthem in 'Golden Streams'[1] and the self-explanatory 'The Man That I Am With My Man'. Closet, what musical closet?

2006: From riot grrrl centre Portland, punk-funk trio the Gossip's album *Standing in the Way of Control* is a surprise hit. Outspoken/out/outsize singer Beth Ditto wins *NME*'s annual 'coolest person in rock' and draws attention from fashion houses and model agencies. Antony [now Anohni] releases his second album *I Am A Bird Now*, a stunning paean to transgender anxiety and desire, which wins the annual Mercury Music prize [for best album of the year].

2007: Starting with the Gossip, Major label giant Sony/Columbia launches label offshoot Music With A Twist, 'A home for gay artists of all genres to experience mainstream success without having to compromise any part of their identity.'

2010: After years of rumour, Kele Okereke of Bloc Party indie rockers comes out and by June is on *Attitude*'s front cover in singlet and gym shorts and making dance music. 'No turning back now,' he tells his publicist. The video for US duo Girls' 'Lust For Life' single is a poly-sexual jamboree featuring a young chap holding another young chap's semi-swollen todger [penis] as a microphone.

2012: According to Grizzly Bear singer Ed Droste, 'There are tons of different types of gay musicians doing music.' Step up, Hercules and Love Affair, Jónsi Birgisson (Sigur Rós) Bradford Cox (Deerhunter), Patrick Wolf, Jamie Stewart (Xiu Xiu), Hunx and his Punx, Nico Muhly, Perfume Genius, John Grant, Rostam Batmanglij (Vampire Weekend), Owen Pallet, Junior Boys, Matmos. And, over in lesbianville, Tegan and Sara, Yo! Majesty, Telepathe, Sia and MEN. Need we go on? The war is over. All rock'n'roll, it seems, is indeed homosexual...

---

1 I was clearly wrong about this, given what I unearthed about Canya Phuckem and Howe when researching this book.

In other words: the twenty-first century has seen many leaps and bounds in LGBTQ representation. Instead of Ray Bourbon being arrested for female impersonation, we've had eight seasons of *RuPaul's Drag Race* on TV, searching for 'the next drag superstar.' Instead of features such as 'Fifty top gay songs' with Abba's 'Dancing Queen' at no. 1, we have 'The fifty most important queer women in music', with country's Chely Wright at no. 50 and Melissa Etheridge at no. 1.[1] Or 'Fifty gay male musicians'[2] with Italian pop singer Tiziano Ferro at no. 50 and Elton John at no. 1.

Band names have included Gay Rodeo, Egyptian Gay Lovers, Gay For Johnny Depp, the Dykeenies, the Gay Blades, Gaye Bykers On Acid, Jason's Gay Haircut, Gay Witch Abortion, The Gay Sportscasters, Lesbian, Gay Beast, Gayrilla Biscuits, Youth of Togay, and Black Fag.

Coming out has become almost commonplace, from boy bands – first, Stephen Gately of Boyzone in 1999 and Lance Bass of *NSYNC in 2006 – to TV competition contestants – first, Will Young in 2002, just months after winning the BBC series *Pop Idol* and *American Idol* runner-up Adam Lambert in 2009. Lambert became the first openly gay singer to top the US album chart with *Trespassing* in 2012[3]. Australian pop singer Sam Sparro was out from the beginning of his career in 2007. Latino superstar Ricky Martin came out to no one's surprise in 2010 and his popularity didn't wane for a second.

Kristian Eivind Espedal, better known as Gaahl of Gorgorth, a popular band on Norway's notoriously violent 'black metal' scene, came out in 2003 and wasn't attacked by any of his rivals.

In this new permissive climate, former closeted rockers emerged, blinking in the daylight of acceptance. First Chuck Panozzo, bassist of AOR rockers Styx in 2001 and, in 2005, Andy Fraser, bassist of UK

---

1 www.afterellen.com/more/79624-the-50-most-important-queer-women-in-music
2 www.newnownext.com/aftereltoncoms-top-50-gay-male-musicians/02/2011
3 Elton John doesn't count as he was closeted when he had all his US no. 1 albums. In 2014, UK singer Sam Smith became the first gay man to top the US and UK charts simultaneously.

hard rock quartet Free and the writer of their classic rock radio staple 'All Right Now'. Both came out as HIV-positive too, to an overwhelmingly supportive reaction. Which artists from the past, given their time again, might have done the same?

Popular music: in transition

Transgender was rock music's last frontier; after all the playing and posturing around gender that drove much of the music's imagery, the artists were actually changing gender. In their former selves, they'd lived as gay men and lesbians had in the sixties, with no established precedent and internalised grief. There were no high profile examples of singers and musicians following the example of trans pioneers Jayne County[1] and Wendy Carlos, who made the decision without the internet to publicise their stories.

Changing gender was no walk on the wild side; no simple story summed up by 'He's A Woman, She's A Man'. Musicians who transitioned also chose to lead a life away from music and the accompanying attention. When Bill 'A Thrill's A Thrill' Amesbury transitioned to Barbra, she retired from music to work alongside her partner, philanthropist Joan Chalmers[2].

When two male rock singers came out as transgender, the reaction was respect and sympathy rather than shock. Mark Free, the lead singer of the hair-metal bands King Kobra and Unruly Child, transitioned to Marcie Free in 1995 and absented herself from music until Unruly Child's 2009 reformation. And when Liam Jason left LA hard rockers Rhino Bucket to become Jackie Enx in 1993, she stopped drumming until 1999 when the band asked her back.

'I tied my hair back, put a *very* baggy sweatshirt with a *very* tight sports bra and went down to the studio, she recalled. 'They hadn't seen

---

1 In 1995, County released her autobiography, *Man Enough to be a Woman*. By the noughties, she was living back in Atlanta and taking care of her aging parents, while periodically fronting a band she called the Electrick Queers.
2 Amesbury was reintroduced to the spotlight in 2002 when Toronto-based duo Collins Pickell released the single 'Can We Talk About Bill?', about an imagined meeting with Barbra: 'In your mind, is he haunting you still? . . . do you remember him still?'

me in a long time and I hoped I would just fly under their radar . . . Near the end of the sessions, they asked if I wanted to come back and play drums. I asked if they would be OK with a girl drummer. They, of course, took that as a refusal on my part, but apparently once I "spilled the beans" – and then revived everyone after they fainted – they decided it was all cool and away we went for the second time. Definitely brave and supportive on their part and it was appreciated.'[1]

South-east Asia had got there first, although reports hadn't reached the west. In South Korea, Lee Kyung-eun, known as Harisu, transitioned to female in the nineties and then Lady, the world's first transfemale pop band, launched in 2005. The same year, Sony BMG launched Venus Flytrap, Thailand's first trans female act.

In the West, the trans torch was carried out of left-field, in the towering six-foot-five form of Anohni. She'd travelled far from New York's Pyramid club; in 2004, she staged two performances at the Whitney Biennale of *Turning*, co-written with video artist Charles Atlas. The focus was thirteen 'remarkable' women, who took turns on a raised podium that rotated slowly as their image appeared on a large video screen behind the Johnsons. Half were queer/trans-identifying, as Anohni 'explored the intersection between trans women and other female artists and icons from New York'.

A year later, Antony and the Johnsons' album *I Am A Bird Now* presented another tableaux of defined queer appeal. Rufus Wainwright sang the Blacklips-era song 'What Can I Do' while Lou Reed (for whom Anohni sang backing vocals in live shows for three years and often duetted on the Velvet Underground classic 'Candy Says') – spoke the intro to 'Fistful Of Love'. Boy George was the co-singer on 'You Are My Sister': 'George was an angel coming down from the imagination of my own childhood,' is how Anohni recalls the session. 'That he manifested in front of me twenty years later, saying that he loved me, by singing my own words. . . I cried for days after he left.'

---

1 http://theheroines.blogspot.co.uk/2015/05/interview-with-jackie-enx.html

George may have been the poster boy for androgyny and trans identity, but *I Am A Bird Now*'s torch songs sang directly about the experience: children 'dreaming of transcendental gender transformations' ('For Today I Am A Boy'), 'My Lady Story' ('. . . is one of annihilation . . . is one of breast amputation'), 'Free At Last'. The album's cover was Peter Hujar's photo of Warhol superstar Candy Darling in 1974, the trans subject of 'Candy Says', looking calm and radiant, but dying of leukaemia.

Anohni's album debut, *Antony And The Johnsons* had crept out, only cultishly appreciated; after winning the UK's annual Mercury Prize, *I Am A Bird Now* was all over television. 'I assumed a song like "For Today I Am A Boy" would have a very marginal appeal. But I was shocked, over and over, to discover how many people were interested in it.'

Anohni remained, at least in public, Antony (and would do so until the end of 2015) and the public had little perception of transgenderism, let alone a musician who had had genital reassignment surgery and hormone therapy. The media section of Wikipedia's entry for 'transsexual' still only lists prominent films and TV and not a single figure from popular music. But in 2006, the first singer of a popular band announced that she would begin the process of changing sex.

Today, Mina Caputo remains the gruff, hollering lead singer of New York's metallic Life Of Agony, as well as a solo artist with a gentler, broader musical disposition. Born Keith Caputo, she grew up with her father and uncle's vinyl, with Queen, Led Zeppelin, the Doors and Bowie among her favourites. 'Rock music doesn't get more feminine than that,' she says. 'Even when I saw [Led Zeppelin singer] Robert Plant, I wasn't sure if he was a he or a she. Their riffs were masculine but the music was graced with femininity.'

By the time she reached high school, rock had gotten tougher and faster; his schoolmates listened to Metallica and punk. Caputo joined Life Of Agony when she was just fifteen. 'I used the band like a bulletproof vest,' she says. 'I knew at a very early age that I was different. I wanted to dress like a girl, but I couldn't share my secrets. So I'd write about pain and heartache but to talk about how lost I was. Which everyone could relate to.'

In 1996, Caputo left Life Of Agony. 'We were getting really popular and I couldn't enjoy it. I was lying to the band and to my own songs and having to live up to the expectations of our fans. There were lots of drugs around too. I thought if I didn't clean up, I'd die. And if I hadn't come out, I would have killed myself.'

It took another ten years, 'of drugs and fear', through which Caputo released two solo albums and rejoined Life Of Agony: 'Unfinished business,' she says. 'I'd grown up with these guys.' In the meantime, Hegarty's *I Am A Bird Now* 'broke my heart, I couldn't believe how beautiful she was.' Finally, while living in Amsterdam and lost in drugs, 'I told myself, I had to get back to the US and do whatever I needed to change my body to match my psychology.' When she confessed to his bandmates, 'They were totally cool, but they were mad because I'd kept it secret our entire relationship.'

Caputo's 'coming out' EP, *Cheat*, included covers of Anohni's 'Today I Am A Boy', Lou Reed's 'Make Up' and Cyndi Lauper's 'Girls Just Want To Have Fun'. His own title track explored the feeling that 'I had cheated myself of a beautiful life that I could have had.' But now, accepted by Life Of Agony and their fans and with Caputo's sexual desires now focused on men (as a result of taking oestrogen), 'It's going great,' she says. 'I have all these tattooed, bruiser guys asking me out on dates, wanting to tell me all their secrets.' The female hormones didn't affect her voice either: 'People were sceptical if I could still sing as I did, but I think I'm better than ever.'

Marissa Martinez-Hoadley, to give Cretin's singer her full married name, has had much the same experience – except the former Dan Martinez is now a woman in death metal, a genre which has a tendency to dwell on 'hacking up women's bodies and having sex with them,' as she puts it. 'Obviously it's offensive and tiresome. But it's done for the entertainment value, the same as horror movies. I don't believe it's hate music. And I have a lot of female death metal fans and friends.'

From San Jose, California, the son of a guitarist in seventies' rock band the Underground Railroad, Martinez also came of age in the era of Metallica. It was the extreme speed, timbre and mindset of death metal that she and her high school friend Matt Widener chose in 1992 for their new band, Cretin.

'I found it exciting that metal kept getting harder, faster and louder,' Martinez recalls. 'It also gave me an easy representation of masculinity to follow. I buried all my trans stuff from adolescence, when I was cross-dressing in private and thinking I was going to hell. But it kept resurfacing.'

Cretin unexpectedly split without releasing a record and Martinez forged a successful career in video game production. By 2005, her marriage was disintegrating but the band reformed and released its debut album *Freakery* in 2006. 'I'd accomplished something with the band that had once seemed impossible,' she says. 'So what about this other nagging impossibility in the back of my head?'

The album track 'Daddy's Little Girl' seemed like a giveaway: 'Little boys have nasty things between their legs/I'd rather have a girl, a dolly I can dress/My pretty little princess, a transgender success.'

But Martinez says that she never intended to transition until couples counselling with her former wife led to solo counselling for gender reassignment. Her bandmates were surprised, but supportive. 'Matt gave me a hug, and said, "Here we go . . ."' It proved a bumpy ride and Martinez had to put Cretin on hold. 'I couldn't do music and relearn everything – to walk, talk, dress – at the same time. It was a huge change from being this metal dude with a scraggly beard.'

In 2008, Martinez came out to *Decibel* magazine, and again faced the press when a reconvened Cretin released the *Stranger* album in 2014. She feels accepted by the world of metal. 'The belief is, "Fuck you, you can't tell me how to live my life," which fans respect.'

In 2009, Sydney, Australia's, 'trans metal band' (according to their website) Mechanical Bride, who dressed in feminine versions of New York Dolls' glam rags, released *Reborn*, 'a concept album about the journey of a transgendered male to female'. The music, 'from speed metal to soft rock, represent various states of mind during the process of transition,' they claimed.

In 2012, Laura Jane Grace did just the same, transitioning as her mainstream-popular rock band Against Me! continued to tour. Grace reinforced the notion that many trans musicians are driven toward the most testosterone-driven of genres: perhaps they're the easiest place to hide, and the most capable of permitting suppressed rage and pain. It's fortunate that the punk, hard rock and metal scenes are united by tightly bound communities that respect artists who project such emotions, while the pop industry is defined more by love. And love was a tortured commodity if you wanted to change gender.

Grace now lives in Chicago, where her daughter goes to school and there is a supporting trans community, but she was born Thomas Gabel in rural Georgia, and partly raised in Italy where her military father had been stationed. Grace was first entranced by Madonna and wanted to *be* Madonna, before becoming a teenage fan of hair metal. 'Poison, Guns N' Roses, Warrant,' she reels off the names. 'Sebastian Bach [of 'AIDS kills fags dead' T-shirt infamy] was more beautiful than some *Vogue* models. I knew how I felt, but I was in deep denial, and the natural response was to go the other way – "I'm not trans, I'm a man, real macho." But punk rock exposed the lie of all that rock-star-excess stuff, beginning with Kurt Cobain. But Queen's "I Want To Break Free", with Freddie in fishnets, that blew me away too!'

Having moved to Florida, Grace turned to bands that sang about anarchy and injustice, especially politicised UK punk bands such as Crass and Poison Girls, which shaped Against Me! Grace's trans issues remained dormant until the band's third album, 2005's *Searching For A Former Clarity*: 'Confessing childhood secrets of dressing up in women's clothes/Compulsions you never knew the reasons to.'

By 2009's *New Wave*, Against Me! had signed to Sire and scored a Top 60 US album. The finale, 'The Ocean', confessed, 'If I could have chosen, I would have been born a woman/My mother once told me she would have named me Laura/I would grow up to be strong and beautiful like her.'

'I thought I was outing myself, but, no!' says Grace. 'I even asked the band if they thought it was weird, but they said, "No, go ahead." But I'd have denied it had anyone asked. I had this live-fast-die-young thing going on, that I might soon be gone and I wouldn't have to explain anything.'

By their 2010 album *White Crosses*, which broke into the US Top 40, Grace was on her second marriage and had become a parent. But after meeting a trans fan of the band, 'I felt ashamed, she was pursuing what I was feeling, but I was so scared, so how could I be up there on the stage? She was the first I reached out to, like, "I don't know any trans people, can I be your friend?"'

She began taking week-long trips to write a new record, checking into hotels dressed as a woman and *Transgender Dysphoria Blues* came out the other end in 2014. She'd already confessed to her wife, sought advice from Mina Caputo and began the process toward transition, going public in *Rolling Stone*. 'Unreal pressure,' she says, which was worsened by a bad reaction to oestrogen when there was no endocrinologist within reach. 'I lost it, like some suicidal breakdown,' she recalls. On tour, fans looked for proof of her transition, while interviewers asked bluntly about operations: 'I hadn't even finished electrolysis on my face, slow the fuck down!'

Fully transitioning; separating from her wife; the delicate matter of having a young daughter; the trials and tribulations of an itinerant lifestyle – despite all this, Grace hasn't, in fact, slowed down. In 2014, alongside *Transgender Dysphoria Blues*, she fronted the documentary series *True Trans With Laura Jane Grace*, talking with trans women and men across the USA, with a book to come at the time of writing, based on the diaries she'd squirreled away all those years.

Grace has been assisted and inspired by the wider acceptance of trans identity, reflected in the high-profile examples of actress Laverne Cox and former Olympic decathlete Caitlyn Jenner. *The Danish Girl* was given a wide release in 2015, the bio-pic of Lili Elbe, one of earlier known cases of sex-reassignment surgery. But the trans narrative remained incomplete. Is it a case of fewer female-to-male transitions? Or that the media still sides with (former) privileged males? Or that trans women provide more photographic glamour, attracting both the male and female gaze?

In 2008, Cher's daughter Chastity Bono, who had identified as transgender in 1995, began the transition into Chaz Bono, but given the celebrity status of his mother and the 2011 TV series *Becoming Chaz*, the press coverage was underwhelming. It was still too early; or was it that the plus-size Bono was not the kind of model-perfect citizen that the media wanted to promote?

Without a raised profile and being Canadian, Lucas Silveira's transition in 2008 was even less documented than Bono's, though he was the first trans man to front a band signed to a major label. Born Lilia Silveira to Portuguese-Canadian parents, Lucas' teenage idols shaped both his gender and musical identity: soul legends Marvin Gaye and Stevie Wonder, Bowie, Chrissie Hynde of the Pretenders and Joan Jett, with her 'hard-edged, masculine energy'. Rough Trade's 'High School Confidential' 'was extremely confusing, but in an exciting way!' says Silveira. 'Anything that showed a hint of queerness felt familiar. But it was also my big secret and something I didn't understand about myself until I was thirty-two. For a long time, transgender was male-to-female and, even now, when I tell people I'm trans, they think I want to transition back to female.'

Silveira first came out as lesbian at eighteen: 'It was the only way to deal with what I was.' But he never wrote about sexuality or gender identity. 'Does Robert Plant write about his sexuality?' he reasons. 'I write about emotion and connections to others and subconscious ramblings that I only work out six months later, not from the fact I have a deep voice or a beard.'

With fiery, sultry vocals and a guitar sound to match, Silveira formed an all-female trio under his old name, 'but I knew I was about to come out and I didn't want my name associated with my music.' So they changed names to the Cliks, a fusion of clit and cock, 'the first trans band name,' he grins. The Cliks were all-lesbian too, though not by design, while 2005's debut album *The Cliks*, resembling a soulful and raunchy Pretenders, was inspired by falling in love with a woman 'who couldn't understand why she had such strong feelings for me too, because she was straight. But she later understood!'

'A *really* messy break-up' with his girlfriend of six years led to the start of therapy and the process of transition. By 2007's *Snakehouse* album, Silveira had a new identity, a new Cliks line-up – his three fellow musicians identified as queer – and a major label deal with Warner Bros (Canada) and Tommy Boy (US).

'The Cliks got signed because *Snakehouse* was a good record,' says Silveira, 'but also because of my story. But I walked into it a bit green. Warners just gave us the money but Tommy Boy got involved. They wanted to exploit the trans side just the right amount so when I thought they were totally accepting and I started being completely myself, they started taking issue. So did my manager, even the band. When I said I needed top surgery before touring, my manager said, "Are you sure? I don't want mental problems on the road." Interviewers wanted to talk about it, but the band said it was taking attention away from the music. Which it partly was, but it was also getting us attention. Trans folks were attending the shows too – one kid said he didn't kill himself because of us, so I was making a change in people's lives. No other musicians in the mainstream were talking about it.'

One high point was joining the *True Colors* tour; a low point was the argument over the artwork for the Cliks' 2009 album *Dirty King*, in which Silveira was topless and wore a crown and boxing gloves. 'It expressed what I was feeling, beaten up by everyone around me. The head of Tommy Boy said, "This is a rock band, not an episode of [plastic surgery hospital drama] *Nip/Tuck*," which was *so* offensive. I stopped giving a shit after that.'

In the aftermath of the Cliks' split, Silveira used the break to start hormone replacement: 'I'd delayed it because I was advised it would ruin my singing voice, which I later discovered wasn't accurate. I just had to take a really low dose of testosterone, sing every day and do vocal training. It made me exhausted and depressed, but I did it.'

Another low was reached after a new Cliks toured 2011's *Black Tie Elevator* album: 'I lost 80 per cent of my fan base because I'd transitioned. Many Cliks fans were lesbian and female and they couldn't identify with me anymore. Some said they felt betrayed. That was a kick in the teeth.'

Rocco Katastrophe had the same experience. 'In the process from a butch gay woman to a less-than-butch straight man, I realised I was losing a community and my place in it was contested,' he says. 'I overheard someone say I was a man rapping about women in a queer space. But I'm gender non-conformist and I was being called out for being a freak! So having found my people after high school, I'd lost them. There's a place now for trans men and a community but I'd never felt so displaced.'

On the plus side, a reader's poll in Canadian music magazine *Chart Attack voted* Silveira 'sexiest Canadian man'. Beside playing Pride events, giving motivational talks and hosting trans features on the Daily Extra's LGBTQ webcast, Silveira has since gained a new musical alias, CHAP and a new R&B/soul sound. 'I feel more authentic doing this because I'm finally more grounded,' he says. His first release, 'Walk Away', featured Minnesota trans rapper Lil One: 'It's the first song I've written from a trans perspective, about a relationship I'd come out of,' says Silveira. 'She turned out to be transphobic, saying I'd only taken hormones because of the pressure to fit into the binary system.'

Silveira (with the Cliks track 'Still') made the cut in *The Advocate*'s 2014 feature 'Thirty-seven alternative trans anthems', as did Caputo, Grace and Schmekel, 'the only out all-trans Jewish folk punk-queercore band,' the magazine claims.[1] Boundaries were only for category-phobes

---

1 www.advocate.com/arts-entertainment/music/2014/12/11/37-alternative-trans-anthems-trans-musicians

and, according to the list, 'Trans, genderqueer, non-binary, two-spirit and gender-nonconforming' were the new spaces in which to express gender identity.

This is where you'll find one of the modern era's most visible of singers, Miley Cyrus, the former teen star of the Disney Channel's *Hannah Montana*, who described herself in *Elle* magazine in 2105 as 'pansexual'[1] and founded the Happy Hippie Foundation, a non-profit organization for homeless and LGBTQ youth. At the same time, Cyrus was writing songs such as 'Bang Me Box' ('You say it tastes like cake with my lips against your face/I want you to eat it, baby').

'I can't even figure out if I'm feeling more like a girl or boy,' she told the *New York Times*. 'It took me talking to enough trans people to realise that I didn't ever have to decide on one.'[2] In her *Elle* interview, Cyrus said her parents 'have learned a lot about LGBT issues from me. They're fifty and from the south, so I don't expect them to understand it all, but I ask them just to accept it for me.' Dad is Billy Ray Cyrus, the man behind 1992's 'Achy Breaky Heart', one of country music's biggest crossover singles. His daughter shows how far pop has come even since his heyday. But country music itself has taken more time and, even after heavy metal had accepted its gay/trans pioneers, Nashville remained one frontier that the LGBTQ marchers had yet to cross.

Country: almost the final frontier

Mainstream country's hostility to same-sex love didn't go as far as hip hop's very public homophobia; it simply ignored it. When artists did unite the two forms, humour was the preferred vehicle, such as that of the Bellamy Brothers' 1997 track 'My Wife Left Me For My Girlfriend' – the duo claimed they were supporting women's empowerment, 'where these two liberated girls really got fed up' – or the Reverend Horton Heat's 'Cowboy Love'.

---

1 www.elleuk.com/now-trending/miley-cyrus-interview-october-2015#!
2 www.nytimes.com/2015/09/01/arts/music/miley-cyrus-and-her-dead-petz.html?smid=tw-share&_r=2

BREAKING DOWN THE WALLS OF HEARTACHE

The pathos and tragedy at the core of 2005's film adaptation of Annie Proulx's short story *Brokeback Mountain* took cowboy love to another level. When country legend Willie Nelson recorded Ned Sublette's comedic 'Cowboys Are Frequently, Secretly (Fond of Each Other)' in tribute to the film, his cover also served to critique Nashville's callous attitude and this, in a genre usually given to sentimentality.

Dolly Parton, the country superstar who has always been fending off rumours about her sexuality, also went out on a limb by recording 'Travelin' Thru' from the pioneering film *Transamerica*, released in 2005. The turnaround in Nashville would not to take much longer.

Shane McAnally was first. The Texan had had some minor country chart hits in 1999 but found the closet too hard to bear and moved to LA's gay mecca, West Hollywood, bartending and writing songs, including a handful for 2007's coming-out indie film *Shelter*. That year, McAnally decided to risk everything and move to Nashville, where he became the city's go-to songwriter for hire (including for hit US TV drama *Nashville*), alongside frequent collaborator Brandy Clark, as openly lesbian as McAnally was openly gay. 'When I stopped hiding who I was,' he said, 'I started writing hits.'[1] Between November 2010 and May 2013, McAnally co-wrote seven US no. 1 country singles and dozens of other hits for artists such as Reba McEntire and Kacey Musgraves.

2010 was gay country's *annus mirabilis* – on both the lesbian and gay fronts. Chely Wright was Nashville's first out lesbian lady. From Kansas City, Missouri, Wright's debut album *Woman In The Moon* had won the Academy of Country Music's top new female vaward in 1995 and the title track of her fourth album, *Single White Female*, topped the country chart in 1997. By 2010, she'd reached both her seventh studio album, *Lifted Off The Ground* and a sudden revelation.

The mournful mood of her album track 'Like Me' exposed her quandary: 'And who's gonna end up holdin' your hand/A beautiful woman or a tall, handsome man?' In Wright's autobiography, *Like Me: Confessions*

---

[1] www.nytimes.com/2013/05/26/arts/music/out-and-riding-high-in-nashville.html?_r=0

of a Heartland Country Singer[1], published at the same time as her album, Wright said she'd been driven to counter the prejudiced views of LGBTQ people, and the personal damage caused by 'lying and hiding'.

In 2004, Wright had started a relationship with a woman, 'the love of my life'. Her girlfriend subsequently married a man and Wright herself continued to date men in relationships that included a high-profile affair with country star Brad Paisley. She admitted that she'd reached the point of putting a gun in her mouth: 'I looked around and realised everything I gained in material wealth meant *nothing* to me. No one knew me. I had no real friends. I couldn't reach out to my friends and say I have a broken heart because they didn't even know I had a relationship. You're gonna come out. You can't do this. You will never have a whole, healthy life and you can't find love.'[2]

So even a 'glossy, mainstream country singer with several hit singles under her belt', as the *Guardian* described her, can be gay. 'The mere fact that someone like me came out is progress,' Wright said. 'But that progress is still slow. I get support from progressive country fans, but in equal measure I'm told that it's a deal-breaker for other fans.'[3] *Lifted Off The Ground* sold half of her usual sales, 'And I'm fine with that,' she said.

Joining her in the frontline was Justin Utley, born in Utah and, he says, 'the prince of Mormon pop,'[4] by the age of fifteen. By by his early twenties, Utley had enrolled in the church's homosexual conversion therapy Evergreen, following his first sexual experience at college. Having met his first boyfriend on the programme – whose death from a heart attack was a sign from God, Utley was told – he abandoned the church.

Rumours had long beset Ty Herndon, the twice-married Texan country singer who had followed a Top 10 chart placing for his 1995

---

1 Pantheon, 2010
2 www.autostraddle.com/chely-wright-country-music-gay-interview-72366
3 www.theguardian.com/music/2014/apr/10/country-music-gay-stars-kicking-closet-door-lavender-country
4 http://raannt.com/justin-utley-out-of-isolation-with-an-ex-mormon-gay-country-music-singer

debut *What Matters Most* by 'doing a George Michael'. He was arrested in a park in Fort Worth, Texas, by an undercover male police officer, though the charge of indecent exposure was dropped when Herndon plea-bargained for drug rehabilitation after being found to be carrying methamphetamine. The story faded away, but not Herndon's addictions. In 2015, he finally came out, gay and sober, on TV's *Entertainment Tonight*. 'I've dreamed about being in country music since I was six years old,' he said. 'It's my life, it's what I do, it's who I am and I went to great lengths to cover up that fact to be a country star.'

Herndon's announcement inspired fellow country singer Billy Gilman to post his own coming-out video the same day. 'It's difficult for me to make this video, not because I'm ashamed of being a gay male artist or a gay artist or a gay person,' he said, 'but it's pretty silly to know that I'm ashamed of doing this knowing that... because I'm in a genre, in an industry that is ashamed of me for being me.'

Gilman was doubly brave in that the former child star, who'd sold five million records, was making a comeback as an adult artist and had found that Nashville didn't want to know. 'I threw a showcase and no major label showed,' he said, supporting Chely's Wright's view that 'a new gay artist being taken around radio stations by a credible record label in Nashville' was still not on the cards.

But Nashville didn't represent the entire country music industry and, under his own steam, Steve Grand managed to break through to a new level, as a country artist openly gay from the start. His 2013 single 'All American Boy', a rousing tour-de-force that was halfway between Nashville and Bruce Springsteen, reached the US Top 50 after the video – funded by Grand – secured a million hits in the first week and, at the time of writing in 2016, now stands at over 5.4 million views on YouTube.

From Lemont, Illinois, Grand survived therapy organised by his Catholic parents to work as a model in the gay lifestyle magazines and then make the leap to music. In the video to 'All American Boy' – whose title could not be more pointed – Grant's character, in standard white

T-shirt and jeans, chances his luck after a drunken Independence Day celebration with another all-American boy. Though straight, the other character doesn't reject Grant's friendship: Bronski Beat's 'Smalltown Boy' comes to mind; the way we were...

Some critics called the video's drunk/unrequited gay-straight storyline a cliché, but Grand had laid down an important marker, using country's traditional images against itself and provocatively using its symbols too, given the fluttering US flag in both the video and the artwork of Grand's debut album *All American Boy*. Subsequent videos showcased gay kisses and togetherness.

Positivity also thrived in country singer Kacey Musgraves's debut single 'Follow Your Arrow' – co-helmed by gay songwriters Brandy Clark and Shane McAnally – that hit the country Top 10 in 2013 with a follow-your-heart message about same-sex love – 'Kiss lots of boys or kiss lots of girls, if that's what you're into.' It won song of the year at the Country Music Awards and crossed over to the national Top 60. Nashville had gone pink – and Tennessee didn't spin off its axis.

Meanwhile, in world news...

This left dancehall reggae as the only musical genre that refused to concede ground to the LGBTQ community, even reneging on written agreements to stop the rot. In 2001, the reggae-based RAS label launched the campaign Slackness Done, 'to sweep away the bad vibes that homophobic, misogynistic and materialistic music has perpetrated on us,' said label partner Brice Rose. He distributed 1200 brooms to labels, media, artists and DJs, 'with a message that it is time for the industry to clean up dancehall music and stop bashing gays.'[1]

That nothing had changed by 2004 showed the ineffectiveness of the initiative. Another campaign, with the more potent title of Stop Murder Music, a term coined in the mid-nineties by UK gay rights activist Peter Tatchell, had the necessary impact. The coordinators were UK activists

---

1 'Is Slackness Done? Cleaning Up The Dancehall', Tasha Joseph, *The Beat* magazine Aug/Sept 2001

OutRage!, the Black Gay Men's Advisory Group and the first Jamaican gay rights organisation, J-Flag.

Stop Murder Music asked LGBTQ organisations to protest against shows by eight Jamaican artists named in a 'dancehall dossier' and to distribute posters that described the eight as 'killer queens'. The campaign succeeded in shutting down concerts and sponsorship deals – Tatchell reckoned £5 million of bookings were lost – and forced the dancehall industry to barter with LGBTQ groups. In 2005, VP Records, Greensleeves and Jet Star, the three principal independent labels promoting dancehall, agreed to stop distributing music that promoted homophobic violence. The tide was stemmed without silencing the artists completely.

The next step was 2007's Reggae Compassionate Act: by signing the contract, dancehall artists agreed not to promote homophobic material. New reports that Beenie Man and Sizzla (alongside Capleton and Banton) had complied were met with the singers' denials; Sizzla sang 'Nah Apologize' and other homophobic songs on his following European tour and Buju Banton made references from the stage to 'Boom Bye Bye'.[1]

Sizzla continued to have concerts cancelled and Beenie Man posted a video in 2012 in which he talked of 'people creating problems for me to work,' but that he 'respect[s] each and every human being.' In an interview on Jamaican TV, he refused to call the clip an apology but agreed to the interviewer's suggestion of it being a 'statement of remorse' if that's what it took to get a US work permit – which was granted.

An authentically sincere apology – on behalf of all Jamaica, it seemed – was issued in 2011 when Mista Majah P released an album, *Tolerance*, in the more accessible and gentle realm of reggae. He might be living in California these days, but his very public stand against homophobia is still profoundly courageous given the state of the opposition.

Majah cites three pivotal incidents. At school in Jamaica's capital

---

[1] Thanks to the Soul Rebels website, established to document homophobia in reggae music, for the summary information, www.soulrebels.org/dancehall.htm

Kingston, he witnessed a boy's beating, 'because he was identified as a "batty boy". I was too young to understand the culture and politics but I knew something was wrong with that picture.' As an adult, he'd seen 'a disgusting, bloody attack on a gay person [in an area] considered a ghetto, where street justice was considered justice before the police show up.' Years later, in California, 'I was discriminated upon by a gay person,' when Majah was branded a supporter of Murder Music because he was Jamaican. 'I felt bad about being stereotyped. Then it hit me – live a day in my shoe and walk a mile, then you will feel how I feel. I knew I had to set the record straight.'

The only other public figure supporting gay rights was, astonishingly, Jamaica's prime minister, Portia Simpson-Miller, but she still lacked the support to change the sodomy laws that Jamaica inherited from the UK, just as Majah hasn't persuaded other reggae artists to support his stand 'for truth and rights'. He does have fellow ex-pat Jamaicans who have appeared alongside him in videos in which he has been brave enough to wear dresses and wigs and send himself up, but also face the camera to deliver diatribes about how dancehall needs to change its ways.

Tolerance was followed by two further albums, *The Closet Is Open* and *Gays Belong In Heaven Too*. Unsurprisingly, Majah has received death threats and he doesn't publicise his visits home to Jamaica to see family. 'It's a lonely road because even promoters say artists won't share the stage with a batty man supporter who they say has damaged reggae,' he notes. 'But the goodness of it outweighs the risk I am taking. Finally, I stand for something. I believe it's making a big difference because I have started a conversation that no one else was willing to. My greatest achievement is an email telling me, "Thank you, because of you and your inspiring music, you save my life."'

The extremity of Jamaica's situation is shared by all countries that lack legal protection for its LGBTQ population, including large swathes of the world, particularly Africa. Homosexuality is illegal in thirty-eight countries of the continent and in Arabic, Caribbean and Asian nations too. While Oscar Wilde was only sent to prison for two years, the death penalty applies in ten countries, including Sudan, the United Arab Emirates, Nigeria and Afghanistan. In other regions, there is extended imprisonment and private retribution, from honour killings to public floggings. But in regions where the laws are less frequently applied, pioneers have emerged.

Outside of Israel, home to Eurovision trans winner Dana International and a thriving LGBTQ scene with many gay and lesbian singers, the Middle East has been particularly starved. The community had one famous advocate in Googoosh (born Faegheh Atashin), Iran's queen of seventies pop, who was unable to work after 1979's Islamic revolution and moved to America in 2000. In 2014 she released *'Behesht'* ('Heaven'), with a video that revealed a love interest between two women and ending on the words, 'Freedom to love for all'. But this was freedom declared from a position of safety; inside the Arab world, there has been just the one voice, Hanned Sinno.

Lebanon is a comparatively liberal Arab nation, with the first gay rights organisation in the Middle East. The law to prosecute homosexual activities – that 'contradict the laws of nature' – was overturned in 2014 and homosexuality declassified as an illness. But for a number of years, since he became the lead singer of the indie-rock/folk band Mashrou' Leila in 2008, Sinno had been openly provoking the country with his views of love, sexuality and politics.

'Mashrou' Leila' translates as 'Leila's Project' and also, 'Night Project', while their 2015 album, *Ibn El Leil* translates as *Son Of The Night*, a term that Sinno says is commonly used to describe 'a party boy. Much of the album revolves around nightlife and escapism and addresses the melancholia of living on the outskirts of society, being submerged and also exiled by those around you or by yourself.'

At night, Lebanon's gay and trans community comes to life but in daylight it has no currency and, until Sinno, no voice. Lacking any role model when he was growing up, Sinno took refuge in grunge and progressive rock, 'which all gave me a sense of self-as-outcast that was easier to digest than my sexual otherness. I identified with artists that wrote about living on the outside – there's an aura about non-mainstream music that makes you feel like your wretchedness is beautiful, like your angst is depth.'

Meeting as students at the American University of Beirut, Mashrou' Leila founder members wanted to provide an alternative to what Sinno calls 'the cookie-cutter artists churned out by the pop industry in Lebanon, which has a monopoly over media outlets. Regionally produced music of dissent was much harder to come across.'

Across Mashrou' Leila's repertoire of three albums, sexuality is represented by *'Shim El Yasmine'* ("Smell The Jasmine'), about a break-up between two men, 'our first song to explicitly use gender-queer language,' says Sinno. *'Ala Babu'* followed suit while *'Skandar Malouf'* satirises homophobic attitudes, in translation: 'Stop checking the lock on your door because you can't hide from the stuff that's happening in your body.' Sinno named the song after two Lebanese men: 'One wrote extremely bigoted and misogynistic songs, like how women should raise their children differently, so that boys grew up to be real men instead of homosexuals. The other ran a TV show that ended up getting sixteen gay men arrested.'

At a time when police raids were common and homosexuality illegal, Sinno knew he was taking a risk. 'I grew up witnessing immense homophobia in local media and I didn't think it would go smoothly, but it has been worth it,' he says. 'And though the status of LGBT acceptance here is deplorable, it is not quite as deplorable as global media makes out.

But if I was to get into trouble,' he concludes, 'again, it'll be well worth it.'

Linking the Middle East with Africa, Egypt is awash with contradictions; while not specifically outlawed under morality laws, homosexuality is punishable with up to seventeen years in prison (with or without hard labour and fines). In 2014, eight men were sentenced to three years for spreading indecent images, following the circulation of a video of a gay marriage ceremony and over twenty men were arrested in a public bathhouse but were acquitted. People were emboldened enough to launch an online LGBT magazine, *Ehna*, but it stayed anonymous and was shut down after just one issue, 'for security reasons'. There have been Egyptian gay pioneers in film and literature, but no music.

It's only when you start heading south in the African continent that a rare chink of light appears. In Angola, the small LGBTQ community has one advocate, the trans singer Titica, born Teca Miguel Garcia, who followed sex reassignment surgery in Brazil and threats and even beatings, to emerge as the queen of Kudoro, Africa's popular brand of electro-rap in the same twerk-friendly vein as New Orleans bounce.

Titica's 2011 single '*Olha O Boneco*' was her pride anthem: 'We are all different but all human, all equal, just "one love",' she declared.[1] By transitioning, Titica has come to be treated more as a woman than as a gay man. Similarly, Iran has a disproportionately high number of trans women while retaining the death penalty for homosexuality. But in Kenya, where you can be imprisoned for fourteen years for homosexuality, the country has a gay male advocate – one who is defiant and vocal.

Jim Chuchu first made music as a member of Just A Band, an enterprising Afro-dance trio formed in 2010 that released three albums and many audio-visual projects. Persisting with photography and film, Chuchu founded the NEST Collective, the ten-strong team behind *Stories Of Our Lives*, a series of five LGBTQ-themed film shorts (funded by UHAI, the East African Sexual Health and Rights Initiative or EASHRI) that Chuchu directed and co-wrote. He also composed the serene soundtrack.

The risks were already high and, initially, the creators of the film were anonymous, before Chuchu, co-writer Njoki Ngumi and executive producer George Gachara all decided to come out in an interview on the eve of the film's premiere at 2014's Toronto Film Festival. *Stories Of Our Lives* continued to be feted internationally but Kenya's film classification board banned it for promoting homosexuality, 'contrary to [Kenya's] national norms and values'. Gachara was subsequently

---

1 https://en.wikipedia.org/wiki/Titica

arrested on charges (later dropped) of violating Kenya's Films and Stage Plays Act.

'I made this film in protest at the bullshit that allows someone like [Kenyan] President Museveni to attack art students for "having no solutions to the country's challenges" – as if the only careers fit for Africans are in the army, construction and finance,' Chuchu said. 'Who will sing our songs if everyone is working in a bank? And when did forming angry mobs to evict and kill gay people become a nation-building activity?'[1]

Like Googoosh in Iran, Namibian artist Shishani was able to find a voice because she was no longer living in her homeland; she was in the Netherlands when she released 'Minority' in 2014, after coming out a year earlier. But her music is widely available in Namibia, where it's still illegal to be gay. 'My music is popular in Namibia. I've made my mark, so I feel stronger, now,' Shishani told Spectra Speaks, the founder of Queer Women of Color Media Wire. 'I may lose some fans, but it's okay. So many others have it way worse than me. So many others activists are risking much more.'

A rainbow riot in the rainbow nation

Like the Middle East axis of Israel and Lebanon, there is one nation on the continent of Africa with an advanced approach to LGBTQ: South Africa. Actually, it's one of *the* most progressive. In 1996, the post-apartheid constitution was the first in the world to outlaw discrimination based on sexual orientation and South Africa was the fifth country to legalise same-sex marriage.

Ironically, it was apartheid that showed homosexuality was not a contributory cause of social and moral decay, but instead it was the racial segregation enforced by the white, English-speaking National Party that governed from 1948 to 1994. This included laws to prohibit marriage between different races that criminalised sexual relations with a person of a different race with sentences of up to seven years for

---

1 www.okayafrica.com/film/stories-of-our-lives-nest-collective-jim-chuchu-kenya-film/

same-sex relations between men. In 1994, the first government of the African National Congress legalised homosexuality and removed all legal obstacles between relationships between races.

No law criminalised sex between women and Brenda Fassie, regarded as South Africa's first black pop star and labelled 'the Madonna of the townships' for her sexually charged performances, was openly bisexual. After her premature death[1], Fassie's heir apparent was Lebo Mathosa who was also bisexual and died young[2].

South Africa's LGBTQ performers seem a little cursed: the first openly gay pop group, the black trio 3Sum, was popular through the noughties; then one member, Jeff Moyo, die of a gastric ulcer and another, Koyo Bala, was diagnosed HIV-positive in 2011. But numerous LGBTQ artists – black and white – are thriving across a spectrum of styles and gender identities.

2013 was a pivotal year, when both Nakhane Touré and Umlilo released their debut records. Touré, from Port Elizabeth, had been thrown out of home by his hardline Christian parents when he came out and continued his battle with God: 'I'd go to gay clubs on Saturdays and imagine the net of fairy lights above me was a ceiling and God couldn't see me. Sundays, I'd pray the guilt away.' It eventually dawned on Touré that the colonialism behind apartheid had also brought Christianity: 'I thought, my ancestors were going to hell until a couple of white guys came over to save us? The Bible has been used to bring us to our knees. To me, it was all a lie.'

Inspired by Brenda Fassie, soul and art rock (Kate Bush and Jeff Buckley), Touré's stunning debut album, *Brave Confusion*, was upfront about his sexuality. 'Christopher' was named after his boyfriend and other song titles also featured male names. The video to Touré's single

---

[1] In 1995, Fassie was discovered in a hotel with the body of her lesbian lover, dead from an apparent overdose and when Fassie died from an overdose in 2004, her lesbian partner was at her bedside.

[2] Mathosa was even younger than Fassie when she died in 2006, aged twenty-nine, in a car crash after successfully weaning herself off the drugs that had brought Fassie down.

'Dark Room' – about his weekend cycles of partying and guilt – was set in a bare, prison-like room with Touré held and caressed by another man. 'It would be a disservice to the songs if we didn't represent its homo-eroticism,' he says. 'I wasn't worried what people would think; in fact, I wanted a reaction.'

Touré's 2015 EP *The Laughing Son* includes 'The Plague', about Africa's problem with HIV, seen from racial and sexual perspectives and 'We Dance Again', an a cappella version of a collaboration with dance DJ Nkosinathi 'Black Coffee' Maphumulo that topped the South Africa chart. 'No one asked me what I was singing when we recorded it,' Touré recalls. 'It's about a man bringing his male lover out of depression via sex. I'm singing, "Come again, come, come, come again . . ." I was so happy that patriarchal and homophobic people were blasting it every morning!'[1]

By comparison, Umlilo (meaning 'fire' in the South African language of Xhosa) is more indebted to African and dance rhythm. Born Siya Ngcobo in Johannesburg, he started performing as Siya Is Your Anarchist: 'He was rougher, angrier, and more political than I am now,' he says. 'Umlilo merges these characteristics with a more open-ended and sensitive side.'

He was fortunate to have an aunt married to the creator/director of the 1998 Broadway musical *Sarafina*, about a group of students involved in the epochal Soweto township riots against apartheid. 'I was four when I got to hang out backstage; all that music and dance was electrifying! I never was interested in action figures and guns.'

Umlilo's music reflects his musical training; jazz and gospel as a child, R&B and kwaito (South Africa's brand of house music), Freddie Mercury and Prince, Brenda Fassie and Lebo Mathosa. The result of these influences is a dramatic, inventive gender-fluid character who writes about 'oppressed or marginalised people finding their own light and the confidence to express it uncompromised.'

---

[1] Touré has also published a novel, *Piggy Boy's Blues*, 'about a young man who lives in the city who goes to live with his uncle in a rural town, who lives with another man. It's also about male rape, dealing or not dealing with what happened . . . it's a light read!'

Anger is Umlilo's prime motivation: 'How did homosexuality become the number one item of agenda in Uganda and Nigeria when people need food and shelter? We're seeing so many of our own getting lynched exactly the way Africans were lynched during slavery and apartheid and civil war and for what? It's not homosexuality that was a western import, it's homophobia.'

He talks about his *Slave To The Beat* EP as 'a more positive look at the future, about marginalised people being comfortable in their skin and exploring and challenging the outside world.'[1]

This growing confidence and pride is shared by 'Zulu pop princess' Toya Delazy, who won newcomer of the year and best pop album award at 2013's South African music awards and was nominated in the best international act for Africa category in the US Afro-American BET Awards. Delazy hasn't declared her sexuality, but her protest at Africa's anti-gay laws in 2014's single 'Forbidden Fruit' – with its images of gay, lesbian and straight couples kissing – spoke for her.

Cape Town's Catherine Jude, who calls herself Dope Saint Jude, has no qualms about declaring herself. 'I do identify with the word "lesbian" but I'm not picky about terms. I like to keep my mind open,' she says. 'I don't know if I fall in love with a trans person . . . you never know if I fall in love with a man.'

Jude's sound – pop, electro, hip hop, kwaito – and vision are equally free of constraints. 'It's limiting to be labelled a conscious or queer or female rapper, I don't have just one narrative,' she says. 'I'm African and a woman, a queer woman, a person of colour . . . my story and our stories, are complex, the way I move between masculine and feminine and comment on race, class, gender, sexuality and pussy power, as a brown person, overcoming limitations.'

Tracey Chapman was an early influence, but riot grrrl too, from

---

[1] Umlilo has also worked as a journalist, TV researcher and wrote and directed a documentary on the South African LGBTQ/AIDS activist Zackie Achmat. At the time of writing in 2016 he is working on a short action film, a theatre script and his debut album.

which Jude appropriated feminist and DIY themes. She also loves the golden age of stage and film musicals: 'I read it as performance art, the way the music, dancing and acting came together so powerfully.' Hip hop is her most problematic love: 'It's the music of the oppressed and they use it to show self-love and empower the listener, but the misogyny and homophobia hurts me. It's like being married to an abuser.'

In 2012, Jude formed Bros B4 Hos, a drag king troupe: 'I would take the beats of Buster Rhymes and Lil Wayne, homophobic guys, and make up my own raps, while the other members would lipsync. My character was based on Lil Wayne, I called him Saint Dude. I realised that gender is a performance, that everything we mark ourselves male and female with are constructs.'

Jude and Umlilo's gender-fluid performances chime with the latest wave of queer rappers in the US, including Mykki Blanco, Angel Haze, Le1f, Azealia Banks and Cakes da Killa, all of whom have made much bigger inroads into the mainstream than the homohop pioneers: their musical fusions are richer, their videos more professional and their aims and visions more complex now that the lines have been blurred between sexualities and genders. It's as if the freedoms of the Harlem Renaissance after slavery weren't curtailed by the Great Depression or McCarthyism, as people have accepted and celebrated their differences.

If only this was the case across the planet, but there have been many steps back too, such as in Russia, where homosexuality between consenting adults in private was decriminalised in 1993 and homegrown pop in the post-cold war nineties was full of queer spirit. But the 'propaganda law' of 2013 banned material that asserted homosexuality was a normal lifestyle – something similar to the UK's Section 28 but fostering a much stronger climate of fear as homophobic violence on the streets has become commonplace.

As in South Africa, other eastern European regions have shown that homosexuality is not a root cause of society ills. For example, the Bulgarian singer Azis used the growing popularity of the Romany/Turkish-influenced electronic pop known as *chalga* to charge his startling gender-fluid persona launched at the start of the noughties. He predated the current trend for bearded drag queens with his blonde goatee and false eyelashes and femme costumes that included a blue bikini. In his videos, Azis would surround himself with muscled men, and yet Bulgarian society hasn't crumbled into anarchy or its children been corrupted.

'I am one of the faces of democracy,' Azis said. 'People saw there was freedom in this country after I appeared on the screen. A lot of people wanted to take me off, a lot of them didn't put me on, they were against me. That's normal, how many years was there communism? For many people, this feeling still remains.'[1]

In Ukraine, the boy band Kazaky are famous for their dashing choreography while wearing high heels. Its popular drag act Verka Serduchka[2] – born Andriy Mykhailovych Danylko – was the country's representative in 2007's Eurovision Song Contest. Just as Russian children haven't wavered because of the Russian band Mokroshelky, who identify as riot grrrl and queercore[3] or their countrymen KGBears, 'the first official Russian bear music project', according to their website. They may carefully avoid printing or saying the word 'homosexual'[4] and they always wear bear masks for their videos and live performance, but tracks such as 'Hungry And Uncut', their Weather Girls parody 'It's Raining Bears' and their suggestion that listeners should 'Shake that hairy ass' in 'Shake That Ass' speaks for their right to freedom. However, their website link now leads to a page that reads, 'This account has been suspended' – and it's not difficult to know why.

While the website was still active, the KGBears posted a video parody of Cochita Wurst, the bearded drag queen who won Eurovision for Austria in 2014 with 'Rise Like A Phoenix'. The culture department of Russia's defence ministry had called Wurst a sign of Europe's 'degrading

---

1 www.publicbroadcasting.net/krvs/.artsmain/article/11/70/976104/Radio/Azis
2 Every country appears to have one camper-than-camp icon, such as Mexico's Juan Gabriel and Turkey's Zeki Muren.
3 http://mokroshelky.bandcamp.com
4 KGBears do feature acts of transgression, such as the hairy bears wearing a wedding dress or leather fetish gear, in the video for 'Shake That Ass'.

moral values'. You wonder what Russia made of their own, the female duo t.A.T.u., who staged a controversial are-they-aren't-they lesbian identity[1] campaign that helped propel their single 'All The Things She Said' to no. 1 across Europe in 2002 and became the first Russian act to reach the US Top 20. Did Russia suffer its own moral collapse when they kissed in the song's video? Did the west?

Perhaps the prevailing Russian officials think that a band such as New York quintet Scissor Sisters (with three openly gay men in its line-up[2] and Top 5 albums stacked with LGBTQ themes), Katy Perry's 'I Kissed A Girl' (seven weeks at US no. 1) or Lady Gaga's 'Born This Way' (no. 1 in twenty-six countries) were a sign of what their country could become? Like Jamaica and many African countries, Russia persists with the belief that homosexuality is a white western import that will only bring destabilisation. Fortunately, there is a wider world in which personal freedoms are not suffocated by nationalism and despots, where personal freedoms are cherished and a hip hop pride anthem can sell over 2 million copies and storm Top 10s around the planet.

Macklemore and Ryan Lewis's 2012 track 'Same Love' was written in support of the campaign for Washington Referendum 74 on the legalisation of same-sex marriage in the state of Washington. Both rappers Macklemore and Lewis were straight and white but the track's featured vocalist, Mary Lambert, was openly gay and black and the media coverage added to the forward momentum.

Back in 2003, the US Supreme Court had invalidated the sodomy laws in the remaining fourteen states that still held them; in 2011, the federal appeals court repealed 'Don't ask don't tell'; in June 2015, DOMA was repealed across the entire US as state-level bans on same-sex marriage were ruled unconstitutional.

---

1 In 2005, Lena Katina said of herself and fellow t.A.T.u member Julia Volkova, 'Our first video was about the love between two girls. We do not pretend to be lesbians – we've never said we were. Julia just had a baby and currently has a girlfriend and we've both always had boyfriends. We share a special bond.'
2 A band named after a sexual position favoured by lesbians. In fact, Dead Lesbian had been Scissor Sisters' first band name.

Hip hop: a rainbow nation?

The relationship between mainstream hip hop and LGBTQ identity also experienced significant change when Frank Ocean came out in 2012. From New Orleans – which might explain his bravery – the singer used his Tumblr account to publish a letter originally intended for the liner notes to his 2012 album *Channel Orange*, to the man he called his 'first love' who had 'changed my life' when Ocean was nineteen. 'I don't know what happens now and that's all right,' Ocean wrote. 'I don't have any secrets I need kept anymore . . . I feel like a free man. If I listen closely . . . I can hear the sky falling too.'[1]

Even if Ocean was more an R&B singer than rapper, he was still part of the hardline LA hip hop collective Odd Future. But the hip hop community was quick to support him, including figures such as the current most popular and iconic black female artist Beyoncé and her equally influential husband Jay Z, and Def Jam label co-founder Russell Simmons, who wrote, 'Today is a big day for hip hop. It is a day that will define who we really are. How compassionate will we be? How loving can we be? How inclusive are we? I am profoundly moved by the courage and honesty of Frank Ocean. Your decision to go public about your sexual orientation gives hope and light to so many young people still living in fear.'[2]

Even Odd Future's leader Tyler, The Creator, a man as fond of the homophobic putdown as Eminem, tweeted his support: 'My big brother finally fucking did that. Proud of that nigga cause I know that shit is difficult or whatever.' Even 50 Cent, another protégé of Dr Dre alongside Eminem, told MTV News, 'Anyone who has an issue with Frank Ocean is an idiot . . . I could care less about what his personal preferences in his actual bedroom.' He added, '[President] Obama is for same-sex marriage . . . If the president is saying that, then who am I to go the other way?'

---

1 http://frankocean.tumblr.com/post/26473798723
2 http://globalgrind.com/2012/07/04/russell-simmons-letter-to-frank-ocean-gay-bi-sexual-comes-out-photos

Less widely documented, but just as significant, was the edging-out of Calvin Lebrun, known as Mister Cee, a pivotal figure in hip hop circles for his role in the rise of rap superstars Big Daddy Kane, Biggie Smalls and Jay Z. He was DJing for New York's revered hip hop station Hot 97 when the police caught him in his car, receiving oral sex from a prostitute that the media identified as a drag queen and a trans woman. When Cee was arrested later, he went on air in 2013 to say he wasn't gay, just that he would get the urge to have fellatio with a man that looks like a woman – and he was having therapy to work through his issues. Talking to the *New York Times*, Cee said, 'It's not that I don't want to say I'm bisexual. It's almost like, you hear a certain record – is this a hip hop record or an R&B record? I'm not so sure. I guess that's where I am.'[1]

Throughout his ordeal, Cee was supported by his close friends in hip hop; their friendship and respect outweighed the homophobia, because this was one of their own. This was revolutionary, given that hip hop had popularised the use of 'No homo', a term that rappers would add to statements that could be construed as 'gay' – and it had been Kanye West who had publicised more understanding for LGBT people, who had started it in 2009 with his verse in Jay Z's 'Run This Town': 'It's crazy how you can go from being Joe Blow/to everybody on your dick – no homo.'

Other 'No homo' examples are Chamillionaire ('No homo, I go hard'), Cam'ron's songtitle 'Silky (No Homo)' and Lil Wayne's, 'Just shot a video with R Kelly, but no homo though'. Yet this was the same Lil Wayne who wore all manner of 'Yes, homo!' outfits and was once photographed kissing his mentor, the rapper Baby, on the lips. But it was Lil B who went as far as naming his 2011 album *I'm Gay* – though his record label reputedly forced the rapper to add the word 'I'm happy' in subtitles.

In his video to 'Unchain Me', Lil B – who had already referred to

---

1 www.nytimes.com/2014/12/22/arts/the-hip-hop-dj-mister-cee-spins-on-after-quitting-hot-97.html?_r=1

himself as 'a princess' – mimed in sparkling, dangling earrings. In an interview with CNN, he said, 'I hope that I can turn some of my fans that might be homophobic or supporters that might be homophobic and say, "You know what, we're all one people. This is love."' When the US legalised same-sex marriage in 2015, he tweeted, 'I'm not gay and I don't want to marry a man or find them attractive but I almost cried for all gays around the world! Progress! Do u – Lil B.'

Whether hip hop is only toying with homosexuality or has come to some enlightened position can't be quantified, but it's clear that raps with the terms 'faggot' and 'No homo' are becoming scarce.

Notably, black Baltimore rapper Yitz Jordan, known as Y-Love, the son of a Christian Ethiopian father and Puerto Rican mother who converted to orthodox Judaism, came out in 2012.

And whether it is all a provocative marketing stunt or a genuine attempt at positivity, Lil B has made his bid, in the same way as David Bowie and Prince, for a more fluid expression; the way Kanye West did by wearing a skirt at the 12-12-12 benefit concert for victims of Hurricane Sandy and Young Thug's fusing of gangsta imagery with painted nails while wearing a lace floral Gucci top, tutu and leopard-print dress in a photoshoot. (He told writer Sam Wolfson, 'I like everything people say about me, "You gay, you a punk, you can't rap, you're the hardest"').[1] In 2010, the then most-wanted female rapper, Nicki Minaj, created a gay male alter ego in Roman Zolanski and even gave him an appearance at the Grammys.

Hip hop and LGBTQ identity has also travelled a long way on TV; debuting in January 2015, *Empire*, the drama series about a hip hop record label dynasty from gay black director Lee Daniels, risked having a gay character as one of its principal male leads. Later that year, the VH1 channel's *Love and Hip Hop: Hollywood* gave gay rap couple Milan Christopher Owens and Miles Brock equal billing alongside their straight counterparts. In 2013, the Fuse channel launched the reality TV

---

1 www.theguardian.com/music/2015/oct/08/young-thug-hits-bring-money-lil-wayne

series *Big Freedia, Queen Of Bounce* – a title that once belonged to her New Orleans friend Katey Red, who appears in the show. Freedia was also a prominent part of Beyoncé's 2016 single 'Formation', set in New Orleans. This particular battle appears to be won . . .

The end, but it begins again . . .

The first images in John Grant's queer history lesson that was his video for 'Glacier' are photographs of same-sex couples taken in secret and evidence of police raids, military discharges and mental health diagnoses. The final images are of two young women kissing and Tyler's tweet to Frank Ocean. Even if it's taken over a hundred years, it's still a notable sign of change.

Released in 2013, Mexican filmmaker-activist Leo Herrara's *The Fortune Teller*, subtitled *50 Yrs of Faggotry in 5 Mins*[1] was a similarly searing and touching history lesson, documenting homosexuality and homophobia. The soundtrack included Sylvester, Cazwell, George Michael and a sissy bounce concert and Herrara cut between 'milestones and icons of the modern gay man . . . from Mapplethorpe to [vlogger] Lohanthony, Uganda to Burning Man, Vogue to Sissy Bounce, AIDS to the Berlin patients' – the last being the name given to the two German men (in 1998 and 2008) who appear to have defeated AIDS.

In 2015, the music video for 'The Father Project' by Iranian-Norwegian artist Tooji tried to push some buttons; an enigmatic stranger walks into a church and proceeds to seduce the priest in front of the altar before spouting angel wings. The conservatives in Russia would have been seething.

In February 2016, official resistance to the video for Kenyan rapper Art Attack's remix of Macklemore And Lewis's 'Same Love' didn't stop it from being freely viewed on YouTube. It was announced as Kenya's first gay music video, with its own hashtag, #kenyangayvideo, setting off a national debate on homosexuality and freedom. The rap began,

---

1 https://vimeo.com/65759516

'This song is dedicated to the new slaves, the new blacks, the new Jews, the new minorities for whom we need a civil rights movement, maybe a sex rights movement. Especially in Africa. Everywhere. This goes out to you. I feel you.'

The video was strong on same-sex couples, featuring bedroom scenes that were more erotic than some western music videos spliced between shots of newspaper headlines (A DISEASE WORSE THAN ALCOHOL), gay pride marches, posters supporting gay marriage and images of Brenda Fassie and Uganda activist Kasha Jacqueline Bombastic Nabagesera. At the end there was a suicide note, like John Grant's 'Glacier' video in reverse.

'We expected that this will create controversy, we expected that a lot of people will talk about it but we didn't expect the amount of publicity it has received,' Art Attack told Reuters. 'The erotic scenes were meant to show that these people also fall in love.'

The same month, Nepal also got its first gay-themed video and song – *'Timile Ta Sajilai'*, by Samir Limbu. True, the video starts with a funeral: a young man has hanged himself after his love was spurned and it ends with the guy who spurned him, heartbroken and turning a gun on himself, in an echo of those pioneering films where gay and lesbian characters met grisly ends. But the conversation has begun.

When the most streamed song of 2014, 'Take Me To Church' by the (straight) Irish singer-songwriter Hozier, has a video depicting a fictional homophobic lynching in Russia with over 314 million views on You Tube, you sense the times are a-changing, even if they remain the same, because the situation in Russia remains real.

'It's horrific and depressing what's happening in other parts of the world. They have as far to go as anyone's ever had to go,' says Indigo Girl Emily Saliers. 'But I think it's really important to celebrate where the evolution has happened, that human beings are capable of broadening their mind and their acceptance. In our miniscule western paradigm, it's huge what's happened. If you have a role model when you're oppressed, it can save your life and music has saved lives. Just look at teen suicide rates in the queer and trans communities.'

One vivid example of representation and validation through the medium of music is the video for Will Young's 2015 single 'Brave Man', which showed a real life trans male teenager walking naked through the streets as different groups of people react.

'I realised that there is often coverage of what it is to be a woman in a man's body but never to my knowledge the documenting of the opposite,' Young wrote on Facebook. 'Almost a perverted kind of patriarchy . . . we see a man determined to be himself in the face of all adversity from inside and outside. This video is about taking a moment in time to explore a section of society who stand up for themselves. To tell a story and offer a window through music into someone's life.'

In 2016 there are enough LGBTQ-related videos, songs and artists to populate a weekly gay music chart, a blog compiled through readers' votes with tracks moving up and down depending on popularity. At the time of writing, no. 1 is 'Look Away', a grand piano ballad sung by two gay men, America's Steve Grand and Israel's Eli Lieb. The heartache is palpable in the lyric, but not in the closet. Meanwhile, John Grant's brazen, profound confessionals are popular enough for him to sell out London's prestigious Royal Albert Hall (capacity: 5,272) in June 2016 and lip-synching of modern pop favourites such as Carly Rae Jepsen's 'Call Me Maybe' by the likes of the Harvard University baseball team and the US Army are knowingly homoerotic. You'd imagine popular music cannot come out any more than it already has.

And yet . . . it's 2016 and North Carolina has passed a law banning anti-discrimination protections based on sexual orientation that requires transgender people in government buildings and public schools to use bathrooms matching their birth gender. Mississippi has also signed legislation allowing individuals and institutions with religious objections to deny services to LGBTQ people. Concerts have been cancelled in those places and new business plans rescinded – but will the US see more conservative backlashes against same-sex marriage and other civil liberties? And will there be more offensives against the LGBTQ population such as the Orlando shooting of June 2016, when forty-nine people were murdered on Latin Night at the gay club Pulse, the deadliest mass shooting by a single gunman in US history?

The LGBTQ community is still fighting back. Jordana LeSesne, the drum and bass producer formerly known as 1.8.7, who transitioned in 1998 and was the victim of a vicious transphobic attack in 2000, is writing the soundtrack for forthcoming film *Free CeCe*, about trans African-American woman Ce Ce McDonald, who killed her attacker in self-defence and yet served nineteen months in (male) prison. A Facebook group, TRANS Entertainment Network, with offices in Atlanta, provides a focal point for hip hop and R&B artists. Six of the estimated 1.9 million transgender women in India have created 6 Pack Band, giving voice to a community that has finally been given equal rights under the law by the country's supreme court.

An album due for release in 2017 underlines the need for giving a voice to those communities still under attack. The project, Rainbow Riots, is being organised by Petter Wallenberg, a Swedish gay producer, songwriter and author who went by the name House of Wallenberg for releases such as 'Be Somebody', which featured ballroom legend Octavia St Laurent and a video with a cast of voguers. His 2016 album, *My House Is Your House*, was his tribute to house music's gay roots in gospel and Frankie Knuckles.

The roots of Rainbow Riot were in a global network that Wallenberg started in protest against a Stockholm booking of dancehall star Sizzla, which has snowballed into a compilation of LGBTQ artists from some of the world's most homophobic and challenging places. It is set to become 'the world's first record label for LGBTQ artists from countries where their human rights are abused,' says Wallenberg.

For the *Rainbow Riot* album, Wallenberg has already recorded a queer rapper from Malawi living in Sweden, Umlilo and a trans Zulu singer in situ, a track with dancehall reformer Mista Majah P and even songs recorded in Uganda featuring rappers Deb and Kay, 'who challenge notions of femininity and express themselves with outspoken lyrics like "All my life I've been called a sinner but that won't bring me down, I'm a winner",' says Wallenberg.

Singer Shivan's dozens of facial piercings are 'not to look cool,' she says. 'It's for self-protection.'

A Ugandan poet speaks the words to 'Unmask', 'about having to hide who you are,' over Wallenberg's music, but the track is credited to Uganda Rainbow Riots because he is not yet willing to reveal his identity. One of Africa's most notoriously homophobic countries, Uganda only narrowly avoided adding the death penalty clause to its Anti-Homosexuality Act.

When Wallenberg visited the capital of Kampala in 2015, he recorded several queer singers and rappers (discovered through private chat groups) and filmed music videos under the watchful eye of the Ugandan police, who believed Wallenberg's explanation that they were making a comedy series. This year, he returned to attend Ugandan Gay Pride, 'the world's most radical Pride festival hidden deep in the jungle!'

As this book went to press, Wallenberg emailed from the Ugandan capital of Kampala, the day after the Mr & Miss Uganda Pride competition was raided by police wielding machine guns, on the pretence of not having the necessary permit. The organisers were arrested, and the guests held hostage, 'including a girl I met at my DJ gig the night before, at Kampala's first ever lesbian club night,' he wrote. 'The police will not be able to prosecute anyone on the suspicion of "being gay" as they have no proof of any "buggery", they basically wanted to terrorise the community.'

'This is the story of the battle between hate and prejudice versus love and freedom,' says Wallenberg. 'Above all, Rainbow Riots is a story of creativity triumphing over adversity.

'This story is only just beginning.'

Acknowledgements

Above all, I want to thank two people. First, JD Doyle, creator of the comprehensive and invaluable online repository Queer Music Heritage, from radio broadcasts and interview transcriptions to photos and articles, an astonishing labour of love: the first to recognise the need for a library, a museum, a narrative, to preserve the sound and vision of a culture and community – especially as many of those he talked to have since died. I couldn't have researched this book without his efforts.

Second, my editor at Constable, Andreas Campomar, is equally important, for believing in this book, and giving me the space to tell the story as I saw it.

Thanks also to my agent Matthew Hamilton at Aitken Alexander and Constable assistant editor Claire Chesser, picture editor Linda Silverman and copy editor Lucian Randall for getting me over the finishing line, and to the team at Hal Leonard for publishing the book in the US.

Special thanks to Jim Fouratt for persistent encouragement, and for his tireless motivation to improve LGBTQ lives over six decades.

Special thanks to Petter Wallenberg. Your commitment to Uganda's besieged LGBTQ community is remarkable.

Special thanks to Jo Kellum and Carla Mandley for the Roc-a-Jets. How you found the courage in 1950s Baltimore to form, and persist with, the band, will always amaze me. And thanks to John Waters for introducing me to Jo, and for his contribution to this book.

For extra enthusiasm, belief and devotion to the musical muse, thanks to Brenda Kelly and Trish Connolly, Patrick Fitzgerald, Craig 4AD Whore Roseberry, Laura Altrock, Ivo Watts-Russell, John-Mark Lapham,

Acknowledgements

Richard Dworkin, Jeffrey Capshew, Mark Eitzel, Jack Fritscher, Jorge Socarras and Tyler Alpern. Thanks to Jon Savage, whose *Queer Noises* compilation, and writing, were more foundations for this book to stand on, and to Guy Blackman for the equally resourceful *Strong Love* compilation. Thanks to Wyndham and Hans Pfister for the refuge in Berlin and to Susan Horton and Eric Rayman for NYC hospitality.

To my families – in London: Mum, David, Penny, Katie, Vicki and Christopher; Tess and the girls; in Michigan, Mom Clum, Doug and family, Liz and family, Nate and Bruce, Mindy and Tom and all the Clum and Crockford relatives.

Many thanks to everyone I interviewed for the book, all ninety-odd of you, but especially Tom Robinson, Paul Southwell, Anohni, Caroline Azar, Frankie Green, Rosemary Schonfeld, Petter Wallenberg, Horse McDonald, Matt Wobensmith, Kristian Hoffman and Marsha Malamet, for dedication to detail. Thanks to the people who led to some of my interviewees, but especially Nathan Clum, Chris Metzier, Chuck Wild, Vicki Wickham, Gerard Koskovich, Larry Roberts, Douglas Macgowan and Matthew Fink.

Thanks to Camilo Rocha for insight into seventies Brazil, and Dom Phillips for the introduction to Camilo. Thanks to Jesper and Christine for the French translation.

Finally, thanks to my nearest-and-dearest: Kurt you old Spratzi, remember the coupe, Mark, Pixie, goddaughter Eloise and James, Sara, Will and goddaughter Harriet, Merle BB PB and Gary, Joanna MLNOV, Yael, Meir, Yas, Lauren and Sam, Duncan, Amanda, Madeleine, Mary Pat, Gordon, Catherine and Arvo, Nicole, Angela, Hop, Sarah and Foster, Cat my foxymoron, Jesper, Christine and family, John and Michael, Kat, Peter, Gabby and Trixie, Clare and Antoine, David, Yvette and family, Christina, Olivia and Bif, Karl, Justin, Lisa and family, Cushla, Dean and Britta, the wonderful Nerva clan but especially Rod, Steph and Elodie, my wonderful Dutch friends, but especially Margriet, keep passing the open windows, cuz Jennie, Mr Stroopy Mumblepants, Steve and Spencer, Bob and Jeff, Patt, Lynn, Siuin, Debbi, Jude, Sigrid, Amy,

BREAKING DOWN THE WALLS OF HEARTACHE

David duP, Laurence, Miriam and Viva, Jane, Richard Boon and my Nunhead pals (Karolina, Lukasz, Hugo and Hannah, Claire, Andrew, Ava and Aiden, Carolyn, Jeremy and Max). Thanks to *MOJO* magazine editorial – Phil Alexander, Jenny Bulley, Danny Eccleston, Ian Harrison and former deputy editor Andrew Male – for all the encouragement and opportunities.

Thanks to Michelangelo Signorite's book *Queer in America; Sex, The Media and the Closets of Power* (1993), a very helpful, and powerful, memoir of AIDS activism through the eighties and nineties.

Finally, thanks to every fourteen-year-old, not just in Tulsa, who will grow up to make this planet a less prejudiced place.

Picture credits

Every effort has been made to obtain the necessary permissions with reference to copyright material, both illustrative and quoted. We apologise for any omissions in this respect and will be pleased to make the appropriate acknowledgements in any future edition.

Early 20th Century
Bessie Smith © The Granger Collection/Topfoto
Fred Barnes © Popperfoto/Getty Images
Vesta Tilley © PastPix /Getty Images

1920s–30s
Gwen Farrar © Sasha/Stringer/Getty Images
Bruz Fletcher, from the collection of Tyler Alpern

1940s
Billy Strayhorn © Jamie Hodgson/ArenaPal/Topfoto
eden ahbez © Peter Stackpole/Getty Images
Sister Rosetta © Michael Ochs Archives/Getty Images
Frances Faye, from the collection of Tyler Alpern

1950s I
Esquerita © Gilles Petard/Getty Images
Little Richard (middle) © Everett/REX/Shutterstock

1950s II
Cornell Gunter © Michael Ochs Archives/Getty Images
Johnnie Ray © Henry Bush/ANL/REX/Shutterstock
Rod McKuen © Michael Ochs Archives Getty Images

BREAKING DOWN THE WALLS OF HEARTACHE

1960s I
Lisa Ben © USC Libraries
Jackie Shane © Jeff Goode/Getty Images
Dusty Springfield © ITV/REX/Shutterstock

1960s II
Cockettes © Jack Mitchell/Getty Images
Long John Baldry © LFI/Photoshot
Polly Perkins © Anthony Nathan

1970s I
Wayne County © Ray Stevenson/REX/Shutterstock

1970s II
Gay Music Spring Night © Danny Nicoletta

1970s III
Jobriath © Michael Ochs Archives /Getty Images
Lou Reed © Michael Ochs Archives/ Getty Images

1980s I
The Bloods © Laura Levine
Phranc © Bleddyn Butcher/REX/Shutterstock
Fifth Column © Jena Von Brucker
Two Nice Girls © Scott Van Osdol

1980s II
Klaus Nomi © Ullstein Bild/Getty Images
Boy George © Richard Young/REX/Shutterstock
Frankie Goes to Hollywood © Getty Images
Michael Callen and Richard Dworkin © Bob Giard
Bronski Beat © Dave Hogan/Getty Images

1990s
David McAlmont © Getty Images
k.d. lang © Paul Natkin/Getty Images
Rob Halford © ITV/REX/Shutterstock
Rainbow Flava © Phat Family Records

540

Picture credits

21st Century
Deep Dickollective © Ayanna U'Dongo
Rocco 'Katastrophe' Kayattios © Amos Mac
Mina Caputo © Michael Loccisano/Getty Images
Rainbow Riots Uganda © Tania Marti

Index

'A Boy Named Sue' (J. Cash) 224–5
A Brand New Me (D. Springfield) 188
'A Certain Smile' (J. Mathis) 96, 99
'A Fairer Tomorrow' (E. Eyde/L. Ben) 88
A Few Loving Women (Lesbian Feminist Liberation group compilation) 208
'A Gay Song' (Everyone Involved) 206, 207
'A Gay Spirit' (C. Murphy) 300
A Girl of the Golden West (R. Bourbon) 86
'A Good Man is Hard to Find' (J. Sarria) 106–7
A Lesbian Portrait . . . (L. Shear) 217
A Man Alone (F. Sinatra) 158
'A Picture of Me Without You' (C. Porter) 34
'A Sad Song' (Everyone Involved) 206–7
A Streetcar Named Desire play/film 68
'A Thing Named Kim' (B. Markie) 411
'A Thrills a Thrill' (J. Baldry) 311
Abelove, Larry 162
Accept 378
'A.C.D.C.' (Sweet) 192
Ace Records 89
'Achilles' Grief' (J. Delgada) 202
'Acid Tracks' (DJ Pierre) 394
A.C.R.O.N.Y.M. Records 490
ACT UP (AIDS Coalition To Unleash Power) 365, 396, 397, 413, 415, 421, 446

Actually (Pet Shop Boys) 374
Adam, Margie 212, 213
Advocate magazine 205, 229, 235, 245, 255, 257, 299, 336, 361, 364, 370, 432, 446, 456, 458, 484, 510
Africa 520–1, 531–2
After Dark magazine 234, 235
Against Me! 506–7
Age of Consent 328, 329
ahbez, eden 57–8
'A.I.D.S' (M.O.D.) 411
AIDS and HIV 3, 361–71, 375–6, 377, 379, 395, 396, 405, 407, 408, 409, 412–14, 415, 421, 422–5, 432–3, 434–5, 440, 467, 468–9, 501
AIDS Quilt 413–14
AIDS Show: Artists Involved With Death and Survival musical 365–6
'Ain't Got No Home' (C. Henry) 92
'Ain't Nobody Straight in LA' (Miracles) 254–5
Akens, Jewel 229
Alcman 4
Aletti, Vince 247–8, 251
Alice Cooper 195, 211, 214
Alice's Restaurant (A. Guthrie) 149
'All American Boy' (S. Grand) 514–15
'All the Girls Love Alice' (E. John) 259
'All the Sad Young Men' (J. Mathis) 99
'All You Need Is Love' (Beatles) 206
Allen, Peter 326, 370
'Alley Cat' (Spivy) 43

Index

Allman, Karen 333–4
Almond, Marc 347–50, 351, 361, 373, 415
Alone After Dark (R. McKuen) 98–9
Altamont Festival 172
'Am I Blue' (Minette) 164–5
A&M Records 295, 408
American Composers League 52–3
American Family TV programme 285, 286, 317–18
'American Way of Love' (The United States of America) 148
'Anarchy in the UK' (Sex Pistols) 271
'And I Moved' (P. Townshend) 330
'And the Boys Lazed on the Verandah' (Fresh) 181
Anderson, Brett 438, 439
Anderson, Casey 107, 108
Andrea True Connection 257
Andrew, Sam 150
'Androgynous' (Replacements) 380
Angels of Light 184, 185, 316
Anger, Kenneth 100, 127, 178
Angola 520
'Angy Atthis' (M. Feldman) 204–5
'Animal Nitrate' (Suede) 439
Anohni 'Fiona Blue' 469–71, 502–3
anti-Semitism 13, 35
Antony and the Johnsons 470–1, 502
'Any Other Way' (J. Shane) 118–19
Anything That Moves magazine 485
Apostles 389
Arden, Don and David 268
'Are You a Boy or a Girl?' (Barbarians) 146–7
Arias, Joey 316, 317, 470
Ariston Hotel, New York City 25
Arlen, Harold 45, 116
Armatrading, Joan 344–5, 418, 427
Armstrong, Billie Joe 445
Army of Lovers 468
Arning, Bill 286
Arnold, Kokomo 22
Ashford, Nick 245–6

Ashmore, Charles 'Blackberri' 299
Ask the Unicorn (Ed Askew) 153
Athletic Model Guild 47, 62
Atlantic Records 87, 247, 462–3, 464
Attack, Art 531–2
Attitude magazine 352, 375, 463, 498–500
Au Pairs 336–7, 339
Automatic Pilot 326, 365
Avenue D 498
Azar, Caroline 384–6
Azis 525–6
Aznavour, Charles 223–4

B-52s 380–1
'B. D. Woman Blues' (B. Jackson) 19
Bach, Sebastian 411
Bachelor magazine 34
'Back in the Closet Again' (Lavender Country) 227
Backstreet Boys 465
Bad Brains 332–3
Baez, Joan 344
Bahiano 13, 192–3
Bailey, Montrea 'Miss Money' 488
Baker, Josephine 27–8
Baldry, John William 'Long John' 156, 157, 260, 272, 310–11, 330
'Ballad of a Thin Man' (B. Dylan) 152, 265
'Ballad of the Sad Young Men' (R. McKuen) 99, 108, 266
Ballard, Pat 95
ballroom scene 399–401, 413, 534
Balls To The Wall (Accept) 378
Bankhead, Tallulah 31, 68
Banton, Buju 455, 516
Barbarians 146–7
Barnes, Fred 11
Barrett, KK 313
Barrow, Keith 290
Bart, Lionel 102, 103
Bassett, Sherwin 37
Bassey, Shirley 167–8, 266

BBC (British Broadcasting Corporation) 154, 159, 197, 223, 275, 348, 352, 355, 428
'Be-In,' Central Park (1967) 160
'Be Prepared' (T. Lehrer) 93
'Be Somebody' (P. Wallenberg) 534
Bean, Archbishop Carl 72, 91, 258–9, 319, 363, 476
'Bean Song' (3 Teens Kill 4) 402
Beastie Boys 409–10, 471
Beat Generation 98
The Beatles 121–3, 136, 137, 153, 206
'Beautiful Soul' (D. Springfield) 310
Beiderbecke, Bix 31–2, 54
Bell, Andy 415–16
Bell, Madeline 132
Bell, William 118
Belolo, Henri 291, 294
Ben, Lisa 87, 88, 105, 108, 113
  see also Eyde, Edith
Benner, Doc 43
Bennett, Tony 125
Bentley, Gladys 19–20, 23, 47, 63, 212
Berlin 14, 27, 179, 196, 218–19, 307–8
Berlin, Irving 47
Bernstein, Leonard 53, 54, 154
Berry, Mike 122
Bertei, Adele 337–40
'Bessie Bell and Mary Gray' (trad. folk ballad) 7
'Better Decide Which Side You're On' (TRB) 271
'Betty Ann and Shirley Cole' (F. Weller) 225
'Bewitched, Bothered and Bewildered' (Rodgers and Hart) 42
'Bewlay Brothers' (D. Bowie) 263
Bi-Coastal (P. Allen) 326
Bianco, Ginger 132, 216
'Big Bad Bruce' (C. Anderson) 107, 108
Big Boys 331–3, 384
'Big Bruce' (S. Greenberg) 173
Big Feedia, Queen of Bounce TV programme 531

'Big Gay Heart' (Lemonheads) 436
'Big Louise' (S. Walker) 159
Bikini Kill 437, 450
Billboard magazine 66–7, 70, 256–7, 318, 414, 464
Billboard R&B chart 70, 73, 76, 78, 89
Billing, Arno 14–15
Billy Budd (B. Britten) 53
Billy Tipton Trio 84
Bingenheimer, Rodney 238
Birtha 214
Bitter Sweet (N. Coward) 33
'Bitterfeast' (M. Cohen) 230
Black Cat, San Francisco 56, 64, 106, 108
'Black Denim Trousers and Motorcycle Boots' (Cheers) 94
'Black Pearl' (Sonny Charles and the Checkmates) 168
'Black Sheep of the Family' (F. Barnes) 11
Blackberri 299
Blacklips 469, 470
Blades, Ruben 409
Blaikley, Alan 123, 141, 192
Blakstone, Nan 50
Blaney, Norah 31
Blatantly Offenzive (Electric Chairs) 282
Blitz, Soho 346
Blondie 327
Bloods 337–41
Bloolips 264
Bloomsbury Group 24
'Blow Away' Jobriath 200
'Blue Blood Blues' (NWLRB) 221
'Blue Moon' (Rodgers and Hart) 42, 89
Blue Thumb Records 295
blues 16–17, 18, 20–2, 70, 72, 86
Blues and Soul magazine 256
'Blues for My Baby' (B. Wright) 73
'Bobby Brown Goes Down' (F. Zappa) 309, 376

544

Body Electric-2: What Whitman's Timeless Words Set to Music (J. Pearson) 293
'Body Squat' (LWLRB) 220
Boettcher, Curt 160
Bogarde, Dirk 114
Bolan, Marc 141, 190, 191, 238
Bomb 437
Bono, Chastity/Chaz 508
'Boom Bye Bye' (B. Banton) 455
Boone, Pat 77–8
Boots and Saddles, New York 327
Bottum, Roddy 457–8, 459, 460
Bouley, Karel 464–5
Bourbon, Ray 30–1, 35, 46, 56, 85, 86
Bowery, Leigh 442
Bowie, Angie 178, 187
Bowie, David 141, 146, 147–8, 159, 177–8, 179–80, 183, 186–7, 189–90, 192, 195, 197, 199, 200, 201, 220, 226, 232, 238, 239, 259, 263, 264, 269, 280, 307, 316–17, 338, 346, 347, 353, 406, 424
'Boy' (Beatles) 122
boy bands 465, 500
Boy George 346–7, 350–2, 356–7, 372, 395, 502–3
'Boy, Girl' (Fifth Column) 385
Boy with Green Hair (film) 58–9
Boys in the Band (film) 134
'Boys Keep Swinging' (D. Bowie) 308, 316–17
'Boys Say Go' (Depeche Mode) 347
Boys Will Be Girls revue 30–1, 35
Boystown Gang 324–5
Boyzone 465, 500
Bradford, Alex 71–2, 74
Brand, Adolf 12
Brandão, Leci 307
Brandt, Jerry 200, 201
Brandt, Pam 215, 367
Brave Confusion (N. Toure) 522–3
'Brave Mulato' (N. Rosa) 193
Brazil 13, 192–4, 306–7, 412–13

Breaking Through (Isis) 216
'Breathing Fear' (KOD) 408, 409
Breedlove, Lynn 447–50
Breen, Joseph 35–6
Brel, Jacques 158–9, 190, 193
Brennan, Jay 26
Bridgers, Aaron 55–6
Bridges, Alicia 305
Brigg, Billy 64, 66, 224
Briggs, John 303
'Bring Me Some Water' (M. Etheridge) 434
Britten, Benjamin 53, 110
Broadnax, Wilmer M. 84
Broadway Melody (film) 28
Brokeback Mountain film 512
Bromley Contingent 277
Bronski Beat 357–61, 364, 372, 396
Brothers Butch 142
Brown, Andrew 301–2
Brown, Danny 43
Bruce, Lenny 242
Bryant, Anita 302, 328
Buckley, Tim 246–7
Buddah Records 216
Buena Vista 298–9, 301–2
'buffet flats' parties 18
Buretti, Freddie 179, 190
Burgess, Wilma 225
Burnel, Jean-Jacques 347
Burns, Pete 372
Burroughs, William 98, 100, 187, 239
Butterick, Brian 402
Buzzcocks 277–8
Byng, Douglas 26

'Ca-the-drals' (DC La Rue) 289–90
Cabaret film 35, 196
cabaret scene 13, 27–8, 196
Cafe Internationale, San Francisco 46
Café Society 265, 309
Calamity Jane (film) 93–4
Callahan, John 327–8
Callen, Michael 366–70, 396, 424–5

Camicia, Jimmy 184–5, 263–4
Camp Records 112–15
Campaign for Homosexual Equality (CHE) 263, 264, 268
Campbell, Robert 263, 273
Candy Ass Records 451
'Candy Says' (Velvet Underground) 171
'Can't Help Lovin' Dat Man' (Kern and Hammerstein II) 28
Can't Stop the Music (film) 305
'Can't Take My Eyes Off You' (F. Valli) 136
'Can't You Hear My Heartbeat' (Goldie and the Gingerbreads) 132
Cantor, Eddie 32
Canya Phuckem and Howe 325–6
Caouette, Jonathan 2
Capote, Truman 52, 164, 288
Capsuto, Steve 106
Captured in the Act (F. Faye) 49
Caputo, Keith/Mina 503–4
Caravan Tonight (S. Grossman) 235, 236, 423
'Careful' (Horse) 427, 428
Carlin, John 422
Carlos, Wendy/Walter 321–2, 501
'Carolyn' (Phranc) 417
Carr, Michael 226
Casablanca Records 291–2, 319, 344
Caserta, Peggy 150
castrati 5
Caswell, Luke 'Cazwell' 478–9, 497, 498
Catholic Discipline 315, 417
Catholicism 35–6, 229
Caushun 490–1, 492
Caviano, Bob 424
Cazuza 412–13
Cazwell 478–9, 497, 498
CBGB, New York 269, 277, 282, 283, 284, 285, 286, 287, 336
Cee, Mister 529
'Cellini (The Menace of Venice)' (J. Rogers) 37

Chaguaramas Club, Soho 277
Chainsaw Records 451, 452
Channel 4 354, 357, 416
Chapman, Tracey 426
Charach, Theodore 143
Charlie and Ray 90
'Cherry Poppin'' (M. Ryder) 310
Chevron, Philip 405–6
Chez Boheme, San Francisco 46
Childers, Leee 170, 186, 198, 279–80
'Children of the Night' (Stylistics) 245
Chopin, Frédéric 5
Chris Robison and His Many Hand Band (C. Robison) 232–4
Christian, Meg 210, 211, 212, 213, 342, 365
Christie, Lou 127–8, 181, 290
'Christopher's Blues' (S. Grossman) 235
Christopherson, Peter 373
Chuchu, Jim 520
Chumbawumba 454
'Cigarettes, Whiskey and Wild, Wild Women' (A. Dobkin) 208
City and the Pillar (G. Vidal) 52
City of Night (J. Rechy) 150–1
Clam House speakeasy 20
classical music 5–6, 10–11, 52, 53, 54, 61, 154
Clay, Andrew Dice 410, 411
Cleveland, James 71
Cliks 509–10
Cline, Patsy 225
Clinton, George 254
'Clitoris in Spanish Town' (J. Ringo) 325
Clooney, Rosemary 80
'Closet Man' (D. Springfield) 310
'Closet Queen' (H. Kennedy) 243
'Closing the Door' (L. Furey) 273, 274, 312
Club Bali, LA 38, 41
Club Laurel, LA 64
Coasters 90–2, 244
Cobain, Kurt 436–7

546

Index

Coccinelle 69
Cockettes 172–3, 183–4, 228, 295
'Cocksucker Blues' (Rolling Stones) 176
Cohen, Michael 229–31, 237
Coil 366, 373, 389, 404
Cole, Jack -52, 79–80
Cole, Nat King 57–8
Coleherne pub, London 267, 268, 279, 353
Collier, Graham 155
Collins, Lecresha 'Tay-Tae' 475–6
Colt, Zebedy 173–5
Columbia Records 29, 66, 73, 109, 124, 150, 160, 200, 409, 430
'Come' (Lick) 453
Come to Me at Tea Time (Minette) 164
'Coming Clean' (Green Day) 445
Communards 395
communism 63, 65, 93, 208
Compton's Cafeteria, San Francisco 165
'Coney Island Baby' (L. Reed) 274
Coney Island Winter (M. Malamet) 162
Confidential magazine 67
Conflict 333–4
Conley, Arthur 119–20
Connor, Chris 87
Connor, William 100
'Constant Craving' (k.d. lang) 432
Continental Baths, New York 246, 288
Contortions 316, 337, 338
Cooke, Sam 134–5
Cooper, Carol 325
Copland, Aaron 53
Cordon, John 58, 237, 238
Cory, George 125–6
Cotton, Josie 334–6
country music 224–9, 233, 240, 424, 431–2, 457, 480–1, 511–15
Country Music AIDS Awareness 424
County, Wayne/Jayne 185, 186, 195, 198, 199, 279–81, 282, 501
Coward, Nöel 32–4, 40, 41, 154, 422

'Cowboys Are Frequently, Secretly Fond of Each Other' (N. Sublette) 327, 512
Cowell, Henry 54
Cowley, Patrick 296–7, 324, 361–2, 423
'Cracked Actor' (D. Bowie) 201
Crash, Darby 314
'Crazy Little Men' (C. Jorgensen) 68
Cretin 504, 505
Crewe, Bob 128–9, 136, 159, 160, 188, 251, 252, 253
'Crime of Passion' (Rough Trade) 344
'Criminal' (Eminem) 484
Crocker, Frankie 247, 256, 259
Crosby, Bing 31–2, 48, 80, 93
Cross, Douglas 125–6
Crouch, Andraé 72
Crowley, Aleister 178
'Cruisin' the Streets' (Boystown Gang) 324–5
'Cruising Down the Boulevard' (L. Ben) 88
Cruising film 343
'Cry' (J. Ray) 66, 67
'Cryin' These Cocksucking Tears' (Lavender Country) 227–9
Culture Club 347, 350–2, 372
Curb, Mike 142–3, 144
Currie, Cherie 285
Curtis, Jackie 170–1, 185, 196, 197
Cyrus, Miley 511

DADT policy (US Military) 457, 483
Dahl, Steve 302
Daily Mirror newspaper 100
Daisy Chain 'buffet flat' 18
Dale, Lennie 193
Dall, John 52
'Damn, I Wish I Was Your Lover' (S.B. Hawkins) 428
Danish Girl film 507–8
D'Aquisto, Steve 251
'Dark Room' (D. Toure) 523
'Dark Slender Boy' (trad. folk ballad) 8

547

Darling, Candy 171, 182, 196, 383, 503
Darnell, Larry 72–3
'Das Lila Lied' (The Lilac Song) (Billing and Schwabach) 14–15, 202
Daughters of Bilitis 86, 88, 100, 105, 165
David Is a Homosexual film 268
'David Watts' (Kinks) 139
Davies, Dave 138, 139
Davies, Miles 155
Davies, Ray 138–9, 182, 265, 309
Davis, Clive 160, 200
Davis, Lena 133, 162
Davis, Madeline 202–3
Davis, Vaginal Crème 388, 403, 437
Day, Doris 93–4, 158
De La Soul 486
Dead Fingers Talk 276
Dead or Alive 372
Deadly Nightshade 215
Dean, Michael W. 437
'Dear John' (Au Pairs) 336–7
'Death to Disco' (J. Lalumia) 287
Decca Records 47, 70, 102, 132, 133, 162, 176, 273
'Dedicated Follower of Fashion' (Kinks) 139
Deen, Howard 482
Deep Dickollective (D/DC) 485, 487–8, 494–5
'Deep In Vogue' (M. McLaren) 400
'Deep Song' (B. Holiday) 125
Def American Recordings 410, 411
Defence of Marriage Act (2010) 379
Defries, Tony 199
Delaney, Sean 319
DeLarverie, Stormé 168
Delazy, Toya 524
Delgada, Johnny 202
Delirium, London 394
D'Ell, Denis 123
Depeche Mode 347, 404
DePino, David 399–400

Derrick, Cowboy Jack 60
'Desperado' (Alice Cooper) 195
Deutsch Amerikanische Freundschaft (DAF) 403
Dew Drop Inn, New Orleans 72–3, 89, 478
Diagnostic and Statistical Manual of Mental Disorders (1959) 63
Diamond Dogs (D. Bowie) 239
Diana Ross and the Supremes 167
Dibango, Manu 247
Dicks 331, 332, 384
Dietrich, Marlene 27
Different from the Others (film) 13
DiFranco, Ani 426
'Diggin' Dykes' (International Sweethearts of Rhythm) 55
Dire Straits 409
'Dirty Dozens' (Speckled Red) 21
disco 242–3, 246, 247–57, 289, 304–6
Disco Demolition Night, Chicago 304
Disco Tex 251–3, 255
'Diseree' (L. Nyro) 217
Divine 184, 260, 343, 391–2, 403
'DNTA' (Smokey) 239, 241
'Do You Come Here Often' (Tornados) 124
'Do You Like Boys?' (Starbuck) 192
'Do You Really Want to Hurt Me' (Culture Club) 351
Dobkin, Alix 67, 68, 84, 86, 93, 208–10, 211, 212, 217–18, 314, 365, 417
'Doctor Doctor' (C. Robison) 233
DOMA 456–7, 490, 527
'Domino Dancing' (Pet Shop Boys) 375
Donovan 152–3, 454
'Don't Bend Down' (L. Lovindeer) 455
'Don't Drink the Orange Juice' (R. McKuen) 302
'Don't Leave Me This Way' (Communards) 395–6
'Don't Stop Me Now' (Queen) 320
'Don't You Want a Man Like Me?' (B. Wright) 73

doo wop 89–90
'Doodle Doodle Doo' (E. Cantor) 85
The Doors 150–1, 237
'Doris the Goddess of Wind' (D. Byng) 26
Double or Nothing film 48
Dover, Eileen 142
'Down in New York' (C. Robison) 233–4
Downing, Al 248–9
'Dr John' (Bronski Beat) 396
drag kings 283, 346, 450, 452–3
drag queens 22–3, 25–6, 30–1, 72, 73, 76, 85, 106, 154, 164–5, 166, 168, 169–70, 193, 224, 226, 264, 280, 295, 313, 387–8, 397–401, 413, 478, 526
  see also Cockettes; County, Wayne/Jayne; Divine; female impersonators; RuPaul
Dragon, Ellyott 450–1
Drake, Nick 231
Dre, Dr 472, 484
'Dreamboy' (R. Campbell) 273
Dresch, Donna 451, 452
The Drifters 90
'Drop the Pilot' (J. Armatrading) 344–5
drugs 148, 152, 163, 164, 183, 240, 241, 280, 394, 438, 439
'Drunk with Love' (B. Fletcher) 38, 39–40, 49
'Dry Dock Dreaming' (S. Grossman) 235
Duplantier, Karla 'Mad Dog' 315, 388
Dupree, Paris 399–400
Durium Dance Band 36
Dutchboy 477–8, 485–6, 488
Dworkin, Richard 92, 228–9, 231, 236, 298, 301, 367–9, 370, 423, 425
Dylan, Bob 152
Dynamic Superiors 244–6, 290
Dzi Croquettes 193–4
Dzubilo, Chloe 469

eastern Europe 525–6
Easy Going 292
'Easy Living' (Coasters) 91–2
Eazy-E 411
Ebony magazine 63
Ecco Productions 174
Echobelly 453
Edens, Roger 45
Edward VIII, King 36–7
Edwards, Bernard 323
Edwards, Richey 435–6
Egan, Rusty 346
Egypt 519–20
Either/Or (Everone Involved) 206
Eitzel, Mark 383, 437, 446
Elbe, Lili 508
Electric Chairs 280, 282
electroclash 497–8
Elektra Records 200, 335
Ellington, Duke 44, 54–5
Eltinge, Julian 25, 26
'Elton's Song' (E. John) 311, 330
Emerson, Eric 195, 199
EMI Records 121, 122, 271, 274, 374, 427, 428
Eminem 471–2, 483–4
'Emmie' (L. Nyro) 161–2, 217
Emmons, EJ 58, 237, 238
Emms, Winifred 'Hetty King' 10
Emotional Rollercoaster (Romanovsky and Phillips) 396
Empire TV programme 530
Empty Glass (P. Townshend) 330
'Endless Masturbation Blues' (Cockettes) 183
English Disco, LA 237, 238
Entertainment Voice magazine 117
Enx, Jackie 501–2
Epic Records 109, 351, 430, 462
'Eppie Morrie' (Lavendar Jane) 209
Epstein, Brian 121–2, 136, 140
Equality Rocks concert 483
Erasure 416
'Eros' (R. McKuen) 108–9

Esquerita 74–5
Esquire magazine 183
Etheridge, Melissa 433–4, 483
Eurythmics 346
Evening Standard newspaper 187
'Ever Fallen in Love...' (Buzzcocks) 278
Everyone Involved 206
'Everyone's a Bigot' (Offs) 315
Everything You Always Wanted to Know About Sex... (D. Rubens) 173
'Evil and Lusty' (M. Cohen) 230
Exploding Plastic Inevitable 145
Extra Fancy 462, 463, 464
Eyde, Edith 51–2, 87–8
   see also Ben, Lisa
'Eyes' (Honeycombs) 123

Face magazine 349–50, 371, 454
Factory, Andy Warhol's 171, 185, 195, 196, 274
   see also Warhol, Andy
Faggots (L. Kramer) 363
'Fairview Mall Story' (Fifth Column) 386
Fame, Georgie 103
Fanny 208, 213–14
Fantasy Records 295
'Farming' (C. Porter) 34
Farrar, Gwendoline 31
Fassie, Brenda 522
Fast 282–3, 392
Faye, Frances 38, 47–9, 86, 133
Fear 334–5
Feeding the Flame... compilation 422
Feldman, Maxine 203–5
female impersonators 8–10, 20–1, 22–3, 25–6, 29, 42–3, 47, 72–3, 74, 85–6, 106, 164
   see also Cockettes; drag queens
Femme Fatale: the Three Faces of Gloria play 185
Ferrick, Melissa 462

Ferron 429
Ferry, Bryan 194–5
Fertile LaToya Jackson fanzine 388
'Fetch Me One More Beer' (Fear) 335
Fields, Danny 160, 284
Fifth Column 384–6
'Fig Man' (Mighty Terror) 135
'Fight Back Rap' (Age of Consent) 328
Fighting For Our Lives march (1983) 364
Finnegan, Mary 178
Firehouse, New York 208, 209, 210, 250
Fireworks film 100
First Amendment, US 100
Fischerspooner 497
Fish, Michael 'Mr Fish of London' 177
Fiske, Dwight 38
Fitzgerald, Patrick 406–9, 416, 442
'Five Years' (D. Bowie) 190
Fixx, Tori 490
Flamingo Club, LA 87
flappers 24
Flawless Sabrina 92–3, 164, 165, 183, 397, 398
Flesh film 171, 197, 383
Fletcher, Bruz 38–41, 49
Floyd, Gary 331, 332, 384
Flying Lesbians 218–19
folk music 97, 105, 107, 108, 149, 152, 154, 230, 234–5, 417, 426
folk tradition 7–8
Folksinger (Phranc) 417
Folkways Records 230, 231, 300
'Foolish Man Blues' (Bessie Smith) 18
Footsteps, New York 399–400
For Women Only (Saul T. Peter) 101
For You (Prince) 328–9
'For You My Love' (L. Darnell) 73
For Your Pleasure (Roxy Music) 194
Fortune Teller video 531
Foster, Jim 203
Foster, Steven 6–7
Four Seasons 128, 129

Fouratt, Jim 90, 150, 151, 160, 172, 205, 236, 288, 343, 419, 420, 425, 426
Foxxjazell 495–7
Framed Youth: Revenge of the Teenage Perverts documentary 357
France 27, 96, 97–8, 158, 179, 224
see also Paris
'France and Friends' (F. Faye) 49
Francis, Connie 124–5
Frank O'Hara Nude With Boots (L. Rivers) 100–1
Frankie and Johnnie duo 37
Frankie Goes To Hollywood (FGTH) 353–7, 372, 377, 394
Frankie Howerd Show TV Programme 159
Frankie Laine Show TV programme 69–70
Fraser, Andy 500–1
'Freakish Man Blues' (G. Hannah) 21–2
Freddie Mercury Tribute Concert (1992) 424
Free CeCe film 534
Free, Mark/Marcie 501
Freed, Alan 70
Freed, Arthur 45
Freed's Fairies 44–5
French, Jim 270
'Frenchie' (Gunther Quint) 299
Fresh 181
Friendship and Freedom magazine 26–7
Fritscher, Jack 57, 59, 66, 67, 68, 93–5, 96, 109, 246–7, 284
Frogs 404–5, 437
Fruit 442
'Fucking Queer' (Apostles) 389
Fugazi 390
Fure, Tret 213, 214, 341–2
Furey, Lewis 273–4, 312
Furies 210
Fyfe, Sir David Maxwell 96

Gaahl of Gorgoroth 500
Gachara, George 520–1
Gahan, Dave 189, 404
Gaiee Records 256–7
Galas, Diamanda 366
Gallery Club, New York 250–1, 288
'Gallery of Love' (A. Timóteo) 306
Gamble, Kenny 244, 248
'Gangsta Gangsta' (N.W.A.) 411
Gardner, Kay 209, 218
Garland, Judy 44, 62, 67, 74, 116, 167
Garrett, Murray 110–12
Gauze 8–9
Gay Activists Alliance (GAA) 173, 208, 305
Gay Artists and Writers Kollective (GAWK) 330
'Gay Bar' (Electric 6) 498
'Gay Boys in Bondage' (Drug Addix) 308
Gay Community Social Services of Seattle 226–7
Gay Dad 454
Gay Freedom Day Parade 303
'Gay Girl' (J. King) 180
'Gay-In', San Francisco 178
Gay Liberation Front (UK) 179, 205, 206, 207, 220, 263, 264, 271, 312
Gay Liberation Front (US) 173, 179, 210–11, 226
'Gay Love' (B. Crosby) 31
Gay magazine 175
Gay Men's Health Crisis (GMHC) 363, 368, 413, 423
Gay News newspaper 234, 263, 271, 358
Gay Pride Marches 179, 202–3, 205, 234, 270–1, 311–12, 479
Gay-Related Immune Deficiency (GRID) 363, 367
Gay Sweatshop 263
'Gay Switchboard Jingle' (Café Society) 265
'Gay Teenager' (B. Topper) 144
Gay Times 138–9, 182
Gaynor, Gloria 250, 288–9, 396
Geffen, David 161, 410–11, 440, 475

Geffen Records 340, 410
gender reassignment
 see trans-genderism/ transexuality
Genet, Jean 98, 148, 407
Gentlemen Prefer Blondes film 79–80
George, Duke of Kent, Prince 32
Georgia Minstrels 9
'Georgie Pie' (Lavender Country) 227
Gerber, Henry 26–7, 65
Germany 10, 11–15, 26, 35, 162–3, 218–19, 274, 378
 see also Berlin
Germs 314, 335
'Get Dancin' (Disco Tex) 251, 252–3
Get Into It (Cazwell) 498
Gil, Gilberto 193, 307
Gilbert, Simon 438
Gillespie, Dizzy 55
Gilman, Billy 514
Ginoli, Jon 443–5
Ginsberg, Allen 98, 100
'Girlfriend' (Queen Pen) 473
'Girls in the Mirror' (P. Perkins) 162
'Glacier' (J. Grant) 3
'Glacier' video 1–3, 531
'Glad to Be Gay' (T. Robinson) 264–5, 309
glam rock 191–2, 194–5, 197–8, 232, 238, 239, 267
 see also Bowie, David
Glassen, Tina 489
'Gloria' (Patti Smith Band) 283–4
Gloria's, New York 47
'Go West' (Pet Shop Boys) 463–4
'Go West' (Village People) 294, 463
God-des and She 489, 494–5
God Is My Co-Pilot 451
'God Save the Queen' 107
Goddard, Geoff 121
Godfrey, Robert John 262
Godin, Dave 256
Goffin, Gerry 210
'Going Home' (P. Cowley) 362
Goldie and the Gingerbreads 132, 216

Goldmine magazine 113–14
Gonna Take a Miracle (L. Nyro) 217
Gooch, Brad 362
Good, Jack 103
Goodbye Yellow Brick Road (E. John) 259–60, 386
Googoosh 518
Gordy, Berry 256, 257–8
Gore, Lesley 129–30, 338
'Gorgeous Love' (KOD) 408
gospel 70, 71–2, 73–4, 89, 258
Gossips, Soho 346
GQ magazine 272
Grace, Laura Jane 506–7
Grainger, Porter 21
Grand, Steve 514–15, 533
Granger, Farley 52
Grant, John 2, 3–4, 531, 533
Grappelli, Stéphane 155
Grasso, Francis 250
Great Depression 23, 35
Great Migration 16
Greece, Ancient 4
'Green Carnation' (N. Coward) 33
Green Day 444–5
Green, Frankie 220, 221–2
Greenberg, Steve 173
Greenfield, Howie 124–5, 126
Greenwich Village Follies 26
Grillo, Brian 462
Grossman, Steven 234–7, 299, 423
groupies 150–1, 237–8
Groupies documentary 237
Grudzien, Peter 240
grunge 436–7
Guns N' Roses 410, 436
Gunther, Cornell 90–2, 244
Guthrie, Arlo 149

Haag, Romy 307–8
Haggerty, Patrick 224, 225–9
Hair musical 149, 200
Halford, Rob 320, 378, 459–61, 480
Hall and Oates 232, 371

INDEX

Hall, Radclyffe 31
'Halloween Parade' (L. Reed) 414
'Hammer' (KOD) 407
Hammerstein II, Oscar 28, 60
Hammerstrom, Robert 226
'Hand In Glove' (Smiths) 382, 406
Handbag 267–8, 269, 281–2
'Handsome Cabin Boy' (folk ballad) 7
'Handsome Devil' (Smiths) 382
'Hanging Around' (Stranglers) 279
'Hanky Panky' (Teddy and Darrel) 143
Hannah, George 21
'Happiness Is a Thing Called Joe' (T. Walker) 116
Happy Mondays 438
Harburg, Yip 45, 116
'Hardy Boys at the Y' (Wainwright) 266–7
Hardy, Françoise 414–15
Hardy, Ron 393–4
Harisu 502
Hark At Her (Fruit) 442
Harlem/Harlem Renaissance 16–17, 20, 21, 22–3, 398
Harrison, Patti 204, 205
'Harry' (Dead Fingers Talk) 276
Harry, Debbie 283
Hart, Lorenz 'Larry' 41–2
'Have I the Right' (Honeycombs) 123
'Have You Seen Your Mother, Baby, Standing in the Shadow?' (Rolling Stones) 137–8
Hawkins, Sophie B. 428
Hay, Harry 65–6, 149
'He Should Have Been A WAC' (US WAC) 50
'Head Over Heals' (Accept) 378
Headbangers Ball TV programme 436
'Heart Is Quick Than The Eye' (Rodgers and Hart) 41
Heartbreakers 278, 279
Heartsong (J. Millington) 341
Heath, Gordon 97
Heaven, London 322, 358

Hedwig and the Angry Itch 469
'Hello Darling' (B. Fletcher) 40
'Hello Hooray' (M. Christian) 211
'Helluva World' (H. Barnes) 224
Hendrix, Jimi 151–2
Hendryx, Nona 253, 254, 427
Henry, Clarence 'Frogman' 92
Henry, Fitzgerald 'Mighty Henry' 135
Henry, Wayman 'Sloppy' 22
Herd 141
Heresey, Harold 44
Herndon, Ty 513–14
Herrara, Leo 531
Hersch, Fred 55, 369, 480
'He's a Woman, She's a Man' (Scorpions) 274
'He's Good for Me' (J. Akens) 229
'He's So Unusual' (H. Kane) 29
'He's the Queen of Fire Island' (S.T. Peter) 101
Hi Fidelity record label 116
Hi-NRG scene 324, 374, 391–3
Hibiscus 171–2, 183, 185
HideZine fanzine 386
High In-Fidelity record label 109, 110
'High School Confidential' (Rough Trade) 342, 343
'Highland Tinker' (folk ballad) 8
'Hilly Brown' (B. Fletcher) 39
Hilton, Alex 491–2, 497
Hindle, Annie 'Charles Ryan' 9
Hip Hop Bee Bop (Man Parrish) 363–4
Hip Hop Homos documentary 489
hippies 160, 161, 163, 169–70, 171–2
Hirschfeld, Magnus 12–13, 14, 27
His New York Diary (N. Rorem) 154
'History Rap' (Age of Consent) 328, 329
Hitfix magazine 285
Hitler, Adolf 35
HIV and AIDS *see* AIDS and HIV
HIV Plus magazine 3
Hockney, David 184–5
Hoffman, Kristian 242, 285, 286, 316, 317–18, 363

553

Hoffman, Wolf 378
Holiday, Billie 86, 93, 125, 295
Holland-Dozier-Holland 243
Hollywood 22, 25, 52, 111, 114
  production code 35–6, 41
Hollywood Harlots 109
'Homo-sexual' (Angry Samoans) 333
'Homo the Range' (B. Peck) 93
Homocore fanzine 389–90
HomoRevolution 495
'Homosapien' (P. Shelley) 352
Homosexual Action West Berlin 179
Homosexual Reform Committees, UK 157, 179
'Homosexuality' (Modern Rocketry) 391
Honeycombs 123
'Honky Tonk Woman' (Rolling Stones) 172
Hood, Sam 208
Hooke, Helen 215
Horn, Trevor 355
Horowitz, Adam 471
Horse 427–8
Horses (Patti Smith Group) 283–4
Hot Peaches 185, 263–4, 269, 273
Hot Wax Records 243
Hotel, Tony 315
'Hound Dog' (W.M. Thornton) 78
House of Latex 413
House of Shame play 102
houses of New York 398–400
How Far Can You Go? . . . (Smokey) 237
How To Destroy Angels (Coil) 404
How to Have Sex in an Epidemic: One Approach safe sex manifesto 368
'How To Say Goodbye to You' (J. Somerville) 414–15
Howard, Gene 110–12
Howard, Ken 123, 141, 192
Howard, Silas 'Flipper' 448, 449
Howdy Club, New York 56
Howl (A. Ginsberg) 100

Hudson, Rock 365
Huff, Leon 244, 248
Huggy Bear 450–1
Hughes, David 327–8
Hughes, Glenn 292
Hunky Dory (D. Bowie) 186, 263, 264
Hunter, Alberta 18
Hunter, Tab 88, 94
Hurrah Club, New York 288, 318
'Hurt' (T. Yuro) 127
Hutchinson, Hutch 34
Hype 177

'I (Who Have Nothing)' (Sylvester) 319
I Am a Bird Now (Anthony and the Johnsons) 502–3
'I Am Curious' (Rough Trade) 344
'I Am What I Am' (Village People) 292
'I, Bloodbrother Be' (Shock Headed Peters) 389
'I Don't Dare' (M. Malamet) 162
'I Don't Want To be Gay' (J. King) 180
'I Feel Love' (D. Summer) 324
'I'm Gonna Dance wit de Guy wot Brung Me' (F. Jaxon) 22
I Know You Know (M. Christians) 211
'I Left My Heart in San Francisco' (Cory and Cross) 125, 126
'I Like the Nightlife' (A. Bridges) 305
'I Love Her Like Mad' (Kit) 416
'I Love My Fruit' (Sweet Violet Boys) 44
'I Only Want to Be With You' (D. Springfield) 131
'I Spent My Last $10.00 (on Birth Control and Beer)' (Two Nice Girls) 419–20
'I Surrender Dear' (B. Crosby) 32
'I Tried to Talk to You' (J. Grant) 3
'I Wanna Be a Homosexual' (Screeching Weasel) 447
'I Want a Millionaire' (Coccinelle) 69
'I Want To Be Good' (R. Bourbon) 30
'I Want To Break Free' (Queen) 376

554

Index

'I Was Born This Way' (C. Bean) 258–9, 319
'I Was Born This Way' (Valentino) 255–7, 258
'I Will Survive' (G. Gaynor) 289
Ian, Janis 153–4, 218, 418, 456, 457
'I'd Like to Make Love With You' (M. Sloan) 208
'I'd Much Rather Be With the Boys' (Rolling Stones) 139
'I'd Rather be Spanish than Mannish' (G. Malin) 29, 37
'(If You Don't Wanna Fuck Me, Baby) Fuck Off!' (Electric Chairs) 282
'I'll be Holding On' (A. Browning) 248–9
'I'll Follow My Secret Heart' (N. Coward) 34
I'll Sing for You (Z. Colt) 174–5
'I'm a Boy' (The Who) 140
'I'm a Gigolo' (C. Porter) 34
'I'm a Lesbian, How About You?' (Flying Lesbians) 219
'I'm a Man' (Macho) 293
'I'm Coming Out' (D. Ross) 323
I'm Gay (Lil B) 529–30
'I'm Gonna Wash That Man Right Outta of My Hair' (Rodgers and Hammerstein) 60
'I'm Illegal' (Team Dresch) 451
'I'm Not a Loser' (Descendants) 333
'I'm the Only One' (M. Etheridge) 434
'I'm Tired' (Savoy Brown) 153
'I'm Unlucky in Gambling' (C. Porter) 34
'I'Maman' Jobriath 200
Imperial Teen 458–9
Improved Sound Ltd 163
'In a Cave' (KOD) 407
In Bed With Madonna documentary 401
In Search of Eros . . . (R. McKuen) 109
'In the Navy' (Village People) 294
In Touch magazine 229, 230, 235

Inclusion For All campaign 360
Indigo Girls 429–30, 532
industrial bands 403–4
Ingénue (k.d. lang) 432
Ingrassia, Tony 185
Inside London (BBC World Service) 223
'Instant Karma' (J. Lennon) 242
Institute of Sexology 13
International, Dana 467–8
International Gay Society 302
International Sweethearts of Rhythm 55
International Times 198
'Invasion' (P. Cowley) 362
Invictus label 243
'Is It All Over My Face?' (Loose Joints) 323–4, 498
Isis 215–16, 217
Island Records 417, 434
Isle of View (J. Spheeris) 234
It Is In the Air musical 27
'It's Dirty But Good' (R. and B. Quillian) 18
'It's My Party' (L. Gore) 129–30
It's Only Right and Natural (Frogs) 404
'It's Raining Men' (Weather Girls) 391
ITV 159
'I've Been To a Marvellous Party' (N. Coward) 33

J-Flag 516
'Jackie' (J.Brel trans. M. Shulman) 158, 159
Jackie Shane Live (J. Shane) 119
Jackson, Antonio Junius 'Tony' 20–1
Jackson, Bessie 19
Jackson, Joe 286–7
Jagger, Mick 137, 138, 172, 177, 288, 309, 330
'Jailhouse Rock' (E. Presley) 79
Jam Today 221–2
Jamaica 454–5, 481, 516–17
James, Billy 160
James, Marion 118

James, Sylvester *see* Sylvester
Jarman, Derek 184–5, 374, 404, 434, 439–40, 442
Jason, Liam (Jackie Enx) 501
Jaxon, Frankie 'Half Pint' 22
jazz 16–17, 54–5, 70, 86, 154–6, 369, 480
Jazz Times magazine 55
J.D.s fanzine 386, 387–8, 389
'Jean Genie' (D. Bowie) 201
Jennings, Tom 389–90
Jeremy magazine 178, 179
Jessie, Obie 244
'Jet Boy Jet Girl' (E. Motello) 308
Jet Records 268
Jett, Joan 285, 418
Jewel Box Revue 43, 44, 47, 56, 168, 397
'Jimmy Row' (C. Robison) 232
'Jimmy's Got a Little Bit of Bitch in Him' (Funkadelic) 254
Jobriath 199–201, 375, 381
John, Elton 156, 191, 197–8, 241–2, 259–60, 269, 272, 311, 330, 366, 369, 406, 412, 424, 440, 484
'John, I'm Only Dancing' (D. Bowie) 190–1
'Johnny, Are You Queer?' (J. Cottons) 335–6
'Johnny Remember Me' (J. Leyton) 121
Johnson, Holly 353–4, 355, 377, 415
Johnson, Marsha P. 168, 173, 178–9, 470
Jolson, Al 32
Jones, Alan 249
Jones, Brian 137, 138, 194, 231
Jones, Bunny 255–6
Jones, G.B. 384, 385, 386–7, 388, 390–1
Jones, Spud 442
Joplin, Janis 149–50, 183, 213, 337, 342
Jordan, Yitz 530
Jorgensen, George 'Christine' 68–9
Journey to the Centre of Uranus show 184
Judas Priest 320, 378, 459–60
Jude, Catherine 524–5

Julius Bar, New York 165, 166
Juvet, Patrick 294
Kaczor, Richie 288–9
Kalamka, Juba 485–6, 487–8, 495
Kandy Lounge, Soho 135
Kane, Helen 28–9
Katastrophe 493–4, 510
Kaufmann, Stefan 378
'Kay, Why?' (Brothers Butch) 142
Kayiatos, Rocco 'Katastrophe' 493–4, 510
Keane, Tommy 380
'Keep An Eye On His Business' (B. Fletcher) 39
Kellum, Jo 80–2, 83
Kemp, Lindsay 147–8, 177, 190
Kempf, Ralf 211
Kennedy, Harrison 243
Kennedy, John 102
Kentucky's Prairie Ramblers 44
Kerbeny, Karl-Maria 12
Kern, Jerome 28
Kerouac, Jack 98
KGBears 526–7
King, Carole 210, 211
King, Hetty 10
King, Jonathan 180
'King's a Queen at Heart' (J. Rees) 36–7
King's X 480
Kinks 138–9, 182–3, 214, 309
   see also Davies, Ray
Kinsey, Dr Alfred 51, 61, 65, 97
'Kiss Me Again' (Dinosaur) 323
Kiss Me, Kate musical 52
'Kiss Me My Dear John' (Homocord Orchestra) 15
Kit 416
Kitchens of Distinction (KOD) 407–9
Kitt, Eartha 92–3
Kitty-Yo Records 497
Knights in White Satin (G. Moroder) 292

Index

Knopfler, Mark 409
Knuckles, Frankie 288, 393, 394, 485, 534
Konk records 265
'Krisco Kisses' (FGTH) 356
Kronstadt, Bettye 197
KRS-One 472

L Word TV programme 494
La Caverne, Soho 102
La Rue, DC 289–90
L'Abbaye club, Paris 97
LaBeija, Crystal 398
Labelle, Patti 253–4, 338
LaBostrie, Dorothy 76
LaBruce, Bruce 386, 387, 388, 390–1, 447
Lace Records 111
Ladder, The magazine 87
Lady 502
'Lady' (M. Christian) 210
Lady Elizabeth 8
'Lady Godiva's Operation' (Velvet Underground) 146
'Lady Marmalade' (P. Labelle) 253, 254
'Lady Stardust' (D. Bowie) 190
Lalumia, Jimi 287
Lambert, Adam 500
Lambert, Kit 139, 140, 141, 180–1
Landesman, Fran 99
Lang, Harold 52
lang, k.d. 430–3
Lao, Meri Franco 219
LaRoche, Pierre 232
Lasley, David 371
'Last Dance' (D. Summer) 304–5
Last Exit To Brooklyn (H. Selby) 145
'Last Pioneers' (S. Grossman) 423
'Late Night' (L. Furey) 273–4
Latifah, Queen 473, 486
Laughner, Peter 338
Laurents, Arthur 52, 94
Lavender Country 226–9, 326–7
Lavender Country (Lavender Country) 226–8

'Lavender Cowboy' (H. Hersey) 44, 224
Lavender Jane 209–10
Lavender Jane Loves Women (Lavender Jane) 209, 211
Lavonne, Princess 74
laws, homophobic 2, 8, 12, 14–15, 27, 35, 46, 47, 54, 67, 74, 83, 85–6, 89–90, 96, 101, 105, 108, 117, 122, 126, 135, 141, 157, 165, 166, 202, 204, 205, 218, 246, 271, 302, 368, 377, 379, 394, 416, 427, 439–40, 517–18, 521–2, 527, 533–4, 535
Le Duce, Soho 135–6, 184, 262
Lear, Amanda 138, 195
'Leather Boys' (Handbag) 268
'Leave This Lesbian World' (Improved Sound Ltd) 163
Lebanon 518
LeBeija, Crystal 398–9
Lebensreform (life reform) movement 57
Lebrun, Calvin 'Mister Cee' 529
Lee, Al 25
Lee, Joseph Thomas 'Deadlee' 489–90, 495
Lehrer, Tom 93
Leiber, Jerry 79, 92
Leitch, Donovan 454
Lennon, John 136, 153, 213, 242
Lennox, Annie 346, 424, 427
Lesbian Feminist Liberation 208
lesbians, Victorian denial of 10
Leslie, Edgar 28
'Let the Heartaches Begin' (J. Baldry) 156
'Let's All Be Fairies' (Durium Dance Band) 36
Let's Dance (D. Bowie) 346
Levan, Larry 288, 323–4, 393, 400
Levine, Bertha 'Spivy' 43
Lewis, Margot 132
Lewis, Rudy 90
Leyton, John 121

557

'Lezzie in Red' (Minette) 163
Liberace 47, 60–1, 62, 67, 68, 100, 112, 375
Liberated Women (P. Perkins) 207
Liberty Music Shop record label 36, 39, 50
License To Ill (Beastie Boys) 409–10, 471
Lick 453
Lieb, Eli 533
'Life at the Outpost' (Skatt Brothers) 320
Life magazine 372
LIFEbeat foundation 424
Lifted Off the Ground (Wright, Chely) 512–13
Lil B 529–30
'Lilac Song' (Billing and Schwabach) 14–15, 202
Lilith 216, 217
Lima, Marina 307
Limelight magazine 5
Limp Bizkit 459
Lion, Margo 27
Lippincott, Edie 81, 83
Little Five Points pub, Toronto 429
Little Richard 73–4, 75–7, 93, 103, 118, 122
'Little Toy Soldier' (D. Bowie) 147
'Little White Cloud That Cried' (J. Ray) 69
Living in the Shadows of a Downtown Movie Show (R. Campbell) 273
'Living In Wartime' (M. Callan) 366, 368
Livingston, Jerry 99
Lockett, Bert 249
Lockwood, Joseph 121, 122
Loft, New York 247–8, 250
'Lola' (Kinks) 182–3
London Records 415
London Women's Liberation Rock Band (LWLRB) 220
'Loneliness' (M. Berry) 122–3

'Long Hot Summer' (TRB) 271, 275
Long John Baldry and the Hoochie Coochie Men (J. Baldry) 157
'Long Tall Sally' (Little Richard) 76
Longtime Companion film 414
Loods, Lesley 337
'Look Away' (S. Grand and E. Lieb) 533
'Looking for a Boy Tonight' (C. Robison) 233
Lopez, Robert 314, 315
Los Angeles (LA) 25, 38, 41, 42, 47, 52, 64, 87, 119, 150, 198, 200, 214, 237–8, 258, 312–13, 387–8
   see also Hollywood
Loud, Lance 285, 317–18, 458
Love and Hip Hop TV programme 530
'Love Child' (Accept) 378
'Love Don't Need A Reason' (Lowlife) 369–70, 425
Love, Gay-Style (Hollywood Harlots) 109
Love is a Drag . . . album 110–12, 115
Love Is Hell (KOD) 407, 408
'Love Potion No. 9' (Clovers) 92
'Love Saves the Day' (MFSB) 248
'Love to Love You Baby' (D. Summer) 257
Lowe, Chris 374
Lowlife 367–8
Ludlam, Charles 170
Lully, Jean-Baptiste 5
Lunch, Lydia 316
'Lush Life' (B. Strayhorn) 56
Lydon, John 'Johnny Rotten' 278–9
Lymon, Frankie 90
The Lyricist (Cyryus) 476–7
Lyte, MC 486

'Ma, He's Making Eyes at Me' (E. Cantor) 32
Ma Rainey 17, 19, 47
MacDonald, Carol 216
'Macho Man' (Village People) 292

Mad About the Boy (Camp Records) 114–15
'Mad About the Boy' (N. Coward) 33, 312
'Madame George' (V. Morrison) 153
Madonna 343, 400–1, 426, 495, 496
Magic Tramps 195–6, 198, 199
Magnetic Fields 446
MainMan 199, 280
Majah P, Mista 516–17, 534
'Make Up' (L. Reed) 196
Malamet, Marsha 162, 370
male impersonators 9–10, 20, 25, 64, 168
'Male Stripper' (Man2Man) 392–3
Malenergy (Man2Man) 392
Malin, Gene 'Jean' 29–30, 36, 37
'Man About Town' (J. Rogers) 37
Man-Boy Love Sickie (Ism) 333
Man Child (C. Robison) 234
'Man Enough to be a Woman' (Electric Chairs) 282
Mancuso, David 247, 248, 251, 255
Mandley, Carla 80
Manic Street Preachers 435–6
Mantley, Carla 82, 83
'March of the Women' (E. Smyth) 11
Marchan, Bobby 89, 478
'Maria' (J. Ian) 218
Marquee club, London 262, 275
Marr, Johnny 382
marriage, gay 226, 379, 451, 456–7, 482, 490, 527
Marriot, Steve 317
Marry Me (T. Fixx) 490
Martin, Andy 389
Martin, Ricky 466, 500
Martin, Scrumbly 183
Martinez, Dan/Marissa 504–5
'Masculine Women! Feminine Men!' (G. Farrar) 31
'Masculine Women, Feminine Men' (Leslie and Monaco) 28
Mashrou' Leila 518, 519

Matador Records 404
Matassa, Cosimo 76
Mathis, Johnny 95–6, 99
Matias, Ivan 492
Matogrosso, Ney 194
Mattachine Society 65, 86, 99–100, 144, 149, 165, 173, 202
Mattea, Kathy 424
Maximum Rocknroll fanzine 390–1
Max's Kansas City, New York 171, 195, 208, 269, 273, 282–3
MCA records 214
McAlinden, Angela 427–8
McAlmont, David 440–2
McAnally, Shane 512
McCarthy, Joseph 63, 64, 85
McCartney, Paul 58, 122, 153
McCulloch, Ian 189
McDonald/Shaw, Carol 132
McDonald, Sheena 'Horse' 427–8
McDonnell, Evelyn 285
McKellen, Ian 420
McKuen, Rod 98–9, 108–9, 158, 159, 292–3, 302
McLaren, Malcolm 270, 271, 279, 350, 400
McNally, Edward 96–7
'Me and Julio Down by the Schoolyard' (P. Simon) 265
Meadmore, Glen 403, 437
Meatmen 333
Mechanical Bride 505–6
Meek, Joe 121, 122–4, 137
Megatron 324
Melly, George 156
Melody Maker 186, 438
'Melpomene Block Party' (Katey Red) 478
'Men of Montrose' (Montrose Men) 319
'Menergy' (Megatron) 324
mental disorder, homosexuality as a 63, 86, 204, 225, 227, 229, 233, 294
Mercer Arts Center 198

Mercury, Freddie 260–1, 320, 376, 412, 423–4, 460
Mercury Records 177, 199, 234, 235, 236
Merritt, Stephen 446
Metro Weekly magazine 491
Mexicana Bar, Miami Beach 56
MGM film studios 44–5
Miami Beach, Florida 56
Michael, George 466–7
Michigan Womyn's Music Festival 'Mitchfest' 212–13
Mickey 7's 242
Middle East 518
Midnight Special TV programme 201
Mighty Terror 135
Mike Cohen (M. Cohen) 230
military, US 457
Milk, Harvey 298, 301, 302, 303, 316, 326, 415
Millennium March 482–3
Miller, Bob 44
Millington, Jean 213
Millington, June 213–14, 217
Minaj, Nicki 530
Mind Warp (P. Cowley) 362
Mineo, Sal 238
Mineshaft, New York 246–7, 284
Minette (Jacques) 85, 163–5, 170
Minnelli, Liza 196, 288
minstrel shows 8–9, 74
Minton, 'Butch' 47
Minty 442
Mira Records 142
Miracles 254–5
Miranda, Carmen 75, 193, 194
Miriam, Faygele ben 226–7
'Miss Amanda Jones' (Rolling Stones) 138
Miss Philadelphia drag pageant 92, 164
Missabu, Rumi 172, 183
Missing Twenty Grand (D. Lasley) 371
'Mister Sandman' (P. Ballard) 94–5
Mitch Ryder and the Detroit Wheels 159–60

Mitchell, John Cameron 469
Mitchell, Joni 160–1, 209–10, 234
Mizer, Bob 62–3
'Moanin' For You' (G. Farrar and N. Blaney) 31
MOJO magazine 58, 75, 76, 273
Mokroshelky 526
Moltke, Kuno Graf von 12
Monaco, James 28
Mona's Club 440, San Francisco 47, 63, 64
'Money' (J. Shane) 119
'Money For Nothing' (Dire Straits) 409
Montagu, Lord 96–7
Montanez Jr, Joseph 'Disco Tex' 251–3, 255
Moon, Keith 238
'Moon Ray' (C. Connor) 87
Moonstone design studio 254
Morali, Jacques 291–2, 294, 393
'More More More' (Andrea True Connection) 257
Morley, Paul 355
Moroder, Giorgio 257, 292, 324
Morplay 478–9
Morris, Eve 226, 228
Morrison, Jan 81, 83
Morrison, Jim 150–1
Morrison, Van 153
Morrissey 381–3, 406, 407
Morrissey, Steven 4
Morton, Jelly Roll 21
Moscone, George 298, 303, 326
Moses Stokes's Travelling Show 17
Moss, Jon 350, 351, 352
Mother Fist and Her Five Daughters (Marc and the Mambas) 373
Motown Records 134, 135, 167, 243, 244–6, 256, 258, 319
Mott the Hoople 190
Mould, Bob 380, 445–6, 458
Moulton, Tom 248–9, 250, 256–7
Mountain Moving Day (Women's Liberation Rock Bands) 207

INDEX

MTV 348, 359, 376, 428, 435, 436, 438, 461, 467, 480–1, 492
Mudd Club, New York City 288, 318, 339
Mumps 285–6
'Munching the Candy' (P. Perkins) 162
Murphy, Charlie 300
'Muscleboys' (Mumps) 286
Musgrave, Kacey 515
'Music Fanzine' (Team Dresch) 451
Music for Mixed Emotions novelty gift 109–10
music hall 11
  see also female impersonators; male impersonators; vaudeville
Music Train (TV programme) 117, 118
Music Week 201
musicologists 5
Muzic Box, Chicago 393–4
'My Daddy Rocks Me with One Steady Roll' (T. Smith) 70
'My Daddy Rocks Me with One Steady Roll' (Tampa Red's Hokum Jazz Band) 22
'My Doctor' (B. Fletcher) 39
'My Funny Valentine' (Rodgers and Hart) 42
'My Grey Boy' (D. McAlmont) 441
'My Heart Has a Mind of Its Own' (C. Francis) 124–5
My Hustler film 197
My Saber is Bent (J. Paar) 105–6
Myers, Pete 184

Na Maria (B. de Romans) 5
Nake Lunch (W. Burroughs) 100
Nancy Boy 454
Napier-Bell, Simon 131, 140, 141, 142, 147, 180–1, 191
Nashville 118, 119, 225, 424, 456, 512
'Nature Boy' (N. K. Cole) 57, 58–9
Naturmensch (natural man) movement 57
Naylor, Liz 450–1

Nazism 35
Ndegéocello 473
Near, Holly 212, 213, 304
Nelson, Willie 512
Nervous Gender 314, 417
'Never Can Say Goodbye' (G. Gaynor) 250, 396
New Christie Minstrels 107, 108
New Gay Life magazine 245
New Musical Express (NME) 103, 197, 253, 265, 269, 277, 374, 407–8, 472
New Orleans 20–1, 72
new romantics 346–7, 352
'New Stovepipe Verses' (H. Blädel) 13
'New York at Night' (D. Parker) 294–5
New York Dolls 198–9, 232, 270, 278, 381
New York Times 104, 236, 361, 479, 491
'Next' (J. Brel trans. M. Shulman) 158, 159
Nice 141
Nicholas, Paul 147
'Night and Day' 49
Night People (R. Burns) 155
Nights of Love in Lesbos album 112
'1984' (D. Bowie) 239
Nirvana 436, 437, 445
Nitzer Ebb 403
No Camping (J. Sarria) 106, 108
No Motive (3 Teens Kill 4) 402
No Skin Off My Ass (film) 388
'Nobody Loves You When You're Old and Gay' (Dead Fingers Talk) 276
'Nobody's Going to Change Me' (Dynamic Superiors) 246
Nocturnal Dream Show, San Francisco 172, 183
Noh Mercy 315
Nolan, Kenny 253
Nomi, Klaus 316, 317–18, 363–4
Normal Heart (play) 366, 370
Norman, Karyl 29, 42
Northern Women's Liberation Rock Band (NWLRB) 221

Novello, Ivor 32
Novoselic, Kris 436, 437
NSYNC 465, 500
Nubin, Rosetta 70
Nuestro Mundo 165
N.W.A. 411
Nyro, Laura 160–2, 215, 217, 234, 253, 338

'Ob-La-Di, Ob-La-Da' (Beatles) 153
O'Brien, Richard 192
Ocean, Frank 528
October, Gene 277
'Ode to Billie Joe' (B. Gentry) 153
Offs 315
O'Grady, Camille 284
Oh Boy TV programme 103
'Oh Shit' (A. Smith) 488–9
'Oh! You Pretty Things' (D. Bowie) 186, 263
O'Hara, Frank 100–1
Okeh records 66, 73
Old Lesbians Organising for Change (OLOC) 212
Oldham, Andrew Loog 137–8, 139, 159, 454
'Olha O Boneco' (Titica) 520
Oliver! musical 102
Oliveros, Pauline 54
Olivia Records 210, 211, 212, 213, 214, 218, 231, 302, 341–2, 433–4, 453
Olivieri, Nicole 313
O'Montis, Paul 35
'On Broadway' (Drifters) 90
'On the Outside' (Kinks) 309
'One' (U2) 435
'One In a Million' (Guns N' Roses) 410
One In Ten 475–6
ONE, Inc. 65, 100
One magazine 65, 88, 100, 112
One20five 496–7
'Only the Strong Survive' (J. Butler) 167
Ono, Yoko 136, 213
opera 10, 101

Orbison, Roy 431
Organisation for Lesbian and Gay Action 420
'Orgasm Addict' (Buzzcocks) 278
Original Plumbing magazine 493
'Orion' (M. Cohen) 230
Orton, Joe 137
Oscar Wilde bookshop, New York 165
Other Voices, Other Rooms (T. Capote) 52
Our Lady of the Flowers (J. Genet) 98, 148
'Out' (S. Grossman) 236
Out In the Country (D. Stevens) 480
Out magazine 336, 446
Out of Borstal rock opera 181
Out of the Slough radio show 229–30
Out On Tuesday TV programme 416
Out Punk Dance Party compilation 450
outing celebrities 410–11
Outpunk records 446–7, 450
'Outside' (G. Michael) 467
OutWeek 410
Ova 222–3
Ova Music Studio 223
'Over the Wall We Go' (D. Bowie) 147

Paar, Jack 105
Paige, Justin 192
Paine, Bobby and Larson 335
Pale Green Ghosts (J. Grant) 3
Panozzo, Chuck 500
Pansy Club, Times Square 29, 35, 42
'pansy craze' 29–31, 38–40, 44
Pansy Division 443, 444–5
Paradise Garage, New York 288, 306, 323–4, 363, 393, 400
Paris 28, 97, 222
Paris Diary of Ned Rorem (N. Rorem) 154
Paris Is Burning documentary 399, 400
Parker, Dennis 294–5
Parnes, Larry 102–3, 120–1
Parrish, Man 363–4, 392–3, 485

Parson, Jeff 276
Parton, Dolly 512
'Patricia Gone With Millicent' (Mighty Terror) 135
Payant, Lee 97
PeaceOUT (World) Homo Hop Festival 488, 495
Peaches 497–8
Peacock Records 78
Pears, Peter 53
Peck, Bob 93
Peduzzi, George Francis 29
Pen, Queen 473–4, 479
Penthouse magazine 77
People in Trouble (S. Schulman) 468–9
Peppermint Lounge, Manhattan 104, 134–5, 246
Perkins, Anthony 88
Perkins, Polly 133–4, 162, 207, 312
Perryman, Rufs 'Speckled Red' 21
'*Pervitida*' (A. Lara) 51
Pervo-Devo (Screeching Weasel) 447
Pet Shop Boys 373–5, 463–4
PETA 432
'Peter and David' (E. Askew) 153
Peter Grimes (B. Britten) 53
Peter, Saul T. 101
Petting parties 24
Phat Family Records 488
Philadelphia film 425
'Philadelphia Freedom' (E. John) 259
Philadelphia International Records (PIR) 244
Philip, Prince of Eulenburg 12, 13
Phillips, Gretchen 418–20
Phoenix, Bobo 276
Phranc 314–15, 417, 426, 451–2
Physique Pictorial magazine 62–3, 292
Pick Up the Mic documentary 491–2, 494
Pidgeon 200
Pierrot in Turquoise play 148
'Pillow Talk' (R. Hudson and D. Day) 158

Pinnick, Doug 480
Pits and Perverts benefit concert 360
Pitt, Ken 141, 146, 147, 178, 180
Pitt-Rivers, Michael 97
Pitts, Charles 229–30
Placebo 453–4
Playboy magazine 322
Playhouse of the Ridiculous 170
Playing With a Different Sex (Au Pairs) 336–7
'Please God Please Help Me' (Morrissey) 381
Pointer Sisters 295
police harassment/raids 101, 135, 166–8, 270–1
politicians/political representatives, gay 108, 203, 298, 301, 302, 303, 316, 326, 415
'Polly Perkins Love Georgia Brown' (P. Perkins) 162
'Polythene Pam' (Beatles) 153
Pop, Iggy 199, 201, 307
Pop-Lore According to the Academy (P. Perkins) 162, 207
Pope, Carole 342–4, 426–7
Popstitutes 389
Pork (play) 185–6
Porter, Cole 34, 40, 41, 49, 52, 422
Positive Force 390
post office, US 100
Poulenc, Francis 52
Powder Box Revue 89, 478
Powell, Louis 37
Power in the Darkness (TRB) 275
Power Plant, Chicago 393
'Pray to Your God' (M. Cohen) 230
Presley, Elvis 70, 77, 78, 79, 103
'Pretty Baby' (A. Jackson) 20
Pretty Boy Entertainment 496
'Pretty Golden Hair' (A. Stewart) 154
Price, Anthony 194–5, 197
Pridgett, Malissa Nix 'Ma Rainey' 17–18, 19
Prince 328–9, 409, 441

'Prince of the Punks' (Kinks) 309
progressive rock 262
Prohibition 17, 23, 35
protests/demonstrations, lesbian and
    gay 165–6, 173, 178–9, 202–3, 204,
    205, 302, 364, 396
    see also ACT UP
'Prove It To Me Blues' (Ma Rainey) 19
Pryor, Richard 155
Public Enemy 454
Pulse, Orlando 534
punk 269–70, 271–2, 277–80, 281, 282,
    285–6, 287, 312–15, 331–4, 384–91,
    446–9
Pure Pleasure (Dynamic Superiors)
    245–6
'Purple Haze' (J. Hendrix) 152
Purple Heart (Lowlife) 369–70
Pyramid Club, New York 401–2, 437,
    469

Quatro, Suzi 191–2
Queen 261, 376, 406, 412, 423–4
'Queen Bitch' (D. Bowie) 186, 263
Queen Elizabeth (band) 198, 199
Queen is in the Closet (Camp Records)
    112–13
'Queen of Compton Street' (Fruit) 442
The Queen 398
Queer Nation 446
'Queer Things (Are Happening)' (R.
    Wallis) 50
queercore 447, 450, 451–2, 453
'Quickie' (T. West) 486, 487
Quillian, Rufus and Ben 18
Quin, Tegan and Sara 481

Radicalesbians 210–11
ragtime scene 20–1
Rail Room, Kansas 84
Rail Runners 84
Rainbow Flava 477–8, 485–6
Rainbow Riot album 534–5
Rainbow Riots 534–5

Raindance (D. Lasley) 371–2
Rainey, Ma 17–18, 19
Rainey, Will 'Pa' 17
Ramones 284
Ranks, Shabba 455
'Rapper's Delight' (Sugarhill Gang) 327
RAS label 5151
Ray, Amy 429–30
Ray, Johnnie 66–8, 69–70, 93, 115
Raye, Martha 48
RCA records 181, 195, 215, 232
Reaction label 141
Read My Lips (J. Somerville) 414–15
'Read My Lips (Enough Is Enough)' (J.
    Somerville) 415
Ready Steady Go! TV programme
    133–4
Reagan, Ronald 332, 366, 377, 402
'Real Men' (J. Jackson) 287
Reavis, John 106
'Rebel, Rebel' (D. Bowie) 239, 280
Rebel Without a Cause (film) 70
Record Mirror 356
Red Hot + Blue 422, 432, 435
Redding, Otis 119, 120
Redwood Records 212
Reed, Lou 144–6, 147, 171, 178, 195,
    196, 232, 274, 307, 308, 414
Reed, Merrill 145
Reeder Jr, Eskew 'Esquerita' 74–5
'Reel Around the Fountain' (Smiths)
    382
Rees, Judd 36–7
Reggae Compassionate Act 516
Rejected documentary 106, 173
'Relax' (FGTH) 353, 354–6, 372, 377
'Relondo Beach' (Patti Smith Group)
    284
R.E.M. 379–80, 381, 406, 434–5, 445
'rent parties' 18
Rent play 468–9
Reprise Records 213
*Research on the Riddle of Man-Manly
    Love* (K.H. Ulrichs) 12

Restless Underwear revue 343
Reuben's, Hollywood 35
Revenge (J. Ian) 457
Revolting Cocks 403
Reynard, Miss Jimmy 47
Reynolds, John 97
Rhapsody by Candlelight (Liberace) 112
Richard, Cliff 103
Richards, Keith 137, 138
Ridiculous Theatrical Company 170–1, 172–3, 184
'Right on Sister' (TRB) 271
'Rimmin' at the Baths' (Automatic Pilot) 326, 365–6
riot grrrl scene 437, 450
Rise and Fall of Ziggy Stardust and the Spiders From Mars (D. Bowie) 189–90, 194
Rising Free (TRB) 274–5
Ritchie Family 292
Rivera, Sylvia 168, 173, 178–9
Rivers, Larry 100–1
Robbins, Jerome 94
Roberts, Casey 38, 39
Robinson, Tom 22, 152, 263–6, 267, 268–9, 270–1, 273, 274–7, 279, 308, 309, 311–12, 360, 394–5, 460
Robison, Chris 152, 231–3, 237
Roc-A-Jets 80–3, 132
Rocca, Robert 59–60, 224
Rock Against Reagan 332
Rock Hudson Sings the Songs of Rod McKuen (R. Hudson) 158
Rock III, Sir Monti 251–3, 255
'Rock Me Tonite' (B. Squier) 376–7
Rocket to Stardom (Mickey 7) 242
Rockland Palace, Harlem 22
rock'n'roll 70–1, 75, 76–9, 80–1, 102
Rocky Horror Show musical 192
Rodgers, Nile 323
Rodgers, Richard 41
Rogers, Jimmie 94
Rogers, Wayne/Jayne 169–70, 171, 185

Rolling Stone magazine 180, 184, 209–10, 216, 235–6, 247, 260, 295, 309, 377, 381, 410, 412, 507
Rolling Stones 127, 137–8, 139, 172, 176–7, 219, 220, 231, 309
Roman Empire 4
Romans, Bieiris de 5
Ronson, Mick 177, 189
Rope film 52, 114
Rorem, Ned 154
Rosa, Noel 192–3
Rose, Axl 410, 424, 436
Rose, Felip 291
Rosenmüller, Johann 5–6
Ross, Diana 251, 323
Rotello, Gabriel 410
'Rough Boys' (P. Townshend) 330
Rough Trade 342–3, 386, 427
Roxy Music 194–5
Roxy, The, Soho 277, 280–1
Ruben, Dr David 173
Rubettes 272–3
'Run Run Run' (Velvet Underground) 146
Runaways 285
Rundgren, Todd 232
Runnalls, Jana 222, 223
RuPaul 402–3, 437–8
Russell, Arthur 323–4, 424, 498
Russell, Jane 80
Russia 2, 24, 525, 526–7, 532
Russo, Renato 413
Rutherford, Paul 353, 354, 355
Ryan, Charles 9
Ryder, Mitch 159–60, 310

Saint club, New York 322, 323, 324
Salliers, Emily 429, 430, 532
'Sally Go 'Round the Roses' (Mitch Ryder and the Detroit Wheels) 159–60, 212
Salmonberries film 432
'Same Love' (Macklemore and R. Lewis) 527, 531

Samwell 498
San Francisco 25, 42, 46, 56, 64, 86, 99, 105, 108, 125, 126, 165, 171–2, 178, 183, 228, 296, 298–9, 303, 315–16, 389, 390, 444, 487
'San Francisco (You Got Me)' (Village People) 291
San Francisco Gay Men's Chorus 303, 326
Sangster, Lynn 416
Santing, Matilde 345
Santos, Manuel Pedro dos 'Bahiano' 13
Sarria, José 106, 108
Sarstedt, Peter 181
'Sartorial Eloquence' (E. John) 311
'Saturday Night at the Bookstore' (Dicks) 332
Saturday Night Fever (film) 289, 304
Saturday Night Live TV programme 316–17
Savoy, Bert 25–6
Savoy Brown 153
'Say I Do It' (W. Henry) 22
'Say There' Teddy and Darrel 143
'Scarecrow' (M. Etheridge) 483
Schiffer, Marcellus 27
Schneider/Schwabach, Kurt 14–15
Schonfeld, Rosemary 222–3
Schubert, Franz 5, 6
Schwartz, Delmore 145
Schwartz, Ignacio 43
Schwul (Warner Südwind) 308
Scientific-Humanitarian Committee 12
Scorpio Rising (film) 127
Scorpions 274
Scott-Heron, Gil 243, 327
Screamers 313
'Screaming' (J. Somerville) 357
SCREW magazine 174
'Searching for Someone Like You' (K. Wells) 83
Seattle 108, 226
Second Unit 384

Second World War (WWII) 44, 45, 46, 50, 54, 60
Secos e Molhado (a.k.a. Dry and Wet) 194
'Secret Life' (Soft Cell) 349
'Secret Love' (D. Day) 93–4, 99
'Secretly' (J. Rogers) 94
Section 28 394, 416, 420, 427, 454
Secunda, Chelita 191
Sedaka, Neil 124–5
'See My Friends' (Kinks) 138, 139
segragation 72, 130
Selby, Hubert 145
'Self-Defence' (Ova) 222
separatism, lesbian 210–11, 217–18, 314–15
'Seven Chinese Brothers' (R.E.M.) 380
Seven Gay Sophisticated Songs (Spivy) 43
SEX boutique 270
'Sex Dwarf' (Soft Cell) 349
Sex Pistols 270, 271, 278
Sexual Freedom League, San Francisco 165
Sexual Offences Act (1967) 157, 178
Sexuality in the Human Male (A. Kinsey) 51
Shane, Jackie 117–19, 342
Shaw, Beverly 63, 87
'She Shook Me Cold' (D. Bowie) 178
Shear, Linda 207, 217
Shelley, Peter 277–8, 352–3
Shephard, Matthew 483
Shepherd, Teri 49
Shepherd, William 101
'Sherry' (Four Seasons) 129
'She's Got Medals' (D. Bowie) 147
Shirelles 122
Shishani 521
Shivans 535
Shocked, Michelle 430
'Shoe Shine Boy' (Dynamic Superiors) 245
Showboat musical 28

Shred of Dignity records 447
Shulman, Mort 158
Siano, Nicky 250–1, 257, 288
Sid Lederman Record Centre 111
Siffre, Labi 440, 472
'Sign O'The Times' (Prince) 409
Signorile, Michelangelo 410
'Silence=Death' campaign 397
Silveira 508–10
Silver, Joy 216
Simone, Nina 86
'Simple Things' (B. Fletcher) 40–1
Simpson, Lillian 19
Simpson, Valerie 246
Simpson, Wallis 36
Sims, Jon Reed 303
Sinatra, Frank 158
'(Sing if You're) Glad to Be Gay' (TRB) 271, 274–6, 308, 311, 395
'Singing for Our Lives' (H. Near) 304
Sinno 518–19
Sioux, Siouxsie 278
'Sip-In' protest (1966) 165, 166
Sire Records 323
'Sissy' (L. Powell) 37
'Sissy Blues' (Ma Rainey) 19
Sissy Man Blues 22
'Sissy Man Blues' (K. Arnold) 22
'Sissy Song' (B. Brigg) 64, 224
'Sister Ray' (Velvet Underground) 146
Sizzla 481, 516, 534
Skafish 318–19
Skatt Brothers 319–20
Skunk Anansie 453
Skyhooks 192
Slash Records 458–9
Sleeze Attack (Canya Phuckem and Howe) 325–6
Slide . . . Easy In (R. McKuen) 292–3
Sloan, Margaret 208
Sly and the Family Stone 167
S&M Label 238
'Smalltown Boy' (Bronski Beat) 358–60, 372

Smash Hits 373–4, 416
Smith, Ada 'Bricktop' 27–8
Smith, Alicia 'God-Des' 488–9, 494
Smith, Bessie 17, 18–19, 21, 47, 149, 295
Smith, Patti 185, 228, 283, 337, 427
Smith, Ruthie 221
Smith, Trixie 70
The Smiths 381–2, 406
The Smiths (The Smiths) 382, 383
Smokie 58, 237, 238–9, 241–2, 268
Smyth, Ethel 10
Snake Anthony's Hot Harlem Revue 72, 73, 78
Snatchin' (Handbag) 281
Snick 58
Socarras, Jorge 296–7, 324, 396–7
Society for Human Rights 27, 65
Society for the Prevention of Cruelty to Long-haired Men 146
'Society's Child' (J. Ian) 153–4
Soft Cell 347–50, 351, 372
'Soft Core' (D. Springfield) 344
'Soft Lesbian Airs' (M.V. White) 10
'Soft Parade' (Doors) 151
Soho 101–2, 135, 262, 277, 346–7
'Some Kinda Love' (Velvet Underground) 171
'Someone Else Will Take Your Place' (A. Hunter) 18
'Someone Saved My Life Tonight' (E. John) 259–60, 406
Somerville, Jimmy 357–9, 364, 373, 375, 395–6, 407, 414–15, 416, 421–2, 427
Something for the Boys musical 52
'Something Strange' (Herd) 141
'Something to Live For' (B. Strayhorn) 44, 56, 58
'Somewhere (There's a Place for Us)' (Sondheim and Bernstein) 94
'Somewhere Over the Rainbow' (Arlen and Harburg) 45, 126
'Song of Dr Hirschfeld' (O. Reutter) 12
Songs of Bilitis (P. Louys) 112
Sonny Charles and Checkmates 168

'Soul Love' (D. Bowie) 190
'Soul Makossa' (M. Dibango) 247
Soul Train TV programme 245
Sound Factory, New York 400, 401
Sounds 191, 221, 313
Sounds, King 455
South Africa 521–4
South Pacific musical 60
Southwell, Paul 267–8, 281
Soviet Union 63, 65
Spandau Ballet 346–7
'Spanish Passion' (R. Bourbon) 30
Sparks, Randy 107–8
speakeasies 17, 18, 20, 23, 47, 50
'(Special Treatment For the) Family Man' (Tuxedomoon) 316
Speckled Red 21
Spector, Phil 121
Spheeris, Jimmie 234
Spierer, Chris 255–6
Spin magazine 425, 445–6
Spivy's Roof, New York 43, 47, 60
Spoliansky, Mischa 'Arno Billing' 14–15, 27
Springfield, Dusty 130–1, 132, 133, 134, 136, 187–9, 215, 222, 310, 338, 344, 374
Squeezebox 469
Squier, Billy 376–7
St Hildegard von Bingen 4–5
St Marks Baths, New York 322–3
St Peters, Crispian 141
Stade, Richardis von 4
Stamp, Chris 139
'Stand' (Sly and the Family Stone) 167
'Stand Up For Your Rights' (International Gay Society) 302
Staples, Kevan 342–3
Starbuck 192
'Starman' (D. Bowie) 187, 189, 194
Starr, Chuck E. 237–8
Stars (Sylvester) 297
State Liquor Authority 165
Stax records 244

Steam 232, 233
Steele, Tommy 102
Stein, Seymour 323
Step II (Sylvester) 297
Stepney Sisters 221
stereotypes on television, gay 64
Stevens, Doug 479–80
Stewart, Al 154
Stewart, Rod 156, 272, 293, 308
Sticky Fingers (Rolling Stones) 176–7
Stigwood, Robert 121, 141, 147, 289
Stipe, Michael 379–80, 381, 383, 434–5, 446, 458
Stoller, Mike 79, 91, 92
Stonewall Inn, West Village 166–8, 173, 192, 204, 225, 241, 250, 328
'Stonewall Nation' (M. Davis) 203, 205, 225
Stooges 199
Stop Murder Music 515–16
Stories of Our Lives film 520–1
'Stout-Hearted Men' (G. Jenkins) 57
Straight Outta Compton (N.W.A.) 411
Straker, Peter 261
'Strange Fruit' (B. Holiday) 93
Strange, Steve 346, 347
'Strange Things Happening Every Day' (R. Tharpe) 70
'Stranger in Paradise' (J. Mathis) 95, 96
'Strangers In the Night' (Teddy and Darrel) 143
Stranglers 279
'Strapping Lad' (whaling ballad) 8
Stratton-Smith, Tony 141
Strayhorn, Billy 44, 54–6, 58, 155
Street Life 265, 266, 272
Street Transvestite Action Revolutionaries (STAR) 179
'Strong Love' (Smokey) 237, 239, 241
Strong Love: Songs of Gay Liberation 1972-1981 compilation album 227, 237
Stroppy Cow Records 222

Student Homophile League, Columbia University 165
Studio 54, New York 288, 323
'Stupid Cupid' (C. Francis) 124
Sublette, Ned 327
Sue label 118
Suede 438–9
Sugar, Jon 329–30
Sugarfoot Sam From Alabam minstrel show 74
Summer, Donna 257, 291–2, 304–5, 324, 361, 364–5
Sunday, Bloody Sunday film 179
sunshine pop 160
'Superdyke' (P. Perkins) 312
'Superman' (G. Gil) 307
'Supermodel (You Better Work)' RuPaul 438
Swanson, Petite 89
Sweet 192
'Sweet Jane' (Velvet Underground) 195
'Sweet Little Sister' (Skid Row) 411
'Sweet Little Sixteen' (C. Berry) 94
'Sweet Soul Music' (A. Conley) 119
'Sweet Surrender' (D. Ross) 251
'Sweet Surrender' (T. Buckley) 247
'Sweet Thing-Candidate-Sweet Thing (Reprise)' (D. Bowie) 239
Sweet Violet Boys 44
'Swinging in the Daisy Chain' (Count Basie) 18
Sylvester 184, 295–8, 317, 319, 362, 375, 415
Sylvester (Sylvester) 295–6
Sylvester and the Hot Band (Sylvester) 295
Symphonia Armonie Celestium Revelationum (St Hildegard) 5

T. Rex 190
'T'ain't Nobody's Business If I Do' (B. Smith) 21
'Tainted Love' (Coil) 366
'Tainted Love' (Soft Cell) 347, 348

Take Fo Records 478
'Take Me To Church' (Hozier) 532
Take That 465
Talking Heads 336
Tallujah 46
Tamla Motown Revue 134
Tampa Red's Hokum Jazz Band 22
Tanega, Norma 188
Tanner, Chris 301
Tapestry (C. King) 211
Tashman, Lilyan 25
t.A.T.u 527
Taupin, Bernie 259
Tavel, Ronald 170
'Taxi Blues' (Little Richard) 75–6
Taylor, Cecil 155
Tchaikovsky, Pyotr 5, 6
Tea Dance (DC La Rue) 290
Teaches of Peaches (Peaches) 497–8
Team Dresch 451
'Tech-No-Logical World' (P. Cowley) 362
Teddy and Darrel 142, 143
Teenage Jesus and the Jerks 316
Teenage Rebellion film 144
Teenagers 90
'Tell Me Something Good' (3 Teens Kill 4) 402
'Tell Tale' (J. Armatrading) 345
'Telstar' (Tornados) 122
Tempest, Florenze 9
Tennant, Neil 373–5, 463
Terence Higgins Trust 366
Terminal Hold (T. Fure) 341
Terry, Helen 372
Test Department 403–4
Testing the Limits documentary 366
Thank God It's Friday (film) 304
'Thanks for Chicago Mr James' (S. Walker) 159
Tharpe, Sister Rosetta 70–1, 73, 74
That Certain Summer film 179
Thatcher, Margaret 394
'That's All Right' (E. Presley) 70

'That's What Friends Are For' (D. Warwick) 366, 370
'That's What's the Matter with Me' (J. Malin) 29
'The Biggest Lie' (Hüsker Dü) 380, 445
'The Boy Can't make It with Girls' (999) 300, 308
The Changer and the Changed . . . (C. Williamson) 211–12, 213
'The Day I Got AIDS' (Frogs) 405
'The Drowners' (Suede) 438–9
'The Father Project' (Tooji) 531
'The Girls Are It Again' (P. Perkins) 133
'The Killing of Georgie' (R. Stewart) 272, 273, 308
'The Letter' (R. Blades) 409
'The Man I Love' (I. & G. Gershwin) 49
The Man Who Sold the World (D. Bowie) 177–8
'The Message' (Grandmaster Flash) 327
'The Mirror' (D. Bowie) 148
'The Ocean' (Against Me!) 506–7
'The Ones Who Aren't Here' (J. Calvi) 365
The Queen documentary 164–5
'The Sex That I Need' (Cazwell and Avenue D) 498
'The Show Must Go On' (Queen) 424
'The Subject Was Faggots' (G. Scott-Heron) 243–4
The Wild Ones (film) 70
'The Wizard' (M. Bolan) 191
'The Young Folk' (Diana Ross and the Supremes) 167
Theatre of the Absurd, Martin Essin's 170
'There Ain't No Sweet Man Worth the Salt of My Tears' (B. Beiderbecke) 31
'There are Fairies at the Bottom of our Garden' (R.A. Fyleman) 32–3

'There is Something on Your Mind (Parts One and Two)' (P. Swanson) 89
There's A Dyke In the Pit compilation 450
These Are the Hits, You Silly Savage (Teddy and Darrel) 142, 143–4
'They all Are' (R. Rocca) 59–60, 224
They Only Come out at Night (E. Winter) 232
'This Charming Man' (Smiths) 382
'This is My Life' (S. Bassey) 167
This Is The Army revue 47
Thomas, Linda Lee 34
Thormahlen, Ernie 197
Thornton, Willi Mae 'Big Mama' 78
3 Teens Kill 4 402
Throbbing Gristle records 403
Thrust Records 142
Tillery, Linda 341
Tilley, Vesta 9–10, 11
Time magazine 173–4, 377
Time Out magazine 283, 442
Times Square, New York 25, 29
'Timile Ta Sajilai' (S. Limbue) 532
Timoteo, Agnaldo 306
Tipton, Billy 84
Titica 520
'To a Woman' (Lavender Country) 228
'To Try for the Sun' (Donovan) 152–3
'Toilet Love' (Electric Chairs) 282
Tom of Finland 353, 388
Tom Robinson Band (TRB) 271–2, 274–6, 308
Tommy rock opera 140–1, 181
Tongue Man 442
Tongues United film 486
'Tooling for Anus' (Meatmen) 333
Toon, Tony 272
Toone, Anderson 338–9, 452–3
Top of the Pops TV programme 152, 189, 347, 348, 355, 391–2, 427
Topper, Burt 144
Tornados 122, 124

Index

Touré, Nakhane 522
Townshend, Pete 139, 140, 141–2, 330–1
Tracks, New York 400
Trailblazers (TV programme) 379
trans-genderism/transexuality 68–9, 84, 140, 146, 159, 164, 165, 171, 203, 274, 280, 282, 307, 321–2, 449, 493, 494–5, 501–11, 533, 534
Transamerica film 512
Transformer (L. Reed) 195, 196
Transgender Dysphoria Blues (L.J. Grace) 507
Trash film 171
Tret Fure (T. Fure) 214
Tribe 8 447, 448–50
'Tribute to Buddy Holly' (M. Berry) 122
tropicalismo 193, 306–7
troubadours 4
'Trouble at the Cup' (Black Randy and the Metrosquad) 284–5
Trout Quintet (F. Schubert) 6
Troy Walker Live (T. Walker) 115–16
'Truck Drivin' Man' (Cowboy Jack Derrick) 60
'Truck Grape' (C. Miranda) 193
True Colours tour 497
Truman, Harry S. 61
The Tube TV programme 354
Tubes 268
Turner, Randy 'Biscuit' 331–2, 384
Turner, Velvert 152
'Tutti Frutti' (Little Richard) 75–6
Tuxedomoon 315–16
12 West Club, New York 251, 260
twelve-inch singles, first 249
'Twinky Insanity' (A. Peterson) 303
Twirling Corps 303
the twist 104, 134–5
'Twistin' the Night Away' (S. Cooke) 134–5
'two 2-4-6-8 Motorway' (TRB) 274
'Two Faces Have I' (L. Christie) 127, 128

Two Nice Girls 418, 419–20, 426
Two Songmakers TV programme 299
'Two Tribes' (FGTH) 356, 372
Tyler, Robin 204, 205

U2 435
Ubangi Club, Harlem 23
Uganda/Ugandan Pride 535
Ulrichs, Karl Heinrich 11–12
Umlilo 522, 523–4, 525
'Uncle Bert' (Creation) 141
'Under Clery's Clock' (Radiators) 405–6
'Under One Roof' (Rubettes) 272–3
Under The Counter Records 85
Undressed (Pansy Division) 444
The Unicorn (P. Grudzien) 241
Unique periodical 12
United States of America (band) 148
Up the Establishment film 163
'Uptown' (Prince) 329
Urnings and Urningins 12
Us magazine 96
US Navy 46
'Useless Man' (Minty) 442–3
Utley, Justin 513

Vadalia, Patsy 72
Vagabond catalogue 114–15
Vail, Tobi 437
Vain Victory: Vicissitudes of the Damned play 196
Valente, Assis 193
Valentine, Hazel 18
'Valentine Stomp' (Fats Waller) 18
Valentino Harris, Charles 255–7
Valli, Frankie 128, 129, 136
Van Halen 239
Van Ronk, Dave 166
van Vechten, Carl 21
Vanguard 165
Vanilla, Cherry 186, 199
Vanity Fair magazine 433
Varga, Chavela 193

571

Variety magazine 17, 29
vaudeville 8, 26, 85
Veloso, Caetano 193, 306–7
Velvet Underground 145–6, 147, 171, 190, 195, 220, 269–70
Velvet Underground & Nico (Velvet Underground) 145–6, 147
'Venus In Furs' (Velvet Underground) 147
Vice Versa pamphlet 51–2
'Vicious' (L. Reed) 196
Vicious, Sid 278
'Vicky's Box' (Throwing Muses) 383
Victim film 114
Victoria, Queen 10
Vidal, Gore 52
videos, music 1–3
'View From Gay Head' (Lavender Jane) 209
VIII, King Edward 36
Village People 290–2, 293–4, 305, 393
Village Voice magazine 174, 218, 336, 364, 418
Ving, Lee 334
Vinyl, Don 315
Visage 247
Vogue magazine 183–4
voguing 399–401

Wace, Robert 182
Wagner, Paul 231
Wainwright 266–7
Wainwright, Rufus 465–6, 502
Wakeman, Alan 205–7
'Wakin'' (Lavender Country) 227
'Walk on the Wild Side' (L. Reed) 196–7
'Walk the Night' (Skatt Brothers) 319–20
Walker, Albertina 71
Walker, Scott 159
Walker, Troy 115–16, 243
'Walking in the Rain' (J. Ray) 69–70
'Walking the Dog' (J. Shane) 117

Wallace, Wally 246
Wallenberg, Petter 534–5
Wallis, Ruth 50
Walls to Roses: Songs of Changing Men (compilation) 299–301
Walsh, Louis 465
Walter, Margaret 382
Ward, Clara 71, 74
Warehouse, Chicago 288, 306, 393, 485
Warhol, Andy 145–6, 164, 170, 171, 176, 185, 195, 285, 288
Warmer Sudwind 308
Warner Bros 200, 213, 345, 445
Washington, Dinah 74, 91, 115, 165
Washington, Maurice 245
Washington, Toni 244–5, 246
Water Under the Bridge (M. Santing) 345
Waters, John 80, 81, 92, 128, 172, 184, 237
Wax Trax! records 403
Waybill, Fee 268
Wayne County at the Trucks show 280
WBAI, New York 229–30
Webster, Paul 99
Wee Wee Pole 402–3
Weinstein, Judy 248
Weinstein, Naomi 207
Welcome To the Pleasuredome (FGTH) 356, 394
Well of Loneliness (R. Hall) 31
Wells, Dicky 155
Wells, Kitty 83
Wenner, Jann 295
'West End Girls' (Pet Shop Boys) 374
West End Records 288, 305, 323, 498
West, Kanye 492
West, Mae 26, 28, 29
West Side Story play/film 94
West, Tim'm 486–7
Westwood, Vivienne 270
'What Did You Do For Feelings, Moritz' 35

Index

What Did You Expect?... (M. Cohen) 230–1
'What Have I Done to Deserve This?' (Pet Shop Boys) 374
What Now My Love (M. Ryder) 159
'When In Heaven' (KOD) 408
'When The Best Friend' 27
'When the Whip Comes Down' (Rolling Stones) 309
'When You Were Mine' (Prince) 329
'Where the Boys Are' (C. Fancis) 125, 126
Whitcomb, Ian 128, 151
White Christmas musical 80
White, Curtis 65
White, Dan 302, 303, 316, 326
White Heat (D. Springfield) 344
White Light/White Heat (Velvet Underground) 146
White, Maude Valérie 10
White Riot Night (MonDello) 303–4
'White Trash Hillbilly Trick' (P. Grudzien) 241
Whitman, Walt 7, 154
The Who 139–41, 142
'Who's to Blame' (Obie Jessie and Seeds of Freedom) 244
'Why' (Bronski Beat) 360
'Why Do Fools Fall in Love' (Teenagers) 90
'Why, No One to Love?' (S. Foster) 7
Wickham, Vicki 131, 132–3, 134, 253, 344
'Width of a Circle' (D. Bowie) 178
Wild Boys (W. Burroughs) 187, 239
Wilde, Marty 102–3
Wilde, Oscar 12, 33, 96, 180
Wildeblood, Peter 96–7
Wilhelm II, Kaiser 12
'Will the World Ever Change for the Better' (Handbag) 268
'Will You Love Me Tomorrow' (M. Berry) 122
Willard, Avery 163

Williams, Marion 74
Williams, Tennessee 68
Williamson, Cris 210, 211–12, 214, 217–18, 231, 236, 342, 365, 429
'Willie O'Winsbury' (folk ballad) 7
Willis, Victor 291–2, 294
Wilson, John C. 52
Wine, Toni 168
Winter, Edgar 232
Wire, Nicky 435, 436
Wiseheart, Susan 212
Wizard Of Oz film 44–5
Wizard of Us 185
WLUP radio 304–5
Wobensmith, Matt 446–7, 450, 475–6, 490
Wolf, Tommy 99
Wolfe, Carole 'Cyryus' 474–7, 479, 488
Wolfenden Report (1957) 96–7, 101, 157
Woman Identified Woman manifesto 211
'Women Don't Need No Men' (L. Bogan) 19
Women on Wheels tour (1976) 212
Women's Army Corps (WAC) 50
Women's Liberation Rock Bands, Chicago and Newhaven 207, 220
Women's Social and Political Union 11
Women's Wax Works Records 209
Wonder, Stevie 256
Woodlawn, Holly 170–1
'Woof, Woof, Oink, Oink' (Canya Phukem and Howe) 326
Word Is Out documentary 107, 302
The Word TV programme 455
World: the Birth of a Nation, the Castration of Man play 185, 186
The Wreckers (E. Smyth) 10
Wright, Billy 72, 73, 74, 75
Wright, Chely 512–13
'Wrong Bathroom' (Tribe 8) 449

Xtravaganza, Luis and Jose 401
XXL magazine 496

'Ya Strugglin'' (KRS-One) 472
Yardbirds 141
Yes I Am (M. Etheridge) 434
'YMCA' (Village People) 291, 293, 294
'You Don't Have to Camp Around' (T. Rundgren) 232
'You Don't Have to Say You Love Me' (D. Springfield) 131, 136
'You Don't Know the Half of It' (Brennan and Savoy) 26
'You Don't Own Me' (L. Gore) 130
'You Know You Want to Be Loved' (K. Barrow) 290
'You Make Me Feel (Mighty Real)' (Sylvester) 297–8, 415
'You Must Come Over' (Brennan and Savoy) 26
'You Spin Me Round' (Dead or Alive) 372
'You Think You're a Man' (Divine) 391–2
'You Turn Me On' (I. Whitcomb) 128
'Young Love' (T. Hunter) 88, 94
Young Men's Christian Organisation (YMCA) 266

Young, Will 500, 533
'You're Kidding Me' (Coccinelle) 69
'You're the Top' (C. Porter) 34
Yours or Mine, London 179
Youth International Party (The Yippies) 160
'You've Got to Hide Your Love Away' (Beatles) 136, 265
Yuro, Timi 127

Zanetta, Tony 186, 199
Zang Tuum Tumb (ZTT) Records 355
Zappa, Frank 309, 375–6, 409
Zelkowitz, Genya 132
Zeros 314
Ziegfeld Follies 25
Ziggy Stardust and the Spiders from Mars 187, 189–90, 192, 199, 201, 232, 263
   see also Bowie, David
Zipper magazine 117
Zone, Miki 392
Zone, Paul 282–3, 392–3